Materials excerpted from

Windows Server® 2008 Network Infrastructure Configuration

Microsoft Certified Technology Specialist
Exam 70-642

Windows Server® 2008 Active Directory® Configuration

Microsoft Certified Technology Specialist
Exam 70-640

Windows Server® 2008 Enterprise
Evaluation Software Inside

⊗WILEY *Custom*
LEARNING SOLUTIONS

To order books or for customer service, please call 1(800)-CALL-WILEY (225-5945).

Printed in the United States of America.

ISBN 978-1-118-27902-1
Printed and bound by Bind Rite.

10 9 8 7 6 5 4 3 2

The content of this text has been taken from

Microsoft® Official Academic Course
Windows Server® 2008
Network Infrastructure Configuration
Microsoft Certified Technology Specialist Exam 70-642

And

Microsoft® Official Academic Course
Windows Server® 2008
Active Directory® Configuration
Microsoft Certified Technology Specialist Exam 70-640

Since this custom text is based on excerpts of the full Microsoft® Official Academic Course textbooks for 70-642 and 70-640, it is not intended to cover the entire objective domain for the Microsoft® certification exams. In that way, this custom text is not meant to be a preparatory text for the Microsoft® 70-642 or 70-640 certification exams.

Custom Table of Contents

Part I

Content from Windows Server 2008 Network Infrastructure Configuration, Exam 70-642

Part II

Content from Windows Server 2008 Active Directory Configuration, Exam 70-640

PART I

Excerpts from:

Microsoft® Official Academic Course
Windows Server® 2008
Network Infrastructure Configuration
Microsoft Certified Technology Specialist Exam 70-642

Microsoft® Official Academic Course

Windows Server® 2008 Network Infrastructure Configuration (70-642)

WILEY

Credits

EXECUTIVE EDITOR	John Kane
DIRECTOR OF MARKETING AND SALES	Mitchell Beaton
MICROSOFT STRATEGIC RELATIONSHIPS MANAGER	Merrick Van Dongen of Microsoft Learning
DEVELOPMENT AND PRODUCTION	Custom Editorial Productions, Inc.
EDITORIAL ASSISTANT	Jennifer Lartz
PRODUCTION MANAGER	Micheline Frederick
PRODUCTION EDITOR	Kerry Weinstein
CREATIVE DIRECTOR	Harry Nolan
COVER DESIGNER	Jim O'Shea
TECHNOLOGY AND MEDIA	Lauren Sapira/Elena Santa Maria

This book was set in Garamond by Aptara, Inc. and printed and bound by Bind Rite Graphics. The covers were printed by Phoenix Color.

ISBN 978-0-470-22515-8

Printed in the United States of America

10 9 8 7 6 5 4 3 2 1

Foreword from the Publisher

Wiley's publishing vision for the Microsoft Official Academic Course series is to provide students and instructors with the skills and knowledge they need to use Microsoft technology effectively in all aspects of their personal and professional lives. Quality instruction is required to help both educators and students get the most from Microsoft's software tools and to become more productive. Thus our mission is to make our instructional programs trusted educational companions for life.

To accomplish this mission, Wiley and Microsoft have partnered to develop the highest quality educational programs for Information Workers, IT Professionals, and Developers. Materials created by this partnership carry the brand name "Microsoft Official Academic Course," assuring instructors and students alike that the content of these textbooks is fully endorsed by Microsoft, and that they provide the highest quality information and instruction on Microsoft products. The Microsoft Official Academic Course textbooks are "Official" in still one more way—they are the officially sanctioned courseware for Microsoft IT Academy members.

The Microsoft Official Academic Course series focuses on *workforce development*. These programs are aimed at those students seeking to enter the workforce, change jobs, or embark on new careers as information workers, IT professionals, and developers. Microsoft Official Academic Course programs address their needs by emphasizing authentic workplace scenarios with an abundance of projects, exercises, cases, and assessments.

The Microsoft Official Academic Courses are mapped to Microsoft's extensive research and job-task analysis, the same research and analysis used to create the Microsoft Certified Technology Specialist (MCTS) exam. The textbooks focus on real skills for real jobs. As students work through the projects and exercises in the textbooks they enhance their level of knowledge and their ability to apply the latest Microsoft technology to everyday tasks. These students also gain resume-building credentials that can assist them in finding a job, keeping their current job, or in furthering their education.

The concept of life-long learning is today an utmost necessity. Job roles, and even whole job categories, are changing so quickly that none of us can stay competitive and productive without continuously updating our skills and capabilities. The Microsoft Official Academic Course offerings, and their focus on Microsoft certification exam preparation, provide a means for people to acquire and effectively update their skills and knowledge. Wiley supports students in this endeavor through the development and distribution of these courses as Microsoft's official academic publisher.

Today educational publishing requires attention to providing quality print and robust electronic content. By integrating Microsoft Official Academic Course products, *WileyPLUS*, and Microsoft certifications, we are better able to deliver efficient learning solutions for students and teachers alike.

Bonnie Lieberman

General Manager and Senior Vice President

Welcome to the Microsoft Official Academic Course (MOAC) program for Microsoft Windows Server 2008. MOAC represents the collaboration between Microsoft Learning and John Wiley & Sons, Inc. publishing company. Microsoft and Wiley teamed up to produce a series of text-books that deliver compelling and innovative teaching solutions to instructors and superior learning experiences for students. Infused and informed by in-depth knowledge from the creators of Windows Server 2008, and crafted by a publisher known worldwide for the pedagogical quality of its products, these textbooks maximize skills transfer in minimum time. Students are challenged to reach their potential by using their new technical skills as highly productive members of the workforce.

Because this knowledgebase comes directly from Microsoft, architect of the Windows Server operating system and creator of the Microsoft Certified Technology Specialist and Microsoft Certified Professional exams (www.microsoft.com/learning/mcp/mcts), you are sure to receive the topical coverage that is most relevant to students' personal and professional success. Microsoft's direct participation not only assures you that MOAC textbook content is accurate and current; it also means that students will receive the best instruction possible to enable their success on certification exams and in the workplace.

▪ The Microsoft Official Academic Course Program

The *Microsoft Official Academic Course* series is a complete program for instructors and institutions to prepare and deliver great courses on Microsoft software technologies. With MOAC, we recognize that, because of the rapid pace of change in the technology and curriculum developed by Microsoft, there is an ongoing set of needs beyond classroom instruction tools for an instructor to be ready to teach the course. The MOAC program endeavors to provide solutions for all these needs in a systematic manner in order to ensure a successful and rewarding course experience for both instructor and student—technical and curriculum training for instructor readiness with new software releases; the software itself for student use at home for building hands-on skills, assessment, and validation of skill development; and a great set of tools for delivering instruction in the classroom and lab. All are important to the smooth delivery of an interesting course on Microsoft software, and all are provided with the MOAC program. We think about the model below as a gauge for ensuring that we completely support you in your goal of teaching a great course. As you evaluate your instructional materials options, you may wish to use the model for comparison purposes with available products.

▪ Pedagogical Features

The MOAC textbook for Windows Server 2008 Network Infrastructure Configuration is designed to cover all the learning objectives for that MCTS exam, which is referred to as its "objective domain." The Microsoft Certified Technology Specialist (MCTS) exam objectives are highlighted throughout the textbook. Many pedagogical features have been developed specifically for *Microsoft Official Academic Course* programs.

Presenting the extensive procedural information and technical concepts woven throughout the textbook raises challenges for the student and instructor alike. The Illustrated Book Tour that follows provides a guide to the rich features contributing to *Microsoft Official Academic Course* program's pedagogical plan. Following is a list of key features in each lesson designed to prepare students for success on the certification exams and in the workplace:

- Each lesson begins with an **Objective Domain Matrix.** More than a standard list of learning objectives, the Domain Matrix correlates each software skill covered in the lesson to the specific MCTS "objective domain."

- Concise and frequent **Step-by-Step** instructions teach students new features and provide an opportunity for hands-on practice. Numbered steps give detailed, step-by-step instructions to help students learn software skills. The steps also show results and screen images to match what students should see on their computer screens.

- **Illustrations:** Screen images provide visual feedback as students work through the exercises. The images reinforce key concepts, provide visual clues about the steps, and allow students to check their progress.

- **Key Terms:** Important technical vocabulary is listed at the beginning of the lesson. When these terms are used later in the lesson, they appear in bold italic type and are defined. The Glossary contains all of the key terms and their definitions.

- Engaging point-of-use **Reader aids,** located throughout the lessons, tell students why this topic is relevant (*The Bottom Line*), provide students with helpful hints (*Take Note*), or show alternate ways to accomplish tasks (*Another Way*). Reader aids also provide additional relevant or background information that adds value to the lesson.

- **Certification Ready?** features throughout the text signal students where a specific certification objective is covered. They provide students with a chance to check their understanding of that particular MCTS objective and, if necessary, review the section of the lesson where it is covered. MOAC offers complete preparation for MCTS certification.

- **Knowledge Assessments** provide three progressively more challenging lesson-ending activities.

▪ Lesson Features

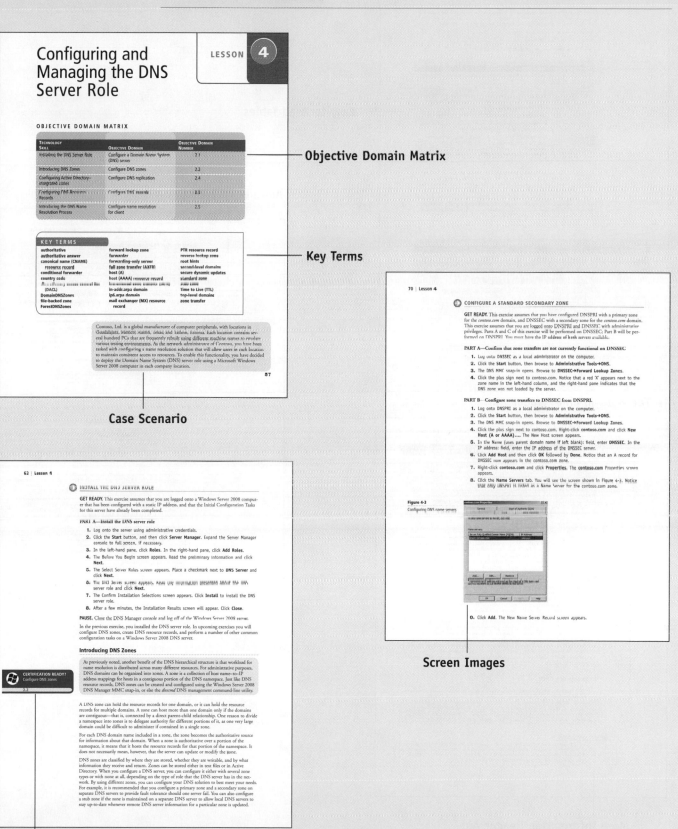

Objective Domain Matrix

Key Terms

Case Scenario

Screen Images

MCTS Certification Objective Alert

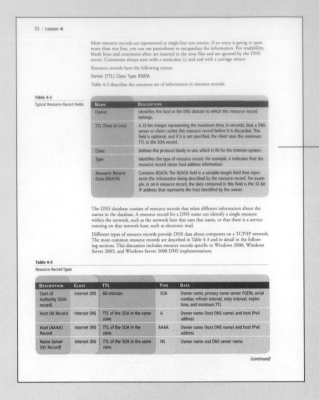

Easy-to-Read Tables

Another Way Reader Aid

The Bottom Line Reader Aid

More Information Reader Aid

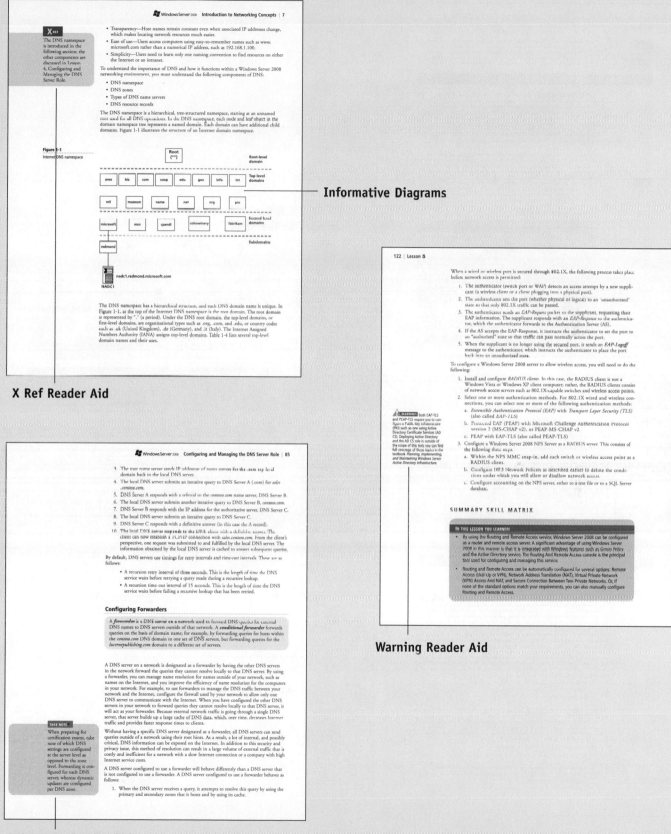

Informative Diagrams

X Ref Reader Aid

Warning Reader Aid

Take Note Reader Aid

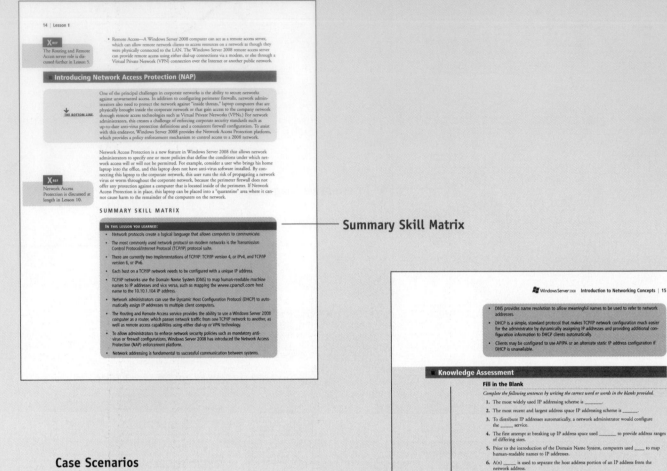

Summary Skill Matrix

Case Scenarios

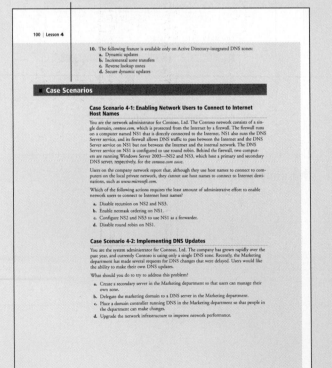

Knowledge Assessment Questions

Conventions and Features Used in This Book

This book uses particular fonts, symbols, and heading conventions to highlight important information or to call your attention to special steps. For more information about the features in each lesson, refer to the Illustrated Book Tour section.

CONVENTION	MEANING
NEW FEATURE	This icon indicates a new or greatly improved Windows feature in this version of the software.
THE BOTTOM LINE	This feature provides a brief summary of the material to be covered in the section that follows.
CLOSE	Words in all capital letters and in a different font color than the rest of the text indicate instructions for opening, saving, or closing files or programs. They also point out items you should check or actions you should take.
CERTIFICATION READY?	This feature signals the point in the text where a specific certification objective is covered. It provides you with a chance to check your understanding of that particular MCTS objective and, if necessary, review the section of the lesson where it is covered.
TAKE NOTE	Reader aids appear in shaded boxes found in your text. *Take Note* provides helpful hints related to particular tasks or topics.
ANOTHER WAY	*Another Way* provides an alternative procedure for accomplishing a particular task.
X REF	These notes provide pointers to information discussed elsewhere in the textbook or describe interesting features of Windows Server 2008 that are not directly addressed in the current topic or exercise.
Alt + Tab	A plus sign (+) between two key names means that you must press both keys at the same time. Keys that you are instructed to press in an exercise will appear in the font shown here.
A *shared printer* can be used by many individuals on a network.	Key terms appear in bold italic.
Key **My Name is**.	Any text you are asked to key appears in color.
Click **OK**.	Any button on the screen you are supposed to click on or select will also appear in color.

Instructor Support Program

The *Microsoft Official Academic Course* programs are accompanied by a rich array of resources that incorporate the extensive textbook visuals to form a pedagogically cohesive package. These resources provide all the materials instructors need to deploy and deliver their courses. Resources available online for download include:

- The **MSDN Academic Alliance** is designed to provide the easiest and most inexpensive developer tools, products, and technologies available to faculty and students in labs, classrooms, and on student PCs. A free 3-year membership is available to qualified MOAC adopters.

  Note: Microsoft Windows Server 2008 can be downloaded from MSDN AA for use by students in this course.

- **Windows Server 2008 Evaluation Software.** DVDs containing an evaluation version of Windows Server 2008 are bundled inside the front cover of this text.

- The **Instructor's Guide** contains Solutions to all the textbook exercises as well as chapter summaries and lecture notes. The Instructor's Guide and Syllabi for various term lengths are available from the Book Companion site (www.wiley.com/college/microsoft) and from *WileyPLUS*.

- The **Test Bank** contains hundreds of questions in multiple-choice, true-false, short answer, and essay formats and is available to download from the Instructor's Book Companion site (www.wiley.com/college/microsoft) and from *WileyPLUS*. A complete answer key is provided.

- **PowerPoint Presentations and Images.** A complete set of PowerPoint presentations is available on the Instructor's Book Companion site (www.wiley.com/college/microsoft) and in *WileyPLUS* to enhance classroom presentations. Tailored to the text's topical coverage and Skills Matrix, these presentations are designed to convey key Windows Server concepts addressed in the text.

  All figures from the text are on the Instructor's Book Companion site (www.wiley.com/college/microsoft) and in *WileyPLUS*. You can incorporate them into your PowerPoint presentations, or create your own overhead transparencies and handouts.

  By using these visuals in class discussions, you can help focus students' attention on key elements of Windows Server and help them understand how to use it effectively in the workplace.

- When it comes to improving the classroom experience, there is no better source of ideas and inspiration than your fellow colleagues. The Wiley Faculty Network connects teachers with technology, facilitates the exchange of best practices, and helps to enhance instructional efficiency and effectiveness. Faculty Network activities include technology training and tutorials, virtual seminars, peer-to-peer exchanges of experiences and ideas, personal consulting, and sharing of resources. For details visit www.WhereFacultyConnect.com.

WileyPLUS

Broad developments in education over the past decade have influenced the instructional approach taken in the Microsoft Official Academic Course program. The way that students learn, especially about new technologies, has changed dramatically in the Internet era. Electronic learning materials and Internet-based instruction is now as much a part of classroom instruction as printed textbooks. *WileyPLUS* provides the technology to create an environment where students reach their full potential and experience academic success that will last them a lifetime!

WileyPLUS is a powerful and highly-integrated suite of teaching and learning resources designed to bridge the gap between what happens in the classroom and what happens at home and on the job. *WileyPLUS* provides instructors with the resources to teach their students new technologies and guide them to reach their goals of getting ahead in the job market by having the skills to become certified and advance in the workforce. For students, *WileyPLUS* provides the tools for study and practice that are available to them 24/7, wherever and whenever they want to study. *WileyPLUS* includes a complete online version of the student textbook, PowerPoint presentations, homework and practice assignments and quizzes, image galleries, test bank questions, gradebook, and all the instructor resources in one easy-to-use Web site.

Organized around the everyday activities you and your students perform in the class, *WileyPLUS* helps you:

- **Prepare & Present** outstanding class presentations using relevant PowerPoint slides and other *WileyPLUS* materials—and you can easily upload and add your own.

- **Create Assignments** by choosing from questions organized by lesson, level of difficulty, and source—and add your own questions. Students' homework and quizzes are automatically graded, and the results are recorded in your gradebook.

- **Offer context-sensitive help to students, 24/7.** When you assign homework or quizzes, you decide if and when students get access to hints, solutions, or answers where appropriate—or they can be linked to relevant sections of their complete, online text for additional help whenever—and wherever they need it most.

- **Track Student Progress.** Analyze students' results and assess their level of understanding on an individual and class level using the *WileyPLUS* gradebook, or export data to your own personal gradebook.

- **Administer Your Course.** *WileyPLUS* can easily be integrated with another course management system, gradebook, or other resources you are using in your class, providing you with the flexibility to build your course, your way.

Please view our online demo at **www.wiley.com/college/wileyplus.** Here you will find additional information about the features and benefits of *WileyPLUS*, how to request a "test drive" of *WileyPLUS* for this title, and how to adopt it for class use.

MSDN ACADEMIC ALLIANCE—FREE 3-YEAR MEMBERSHIP AVAILABLE TO QUALIFIED ADOPTERS!

The Microsoft Developer Network Academic Alliance (MSDN AA) is designed to provide the easiest and most inexpensive way for universities to make the latest Microsoft developer tools, products, and technologies available in labs, classrooms, and on student PCs. MSDN AA is an annual membership program for departments teaching Science, Technology, Engineering, and Mathematics (STEM) courses. The membership provides a complete solution to keep academic labs, faculty, and students on the leading edge of technology.

Software available in the MSDN AA program is provided at no charge to adopting departments through the Wiley and Microsoft publishing partnership.

As a bonus to this free offer, faculty will be introduced to Microsoft's Faculty Connection and Academic Resource Center. It takes time and preparation to keep students engaged while giving them a fundamental understanding of theory, and the Microsoft Faculty Connection is designed to help STEM professors with this preparation by providing articles, curriculum, and tools that professors can use to engage and inspire today's technology students.

* Contact your Wiley rep for details.

For more information about the MSDN Academic Alliance program, go to:

msdn.microsoft.com/academic/

Note: Microsoft Windows Server 2008 can be downloaded from MSDN AA for use by students in this course.

Important Web Addresses and Phone Numbers

To locate the Wiley Higher Education Rep in your area, go to the following Web address and click on the "*Who's My Rep?*" link at the top of the page.

www.wiley.com/college

Or Call the MOAC Toll Free Number: 1 + (888) 764-7001 (U.S. & Canada only).

To learn more about becoming a Microsoft Certified Professional and exam availability, visit www.microsoft.com/learning/mcp.

Book Companion Web Site (www.wiley.com/college/microsoft)

The students' book companion site for the MOAC series includes any resources, exercise files, and Web links that will be used in conjunction with this course.

WileyPLUS

WileyPLUS is a powerful and highly-integrated suite of teaching and learning resources designed to bridge the gap between what happens in the classroom and what happens at home and on the job. For students, *WileyPLUS* provides the tools for study and practice that are available 24/7, wherever and whenever they want to study. *WileyPLUS* includes a complete online version of the student textbook, PowerPoint presentations, homework and practice assignments and quizzes, image galleries, test bank questions, gradebook, and all the instructor resources in one easy-to-use Web site.

WileyPLUS provides immediate feedback on student assignments and a wealth of support materials. This powerful study tool will help your students develop their conceptual understanding of the class material and increase their ability to answer questions.

- A **Study and Practice** area links directly to text content, allowing students to review the text while they study and answer.

- An **Assignment** area keeps all the work you want your students to complete in one location, making it easy for them to stay on task. Students have access to a variety of interactive self-assessment tools, as well as other resources for building their confidence and understanding. In addition, all of the assignments and quizzes contain a link to the relevant section of the multimedia book, providing students with context-sensitive help that allows them to conquer obstacles as they arise.

- A **Personal Gradebook** for each student allows students to view their results from past assignments at any time.

Please view our online demo at www.wiley.com/college/wileyplus. Here you will find additional information about the features and benefits of *WileyPLUS*, how to request a "test drive" of *WileyPLUS* for this title, and how to adopt it for class use.

Wiley Desktop Editions

Wiley MOAC Desktop Editions are innovative, electronic versions of printed textbooks. Students buy the desktop version for 50% off the U.S. price of the printed text, and get the added value of permanence and portability. Wiley Desktop Editions provide students with numerous additional benefits that are not available with other e-text solutions.

Wiley Desktop Editions are NOT subscriptions; students download the Wiley Desktop Edition to their computer desktops. Students own the content they buy to keep for as long as they want. Once a Wiley Desktop Edition is downloaded to the computer desktop, students have instant access to all of the content without being online. Students can also print out the sections they prefer to read in hard copy. Students also have access to fully integrated resources within their Wiley Desktop Edition. From highlighting their e-text to taking and sharing notes, students can easily personalize their Wiley Desktop Edition as they are reading or following along in class.

Windows Server 2008 Evaluation Edition

All MOAC Windows Server 2008 textbooks are packaged with an evaluation edition of Windows Server 2008 on the companion DVDs. Installing the Windows Server Evaluation Edition provides students with the state-of-the-art system software, enabling them to use a full version of Windows Server 2008 for the course exercises. This also promotes the practice of learning by doing, which can be the most effective way to acquire and remember new computing skills.

Evaluating Windows Server 2008 software does not require product activation or entering a product key. The Windows Server 2008 Evaluation Edition provided with this textbook may be installed without activation and evaluated for an initial 60 days. If you need more time to evaluate Windows Server 2008, the 60-day evaluation period may be reset (or re-armed) three times, extending the original 60-day evaluation period by up to 180 days for a total possible evaluation time of 240 days. After this time, you will need to uninstall the software or upgrade to a fully licensed version of Windows Server 2008.

System Requirements

The following are estimated system requirements for Windows Server 2008. If your computer has less than the minimum requirements, you will not be able to install this product correctly. Actual requirements will vary based on your system configuration and the applications and features you install.

PROCESSOR

Processor performance depends not only on the clock frequency of the processor, but also on the number of processor cores and the size of the processor cache. The following are the processor requirements for this product:

- Minimum: 1 GHz (for x86 processors) or 1.4 GHz (for x64 processors)
- Recommended: 2 GHz or faster

RAM

The following are the RAM requirements for this product:

- Minimum: 512 MB
- Recommended: 2 GB or more
- Maximum (32-bit systems): 4 GB (for Windows Server 2008 Standard) or 64 GB (for Windows Server 2008 Enterprise or Windows Server 2008 Datacenter)
- Maximum (64-bit systems): 32 GB (for Windows Server 2008 Standard) or 2 TB (for Windows Server 2008 Enterprise, Windows Server 2008 Datacenter, or Windows Server 2008 for Itanium-Based Systems)

TAKE NOTE*

An Intel Itanium 2 processor is required for Windows Server 2008 for Itanium-Based Systems.

www.wiley.com/college/microsoft *or*
call the MOAC Toll-Free Number: 1+(888) 764-7001 (U.S. & Canada only)

Disk space requirements

The following are the approximate disk space requirements for the system partition. Itanium-based and x64-based operating systems will vary from these estimates. Additional disk space may be required if you install the system over a network. For more information, see www.microsoft.com/windowsserver2008.

- Minimum: 10 GB
- Recommended: 40 GB or more
- DVD-ROM drive
- Super VGA (800 x 600) or higher-resolution monitor
- Keyboard and Microsoft mouse (or other compatible pointing device)

Important Considerations for Active Directory Domain Controllers

The upgrade process from Windows Server 2003 to Windows Server 2008 requires free disk space for the new operating system image, for the Setup process, and for any installed server roles.

For the domain controller role, the volume or volumes hosting the following resources also have specific free disk space requirements:

- Application data (%AppData%)
- Program files (%ProgramFiles%)
- Users' data (%SystemDrive%\Documents and Settings)
- Windows directory (%WinDir%)

The free space on the %WinDir% volume must be equal or greater than the current size of the resources listed above and their subordinate folders when they are located on the %WinDir% volume. By default, dcpromo places the Active Directory database and log files under %Windir%—in this case, their size would be included in the free disk space requirements for the %Windir% folder.

However, if the Active Directory database is hosted outside of any of the folders above, then the hosting volume or volumes must only contain additional free space equal to at least 10% of the current database size or 250 MB, whichever is greater. Finally, the free space on the volume that hosts the log files must be at least 50 MB.

A default installation of the Active Directory directory service in Windows Server 2003 has the Active Directory database and log files under %WinDir%\NTDS. With this configuration, the NTDS.DIT database file and all the log files are temporarily copied over to the quarantine location and then copied back to their original location. This is why additional free space is required for those resources. However, the SYSVOL directory, which is also under %WinDir% (%WinDir%\SYSVOL), is moved and not copied. Therefore, it does not require any additional free space.

After the upgrade, the space that was reserved for the copied resources will be returned to the file system.

Installing and Re-Arming Windows Server 2008

Evaluating Windows Server 2008 software does not require product activation. The Windows Server 2008 Evaluation Edition may be installed without activation, and it may be evaluated for 60 days. Additionally, the 60-day evaluation period may be reset (re-armed) three times. This action extends the original 60-day evaluation period by up to 180 days for a total possible evaluation time of 240 days.

How To Install Windows Server 2008 Without Activating It

TAKE NOTE*

After Windows Server 2008 is installed, the edition cannot be changed without reinstalling it.

1. Run the Windows Server 2008 Setup program.

2. When you are prompted to enter a product key for activation, do not enter a key. Click No when Setup asks you to confirm your selection.

3. You may be prompted to select the edition of Windows Server 2008 that you want to evaluate. Select the edition that you want to install.

4. When you are prompted, read the evaluation terms in the Microsoft Software License Terms, and then accept the terms.

5. When the Windows Server 2008 Setup program is finished, your initial 60-day evaluation period starts. To check the time that is left on your current evaluation period, run the Slmgr.vbs script that is in the System32 folder. Use the **-dli** switch to run this script. The **slmgr.vbs -dli** command displays the number of days that are left in the current 60-day evaluation period.

How To Re-Arm the Evaluation Period

This section describes how to extend, or re-arm, the Windows Server 2008 evaluation period. The evaluation period is also known as the "activation grace" period.

When the initial 60-day evaluation period nears its end, you can run the Slmgr.vbs script to reset the evaluation period. To do this, follow these steps:

1. Click **Start**, and then click **Command Prompt**.

2. Type **slmgr.vbs -dli**, and then press **ENTER** to check the current status of your evaluation period.

3. To reset the evaluation period, type **slmgr.vbs –rearm**, and then press **ENTER**.

4. Restart the computer.

This resets the evaluation period to 60 days.

How To Automate the Extension of the Evaluation Period

You may want to set up a process that automatically resets the evaluation period every 60 days. One way to automate this process is by using the Task Scheduler. You can configure the Task Scheduler to run the Slmgr.vbs script and to restart the server at a particular time. To do this, follow these steps:

1. Click **Start**, point to **Administrative Tools**, and then click **Task Scheduler**.

2. Copy the following sample task to the server, and then save it as an .xml file. For example, you can save the file as **Extend.xml**.

```xml
<?xml version="1.0" encoding="UTF-16"?> <Task version="1.2"
xmlns="http://schemas.microsoft.com/windows/2004/02/mit/task">
<RegistrationInfo> <Date>2007-09-17T14:26:04.433</Date>
<Author>Microsoft Corporation</Author> </RegistrationInfo>
<Triggers> <TimeTrigger id="18c4a453-d7aa-4647-916b-
af0c3ea16a6b"> <Repetition> <Interval>P59D</Interval>
<StopAtDurationEnd>false</StopAtDurationEnd> </Repetition>
<StartBoundary>2007-10-05T02:23:24</StartBoundary>
<EndBoundary>2008-09-17T14:23:24.777</EndBoundary>
<Enabled>true</Enabled> </TimeTrigger> </Triggers>
<Principals> <Principal id="Author">
<UserId>domain\alias</UserId>
```

```
<LogonType>Password</LogonType>
<RunLevel>HighestAvailable</RunLevel> </Principal>
</Principals> <Settings> <IdleSettings>
<Duration>PT10M</Duration> <WaitTimeout>PT1H</WaitTimeout>
<StopOnIdleEnd>true</StopOnIdleEnd>
<RestartOnIdle>false</RestartOnIdle> </IdleSettings>
<MultipleInstancesPolicy>IgnoreNew</MultipleInstancesPolicy>
<DisallowStartIfOnBatteries>true</DisallowStartIfOnBatteries>
<StopIfGoingOnBatteries>true</StopIfGoingOnBatteries>
<AllowHardTerminate>true</AllowHardTerminate>
<StartWhenAvailable>false</StartWhenAvailable>
<RunOnlyIfNetworkAvailable>false</RunOnlyIfNetworkAvailable>
<AllowStartOnDemand>true</AllowStartOnDemand>
<Enabled>true</Enabled> <Hidden>false</Hidden>
<RunOnlyIfIdle>false</RunOnlyIfIdle>
<WakeToRun>true</WakeToRun>
<ExecutionTimeLimit>P3D</ExecutionTimeLimit>
<DeleteExpiredTaskAfter>PT0S</DeleteExpiredTaskAfter>
<Priority>7</Priority> <RestartOnFailure>
<Interval>PT1M</Interval> <Count>3</Count>
</RestartOnFailure> </Settings> <Actions Context="Author">
<Exec> <Command>C:\Windows\System32\slmgr.vbs</Command>
<Arguments>-rearm</Arguments> </Exec> <Exec>
<Command>C:\Windows\System32\shutdown.exe</Command>
<Arguments>/r</Arguments> </Exec> </Actions> </Task>
```

3. In the sample task, change the value of the following "UserID" tag to contain your domain and your alias:

   <UserId>domain\alias</UserId>

4. In the Task Scheduler, click **Import Task** on the **Action** menu.
5. Click the sample task .xml file. For example, click **Extend.xml**.
6. Click **Import**.
7. Click the **Triggers** tab.
8. Click the **One Time** trigger, and then click **Edit**.
9. Change the start date of the task to a date just before the end of your current evaluation period.
10. Click **OK**, and then exit the Task Scheduler.

The Task Scheduler will now run the evaluation reset operation on the date that you specified.

Preparing to Take the Microsoft Certified Technology Specialist (MCTS) Exam

The Microsoft Certified Technology Specialist (MCTS) certifications enable professionals to target specific technologies and to distinguish themselves by demonstrating in-depth knowledge and expertise in their specialized technologies. Microsoft Certified Technology Specialists are consistently capable of implementing, building, troubleshooting, and debugging a particular Microsoft Technology.

For organizations, the new generation of Microsoft certifications provides better skills verification tools that help with assessing not only in-demand skills on Windows Server, but also the ability to quickly complete on-the-job tasks. Individuals will find it easier to identify and work towards the certification credential that meets their personal and professional goals.

To learn more about becoming a Microsoft Certified Professional and exam availability, visit www.microsoft.com/learning/mcp.

Microsoft Certifications for IT Professionals

The new Microsoft Certified Technology Specialist (MCTS) and Microsoft Certified IT Professional (MCITP) credentials provide IT professionals with a simpler and more targeted framework to showcase their technical skills in addition to the skills that are required for specific developer job roles.

The Microsoft Certified Database Administrator (MCDBA), Microsoft Certified Desktop Support Technician (MCDST), Microsoft Certified System Administrator (MCSA), and Microsoft Certified Systems Engineer (MCSE) credentials continue to provide IT professionals who use Microsoft SQL Server 2000, Windows XP, and Windows Server 2003 with industry recognition and validation of their IT skills and experience.

Microsoft Certified Technology Specialist

The new Microsoft Certified Tehnology Specialist (MCTS) credential highlights your skills using a specific Microsoft technology. You can demonstrate your abilities as an IT professional or developer with in-depth knowledge of the Microsoft technology that you use today or are planning to deploy.

The MCTS certifications enable professionals to target specific technologies and to distinguish themselves by demonstrating in-depth knowledge and expertise in their specialized technologies. Microsoft Certified Technology Specialists are consistently capable of implementing, building, troubleshooting, and debugging a particular Microsoft technology.

You can learn more about the MCTS program at www.microsoft.com/learning/mcp/mcts.

Microsoft Certified IT Professional

The new Microsoft Certified IT Professional (MCITP) credential lets you highlight your specific area of expertise. Now, you can easily distinguish yourself as an expert in database administration, database development, business intelligence, or support.

By becoming certified, you demonstrate to employers that you have achieved a predictable level of skill not only in the use of the Windows Server operating system, but with a comprehensive set of Microsoft technologies. Employers often require certification either as a condition of employment or as a condition of advancement within the company or other organization.

You can learn more about the MCITP program at www.microsoft.com/learning/mcp/mcitp.

The certification examinations are sponsored by Microsoft but administered through Microsoft's exam delivery partner Prometric.

Preparing to Take an Exam

Unless you are a very experienced user, you will need to use a test preparation course to prepare to complete the test correctly and within the time allowed. The *Microsoft Official Academic Course* series is designed to prepare you with a strong knowledge of all exam topics, and with some additional review and practice on your own, you should feel confident in your ability to pass the appropriate exam.

After you decide which exam to take, review the list of objectives for the exam. You can easily identify tasks that are included in the objective list by locating the Objective Domain Matrix at the start of each lesson and the Certification Ready sidebars in the margin of the lessons in this book.

To take the MCTS test, visit www.microsoft.com/learning/mcp/mcts to locate your nearest testing center. Then call the testing center directly to schedule your test. The amount of advance notice you should provide will vary for different testing centers, and it typically depends on the number of computers available at the testing center, the number of other testers who have already been scheduled for the day on which you want to take the test, and the number of times per week that the testing center offers MCTS testing. In general, you should call to schedule your test at least two weeks prior to the date on which you want to take the test.

When you arrive at the testing center, you might be asked for proof of identity. A driver's license or passport is an acceptable form of identification. If you do not have either of these items of documentation, call your testing center and ask what alternative forms of identification will be accepted. If you are retaking a test, bring your MCTS identification number, which will have been given to you when you previously took the test. If you have not prepaid or if your organization has not already arranged to make payment for you, you will need to pay the test taking fee when you arrive.

Student CD

The CD-ROM included with this book contains five practice exams that will help you hone your knowledge before you take the MCTS Windows Server 2008 Network Infrastructure, Configuring (Exam 70-642) certification examination. Each exam has between 40 and 50 questions and is timed for 90 minutes. The exams are meant to provide practice for your certification exam and are also good reinforcement of the material covered in the course.

The enclosed Student CD will run automatically. Upon accepting the license agreement, you will proceed directly to the exams. The exams also can be accessed through the Assets folder located within the CD files.

Acknowledgments

MOAC Instructor Advisory Board

We would like to thank our Instructor Advisory Board, an elite group of educators who has assisted us every step of the way in building these products. Advisory Board members have acted as our sounding board on key pedagogical and design decisions leading to the development of these compelling and innovative textbooks for future Information Workers. Their dedication to technology education is truly appreciated.

Charles DeSassure, Tarrant County College

Charles DeSassure is Department Chair and Instructor of Computer Science & Information Technology at Tarrant County College Southeast Campus, Arlington, Texas. He has had experience as a MIS Manager, system analyst, field technology analyst, LAN Administrator, microcomputer specialist, and public school teacher in South Carolina. DeSassure has worked in higher education for more than ten years and received the Excellence Award in Teaching from the National Institute for Staff and Organizational Development (NISOD). He currently serves on the Educational Testing Service (ETS) iSkills National Advisory Committee and chaired the Tarrant County College District Student Assessment Committee. He has written proposals and makes presentations at major educational conferences nationwide. DeSassure has served as a textbook reviewer for John Wiley & Sons and Prentice Hall. He teaches courses in information security, networking, distance learning, and computer literacy. DeSassure holds a master's degree in Computer Resources & Information Management from Webster University.

Kim Ehlert, Waukesha County Technical College

Kim Ehlert is the Microsoft Program Coordinator and a Network Specialist instructor at Waukesha County Technical College, teaching the full range of MCSE and networking courses for the past nine years. Prior to joining WCTC, Kim was a professor at the Milwaukee School of Engineering for five years where she oversaw the Novell Academic Education and the Microsoft IT Academy programs. She has a wide variety of industry experience including network design and management for Johnson Controls, local city fire departments, police departments, large church congregations, health departments, and accounting firms. Kim holds many industry certifications including MCDST, MCSE, Security+, Network+, Server+, MCT, and CNE.

Kim has a bachelor's degree in Information Systems and a master's degree in Business Administration from the University of Wisconsin Milwaukee. When she is not busy teaching, she enjoys spending time with her husband Gregg and their two children—Alex, 14, and Courtney, 17.

Penny Gudgeon, Corinthian Colleges, Inc.

Penny Gudgeon is the Program Manager for IT curriculum at Corinthian Colleges, Inc. Previously, she was responsible for computer programming and web curriculum for twenty-seven campuses in Corinthian's Canadian division, CDI College of Business, Technology and Health Care. Penny joined CDI College in 1997 as a computer programming instructor at one of the campuses outside of Toronto. Prior to joining CDI College, Penny taught productivity software at another Canadian college, the Academy of Learning, for four years. Penny has experience in helping students achieve their goals through various learning models from instructor-led to self-directed to online.

**www.wiley.com/college/microsoft or
call the MOAC Toll-Free Number: 1+(888) 764-7001 (U.S. & Canada only)**

Before embarking on a career in education, Penny worked in the fields of advertising, marketing/sales, mechanical and electronic engineering technology, and computer programming. When not working from her home office or indulging her passion for lifelong learning, Penny likes to read mysteries, garden, and relax at home in Hamilton, Ontario, with her Shih-Tzu, Gracie.

Margaret Leary, Northern Virginia Community College

Margaret Leary is Professor of IST at Northern Virginia Community College, teaching Networking and Network Security Courses for the past ten years. She is the co-Principal Investigator on the CyberWATCH initiative, an NSF-funded regional consortium of higher education institutions and businesses working together to increase the number of network security personnel in the workforce. She also serves as a Senior Security Policy Manager and Research Analyst at Nortel Government Solutions and holds a CISSP certification.

Margaret holds a B.S.B.A. and MBA/Technology Management from the University of Phoenix, and is pursuing her Ph.D. in Organization and Management with an IT Specialization at Capella University. Her dissertation is titled "Quantifying the Discoverability of Identity Attributes in Internet-Based Public Records: Impact on Identity Theft and Knowledge-based Authentication." She has several other published articles in various government and industry magazines, notably on identity management and network security.

Wen Liu, ITT Educational Services, Inc.

Wen Liu is Director of Corporate Curriculum Development at ITT Educational Services, Inc. He joined the ITT corporate headquarters in 1998 as a Senior Network Analyst to plan and deploy the corporate WAN infrastructure. A year later he assumed the position of Corporate Curriculum Manager supervising the curriculum development of all IT programs. After he was promoted to the current position three years ago, he continued to manage the curriculum research and development for all the programs offered in the School of Information Technology in addition to supervising the curriculum development in other areas (such as Schools of Drafting and Design and Schools of Electronics Technology). Prior to his employment with ITT Educational Services, Liu was a Telecommunications Analyst at the state government of Indiana working on the state backbone project that provided Internet and telecommunications services to the public users such as K-12 and higher education institutions, government agencies, libraries, and healthcare facilities.

Wen Liu has an M.A. in Student Personnel Administration in Higher Education and an M.S. in Information and Communications Sciences from Ball State University, Indiana. He used to be the director of special projects on the board of directors of the Indiana Telecommunications User Association, and used to serve on Course Technology's IT Advisory Board. He is currently a member of the IEEE and its Computer Society.

Jared Spencer, Westwood College Online

Jared Spencer has been the Lead Faculty for Networking at Westwood College Online since 2006. He began teaching in 2001 and has taught both on-ground and online for a variety of institutions, including Robert Morris University and Point Park University. In addition to his academic background, he has more than fifteen years of industry experience working for companies including the Thomson Corporation and IBM.

Jared has a master's degree in Internet Information Systems and is currently ABD and pursuing his doctorate in Information Systems at Nova Southeastern University. He has authored several papers that have been presented at conferences and appeared in publications such as the Journal of Internet Commerce and the Journal of Information Privacy and Security (JIPC). He holds a number of industry certifications, including AIX (UNIX), A+, Network+, Security+, MCSA on Windows 2000, and MCSA on Windows 2003 Server.

MOAC Windows Server Reviewers

We also thank the many reviewers who pored over the manuscript, providing invaluable feedback in the service of quality instructional materials.

Windows Server® 2008 Network Infrastructure Configuration Exam 70-642

Fidelis Ngang, Houston Community College

John Crowley, Bucks County Community College

Brian Bridson, Baker College of Flint

Focus Group and Survey Participants

Finally, we thank the hundreds of instructors who participated in our focus groups and surveys to ensure that the Microsoft Official Academic Courses best met the needs of our customers.

Jean Aguilar, Mt. Hood Community College

Konrad Akens, Zane State College

Michael Albers, University of Memphis

Diana Anderson, Big Sandy Community & Technical College

Phyllis Anderson, Delaware County Community College

Judith Andrews, Feather River College

Damon Antos, American River College

Bridget Archer, Oakton Community College

Linda Arnold, Harrisburg Area Community College–Lebanon Campus

Neha Arya, Fullerton College

Mohammad Bajwa, Katharine Gibbs School–New York

Virginia Baker, University of Alaska Fairbanks

Carla Bannick, Pima Community College

Rita Barkley, Northeast Alabama Community College

Elsa Barr, Central Community College–Hastings

Ronald W. Barry, Ventura County Community College District

Elizabeth Bastedo, Central Carolina Technical College

Karen Baston, Waubonsee Community College

Karen Bean, Blinn College

Scott Beckstrand, Community College of Southern Nevada

Paulette Bell, Santa Rosa Junior College

Liz Bennett, Southeast Technical Institute

Nancy Bermea, Olympic College

Lucy Betz, Milwaukee Area Technical College

Meral Binbasioglu, Hofstra University

Catherine Binder, Strayer University & Katharine Gibbs School–Philadelphia

Terrel Blair, El Centro College

Ruth Blalock, Alamance Community College

Beverly Bohner, Reading Area Community College

Henry Bojack, Farmingdale State University

Matthew Bowie, Luna Community College

Julie Boyles, Portland Community College

Karen Brandt, College of the Albemarle

Stephen Brown, College of San Mateo

Jared Bruckner, Southern Adventist University

Pam Brune, Chattanooga State Technical Community College

Sue Buchholz, Georgia Perimeter College

Roberta Buczyna, Edison College

Angela Butler, Mississippi Gulf Coast Community College

Rebecca Byrd, Augusta Technical College

Kristen Callahan, Mercer County Community College

Judy Cameron, Spokane Community College

Dianne Campbell, Athens Technical College

Gena Casas, Florida Community College at Jacksonville

Jesus Castrejon, Latin Technologies

Gail Chambers, Southwest Tennessee Community College

Jacques Chansavang, Indiana University–Purdue University Fort Wayne

Nancy Chapko, Milwaukee Area Technical College

Rebecca Chavez, Yavapai College

Sanjiv Chopra, Thomas Nelson Community College

Greg Clements, Midland Lutheran College

Dayna Coker, Southwestern Oklahoma State University–Sayre Campus

Tamra Collins, Otero Junior College

Janet Conrey, Gavilan Community College

Carol Cornforth, West Virginia Northern Community College

Gary Cotton, American River College

Edie Cox, Chattahoochee Technical College

Rollie Cox, Madison Area Technical College

David Crawford, Northwestern Michigan College

J.K. Crowley, Victor Valley College

Rosalyn Culver, Washtenaw Community College

Sharon Custer, Huntington University

Sandra Daniels, New River Community College

Anila Das, Cedar Valley College

Brad Davis, Santa Rosa Junior College

Susan Davis, Green River Community College

Mark Dawdy, Lincoln Land Community College

Jennifer Day, Sinclair Community College

Carol Deane, Eastern Idaho Technical College

Julie DeBuhr, Lewis-Clark State College

Janis DeHaven, Central Community College

Drew Dekreon, University of Alaska–Anchorage

Joy DePover, Central Lakes College

Salli DiBartolo, Brevard Community College

Melissa Diegnau, Riverland Community College

Al Dillard, Lansdale School of Business

Marjorie Duffy, Cosumnes River College

Sarah Dunn, Southwest Tennessee Community College

Shahla Durany, Tarrant County College– South Campus

Kay Durden, University of Tennessee at Martin

Dineen Ebert, St. Louis Community College–Meramec

Donna Ehrhart, State University of New York–Brockport

Larry Elias, Montgomery County Community College

Glenda Elser, New Mexico State University at Alamogordo

Angela Evangelinos, Monroe County Community College

Angie Evans, Ivy Tech Community College of Indiana

Linda Farrington, Indian Hills Community College

Dana Fladhammer, Phoenix College

Richard Flores, Citrus College

Connie Fox, Community and Technical College at Institute of Technology West Virginia University

Wanda Freeman, Okefenokee Technical College

Brenda Freeman, Augusta Technical College

Susan Fry, Boise State University

Roger Fulk, Wright State University–Lake Campus

Sue Furnas, Collin County Community College District

Sandy Gabel, Vernon College

Laura Galvan, Fayetteville Technical Community College

Candace Garrod, Red Rocks Community College

Sherrie Geitgey, Northwest State Community College

Chris Gerig, Chattahoochee Technical College

Barb Gillespie, Cuyamaca College

Jessica Gilmore, Highline Community College

Pamela Gilmore, Reedley College

Debbie Glinert, Queensborough Community College

Steven Goldman, Polk Community College

Bettie Goodman, C.S. Mott Community College

Mike Grabill, Katharine Gibbs School– Philadelphia

Francis Green, Penn State University

Walter Griffin, Blinn College

Fillmore Guinn, Odessa College

Helen Haasch, Milwaukee Area Technical College

John Habal, Ventura College

Joy Haerens, Chaffey College

Norman Hahn, Thomas Nelson Community College

Kathy Hall, Alamance Community College

Teri Harbacheck, Boise State University

Linda Harper, Richland Community College

Maureen Harper, Indian Hills Community College

Steve Harris, Katharine Gibbs School–New York

Robyn Hart, Fresno City College

Darien Hartman, Boise State University

Gina Hatcher, Tacoma Community College

Winona T. Hatcher, Aiken Technical College

BJ Hathaway, Northeast Wisconsin Tech College

Cynthia Hauki, West Hills College – Coalinga

Mary L. Haynes, Wayne County Community College

Marcie Hawkins, Zane State College

Steve Hebrock, Ohio State University Agricultural Technical Institute

Sue Heistand, Iowa Central Community College

Heith Hennel, Valencia Community College

Donna Hendricks, South Arkansas Community College

Judy Hendrix, Dyersburg State Community College

Gloria Hensel, Matanuska-Susitna College University of Alaska Anchorage

Gwendolyn Hester, Richland College

**www.wiley.com/college/microsoft or
call the MOAC Toll-Free Number: 1+(888) 764-7001 (U.S. & Canada only)**

Tammarra Holmes, Laramie County Community College

Dee Hobson, Richland College

Keith Hoell, Katharine Gibbs School–New York

Pashia Hogan, Northeast State Technical Community College

Susan Hoggard, Tulsa Community College

Kathleen Holliman, Wallace Community College Selma

Chastity Honchul, Brown Mackie College/ Wright State University

Christie Hovey, Lincoln Land Community College

Peggy Hughes, Allegany College of Maryland

Sandra Hume, Chippewa Valley Technical College

John Hutson, Aims Community College

Celia Ing, Sacramento City College

Joan Ivey, Lanier Technical College

Barbara Jaffari, College of the Redwoods

Penny Jakes, University of Montana College of Technology

Eduardo Jaramillo, Peninsula College

Barbara Jauken, Southeast Community College

Susan Jennings, Stephen F. Austin State University

Leslie Jernberg, Eastern Idaho Technical College

Linda Johns, Georgia Perimeter College

Brent Johnson, Okefenokee Technical College

Mary Johnson, Mt. San Antonio College

Shirley Johnson, Trinidad State Junior College–Valley Campus

Sandra M. Jolley, Tarrant County College

Teresa Jolly, South Georgia Technical College

Dr. Deborah Jones, South Georgia Technical College

Margie Jones, Central Virginia Community College

Randall Jones, Marshall Community and Technical College

Diane Karlsbraaten, Lake Region State College

Teresa Keller, Ivy Tech Community College of Indiana

Charles Kemnitz, Pennsylvania College of Technology

Sandra Kinghorn, Ventura College

Bill Klein, Katharine Gibbs School–Philadelphia

Bea Knaapen, Fresno City College

Kit Kofoed, Western Wyoming Community College

Maria Kolatis, County College of Morris

Barry Kolb, Ocean County College

Karen Kuralt, University of Arkansas at Little Rock

Belva-Carole Lamb, Rogue Community College

Betty Lambert, Des Moines Area Community College

Anita Lande, Cabrillo College

Junnae Landry, Pratt Community College

Karen Lankisch, UC Clermont

David Lanzilla, Central Florida Community College

Nora Laredo, Cerritos Community College

Jennifer Larrabee, Chippewa Valley Technical College

Debra Larson, Idaho State University

Barb Lave, Portland Community College

Audrey Lawrence, Tidewater Community College

Deborah Layton, Eastern Oklahoma State College

Larry LeBlanc, Owen Graduate School– Vanderbilt University

Philip Lee, Nashville State Community College

Michael Lehrfeld, Brevard Community College

Vasant Limaye, Southwest Collegiate Institute for the Deaf – Howard College

Anne C. Lewis, Edgecombe Community College

Stephen Linkin, Houston Community College

Peggy Linston, Athens Technical College

Hugh Lofton, Moultrie Technical College

Donna Lohn, Lakeland Community College

Jackie Lou, Lake Tahoe Community College

Donna Love, Gaston College

Curt Lynch, Ozarks Technical Community College

Sheilah Lynn, Florida Community College– Jacksonville

Pat R. Lyon, Tomball College

Bill Madden, Bergen Community College

Heather Madden, Delaware Technical & Community College

Donna Madsen, Kirkwood Community College

Jane Maringer-Cantu, Gavilan College

Suzanne Marks, Bellevue Community College

Carol Martin, Louisiana State University– Alexandria

Cheryl Martucci, Diablo Valley College

Roberta Marvel, Eastern Wyoming College

Tom Mason, Brookdale Community College

Mindy Mass, Santa Barbara City College

Dixie Massaro, Irvine Valley College

Rebekah May, Ashland Community & Technical College

Emma Mays-Reynolds, Dyersburg State Community College

Timothy Mayes, Metropolitan State College of Denver

Reggie McCarthy, Central Lakes College

Matt McCaskill, Brevard Community College

Kevin McFarlane, Front Range Community College

Donna McGill, Yuba Community College

Terri McKeever, Ozarks Technical Community College

Patricia McMahon, South Suburban College

Sally McMillin, Katharine Gibbs School–Philadelphia

Charles McNerney, Bergen Community College

Lisa Mears, Palm Beach Community College

Imran Mehmood, ITT Technical Institute–King of Prussia Campus

Virginia Melvin, Southwest Tennessee Community College

Jeanne Mercer, Texas State Technical College

Denise Merrell, Jefferson Community & Technical College

Catherine Merrikin, Pearl River Community College

Diane D. Mickey, Northern Virginia Community College

Darrelyn Miller, Grays Harbor College

Sue Mitchell, Calhoun Community College

Jacquie Moldenhauer, Front Range Community College

Linda Motonaga, Los Angeles City College

Sam Mryyan, Allen County Community College

Cindy Murphy, Southeastern Community College

Ryan Murphy, Sinclair Community College

Sharon E. Nastav, Johnson County Community College

Christine Naylor, Kent State University Ashtabula

Haji Nazarian, Seattle Central Community College

Nancy Noe, Linn-Benton Community College

Jennie Noriega, San Joaquin Delta College

Linda Nutter, Peninsula College

Thomas Omerza, Middle Bucks Institute of Technology

Edith Orozco, St. Philip's College

Dona Orr, Boise State University

Joanne Osgood, Chaffey College

Janice Owens, Kishwaukee College

Tatyana Pashnyak, Bainbridge College

John Partacz, College of DuPage

Tim Paul, Montana State University–Great Falls

Joseph Perez, South Texas College

Mike Peterson, Chemeketa Community College

Dr. Karen R. Petitto, West Virginia Wesleyan College

Terry Pierce, Onandaga Community College

Ashlee Pieris, Raritan Valley Community College

Jamie Pinchot, Thiel College

Michelle Poertner, Northwestern Michigan College

Betty Posta, University of Toledo

Deborah Powell, West Central Technical College

Mark Pranger, Rogers State University

Carolyn Rainey, Southeast Missouri State University

Linda Raskovich, Hibbing Community College

Leslie Ratliff, Griffin Technical College

Mar-Sue Ratzke, Rio Hondo Community College

Roxy Reissen, Southeastern Community College

Silvio Reyes, Technical Career Institutes

Patricia Rishavy, Anoka Technical College

Jean Robbins, Southeast Technical Institute

Carol Roberts, Eastern Maine Community College and University of Maine

Teresa Roberts, Wilson Technical Community College

Vicki Robertson, Southwest Tennessee Community College

Betty Rogge, Ohio State Agricultural Technical Institute

Lynne Rusley, Missouri Southern State University

Claude Russo, Brevard Community College

Ginger Sabine, Northwestern Technical College

Steven Sachs, Los Angeles Valley College

Joanne Salas, Olympic College

Lloyd Sandmann, Pima Community College–Desert Vista Campus

Beverly Santillo, Georgia Perimeter College

Theresa Savarese, San Diego City College

Sharolyn Sayers, Milwaukee Area Technical College

Judith Scheeren, Westmoreland County Community College

Adolph Scheiwe, Joliet Junior College

Marilyn Schmid, Asheville-Buncombe Technical Community College

Janet Sebesy, Cuyahoga Community College

Phyllis T. Shafer, Brookdale Community College

Ralph Shafer, Truckee Meadows Community College

Anne Marie Shanley, County College of Morris

Shelia Shelton, Surry Community College

Merilyn Shepherd, Danville Area Community College

Susan Sinele, Aims Community College

Beth Sindt, Hawkeye Community College

Andrew Smith, Marian College

Brenda Smith, Southwest Tennessee Community College

Lynne Smith, State University of New York–Delhi

Rob Smith, Katharine Gibbs School–Philadelphia

Tonya Smith, Arkansas State University–Mountain Home

Del Spencer – Trinity Valley Community College

Jeri Spinner, Idaho State University

Eric Stadnik, Santa Rosa Junior College

Karen Stanton, Los Medanos College

Meg Stoner, Santa Rosa Junior College

Beverly Stowers, Ivy Tech Community College of Indiana

Marcia Stranix, Yuba College

Kim Styles, Tri-County Technical College

Sylvia Summers, Tacoma Community College

Beverly Swann, Delaware Technical & Community College

Ann Taff, Tulsa Community College

Mike Theiss, University of Wisconsin–Marathon Campus

Romy Thiele, Cañada College

Sharron Thompson, Portland Community College

Ingrid Thompson-Sellers, Georgia Perimeter College

Barbara Tietsort, University of Cincinnati–Raymond Walters College

Janine Tiffany, Reading Area Community College

Denise Tillery, University of Nevada Las Vegas

Susan Trebelhorn, Normandale Community College

Noel Trout, Santiago Canyon College

Cheryl Turgeon, Asnuntuck Community College

Steve Turner, Ventura College

Sylvia Unwin, Bellevue Community College

Lilly Vigil, Colorado Mountain College

Sabrina Vincent, College of the Mainland

Mary Vitrano, Palm Beach Community College

Brad Vogt, Northeast Community College

Cozell Wagner, Southeastern Community College

Carolyn Walker, Tri-County Technical College

Sherry Walker, Tulsa Community College

Qi Wang, Tacoma Community College

Betty Wanielista, Valencia Community College

Marge Warber, Lanier Technical College–Forsyth Campus

Marjorie Webster, Bergen Community College

Linda Wenn, Central Community College

Mark Westlund, Olympic College

Carolyn Whited, Roane State Community College

Winona Whited, Richland College

Jerry Wilkerson, Scott Community College

Joel Willenbring, Fullerton College

Barbara Williams, WITC Superior

Charlotte Williams, Jones County Junior College

Bonnie Willy, Ivy Tech Community College of Indiana

Diane Wilson, J. Sargeant Reynolds Community College

James Wolfe, Metropolitan Community College

Marjory Wooten, Lanier Technical College

Mark Yanko, Hocking College

Alexis Yusov, Pace University

Naeem Zaman, San Joaquin Delta College

Kathleen Zimmerman, Des Moines Area Community College

We also thank Lutz Ziob, Jim DiIanni, Merrick Van Dongen, Jim LeValley, Bruce Curling, Joe Wilson, Rob Linsky, Jim Clark, Jim Palmeri, and Scott Serna at Microsoft for their encouragement and support in making the Microsoft Official Academic Course programs the finest instructional materials for mastering the newest Microsoft technologies for both students and instructors.

CONTENTS

Introduction to Networking Concepts

OBJECTIVE DOMAIN MATRIX

TECHNOLOGY SKILL	OBJECTIVE DOMAIN	OBJECTIVE DOMAIN NUMBER
Configuring IPv4 and IPv6 addressing	Configure IPv4 and IPv6 addressing	1.1

KEY TERMS

Automatic Private IP Addressing (APIPA)
CIDR notation
classful addressing
Classless Inter-Domain Routing (CIDR)
default gateway
DHCP relay agent above
dotted-decimal notation
Dynamic Host Configuration Protocol (DHCP)
fully qualified domain name (FQDN)

host
host address
HOSTS files
Internet Service Providers (ISPs)
IP address
IP version 4 (IPv4)
IP version 6 (IPv6)
name resolution
network address
network address translation (NAT)
network protocols

octets
routing
static IP address
subnet mask
subnets
subnetting
Transmission Control Protocol/Internet Protocol (TCP/IP)

Engulf & Devour (E&D) is a fast-growing, venture-funded new media company, specializing in acquiring smaller, technology-based media companies and integrating their operations to benefit from economies of scale. As a network-based, consumer market–driven enterprise, E&D must manage the assimilation of technical environments from acquired companies without disrupting network operations and still provide the efficiencies promised to the venture capitalists backing the corporation. Network accessibility must be maintained to provide service levels expected by consumers, while adding new systems, retiring obsolete systems, and redeploying existing systems. Network address management and name resolution tools are fundamental requirements for this situation. In this lesson you will learn the basic concepts of network address management and name resolution.

In this lesson we will begin our discussion of Windows Server 2008 with an overview of general TCP/IP networking concepts. The lesson begins with a discussion of the TCP/IP protocol, focusing on how IPv4 and IPv6 IP addresses are managed and configured. Once we have concluded our overview of TCP/IP addressing, we will take an introductory look at a number of networking services offered by Windows Server 2008, including the Domain Name System (DNS), the Dynamic Host Configuration Protocol (DHCP), the Routing & Remote Access (RRAS) service, and the Network Access Protection (NAP) service. This lesson is meant to provide an introduction only to DNS, DHCP, RRAS, and NAP; each of these will be discussed at length in later lessons in this text.

■ Understanding TCP/IP Addressing

THE BOTTOM LINE

From as early as the 1950s, one of the main challenges in the field of computer science has been finding ways to allow different computers to communicate with one another. Before networking technologies became prevalent, files would be transferred manually from one computer to another using portable media such as a floppy disk. Over time, this process was replaced by various networking technologies that allowed computers to communicate using different types of network cables, which are the physical means of communicating, as well as *network protocols*, which provide the logical "language" for communication. Just like two human beings must speak the same language in order to communicate, two computers must be configured with the same network protocols in order to communicate and transfer information. Numerous networking protocols have gained varying levels of prevalence over the years, but the most common networking protocol in use today is *Transmission Control Protocol/Internet Protocol (TCP/IP)*. Rather than a single network protocol, TCP/IP consists of a suite of different protocols that work in concert to allow computers to communicate on a TCP/IP network. TCP/IP networks are arranged in a hierarchical fashion that allows for a great deal of flexibility and scalability; by subdividing TCP/IP networks into smaller groupings called *subnets*, the administration of a TCP/IP network can be as centralized or as decentralized as the needs of a particular organization might dictate. (You can see this in action in the largest TCP/IP network in the world, which is "owned" and administered by hundreds and thousands of separate entities. The name of this TCP/IP network? The Internet.) This lesson introduces fundamental concepts related to TCP/IP networking, including the fundamentals of IP network addressing, and the distinction between IPv4 and IPv6. The lesson also introduces the basic concepts of various TCP/IP network services such as DHCP, DNS, and *routing*, the process of transferring data across a network from one LAN to another.

In order for any computer or *host*, a computer, printer, or other device configured with a network interface, to communicate on a TCP/IP network, it must be configured with a valid *IP address*. This IP address, analogous to the postal address of a house or an office building, provides a way to identify a device that is connected to a TCP/IP network and provides a means for one computer to contact another in order to transmit information. Each IP address consists of two components:

- *network address*—This portion of the IP address is shared by all TCP/IP hosts on a particular network or subnet.
- *host address*—This comprises the portion of the IP address that is unique to a particular computer or host. The combination of the network address plus the host address creates the IP address as a whole, each of which must be unique across an entire TCP/IP network.

In addition to the IP address, each TCP/IP host must be configured with the following:

- *subnet mask*—Used to identify which network the TCP/IP host resides on by defining where the network address stops and the host address begins.
- *default gateway*—Allows a host to communicate with devices that reside on a remote network or location. (On the extremely rare occasion when you are configuring hosts that never need to communicate outside of their own subnet, a default gateway is not required; however, with the prevalence of Internet connectivity, you will almost always find a default gateway configured on TCP/IP-enabled devices.)

Router ←

Introducing TCP/IP Addressing

The TCP/IP protocol suite has undergone several revisions since it was first developed in the 1960s. The version of TCP/IP that is most commonly used on modern networks is *IP version 4(IPv4)*. *IP version 6 (IPv6)* is a new TCP/IP implementation that is increasing in prevalence, as it addresses a number of shortcomings that have appeared in IPv4 over time. IPv4 was the first implementation of the Internet Protocol (IP) to be widely deployed, predating the public Internet. It uses 32 bits (four bytes, or *octets*) for addressing, thus providing a mathematical limit of 2^{32} possible addresses. Some of the possible addresses are reserved (for example, for private networks or multicast addresses), so that the maximum number of possible network addresses is somewhat less than the theoretical maximum. IPv4 addresses are commonly represented using what is called *dotted-decimal notation*, in which the decimal value of each byte is shown, using periods to separate the bytes; for example, 192.1.120.84 or 192.5.18.102 would be IPv4 addresses in dotted-decimal notation.

When IPv4 was first introduced, only the first octet was used for the network number and the remaining three octets were used for the host number. This limited the number of possible networks to a maximum of 254, which was quickly seen to be inadequate. The next revision defined what is termed *classful addressing*, in which the field for the network number was a different length for different classes of network, and the remaining bits were used for the host number, so each network class had a different maximum number of nodes. As shown in Table 1-1, the first one to four bits identified the network class, and the remaining bits comprised the network and host address fields. Class A networks had the most significant bit as "0" and used the remainder of the first octet for the network number. Thus there were 126 Class A networks, with a maximum of 16,777,214 hosts in each. Note that the number of valid networks and hosts available is always $2^N - 2$ (where N is the number of bits used, and the 2 adjusts for the special function of the first and last address in each network). Class B networks had the two most significant bits as "10," with the remainder of the first two octets, or fourteen bits, representing the network number. Thus there were 16,384 Class B networks, with a maximum of 65,534 hosts in each. Class C networks had the three most significant bits as "110," with the remainder of the first three octets as the network number and the last octet as the host number. Thus there were 2,097,152 Class C networks, each with a maximum of 254 host addresses. Network addresses with the four most significant bits "1110" (Class D, multicast) and "1111" (Class E, reserved) were also defined.

Table 1-1

IP Network Classes

Network Class	Leading Bits	Bits for Network Number	Number of Networks	Bits for Host Number	Maximum Hosts
Class A	0	7	126	24	16,777,214
Class B	10	14	16,384	16	65,534
Class C	110	21	2,097,152	8	254
Class D (multicast)	1110				
Class E (reserved)	1111				

Using this classful addressing scheme created a few large networks with many possible host addresses, and a much larger number of small networks with fewer possible host addresses, so it was considerably more flexible. However, there were still problems and limitations in this design. Some networks required more host addresses than their network class allowed, and other networks had many more host addresses than they used.

To overcome these issues and to improve flexibility for public *Internet Service Providers (ISPs)* to allocate many small networks to their customers, *Classless Inter-Domain Routing (CIDR)* evolved. CIDR creates a hierarchical addressing structure by breaking the network address space into CIDR blocks, which are identified by the leading bit string, similar to the classful addressing just described. However, the length of the bit string identifying a CIDR block is specified as part of the block name, using *CIDR notation*. CIDR notation describes a network by specifying the base address and the number of bits used for the network portion; i.e., 10.0.0.0/8 would describe a network using 24 bits for host numbering and thus having a maximum of $2^{24} -2$ possible host addresses. The CIDR notation can be viewed as representing a bitmask dividing the routing (network) information and a block of local addresses. The classful networking address structure can also be described using CIDR notation, as shown in Table 1-2.

Table 1-2

CIDR Representation of Classful Addresses

NETWORK CLASS	STARTING ADDRESS	ENDING ADDRESS	CIDR BLOCK	BITMASK
Class A	0.0.0.0	127.255.255.255	/8	255.0.0.0
Class B	128.0.0.0	191.255.255.255	/16	255.255.0.0
Class C	192.0.0.0	223.255.255.255	/24	255.255.255.0
Class D (multicast)	224.0.0.0	239.255.255.255	/4	
Class E (reserved)	240.0.0.0	255.255.255.255	/4	

This hierarchical structure can be even further divided by *subnetting*. Subnetting refers to the logical partitioning of an organization's network address range into smaller blocks, by using a subnet mask to further distinguish the contents of the network address as a subnet number and a subnet address block. CIDR can be viewed as a method of subnetting the entire public IP address space, essentially carving it up into blocks that can be managed by service providers. A subnet mask is analogous to defining CIDR blocks within internal networks, allowing ISPs to delegate address management within the blocks assigned to their customers. Thus the CIDR block number contains information required for external routing, and the subnet mask distinguishes information required for routing internally from the host numbers (or hierarchical subnet addresses) contained within the subnet.

A big advantage of subnetting is that systems within a subnet need not be burdened with information about external network addressing. Systems within the same subnet share the same network address, so they can communicate directly without additional information about the external network. A default gateway is then used to route traffic for addresses outside the local subnet. Only the gateway requires any information about external network addressing.

For convenience, several network address blocks were reserved for private networks, and they were defined to be non-routable outside of the private network. Hosts using private network addresses can communicate with public networks only by using *network address translation (NAT)*, which enables routing by mapping their private network address to a different, routable network address. The private IPv4 network address ranges are shown in Table 1-3.

Table 1-3

Private Network Address Ranges

ADDRESS RANGE	DESCRIPTION	MAXIMUM ADDRESSES	CLASSFUL DESCRIPTION	CIDR DESCRIPTION
10.0.0.0 – 10.255.255.255	24-bit block	16,777,216	Single Class A network	10.0.0.0/8
172.16.0.0 – 172.31.255.255	20-bit block	1,048,576	16 contiguous Class B networks	172.16.0.0/12
169.254.0.0 – 169.254.255.255	16-bit block	65,536	256 contiguous Class C networks	169.254.0.0/16
192.168.0.0 – 192.168.255.255	16-bit block	65,536	256 contiguous Class C networks	192.168.0.0/16

Introducing IP version 6 (IPv6)

With the popularization of the public Internet, the limitations of the address space, that is, the list of usable TCP/IP addresses, provided by IPv4 became a concern. When IPv4 reached prevalence in the 1960s, no one foresaw the Internet explosion of the 1990s that would threaten to exhaust even the 4-billion-plus IP addresses available through IPv4. While the use of private IP networks and NAT have alleviated the problem somewhat, a long-term solution is still required. To this end, *IPv6*, the next generation of the TCP/IP protocol, was developed to provide a significantly larger address space for current and future implementations of TCP/IP networks.

IPv6 uses 128 bits, or 16 bytes, for addressing, thus providing 2^{128} (about 340 billion) unique addresses. To put this in perspective, the IPv6 address space would allow each human being on the planet Earth to possess multiple IPv6 IP addresses that were assigned only to them, without ever being re-used.

IPv6 address notation is noticeably different from the dotted-decimal of IPv4, using eight groups of four hexadecimal digits, separated by colons. IPv6 includes a few other enhancements for performance and security. Notably, IP security through the use of IPSec is an integral part of IPv6, whereas it was an optional feature under IPv4.

XREF

IPSec is a suite of protocols for establishing cryptographic keys and using them to secure IP communications, which we will discuss at length later in this text.

Unlike IPv4 addresses, which are 32 bits in length and expressed in dotted-decimal notation, IPv6 addresses are 128 bits in length and expressed in hexadecimal notation. For example, `192.168.1.101` is an example of an IPv4 IP address, while `2001:0db8:85a3:08d3:13 19:8a2e:0370:7334` is an example of an IPv6 IP address. If an IPv6 address contains a series of sequential zeroes, the address can be shortened to use a single zero in each group, or else the entire grouping can be represented using a double colon (`::`). So the following three strings all represent the same IPv6 address:

- `2001:0000:0000:0000:0000:0000:0000:7334`
- `2001:0:0:0:0:0:0:7334`
- `2001::7334`

TAKE NOTE*

The loopback address in IPv4 is written as `127.0.0.1`; in IPv6 it is written as `::1`.

IPv6 addresses have retained from IPv4 the delineation between host address and network address, and IPv6 networks can be expressed using CIDR notation such as `2001:0db8:1234::/48` to represent the `2001:0db8:1234` network configured with a 48-bit subnet mask.

CERTIFICATION READY?
Configure IPv4 and IPv6 addressing
1.1

IPv6 has been supported in the Windows operating systems since Windows Server 2003; however, Windows Vista and Windows Server 2008 are the first Microsoft operating systems to have IPv6 support turned on right out of the box. IPv6 can be managed using the Network and Sharing Center graphical user interface, or using the netsh command-line utility.

■ Introducing the Domain Name System (DNS)

For network devices, such as computers and printers, to communicate on the Internet or within your organization's TCP/IP network, they must be able to locate one another. This ability is provided by the IP address, as we discussed in the previous section. But it is cumbersome to use IP addresses as the only means of identifying systems. A more common practice is to use human-readable names as a more convenient way for humans to refer to systems. Thus, in order for Computer A to communicate with Computer B using TCP/IP, Computer A must obtain the IP address of Computer B. It is also convenient to be able to refer to a network, or part of a network, by its name instead of its address range.

The Domain Name System (DNS) provides the mechanism for associating meaningful host names with network addresses. Because DNS plays such a key role in Microsoft Windows Server 2008 and the public Internet, it is critical that you have a strong grasp of its concepts, processes, and methods of configuration. Without DNS, your network will most likely not function—clients won't be able to resolve names to Internet Protocol (IP) addresses. In addition, Active Directory clients use DNS to locate domain controllers; therefore, it is important that you understand key DNS concepts and how to properly configure DNS for your network.

The process of obtaining an IP address for a computer name (for example, "ComputerA") is called *name resolution*. Originally, before the evolution of what we now know as the Internet, name resolution was handled by text files called ***HOSTS files***. The text file listed each name of the host and its corresponding IP address within the HOSTS file. Whenever a new host was added to the network, the HOSTS file was updated with the host name and IP address. Periodically, all systems would download and then use the updated HOSTS file. Because the HOSTS file was flat, rather than hierarchical, every host name using this system had to be unique. There was no method for creating namespaces such as DNS domains like *www.adatum.com*.

Another problem with HOSTS files was an inability to distribute the workload that resulted from parsing this file across multiple computers. Every HOSTS file listed every available host, which meant that every computer that parsed the HOSTS file did all of the work to resolve client names into IP addresses. Clearly, this was inefficient, and a better name resolution system had to be devised.

Using DNS for Name Resolution

DNS was developed to provide a method of associating such names with network addresses. DNS provides mechanisms for communicating names and network addresses publicly, so that system names can be resolved to network addresses from anywhere that the address would be reachable. Because DNS is designed as a distributed database with a hierarchical structure, it can serve as the foundation for host name resolution in a TCP/IP network of any size, including the Internet. The distributed nature of DNS enables the name resolution workload to be shared among many computers. Today, most internetworking software, such as e-mail programs and Web browsers, use DNS for name resolution. Also, because of the hierarchical design of DNS, it provides a means of naming networks as well as end devices.

In a Windows Server 2008 network, the primary means of identifying network devices and network services is through the use of DNS. Although DNS is most commonly associated with the Internet, private networks also use DNS because of the following benefits:

- Scalability—Because DNS is capable of distributing workload across several databases or computers, it can scale to handle any level of name resolution required.

X REF

The DNS namespace is introduced in the following section; the other components are discussed in Lesson 4, Configuring and Managing the DNS Server Role.

- Transparency—Host names remain constant even when associated IP addresses change, which makes locating network resources much easier.
- Ease of use—Users access computers using easy-to-remember names such as www.microsoft.com rather than a numerical IP address, such as 192.168.1.100.
- Simplicity—Users need to learn only one naming convention to find resources on either the Internet or an intranet.

To understand the importance of DNS and how it functions within a Windows Server 2008 networking environment, you must understand the following components of DNS:

- DNS namespace
- DNS zones
- Types of DNS name servers
- DNS resource records

The DNS namespace is a hierarchical, tree-structured namespace, starting at an unnamed root used for all DNS operations. In the DNS namespace, each node and leaf object in the domain namespace tree represents a named domain. Each domain can have additional child domains. Figure 1-1 illustrates the structure of an Internet domain namespace.

Figure 1-1

Internet DNS namespace

The DNS namespace has a hierarchical structure, and each DNS domain name is unique. In Figure 1-1, at the top of the Internet DNS namespace is the root domain. The root domain is represented by "." (a period). Under the DNS root domain, the top-level domains, or first-level domains, are organizational types such as .org, .com, and .edu, or country codes such as .uk (United Kingdom), .de (Germany), and .it (Italy). The Internet Assigned Numbers Authority (IANA) assigns top-level domains. Table 1-4 lists several top-level domain names and their uses.

Table 1-4

Generic Top-Level Domain Names

Domain Name	Use
.aero	Exclusively reserved for the aviation community
.biz	A top-level domain that is aimed at large and small companies around the world
.com	Commercial organizations, such as microsoft.com for the Microsoft Corporation
.coop	A top-level domain for cooperatives
.edu	Educational institutions, now mainly four-year colleges and universities, such as wustl.edu for Washington University in St. Louis
.gov	Agencies of the U.S. federal government, such as fbi.gov for the U.S. Federal Bureau of Investigation
.info	An unrestricted domain aimed at providing information for worldwide consumption
.int	Organizations established by international treaties, such as nato.int for NATO
.mil	U.S. military, such as af.mil for the U.S. Air Force
.museum	A domain restricted to museums and related organizations and individuals
.name	A global domain for use by individuals that possibly develops into a global digital identity for users
.net	Computers of network providers, organizations dedicated to the Internet, Internet service providers (ISPs), and so forth, such as internic.net for the Internet Network Information Center (InterNIC)
.org	A top-level domain for groups that do not fit anywhere else, such as nongovernmental or nonprofit organizations (for example, w3.org, which is the World Wide Web Consortium)
.pro	A top-level domain for professionals, such as doctors, lawyers, and accountants

DNS uses a ***fully qualified domain name (FQDN)*** to map a host name to an IP address. The FQDN describes the exact relationship between a host and its DNS domain. For example, *computer1.sales.adatum.com* represents a host name, *computer1*, in the *sales* domain, in the *adatum* second-level domain, and in the *.com* top-level domain, which is under the "." root domain.

Second-level DNS domains are registered to individuals or organizations, such as *microsoft.com*, the Microsoft Corporation in the corporate (.com) domain; or *wustl.edu*, which is Washington University of St. Louis in the education (.edu) domain; or *gov.au*, the domain for the Australian government. Second-level DNS domains can have many subdomains, and any domain can have hosts. A host is a specific computer or other network device within a domain, such as *computer1* in the *sales* subdomain of the *microsoft.com* domain.

One benefit of the hierarchical structure of DNS is that it is possible to have two hosts with the same host names that are in different locations in the hierarchy. For example, two hosts named computer1—*computer1.sales.adatum.com* and *computer1.cpandl.microsoft.com*—can both exist without conflict because they are in different locations in the namespace hierarchy.

As previously noted, another benefit of the DNS hierarchical structure is that workload for name resolution is distributed across many different resources, through the use of DNS caching, DNS zones, and delegation of authority through the use of appropriate resource records. DNS zones, name servers, and resource records are discussed in more detail later in this book. For now, it is sufficient to understand that DNS is the way that IP addresses can be given a unique name.

■ Introducing the Dynamic Host Configuration Protocol (DHCP)

↓
THE BOTTOM LINE

It is very important to understand that address assignments are not arbitrary. The address specifies both the system identification and also its location within the network. Thus, each IP address must be both valid and unique within the host's entire internetwork. This requirement presents a challenge for network administrators. The process of assigning, changing, retiring, and reassigning addresses must be carefully monitored to ensure that each host has a unique IP address. Private network address ranges help, but addresses within private networks must still be unique within that network. The *Dynamic Host Configuration Protocol (DHCP)* provides a mechanism for conveniently assigning network addresses and other network configuration parameters to a system upon request, usually when it is first bootstrapped or attached to the network. This greatly simplifies network management.

When administering TCP/IP hosts, you can assign *static IP addresses*, which must be configured and maintained manually. This can become a daunting, tedious task as the number of systems grows to larger numbers. Organizations with significant numbers of workstations requiring IP address configurations would have great difficulty managing IP addressing manually. Dynamic Host Configuration Protocol (DHCP) simplifies the problem by automating the assigning, tracking, and reassigning of IP addresses.

DHCP allows administrators to configure TCP/IP by automatically assigning unique IP addresses while preventing duplicate address assignment and also to provide other important settings such as the default gateway, subnet mask, DNS, etc. Ideally, this would be accomplished without having to manually list every device on the network. DHCP is based heavily on the Bootstrap Protocol (BOOTP), a protocol still in use today that provides IP configuration information to diskless workstations that cannot store information locally and need to store their IP information in volatile memory upon each system boot. DHCP may be based on BOOTP, but it extends its predecessor in several ways. Rather than push preconfigured parameters to expected clients, DHCP can dynamically allocate an IP address from a pool of addresses and then reclaim it when it is no longer needed. Because this process is dynamic, no duplicate addresses are assigned by a properly configured DHCP server and administrators can move computers between subnets without manually configuring them. In addition, a large number of standard configuration and platform-specific parameters can be specified and dynamically delivered to the client. Thus, DHCP provides important functions beyond simply bootstrapping diskless workstations, and it is often used to automatically configure networking after systems are booted.

Understanding DHCP

DHCP is an open, industry-standard protocol that reduces the complexity of administering networks based on TCP/IP. It provides a mechanism for automatically assigning IP addresses and reusing them when they are no longer needed by the system to which they were assigned. It also provides mechanisms for providing associated configuration information when systems are first assigned IP addresses. DHCP is defined by the Internet Engineering Task Force (IETF) Requests for Comments (RFCs) 2131 and 2132.

➕ MORE INFORMATION

DHCP is an IETF standard and is defined in RFCs 2131 and 2132, which can be looked up at www.rfc-editor.org/rfcsearch.html. Requests For Comments (usually referred to in abbreviated form as RFC) is the process by which the IETF arrives at a consensus standard for fundamental internet technologies. New RFC numbers are assigned sequentially, and are conventionally used to identify the resulting standard.

IP addressing is complex, in part because each host connected to a TCP/IP network must be assigned at least one unique IP address and subnet mask in order to communicate on the network. Additionally, most hosts will require additional information, such as the IP addresses of the default gateway and the DNS servers. DHCP frees system administrators from manually configuring each host on the network. The larger the network, the greater the benefit of using DHCP. Without dynamic address assignment, each host has to be configured manually and IP addresses must be carefully managed to avoid duplication or misconfiguration.

Managing IP addresses and host options is much easier when configuration information can be managed from a single location rather than coordinating information across many locations. DHCP can automatically configure a host while it is booting on a TCP/IP network, as well as change settings while the host is connected to the network. All of this is accomplished using settings and information from a central DHCP database. Because settings and information are stored centrally, you can quickly and easily add or change a client setting (for example, the IP address of an alternate DNS server) for all clients on your network from a single location. Without a centralized database of configuration information, it is difficult to maintain a current view of the host settings or to change them.

All Microsoft Windows clients automatically install the DHCP Client service as part of TCP/IP, including Microsoft Windows Vista, Microsoft Windows XP, Microsoft Windows 2000, Microsoft Windows NT 4, Microsoft Windows Millennium Edition (Windows Me), and Microsoft Windows 98.

In brief, DHCP provides five key benefits to those managing and maintaining a TCP/IP network:

- Centralized administration of IP configuration—DHCP IP configuration information can be stored in one location, enabling the administrator to centrally manage it. A DHCP server tracks all leased and reserved IP addresses and lists them in the DHCP console. You can use the DHCP console to determine the IP addresses of all DHCP-enabled devices on your network. Without DHCP, not only would you need to manually assign addresses, but you would also be required to devise a method of tracking and updating them.
- Dynamic host configuration—DHCP automates the host configuration process for key configuration parameters. This eliminates the need to manually configure individual hosts when TCP/IP is first deployed or when IP infrastructure changes are required.
- Seamless IP host configuration—The use of DHCP ensures that DHCP clients get accurate and timely IP configuration parameters, such as the IP address, subnet mask, default gateway, IP address of the DNS server, and so on, without user intervention. Because the configuration is automatic, troubleshooting of misconfigurations, such as mistyped numbers, is largely eliminated.
- Scalability—DHCP scales from small to large networks. DHCP can service networks with ten clients as well as networks with thousands of clients. For very small, isolated networks, Automatic Private IP Addressing (APIPA) can be used, which is a component of Windows networking that automatically determines the client IP configuration without access to an external DHCP server.
- Flexibility—Using DHCP gives the administrator increased flexibility, allowing the administrator to more easily change IP configurations when the infrastructure changes.

X REF

APIPA is defined and discussed in more detail later in this lesson.

USING THE DHCP RELAY AGENT

DHCP relies heavily on broadcast messages. Broadcast messages are generally limited to the subnet in which they originate and are not forwarded to other subnets. This poses a problem if a client is located on a different subnet from the DHCP server. A DHCP relay agent can solve this problem.

A *DHCP relay agent* is either a host or an IP router that listens for DHCP (and BOOTP) client messages being broadcast on a subnet and then forwards those DHCP messages to a DHCP server on a remote subnet. The DHCP server sends DHCP response messages back to the relay agent, which then broadcasts them onto the local subnet for the DHCP client. Using DHCP relay agents eliminates the need to have a DHCP server on every subnet.

To support and use the DHCP service across multiple subnets, routers connecting each subnet should comply with the DHCP/BOOTP relay agent capabilities described in RFC 1542. To comply with RFC 1542 and provide relay agent support, each router must be able to recognize BOOTP and DHCP protocol messages and relay them appropriately. Because routers typically interpret DHCP messages as BOOTP messages, a router with only BOOTP relay agent capability relays DHCP packets and any BOOTP packets sent on the network.

The DHCP relay agent is configured with the address of a DHCP server. The DHCP relay agent listens for DHCPDISCOVER, DHCPREQUEST, and DHCPINFORM messages that are broadcast from the client. The DHCP relay agent then waits a previously configured amount of time and, if no response is detected, sends a unicast message to the configured DHCP server. The server then acts on the message and sends the reply back to the DHCP relay agent. The relay agent then broadcasts the message on the local subnet, allowing the DHCP client to receive it. This is depicted in Figure 1-2.

Figure 1-2

DHCP messages are forwarded by a DHCP relay agent

1. Client 1 Broadcasts a DHCPDISCOVER packet
2. Relay agent forwards DHCPDISCOVER packet to DHCP server
3. Server sends a DHCPOFFER packet to the DHCP relay agent
4. Relay agent broadcasts the DHCPOFFER packet
5. Client 1 broadcasts a DHCPREQUEST packet
6. Relay agent forwards the DHCPREQUEST packet to the DHCP server
7. Server broadcasts a DHCPACK packet which is picked up by the DHCP relay agent
8. Relay agent broadcasts the DHCPACK packet

CONFIGURING CLIENTS WITHOUT DHCP

Client systems need to obtain an IP address in order to join the network. DHCP is the usual solution, but it is possible that no DHCP server would be accessible (for example, a remote server could become inaccessible if the relay agent went down). As mentioned previously, clients can be configured automatically determine their IP configuration in cases where they cannot access an external DHCP server. This automatic configuration facility is called *Automatic Private IP Addressing (APIPA)*.

In most cases, DHCP clients find a server either on a local subnet or through a relay agent. To allow for the possibility that a DHCP server is unavailable, Windows Vista, Windows Server 2008, Windows Server 2003, Windows XP, Windows 2000, and Windows 98 provide Automatic Private IP Addressing (APIPA). APIPA is a facility of the Windows TCP/IP implementation that allows a computer to determine IP configuration information without a DHCP server or manual configuration.

APIPA avoids the problem of IP hosts being unable to communicate if for some reason the DHCP server is unavailable. Figure 1-3 illustrates different IP address assignment outcomes

Figure 1-3

How IP addresses are assigned
using APIPA or an alternate
configuration

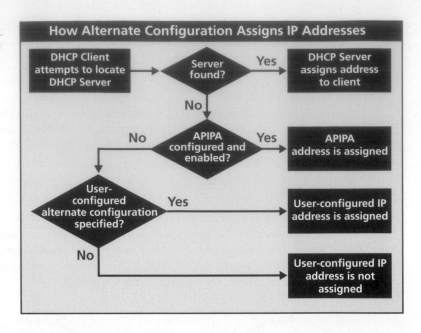

when a DHCP client attempts to find a DHCP server. In the case where a DHCP server is
not found and APIPA is configured and enabled, an APIPA address is assigned. APIPA is useful for small workgroup networks where no DHCP server is implemented. Because autocon-
figuration does not support a default gateway, it works only with a single subnet and is not
appropriate for larger networks.

If the DHCP client is unable to locate a DHCP server and is not configured with an alternate configuration (as shown in Figure 1-4), the computer configures itself with an IP address
randomly chosen from the Internet Assigned Numbers Authority (IANA)–reserved class B
network 169.254.0.0 and with the subnet mask 255.255.0.0. The autoconfigured computer then tests to verify that the IP address it has chosen is not already in use by using a
gratuitous ARP broadcast. If the chosen IP address is in use, the computer randomly selects
another address. The computer makes up to ten attempts to find an available IP address.

Figure 1-4

Alternate configuration
properties page

Once the selected address has been verified as available, the client is configured to use that
address. The DHCP client continues to check for a DHCP server in the background every five
minutes, and if a DHCP server is found, the configuration offered by the DHCP server is used.

Windows Vista, Windows XP, Windows Server 2008, and Windows Server 2003 clients can be configured to use an alternate configuration, which the DHCP client uses if a DHCP server cannot be contacted. The alternate configuration includes an IP address, a subnet mask, a default gateway, DNS, and additional configuration information.

One purpose of the alternate configuration is as a solution for portable computers that move between a corporate, DHCP-enabled network and a home network where static IP addressing is used. For example, Janice has a portable computer she uses at work and at home. At work, her portable computer obtains IP address information using DHCP, but she does not use a DHCP server at home. Janice can use alternate configuration to hold her home IP address, subnet mask, default gateway, and DNS server information so that when she connects her portable computer to her home network, it is configured automatically.

If you use DHCP with an alternate configuration, and the DHCP client cannot locate a DHCP server, the alternate configuration is used to configure the network adapter. No additional discovery attempts are made except under the following conditions:

- The network adapter is disabled and then enabled again.
- Media (such as network cabling) is disconnected and then reconnected.
- The TCP/IP settings for the adapter are changed, and DHCP remains enabled after these changes.

If a DHCP server is found, the network adapter is assigned a valid DHCP IP address lease.

To display the Alternate Configuration tab shown in Figure 1-4, the network adapter must be configured to obtain an IP address automatically. To view the Alternate Configuration tab, follow these steps:

1. Open the Control Panel, and double-click Network and Internet.
2. Double-click Network and Sharing Center.
3. In the Network Connections window, right-click Local Area Connection, and then click Properties.
4. In the Local Area Connection Properties page, click Internet Protocol (TCP/IP), and then click Properties.
5. In the Alternate Configuration tab, specify your IP address settings.

■ Using the Routing and Remote Access Service (RRAS)

THE BOTTOM LINE

Routing, or the process of transferring data across a network from one LAN to another, provides the basis for TCP/IP communications on the Internet and nearly all other corporate networks. Routing plays a key role in every organization that is connected to the Internet or that has more than one network segment. Routing can be a complex process, but if you understand some key concepts such as authentication, authorization, static routing, and policies, you can effectively configure, monitor, and troubleshoot routing and remote access for your organization.

As the name implies, the RRAS server role provides two key services for your network clients:

- Routing—By configuring two network interface cards (NICs) within a Windows Server 2008 server, the server can provide a means of transmitting data from one network to another.

TAKE NOTE*

For larger networks, the processing demands of network routing are typically handled by dedicated hardware-based routers. The routing service included with Windows Server 2008 is better suited for a smaller network or one with a small amount of network traffic that needs to pass between subnets.

X REF

The Routing and Remote Access server role is discussed further in Lesson 5.

• Remote Access—A Windows Server 2008 computer can act as a remote access server, which can allow remote network clients to access resources on a network as though they were physically connected to the LAN. The Windows Server 2008 remote access server can provide remote access using either dial-up connections via a modem, or else through a Virtual Private Network (VPN) connection over the Internet or another public network.

■ Introducing Network Access Protection (NAP)

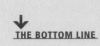

THE BOTTOM LINE

One of the principal challenges in corporate networks is the ability to secure networks against unwarranted access. In addition to configuring perimeter firewalls, network administrators also need to protect the network against "inside threats," laptop computers that are physically brought inside the corporate network or that gain access to the company network through remote access technologies such as Virtual Private Networks (VPNs.) For network administrators, this creates a challenge of enforcing corporate security standards such as up-to-date anti-virus protection definitions and a consistent firewall configuration. To assist with this endeavor, Windows Server 2008 provides the Network Access Protection platform, which provides a policy enforcement mechanism to control access to a 2008 network.

X REF

Network Access Protection is discussed at length in Lesson 10.

Network Access Protection is a new feature in Windows Server 2008 that allows network administrators to specify one or more policies that define the conditions under which network access will or will not be permitted. For example, consider a user who brings his home laptop into the office, and this laptop does not have anti-virus software installed. By connecting this laptop to the corporate network, this user runs the risk of propagating a network virus or worm throughout the corporate network, because the perimeter firewall does not offer any protection against a computer that is located inside of the perimeter. If Network Access Protection is in place, this laptop can be placed into a "quarantine" area where it cannot cause harm to the remainder of the computers on the network.

SUMMARY SKILL MATRIX

IN THIS LESSON YOU LEARNED:

• Network protocols create a logical language that allows computers to communicate.

• The most commonly used network protocol on modern networks is the Transmission Control Protocol/Internet Protocol (TCP/IP) protocol suite.

• There are currently two implementations of TCP/IP: TCP/IP version 4, or IPv4, and TCP/IP version 6, or IPv6.

• Each host on a TCP/IP network needs to be configured with a unique IP address.

• TCP/IP networks use the Domain Name System (DNS) to map human-readable machine names to IP addresses and vice versa, such as mapping the *www.cpandl.com* host name to the 10.10.1.104 IP address.

• Network administrators can use the Dynamic Host Configuration Protocol (DHCP) to automatically assign IP addresses to multiple client computers.

• The Routing and Remote Access service provides the ability to use a Windows Server 2008 computer as a router, which passes network traffic from one TCP/IP network to another, as well as remote access capabilities using either dial-up or VPN technology.

• To allow administrators to enforce network security policies such as mandatory anti-virus or firewall configurations, Windows Server 2008 has introduced the Network Access Protection (NAP) enforcement platform.

• Network addressing is fundamental to successful communication between systems.

- DNS provides name resolution to allow meaningful names to be used to refer to network addresses.

- DHCP is a simple, standard protocol that makes TCP/IP network configuration much easier for the administrator by dynamically assigning IP addresses and providing additional configuration information to DHCP clients automatically.

- Clients may be configured to use APIPA or an alternate static IP address configuration if DHCP is unavailable.

■ Knowledge Assessment

Fill in the Blank

Complete the following sentences by writing the correct word or words in the blanks provided.

1. The most widely used IP addressing scheme is _____.

2. The most recent and largest address space IP addressing scheme is _____.

3. To distribute IP addresses automatically, a network administrator would configure the _____ service.

4. The first attempt at breaking up IP address space used _____ to provide address ranges of differing sizes.

5. Prior to the introduction of the Domain Name System, computers used _____ to map human-readable names to IP addresses.

6. A(n) _____ is used to separate the host address portion of an IP address from the network address.

7. The subnet mask within the TCP/IP configuration is used to distinguish the _____ from the host address.

8. In dotted-decimal notation, each IPv4 address is broken up into four _____.

9. Server computers and other systems that need to be accessed reliably by network clients should be configured with a(n) _____.

10. The method of breaking up IP address space into address ranges of flexible size is called _____.

Multiple Choice

Circle the correct choice.

1. What must each host on a TCP/IP network be configured with in order to communicate with other hosts?
   a. Preferred DNS server
   b. Preferred WINS server
   c. IP address
   d. Default gateway

2. What is the process of transmitting TCP/IP traffic from one IP subnet to another?
   a. Subnetting
   b. Routing
   c. Transmitting
   d. Broadcasting

3. An IP network that is formatted such as 192.168.1.0/24 is referred to as what type of notation?
   a. CIDR notation
   b. NAT notation
   c. IPv4 notation
   d. IPv6 notation

4. What is the default network protocol of the Internet and most modern corporate networks?
   a. IPX/SPX
   b. NetBEUI
   c. AppleTalk
   d. TCP/IP

5. What was used by TCP/IP networks to perform name resolution prior to the introduction of the Domain Name System (DNS)?
   a. HOSTS files
   b. HOST files
   c. LM files
   d. WINS files

6. What is the process of dividing a large TCP/IP address space into multiple smaller networks called?
   a. Routing
   b. NATting
   c. Subnetting
   d. Supernetting

7. What technology is used by private network ranges that has extended the useful life of IPv4 addressing and slowed the adoption rate of IPv6?
   a. Subnetting
   b. NAT
   c. Routing
   d. CIDR

8. Which TCP/IP configuration item allows client computers to communicate with other computers that are located on remote networks?
   a. Default gateway
   b. Router
   c. Hub
   d. Switch

9. On a TCP/IP network that uses the Domain Name System (DNS) for name resolution, what unique configuration item must each TCP/IP host possess?
   a. HOSTS file
   b. LMHOSTS file
   c. Fully-qualified domain name
   d. UNC name

10. In what format are IPv4 IP addresses most commonly written?
    a. Hexadecimal
    b. Binary
    c. Dotted-decimal
    d. Dotted-hexadecimal

■ Case Scenarios

Scenario 1-1: Designing Windows Server 2008 Network Services

Lucerne Publishing is a publishing company based in New York City, New York, which produces science textbooks for colleges and medical schools. In recent months, Lucerne Publishing has been planning a move towards a "virtual office," where over 300 writers, editors, and graphics personnel will transition to working out of their homes instead of working in traditional "brick-and-mortar" offices. The main office in New York City will continue to house roughly 200 employees working in centralized functions such as Payroll, Accounting, and Human Resources. Each of these departments maintains a number of file and application servers that house sensitive personal and financial data, all of which require extensive security for their sensitive data. As the network administrator for Lucerne Publishing, you are tasked with configuring remote access for these new virtual office employees, while still maintaining the overall security of the Lucerne Publishing network.

Based on this information, answer the following questions:

1. In order to support access for remote employees, you have been authorized to upgrade Internet access at the Lucerne Publishing corporate office. You expect a significant increase in both inbound and outbound traffic as Lucerne Publishing makes the transition to a virtual office environment. You need to choose a method for routing traffic to and from the Internet and the corporate offices. Should you configure a Windows Server 2008 computer to act as your Internet router, or select another option?

2. What types of access can you support for virtual office staff members to access corporate resources, and how will you provide this access?

3. Lucerne Publishing's Chief Security Officer has expressed a concern over the security risks posed by allowing access to internal networks by virtual office computers, given that these computers will not be closely monitored by corporate IT staff. What can you do to minimize the risks to Lucerne Publishing's internal resources?

Installing Microsoft Windows Server 2008

KEY TERMS

basic disks
boot volume
dynamic disks
GPT (GUID Partition Table)
Initial Configuration Tasks
Internet Connection Sharing (ICS)
Key Management Service (KMS)
MBR (Master Boot Record)
mirrored volume

mount point
Multiple Activation Key (MAK)
NetBIOS
Network and Sharing Center
network discovery
network location
RAID-5 volume
repair mode
Server Core
simple volume
spanned volume

striped volume
system volume
volume
Volume Activation
Volume Activation Management Tool (VAMT)
Windows Firewall
Windows Server Backup
WINS Server
Wireless Networking

Engulf & Devour (E&D) is preparing to deploy new Windows Server 2008 computers to upgrade the network infrastructure of several small companies they have recently acquired. In order to facilitate this process, E&D's IT department must determine the appropriate server installation option for each server as well as manage the process of licensing and activating the new operating system licenses.

In this lesson, we will describe the activities associated with installing the Microsoft Windows Server 2008 operating system. We will begin by describing the steps involved in installing the Windows Server 2008 software. Next we will take a look at Server Manager, a new administrative console that provides a "one-stop shop" for server administration tasks in Windows Server 2008. We will then examine configuring hard disk storage options in Windows Server 2008, as well as the new Server Core installation option in Windows Server 2008. Finally, we will describe the new process of Windows Activation, which is used to manage software licensing and activation within an enterprise environment.

■ Installing the Software

↓ THE BOTTOM LINE
Installing the Microsoft Windows Server 2008 operating system software is the cornerstone to building a working network environment. Any unresolved errors or other issues during the installation process can cause significant problems and headaches both immediately and in the future. A good grasp of the fundamentals is important for a smooth installation.

Installation of Windows Server 2008 software can produce a system configuration containing only the specific facilities required for a specific role, called **Server Core,** or a full server installation containing all of the available Windows Server 2008 functionality.

When installing Windows Server 2008, you have the option of installing onto fresh media that has never been used before or onto previously used media containing existing files. If

TAKE NOTE*

Always back up existing files before performing any software installation! The installation procedures for Windows Server 2008 may be run standalone by booting the distribution DVD, or online running under an existing Windows software environment.

TAKE NOTE*

The online installation procedure requires Microsoft Windows Vista or Windows Server 2008. It will not run under Microsoft Windows XP or previous versions. When upgrading such systems, it will be necessary to boot the Windows Server 2008 distribution media and perform a standalone install.

WARNING Existing data will most likely be irretrievably lost by deleting the partition containing it (recovery is sometimes possible, but don't count on it!), so proceed with caution.

Windows Server 2008 is installed onto a disk partition containing a previous version of Windows, the files will be preserved but the software may or may not be usable.

Software installation is an essential step in preparing a new hardware system for use. To accomplish this, the Windows Server 2008 software distribution media includes a completely self-contained installation procedure that will run in a standalone manner without requiring any additional resources. The standalone installation software also provides a *repair mode,* which provides a minimal execution environment to allow running software that may be required or useful in attempting to recover a damaged Windows system.

When Windows Server 2008 is installed onto previously used media, the contents may be preserved or the media may be reinitialized and treated as though it is new, which will result in the previous contents being irretrievably destroyed. If the contents of previously used media are preserved, some of the initialization to prepare new hardware for use is not required, and some additional provisions to protect and preserve existing file contents are required.

When Windows Server 2008 software is installed onto previously unused hardware (or previously used hardware that is being completely reinitialized), several actions must be taken to initialize the hardware and prepare it for use. At the lowest level, a partition structure must be created on the physical hard drive to provide a logical addressing structure that organizes it into usable storage areas, and then a file volume structure must be created to manage the contents of a partition to allow storing files within it.

Traditionally, a disk could contain up to four primary partitions, one of which could be designated as an extended partition containing logical partitions (or logical drives). Originally the partition structure was associated with a single physical disk with a maximum of four logical partitions in the extended partition, but most modern systems have extended these limitations. Although some low-level disk utilities do allow modifying existing partition parameters, this entails a high risk of data loss, so in practice it is safest to assume that all disk partitions should be backed up before attempting to perform any type of modification such as deleting or extending them. Deleting a partition destroys the contents, so any files or data stored in it will be lost. Partitions provide a convenient mechanism for isolating different file systems. For example, legacy FAT and modern NTFS file systems can both be provided on a single disk, or one partition can be used to contain data files with another containing system software.

Windows Server 2008 software will be installed into a single partition designated during the installation process. Because the software is installed into a single partition, the specified minimum storage requirements actually apply to the space within the partition being used, not the total drive size. The installation process will allow installation to any hard drive attached to the system. It will also allow deleting previously existing partitions and creating new ones on any hard drive.

⊕ INSTALL WINDOWS SERVER 2008

GET READY. This exercise assumes that you have configured a physical computer (or a virtual guest using virtualization software such as Microsoft Virtual Server 2005 R2 or Microsoft Virtual PC) with a single hard drive configured as a single partition.

1. Insert a bootable Windows Server 2008 media and power on the physical or virtual server.
2. You can see the opening installation screen in Figure 2-1. Here you are prompted to configure the following three items:
   - Language to install—for example, English or German
   - Time and currency format—for example, English (United States) or French (Switzerland)
   - Keyboard or input method—for example, US or United Kingdom

Figure 2-1

Beginning the Windows Server
2008 installation

3. Click **Next**, followed by **Install Now**.

4. Next you will see the screen shown in Figure 2-2, where you will be prompted to enter the Windows product key. Enter a legitimate Windows product key and click **Next**.

Figure 2-2

Entering the Windows product
key

Type your product key for activation

You can find your product key on your computer or on the installation disc holder inside the Windows package. Although you are not required to enter your product key now to install, failure to enter it may result in the loss of data, information, and programs. You may be required to purchase another edition of Windows. We strongly advise that you enter your product identification key now.

The product key sticker looks like this:

XXXXX-XXXXX-XXXXX-XXXXX-XXXXX

Product key (dashes will be added automatically):

☑ Automatically activate Windows when I'm online

What is activation?

Read our privacy statement   Next

5. Next you will be prompted either to install the full version of Windows Server 2008 or perform a Server Core installation. For now, select a **full install**; we'll discuss Server Core in a later section. Click **Next** to continue.

6. On the following screen, you'll be prompted to accept the Windows Server 2008 license terms. Read the license terms and then place a check mark next to **I accept the license terms**. Click **Next** to continue the installation.

7. Next you'll see the screen shown in Figure 2-3, which will prompt you to select between an upgrade installation or a clean install. Since we are installing Windows onto brand-new hardware, notice that the Upgrade option is grayed out and only the Custom option is available. Select the **Custom** installation option.

Figure 2-3

Selecting an installation
method

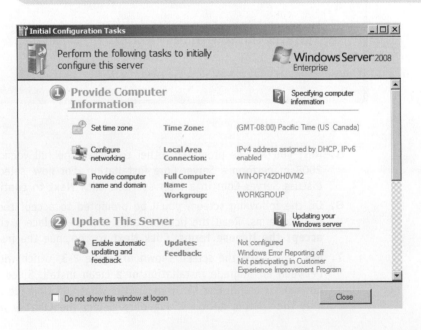

8. On the following screen, you'll be prompted to select the hard drive partition on which you wish to install Windows. Select the appropriate partition and click **Next**.

9. At this point the installation process will begin. The remainder of the installation will run largely automated until it completes.

10. To improve the security of a Windows Server 2008 installation, on final reboot you will be prompted to establish a complex password.

STOP. We will use this Windows Server 2008 installation for future exercises in this and other lessons.

Performing Initial Configuration Tasks

The freshly installed Windows Server 2008 software will automatically launch the **Initial Configuration Tasks** screen at startup, as shown in Figures 2-4 and 2-5. Many of these tasks are straightforward, such as setting the administrator password or the time zone, and these tasks are not discussed in detail here. You should, however, step through all of the tasks presented in the initial configuration screen for your system.

Figure 2-4

Viewing the Initial
Configuration Tasks screen

It is especially important to download and apply any updates that have been released since the installation media was created, as shown in the second section of the configuration tasks in Figure 2-5.

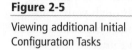

Figure 2-5

Viewing additional Initial Configuration Tasks

Configuring Basic Network Settings

To simplify the configuration process, Windows Server 2008 introduces the Initial Configuration Tasks screen, which will appear by default on each newly configured 2008 computer. As you've seen, this interface provides a single administrative point to configure common items such as the server clock, time zone, Windows Update settings, and basic network settings before moving on to more advanced configuration options. On any Windows Server 2008 computer that will participate on a corporate network, it is critical to configure network settings correctly to allow it to communicate with other hosts on local or remote networks.

For more information on TCP/IP addressing, refer to Lesson 1.

As discussed in Lesson 1, each host on a TCP/IP network should be configured with a number of mandatory and optional configuration items, including:

- IPv4 or IPv6 address
- Subnet mask
- Default gateway
- DNS/WINS servers

The option to configure networking allows you to view and set the networking parameters for your Windows Server 2008 system and the network it serves. This is where you set the IP address or specify the system is to be a DHCP client, and the DNS servers it will use. If this system will be a DHCP server, you should set a static IP address, because that will be required when you try to set up the DHCP server role. If the system is used on multiple networks, you can set an alternate configuration to be used when a DHCP server is unavailable (by using either Automatic Private IP Addressing, or providing a fixed IP address as a fallback option). To set these values, open the Properties screen for the connection you want to set, choose the item for TCP/IPv4, and click the Properties button. This allows you to set the IP addressing mechanism for the system, and when DHCP is used (*Obtain an IP address automatically* is selected), a tab is provided to allow the alternate configuration to be specified as a fallback option.

If you set the IP address manually, you will also need to provide DNS server information manually. Otherwise, the DHCP server will provide the DNS server information as part of setting the client parameters.

You can also use the Connection Properties screen to control **Internet Connection Sharing (ICS),** which allows other users on your network to access the Internet through your computer. This requires your computer to have two network connections, one to the Internet and the other to a local network. Essentially, ICS turns your computer into a router so that other computers on the local network can access its Internet connection. You should note that the default setting allows other network users to control or disable the shared Internet connection. This avoids the need for them to have access to your computer in order to manage the shared Internet connection, but it could allow anybody on your network to manage the connection (unless you take care to set up other security facilities).

The *View Status* display for the connection provides access to many details of the connection, including DHCP lease details, network gateway information, the device Media Access Control (MAC) or physical address, and much more, as shown in Figure 2-6.

Figure 2-6

Viewing the status of a network connection

You can configure network settings on a Windows Server 2008 computer using a number of different tools, including the Initial Configuration Tasks or the new Server Manager consoles, as well as the Windows command line.

⊙ CONFIGURE BASIC NETWORK SETTINGS

GET READY. This exercise will use a mixture of GUI interfaces and command-line utilities to configure network settings.

1. Log onto the Windows Server 2008 computer using administrative credentials.

2. On a newly installed server, the Initial Configuration Tasks screen appears. To configure the IP address, subnet mask, and default gateway from the Initial Configuration Tasks screen, click **Configure Networking**. The Network Connections screen will open. Right-click the **Local Area Connection** icon and click **Properties** as shown in Figure 2-7.

Figure 2-7

Local Area Network
Connection Properties

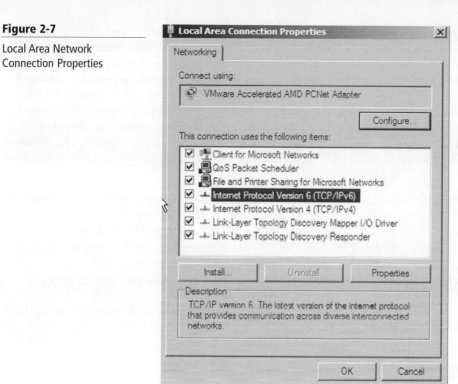

3. Double-click **Internet Protocol version 4 (IPv4).** To configure the server with a static IP address, select **Use the following IP address.** Enter an appropriate IP address, subnet mask, and default gateway for your environment. Click **OK**, and then click **OK** again.

4. To add a preferred and alternate DNS server from the command line, click the **Start** button, then click **All Programs→Accessories→Command Prompt.**

5. Key the command **netsh interface ipv4 add dnsserver "Local Area Connection"** *<DNS server IP address>.address>.address>,* using the IP address of your preferred DNS server, and then press ⟨**Enter**⟩. Repeat this command, inserting the IP address of your alternate DNS server, and then press ⟨**Enter**⟩.

6. Key **exit** and press ⟨**Enter**⟩ to close the command prompt window.

PAUSE. You can log off of the Windows Server 2008 computer, or remain logged on for the next exercise.

Configuring the Windows Firewall

The final task in the initial configuration task list is to configure the *Windows Firewall.* Initially, the Windows Firewall is on by default, and this allows you to turn it off (not recommended!) or to change the settings.

The *network location* setting characterizes the network environment to which you are connected—for example "work" or "public network." The important effect of this setting is to control network discovery, which is the process by which other computers on the network can find (and perhaps access) your computer, and the shared resources it provides. *Network discovery* finds and accesses other computers and shared resources on the network. File and printer sharing would be examples of a service affected by this setting. If you inappropriately allowed network discovery in a public network environment (for example, an Internet café), you would allow total strangers to see and access any file shares on your system. The *Network and Sharing Center* allows you to set the network location, and the Windows Firewall screen has a link to access the Network Center.

The Windows Firewall Settings screen shown in Figure 2-8 allows you to turn the firewall on or off, and to control the connections it will allow when it is running. The most restrictive option is to block all incoming connections when Windows Firewall is on. This prevents any inbound connection attempts from succeeding, and it is intended for situations in which you are connected to an insecure network and inbound connections are more likely to be attacks from malicious users or hackers. There will be no notification of blocked attempts to connect, even for connections that you have indicated should be allowed normally. The normal mode for Windows Firewall is on, which blocks all connection requests except those explicitly allowed on the Exceptions tab.

Figure 2-8

Configuring the Windows Firewall

The Exceptions tab lists some of the exceptions that are frequently encountered in network environments, so that they can be explicitly allowed through the Windows Firewall. This is useful for enterprise environments in which the network itself is protected by firewalls and other security measures. In such an environment, the facilities listed would commonly be needed for asset management, distributed applications, and other business imperatives, so allowing them through the Windows Firewall is necessary. For maximum security, however, you should enable only those required in your particular environment. The Exceptions tab also allows enabling access by a specific program, or by specifying a particular port. Specifying a particular port is less desirable because it opens that port permanently, whereas specifying a program allows access only when that program is running.

Configuring Server Roles

To improve the security and manageability of Windows Server 2008 computers, you can use the Server Manager console to install one or multiple Server Roles, which define a particular duty that a server might perform on a 2008 network. For example, installing the Active Directory Domain Services role will step you through adding all of the services needed to configure a server as an Active Directory domain controller. To reduce the attack surface on Windows Server 2008 computers, system files (such as executables and DLL files) associated with a particular role will not be installed on a server until the role is installed, instead of leaving unused software lying dormant on the server as a potential target for a network virus or worm.

The default installation of Windows Server 2008 Enterprise Edition allows you to install 17 different server roles:

- Active Directory Certificate Services
- Active Directory Domain Services
- Active Directory Federation Services
- Active Directory Lightweight Directory Services
- Active Directory Rights Management Services
- Application Server
- DHCP Server
- DNS Server
- Fax Server
- File Services
- Network Policy and Access Services
- Print Services
- Terminal Services
- UDDI Services
- Web Server (IIS)
- Windows Deployment Services
- Windows SharePoint Services

When adding a server role using Server Manager, you are presented with a number of informational screens describing the role being installed, as well as any prerequisites to install the role and checklists to follow to configure the role once it has been installed. You can also use Server Manager to cleanly remove a role if it is no longer in use on a particular server.

CONFIGURE SERVER ROLES ON WINDOWS SERVER 2008

GET READY. This exercise assumes that you have installed Windows Server 2008, Enterprise Edition, and are logged on as a local Administrator of the server.

1. If the Server Manager screen does not appear automatically, click the **Start** button and then click **Server Manager**.
2. In the left-hand pane, double-click the **Roles** node.
3. In the right-hand pane, click **Add role**. Click **Next** to bypass the initial Welcome Screen.

4. You will see the Select Server Roles screen shown in Figure 2-9. Here you will select the role that you want to install on the server. For this exercise we will install the DNS Server role. Place a check mark next to DNS Server and click **Next**.

Figure 2-9

Selecting Server Roles to install

5. On the following screen you will see an introduction to the DNS Server role, including links to additional information in the Windows Help files. Click **Next** to continue.

6. The Confirm Installation Selections screen appears. Click **Install** to begin the installation.

7. After a few minutes, the Installation Results screen will appear. Click **Close** to return to the Server Manager console, shown in Figure 2-10. Notice that the DNS Server role is now listed in the Roles Summary section.

Figure 2-10

Viewing Server Manager

PAUSE. Log off of the Windows Server 2008 computer, or remain logged on for the next exercise.

In the previous exercise, you configured the DNS Server role using the Server Manager console. The following section describes configuring hard drives and storage options for Windows Server 2008.

Adding Windows Server 2008 Features

The Add features option allows adding various features and facilities that may be useful or necessary, depending on your network environment and requirements..

Some of the features that may be relevant in the context of this tutorial include:

- Remote Server Administration Tools—The Remote Server Administration Tools allow the Windows Server 2008 system to be used to remotely administer another server. Installation of these tools installs the ability to administer the remote server's software, not to use the remote server's software. This enables outbound connections from your system to manage other servers.
- *Windows Server Backup*—The Windows Server Backup feature allows recovery of operating system state, files, folders, and application data by periodically creating a snapshot of the full server, or selected volumes.
- *WINS Server*—The WINS Server feature provides the ability to run a WINS (Windows Internet Name Service) server, which provides a *NetBIOS* Name Server facility. NetBIOS name resolution was the primary means of name resolution prior to the introduction of Active Directory in Windows 2000 Server, which relied on DNS as its primary means of resolving human-readable names to IP addresses. Essentially, WINS is to NetBIOS names as DNS is to domain names, providing a mapping of a computer's NetBIOS name to a corresponding IP address.
- *Wireless Networking* The Wireless Networking feature installs and configures wireless connections and wireless LAN profiles.

Configuring Storage in Windows Server 2008

Once you have installed the Windows Server 2008 operating system, you can add and remove physical hard disks and logical partitions to increase or modify the available storage on your server. Similar to other administrative tasks in Windows Server 2008, you can manage storage options using either a Graphical User Interface or a command-line interface. In this section we will discuss the terminology that you will need to understand to manage storage on a Windows Server 2008 computer, as well as the tools that you can use to do so.

Windows Server 2008 (and all Microsoft operating systems going back to Windows 2000) supports two types of hard disks:

- *Basic disks* use partition tables that are recognized and supported by older operating systems such as MS-DOS, Windows 95, Windows 98, and Windows Me. Basic disks do not support advanced storage options such as striped volumes, spanned volumes, and RAID-5 volumes. All disk drives in a Windows Server 2008 computer begin as basic disks until they are converted to dynamic disks.
- *Dynamic disks* provide access to more advanced configuration features. Once a basic disk is converted to a dynamic disk, that disk can be accessed only by operating systems that support dynamic disks: Windows 2000 Professional, Windows XP Professional, Windows Vista Business, Enterprise or Ultimate, Windows 2000 Server, Windows Server 2003, and Windows Server 2008.

When working with dynamic disks, you will need to be familiar with the following terms:

- A *volume* describes a logical unit of disk space that is made up of space contained on one or more physical disks. Volumes on a dynamic disk can be configured as simple, spanned, mirrored, striped, or RAID-5 volumes.

- A *simple volume* consists of free space contained on a single physical disk. You can configure all of the available space on a disk as a simple volume, or you can configure multiple simple volumes using the space on a single disk.

- A *spanned volume* is made up of free space from multiple physical disks. For example, if you have two physical disks in a server that are each 500GB in size, you can combine them into a single spanned volume that is 1TB in size. Spanned volumes are not fault-tolerant, which means that if you lose one disk in the volume, you will lose all data contained on all disks. A spanned volume can be created on a minimum of 2 disks and a maximum of 32 disks.

- A *striped volume* is similar to a spanned volume in that it is made up of free space from multiple disks. Unlike a spanned volume, though, a striped volume uses RAID-0 striping to interleave the data across the disks, thus improving the read performance of the volume. Striped volumes are also not fault-tolerant and will not withstand the loss of a disk in the volume. A striped volume can be created on a minimum of 2 disks and a maximum of 32 disks.

- A *mirrored volume* is a fault-tolerant volume consisting of two physical disks, in which the data on one disk is copied exactly onto the second disk. This provides data redundancy, such that if one disk in the mirror fails, the other disk will continue to function without loss of data.

- A *RAID-5 volume* is a fault-tolerant volume where data is interleaved across three or more disks much in the same way as in a striped volume, but with additional information known as *parity*. If one disk in a RAID-5 volume fails, the data contained on the failed disk can be rebuilt using the parity information stored on the disks in the rest of the volume. A RAID-5 volume can be created using a minimum of three disks and a maximum of 32 disks.

When you create a new partition, you can either assign the partition a drive letter, or else you can configure it as a *mount point* that will appear as a folder within an existing drive letter. For example, creating a 500MB partition and assigning it to a mount point to the E:\EXCHANGE\DATA directory will add a folder called DATA containing 500MB of space.

You can manage disks and partitions in Windows Server 2008 using the Disk Management GUI tool, or the diskpart command-line utility. In the following exercise, we will perform various tasks associated with managing storage in Windows Server 2008.

Before you can manage a disk drive in Windows Server 2008, the disk needs to be initialized. All new disks are initialized as basic disks, and can be initialized using one of two partition styles:

- *MBR (Master Boot Record)*—This partition style is recognized by down-level operating systems.

- *GPT (GUID Partition Table)*—This partition style is recommended for disks larger than 2TB, or disks that are used in Itanium computers.

TAKE NOTE*

While not specific to basic or dynamic disks, there are two other volume designations that you should be aware of: the *system volume* contains files necessary to boot the computer, and the *boot volume* contains the Windows operating system files. The system volume and the boot volume can, but do not necessarily need to be, the same volume.

CONFIGURE STORAGE IN WINDOWS SERVER 2008

GET READY. This exercise assumes that you have added three additional disks to your Windows Server 2008 computer, each with unallocated space available to create new partitions. If you are using a virtual environment to perform these steps, you can add additional disks using the administrative console of your virtualization software.

1. Log onto the Windows Server 2008 computer using credentials that have administrative rights to the local computer.

2. If the Server Manager console does not appear automatically, click the **Start** button, and then click **Server Manager**.

3. In the left-hand pane, drill down to **Storage→Disk Management**.

4. You will see a screen similar to Figure 2-11. If the new disks are listed as *Offline*, right-click each disk and click **Online**. The disk status will change to *Not Initialized*.

Figure 2-11

Viewing Disk Management

5. Right-click one new disk and click **Initialize Disk**. You will see the screen shown in Figure 2-12. Select the **MBR** partition style and click **OK**. All new disks will list a status of *Online* and are initialized as basic disks.

Figure 2-12

Initializing a newly installed disk

6. Right-click a newly added disk and click **Convert to dynamic disk**. Select one or more disks to convert. Click **OK**.

7. To demonstrate creating a new partition in Disk Management, we will create a simple volume. Right-click a disk containing unallocated space and click **New Simple Volume**. The New Simple Volume Wizard appears. Click **Next**.

8. The Specify Volume Size screen appears. Enter **50** to create a 50MB partition and click **Next**.

9. The Assign Drive Letter or Path screen appears. Assign the new partition an available drive letter and click **Next**.

10. The Format Partition screen appears. Select the option to format this drive using the NTFS file system and click **Next**.

11. Click **Finish** to create the partition. The new partition will show a status of *Formatting*, followed by a status of *Healthy* when the format has completed.

Next we will create a RAID 5 partition using the diskpart command-line utility.

12. Click **Start**, key **cmd** in the Run line, and click **OK**.

13. To create a 50MB RAID-5 partition across three disks, enter the command **diskpart create volume raid size=50 disk=1,2,3** and then press (Enter).

14. Key **exit** and press (Enter) to close the command prompt.

15. Confirm that the newly configured RAID partition is displayed in the Disk Management console.

PAUSE. You can close Server Manager or leave it open for a subsequent exercise.

Installing Server Core

Windows Server 2008 introduces a new option for installing only the services required for a specific function, creating a server installation that possesses an extremely small installation footprint. This feature is called Server Core and it provides only the services required to perform specific roles such as the DHCP, DNS, file server, or domain controller roles.

Rather than being a separate product (or SKU in licensing terms), Server Core is simply an installation option that is available with all Windows Server 2008 media; you can use the 2008 media to install either Server Core or a full installation of the operating system as your needs dictate. Server Core creates a small installation footprint as well as a limited attack surface from a network security perspective. Since it does not install nonessential services and applications, it includes only a limited GUI. For example, a Server Core computer will allow you to launch the Windows Registry Editor, Notepad, and a number of Control Panel applets; but it does not include a Start Menu and it does not allow you to install or run any of the MMC consoles such as Computer Management or Active Directory Users and Computer. Even more interesting from a security standpoint is that a Server Core installation does not include programs that were previously standard components on a server operating system, such as Windows Explorer and Outlook Express, since their presence created additional opportunities for security compromises of the server.

There are several advantages to installing Server Core. Because it includes only what is required for the designated roles, a Server Core installation will typically require less maintenance and fewer updates as there are fewer components to manage. Security is improved. Since there are fewer programs and components installed and running on the server, there are fewer attack vectors exposed to the network, resulting in a reduced attack surface. Because there are fewer components installed, the minimum resources required will be less than for a full installation, and there may be less overhead during normal processing.

On the other hand, there are some disadvantages associated with the Server Core configuration. Most noticeable is the inconvenience of not having the familiar GUI options available during system administration. Server Core installations are also designed for a specific set of limited roles, so they might not be as well suited for small networks where a single server might be used for several roles.

The installation process for Server Core is identical to the installation of a full version of Windows Server 2008. Once a Server Core computer is installed, however, it can be managed locally using only command-line utilities and the limited GUI facilities installed on a Server Core computer. When a computer running Windows Server 2008 Server Core is initially installed, you will see the interface shown in Figure 2-13. As you can see, there is only a command prompt available to you to begin administering the computer.

Figure 2-13

Administering a Server Core computer

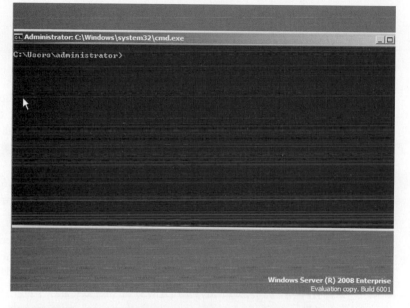

Managing Server Core from the Command Line

Since a Server Core installation includes only the most limited GUI capabilities, local administration of a Server Core computer requires a thorough knowledge of the command-line utilities that are available within Windows Server 2008. Using these utilities, you can perform an almost identical set of administrative functions as you can using the graphical user interface in a full installation of 2008, including modifying network settings, joining a Server Core computer to an Active Directory domain, and more.

MANAGE SERVER CORE FROM THE COMMAND LINE

GET READY. This exercise assumes that you have configured a Windows Server 2008 Server Core using the default installation settings, using the steps described in the "Install Windows Server 2008" exercise.

1. To list the current TCP/IP configuration, key the command string **netsh interface ipv4 show config** in the command prompt and press (Enter).

2. To configure a static IPv4 IP address, key the command string **netsh interface ipv4 add address "Local Area Connection"** *<IP Address> <Subnet Mask> <Default Gateway>* and press (Enter).

3. To add a DNS resolver, key the command string **netsh interface ipv4 add dns server "Local Area Connection"** *<DNS Server IP Address>* and press (Enter).

4. To confirm that your changes were made, key **netsh interface ipv4 show config** again and press (Enter).

5. To set the correct time zone for the Server Core computer, (Enter) **timedate .cpl.** and press (Enter). The familiar Date and Time Control Panel applet appears.

6. To see the limited GUI functionality of Server Core in action, key **explorer.exe** and press (Enter). Notice that the Server Core installation does not recognize explorer. exe as a valid command.

STOP. You have completed the exercise.

In the previous exercise, you performed some common administrative tasks on a Server Core computer using both command-line tools and limited GUI functionality that is available within Server Core. For a full listing of command-line utilities at your disposal, search the Microsoft TechNet Web site for the phrase "Command-Line Reference A-Z."

Configuring Windows Activation

To help address the ongoing issue of software piracy, Windows Vista and Windows Server 2008 include tools to assist administrators in automating and managing the licensing process for operating system software on their network. In particular, *Volume Activation* is used to manage the licensing process for volume licenses of both Vista as well as Windows Server 2008. Volume Activation can eliminate the need to manually enter a product key when the operating system software is installed, and it allows you to protect and manage volume license keys throughout an organization.

Microsoft offers two types of software keys for a Windows Vista or Windows Server 2008 network, depending on the needs of your specific situation:

- A *Multiple Activation Key (MAK)* is used for a one-time activation with Microsoft's hosted activation service. A MAK key can be activated via the Internet, over the phone, or by using the *Volume Activation Management Tool (VAMT)*.

- A *Key Management Service (KMS)* license key allows you to host an activation service locally within your own network. Rather than contacting the Microsoft-hosted activation service each time a new instance of Vista or Windows Server 2008 needs to be activated on your network, KMS allows you to contact the Microsoft activation service one time to activate your KMS host, after which all activation traffic is managed locally. The minimum number of physical computers required to allow you to use a KMS key is 25 Vista computers and five Windows Server 2008 computers. Any computer on your network that has been activated by an internal KMS host will attempt to "check in" with the KMS host every seven days, and will be required to connect to that host at least once every 180 days to maintain its license.

When working in a corporate network or other production environment, you can obtain more information about Microsoft Licensing from the Microsoft Web site, or by contacting an authorized reseller of Microsoft products.

SUMMARY SKILL MATRIX

IN THIS LESSON YOU LEARNED:

- The Windows Server 2008 distribution media contains a bootable system that can be used for a standalone software installation or to repair an existing installation.

- Windows Server 2008 will be installed on a single partition specified at the start of the installation process.

- Existing files may be preserved, or they can be destroyed by reinitializing the partition to which Windows Server 2008 is installed.

- Initial configuration tasks must be performed after the Windows Server 2008 software is installed, to finish preparing it for use. These tasks include setting system parameters and passwords, adding server roles, adding server features, and setting up Windows Firewall.

- Network addressing is fundamental to successful communication between systems.

- DNS provides name resolution to allow meaningful names to be used to refer to network addresses.

- DHCP is a simple, standard protocol that makes TCP/IP network configuration much easier for the administrator by dynamically assigning IP addresses and providing additional configuration information to DHCP clients automatically.

- Clients may be configured to use APIPA or an alternate static IP address configuration if DHCP is unavailable.

- Windows Server 2008 allows you to configure various types of storage, including RAID-0, RAID-1, and RAID-5 storage arrays.

- Windows Vista and Windows Server 2008 use activation technology to help combat piracy of Microsoft software.

Knowledge Assessment

Fill in the Blank

Complete the following sentences by writing the correct word or words in the blanks provided.

1. The ability to use the installation process to fix problems with an existing Windows Server system is called _____.

2. Installation of just the necessary components for a particular server role, without the GUI and other software features, is called _____.

3. The _____ screen appears by default when the Windows Server 2008 operating system is first installed.

4. A _____ offers the best performance of any multi-disk configuration option within the Disk Management MMC, but does so at the expense of fault tolerance.

5. The feature that allows users on different computers to access the Internet through a single connection is called _____.

6. The _____ provides a single point of administration to configure networking and firewall configuration tasks on a Windows Server 2008 computer.

7. The setting describing the network environment, such as home or public network, is called the _____.

8. Unsolicited inbound traffic can be blocked through the use of the _____.

9. The network location setting controls the behavior of _____.

10. Once a disk is converted from a basic disk to a(n) _____, it can be accessed only by operating systems that support dynamic disks: Windows 2000 Professional, Windows XP Professional, Windows Vista Business, Enterprise or Ultimate, Windows 2000 Server, Windows Server 2003, and Windows Server 2008.

Multiple Choice

Circle the correct choice.

1. What type of license key allows you to host an activation service locally within your own network?
   - **a.** Multiple Activation Key (MAK)
   - **b.** Key Management System (KMS)
   - **c.** Key Activation System (KAS)
   - **d.** Multiple Management System (MMS)

2. What type of volume uses 50% of available drive space to provide fault tolerance for the volume?
   - **a.** RAID-0
   - **b.** RAID-1
   - **c.** RAID-5
   - **d.** RAID-6

3. Which disk formatting option will cause a disk to appear as a folder within an existing volume?
   a. Mount point
   b. Mirrored volume
   c. Striped volume
   d. GPT point

4. Which Windows Server 2008 feature installs and configured wireless connections and wireless LAN profiles?
   a. Network and Sharing Center
   b. Windows Firewall with Advanced Security
   c. Wireless Networking
   d. Network Access Protection

5. What was the primary means of name resolution on Windows networks prior to the introduction of Windows 2000 and Active Directory?
   a. AppleTalk
   b. Domain Name System (DNS)
   c. HOSTS files
   d. NetBIOS

6. Which feature is used to perform backups and restores of Windows volumes?
   a. NTBackup
   b. Windows Server Backup
   c. Windows Backup
   d. Windows NT Backup

7. Which networking service is used to automatically associate NetBIOS names with IP addresses?
   a. DNS
   b. NetBEUI
   c. WINS
   d. AppleTalk

8. Which disk partition style is recommended for disks larger than 2TB, or disks that are used in Itanium computers?
   a. Master Boot Record (MBR)
   b. GUID Partition Table (GPT)
   c. Master Partition Table (MPT)
   d. GUID Boot Record (GBR)

9. What is used to manage the licensing process for volume licenses of Windows Vista and Windows Server 2008?
   a. Volume Activation
   b. Activation keys
   c. Microsoft Select
   d. Enterprise Agreement

10. Which volume contains the operating system files on a Windows computer?
    a. System volume
    b. Boot volume
    c. Mirrored volume
    d. Striped volume

■ Case Scenarios

Scenario 2-1: Planning for Windows Server 2008

Contoso, Ltd. is a research company located in Palo Alto, California. It is in the midst of a significant upgrade to its network infrastructure, including an upgrade of all server computers to Windows Server 2008. The team leader for the server upgrade project is gathering information to determine the optimum configuration for each server computer. Based on the information in this lesson, answer the following questions.

1. You have a SQL Server 2005 database against which clients perform numerous read-intensive operations. You have been tasked with optimizing the performance of this database as much as possible. Based on this requirement, how should you configure the disks on which the database files will be installed?

2. Contoso, Ltd. has a number of satellite offices where researchers work locally on client projects. These offices are minimally staffed and do not usually have on-site IT staff available to administer any locally housed servers. You are concerned with installing only the minimum necessary services and creating the most secure possible installation footprint on servers that are housed at these remote offices. What new feature of Windows Server 2008 can you use to increase the security of these servers?

Configuring and Managing the DHCP Server Role

OBJECTIVE DOMAIN MATRIX

Technology Skill	Objective Domain	Objective Domain Number
Configuring the DHCP Server Role	Configure Dynamic Host Configuration Protocol (DHCP)	1.2

KEY TERMS

Address Resolution Protocol (ARP)
Application Layer
authorize
automatic restores
available address pool
checkpoint file
class options
compacted
DHCPACK
DHCPDECLINE
DHCPDISCOVER

DHCPINFORM
DHCPNACK
DHCPOFFER
DHCPRELEASE
DHCPREQUEST
exclusion range
Joint Engine Technology (JET)
Media Access Control (MAC)
multinets
Open System Interconnection (OSI)
reconciliation

Request for Comments (RFC)
reservations
rogue DHCP server
superscope
T1
T2
Trivial File Transfer Protocol (TFTP)
User Datagram Protocol (UDP)

Adventure Works (*http://www.adventure-works.com*) is a worldwide company specializing in providing hiking, scuba, and other outdoor excursions. Their corporate headquarters, located in Boulder, Colorado, has just undergone a significant upgrade to its network infrastructure to support recent expansion in the number of administrative staff required in Boulder to support the efforts of the tour organizers and leaders. Before the infrastructure upgrade, Adventure Works' network administrators configured each server and workstation with a static IP address, using a Microsoft Access database to keep track of which IP addresses were assigned to which computers. To improve the efficiency of managing the recent staff expansion, Adventure Works IT management has decided to deploy a DHCP server using Microsoft Windows Server 2008.

By the end of this lesson, you will have a detailed understanding of the Dynamic Host Configuration Protocol (DHCP) server role within Microsoft Windows Server 2008. DHCP can be used to automatically assign a computer's IP address, subnet mask, and default | gateway, as well as such optional configuration items as a preferred and alternate DNS server or WINS server. This lesson will cover the steps required to install and configure the DHCP server as well as related components such as the DHCP Relay Agent.

■ Configuring the DHCP Server Role

THE BOTTOM LINE

In order to communicate with other hosts on a network, all Transmission Control Protocol/Internet Protocol (TCP/IP) hosts must be correctly configured. Each host must have an Internet Protocol (IP) address and a subnet mask, and if communicating outside the local subnet, each must also have a default gateway. Each IP address must be valid and unique within the host's internetwork. This requirement can present a challenge for network administrators. If it is done manually, accurate and timely records must be kept of each host, noting where the host is located and what IP address and subnet mask have been assigned to it. This can quickly become a daunting, tedious task. Organizations with large numbers of workstations requiring IP addresses would have great difficulty managing IP addressing manually. The Dynamic Host Configuration Protocol (DHCP) simplifies this process by automating the assigning, tracking, and reassigning of IP addresses.

CERTIFICATION READY?
Configure Dynamic Host
Configuration Protocol
(DHCP)
1.2

IP addressing is complex, in part because each host (a computer, printer, or other device with a network interface) connected to a TCP/IP network must be assigned at least one unique IP address and subnet mask in order to communicate on the network. Additionally, most hosts will require additional information, such as the IP addresses of the default gateway and the DNS servers. DHCP frees system administrators from manually configuring each host on the network. The larger the network, the greater the benefit of using a dynamic address assignment. Without this, each host must be configured manually and IP addresses must be carefully managed to avoid duplication or misconfiguration.

Since the advent of TCP/IP, several solutions have been developed to address the challenge of configuring TCP/IP settings for organizations with a large number of workstations. The *Reverse Address Resolution Protocol (RARP)* was designed for diskless workstations that had no means of permanently storing their TCP/IP settings. RARP, as its name suggests, was essentially the opposite of ***Address Resolution Protocol (ARP)***. ARP was used to discover the Media Access Control (MAC) address (an address unique to a Network Interface Card) that corresponds to a particular IP address. RARP clients broadcast the MAC address. A RARP server then responds by transmitting the IP address assigned to the client computer.

Because RARP failed to provide other much-needed settings to the client, such as a subnet mask and a default gateway, it gave way to another solution, the Bootstrap Protocol (BOOTP). BOOTP, which is still in use today, enables a TCP/IP workstation to retrieve settings for all the configuration parameters it needs to run, including an IP address, a subnet mask, a default gateway, and Domain Name System (DNS) server addresses. Using ***Trivial File Transfer Protocol (TFTP)***, a lightweight version of FTP that uses the UDP protocol, a workstation also can download an executable boot file from a BOOTP server. The major drawback of BOOTP is that an administrator still must specify settings for each workstation on the BOOTP server. A better way to administer TCP/IP would be to automatically assign unique IP addresses while preventing duplicate address assignment and while providing other important settings such as the default gateway, subnet mask, DNS, Windows Internet Naming Service (WINS) server, and so on. Ideally, this would be accomplished without having to manually list every device on the network. To address this issue, server administrators can deploy DHCP.

DHCP is based heavily on BOOTP, but rather than pushing preconfigured parameters to expected clients, DHCP can dynamically allocate an IP address from a pool of addresses and then reclaim it when it is no longer needed. Because this process is dynamic, no duplicate addresses are assigned by a properly configured DHCP server, and administrators can move computers between subnets without manually configuring them. In addition, a large number of standard configuration and platform-specific parameters can be specified and dynamically delivered to the client. DHCP is an open, industry-standard protocol that reduces the complexity of administering networks based on TCP/IP. It is defined by the *Internet Engineering Task Force (IETF)* in **Requests for Comments (RFCs)** 2131 and 2132.

Managing IP addresses and host options is much easier when configuration information can be managed from a single location rather than coordinating information across many locations. DHCP can automatically configure a host while it is booting on a TCP/IP network, as well as change settings while the host is connected to the network. All of this is accomplished using settings and information from a central DHCP database. Because settings and information are stored centrally, you can quickly and easily add or change a client setting (for example, the IP address of an alternate DNS server) for all clients on your network from a single location. Without a centralized database of configuration information, it is difficult to maintain a current view of the host settings or to change them.

Each Microsoft Windows Server 2008 edition (the Standard Edition, Enterprise Edition, and Datacenter Edition) include the DHCP Server service, which is an optional installation. All Microsoft Windows clients automatically install the DHCP Client service as part of TCP/IP, including Windows Server 2008, Windows Server 2008, Microsoft Windows Vista, and Microsoft Windows XP.

In brief, DHCP provides four key benefits to those managing and maintaining a TCP/IP network:

- Centralized administration of IP configuration—DHCP IP configuration information can be stored in a single location and enables the administrator to centrally manage all IP configuration information. A *DHCP server* tracks all leased and reserved IP addresses and lists them in the DHCP console. You can use the DHCP console to determine the IP addresses of all DHCP-enabled devices on your network. Without DHCP, not only would you need to manually assign addresses, you would also need to devise a method of tracking and updating them.

- Dynamic host configuration—DHCP automates the host configuration process for key configuration parameters. This eliminates the need to manually configure individual hosts when TCP/IP is first deployed or when IP infrastructure changes are required.

- Seamless IP host configuration—The use of DHCP ensures that DHCP clients get accurate and timely IP configuration parameters, such as the IP address, subnet mask, default gateway, IP address of the DNS server, and so on, without user intervention. Because the configuration is automatic, troubleshooting of misconfigurations, such as mistyped numbers, is largely eliminated.

- Flexibility and scalability—Using DHCP gives the administrator increased flexibility, allowing the administrator to more easily change IP configurations when the infrastructure changes. DHCP also scales from small to large networks. DHCP can service networks with ten clients as well as networks with thousands of clients. For very small, isolated networks, Automatic Private IP Addressing (APIPA) can be used. (APIPA is discussed later in this lesson.)

Understanding How DHCP Works

The core function of DHCP is to assign addresses. DHCP functions at the **Application Layer** of the **Open System Interconnection (OSI)** reference model, as defined by the International Organization for Standardization (ISO) and the Telecommunication Standards Section of the International Telecommunications Union (ITU-T). The OSI model is used for reference and teaching purposes; it divides computer networking functions into seven layers. From top to bottom, the seven layers are application, presentation, session, transport, network, data-link, and physical. For more information about the OSI reference model, see the *Network + Certification Training Kit,* Second Edition (Microsoft Press, 2001).

As discussed previously, the key aspect of the DHCP process is that it is dynamic. What this means to the network administrator is that the network can be configured to allocate an IP address to any device that is connected anywhere on the network. This allocation of addresses is achieved by sending messages to, and receiving application layer messages (messages from the Application Layer of the OSI model) from, a DHCP server. All DHCP messages are carried in *User Datagram Protocol (UDP)* datagrams using the well-known port numbers 67 (from the server) and 68 (to the client). UDP operates at the Transport Layer of the OSI model and is a low-overhead protocol because it does not use any type of packet acknowledgement.

Before learning how address allocation works, you should understand some terminology related to the DHCP server role: DHCP clients, servers, and leases. These terms are defined as follows.

* *DHCP client*—A computer that obtains its configuration information from DHCP.
* *DHCP server*—A computer that provides DHCP configuration information to multiple clients; the IP addresses and configuration information that the DHCP server makes available to the client are defined by the DHCP administrator.
* *DHCP lease*—This defines the duration for which a DHCP server assigns an IP address to a DHCP client. The lease duration can be any amount of time between 1 minute and 999 days, or it can be unlimited. The default lease duration is eight days.

In addition to this terminology, you should also be familiar with the various *DHCP message types* that are used by DHCP clients and servers on a TCP/IP network.

* **DHCPDISCOVER**—Sent by clients via broadcast to locate a DHCP server. Per RFC 2131, the DHCPDISCOVER message may include options that suggest values for the network address and lease duration.
* **DHCPOFFER**—Sent by one or more DHCP servers to a DHCP client in response to DHCPDISCOVER, along with offered configuration parameters.
* **DHCPREQUEST**—Sent by the DHCP client to signal its acceptance of the offered address and parameters. The client generates a DHCPREQUEST message containing the address of the server from which it is accepting the offer, along with the offered IP address. Because the client has not yet configured itself with the offered parameters, it transmits the DHCPREQUEST message as a broadcast. This broadcast notifies the server that the client is accepting the offered address and also notifies the other servers on the network that the client is rejecting their offers.
* **DHCPDECLINE**—Sent by a DHCP client to a DHCP server, informing the server that the offered IP address has been declined. The DHCP client will send a DHCPDECLINE message if it determines that the offered address is already in use. After sending a DHCPDECLINE, the client must begin the lease or renewal process again.
* **DHCPACK**—Sent by a DHCP server to a DHCP client to confirm an IP address and to provide the client with those configuration parameters that the client has requested and the server is configured to provide.
* **DHCPNACK**—Sent by a DHCP server to a DHCP client to deny the client's DHCPREQUEST. This might occur if the requested address is incorrect because the client was moved to a new subnet or because the DHCP client's lease expired and cannot be renewed. After receiving a DHCPNACK message, the client must begin the lease or renewal process again.
* **DHCPRELEASE**—Sent by a DHCP client to a DHCP server to relinquish an IP address and cancel the remaining lease. This message type is sent to the server that provided the lease.
* **DHCPINFORM**—Sent from a DHCP client to a DHCP server to ask only for additional local configuration parameters; the client already has a configured IP address. This message type is also used to detect unauthorized DHCP servers.

The initial DHCP lease process is accomplished using a series of exchanges between a DHCP client and DHCP server that utilize four messages, DHCPDISCOVER, DHCPOFFER,

DHCPREQUEST, and DHCPACK, as shown in Figure 3-1. You can remember this four-step sequence of the DHCP lease process with the acronym DORA, for "Discover, Offer, Request, Acknowledgement," as described here:

Figure 3-1

The DHCP lease process

1. DHCPDISCOVER. The client broadcasts a DHCPDISCOVER message to find a DHCP server. Because the client does not already have an IP address or know the IP address of the DHCP server, the DHCPDISCOVER message is sent as a local area broadcast, with 0.0.0.0 as the source address and 255.255.255.255 as the destination address. The DHCPDISCOVER message is a request for the location of a DHCP server and IP addressing information. The request contains the client's MAC address and computer name so that the DHCP servers know which client sent the request. After broadcasting its DHCPDISCOVER message, the DHCP client waits 1 second for an offer. If an offer is not received, the client will not be able to initialize, and the client will rebroadcast the request three times (at 9-, 13-, and 16-second intervals, plus a random offset between 0 milliseconds and 1 second). If an offer is not received after four tries, the client continuously retries in five-minute intervals. If DHCP fails, Windows Server 2008, Windows Vista, Windows XP, and Windows Server 2003 can use APIPA to obtain a dynamically assigned IP address and subnet mask. Clients can also use an alternate configuration, which assigns predefined settings if a DHCP server cannot be located. APIPA and alternate configurations are described in the "Using APIPA and Alternate Configurations" section later in this lesson.

2. All DHCP servers that receive the DHCPDISCOVER message and that have a valid configuration for the client will broadcast a DHCPOFFER message with the following information:

   • Source (DHCP server) IP address

   • Physical (MAC) address of the requesting client (this is sent to the broadcast IP address of 255.255.255.255 because the client has not yet been configured with IP information)

   • An offered IP address

   • Client hardware address

   • Subnet mask

   • Length of lease

   • A server identifier (the IP address of the offering DHCP server)

3. After the client receives an offer from at least one DHCP server, it broadcasts a DHCPREQUEST message to all DHCP servers with 0.0.0.0 as the source address and 255.255.255.255 as the destination address. The broadcast DHCPREQUEST message contains the following information:

   • The IP address of the DHCP server chosen by the client

   • The requested IP address for the client

   • A list of requested parameters (subnet mask, router, DNS server list, domain name, vendor-specific information, WINS server list, NetBIOS node type, NetBIOS scope)

TAKE NOTE*

When DHCP servers whose offers were not accepted receive the DHCPREQUEST message, they retract their offers.

4. The DHCP server with the accepted offer sends a successful acknowledgement to the client in the form of a DHCPACK message. This message contains a valid lease for an IP address, including the renewal times (T1 and T2, which are discussed next) and the duration of the lease (in seconds).

A DHCP client will perform the initial lease process in the following situations:

- The very first time the client boots
- After releasing its IP address
- After receiving a DHCPNACK message, in response to the DHCP client attempting to renew a previously leased address

Because each DHCP lease has a finite lifetime, the client must periodically renew the lease after obtaining it. Windows DHCP clients attempt to renew the lease either at each reboot or at regular intervals after the DHCP client has initialized. The lease renewal involves just two DHCP messages, as shown in Figure 3-2—DHCPREQUEST (either broadcast or unicast) and DHCPACK. If a Windows DHCP client renews a lease while booting, these messages are sent through broadcast IP packets. If the lease renewal is made while a Windows DHCP client is running, the DHCP client and the DHCP server communicate using unicast messages. (In contrast with broadcast messages, unicast messages are point-to-point messages between two hosts.)

Figure 3-2

The DHCP lease renewal process

DHCP client   DHCP server

A DHCP client first attempts to reacquire its lease at half the lease time, which is known as *T1*. The DHCP client obtains the value of T1 from the DHCPACK message that confirmed the IP lease. If the lease reacquisition fails at T1, the DHCP client attempts a further lease renewal at 87.5 percent of the lease time, which is known as *T2*. Like T1, T2 is specified in the DHCPACK message. If the lease is not reacquired before it expires (if, for example, the DHCP server is unreachable for an extended period of time), the client immediately releases the IP address as soon as the lease expires and attempts to acquire a new lease.

If the DHCP client requests a lease through a DHCPREQUEST message that the DHCP server cannot fulfill (for example, when a portable computer is moved to a different subnet, as shown in Figure 3-3), the DHCP server sends a DHCPNACK message to the client. This informs the client that the requested IP lease will not be renewed. The client then begins the acquisition process again by broadcasting a DHCPDISCOVER message. When a Windows DHCP client boots in a new subnet, it broadcasts a DHCPREQUEST message to renew its lease. The DHCP renewal request is broadcast on the subnet so all DHCP servers that provide DHCP addresses will receive the request. This DHCP server responding on the new subnet is different from the server that provided the initial lease. When the DHCP server receives the broadcast, it compares the address the DHCP client is requesting with the scopes configured on the server and the subnet.

Figure 3-3

A DHCP client booting in a
new subnet

If it is not possible to satisfy the client request, the DHCP server issues a DHCPNACK message, and the DHCP client then begins the lease acquisition process again. If the DHCP client is unable to locate any DHCP server when rebooting, it issues an ARP broadcast for the default gateway that was previously obtained, if one was provided. If the IP address of the gateway is successfully resolved, the DHCP client assumes that it remains located on the same network from which it obtained its current lease and continues to use its lease. Otherwise, if the IP address of the gateway is not resolved, the client assumes that it has been moved to a network that has no DHCP services currently available (such as a home network), and it configures itself using either APIPA or an alternate configuration. Once it configures itself, the DHCP client tries to locate a DHCP server every five minutes in an attempt to renew its lease.

Using the DHCP Relay Agent

DHCP relies heavily on broadcast messages. Broadcast messages are generally limited to the subnet in which they originate and are not forwarded to other subnets. This poses a problem if a client is located on a different subnet from the DHCP server. A *DHCP relay agent* is either a host or an IP router that listens for DHCP (and BOOTP) client messages being broadcast on a subnet and then forwards those DHCP messages to a DHCP server. The DHCP server sends DHCP response messages back to the relay agent, which then broadcasts them onto the subnet for the DHCP client. Using DHCP relay agents eliminates the need to have a DHCP server on every subnet.

To support and use the DHCP service across multiple subnets, routers connecting each subnet should comply with the DHCP/BOOTP relay agent capabilities described in RFC 1542. To comply with RFC 1542 and provide relay agent support, each router must be able to recognize BOOTP and DHCP protocol messages and relay them appropriately. Because routers typically interpret DHCP messages as BOOTP messages, a router with only BOOTP relay agent capability relays DHCP packets and any BOOTP packets sent on the network.

The DHCP relay agent is configured with the address of a DHCP server. The DHCP relay agent listens for DHCPDISCOVER, DHCPREQUEST, and DHCPINFORM messages that are broadcast from the client. The DHCP relay agent then waits a previously configured amount of time and, if no response is detected, sends a unicast message to the configured DHCP server. The server then acts on the message and sends the reply back to the DHCP relay agent. The relay agent then broadcasts the message on the local subnet, allowing the DHCP client to receive it.

Using APIPA and Alternate Configurations

In most cases, DHCP clients find a server either on a local subnet or through a relay agent. To allow for the possibility that a DHCP server is unavailable, Windows clients can obtain their IP configuration using Automatic Private IP Addressing (APIPA). APIPA is a feature of the Windows TCP/IP implementation that allows a computer to determine IP configuration information without a DHCP server without relying on manual configuration of the TCP/IP stack.

APIPA avoids the problem of IP hosts being unable to communicate if for some reason the DHCP server is unavailable. In the case where a DHCP server is not found and APIPA is configured and enabled, an APIPA address is assigned. APIPA is useful for small workgroup networks where no DHCP server is implemented.

If the DHCP client is unable to locate a DHCP server and is not configured with an alternate configuration (discussed next), the computer configures itself with an IP address randomly chosen from the Internet Assigned Numbers Authority (IANA)–reserved class B network 169.254.0.0 and with the subnet mask 255.255.0.0. The auto-configured computer then tests to verify that the IP address it has chosen is not already in use by using a gratuitous ARP broadcast. If the chosen IP address is in use, the computer randomly selects another address. The computer makes up to ten attempts to find an available IP address.

Once the selected address has been verified as available, the client is configured to use that address. The DHCP client continues to check for a DHCP server in the background every five minutes, and if a DHCP server is found, the configuration offered by the DHCP server is used.

Windows clients can also be configured to use an alternate configuration, which the DHCP client uses instead of APIPA if a DHCP server cannot be contacted. The alternate configuration includes an IP address, a subnet mask, a default gateway, DNS, and WINS server addresses.

One purpose of the alternate configuration is as a solution for portable computers that move between a corporate, DHCP-enabled network and a home network where static IP addressing is used. For example, Janice has a portable computer she uses at work and at home. At work, her portable computer obtains IP address information using DHCP, but she does not use a DHCP server at home. Janice can use alternate configuration to hold her home IP address, subnet mask, default gateway, and DNS server information so that when she connects her portable computer to her home network, it is configured automatically.

If you use DHCP with an alternate configuration and the DHCP client cannot locate a DHCP server, the alternate configuration is used to configure the network adapter. No additional discovery attempts are made except under the following conditions:

- The network adapter is disabled and then enabled again
- Media (such as network cabling) is disconnected and then reconnected
- The TCP/IP settings for the adapter are changed, and DHCP remains enabled after these changes

If a DHCP server is found, the network adapter is assigned a valid DHCP IP address lease.

To display the Alternate Configuration tab in Windows Server 2008, as shown in Figure 3-4, the network adapter must be configured to obtain an IP address automatically. To view the Alternate Configuration tab, follow these steps:

1. Open the Control Panel, and double-click Network and Sharing Center. In the Network and Sharing section, click Manage Network Connections.
2. In the Network Connections window, right-click Local Area Connection, and then click Properties.
3. In the Local Area Connection Properties page, click Internet Protocol version 4 (TCP/IPv4), and then click Properties.
4. Ensure that the Obtain an IP Address Automatically radio button is selected. In the Alternate Configuration tab, specify your IP address settings.

Figure 3-4

Viewing the Alternate
Configuration screen

Installing the DHCP Server Role

Windows Server 2008 has introduced the Server Manager utility as a single point of reference for managing all components of the Windows operating system, as well as installing, managing, and uninstalling various server roles such as Active Directory Domain Services, DHCP, DNS, and others. Adding the DHCP server role is largely wizard-driven, and allows you to configure basic DHCP settings at the same time that you install the role.

INSTALL THE DHCP SERVER ROLE

GET READY. This exercise assumes that you have installed Windows Server 2008, Enterprise Edition, and that you have local administrator access to the computer. In Part A we will add the DHCP server role on a full installation of Windows Server 2008. In Part B we will add the DHCP server role on a Server Core installation of Windows Server 2008.

PART A—Adding the DHCP Server Role on a Full Installation of Windows Server 2008

1. Press (Ctrl) + (Alt) + (Del) on the Windows Server 2008 computer and log on as the default administrator of the local computer.

2. The Server Manager screen will appear automatically. Expand the Server Manager window to full-screen if necessary.

3. In the left-hand pane of Server Manager, double-click **Roles**.

4. Click **Add Role**. Click **Next** to bypass the initial Welcome screen.

5. The Select Server Roles screen appears. Place a checkmark next to **DHCP Server**. Click **Next**.

6. The Introduction to DHCP Server screen appears. Read the information about the DHCP Server role and click **Next**.

7. The Specify IPv4 DNS Server Settings screen appears. Enter the appropriate information for your network configuration and click **Next**.

8. The Specify IPv4 WINS Server Settings screen appears. Select the appropriate configuration for your network and click **Next**.

9. The Add or Edit DHCP Scopes screen appears. Click **Add** to create a DHCP scope for your network.

10. The Add Scope screen appears. Enter the appropriate information for your network configuration, for example:

- *Name:* 70-642 Lab Network
- *Starting IP Address:* 192.168.1.100
- *Ending IP Address:* 192.168.1.254
- *Subnet Mask:* 255.255.255.0
- *Default Gateway:* 192.168.1.1
- *Subnet type:* Wired

11. Ensure that there is a checkmark next to **Activate this scope**, and then click **OK**.

12. Click **Next**. The Configure DHCPv6 Stateless Mode screen appears. Select **Enable DHCPv6 stateless mode** and click **Next**.

13. The Specify IPv6 DNS Server Settings screen appears. Enter the appropriate information for your network configuration and click **Next**.

14. The Authorize DHCP Server screen appears. Select **Skip authorization of this DHCP server in AD DS** and click **Next**.

15. The Confirm Installation Selections screen appears. Click **Install**.

PART B—Adding the DHCP Server Role on a Server Core Installation of Windows Server 2008

1. Press Ctrl + Alt + Del on the Server Core computer and log on as the default administrator of the local computer.

2. From the command prompt, enter the following command and press **Enter**:

Start /w ocsetup DHCPServerCore

STOP. When the installation is completed, log off of the Windows Server 2008 computer.

In the previous exercise, you installed the DHCP Server role on a Windows Server 2008 computer. In the next section, we will discuss the process of authorizing DHCP servers within Active Directory.

Authorizing a DHCP Server

In implementations of DHCP prior to Windows 2000, any user could create a DHCP server on the network, an action that could lead to conflicts in IP address assignments. For example, if a client obtains a lease from an incorrectly configured DHCP server, the client might receive an invalid IP address, which prevents it from communicating on the network. This can prevent users from logging on. In Windows Server 2000 and later, an unauthorized DHCP server (also referred to as a *rogue DHCP server*) is simply a DHCP server that has not been explicitly listed in the Active Directory Domain Service as an authorized server. You must *authorize* a DHCP server in Active Directory before the server can issue leases to DHCP clients.

At the time of initialization, the DHCP server contacts Active Directory to determine whether it is on the list of servers that are currently authorized to operate on the network. One of the following actions then occurs:

- If the DHCP server is authorized, the DHCP Server service starts.
- If the DHCP server is not authorized, the DHCP Server service logs an error in the system event log, does not start, and, of course, will not respond to client requests.

Let's examine two scenarios. In the first scenario, the DHCP server is part of a domain and is authorized. In the second scenario, the DHCP server is not in a domain and, consequently, not authorized.

In the first scenario, the DHCP server initializes and determines if it is part of the directory domain. Since it is, it contacts the directory service to verify that it is authorized. The directory service confirms the server is authorized. After receiving this confirmation, the server broadcasts a DHCPINFORM message to determine if other directory services are available and repeats the authorization process with each directory service that responds. After this is completed, the server begins servicing DHCP clients accordingly.

In the second scenario, the server is not a part of a domain. When the server initializes, it checks for DHCP member servers. If no DHCP member servers are located, the server begins servicing DHCP clients and continues to check for member servers by sending a DHCPINFORM message every five minutes. If a DHCP member server is located, the server shuts down its DHCP service and, of course, stops servicing DHCP clients.

Active Directory must be present to authorize DHCP servers and block unauthorized servers. If you install a DHCP server on a network without Active Directory, no authorization will take place. If you subsequently add Active Directory, the DHCP server will sense the presence of Active Directory; however, if it has not been authorized, the server will shut itself down. DHCP servers are not authorized by default; they must be explicitly authorized.

When a DHCP server that is not a member server of the domain (such as a member of a workgroup) initializes, the following happens:

1. The server broadcasts a DHCPINFORM message on the network.
2. Any other server that receives this message responds with a DHCPACK message and provides the name of the directory domain it is part of.
3. If a workgroup DHCP server detects a member DHCP server of a domain on the network, the workgroup DHCP server assumes itself to be unauthorized on that network and shuts itself down.
4. If the workgroup DHCP server detects the presence of another workgroup server, it ignores it; this means multiple workgroup servers can be active at the same time as long as there is no directory service.

TAKE NOTE*

To authorize a DHCP server, a user must be a member of the Enterprise Admins group, which exists in the root domain of the forest.

Even when a workgroup server initializes and becomes authorized (because no other domain member server or workgroup server is on the network), it continues to broadcast DHCPINFORM every five minutes. If an authorized domain member DHCP server initializes later, the workgroup server becomes unauthorized and stops servicing client requests.

➔ AUTHORIZE A DHCP SERVER

GET READY. This exercise assumes that you have installed the DHCP Server role on a Windows Server 2008 computer in an Active Directory domain, and that you have local administrator rights to the DHCP server.

1. Press (**Ctrl**) + (**Alt**) + (**Del**) on the Windows Server 2008 computer and log on as the default administrator of the local computer.
2. Click **Start→Administrative Tools→DHCP**.
3. In the console tree, right-click **DHCP**, and then click **Manage Authorized Servers**.
4. In the Manage Authorized Servers dialog box, select **Authorize**.
5. In the Authorize DHCP Server dialog box, key the name or IP address of the DHCP server to be authorized, and then click **OK**.
6. The computer will list the IP and full computer name and then ask for confirmation. Click **OK** to continue.

STOP. You can close the DHCP administrative console or leave it open for a subsequent exercise. To authorize a DHCP server from a Server Core computer, use the netsh command using the following syntax: **netshdhcp add server <Server IP Address>**

In this exercise, you authorized a DHCP server within an Active Directory domain. In the next section we will discuss creating and configuring DHCP scopes to issue specific DHCP configurations to your network clients.

Configuring DHCP Scopes

A DHCP scope determines which IP addresses are allocated to clients. A scope defines a set of IP addresses and associated configuration information that can be supplied to a DHCP client. A scope must be defined and activated before DHCP clients can use the DHCP server for dynamic TCP/IP configuration. You can configure as many scopes on a DHCP server as needed for your network environment.

A DHCP administrator can create one or more scopes on one or more Windows Server 2008 servers running the DHCP Server service. However, because DHCP servers do not communicate scope information with each other, you must be careful to define scopes so that multiple DHCP servers are not assigning the same IP address to multiple clients or assigning addresses that are statically assigned to existing IP hosts.

The IP addresses defined in a DHCP scope must be contiguous and are associated with a subnet mask. If the addresses you want to assign are not contiguous, you must create a scope encompassing all the addresses you want to assign and then exclude specific addresses or address ranges from the scope. You can create only one scope per subnet on a single DHCP server. To allow for the possibility that some IP addresses in the scope might have been already assigned and are in use, the DHCP administrator can specify an *exclusion range*—one or more IP addresses in the scope that are not handed out to DHCP clients. An exclusion range is a limited sequence of IP addresses within a scope range that are to be excluded from DHCP service offerings. Where exclusion ranges are used, they ensure that any addresses within the defined exclusion range are not offered to clients of the DHCP server. You should exclude all statically configured IP addresses within a particular IP address range.

Once a DHCP scope is defined and exclusion ranges are applied, the remaining addresses form what is called an *available address pool* within the scope. Pooled addresses can then be dynamically assigned to DHCP clients on the network.

⊕ CONFIGURE A DHCP SCOPE

GET READY. This exercise assumes that you have installed the DHCP Server role on a Windows Server 2008 computer, and that you have administrative rights to that server.

1. Press (Ctrl) + (Alt) + (Del) on the Windows Server 2008 computer and log on as the default administrator of the local computer.

2. Click **Start→Administrative Tools→DHCP**.

3. To configure an IPv4 DHCP scope, drill down to the server name, followed by IPv4.

4. Right-click **IPv4** and select **New scope**. Click **Next** to bypass the initial Welcome screen.

5. The Scope Name screen appears. Enter a name and description for the DHCP scope and then click **Next**.

6. The IP Address Range screen appears. Enter the starting and ending IP address and the subnet mask for the scope and then click **Next**.

7. The Add Exclusions screen appears. Enter any necessary exclusions and then click **Next**.

8. The Lease Duration screen appears. Enter the length of the DHCP lease and click **Next**.

9. The Configure DHCP Options screen appears. Click **Yes, I want to configure these options now** and click **Next**.

10. The Router (Default Gateway) screen appears. Enter the default gateway for the scope, click **Add,** and then click **Next**.

11. The Domain Name and DNS Servers screen appears. Enter the DNS domain and DNS servers as appropriate for the scope. Click **Next**.

12. The WINS Servers screen appears. Enter the WINS servers as appropriate for the scope and then click **Next**.

13. The Activate Scope screen appears. Click **Yes, I want to activate this scope now** and then click **Next**.

14. Click **Finish** to complete creating the DHCP scope.

PAUSE. You can close the DHCP management console or else leave it open for a subsequent exercise. To configure a DHCP scope from a Server Core computer, use the netsh command.

In the previous exercise you created and configured a DHCP server on a Windows Server 2008 computer. In the next section we will discuss creating DHCP reservations within a DHCP scope.

TAKE NOTE *

A DHCP *superscope* is an administrative grouping of scopes that is used to support *multinets*, or multiple logical subnets (subdivisions of an IP network) on a single network segment (a portion of the IP internetwork bounded by IP routers). Multinetting commonly occurs when the number of hosts on a network segment grows beyond the capacity of the original address space. By creating a logically distinct second scope and then grouping these two scopes into a single superscope, you can double your physical segment's capacity for addresses. (In multinet scenarios, routing is also required to connect the logical subnets.) In this way, the DHCP server can provide clients on a single physical network with leases from more than one scope. Superscopes contain only a list of member scopes or child scopes that can be activated together; they are not used to configure other details about scope use.

Configuring a DHCP Reservation

Network administrators can use DHCP *reservations* for DHCP-enabled hosts that need to have static IP addresses on your network. Examples of hosts that require static IP addresses are e-mail servers and application servers. File and print servers may also require static or reserved IP addresses if they are accessed by their IP addresses.

DHCP reservations enable permanent address lease assignment by the DHCP server. Where reservations are used, they ensure that a specified hardware device on the network can always use the same IP address. Reservations must be created within a scope and must not be excluded from the scope. Excluded addresses are not available for assignment to clients even if reserved for a client. An IP address is set aside, or reserved, for a specific network device that has the *Media Access Control (MAC)* address (the hard-coded hexadecimal hardware address associated with a Network Interface Card) associated with that IP address. Therefore, when creating a reservation, you must know the MAC address for each device for which you are reserving an address. The MAC address can be obtained by keying **ipconfig /all** at the command line, which will result in output similar to the following:

```
Ethernet adapter Wireless Network Connection:
Connection-specific DNS Suffix.:
Description........................:  Dell Wireless 1390 WLAN Mini-Card
Physical Address.................:  00-1A-92-9F-D7-DC
```

Dhcp Enabled.......................:	Yes
Autoconfiguration Enabled...:	Yes
IP Address..........................:	192.168.1.100
Subnet Mask.......................:	255.255.255.0
Default Gateway.................:	192.168.1.1
DHCP Server......................:	192.168.1.1
DNS Servers.......................:	192.168.1.210
	192.168.1.215
Lease Obtained.................:	Sunday, December 02, 2007 4:54:47 PM
Lease Expires...................:	Monday, December 03, 2007 4:54:47 PM

The MAC address in this example is 00-1A-92-9F-D7-DC.

⊘ CONFIGURE A DHCP RESERVATION

GET READY. This exercise assumes that you have configured a DHCP Server on a Windows Server 2008 computer and have configured at least one DHCP scope.

1. Press **Ctrl** + **Alt** + **Del** on the Windows Server 2008 computer and log on as the default administrator of the local computer.
2. Click **Start→Administrative Tools→DHCP**.
3. To configure an IPv4 DHCP scope, drill down to the server name, followed by IPv4, followed by the scope name, and then expand the **Reservations** node.
4. Right-click the **Reservations** node and click **New Reservation....**
5. The New Reservation screen appears. Enter a descriptive name for the reservation, followed by the desired IP address.
6. Enter the MAC address of the computer that should receive this reservation, and an optional description.
7. Click **Add** and then click **Close.**

PAUSE. You can close the DHCP administration console, or else leave it open for a subsequent exercise. To configure a DHCP scope from a Server Core computer, use the netsh command.

In the previous exercise, you configured a DHCP reservation within a DHCP scope. In the next exercise, we will discuss configuring DHCP options to fine-tune the configuration of computers receiving their IP address configuration from a Windows Server 2008 DHCP server.

Configuring DHCP Options

DHCP options are additional client-configuration parameters that a DHCP server can assign when serving leases to DHCP clients. DHCP options are configured using the DHCP console and can apply to scopes and reservations. For example, IP addresses for a router or default gateway, WINS servers, or DNS servers are commonly provided for a single scope or globally for all scopes managed by the DHCP server.

Many DHCP options are predefined through RFC 2132, but the Microsoft DHCP server also allows you to define and add custom options. Table 3-1 describes some of the options that can be configured.

Table 3-1

DHCP Options

Option	Description
Router (default gateway)	The addresses of any default gateway or router. This router is commonly referred to as the default gateway.
Domain name	A DNS domain name defines the domain to which a client computer belongs. The client computer can use this information to update a DNS server so that other computers can locate the client.
DNS and WINS servers	The addresses of any DNS and WINS servers for clients to use for network communication.

DHCP options can be assigned to all scopes, one specific scope, or to a specific machine reservation. There are four types of DHCP options in Windows Server 2008:

- *Server options*—apply to all clients of the DHCP server. Use these options for parameters common across all scopes on the DHCP server.
- *Scope options*—apply to all clients within a scope and are the most often used set of options. Scope options override server options.
- ***Class options***—provide DHCP parameters to DHCP clients based on type—either vendor classes or user classes.
- *Client options*—apply to individual clients. Client options override all other options (server, scope, and class).

User classes are created at the discretion of the DHCP administrator. Vendor classes are defined by the machine's vendor and cannot be changed. Using vendor and user classes, an administrator can then configure the DHCP server to assign different options, depending on the type of client receiving them. For example, an administrator can configure the DHCP server to assign different options based on type of client, such as desktop or portable computer. This feature gives administrators greater flexibility in configuring clients. If client class options are not used, default settings are assigned. Vendor class and vendor options are described in RFC 2132 and can be looked up at *http://www.rfc-editor.org/rfcsearch.html*.

Configuring the DHCP Relay Agent

When the DHCP client and the DHCP server are on the same subnet, the DHCPDISCOVER, DHCPOFFER, DHCPREQUEST, and DHCPACK messages are sent by means of broadcast traffic. When the DHCP server and DHCP client are not on the same subnet, the connecting router or routers must support the forwarding of DHCP messages between the DHCP client and the DHCP server, or a BOOTP/DHCP relay agent must be installed on the subnet where the client is located. This is because BOOTP and DHCP protocols rely on network broadcasts to perform their work, and routers in normal routed environments do not automatically forward broadcasts from one interface to another.

In this section, we will discuss the two options available to you to allow a DHCP server on one subnet to service client requests from remote subnets. First, if the routers separating the DHCP server and clients are RFC 1542 compliant, the routers can be configured for BOOTP forwarding. Through BOOTP forwarding, routers forward DHCP broadcasts between clients and servers and inform servers on the originating subnet of the DHCP requests. This process allows DHCP servers to assign addresses to the remote clients from the appropriate scope.

The second way to allow remote communication between DHCP servers and clients is to configure a DHCP relay agent on the subnet containing the remote clients. DHCP relay agents intercept DHCPDISCOVER packets and forward them to a remote DHCP server whose address has been pre-configured. A DHCP relay agent is either a router or a host computer configured to listen for DHCP/BOOTP broadcast messages and direct them to a specific DHCP server or servers. Using relay agents eliminates the necessity of having a DHCP server on each physical network segment or having RFC 2131–compliant routers. Relay agents not only direct local DHCP client requests to remote DHCP servers, but also return remote DHCP server responses to the DHCP clients. Although the DHCP relay agent is configured through the Routing and Remote Access server role, the computer that is hosting the agent does not need to be functioning as an actual router between subnets. RFC 2131–compliant routers (supersedes RFC 1542) contain relay agents that allow them to forward DHCP packets.

Let's examine a scenario in which a DHCP client on Subnet 2 attempts to obtain its IP address from a DHCP server on Subnet 1:

1. The DHCP client broadcasts a DHCPDISCOVER message on Subnet 2 as a UDP datagram over UDP port 67, which is the port reserved and shared for BOOTP and DHCP server communication.

2. The relay agent, in this case a DHCP/BOOTP relay–enabled router, examines the gateway IP address field in the DHCP/BOOTP message header. If the field has an IP address of 0.0.0.0, the relay agent fills it with its own IP address and forwards the message to Subnet 1, where the DHCP server is located.

3. When the DHCP server on Subnet 1 receives the DHCPDISCOVER message, it examines the gateway IP address field for a DHCP scope to determine whether it can supply an IP address lease. If the DHCP server has multiple DHCP scopes, the address in the gateway IP address field identifies the DHCP scope from which to offer an IP address lease.

For example, if the gateway IP address field has an IP address of 192.168.45.2, the DHCP server checks its DHCP scopes for a scope range that matches the Class C IP network that includes the gateway IP address of the computer. In this case, the DHCP server checks to see which scope includes addresses between 192.168.45.1 and 192.168.45.254. If a scope exists that matches this criterion, the DHCP server selects an available address from the matched scope to use in an IP address lease offer (DHCPOFFER) response to the client. The DHCP Relay Agent process continues as follows:

4. The DHCP server sends a DHCPOFFER message directly to the relay agent identified in the gateway IP address field.

5. The router relays the address lease offer (DHCPOFFER) to the DHCP client as a broadcast since the client's IP address is still unknown.

After the client receives the DHCPOFFER, a DHCPREQUEST message is relayed from client to server, and a DHCPACK message is relayed from server to client in accordance with RFC 1542.

Managing the DHCP Database

DHCP plays a key role in an organization's network infrastructure. Without an accessible DHCP server, most clients completely lose network connectivity. Therefore, like any key resource in your organization, you must carefully manage the DHCP server. Proper management of a DHCP server helps prevent server downtime and aids in quick recovery after a server failure.

Your network is constantly changing. New servers are added and existing servers are changing roles or are removed from the network altogether. Because of this, you must both monitor and manage the DHCP service to ensure it is meeting the needs of the organization. Specifically, you must manage the DHCP database by performing the following database functions:

- Backup and restore
- Reconciliation
- Compacting the database
- Removing the database

The DHCP server database is a dynamic database, which is a data store that is updated as DHCP clients are assigned or as they release their TCP/IP configuration parameters. Because the DHCP database is not a distributed database like the DNS server database, maintaining the DHCP server database is less complex. DNS is stored hierarchically across many different servers, with each server containing a part of the overall database. DHCP, by contrast, is contained in a few files on one server.

The DHCP server database in the Windows Server 2008 family uses the *Joint Engine Technology (JET)* storage engine. When you install the DHCP service, the files shown in Table 3-2 are automatically created in the %systemroot%\System32\Dhcp directory.

Table 3-2

DHCP Service Database Files

FILE	DESCRIPTION
Dhcp.mdb	The DHCP server database file.
Temp.edb	A file used by the DHCP database as a temporary storage file during database index maintenance operations. This file sometimes resides in the %systemroot%\System32\Dhcp directory after a system failure.
J50.log and J50#####.log	A log of all database transactions. The DHCP database uses this file to recover data when necessary.
J50.chk	A *checkpoint file* indicates the location of the last information that was successfully written from the transaction logs to the database. In a data recovery scenario, the checkpoint file indicates where the recovery or replaying of data should begin. The checkpoint file is updated when data is written to the database file (Dhcp.mdb).

There is virtually no limit to the number of records a DHCP server stores; the size of the database is primarily dependent upon the number of DHCP clients on the network. The size of the DHCP database is not directly proportional to the number of active client lease entries, though, because over time some DHCP client entries become obsolete or deleted. This space is not immediately reclaimed and therefore some space remains unused. To recover the unused space, the DHCP database must be *compacted*; that is, the database must be optimized to reclaim unused space that has been left by adding and removing records. Dynamic database compaction occurs on DHCP servers as an automatic background process during idle time or after a database update.

Backing Up and Restoring the DHCP Database

Windows Server 2008 DHCP servers support automatic and manual backups. To provide fault tolerance in the case of a failure, it is important to back up the DHCP database. This enables you to restore the database from the backup copy if the hardware fails.

When you perform a backup, the entire DHCP database is saved, including the following:

- Scopes, including superscopes and multicast scopes
- Reservations
- Leases
- Options, including server options, scope options, reservation options, and class options

By default, the DHCP service automatically backs up the DHCP database and related registry entries to a backup directory on the local drive. This occurs every 60 minutes. By default, automatic backups are stored in the %systemroot%\System32\Dhcp\Backup directory. The administrator can also change the backup location. Automatic backups can use only *automatic restores*, which are performed by the DHCP service when corruption is detected.

You can also back up the DHCP database manually. By default, manual backups are stored in the %systemroot%\System32\Dhcp\Backup\ directory, or you can specify an alternate location. You can manually back up the DHCP database while the DHCP service is running. The backup destination must be on the local disk; remote paths are not allowed, and the backup directory is created automatically if it does not already exist. The administrator can then copy the backed up DHCP files to an offline storage location such as a tape or a disk.

⟶ BACK UP AND RESTORE THE DHCP DATABASE

GET READY. This exercise assumes that you have installed the DHCP Server role on a Windows Server 2008 computer, and that you have administrative rights to that server.

1. In the DHCP console, in the console tree, select the appropriate DHCP server.
2. Right-click the server and click **Backup**.
3. In the Browse For Folder dialog box, select the appropriate folder to back up to, and then click **OK**.
4. To restore the DHCP database, right-click the server and click **Restore**.
5. In the Browse For Folder dialog box, select the folder where the backup resides and then click **OK**.
6. In the DHCP dialog box, click **Yes** to stop and then restart the service.
7. If the status of the service does not update, press **F5** to refresh the DHCP console.

PAUSE. You can close the DHCP administrator console, or else leave it open for subsequent exercises.

In the previous exercise you performed a manual backup and restore of the DHCP database. Next we will discuss reconciling the DHCP database.

Reconciling the DHCP Database

When you reconcile a server or a scope, the DHCP service uses both the summary information in the registry and the detailed information in the DHCP database to reconstruct the most current view of the DHCP service. You can choose to reconcile all scopes on the server by selecting the DHCP server, or you can reconcile one scope by selecting the appropriate scope.

Reconciliation is the process of verifying DHCP database values against DHCP registry values. You should reconcile your DHCP database in the following scenarios:

- The DHCP database values are configured correctly, but they are not displayed correctly in the DHCP console.
- After you have restored a DHCP database, but the restored DHCP database does not have the most recent values.

For example, assume your existing database was deleted and you have to restore an older version of the database. If you start DHCP and open the console, you will notice that the scope and options display, but the active leases do not. Reconciliation populates the client lease information from the registry to the DHCP database.

Before using the Reconcile feature to verify client information for a DHCP scope from the registry, the server computer needs to meet the following criteria:

- You must restore the DHCP server registry keys, or they must remain intact from previous service operations on the server computer.
- You must generate a fresh copy of the DHCP server database file in the %systemroot%\ System32\Dhcp folder on the server computer.

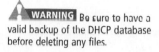 **WARNING** Be sure to have a valid backup of the DHCP database before deleting any files.

You can generate a fresh copy of the DHCP server database file by stopping the DHCP server service, deleting all of the database files in the current database path folder, and then restarting the DHCP server service.

Once the registry and database meet the previous criteria, you can restart the DHCP service. Upon opening the DHCP console, you might notice that scope information is present, but that there are no active leases displayed. To regain your active leases for each scope, use the Reconcile feature. You can reconcile a single scope or the entire server by right-clicking on the appropriate node and then clicking Reconcile.

When viewing properties for individual clients displayed in the list of active leases, you might notice client information displayed incorrectly. When the scope clients renew their leases, the DHCP Manager corrects and updates this information.

SUMMARY SKILL MATRIX

IN THIS LESSON YOU LEARNED:

- DHCP is a simple, standard protocol that makes TCP/IP network configuration much easier for the administrator by dynamically assigning IP addresses and providing additional configuration information to DHCP clients automatically.

- Additional configuration information is provided in the form of options and can be associated with reserved IPs, to a vendor or user class, to a scope, or to an entire DHCP server.

- Because DHCP is a key component in your organization, you must manage and monitor it.

- DHCP management consists of backing up and restoring the database as well as reconciling, compacting, and, in some cases, removing the database.

- APIPA is useful for providing addresses to single-segment networks that do not have a DHCP server.

Knowledge Assessment

Matching

Match the term in Column 1 to its description in Column 2.

a. authorize

b. automatic restore

c. class options

d. DHCPDECLINE

e. DHCPRELEASE

f. exclusion range

g. Joint Engine Technology (JET)

h. reservation

i. rogue DHCP server

j. T2

_____ 1. This DHCP message type is sent by a DHCP client when it no longer requires the use of an IP address that it has leased from a DHCP server.

_____ 2. You can configure one of these to ensure that a DHCP client always eceives the same IP address from a particular DHCP server.

_____ 3. This is used to ensure that a particular address or block of addresses within a scope is not assigned to DHCP clients by a DHCP server.

_____ 4. You must do this to any DHCP server that needs to function within an Active Directory domain.

_____ 5. A DHCP client will send this message type if it determines that an IP address offered by a DHCP server is already in use.

_____ 6. This is performed by a DHCP server when corruption is detected within the DHCP database.

_____ 7. The DHCP database is based on this database technology.

_____ 8. Authorizing DHCP servers in Active Directory is designed to prevent against these.

_____ 9. These provide DHCP parameters to DHCP clients based on vendor or user type.

_____10. This defaults to 87.5% of the total DHCP lease.

Multiple Choice

Select all answers that apply for the following questions.

1. Which of the following DHCP message types is sent first in the process of obtaining an address lease?
   a. DHCPOFFER
   b. DHCPACK
   c. DHCPDISCOVER
   d. DHCPREQUEST

2. At which layer of the OSI model does DHCP operate?
   a. Session layer
   b. Network layer
   c. Application layer
   d. Presentation layer

3. What protocol is used by the Trivial File Transfer Protocol (TFTP)?
   a. User Datagram Protocol (UDP)
   b. Transmission Control Protocol (TCP)
   c. Internet Protocol (IP)
   d. Internet Message Control Protocol (ICMP)

4. A DHCP client first attempts to reacquire its lease at half the lease time, which is known as:
   a. DHCP reservation
   b. T1
   c. T2
   d. DHCP lease

5. The _____ is composed of the remaining addresses within a DHCP scope once all exclusion ranges have been applied.
   a. total address pool
   b. available address pool
   c. net address pool
   d. remaining address pool

6. The following is a lightweight version of FTP that uses the UDP protocol, which is used by the BOOTP protocol to transmit network configuration information:
   a. TCP
   b. IP
   c. TFTP
   d. SNMP

7. The following process will populate DHCP client lease information from the registry to the DHCP database:
   a. Backup
   b. Automatic restore
   c. Reconciliation
   d. Discovery

8. The following is an administrative grouping of scopes that is used to support multiple logical subnets on a single network segment:
   a. host
   c. superscope
   b. scope
   d. multinet

9. This indicates the location of the last information that was successfully written from transaction logs to a database file such as a DHCP database.
   a. Log file
   b. JET file
   c. Checkpoint file
   d. Check file

10. The following is a hexadecimal address that is uniquely associated with a specific Network Interface Card (NIC):
    a. MAC
    b. JET
    c. BOOTP
    d. IETF

■ Case Scenarios

Scenario 3-1: Obtaining an IP Address

Last month, a server was configured for DHCP and was functioning normally. Five days ago, a test server on the same network segment was promoted to be the first domain controller on the network. Today several users on the same subnet as the original DHCP server have complained that they are unable to obtain an IP address using DHCP. What is the most likely reason users are unable to obtain an IP address?

    a. The users' IP address leases have expired.

    b. A DHCP relay agent is missing or incorrectly configured.

    c. There are duplicate IP addresses on the network.

    d. The DHCP server must be authorized and is not.

Scenario 3-2: Maximizing Lease Availability

You are configuring DHCP scope options for Contoso, Ltd. The company has a limited number of IP addresses available for clients, and it wants to configure DHCP to maximize IP address availability. Choose all of the following actions that will accomplish this objective:

    a. Set long lease durations for IP addresses.

    b. Set short lease durations for IP addresses.

    c. Configure a DHCP option to automatically release an IP address when the computer shuts down.

    d. Create DHCP reservations for all portable computers.

Configuring and Managing the DNS Server Role

OBJECTIVE DOMAIN MATRIX

TECHNOLOGY SKILL	OBJECTIVE DOMAIN	OBJECTIVE DOMAIN NUMBER
Installing the DNS Server Role	Configure a Domain Name System (DNS) server	2.1
Introducing DNS Zones	Configure DNS zones	2.2
Configuring Active Directory–Integrated Zones	Configure DNS replication	2.4
Configuring DNS Resource Records	Configure DNS records	2.3
Introducing the DNS Name Resolution Process	Configure name resolution for client	2.5

KEY TERMS

authoritative
authoritative answer
canonical name (CNAME) resource record
conditional forwarder
country code
discretionary access control list (DACL)
DomainDNSZones
file-backed zone
ForestDNSZones

forward lookup zone
forwarder
forwarding-only server
full zone transfer (AXFR)
host (A)
host (AAAA) resource record
incremental zone transfer (IXFR)
in-addr.arpa domain
ip6.arpa domain
mail exchanger (MX) resource record

PTR resource record
reverse lookup zone
root hints
second-level domains
secure dynamic updates
standard zone
stub zone
Time to Live (TTL)
top-level domains
zone transfer

Contoso, Ltd. is a global manufacturer of computer peripherals, with locations in Guadalajara, Mexico; Austin, Texas; and Tallinn, Estonia. Each location contains several hundred PCs that are frequently rebuilt using different machine names to emulate various testing environments. As the network administrator of Contoso, you have been tasked with configuring a name resolution solution that will allow users in each location to maintain consistent access to resources. To enable this functionality, you have decided to deploy the Domain Name System (DNS) server role using a Microsoft Windows Server 2008 computer in each company location.

In this lesson we will discuss the Domain Name System (DNS), the primary means of name resolution in Active Directory and on major TCP/IP networks such as the Internet. We will begin with a discussion of the components of DNS. Once you have a grounding in the overall concepts of DNS, we will walk through the steps required to implement this service on a Windows Server 2008 network.

■ Configuring the Domain Name System (DNS) Service

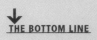

THE BOTTOM LINE

This lesson introduces fundamental concepts related to Domain Name System (DNS) name resolution in Microsoft Windows Server 2008. The lesson also explains key DNS concepts such as the DNS namespace, DNS zones, types of DNS servers, DNS resource records, and DNS resolvers. Also discussed is the process of configuring DNS servers, the types and process of DNS queries, and forwarding. Because DNS plays such a key role in Windows Server 2008, it is critical that you have a strong grasp of its concepts, processes, and methods of configuration. Without DNS, your network will most likely not function— clients won't be able to resolve names to Internet Protocol (IP) addresses. In addition, Active Directory clients use DNS to locate domain controllers; therefore, it is important that you understand key DNS concepts and how to properly configure DNS for your network.

For network devices such as computers and printers to communicate on the Internet or within your organization's network, they must be able to locate one another. In a Windows Server 2008 network, the primary means of locating network devices and network services is through the use of the Domain Name System, or DNS. For example, in order for COMPUTERA to communicate with COMPUTERB over a Transmission Control Protocol/Internet Protocol (TCP/IP) network, COMPUTERA must obtain the IP address of COMPUTERB. The process of mapping an IP address to a computer name (for example, COMPUTERA) is called *name resolution*. Windows Server 2008 includes both the DNS and Windows Internet Naming System (WINS) name resolution services to allow 2008 computers to translate between human-readable names, which are easy for users to understand, and numerical IP addresses, which are difficult for users to comprehend but are necessary for TCP/IP communications.

Before you can design and configure DNS for your Windows Server 2008 network, it is important to have an understanding of how DNS name resolution was developed for use on TCP/IP networks. Before the growth of the ARPANET into what we now know as the Internet, name resolution was handled through the use of text files called *HOSTS files* that were stored locally on each computer. The HOSTS file listed each name of the host and its corresponding IP address. Whenever a new host was added to the network, an administrator would manually update the HOSTS file with the new host name or IP address information. Periodically, all ARPANET users would then download and use the updated HOSTS file. Because the HOSTS file was flat, rather than hierarchical, it was impossible to organize hosts into separate domain structures. There was no method for creating hierarchical namespaces such as domains.

Another problem with HOSTS files was the size of the file and the inability to distribute the workload that resulted from parsing this file across multiple computers. Every HOSTS file listed every available ARPANET host, which meant that every computer that parsed the HOSTS file did 100 percent of the work to resolve client names into IP addresses. Clearly, this was inefficient and a better name resolution system had to be devised. In 1984, when the number of hosts on ARPANET reached 1,000, DNS was introduced. Because DNS is designed as a distributed database with a hierarchical structure, it can serve as the foundation for host name resolution in a TCP/IP network of any size, including the Internet. The distributed nature of DNS enables the name resolution workload to be shared among many computers. Today, most internetworking software, such as electronic mail programs and Web browsers, uses DNS for name resolution.

Although DNS is most commonly associated with the Internet, private networks also use DNS because of the following benefits:

- Scalability—Because DNS is capable of distributing workload across several databases or computers, it can scale to handle any level of name resolution required.

- Constancy—Host names remain constant even when associated IP addresses change, which makes locating network resources much easier.

- Ease of Use—Users access computers using easy-to-remember names such as *www. microsoft.com* rather than a numerical IP address, such as 192.168.1.100.

- Simplicity—Users need to learn only one naming convention to find resources on either the Internet or an intranet.

To understand the importance of DNS and how it functions within a Windows Server 2008 environment, you must understand a number of different components within DNS.

Introducing DNS Namespaces

A *DNS namespace* is a hierarchical, tree-structured list of DNS host names, starting at an unnamed root that is used for all DNS operations. Each domain can have additional child domains: a typical DNS namespace might be the *contoso.com* domain, which contains the *us.contoso.com* and *ee.contoso.com* child domains within the same namespace, and host names (also called *leaf objects*) representing individual TCP/IP-enabled devices such as *server1.austin.us.contoso.com*, *hplaserjet.sales.ee.contoso.com*, or *www.us.contoso.com*. Figure 4-1 illustrates the structure of a typical DNS namespace that you might find on the Internet.

Figure 4-1

Viewing a typical DNS namespace

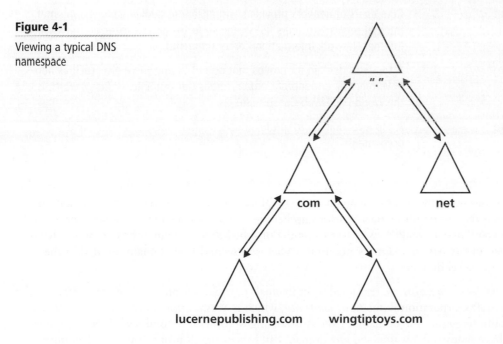

The DNS namespace has a hierarchical structure, and each DNS domain name is unique within a namespace. In Figure 4-1, at the top of the Internet DNS namespace is the root domain. The root domain is represented by "." (a period). Under the DNS root domain, the **top-level domains**, or first-level domains, are organizational types such as .org, .com, and .edu. There are three types of top-level domains:

- Generic—See Table 4-1 for examples of generic, top-level domain names.
- **Country code**—Examples of country code domain names are .uk., .jp, and .us.
- Infrastructure domain—.arpa is the Internet's infrastructure domain name.

Table 4-1

Generic Top-Level Domain
Names

Domain Name	Use
.aero	Exclusively reserved for the aviation community
.biz	A top-level domain that is aimed at large and small companies around the world
.com	Commercial organizations, such as *microsoft.com* for the Microsoft Corporation
.coop	A top-level domain for cooperatives
.edu	Educational institutions, now mainly four-year colleges and universities, such as *wustl.edu* for Washington University in St. Louis.
.gov	Agencies of the U.S. federal government, such as *fbi.gov* for the U.S. Federal Bureau of Investigation
.info	An unrestricted domain aimed at providing information for worldwide consumption
.int	Organizations established by international treaties, such as *nato.int* for NATO
.mil	U.S. military, such as *af.mil* for the U.S. Air Force
.museum	A domain restricted to museums and related organizations and individuals
.name	A global domain for use by individuals that possibly develops into a global digital identity for users
.net	Computers of network providers, organizations dedicated to the Internet, Internet service providers (ISPs), and so forth, such as *internic.net* for the Internet Network Information Center (InterNIC)
.org	A top-level domain for groups that do not fit anywhere else, such as non-governmental or nonprofit organizations (for example, *w3.org*, which is the World Wide Web Consortium)
.pro	A top-level domain for professionals, such as doctors, lawyers, and accountants

DNS uses the fully qualified domain name (FQDN) to map a host name to an IP address. An FQDN describes the exact relationship between a host and its DNS domain. For example, *computer1.sales.microsoft.com* represents a fully qualified domain name: the computer1 host, located in the sales domain, located in the Microsoft second-level domain, located in the .com top-level domain.

Second-level domains are registered to individuals or organizations, such as *microsoft.com*, the Microsoft Corporation domain; or *wustl.edu*, which is Washington University in the St. Louis domain; or *gov.au*, the domain for the Australian government. Second-level DNS domains can have many *subdomains*, and any domain can have hosts. A host is a specific computer or other network device within a domain, such as *computer1* in the *sales* subdomain of the *microsoft.com* domain.

One benefit of the hierarchical structure of DNS is that it is possible to have two hosts with the same host name that are in different locations in the hierarchy. For example, two hosts named *computer1*—*computer1.sales.microsoft.com* and *computer1.cpandl.microsoft.com*—can both exist without conflict because they are in different locations in the namespace hierarchy.

Deploying DNS Servers

As you might expect from the name, *DNS servers* are Windows Servers that host the DNS server role and are classified by the type of zones that they host. A DNS server can host primary zones, secondary zones, stub zones, or no zones. (A DNS *zone* is a collection of host name–to–IP address mappings for hosts in a contiguous portion of the DNS namespace, such as *contoso.com* or *austin.contoso.com*.) A DNS server is called the *primary name server* for any primary zones it hosts and a *secondary name server* for the secondary zones it hosts. A *caching-only server* hosts no zones.

 REF   DNS zones will be discussed more fully in the next section: "Introducing DNS zones."

DNS server types are determined by the type of zone or zones they host, and by the functions they perform. A DNS server may host either primary or secondary zones or both. If the server doesn't host any zones, it is referred to a *caching-only server*. A server is said to be **authoritative** for a particular zone if it hosts a primary or secondary zone for a particular DNS domain. These three types of servers are supported in Windows Server 2003 and Windows Server 2008, and are discussed as follows:

- Primary name server—Primary name servers have been configured with one or more primary DNS zones. In the case of standard or file-backed zones, when a change is made to the zone data, such as adding resource records to the zone, the changes must be made on the primary server for that zone; these changes will then propagate to secondary name servers. In the case of AD-integrated zones, there is no distinction between primary and secondary servers.
- Secondary name server—A secondary name server hosts one or more secondary zone databases. Because a zone transfer is used to create a secondary zone, the primary name server and zone already must exist to create a secondary name server.
- Caching-only server—Caching-only servers do not host any zones and are not authoritative for any domain. Caching-only DNS servers start with an empty cache, and then add resource record entries as the server fulfills client requests. This information is then available from its cache when answering subsequent client queries. A caching-only DNS server is valuable at a site when DNS functionality is needed locally but when creating a separate domain or zone is not desirable.

Installing the DNS Server Role

To enjoy the benefits of DNS, you must, of course, install DNS. Before you install DNS, it is recommended that you configure your computer to use a static IP address. If the DNS server is assigned its IP address from Dynamic Host Configuration Protocol (DHCP), its IP address may change. If the DNS server's IP address changes, queries sent by DNS clients configured with the old IP address will fail. Windows Server 2008 provides several wizards and other tools to install DNS quickly and easily. One method of installing DNS is by using the Server Manager page. The Server Manager page enables you to add or remove server roles, such as file server, print server, DHCP server, and DNS server. The following procedure explains how to use the Server Manager console to add the DNS server role. It will also cover the steps needed to create a zone and one or more resource records within a zone, now that we have covered the theory behind each of these concepts.

→ **INSTALL THE DNS SERVER ROLE**

GET READY. This exercise assumes that you are logged onto a Windows Server 2008 computer that has been configured with a static IP address, and that the Initial Configuration Tasks for this server have already been completed.

Install the DNS server role

1. Log onto the server using administrative credentials.
2. Click the **Start** button, and then click **Server Manager**. Expand the Server Manager console to full-screen, if necessary.
3. In the left-hand pane, click **Roles**. In the right-hand pane, click **Add Roles**.
4. The Before You Begin screen appears. Read the preliminary information and click **Next**.
5. The Select Server Roles screen appears. Place a checkmark next to **DNS Server** and click **Next**.
6. The DNS Server screen appears. Read the information presented about the DNS server role and click **Next**.
7. The Confirm Installation Selections screen appears. Click **Install** to install the DNS server role.
8. After a few minutes, the Installation Results screen will appear. Click **Close**.

PAUSE. Close the DNS console and log off of the Windows Server 2008 server.

In the previous exercise, you installed the DNS server role. In upcoming exercises you will configure DNS zones, create DNS resource records, and perform a number of other common configuration tasks on a Windows Server 2008 DNS server.

Introducing DNS Zones

CERTIFICATION READY?
Configure DNS zones
2.2

As previously noted, another benefit of the DNS hierarchical structure is that workload for name resolution is distributed across many different resources. For administrative purposes, DNS domains can be organized into zones. A zone is a collection of host name–to–IP address mappings for hosts in a contiguous portion of the DNS namespace. Just like DNS resource records, DNS zones can be created and configured using the Windows Server 2008 DNS MMC snap-in, or else the *dnscmd* DNS management command-line utility.

A DNS zone can hold the resource records for one domain, or it can hold the resource records for multiple domains. A zone can host more than one domain only if the domains are contiguous—that is, connected by a direct parent-child relationship. One reason to divide a namespace into zones is to delegate authority for different portions of it, as one very large domain could be difficult to administer if contained in a single zone.

For each DNS domain name included in a zone, the zone becomes the authoritative source for information about that domain. When a zone is authoritative over a portion of the namespace, it means that it hosts the resource records for that portion of the namespace. It does not necessarily mean, however, that the server can update or modify the zone.

DNS zones are classified by where they are stored, whether they are writable, and by what information they receive and return. Zones can be stored either in text files or in Active Directory. When you configure a DNS server, you can configure it either with several zone types or with none at all, depending on the type of role that the DNS server has in the network. By using different zones, you can configure your DNS solution to best meet your needs. For example, it is recommended that you configure a primary zone and a secondary zone on separate DNS servers to provide fault tolerance should one server fail. You can also configure a stub zone if the zone is maintained on a separate DNS server to allow local DNS servers to stay up-to-date whenever remote DNS server information for a particular zone is updated.

In brief, zone data is maintained on a DNS name server and is stored in one of two ways:

- As a text-based zone file containing lists of mappings, called a *standard zone* or a *file-backed zone*
- Within an Active Directory database, called an *Active Directory–integrated zone*

In terms of the types of queries that a DNS zone (either standard or AD-integrated) can respond to, each zone can be either a *forward lookup zone* or a *reverse lookup zone*. In turn, each forward or reverse lookup zone can be one of three types:

- Primary zone
- Secondary zone
- Stub zone

As you can see, there are numerous possible combinations of each zone type that you can configure on a DNS server. For example, a single DNS server can host:

- A standard primary forward lookup zone
- A standard secondary forward lookup zone
- An Active Directory–integrated stub zone
- A standard secondary reverse lookup zone

…and so on.

When configuring a DNS server, you can configure a single server to host multiple zones if desired, and you can mix and match between different zone types. For example, a single DNS server might host a primary zone for *contoso.com*, as well as a secondary zone for *lucernepublishing.com* to allow improved name resolution for a remote network's resources, as might be necessary in the case of cross-departmental or cross-organizational projects that require access to resources across multiple organizations.

Configuring Standard Zones

You can configure DNS zones in a number of different ways to meet the requirements of your network topology, administrative model, and the size of your DNS namespace. Typical DNS server operation involves three standard zones (primary, secondary, and in-addr.arpa). Windows Server 2003 and Windows Server 2008 provide a fourth option, stub zones.

Let's look at each of the standard zone types that can be configured on a Windows Server 2008 server.

- Standard primary zone—A standard primary zone hosts a read/write copy of the DNS zone in which resource records are created and managed. Only one server can host and load the master copy of the zone; no additional primary servers for the zone are permitted, and only the server hosting the primary zone is allowed to accept dynamic updates and process zone changes. When setting up DNS servers to host the zones for a domain, the primary server normally is located where it will be accessible for administering the zone file.
- Standard secondary zone—A copy of the zone file may be stored on one or more servers to balance network load, provide fault tolerance, or avoid forcing queries across a slow, wide area network (WAN) link. This standard secondary zone is a read-only copy of the standard primary DNS zone. In standard zones, information from a primary zone is transmitted to a secondary zone by performing a **zone transfer**, which is done by copying the zone file from the primary server to a secondary server. A zone transfer can be a **full zone transfer** (called an **AXFR**), in which the entire contents of the zone is copied from the primary server to the secondary server during each zone transfer, or an **incremental zone transfer** (called an **IXFR**), in which only changed information is transmitted after an initial AXFR, in order to cut down on bandwidth usage between

primary and secondary servers. When a secondary zone is created, you must specify the IP address of one or more master DNS servers from which you want to copy the zone; these can be the Primary DNS server for the zone or another Secondary DNS server. These copies are referred to as *secondary zone database files*. The secondary zone database files are updated regularly from the primary zone database.

• Reverse lookup zone—Most queries sent to a DNS server are forward queries; that is, they request an IP address based on a DNS name. DNS also provides a reverse lookup process, which enables a host to determine another host's name based on its IP address. For example, a query contains the equivalent of "What is the DNS domain name of the host at IP address 192.168.100.1?" To answer this query, the **in-addr.arpa domain** is consulted in combination with the IP address in question. As you read the IP address from left to right, the network portion is some number of bits on the left, and the host portion is some number of bits on the right, based on the subnet mask. For example, 192.168.100.2, with a default subnet mask of 255.255.255.0, means the network portion is 192.168.100, and the host address is 2. Because the higher-level portion of the address is on the right, it must be reversed when building the domain tree. In short, because FQDNs go from specific to general, and IP addresses go from general to specific, that is, reading left to right, to facilitate reverse lookup, the IP address is reversed when concatenated with the in-addr.arpa domain. For example, the reverse lookup zone for the subnet 192.168.100.0 is 100.168.192.in-addr.arpa. The in-addr.arpa domain tree makes use of the *pointer (PTR) resource record*, which is used to associate the IP address with the host name. This lookup should correspond to an *address (A) resource record* for the host in a forward lookup zone. Reverse lookup queries often are used by network applications for verification rather than identification or as a tool for monitoring and troubleshooting the DNS service. The in-addr.arpa domain is used only for Internet Protocol version 4 (IPv4)-based networks. In the DNS console for Windows Server 2003, the DNS server's New Zone Wizard uses this domain when it creates a new reverse lookup zone. Internet Protocol version 6 (IPv6)-based reverse lookup zones are based on the **ip6.arpa domain**, which provides the same functionality as the in-addr.arpa domain for IPv6 networks.

• Stub zone—A DNS server running Windows Server 2003 or Windows Server 2008 also supports a new type of zone called a **stub zone**. A stub zone is a copy of a zone that contains only those resource records necessary to identify the authoritative DNS servers for that zone. A stub zone is a pointer to the DNS server that is authoritative for that zone, and it is used to maintain or improve DNS resolution efficiency. The stub zone contains a subset of zone data consisting of an SOA, an NS, and an A record. Like a standard secondary zone, resource records in the stub zone cannot be modified; they must be modified at the primary zone. Stub zones enable a DNS server to resolve DNS queries by using the stub zone's list of name servers without needing to query the Internet or internal root server for the DNS namespace. Using stub zones throughout your DNS infrastructure enables you to distribute a list of the authoritative DNS servers for a zone without using secondary zones. However, stub zones do not serve the same purpose as secondary zones and should not be considered as a solution to address redundancy and load sharing.

In the following exercises, we will configure a standard primary zone, secondary zone, and stub zone.

➡ CONFIGURE A STANDARD PRIMARY ZONE

GET READY. This exercise assumes that you have installed the DNS server role as described in a previous exercise, and that you are logged onto the Windows Server 2008 computer with administrative privileges. In this exercise, we will create a forward lookup zone for the *contoso. com* domain on a server named DNSPRI.

1. Click the **Start** button, then click **Administrative Tools** and then **DNS**.
2. Expand the DNS console to full-screen, if necessary.
3. Drill down to **DNSPRI→Forward Lookup Zones**.

4. Right-click **Forward Lookup Zones** and click **New Zone**....

5. The Welcome to the New Zone Wizard screen appears. Click **Next**.

6. The Zone Type screen appears. Select the **Primary zone** radio button and click **Next**.

7. The Zone Name screen appears. In the *Zone name:* text box, enter **contoso.com** and then click **Next**.

8. The Zone File screen appears. Ensure that the *Create a new file with this file name:* radio button is selected and then click **Next**.

9. The Dynamic Update screen appears. Ensure that the *Do not allow dynamic updates* radio button is selected and then click **Next**.

10. The Completing the New Zone Wizard appears. Click **Finish**.

PAUSE. Close the DNS MMC snap-in and log off of the DNSPRI Windows Server 2008 server.

In the previous exercise, you configured a standard primary zone for the *contoso.com* DNS domain. In the next exercise, you will configure a secondary zone for load balancing on a second Windows Server 2008 computer called DNSSEC.

➔ CONFIGURE A STANDARD SECONDARY ZONE

GET READY. This exercise assumes that you have installed the DNS server role on a Windows Server 2008 computer called DNSSEC that has been configured with a static IP address, and that the Initial Configuration Tasks for this server have already been completed, This exercise assumes that you are logged onto DNSSEC with administrative privileges. You must also have the IP address of the DNSPRI server available.

1. Click the **Start** button, then click **Administrative Tools** and then **DNS**.

2. Expand the DNS console to full-screen, if necessary.

3. Drill down to **DNSSEC→Forward Lookup Zones**.

4. Right-click **Forward Lookup Zones** and click **New Zone**....

5. The Welcome to the New Zone Wizard screen appears. Click **Next**.

6. The Zone Type screen appears. Select the **Secondary zone** radio button and click **Next**.

7. The Zone Name screen appears. In the *Zone name:* text box, enter **contoso.com** and then click **Next**.

8. The Zone File screen appears. Ensure that the *Create a new file with this file name:* radio button is selected and then click **Next**.

9. The Master DNS Servers screen appears. Key the IP address of **DNSPRI** and then press (Enter). Ensure that the Validated column shows a status of "OK," and then click **Next**.

10. The Completing the New Zone Wizard appears. Click **Finish**.

PAUSE. Close the DNS MMC snap-in and log off of the DNSSEC Windows Server 2008 server.

In the previous exercise, you configured a standard secondary zone for the *contoso.com* DNS domain. In the next exercise, you will configure a stub zone on a Windows Server 2008 computer called DNSSEC.

➔ CONFIGURE A STUB ZONE

GET READY. This exercise assumes that you have installed the DNS server role on a Windows Server 2008 computer called DNSSEC that has been configured with a static IP address, and that the Initial Configuration Tasks for this server have already been completed, This exercise assumes that you are logged onto DNSSEC with administrative privileges. You must also have the IP address of the DNSPRI server available.

1. Click the **Start** button, then click **Administrative Tools** and then **DNS**.
2. Expand the DNS console to full-screen, if necessary.
3. Drill down to **DNSSEC→Forward Lookup Zones**.
4. Right-click **Forward Lookup Zones** and click **New Zone**....
5. The Welcome to the New Zone Wizard screen appears. Click **Next**.
6. The Zone Type screen appears. Select the **Stub zone** radio button and click **Next**.
7. The Zone Name screen appears. In the *Zone name:* text box, enter **contoso.com** and then click **Next**.
8. The Master DNS Servers screen appears. Key the IP address of **DNSPRI** and then press (Enter). Ensure that the Validated column shows a status of "OK," and then click **Next**.
9. The Completing the New Zone Wizard appears. Click **Finish**.

PAUSE. Close the DNS MMC snap-in and log off of the DNSSEC Windows Server 2008 server.

In the previous exercise, you configured a standard stub zone for the *contoso.com* DNS domain. In the next section, we will discuss configuring Active Directory–integrated DNS zones to improve the replication efficiency and security of your DNS data.

Configuring Active Directory–Integrated Zones

Storing zones in Active Directory is a Microsoft proprietary method of managing, securing, and replicating DNS zone information. An Active Directory–integrated zone is a DNS zone contained within Active Directory. Zones stored in text files are typically referred to as *standard* or *file-backed zones*, while zones that are stored in Active Directory are referred to as *Active Directory–integrated zones*.

Storing a zone in Active Directory has the following benefits:

- Fault tolerance—Redundant copy of DNS zone information can be stored on multiple servers.
- Security—DNS zones stored in Active Directory can take advantage of increased security by modifying its **discretionary access control list (DACL)**. The DACL enables you to specify which users and groups may modify the DNS zones. You can also configure **secure dynamic updates** for Active Directory–integrated zones, which will only allow records to be updated by the client that first registered the record.
- Zones are multimaster—This means that zones can be updated in more than one location, i.e., from more than one server. All domain controllers where the zone is stored can modify the zone, and changes to the zone are then replicated to the other domain controllers that contain the zone file.
- Efficient replication—Zone transfers are replaced by more efficient Active Directory replication. This can be especially important over networks with slow links because Active Directory compresses replication data that passes between sites.
- Maintain use of secondary zones—Zones that are stored in Active Directory can also be transferred to standard secondary servers to create secondary zones in the same way that file-backed secondary zones are transferred.

Windows Server 2003 and Windows Server 2008 provide a more efficient method of replicating DNS zone information than does Microsoft Windows 2000 Server. In Microsoft

Windows 2000, updates to Active Directory zones were replicated to all domain controllers in that domain, whether or not they were also configured as DNS servers.

With Windows Server 2003 and Windows Server 2008, Active Directory–integrated zones can be configured with one of three different *replication scopes*, which is to say that their information can be replicated in three different ways:

- To all domain controllers in the domain (this is the only replication scope available that was available in Windows 2000)
- To all domain controllers that are DNS servers in the local domain, also known as the **DomainDNSZones** application partition
- To all domain controllers that are also DNS servers in the entire forest, also known as the **ForestDNSZones** application

You can create two types of Active Directory–integrated zones: forward lookup zones and reverse lookup zones.

An *Active Directory–integrated forward lookup zone* is similar to a standard primary zone. Outside of Active Directory, primary and secondary servers are necessary because they follow a single-master update model, where only one server contains a writable copy of the zone database. However, Active Directory–integrated zones follow a multimaster update model, meaning all Active Directory–integrated zones contain a read/write copy of the zone and can make changes to the zone information. Therefore, primary and secondary distinctions are not necessary.

An *Active Directory–integrated reverse lookup zone* is used for resolving an IP address to a name and is similar to the standard in-addr.arpa zone. The reverse lookup zone is stored and updated in the same manner as the Active Directory–integrated forward lookup zone.

Configuring DNS Delegation

Initially, a zone stores information about a single DNS domain name. As other domains are added, you must make a decision about whether or not the domain will be part of the same zone. If you choose to add the subdomain, you may manage the subdomain as part of the original zone, or else delegate management of the subdomain to a different zone.

For example, Figure 4-2 shows the *contoso.com* domain, which contains domain names for Contoso, Ltd. When the *contoso.com* domain is first created at a single server, it is configured as a single zone for all of the Contoso DNS namespace. If, however, the *contoso.com* domain needs to use subdomains, those subdomains must be included in the zone or delegated away to another zone.

Figure 4-2

Viewing a DNS zone configuration

CONTOSO.COM ZONE

SALES.CONTOSO.COM ZONE.　　DEV.CONTOSO.COM

In this example, the *contoso.com* domain shows a new subdomain—the *sales.contoso.com* domain—delegated away from the *contoso.com* zone and managed in its own zone. However, the *contoso.com* zone needs to contain a few resource records to provide the delegation information that references the DNS servers that are authoritative for the delegated *sales.contoso. com* subdomain. If the *contoso.com* zone does not use delegation for a subdomain, the data for the subdomain remains part of the *contoso.com* zone. For example, the subdomain *dev.contoso. com* is not delegated away, but is managed by the *contoso.com* zone.

Configuring DNS Zone Transfers

Zone transfers are the complete or partial transfer of all data in a zone from the primary DNS server hosting the zone to a secondary DNS server hosting a copy of the zone. The copy of the zone hosted on a secondary DNS server is initially created using a zone transfer. When changes are made to the zone on a primary DNS server, the primary DNS server notifies the secondary DNS servers that changes have occurred and the changes are replicated to all the secondary DNS servers for that zone using zone transfers.

In the original DNS specifications, only one form of zone transfer was available, the full zone transfer (AXFR). Windows 2000, Windows Server 2003, and Windows Server 2008 DNS also support incremental zone transfers in addition to full zone transfers. This section describes both types of zone transfers, as well as the notification process known as *DNS Notify*.

The following events trigger zone transfers:

- A transfer is manually initiated using the console at the secondary server.
- The zone refresh interval expires.
- The DNS Server service is started at the secondary server.
- The master server notifies the secondary server of a zone change or changes.

Zone transfers are always initiated at the secondary server for a zone and sent to the server's configured master server, which acts as its source for the zone. A master server can be any other DNS server that loads the zone, such as either the primary server for the zone or another secondary server. When the master server receives the request for the zone, it can reply with either an incremental (IXFR) or full (AXFR) transfer of the zone to the secondary server.

In a full zone transfer, the primary DNS server hosting the primary zone transfers a copy of the entire zone database to the secondary DNS server hosting a copy of the zone. Whether a full or incremental transfer, the following process takes place:

X REF

See the "Configuring DNS Resource Records" section of this lesson for information about the Start of Authority (SOA) record.

1. When the value of the Refresh field in the Start of Authority (SOA) resource record for the zone hosted on the secondary DNS server expires, the secondary DNS server queries the primary DNS server for the SOA record of the primary zone.

2. The primary DNS server for the zone replies to the query with the SOA resource record.

3. The secondary DNS server for the zone compares the serial number in the returned SOA record to the serial number in the SOA record for the local copy of the zone. If the serial number sent by the primary DNS server for the zone is higher than the serial number for its local zone, the zone needs to be updated, and the secondary DNS server sends an AXFR request (a request for a full zone transfer) to the primary DNS server.

4. The primary DNS server receives the request for the zone transfer and sends the full zone database to the secondary DNS server, essentially re-creating the copy of the zone while maintaining any zone settings.

If the primary DNS server for the zone does not respond to the request for a zone transfer sent from the secondary DNS server, the secondary DNS server continues to retry for the interval specified in the Retry field in the SOA resource record for the zone. If there is still no answer after the interval specified in the Expire field in the SOA resource record for the zone expires, the secondary DNS server discards its zone.

Incremental zone transfers were designed to reduce the amount of network traffic generated by full zone transfers. Rather than sending a copy of the entire zone file, an incremental zone transfer sends only records that have changed since the last zone update. Windows 2000, Windows Server 2003, and Windows Server 2008 all support incremental zone transfers.

Although an incremental zone transfer saves network bandwidth, it uses additional disk space on the server to record the version history. The primary DNS server for the zone maintains a recent version history of the zone, which observes any record changes that occurred in the most recent version updates of the zone. To conserve disk space, DNS servers store only the most recent updates. The Windows Server 2008 DNS Server service stores these updates in a log file that resides in *the %systemroot%\System32\Dns* folder. The log file is named by using the name of the zone file with .log appended. For example, if the zone file for the *contoso.com* domain is stored in the file *Contoso.com.dns,* the log file is named *Contoso.com.dns.log*.

An incremental zone transfer uses the following process:

1. Initially, when a secondary server is first configured, it sends a full zone transfer request (AXFR) to its master DNS server. The master (source) server responds by sending a full copy of the zone to the secondary (destination) server.

2. Each zone delivery has a version indicated by a serial number in the properties of the SOA resource record and a refresh interval (by default, 900 seconds). The refresh interval indicates at what interval the secondary server should request another copy of the zone from the source server.

3. After the interval expires, the destination server submits an SOA query to request an incremental zone transfer.

4. The source server answers the query by sending its SOA record, which contains the aforementioned serial number.

5. The destination server compares the serial number from the SOA record to its current local serial number. If the numbers are equal, no transfer is requested, and the refresh interval is reset.

6. If the value of the serial number in the SOA response is higher than its current local serial number, records on the source are newer than the local records and an IXFR query is sent to the source server. This query contains the local serial number so the source server can determine which records the destination server needs.

7. Depending on several factors, the source server responds with either an incremental or full transfer of the zone. The primary DNS server for a zone is not required to perform an incremental zone transfer. It can choose to perform a full zone transfer under the following conditions:

   • The primary DNS server does not support incremental zone transfers.

   • The primary DNS server does not have all the necessary data for performing an incremental zone transfer.

   • An incremental zone transfer uses more network bandwidth than a full zone transfer.

When the secondary DNS server receives an incremental zone transfer, it creates a new version of the zone and begins replacing outdated resource records with the updated resource records from the source server, applying oldest to newest. When all the updates are completed, the secondary DNS server replaces its old version of the zone with the new version of the zone.

By default, Windows Server 2008 will only permit zone transfers on standard zones to those servers that have been configured as name servers for the zone in question. Before you can configure an additional name server, it must be configured with a valid FQDN that is resolvable by the server in question.

In the following exercise, we will configure DNSPRI to permit zone transfers to take place to the secondary zone configured on DNSSEC, and we will then force a zone transfer to take place between DNSPRI and DNSSEC.

➔ CONFIGURE A STANDARD SECONDARY ZONE

GET READY. This exercise assumes that you have configured DNSPRI with a primary zone for the *contoso.com* domain, and DNSSEC with a secondary zone for the *contoso.com* domain. This exercise assumes that you are logged onto DNSPRI and DNSSEC with administrative privileges. Parts A and C of this exercise will be performed on DNSSEC; Part B will be performed on DNSPRI. You must have the IP address of both servers available.

PART A—Confirm that zone transfers are not currently functional on DNSSEC

1. Log onto DNSSEC as a local administrator on the computer.
2. Click the **Start** button, then browse to **Administrative Tools→DNS**.
3. The DNS MMC snap-in opens. Browse to **DNSSEC→Forward Lookup Zones**.
4. Click the plus sign next to contoso.com. Notice that a red 'X' appears next to the zone name in the left-hand column, and the right-hand pane indicates that the DNS zone was not loaded by the server.

PART B—Configure zone transfers to DNSSEC from DNSPRI.

1. Log onto DNSPRI as a local administrator on the computer.
2. Click the **Start** button, then browse to **Administrative Tools→DNS**.
3. The DNS MMC snap-in opens. Browse to **DNSSEC→Forward Lookup Zones**.
4. Click the plus sign next to contoso.com. Right-click **contoso.com** and click **New Host (A or AAAA)....** The New Host screen appears.
5. In the Name (uses parent domain name if left blank): field, enter **DNSSEC**. In the IP address: field, enter the IP address of the DNSSEC server.
6. Click **Add Host** and then click **OK** followed by **Done**. Notice that an A record for DNSSEC now appears in the contoso.com zone.
7. Right-click **contoso.com** and click **Properties**. The **contoso.com** Properties screen appears.
8. Click the **Name Servers** tab. You will see the screen shown in Figure 4-3. Notice that only DNSPRI is listed as a Name Server for the contoso.com zone.

Figure 4-3

Configuring DNS name servers

9. Click **Add**. The New Name Server Record screen appears.

10. In the Server fully qualified domain name (FQDN): text box, enter **DNSSEC.contoso.com**. Click **Resolve**.

11. Click **OK** twice to save your changes.

PART C—Confirm that zone transfers are now taking place on DNSSEC

1. Log onto DNSSEC as a local administrator on the computer.

2. Click the **Start** button, then browse to **Administrative Tools→DNS**.

3. The DNS MMC snap-in opens. Browse to **DNSSEC→Forward Lookup Zones**.

4. Click the plus sign next to contoso.com. Notice that the contents of the contoso .com zone have been transferred to DNSSEC.

PAUSE. Close the DNS MMC snap-in on each server, and then log off of both servers.

Using DNS Notify

Windows-based DNS servers support DNS Notify, an update to the original DNS protocol specification that permits a means of initiating notification to secondary servers when zone changes occur (RFC 1996). Servers that are notified can then initiate a zone transfer as described previously to request zone changes from their master servers and update their local replicas of the zone. This process improves consistency of zone data.

The list of secondary DNS servers that a primary DNS server will notify is maintained in the notify list, which is a list of the IP addresses for those secondary servers. When the zone is updated, the primary DNS server for the zone notifies only DNS servers on the notify list. For secondary DNS servers to be notified by the DNS server acting as their configured source for a zone, each secondary server must first have its IP address in the notify list of the source server. In Windows Server 2008 DNS, you can use the DNS Notify dialog box to set the notify list.

In addition to notifying the listed servers, the DNS console permits you to use the contents of the notify list as a means to restrict or limit zone transfer access to only those secondary servers specified in the list. This can help prevent an undesired attempt by an unknown or unapproved DNS server to pull, or request, zone updates.

When the zone on a primary DNS server is updated, the following events occur:

- The Serial Number field in the SOA record is incremented to indicate that a new version of the zone is written to a disk.
- The primary DNS server sends a notify message to the DNS servers that are specified in its notify list.
- A secondary DNS server for the zone that receives the notify message responds by sending an SOA-type query back to the notifying primary DNS server to determine if the zone on the primary DNS server is a later version than the copy of the zone currently stored on the secondary DNS server.
- If a notified secondary DNS server determines that the serial number specified in the SOA record of the zone on the primary DNS server is higher than the serial number specified in the SOA record for its current zone copy (the zone contains more recent updates), the notified secondary DNS server requests a zone transfer (AXFR or IXFR).

Configuring DNS Resource Records

A DNS *resource record* is information that is related to a DNS domain; for example, the host record defining a host IP address. Resource records are represented in binary form in packets when queries and responses are made using DNS. In DNS zone files, however, resource records are represented as text entries. In Windows Server 2008, resource records can be created using the DNS console or the dnscmd command-line utility.

Most resource records are represented as single-line text entries. If an entry is going to span more than one line, you can use parentheses to encapsulate the information. For readability, blank lines and comments often are inserted in the zone files and are ignored by the DNS server. Comments always start with a semicolon (;) and end with a carriage return.

Resource records have the following syntax:

Owner [TTL] Class Type RDATA

Table 4-2 describes the common set of information in resource records.

Table 4-2

Typical Resource Record Fields

NAME	DESCRIPTION
Owner	Identifies the host or the DNS domain to which this resource record belongs.
TTL (Time to Live)	A 32-bit integer representing the maximum time, in seconds, that a DNS server or client caches this resource record before it is discarded. This field is optional, and if it is not specified, the client uses the minimum TTL in the SOA record.
Class	Defines the protocol family in use, which is IN for the Internet system.
Type	Identifies the type of resource record. For example, A indicates that the resource record stores host address information.
Resource Record Data (RDATA)	Contains RDATA. The RDATA field is a variable-length field that represents the information being described by the resource record. For example, in an A resource record, the data contained in this field is the 32-bit IP address that represents the host identified by the owner.

The DNS database consists of resource records that relate different information about the names in the database. A resource record for a DNS name can identify a single resource within the network, such as the network host that uses that name, or that there is a service running on that network host, such as electronic mail.

Different types of resource records provide DNS data about computers on a TCP/IP network. The most common resource records are described in Table 4-3 and in detail in the following sections. This discussion includes resource records specific to Windows 2000, Windows Server 2003, and Windows Server 2008 DNS implementations.

Table 4-3

Resource Record Types

DESCRIPTION	CLASS	TTL	TYPE	DATA
Start of Authority (SOA record)	Internet (IN)	60 minutes	SOA	Owner name, primary name server FQDN, serial number, refresh interval, retry interval, expire time, and minimum TTL
Host (A) Record	Internet (IN)	TTL of the SOA in the same zone	A	Owner name (host DNS name) and host IPv4 address
Host (AAAA) Record	Internet (IN)	TTL of the SOA in the zone	AAAA	Owner name (host DNS name) and host IPv6 address
Name Server (NS Record)	Internet (IN)	TTL of the SOA in the same zone	NS	Owner name and DNS server name

(continued)

Table 4-3 *(continued)*

Description	Class	TTL	Type	Data
Mail Exchanger (MX Record)	Internet (IN)	TTL of the SOA in the same zone	MX	Owner name, Mail Exchanger (MX) server DNS name, and preference number
Canonical Name (CNAME Record, alias record)	Internet (IN)	TTL of the SOA in the same zone	CNAME	Owner name (alias name) and host DNS name
Service Locator Record (SRV)	Internet (IN)	TTL of the SOA in the same zone	SRV	Domain name associated with the service, Service Name (LDAP, KDC, etc.), Protocol, Weight, Priority, Port number

Start of Authority (SOA) Resource Record

Every zone contains an SOA resource record at the top of the zone file. An SOA resource record indicates the starting point or original point of authority for information stored in a zone. It contains all the zone-specific information for the DNS server to use when maintaining the zone. The SOA resource record is the first resource record that is created when creating a new zone.

The RDATA field for the SOA resource record contains the fields shown in Table 4-4.

Table 4-4

RDATA Fields for the SOA Resource Record

RDATA Fields	Description
Authoritative server	Contains the name of the primary DNS server authoritative for the zone.
Responsible person	Shows the e-mail address of the administrator who is responsible for the zone. This field takes a period (.) instead of an at (@) sign.
Serial number	Shows how many times the zone is updated. When a zone's secondary server contacts its master server to determine whether it needs to initiate a zone transfer, the zone's secondary server compares its own serial number with that of the master. If the serial number of the master server is higher, the secondary server initiates a zone transfer.
Refresh	Shows how often the secondary server for the zone checks to see whether the zone data is changed.
Retry	After sending a zone transfer request, shows how long (in seconds) the zone's secondary server waits before sending another request.
Expire	After a zone transfer, shows how long (in seconds) the zone's secondary server continues to respond to zone queries before discarding its own zone as invalid.
Minimum TTL	Applies to all the resource records in the zone whenever a TTL value is not specified in a resource record or is shorter than the minimum TTL specified in the zone's SOA record. Whenever a DNS client queries the server, the server sends back resource records containing a record-specific TTL or the minimum TTL. Negative responses are cached for the minimum TTL of the SOA resource record of the authoritative zone.

The following output is an example of an SOA resource record:

```
na.contoso.com. IN SOA (
nadc1.na.contoso.com.; authoritative server for the zone
administrator.na.contoso.com.; zone admin e-mail;
(responsible person)
5099;    serial number
3600;    refresh (1 hour)
600;     retry (10 mins)
86400;   expire (1 day)
60 );    minimum TTL (1 min)
```

Name Server (NS) Resource Record

The name server (NS) resource record identifies a DNS server that is authoritative for a zone; that is, a DNS server that hosts a primary or secondary copy of the DNS zone in question. The name of the DNS server that is authoritative for a zone is stored in the RDATA field. NS records are used to indicate both primary and secondary DNS servers for the zone specified in the SOA resource record and to indicate the DNS servers for any delegated zones. If a zone has multiple authoritative servers (for example, a primary server and one or more secondary servers), you need to have an NS record for each server.

TAKE NOTE*

Every zone must contain at least one NS record.

The Windows Server 2008 DNS Server service automatically creates the first NS record for a zone when the zone is created. You can add additional NS records by using DNS or the dnscmd command-line tool.

For example, if the administrator for *contoso.com* delegates authority for the *us.contoso.com* subdomain to the *usdc1.us.contoso.com* server, the following line is added to the *contoso.com* and *na.contoso.com* zones:

```
us.contoso.com. IN NS usdc1.us.contoso.com.
```

Using Delegation and Glue Records

Delegation and glue records are resource records that you add to a zone to delegate a subdomain to a separate zone hosted on a different DNS server. A delegation record is represented by the NS record in the parent zone that lists the authoritative DNS server hosting the child zone for the delegated subdomain. A glue record is the A record in the parent zone for the authoritative DNS server hosting the child zone for the delegated subdomain.

For example, the DNS server that hosts the zone for the domain *contoso.com* will delegate authority for the subdomain *us.contoso.com* to the DNS server *ns2.us.contoso.com*, which is where a zone for the domain *us.contoso.com* is hosted. To create this delegation, the following records are added to the parent zone *contoso.com*:

```
us.contoso.com.           IN NS ns2.us.contoso.com
ns2.us.contoso.com.       IN A 172.16.54.1
```

When a DNS client submits a query for a name in the child zone to the DNS server that is authoritative for the parent zone, the authoritative DNS server for the parent zone checks its zone. The delegation resource records tell it which DNS server is authoritative for the child zone. The authoritative DNS server for the parent zone can then return a referral containing the delegation records to the DNS client.

A glue record is necessary in this example because *ns2.us.contoso.com* is a member of the delegated domain *us.contoso.com*. However, if it was a member of a different domain, such as *lucernepublishing.com*, the DNS client can perform standard name resolution to resolve the name of the authoritative DNS server to an IP address, in which case a glue record is not required. Separate domain configurations are less common.

Incorrect delegations are a major source of name resolution failure for DNS because an incorrect delegation removes a branch of the DNS namespace tree, and the other nodes in the tree cannot locate the DNS names in and under the branch. For this reason, it is recommended that you verify delegations periodically, and that administrators responsible for parent and child zones communicate any modifications that can affect delegation.

IPv4 Host Records (A) and IPv6 Host Records (AAAA)

The IPv4 *host (A)* resource record maps a FQDN to an IPv4 address. The IPv6 *host (AAAA) resource record* performs the same function, except that it maps an FQDN to an IPv6 address.

For example, the following A resource record is located in the zone *us.contoso.com* and maps the FQDN of a server to its IP address:

```
usdc1.us.contoso.com.    IN A 172.16.48.1
```

The A resource record contains the following fields:

- The Owner, TTL, Class, and Type fields, which are described in Table 4-2, "Typical Resource Record Fields," earlier in this lesson.
- The RDATA field is the IP address of the owner.

PTR Resource Record

The *PTR resource record* performs the reverse function of the A resource record by mapping an IP address to an FQDN. For example, the following PTR resource record maps the IP address 172.16.48.1 of *usdc1.us.contoso.com* to its FQDN:

```
1.48.16.172.in-addr.arpa. IN PTR usdc1.us.contoso.com.
```

PTR resource records contain the following fields:

- The Owner, TTL, Class, and Type fields, which are described in Table 4-2, "Typical Resource Record Fields," earlier in this lesson.
- The RDATA field is the host name of the host with the IP address contained in the Owner field.

Canonical Name (CNAME) Resource Record

The *canonical name (CNAME) resource record* creates an alias for a specified FQDN. You can use CNAME records to hide the implementation details of your network from the clients that connect to it. For example, if you want to put a File Transfer Protocol (FTP) server named *ftp1.us.contoso.com* on your *us.contoso.com* subdomain, but you know that in six months you might move it to a computer named *ftp2.us.contoso.com* and you do not want your users to have to know about the change, do the following: create an alias called *ftp.us.contoso.com* that points to *ftp1.us.contoso.com*. When you move your computer, you need to change only the CNAME record to point to *ftp2.us.contoso.com*.

For example, the following CNAME resource record creates an alias for *ftp1.na.contoso.com*:

```
ftp.us.contoso.com. IN CNAME ftp1.us.contoso.com.
```

After a DNS client queries for the name for *ftp.na.contoso.com*, the DNS server finds the CNAME resource record, resolves the query for *ftp1.us.contoso.com*, and returns both the A and CNAME resource records to the client.

CNAME resource records contain the following fields:

- The Owner, TTL, Class, and Type fields. The Owner field for CNAME records is the alias.
- The RDATA field is the name of the host to which the alias points. (A CNAME record cannot be created unless the A record that it is pointing to already exists.)

Mail Exchanger (MX) Resource Record

The ***mail exchanger (MX) resource record*** specifies a server that is configured to act as a mail server for a DNS name. The mail server identified by an MX record is a host that either processes or forwards mail for a DNS domain name. Processing the mail means either delivering it to the addressee or passing it to a different type of mail transport. Forwarding the mail means sending it to its final destination server, sending it by using Simple Mail Transfer Protocol (SMTP) to another mail exchange server that is closer to the final destination, or queuing it for a specified amount of time.

To improve the reliability of the mail service for a domain, you can designate secondary mail servers that can store mail for a domain. If the primary mail server stops responding, the secondary servers can hold the mail and then forward it when the mail server comes back into service. An SMTP smart host (a host capable of using MX records) uses multiple mail servers, provided you configure multiple MX resource records.

The following example shows MX resource records for the mail servers for the domain *na.contoso.com*:

```
@ IN MX 5 mailserver1.us.contoso.com.
@ IN MX 10 mailserver2.us.contoso.com.
@ IN MX 20 mailserver3.us.contoso.com.
```

MX resource records contain the following fields:

- The Owner, TTL, Class, and Type fields, which are described in Table 4-2, "Typical Resource Record Fields," earlier in this lesson.

The following data is stored in the RDATA field of the MX resource record:

- The fourth field in the MX record is the mail server preference value. The preference value specifies the preference given to the MX record among other MX records. Records with lower priority numbers (which are higher priority) are preferred. Thus, when a mail client needs to send mail to a certain DNS domain, it first contacts a DNS server for that domain and retrieves all the MX records. It then contacts the mailer with the lowest preference value.
- The final field is the name of the mail server to contact.

For more information about how mail is routed in the domain system, see RFC 974, which can be accessed at *http://www.rfc-editor.org/rfcsearch.html*.

For example, suppose Holly Holt sends an e-mail message to *loviatt@us.contoso.com* on a day that mailserver1 is down, but mailserver2 is working. Her e-mail client tries to deliver the message to mailserver1 because it has the lowest preference value, but it fails because mailserver1 is down. In this case, Holly's e-mail client chooses mailserver2 because its preference value is the second lowest. If mailserver2 is operating, the mail is successfully delivered to mailserver2.

To prevent mail loops, if the e-mail client is on a host that is listed as an MX for the destination host, the e-mail client can deliver only to an MX with a lower preference value than its own host. If a mail server receives multiple MX records with equal priority, the choice of which MX record to use depends on implementation.

Service Locator (SRV) Resource Record

Service locator (SRV) resource records enable you to specify the location of servers that provide a specific network service over a specific protocol and in a specific domain. SRV records allow you to have several servers offering a network service and to move services between servers without changing the client configuration. For example, if you have two application servers in your domain, you can create SRV resource records in DNS that specify which hosts serve as application servers. Client applications that support SRV records will use DNS to retrieve the SRV resource records for the application servers.

Active Directory is an example of an application that relies on SRV resource records. An example of an application that supports SRV resource records is the Windows 2000, Windows Server 2003, and Windows Server 2008 Netlogon service. On Windows 2000, Microsoft Windows XP, Windows Server 2003, Windows Server 2008, and Windows Vista, client computers use SRV resource records to locate domain controllers for an Active Directory domain.

The format for an SRV record is as follows:

`_Service_Protocol.Name [TTL] Class SRV Priority Weight Port Target`

Table 4-5 outlines the SRV resource record fields.

Table 4-5

SRV Resource Record Fields

FIELD NAME	DESCRIPTION
Service	Specifies the name of the service, such as http or telnet.
Protocol	Specifies the protocol, such as Transmission Control Protocol (TCP) or User Datagram Protocol (UDP).
Name	Specifies the domain name to which the resource record refers.
TTL	Uses a 32-bit integer to represent the maximum time, in seconds, that a DNS server or client caches this entry before it is discarded. This field is optional, and if it is not specified, the client uses the minimum TTL in the SOA record.
Class	Defines the protocol family in use, which is usually IN for the Internet system. The other value defined in RFC 1034 is CH for the Chaos system, which was used experimentally at the Massachusetts Institute of Technology.

Table 4-6 describes the data stored in the RDATA field of the SRV resource record.

Table 4-6

SRV Record RDATA Fields

FIELD NAME	DESCRIPTION
Priority	Specifies the priority of the host. Clients attempt to contact the host with the lowest priority number.
Weight	Performs load balancing. When the Priority field is the same for two or more records in the same domain, clients must try records with higher weights more often, unless the clients support some other load-balancing mechanism.
Port	Shows the port for the service on this host.
Target	Shows the FQDN for the host providing the service.

The following example shows SRV records for two domain controller servers:

```
_ldap._tcp.contoso.com.  IN SRV 0 0 389 dc1.contoso.com.
_ldap._tcp.contoso.com.  IN SRV 10 0 389 dc2.contoso.com.
```

This example does not specify a TTL. Therefore, the DNS client uses the minimum TTL specified in the SOA resource record.

If a computer needs to locate a Lightweight Directory Access Protocol (LDAP) server in the *contoso.com* domain, the DNS client sends an SRV query for the following name:

```
_ldap._tcp.contoso.com.
```

The DNS server replies with the SRV records listed in the previous example. The DNS client then chooses between DC1 and DC2 by looking at their priority values. Because DC1 has the lower priority value, the LDAP client chooses DC1. In this example, if the priority values were the same but the weight values were different, the client would choose a domain controller randomly with a probability proportional to the Weight field value.

Next, the DNS client requests the A record for *DC1.contoso.com*, and the DNS server sends the A record. Finally, the client attempts to contact the domain controller using the IP address in the A record.

Using Wildcard Resource Records

In some DNS designs, you might need to use a large number of resource records in a zone. However, you might find it difficult to manually add the records. In such cases, you can define a wildcard DNS resource record.

The following is an example of a wildcard address from the *contoso.com* domain:

```
* IN A 172.16.54.1
```

If the preceding A record is in DNS, all queries for a host in the *contoso.com* domain not explicitly defined in the zone file receive a reply for 172.16.54.1. Windows 2000, Windows Server 2003, and Windows Server 2008 DNS support wildcard resource records.

→ CONFIGURE DNS RESOURCE RECORDS

GET READY. This exercise assumes that you have configured DNSPRI with a primary zone for the *contoso.com* domain. This exercise assumes that you are logged onto DNSPRI with administrative privileges.

1. In the DNS console, drill down to **DNSPRI→Forward Lookup Zones→contoso.com**.
2. Right-click **contoso.com** and click **New Host Record (A or AAAA)....**
3. The New Host window appears. In the Name (uses parent domain name if blank): field, enter **SERVER1**. In the IP Address field, enter an IP address appropriate for your environment, such as *192.168.52.150*.
4. Click **Add Host**. Read the DNS window that appears. Click **OK** and then click **Done**.
5. Right-click **contoso.com** and click **New Mail Exchanger (MX)....**
6. The New Resource Record window appears. In the host or child domain: text box, enter **mail.** In the Fully Qualified Domain Name (FQDN) of mail server: text box, enter *SERVER1.contoso.com*.
7. Click **OK**.

PAUSE. Close the DNS MMC snap-in and log off of the Windows Server 2008 computer before continuing.

In the previous exercise, you configured DNS resource records on a Windows Server 2008 computer. In the following section, you will learn about the process of allowing clients to dynamically update their own resource records on a Windows Server 2008 DNS server.

Configuring DNS Dynamic Updates

Windows Server 2008 DNS supports the DNS dynamic update protocol (RFC [Request for Comments] 2136), which enables DNS clients to dynamically update their resource records in DNS zones. You can specify that the DHCP server in your network dynamically update DNS when it configures a DHCP client computer. This reduces the administration time that is necessary when manually administering zone records. You use the dynamic update feature in conjunction with DHCP to update resource records when a computer releases or updates its IP address.

Client computers running Windows 2000 or later attempt to update address (A) resource records directly, but they utilize the DHCP server to dynamically update their pointer (PTR) resource records. DHCP-enabled client computers running earlier versions of Microsoft operating systems are unable to update or register their DNS resource records directly. These DHCP clients must use the DHCP service provided with Windows 2000, Windows Server 2003, and Windows Server 2008 to register and update both their A and PTR resource records on behalf of these down-level clients.

Although dynamic updates allow clients to update DNS resource records, this is not a secure method. A more secure way of updating DNS resource records is using secure dynamic updates. The server attempts the update only if the client can prove its identity and has the proper credentials to make the update. Secure dynamic updates are available only through Active Directory domain service and when Active Directory–integrated DNS is enabled. By default, Active Directory–integrated zones only allow secure dynamic updates, though this setting can be modified when you create the zone. If you created the zone as a standard primary zone, and then you converted it into an Active Directory–integrated zone, it preserves the primary zone dynamic update configuration, which can be changed using the DNS MMC console.

You can configure dynamic updates for a DNS zone to use one of the following options:

- None—No dynamic updates permitted, all DNS entries must be created manually. This is the default dynamic updates setting for a standard DNS zone.
- Nonsecure and secure—Allows clients to first attempt a nonsecure dynamic update, and only if that fails to attempt a secure dynamic update. Because clients will attempt a nonsecure update first, configuring this setting is effectively the same as permitting all dynamic updates to occur in a nonsecure fashion.
- Secure only—This option is only available on DNS zones that have been configured on Active Directory domain controllers.

Configuring Aging and Scavenging of DNS Records

Traditionally, the DNS administrator manually added or deleted resource records from DNS zone files as required. With dynamic update, individual computers and services are able to automatically add, update, and delete DNS resource records. For example, the Windows XP, Windows Vista, Windows 2000, Windows Server 2003, and Windows Server 2008 DNS Client services register their clients' A and pointer (PTR) resource records in DNS at start time and every 24 hours thereafter. Dynamic update ensures that the records are up-to-date and guards against accidental deletion of resource records by the DNS administrator.

Over time, stale resource records accumulate in the DNS database. Records become stale, for example, when computers, especially those of mobile users, abnormally disconnect from the network. Stale records provide outdated and inaccurate information to clients, take up unnecessary space, and can possibly degrade server performance. Windows Server 2008 provides a mechanism called *scavenging* to remove these records as they become out-of-date.

Windows Server 2008 adds a time stamp to dynamically added resource records in primary zones where aging and scavenging are enabled. Records added manually are time stamped with a value of zero, which indicates those records should be excluded from the aging and scavenging process. Since secondary name servers receive a read-only copy of the zone data from primary name servers, only primary zones are eligible to participate in this process (or Active Directory–integrated zones, in the case of AD-integrated DNS). Servers can be configured to perform recurring scavenging operations automatically, or you can initiate a manual and immediate scavenging operation at the server.

DNS Scavenging depends on the following two settings:

- No-Refresh Interval—The time between the most recent refresh of a record time stamp and the moment when the time stamp may be refreshed again. When scavenging is enabled, this is set to 7 days by default.
- Refresh Interval—The time between the earliest moment when a record time stamp can be refreshed and the earliest moment when the record can be scavenged. The refresh interval must be longer than the maximum record refresh period. When scavenging is enabled, this is set to 7 days by default.

A DNS record becomes eligible for scavenging after both the no-refresh and refresh intervals have elapsed, for a total of 14 days by default. Scavenging is enabled on a per-zone basis, and is disabled by default. You should not enable DNS resource record scavenging unless you are absolutely certain that you understand all the parameters and have configured them correctly. Otherwise, you might accidentally configure the server to delete records that it should retain. If a name is accidentally deleted, not only do users fail to resolve queries for that name, but also a different user can create and own that name, even on zones configured for secure dynamic update.

Introducing the DNS Name Resolution Process

The DNS *resolver* refers to the DNS client software that exists on a Windows computer regardless of whether it is running a client or a server operating system. In this way it is important not to confuse the notion of a DNS client resolver with a client operating system such as Windows XP or Windows Vista; a Windows Server 2008 computer contains DNS client software and will often function as a DNS client when attempting to resolve DNS queries. When any DNS client needs to look up a fully qualified domain name to obtain its corresponding IP address, it forms a *DNS query* that contains the DNS domain name (stated as an FQDN), the query type specifying the resource records to be returned (A, SRV, and so on), and the DNS domain name class, which is IN for the Internet system. The query is first passed to the local DNS resolver client service for resolution. If the query cannot be resolved locally, it is sent to the preferred DNS server as configured in the client's TCP/IP properties. If the query does not match an entry in the cache, the resolution process continues with the client querying a DNS server to resolve the name.

CERTIFICATION READY?
Configure name resolution for clients
2.5

When a query is sent to a DNS server, the server can respond in a number of ways. Following are the most common responses to DNS queries:

- An ***authoritative answer***—An authoritative answer is a positive answer returned to the client and delivered with the authority bit set in the DNS message to indicate the answer was obtained from a server with direct authority for the queried name.
- A positive answer—A positive answer can consist of the queried resource record or a list of resource records (also known as a *resource record set*) that fits the queried DNS domain name and record type specified in the query message. Positive answers may or may not be authoritative.

- A referral answer—A referral answer contains additional resource records not specified by the name or type in the query. This type of answer is returned to the client if the recursion process is not supported. The records are meant to act as helpful reference answers that the client can use to continue the query using iteration. A referral answer contains additional data, such as resource records, that are other than the type queried. For example, if the queried host name was "www" and no A resource records for this name were found in this zone, but a CNAME resource record for "www" was found instead, the DNS server can include that information when responding to the client. If the client is able to use iteration, it can make additional queries using the referral information in an attempt to fully resolve the name.

- A negative answer—A negative answer from the server can indicate that one of two possible results was encountered while the server attempted to process and recursively resolve the query fully and authoritatively: An authoritative server reported that the queried name does not exist in the DNS namespace, or an authoritative server reported that the queried name exists but no records of the specified type exist for that name. The resolver passes the query response back to the requesting program and caches the response.

In addition to the zones configured on a DNS server, a server can also use two additional methods to respond to a client query. These additional name resolution methods involve the use of root hints, and the *DNS server cache*, described in the following sections.

Using Root Hints

DNS servers resolve DNS queries using local authoritative or cached data. But if the server does not contain the requested data and is not authoritative for the name in a query, it may perform recursive resolution or return a referral to another DNS server depending on whether the client requested recursion. The DNS Server service must be configured with *root hints* to resolve queries for names that it is not authoritative for or for which it contains no delegations. Root hints contain the names and IP addresses of the DNS servers authoritative for the root zone. You can use the DNS console to manage the list of root servers, as well as the dnscmd command-line utility.

By default, DNS servers use a root hints file, called *cache.dns*, on Microsoft DNS servers. The cache.dns file is stored in the *%systemroot%\System32\Dns* folder on the server computer. When the server starts, cache.dns is preloaded into server memory. By using root hints to find root servers, a DNS server is able to complete recursive queries. This process is designed to enable any DNS server to locate the servers that are authoritative for any other DNS domain name used at any level in the namespace tree.

When you use the Windows Server 2008 GUI to configure a DNS server, it sends an NS query for the root domain (.) to the preferred and alternate DNS servers for the server. The query response is placed into the root hints of the DNS server. If no root servers are detected, the wizard sends the same query to the DNS servers specified in the cache.dns file that correspond to the root servers on the Internet. If no root servers are detected, the wizard prompts the user to either make the server a root server or to manually specify root hints. Updating root hints enables the server to function more efficiently. You should update root hints whenever a new server is added or changed.

Configuring Name Server Caching

As DNS servers make recursive queries on behalf of clients, they temporarily cache resource records. Cached resource records contain information obtained from DNS servers that are authoritative for DNS domain names learned while making iterative queries (discussed in the next section) to search and fully answer a recursive query performed on behalf of a client. Later, when other clients place new queries that request resource record information matching cached resource records, the DNS server can use the cached resource record information to answer them.

Caching provides a way to speed the performance of DNS resolution for subsequent queries of popular names, while substantially reducing DNS-related query traffic on the network. When information is cached, a *Time to Live (TTL)* value applies to all cached resource records. As long as the TTL for a cached resource record does not expire, a DNS server can continue to cache and use the resource record again when answering queries by its clients that match these resource records. Caching TTL values used by resource records in most zone configurations are assigned the minimum (default) TTL, which is set in the zone's SOA resource record. By default, the minimum TTL is 3,600 seconds (one hour) but can be adjusted, or, if needed, individual caching TTLs can be set at each resource record.

To reduce the amount of traffic to the DNS server or servers, the DNS resolver on each client will cache resource records that are obtained from query responses. These resource records are used to resolve repeated client queries and reduce redundant queries to the DNS server. Each entry in the cache has a specified TTL, typically set by the query response. When the TTL expires, the entry is purged from the cache. When the resolver is unable to answer a query using its own cache, the resolver sends the query to one or more DNS servers configured in the TCP/IP properties of the server. If a HOSTS file is configured on the client, it is preloaded into the resolver cache.

To view the DNS resolver cache on any Windows computer, key the following at a command prompt:

`ipconfig /displaydns`

To purge the cache, key the following at a command prompt:

`ipconfig /flushdns`

Using Iterative and Recursive DNS Queries

Queries from DNS resolvers (whether originating from a client or a server-based operating system) can take one of two forms: an *iterative query* or a *recursive query*. An iterative query is a DNS query sent to a DNS server in which the querying host requests it to return the best answer it can provide using its own information, and without seeking further assistance from other DNS servers.

WARNING Do not confuse *recursion*, which is used by *iterative queries*, with *recursive queries*, which are discussed next!

For example, in Figure 4-4, a host queries the primary DNS server, which checks its records and refers the client to Server A. Server A checks its names cache, does not find an answer, and sends a referral to Server B instead. The host receives the response and submits a query to Server B, which responds with a referral to Server C. The original host queries Server C and receives a response. The process of a DNS server performing this "tree-walking" of DNS servers to locate the answer to a query is referred to as *recursion*.

As shown in Figure 4-4, the querying host is responsible for issuing additional queries until it obtains a definitive answer. In the example that follows, the host issues three queries before receiving the requested information. The process is as follows:

1. The first step of the query process is to convert a name request into a query and then pass it to the DNS Client service for resolution that uses locally cached information.

Figure 4-4

Viewing a typical iterative query

DNS SERVER A   **DNS SERVER B**   **DNS SERVER C**

3: Are you authoritative for contoso.com?
4: No, referral to server B

5: Are you authoritative for contoso.com?
6: No, referral to server C

7: Are you authoritative for contoso.com?
8: Yes, here is the answer to your query

1: Is sales contoso.com cached?
2: No, referral to server A

CLIENT   **PRIMARY DNS**

If the query can be answered from the local cache, the process is complete. Otherwise, the client submits an iterative query to its preferred DNS server.

2. The primary DNS server checks to see if it has authority for that domain. In this example, it does not have authority, but it does contain information that points to the .com top-level domain DNS servers. The primary server responds with a referral to the .com top-level domain servers.

3. The DNS client submits an iterative query to DNS Server A.

4. DNS Server A responds with a referral to DNS Server B.

5. The client submits an iterative query to DNS Server B for *sales.contoso.com*.

6. DNS Server B responds with a referral to DNS Server C.

7. The client submits an iterative query to DNS Server C.

8. DNS Server C is authoritative for the *sales.contoso.com* domain and responds with a definitive answer to the client query (in this case, the A record for *sales.contoso.com*).

A recursive query is a DNS query sent to a DNS server in which the querying host asks the DNS server to provide a definitive answer to the query, even if that means contacting other servers to provide the answer. When sent a recursive query, the DNS server iteratively queries other DNS servers to obtain an answer. In Figure 4-5, the querying host issues only one query before receiving the requested information.

To centralize the workload and reduce network traffic, host computers typically issue recursive queries to DNS servers. A network of 1,000 clients iteratively querying DNS servers is clearly less efficient than centralizing queries to a handful of DNS servers. Centralizing queries means each client sends a single recursive query rather than each client sending multiple iterative queries. DNS servers generally issue iterative queries against other DNS servers if they are unable to answer a recursive query from cached information. By using recursive queries, the workload of resolving DNS names can be concentrated to a few servers and thereby achieve much greater efficiency. Figure 4-5 illustrates the client submitting a recursive query and receiving a definitive answer. The process is as follows:

Figure 4-5

Viewing the recursive query process

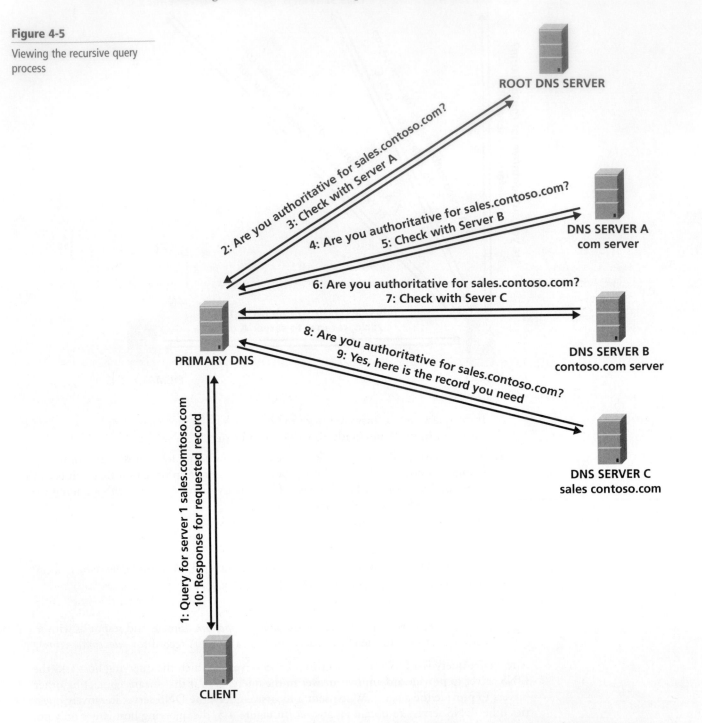

1. The first step of the query process is to convert a name request into a query and then pass it to the DNS Client service for resolution using locally cached information. If the query can be answered from the local cache, the process is complete. Otherwise, the query is passed to the local DNS server.

2. The local name server checks to see if it has authority for that domain. In this example, it does not have authority, but it does contain root hints. The local name server uses the root hints to begin a search for the name server that has authority for the domain *sales.contoso.com*. It then queries the root name server.

3. The root name server sends IP addresses of name servers for the .com top-level domain back to the local DNS server.

4. The local DNS server submits an iterative query to DNS Server A (.com) for *sales .contoso.com*.

5. DNS Server A responds with a referral to the *contoso.com* name server, DNS Server B.

6. The local DNS server submits another iterative query to DNS Server B, *contoso.com*.

7. DNS Server B responds with the IP address for the authoritative server, DNS Server C.

8. The local DNS server submits an iterative query to DNS Server C.

9. DNS Server C responds with a definitive answer (in this case the A record).

10. The local DNS server responds to the DNS client with a definitive answer. The client can now establish a TCP/IP connection with *sales.contoso.com*. From the client's perspective, one request was submitted to and fulfilled by the local DNS server. The information obtained by the local DNS server is cached to answer subsequent queries.

By default, DNS servers use timings for retry intervals and time-out intervals. These are as follows:

- A recursion retry interval of three seconds. This is the length of time the DNS service waits before retrying a query made during a recursive lookup.

- A recursion time-out interval of 15 seconds. This is the length of time the DNS service waits before failing a recursive lookup that has been retried.

Configuring Forwarders

A **forwarder** is a DNS server on a network used to forward DNS queries for external DNS names to DNS servers outside of that network. A **conditional forwarder** forwards queries on the basis of domain name; for example, by forwarding queries for hosts within the *contoso.com* DNS domain to one set of DNS servers, but forwarding queries for the *luvernepublishing.com* domain to a different set of servers.

A DNS server on a network is designated as a forwarder by having the other DNS servers in the network forward the queries they cannot resolve locally to that DNS server. By using a forwarder, you can manage name resolution for names outside of your network, such as names on the Internet, and you improve the efficiency of name resolution for the computers in your network. For example, to use forwarders to manage the DNS traffic between your network and the Internet, configure the firewall used by your network to allow only one DNS server to communicate with the Internet. When you have configured the other DNS servers in your network to forward queries they cannot resolve locally to that DNS server, it will act as your forwarder. Because external network traffic is going through a single DNS server, that server builds up a large cache of DNS data, which, over time, decreases Internet traffic and provides faster response times to clients.

Without having a specific DNS server designated as a forwarder, all DNS servers can send queries outside of a network using their root hints. As a result, a lot of internal, and possibly critical, DNS information can be exposed on the Internet. In addition to this security and privacy issue, this method of resolution can result in a large volume of external traffic that is costly and inefficient for a network with a slow Internet connection or a company with high Internet service costs.

A DNS server configured to use a forwarder will behave differently than a DNS server that is not configured to use a forwarder. A DNS server configured to use a forwarder behaves as follows:

1. When the DNS server receives a query, it attempts to resolve this query by using the primary and secondary zones that it hosts and by using its cache.

TAKE NOTE *

When preparing for certification exams, take note of which DNS settings are configured at the server level as opposed to the zone level. Forwarding is configured for each DNS server, whereas dynamic updates are configured per DNS zone.

2. If the query cannot be resolved using this local data, it will forward the query to the DNS server designated as a forwarder.

3. The DNS server will wait briefly for an answer from the forwarder before attempting to contact the DNS servers specified in its root hints.

4. Rather than send the standard iterative query, when a DNS server forwards a query to a forwarder, by default, it sends a recursive query to the forwarder.

Each domain name used for forwarding on a DNS server is associated with the IP addresses of one or more DNS servers. A DNS server configured for forwarding will use its forwarders list after it has determined that it cannot resolve a query using its authoritative data (primary or secondary zone data) or cached data. If the server cannot resolve a query using forwarders, it may attempt recursion to the root hint servers.

The order of the IP addresses listed determines the sequence in which the IP addresses are used. After the DNS server forwards the query to the forwarder with the first IP address associated with the domain name, it waits a short period for an answer from that forwarder (according to the DNS server's time-out setting) before resuming the forwarding operation with the next IP address associated with the domain name. It continues this process until it receives a positive answer from a forwarder or until it has tried all addresses in the list.

When a DNS server configured to use conditional forwarding receives a query for a domain name, it compares that domain name with its list of domain name conditions and uses the longest domain name condition that corresponds to the domain name in the query. For example, a DNS server receives a query for *www.qualitycontrol.research.wingtiptoys.com*.

It compares that domain name with both *wingtiptoys.com* and *research.wingtiptoys.com*. The DNS server determines that *research.wingtiptoys.com* is the domain name that more closely matches the original query.

Conditional forwarding enables a DNS server to forward queries to other DNS servers based on the DNS domain names in the queries. With conditional forwarding, a DNS server could be configured to forward all the queries it receives for names ending with *research.wingtiptoys .com* to a specific DNS server's IP address or to the IP addresses of multiple DNS servers.

For example, when two companies, *fabrikam.com* and *wingtiptoys.com*, merge or collaborate, they may want to allow clients from the internal namespace of one company to resolve the names of the clients from the internal namespace of another company.

The administrators from one organization (*fabrikam.com*) may inform the administrators of the other organization (*wingtiptoys.com*) about the set of DNS servers that they can use to send DNS queries for name resolution within the internal namespace of the first organization. In this case, the DNS servers in the *wingtiptoys.com* organization will be configured to forward all queries for names ending with *fabrikam.com* to the designated DNS servers.

One important configuration item to note is that a DNS server cannot perform conditional forwarding for any domain names for which that server is authoritative. For example, the authoritative DNS server for the zone *widgets.microsoft.com* cannot forward queries according to the domain name *widgets.microsoft.com*. If the DNS server were allowed to do this, it would nullify the server's capability to respond to queries for the domain name *widgets.microsoft.com*. The DNS server authoritative for *widgets.microsoft.com* can forward queries for DNS names that end with *hr.widgets.microsoft.com*, if *hr.widgets.microsoft.com* is delegated to another DNS server.

The conditional forwarder setting consists of the following:

- The domain names for which the DNS server will forward queries
- One or more DNS server IP addresses for each domain name specified

A DNS server can also be configured as a ***forwarding-only server***, which will not perform recursion after the forwarders fail; if it does not get a successful query response from any of the servers configured as forwarders, it sends a negative response to the DNS client. This option to prevent recursion can be set for each conditional forwarder in Windows Server 2008. For example, a DNS server can be configured to perform recursion for the domain name *research .wingtiptoys.com*, but not to perform recursion for the domain name *wingtiptoys.com*.

A new feature of Windows Server 2008 is that conditional forwarder information can be integrated into Active Directory when DNS is installed on a domain controller. This allows you to replicate conditional forwarder information among multiple DNS servers on your network. A conditional forwarder in an Active Directory environment can be replicated to any of the following:

- All DNS servers in the forest
- All DNS servers in the domain
- All domain controllers in the domain

In the following exercise, we will configure both forwarders and conditional forwarders on a Windows Server 2008 DNS server.

CONFIGURE FORWARDERS

GET READY. This exercise assumes that you have configured DNSPRI with a primary zone for the *contoso.com* domain. This exercise assumes that you are logged onto DNSPRI with administrative privileges. In Part A you will configure a DNS forwarder; in Part B you will configure conditional forwarders based on domain name.

PART A—Configure a forwarder for a DNS Server

1. Click the **Start** button, then browse to **Administrative Tools→DNS**.
2. Click the plus sign (+) next to DNSPRI. Right-click **DNSPRI** and select **Properties**.
3. Click the **Forwarders** tab. You will see the screen shown in Figure 4-6.

Figure 4-6

Configuring DNS forwarders

4. Click **Edit**. Enter the IP address of a remote DNS server and click **OK**.
5. To prevent this DNS server from using recursion, remove the checkmark next to Use root hints if no forwarders are available, and then click **OK**.

PART B—Configure a conditional forwarder

1. In the left-hand pane of the DNS MMC snap-in, select the **Conditional Forwarders** node.

2. Right-click the **Conditional Forwarders** node and click **New Conditional Forwarder....**
You will see the screen shown in Figure 4-7.

Figure 4-7

Configuring conditional
forwarders

3. In the DNS Domain: text box, enter the name of the remote domain for which you wish to set up conditional forwarding; for example, enter *lucernepublishing.com*.

4. In the IP addresses of the master servers: field, enter the IP address of a server that is authoritative for the lucernepublishing.com zone and press (Enter).

5. Click **OK** to save your changes.

PAUSE. Close the DNS MMC snap-in and log off of the Windows Server 2008 computer before continuing.

In the previous exercise, you configured forwarders and conditional forwarders on a Windows Server 2008 DNS server. In the next section, we will discuss the ongoing administration and troubleshooting of the DNS server role using both graphical user interface (GUI) and command-line tools.

Troubleshooting DNS and the Name Resolution Process

DNS is a key service in Microsoft Windows Server 2008 networks. If DNS fails, clients often lose connectivity to the Internet or to other clients and Active Directory fails. Effective management and monitoring procedures mitigate the possibility of DNS server failure. This section introduces you to the tools, concepts, and procedures necessary to manage and monitor DNS name resolution. Topics in this lesson include securing DNS, monitoring and troubleshooting DNS with tools such as the DNS Event Viewer and DNS debug log, and using tools such as Nslookup and Dnscmd.

Several tools are useful for managing and monitoring DNS services. These tools include the following:

- The DNS MMC snap-in, which is part of Administrative Tools. The DNS console is the primary tool for configuring DNS.

- Nslookup, which can be used to query DNS zone information to verify existing and proper configuration of resource records.

- Logging features, such as DNS events that are logged to the Windows Event Viewer, which you can view with the DNS MMC snap-in, Server Manager, or the Windows Event Viewer. File-based logs also can be used temporarily as an advanced debugging option to log and trace selected service events.

- Dnscmd, which enables you to use the command line to perform most of the tasks you can perform using the DNS console.

You can use the DNS console to manually or automatically test DNS servers by submitting two different types of queries:

- A simple query, or iterative query. The DNS resolver (client) on the server computer queries the local DNS servers, which are located on the same computer.

- A recursive query to other DNS servers. The DNS resolver (client) on the server computer queries the local DNS server, but instead of submitting an iterative query, it submits a recursive query. Specifically, the client asks the server to use recursion to resolve a name server (NS)–type query for the root of the DNS domain namespace. This type of query typically requires additional recursive processing and can be helpful in verifying that server root hints or zone delegations are properly set.

These settings are accessed by clicking the Monitoring tab in the DNS server properties window. You can perform the test by clicking the Test Now button or specify an interval for performing the test.

Using NsLookup

Nslookup is a command-line tool built into TCP/IP that is available in Windows Server 2008 to perform DNS queries and enable examination of the content of zone files on local and remote servers. Nslookup is often used to verify the configuration of DNS zones and to diagnose and solve name resolution problems. In order for Nslookup to be used to troubleshoot DNS name resolution, a reverse lookup zone must be configured for the DNS domain that is being queried.

Nslookup can be run at the command prompt (in command prompt mode) or as a program that accepts serial commands and queries (in interactive mode). To look up a single host name, you would typically enter a single command at the command prompt. For example, executing the following command at the command prompt returns the Internet Protocol (IP) addresses associated with the fully qualified domain name (FQDN) *www.microsoft.com* (output results will vary):

```
C:\.nslookup www.microsoft.com
Server: usdc1.us.contoso.com
Address: 192.168.0.100
Non-authoritative answer:
Name: www.microsoft.akadns.net
Addresses: 207.46.134.155,   207.46.134.190, 207.46.249.222,
207.46.249.27
207.46.249.190
Aliases: www.microsoft.com
```

To resolve the query, the Nslookup utility submits the name to the DNS server specified for the primary connection on the local client computer. This DNS server can then answer the query from its cache or through recursion.

If you submit a query for a host name that does not exist, you receive the following response:

```
C:\.nslookup thisdoesnotexist.contoso.com
Server: usdc1.us.contoso.com
Address: 192.168.0.100
*** usdc1.us.contoso.com can't find thisdoesnotexist.contoso.com:
Non-existent domain
```

If you troubleshoot a specific DNS server instead of the one specified for the primary connection on the local client computer, you can specify that DNS server using the Nslookup command. For example, the following command executed at the command prompt queries the DNS server at 192.168.52.141 for the name *www.microsoft.com*:

```
C:\.nslookup www.microsoft.com 192.168.52.141
```

You can also use Nslookup to resolve IP addresses to host names. For example, the following command executed at the command prompt returns the FQDN associated with the address 192.168.141.22, as shown in this output:

```
C:\.nslookup 192.168.141.22
Server: localhost
Address: 127.0.0.1

Name: www.contoso.com
Address: 192.168.141.22
```

Use the following syntax for Nslookup in the command prompt mode:

```
nslookup [-opt...] [{Host| [Server]}]
```

The Nslookup command uses the following switches:

- -opt—Specifies one or more Nslookup subcommands as a command-line option.
- Host—Looks up information for Host using the current default DNS name server (NS), if no other server is specified. To look up a computer not in the current DNS domain, append a period to the name.
- Server—Specifies to use this server as the DNS name server. If you omit Server, the default DNS name server is used.

When issuing multiple Nslookup commands, it is generally more efficient to use Nslookup in interactive mode. To enter interactive mode, open a command prompt, key nslookup, and press Enter. In interactive mode, Nslookup accepts commands that allow the program to perform a variety of functions, such as displaying the specific contents of messages included in DNS exchanges, simulating a zone transfer, or searching for records of a specific type on a given server. These commands can be displayed by keying the help or ? command.

When you are in interactive mode, you can also use the Set command to configure Nslookup options that determine how the resolver carries out queries. One option is to use the debug command. By default, Nslookup is set to nodebug. Keying set debug while in interactive mode enters debug mode, which enables Nslookup to display the DNS response messages communicated from the DNS server. You can view the options currently configured for Nslookup by running the *set all* command.

⚠️ **WARNING** Nslookup commands entered while in interactive mode are case-sensitive and must be keyed in lowercase.

Table 4-7 describes the most common options configured with the Set command.

Table 4-7

Command-Line Options Available with the Set Command

OPTION	PURPOSE	EXAMPLE (INTERACTIVE MODE)
set all	Shows the configuration status of all options.	>set all
set [no]debug	Puts Nslookup in debug mode. With debug mode turned on, more information is printed about the packet sent to the server and the resulting answer.	>set debug Or >set nodebug
set [no]d2	Puts Nslookup in verbose debug mode so you can examine the query and response packets between the resolver and the server.	>set d2 Or >set nod2

(continued)

Table 4-7 (continued)

OPTION	PURPOSE	EXAMPLE (INTERACTIVE MODE)
set domain=<domain name>	Tells the resolver which domain name to append for unqualified queries (for example, sales is an unqualified query as opposed to *sales.fabrikam.com*), including all queried names not followed by a trailing dot.	>set domain=bottinc.com
set timeout=<time-out value>	Tells the resolver what time-value to use, in seconds. This option is useful for slow links on which queries frequently time out and the wait time must be lengthened.	>set timeout=5
set type=<record type> or set querytype=<record type> or set q=<record type>	Tells the resolver which type of resource records to search for (for example, address [A], pointer [PTR], or service locator [SRV] records). If you want the resolver to query for all types of resource records, key set type=all.	>set type=A >set q=MX

By default, names queried for in Nslookup return only matching host address (A) resource records. To look up different data types within the domain namespace, use the Set Type command or set querytype (set q) command at the command prompt. For example, to query for mail exchanger (MX) resource records only instead of A resource records, key set q=mx. To query for a record of any type, execute the Nslookup command set q=any.

TAKE NOTE*

The first time a query is made for a remote name, the answer is authoritative, but subsequent queries are nonauthoritative. This pattern appears for the following reason: the first time a remote host is queried, the local DNS server contacts the DNS server that is authoritative for that domain. The local DNS server then caches that information so that subsequent queries are answered nonauthoritatively out of the local server's cache.

To query another name server directly, use the *server* or *lserver* commands to switch to that name server. The *lserver* command uses the local server to get the address of the server to switch to, whereas the *server* command uses the current default server to get the address.

After you execute either of these commands, all subsequent lookups in the current Nslookup session are performed at the specified server until you switch servers again. The following syntax illustrates what you would key to initiate a server switch:

```
C:\> nslookup
Default Server: nameserver1.contoso.com
Address: 10.0.0.1
> server nameserver2
Default Server: nameserver2.contoso.com
Address: 10.0.0.2
```

You can use the Nslookup subcommand ls to list information for a DNS domain. However, when you issue an Nslookup command with the ls subcommand, you effectively are requesting a zone transfer, so if the DNS server does not permit zone transfers to the IP address that you are running Nslookup from, this command will fail. The syntax for the ls command is as follows:

```
ls [- a | d | t type] domain [> filename]
```

Table 4-8 lists valid options for the ls subcommand.

Table 4-8

Nslookup ls Options

OPTION	PURPOSE	EXAMPLE
-t QueryType	Lists all records of a specific type.	>ls –t cname contoso.com
-a	Lists aliases of computers in the DNS domain (equivalent to -t CNAME).	>ls –a contoso.com
-d	Lists all records for the DNS domain (equivalent to -t ANY).	>ls –d contoso.com
-h	Lists central processing unit (CPU) and operating system information for the DNS domain (equivalent to—t HINFO).	>ls –h contoso.com
-s	Lists well-known services of computers in the DNS domain (equivalent to -t WKS).	>ls –s contoso.com

The following output demonstrates the use of the ls command in interactive mode:

```
>ls contoso.com
[nameserver1.contoso.com]
nameserver1.contoso.com.   NS server = ns1.contoso.com
nameserver2.contoso.com    NS server = ns2.contoso.com
nameserver1                A 10.0.0.1
nameserver2                A 10.0.0.2
```

Using Dnscmd

You can use the Dnscmd command-line tool to perform most of the tasks that you can do from the DNS console. This tool can be used to script batch files, to help automate the management and updates of existing DNS server configurations, or to perform setup and configuration of DNS servers.

Dnscmd is provided as a built-in command-line tool for managing DNS servers in Windows Server 2008. The Dnscmd command allows you to perform a large number of DNS-related tasks, including the following:

- Create, delete, and view zones and records.
- Reset server and zone properties.
- Perform zone maintenance operations, such as updating the zone, reloading the zone, refreshing the zone, writing the zone back to a file or to Active Directory, and pausing or resuming the zone.
- Clear the cache.
- Stop and start the DNS service.
- View statistics.

For example, to display a complete list of the zones configured on a DNS server by using Dnscmd, at the command prompt, key dnscmd [ComputerName] /enumzones. A sample output of this command follows:

```
C:\>dnscmd localhost /enumzones
Enumerated zone list:
Zone count = 5
```

```
Zone name                   Type            Storage Properties
.                           Cache           AD-Legacy
_msdcs.contoso01.com        Primary         AD-Forest Secure
1.1.10.in-addr.arpa         Primary         AD-Legacy Secure Rev
computer01.contoso.com      Primary         AD-Legacy
contoso01.com               Primary         AD-Domain Secure

Command completed successfully.
```

To display information about a specific zone that is configured on a DNS server by using Dnscmd, at the command prompt, key the following:

```
dnscmd [ComputerName] /zoneinfo [zone]
```

Sample output of this command follows below:

```
C:\>dnscmd localhost /zoneinfo contoso01.com
Zone query result:
Zone info:

        ptr                 = 00083050
        zone name           = contoso01.com
        zone type           = 1
        update              = 2
        DS integrated       = 1
        data file           - (null)
        using WINS          = 0
        using Nbstat        = 0
        aging               = 0
        refresh interval    = 168
        no refresh          - 168
        scavenge available  = 3529116
        Zone Masters
        NULL IP Array.
        Zone Secondaries
        NULL IP Array.
        secure secs         = 3
        directory partition = AD-Domain flags 00000015
        zone DN             = DC=contoso01.com,cn=MicrosoftDNS,
                              DC=DomainDnsZones, DC=contoso01,
                              DC=com


              Command completed successfully.
```

Configuring Advanced DNS Server Properties

Advanced DNS server properties refer to the settings that can be configured in the Advanced tab of the DNS Server Properties dialog box (shown in Figure 4-8). These properties relate to server-specific features, such as disabling recursion, handling resolution of multi-homed hosts, and achieving compatibility with non-Microsoft DNS servers.

Figure 4-8

Viewing advanced DNS server
properties

The default installation settings of the DNS server role include six server options, which are
either on or off, and three other server features with various selections for configuration. Table
4-9 shows the default settings for all nine features.

Table 4-9

Default DNS Installation Settings

PROPERTY	SETTING
Disable Recursion (also disables forwarders)	Off
BIND Secondaries	Off
Fail On Load If Bad Zone Data	Off
Enable Round Robin	On
Enable Netmask Ordering	On
Secure Cache Against Pollution	On
Name Checking	Multibyte (UTF-8)
Load Zone Data On Startup	From Active Directory And Registry
Enable Automatic Scavenging Of Stale Records	Off (requires configuration when enabled)

In most situations, these installation defaults are acceptable and do not require modification.
However, when needed, you can use the DNS console to modify these advanced parameters and
accommodate special deployment needs and situations. You can restore these default settings at
any time using the Advanced tab by clicking the Reset To Default button on the Advanced tab.

We'll now describe each available configuration option in more detail.

- Disable Recursion—The Disable Recursion server option is disabled by default (meaning
  that recursion is enabled). When the Disable Recursion option is enabled, the DNS Server
  service does not answer queries for which it is not authoritative or which it has not already
  answered and placed in its cache. Instead, the DNS Server service provides the client with
  referrals, which are resource records that allow a DNS client to perform iterative queries to
  resolve an FQDN. Do not disable recursion on a server if any other name servers are using
  this server as a forwarder. You should only disable recursion when you want to create a
  server that does not query any other servers to resolve client DNS queries.

- BIND Secondaries—The BIND Secondaries option controls whether a fast transfer format is used during a DNS zone transfer. Berkeley Internet Name Domain (BIND) is a common implementation of DNS written and ported to most available versions of the UNIX operating system. Fast transfer format is an efficient means of transferring zone data that provides data compression and allows multiple records to be transferred per individual Transmission Control Protocol (TCP) message. Fast zone transfer is always used among Windows-based DNS servers, so the BIND Secondaries option does not affect communications among Windows servers. However, only BIND versions 4.9.4 and later can handle these fast zone transfers. For BIND versions earlier than 4.9.4, DNS servers running Windows Server 2003 can be configured to transfer a zone using the slower, uncompressed transfer format. When you select the BIND Secondaries check box in the Advanced tab of the Server Properties dialog box, no fast transfers are made. If you know your DNS server will be performing zone transfers with DNS servers using BIND version 4.9.4 or later, you should disable this option to allow fast zone transfers to occur.

TAKE NOTE*

BIND version 9.1 was released January 17, 2001, so this option should not see much use on a production network.

- Fail On Load If Bad Zone Data—DNS servers running on Windows Server 2008 will, by default, load a zone even if that zone contains errors. In that scenario, errors are logged and ignored. Enabling Fail On Load If Bad Zone Data prevents a zone with errors from being loaded.
- Enable Round Robin—*DNS round robin* is a load balancing mechanism used by DNS servers to share and distribute network resource loads. If multiple resource records satisfy a query, you can use round robin to rotate the order of resource record types returned to the client. By default, DNS uses round robin to rotate the order of resource record data returned in query answers in which multiple resource records of the same type exist for a queried DNS domain name. This feature provides a simple method for load balancing client use of Web servers and other frequently queried multi-homed computers.

Consider this example of DNS round robin: The Web server named *server1.contoso.com* has three network adapters and three distinct IP addresses. In the stored zone (either in a database file or in Active Directory), the three A resource records mapping the host name to each of its IP addresses appear in this fixed order:

```
server1 IN A 10.0.0.1
server1 IN A 10.0.0.2
server1 IN A 10.0.0.3
```

The first DNS client—Client1—that queries the server to resolve this host's name receives the list in this default order. However, when a second client—Client2—sends a subsequent query to resolve this name, the list is rotated as follows:

```
server1 IN A 10.0.0.2
server1 IN A 10.0.0.3
server1 IN A 10.0.0.1
```

When you clear the Enable Round Robin check box, round robin is disabled for the DNS server. If round robin is disabled for a DNS server, the order of the response for these queries is based on a static ordering of resource records in the answer list as they are stored in the zone (either its zone file or Active Directory).

- Enable Netmask Ordering—Netmask ordering is a method DNS uses to give ordering and preference to IP addresses on the same network when a requesting client queries for a host name that has multiple A resource records. This is designed so that the client program will attempt to connect to a host using the closest (and, therefore, presumably fastest) IP address available. When returning more than one IP address to a client when Netmask Ordering is enabled, IP addresses most closely matching the client's subnet mask are placed at the top of the response list. The Enable Netmask Ordering option is selected by default.

For an example of netmask ordering in action, consider the following scenario: a multihomed computer, *server1.contoso.com*, has three A resource records for each of its three IP addresses in the *contoso.com* zone. These three records appear in the following order in the zone—either in the zone file or in Active Directory:

```
server1 IN A 192.168.1.27
server1 IN A 10.0.0.14
server1 IN A 172.16.20.4
```

When a DNS client resolver at IP address 10.4.3.2 queries the server for the IP addresses of the host *server1.contoso.com*, the DNS Server service notes that the originating IP network address (10.0.0.0) of the client matches the network (class A) ID of the 10.0.0.14 address in the answer list of resource records. The DNS Server service then reorders the addresses in the response list as follows:

```
server1 IN A 10.0.0.14
server1 IN A 192.168.1.27
server1 IN A 172.16.20.4
```

If the network ID of the IP address of the requesting client does not match any of the network IDs of the resource records in the answer list, the list is not reordered.

- Secure Cache Against Pollution—By default, the Secure Cache Against Pollution option is enabled. This setting allows the DNS server to protect its cache against referrals that are potentially polluting or nonsecure. When the setting is enabled, the server caches only those records with a name that corresponds to the domain for which the original queried name was made. Any referrals received from another DNS server along with a query response are simply discarded. For example, if a query is originally made for the name *example.lucernepublishing.com*, and a referral answer provides a record for a name outside the *lucernepublishing.com* domain name tree (such as *msn.com*), that name is discarded if the Secure Cache Against Pollution option is enabled. This setting helps prevent unauthorized computers from impersonating another network server. When this option is disabled, however, the server caches all the records received in response to DNS queries—even when the records do not correspond to the queried-for domain name.

- Name Checking—By default, the Name Checking dropdown list box in the Advanced tab of the DNS Server Properties dialog box is set to Multibyte (UTF-8). Thus, the DNS service, by default, verifies that all domain names handled by the DNS service conform to the UCS Transformation Format (UTF). Unicode is a 2-byte encoding scheme, compatible with the traditional 1-byte American Standard Code for Information Interchange (ASCII) format, that allows for binary representation of most human languages. Table 4-10 lists and describes the four name-checking methods.

Table 4-10

Name-Checking Methods

METHOD	DESCRIPTION
Strict RFC (American National Standards Institute [ANSI])	Uses strict checking of names. These restrictions, set in Request for Comments (RFC) 1123, include limiting names to uppercase and lowercase letters (A–Z, a–z), numbers (0–9), and hyphens (-). The first character of the DNS name can be a number.
Non RFC (ANSI)	Permits names that are nonstandard and that do not follow RFC 1123 Internet host naming specifications.
Multibyte (UTF-8)	Permits recognition of characters other than ASCII, including Unicode, which is normally encoded as more than one octet (8 bits) in length. With this option, multibyte characters can be transformed and represented using UTF-8 support, which is provided with Windows Server 2003.

(continued)

Table 4-10 *(continued)*

METHOD	DESCRIPTION
	Names encoded in UTF-8 format must not exceed the size limits stated in RFC 2181, which specifies a maximum of 63 octets per label and 255 octets per name. Character count is insufficient to determine size because some UTF-8 characters exceed one octet in length. This option allows for domain names using non-English alphabets.
All Names	Permits any naming conventions.

Despite the flexibility of the UTF-8 name-checking method, you should consider changing the Name Checking option to Strict RFC when your DNS servers perform zone transfers to non-Windows servers that are not UTF-8-aware. Although DNS server implementations that are not UTF-8-aware might be able to accept the transfer of a zone containing UTF-8-encoded names, these servers might not be capable of writing back those names to a zone file or reloading those names from a zone file.

You should use the other two name-checking options, Non RFC and All Names, only when a specific application requires them.

- Load Zone Data On Startup—By default, the Load Zone Data On Startup property is set to the From Active Directory And Registry option. Thus, by default, DNS servers in Windows Server 2003 initialize with the settings specified in the Active Directory database and the server registry. You can also load zone data using two other settings: From Registry and From File. The From Registry option forces the DNS server to initialize by reading parameters stored in the Windows registry. The From File option forces the DNS server to initialize by reading parameters stored in a boot file. The boot file must be a text file named Boot located on the local computer in the *%systemroot%\System32\Dns* folder. When a boot file is used, settings in the file are applied to the server, overriding the settings stored in the registry on the DNS server. However, for parameters that are not configurable using boot file directives, registry defaults (or stored reconfigured server settings) are applied by the DNS Server service.

> **TAKE NOTE ***
>
> Windows Server 2008 has made improvements in the way that Active Directory–integrated zones are loaded when a domain controller that's running the DNS Server role starts up. This improvement, called *background zone loading*, allows DNS servers in large organizations to begin responding to DNS queries much earlier in the boot process than in previous versions of the Windows server operating systems.

SUMMARY SKILL MATRIX

IN THIS LESSON YOU LEARNED:

- DNS names and the DNS protocol are required for Active Directory domains and for compatibility with the Internet.

- The DNS namespace is hierarchical and based on a unique root that can have any number of subdomains. An FQDN is the name of a DNS host in this namespace that indicates the host's location relative to the root of the DNS domain tree. An example of an FQDN is *host1.subdomain.microsoft.com.*

- A DNS zone is a contiguous portion of a namespace for which a server is authoritative. A server can be authoritative for one or more zones, and a zone can contain one or more contiguous domains. A DNS server is authoritative for a zone if it hosts the zone, either as a primary or secondary DNS server. Each DNS zone contains the resource records it needs to answer queries for its portion of the DNS namespace.

- There are several types of DNS servers: primary, secondary, master name, and caching-only.

  - A DNS server that hosts a primary DNS zone is said to act as a primary DNS server. Primary DNS servers store original source data for zones. With Windows Server 2003, you can implement primary zones in one of two ways: as standard primary zones, in which zone data is stored in a text file, or as an Active Directory–integrated zone, in which zone data is stored in the Active Directory database.

- A DNS server that hosts a secondary DNS server is said to act as a secondary DNS server. Secondary DNS servers are authoritative backup servers for the primary server. The servers from which secondary servers acquire zone information are called masters.

- A caching-only server forwards requests to other DNS servers and hosts no zones, but builds a cache of frequently requested records.

- Recursion is one of the two process types for DNS name resolution. A DNS client will request that a DNS server provide a complete answer to a query that does not include pointers to other DNS servers, effectively shifting the workload of resolving the query from the client to the DNS server. For the DNS server to perform recursion properly, the server needs to know where to begin searching for names in the DNS namespace. This information is provided by the root hints file, *cache.dns,* which is stored on the server computer.

- A DNS server on a network is designated as a forwarder by having the other DNS servers in the network forward the queries they cannot resolve locally to that DNS server. Conditional forwarding enables a DNS server to forward queries to other DNS servers based on the DNS domain names in the queries.

■ Knowledge Assessment

Fill in the Blank

Complete the following sentences by writing the correct word or words in the blanks provided.

1. A(n) _____ will transfer all records within a zone from a primary server to a secondary server.

2. A(n) _____ creates an alias for an existing A record.

3. A(n) _____ is used by e-mail systems such as Microsoft Exchange to locate mail servers in different networks.

4. The _____ allows IPv6 hosts to map host names to IP addresses.

5. *contoso.com* is an example of a(n) _____ within the .com top-level domain.

6. The _____ application scope will replicate DNS data to all DNS servers within a domain.

7. A(n) _____ stores DNS data in a text file on the server hard drive, rather than as part of Active Directory.

8. Each DNS record has a(n) _____ that indicates the maximum time that a record will be cached by a DNS server before it is discarded.

9. A DNS server is considered _____ for each zone that it hosts.

10. A DNS domain name like *.uk* or *.it* is an example of a(n) _____ domain.

Multiple Choice

Select all answers that apply for the following questions.

1. This DNS configuration item will forward DNS queries to different servers based on the domain name of the query.
   a. Iterative forwarder
   b. Recursive forwarder
   c. Conditional forwarder
   d. IPv6 forwarder

2. This type of zone takes human-readable FQDNs and translates them into IP addresses.
   a. Standard zone
   b. Forward lookup zone
   c. Reverse lookup zone
   d. Inverse lookup zone

3. This zone is used in conjunction with IPv4 IP addresses to resolve queries for IPv4 IP addresses to resolve queries for FQDNs.
   a. In.addr-arpa
   b. In.addr-ipv4
   c. In.addr-ipv4.arpa
   d. In.ipv4.arpa

4. The IPv6 DNS host record is referred to as a(n):
   a. A record
   b. AA record
   c. AAA record
   d. AAAA record

5. A DNS server that hosts a primary or secondary zone containing a particular record can issue the following response to a query for that record:
   a. Authoritative answer
   b. Non-authoritative answer
   c. Referral answer
   d. Non-referral answer

6. You can secure an Active Directory–integrated DNS server, zone, or record by applying the following to it:
   a. System Access Control List
   b. Security Access Control List
   c. Discretionary Access Control List
   d. Distributed Access Control List

7. This zone type contains only SOA, name server, and glue records for the relevant zone.
   a. Secondary zone
   b. Stub zone
   c. Primary zone
   d. Caching-only zone

8. Data from a primary zone is transmitted to secondary zones using the following:
   a. Zone transfer
   b. Zone transmission
   c. DNS Zone
   d. Active Directory replication

9. These contain the names and IP addresses of the DNS servers authoritative for the root zone.
   a. "." zone
   b. Top-level zone
   c. Root Hints
   d. Root Cache

10. The following feature is available only on Active Directory–integrated DNS zones:
    a. Dynamic updates
    b. Incremental zone transfers
    c. Reverse lookup zones
    d. Secure dynamic updates

Case Scenarios

Scenario 4-1: Enabling Network Users to Connect to Internet Host Names

You are the network administrator for Contoso, Ltd. The Contoso network consists of a single domain, *contoso.com*, which is protected from the Internet by a firewall. The firewall runs on a computer named NS1 that is directly connected to the Internet. NS1 also runs the DNS Server service, and its firewall allows DNS traffic to pass between the Internet and the DNS Server service on NS1 but not between the Internet and the internal network. The DNS Server service on NS1 is configured to use round robin. Behind the firewall, two computers are running Windows Server 2003—NS2 and NS3, which host a primary and secondary DNS server, respectively, for the *contoso.com* zone.

Users on the company network report that, although they use host names to connect to computers on the local private network, they cannot use host names to connect to Internet destinations, such as *www.microsoft.com*.

Which of the following actions requires the least amount of administrative effort to enable network users to connect to Internet host names?

- a. Disable recursion on NS2 and NS3.
- b. Enable netmask ordering on NS1.
- c. Configure NS2 and NS3 to use NS1 as a forwarder.
- d. Disable round robin on NS1.

Scenario 4-2: Implementing DNS Updates

You are the system administrator for Contoso, Ltd. The company has grown rapidly over the past year, and currently Contoso is using only a single DNS zone. Recently, the Marketing department has made several requests for DNS changes that were delayed. Users would like the ability to make their own DNS updates.

What should you do to try to address this problem?

- a. Create a secondary server in the Marketing department so that users can manage their own zone.
- b. Delegate the marketing domain to a DNS server in the Marketing department.
- c. Place a domain controller running DNS in the Marketing department so that people in the department can make changes.
- d. Upgrade the network infrastructure to improve network performance.

MATRIX SKILL	SKILL NUMBER	LESSON NUMBER
Configure IPv4 & IPv6 addressing	1.1	1
Configure Dynamic Host Configuration Protocol (DHCP)	1.2	3
Configure routing	1.3	5
Configure IPsec	1.4	9
Configure a Domain Name System (DNS) server	2.1	4
Configure DNS zones	2.2	4
Configure DNS records	2.3	4
Configure DNS replication	2.4	4
Configure name resolution for client	2.5	4
Configure remote access	3.1	5
Configure Network Access Protection (NAP)	3.2	10
Configure network authentication	3.3	9
Configure wireless access	3.4	5
Configure firewall settings	3.5	9
Configure a file server	4.1	6
Configure Distributed File System (DFS)	4.2	6
Configure shadow copy services	4.3	11
Configure backup and restore	4.4	11
Manage disk quotas	4.5	11
Configure and monitor print services	4.6	7
Configure Windows Server Update Services (WSUS) server settings	5.1	8
Capture performance data	5.2	8
Monitor event logs	5.3	8
Gather network data	5.4	8

■ Getting Started

The *Windows Server 2008 Network Infrastructure Configuration* title of the Microsoft Official Academic Course (MOAC) series includes two books: a textbook and a lab manual. The exercises in the lab manual are designed for classroom use under the supervision of an instructor or a lab aide. In an academic setting, the computer classroom might be used by a variety of classes each day, so you must plan your setup procedure accordingly. For example, consider automating the classroom setup procedure and using removable fixed disks in the classroom. Use the automated setup procedure to rapidly configure the classroom environment and remove the fixed disks after teaching this class each day.

■ Classroom Setup

This course should be taught in a classroom containing networked computers where students can develop their skills through hands-on experience with Microsoft Windows Server 2008. The exercises in the lab manual require the computers to be installed and configured in a specific manner. Failure to adhere to the setup instructions in this document can produce unanticipated results when the students perform the exercises.

TAKE NOTE*

You can either use multiple physical machines for each student, or you can install the server and client as virtual machines on a single physical machine using Microsoft Virtual PC or a similar virtual machine environment. If you use Virtual PC, your physical machine must comply with the minimum requirements for Windows Server 2008. Virtual PC also requires 1.6GHz processor speed or faster and 640MB RAM (1GB recommended) over and above the RAM required by the hosting operating system for each virtual guest that will be running on the host computer.

Windows Server 2008 Requirements

A physical computer running Windows Server 2008 requires the following hardware and software.

HARDWARE REQUIREMENTS

All hardware must be on the Microsoft Windows Server 2008 Windows Catalog.
- One 1GHz processor (2GHz or greater recommended)
- 512MB RAM (2GB or greater recommended)
- 10GB hard disk minimum (40GB or greater recommended)
- One DVD-ROM drive
- One mouse
- One Super VGA display adapter and monitor
- One Ethernet network interface adapter

SOFTWARE REQUIREMENTS

The software listed below is required for the course.

- Microsoft Windows Server 2008 (Evaluation edition available as a free download from Microsoft's Web site at *http://technet.microsoft.com*)

In order to perform several optional labs, the software listed below is required:

- Microsoft Windows Vista Ultimate (evaluation edition available as a free download from Microsoft's Web site at *http://technet.microsoft.com*)

Classroom Configuration and Network Considerations

Each student's server is configured as a Windows Server 2008 stand-alone server in a work-group configuration. The instructor's computer is configured as a Windows Server 2008 domain controller for the purposes of the first Lab exercise, using the following configuration:

- Active Directory domain name: lucernepublishing.com
- Computer name: INSTRUCTOR01
- Fully qualified domain name (FQDN): instructor01.lucernepublishing.com

For several optional exercises, each student will require two additional server computers—one running the Windows Server 2008 Server Core installation and one running Windows Vista, Enterprise Edition.

TAKE NOTE*

To maintain consistency with the order of the textbook that this lab manual accompanies, Lab 1 will address configuring TCP/IP addressing on one or more already-installed Windows Server 2008 computers. Lab 2 will then require you to remove the 2008 installations that were used in Lab 1 in order to perform actual installations of the Windows Server 2008 operating system. Depending on the pre-existing skill set of your students, instructors may wish to reverse the order of Labs 1 and 2 to reduce the setup/teardown required between the two labs. Sidebars in Lab 1 indicate any necessary changes if the instructor chooses to reverse the order of Labs 1 and 2.

A Note on the Use of Virtualization

The lab exercises were written using Windows Server 2008 and Windows Vista installed as virtual guests in Microsoft Virtual Server 2005 R2 and the exercises were tested with virtual guests in Microsoft Virtual PC. Depending on your needs, you can install multiple guests using Virtual Server, Virtual PC, or VMWare. Keep in mind that running multiple virtual "guests" on a single physical "host" can greatly increase the hardware requirements needed by the physical host; be sure to test these configurations before attempting to use virtual guests to teach in an actual classroom environment in order to ensure that performance is acceptable.

Additionally, you may wish to use advanced virtualization features such as snapshots, undo disks, and differencing disks to decrease the amount of time needed to deploy multiple virtual servers, as well as the time required to roll back the changes made in each individual lab. The use of these advanced virtualization features is beyond the scope of this document; consult the documentation for your virtualization software of choice to determine if this would prove valuable in your environment.

Installing Windows Server 2008

If your computer has an existing 32-bit operating system installed, start the computer as usual and insert the Windows Server 2008 Installation disk. The Microsoft Windows 2008 window opens automatically. In the left pane of the window, select Install Windows Server 2008. If the Microsoft Windows 2008 window does not open automatically, double-click the CD-ROM drive in Windows Explorer to launch the auto-play feature.

If your computer does not have an operating system installed, you will need to boot your computer from the Windows Server 2008 Installation disk. When you boot from the disk, the Windows Server 2008 Setup program starts automatically.

After Windows Server 2008 Setup is launched, follow the steps below to continue the installation.

TAKE NOTE *

The steps below assume that you are performing a new installation; the steps to upgrade to Windows Server 2008 from an existing operating system will differ slightly.

INSTALL WINDOWS SERVER 2008

TAKE NOTE *

Depending on how your school's network is set up, you might need to use different values for settings, such as IP addresses, to match your actual networking environment.

GET READY. You will now install the Windows Server 2008 operating system. These steps require the Windows Server 2008 installation media, as well as a valid product key if appropriate to your lab environment.

1. Insert the Windows Server 2008 installation media and power on the physical or virtual server.

2. You will see the initial installation screen. Here you are prompted to configure the following three items:
   - Language to install: for example, English or German
   - Time and currency format: for example, English (United States) or French (Switzerland)
   - Keyboard/input layout: for example, US or United Kingdom

3. Click **Next**, followed by **Install Now**.

4. Depending on the type of media you are using to install the software, you might be prompted to enter the Windows product key. If prompted, enter a legitimate Windows product key and click **Next**.

5. Next you will be prompted to install either the full version of Windows Server 2008 or Server Core. Select a full install or a Server Core install as appropriate for the particular image that you are building. Click **Next** to continue.

6. On the subsequent screen, you will be prompted to accept the Windows Server 2008 license terms. Read the licensing terms and then place a checkmark next to **I accept the license terms**. Click **Next** to continue the installation.

7. You will be prompted to select an upgrade installation or a clean install. If you are installing Windows onto brand new hardware, you will notice that the Upgrade option is grayed out and only the Custom option is available. Select the **Custom** installation option.

8. On the subsequent screen, you will be prompted to select the hard drive partition on which to install Windows. Select the appropriate partition and click **Next**. At this point, the installation process will begin. The remainder of the installation is largely automated. To improve the security of a Windows Server 2008 installation, you will be prompted to establish a complex password on the final reboot.

PAUSE. In this exercise, you performed the initial installation of the Windows Server 2008 operating system on a newly formatted computer.

TAKE NOTE *

After Windows Server 2008 Setup restarts, the computer might try to boot from the Windows Server 2008 DVD. If this happens, you will be prompted to press a key to boot from the DVD; if you do not press a key, Windows Server 2008 should start normally. However, if the Windows Server 2008 Setup routing restarts automatically, simply remove the installation media and then restart the computer.

COMPLETE POST-INSTALLATION TASKS ON THE SERVER

GET READY. After the installation is complete and the computer has restarted, you should see the Welcome To Windows dialog box. In this exercise, you will install the Virtual Machine Additions onto the Virtual PC instance in question. (If you are using separate physical machines rather than VM instances, skip this section.)

1. Press (Ctrl) + (Alt) + (Delete) and enter the username and password you specified earlier to log on *(Administrator/MSPress#1)*. The Initial Configuration Tasks dialog box is displayed. Leave this page displayed, because students will use this interface during the first lab exercise.

2. If you are using Virtual PC, install Virtual Machine Additions. To do so, select **Install Or Update Virtual Machine Additions** from the Actions menu of the Virtual PC menu, and then follow the prompts. After the installation, you will be prompted to restart Windows Server 2008. After restarting, repeat step 1 of this section to log on.

PAUSE. In this exercise, you installed the Virtual Machine Additions onto one or more Virtual PC or Microsoft Virtual Server instances of the Windows Server 2008 operating system. In the next exercise, you will install and configure the Active Directory Domain Services role on the instructor computer in order to demonstrate Active Directory integration during several lab exercises.

> **TAKE NOTE***
>
> At some point, the operating system will prompt you to activate the server. When that happens, follow the steps to activate the server.

Installing Active Directory on the Instructor's Computer

INSTALL ACTIVE DIRECTORY ON THE INSTRUCTOR'S COMPUTER

GET READY. In this exercise you will configure a single-forest Active Directory domain named *lucernepublishing.com*. This exercise assumes that the server in question has been configured with a static IP address.

1. Press (Ctrl) + (Alt) + (Delete) on the instructor's computer and log on as the default administrator of the local computer. Your username will be *Administrator*. The password will be *MSPress#1* or the password that you configured when the server was built. The Initial Configuration Tasks screen will be displayed automatically.

2. Configure the following items prior to installing Active Directory:

   • Time zone and current time

   • Network configuration: Static IP address, subnet mask, default gateway

   • Enable automatic updates and feedback

   • Computer name: INSTRUCTOR01

3. Reboot the computer when instructed. After it reboots, log on using administrative credentials.

4. Close the Initial Configuration Tasks screen.

5. If the Server Manager screen does not appear automatically, click the **Start** button, and then click **Server Manager**.

6. Expand the Server Manager window to full screen if necessary.

7. In the left pane of Server Manager, double-click **Roles**.

8. Click **Add Role**. Click **Next** to bypass the initial Welcome screen. The Select Server Roles screen is displayed.

9. Place a checkmark next to **Active Directory Domain Services**. Click **Next**. The Active Directory Domain Services screen is displayed.

10. Read the introductory information to Active Directory Domain Services and click **Next**. The Confirm Installation Selections screen is displayed.

11. Read the confirmation information to prepare for the installation. Click **Install** to install the AD Domain Services role. The Installation Results screen is displayed.

12. Click **Close this wizard** and launch the **Active Directory Domain Services Installation Wizard (dcpromo.exe)**. The Welcome to the Active Directory Domain Services Installation Wizard screen is displayed.

13. Click **Next** twice to continue. The Choose a Deployment Configuration screen is displayed.

14. Click the **Create a new domain in a new forest** radio button, then click **Next.** The Name the Forest Root domain screen is displayed.

15. Key **lucernepublishing.com** as the name of the new domain and click Next. The Domain NetBIOS Name screen appears.

16. Key **LP** and click **Next.** The Set Forest Functional Level screen is displayed.

17. Select **Windows Server 2008** and click **Next.** The Additional Domain Controller Options screen is displayed.

18. Verify that the DNS Server checkbox is selected, and then click **Next.** A warning message is displayed concerning DNS delegations. Read the warning message and click **Yes** to continue. The Location for Database, Log Files, and SYSVOL screen is displayed.

19. Accept the default selections and click **Next** to continue. The Directory Services Restore Mode Administrator Password screen is displayed.

20. Enter **MSPress#1** into the Password and Confirm Password text boxes and click **Next** to continue. The Summary screen is displayed.

21. Review your installation choices and click **Next** to continue. The Active Directory Domain Services Installation Wizard screen is displayed, indicating that the Active Directory DS service is being installed. The Completing the Active Directory Domain Services Installation Wizard screen is displayed.

22. Click **Finish.** When prompted, click **Restart Now** to restart the newly configured domain controller.

PAUSE. In this exercise, you configured the instructor's computer as a domain controller in the lucernepublishing.com domain. In the next exercise, you will configure a DHCP server to allow the lab computers to obtain IP addresses automatically. If your lab network uses DHCP through another mechanism, such as a hardware-based router, you can skip this section.

INSTALL AND CONFIGURE THE DHCP SERVER

GET READY. In this exercise you will install and configure a DHCP server on the INSTRUCTOR01 computer.

1. Press (Ctrl) + (Alt) + (Delete) on the instructor's computer and log on as the default administrator of the local computer. Your username will be *Administrator.* The password will be *MSPress#1* or the password that you configured when the server was built. The Server Manager screen will be displayed automatically.

2. Expand the Server Manager window to full screen if necessary.

3. In the left pane of Server Manager, double-click **Roles**.

4. Click **Add Roles.** Click **Next** to dismiss the initial Welcome screen. The Select Server Roles screen is displayed.

5. Place a checkmark next to **DHCP Server.** Click **Next.** The Introduction to DHCP Server screen is displayed.

6. Read the information about the DHCP Server role and click **Next.** The Specify IPv4 DNS Server Settings screen is displayed.

7. Leave all text boxes as is and click **Next.** The Specify IPv4 WINS Server Settings screen is displayed.

8. Leave the default radio button selected and click **Next.** The Add or Edit DHCP Scopes screen is displayed.

9. Click **Add** to create a DHCP scope for your network. The Add Scope screen is displayed.

10. Enter the following information, customized as appropriate for your classroom setup:

   - Scope Name: **70-642 Lab**
   - Starting IP address: **192.168.1.100**
   - Ending IP address: **192.168.1.254**
   - Subnet mask: **255.255.255.0**
   - Default gateway: **192.168.1.1**
   - Subnet type: **Wired**

11. Verify that there is a checkmark next to **Activate this scope**, and then click **OK**.

12. Click **Next**. The Configure DHCPv6 Stateless Mode screen is displayed.

13. Leave the default radio button selected and click **Next**. The Specify IPv6 DNS Server Settings screen is displayed.

14. Leave all text boxes blank and click **Next.** The Authorize DHCP Server screen is displayed.

15. Leave the default radio button selected and click **Next**. The Confirm Installation Selections screen is displayed.

16. Click **Install**. When the installation is completed, click **Close**.

STOP. You have now completed all the necessary steps to set up the instructor's computer and all the student computers to use the *Windows Server 2008 Network Infrastructure Configuration* Lab Manual. This includes installing Windows Server 2008 on all student computers, as well as configuring the instructor's computer as a DHCP server and as a domain controller in the lucernepublishing.com domain.

Additional Setup Considerations for Individual Labs

In Lab 5, performing exercises involving the Routing & Remote Access service will require each computer to be configured with a second network interface card (NIC) to simulate network routing within the lab environment. This can either be accomplished by installing a second NIC within the physical machines, or by configuring Virtual Networking within the virtualization product. To assist students in completing this lab, prepare a diagram of the network in which they will be working, similar to the one shown in Figure 1.

Lab 7 involves creating and configuring printers on a Windows Server 2008 computer. The lab instructions involve setting up a "dummy" HP LaserJet 4 printer; however, if your lab environment has a physical printer available that students can work with, you may modify the

Figure 1

Sample network diagram for Lab 5

192.168.10.0/24   192.168.11.0/24   192.168.12.0/24

W2K8*xx*   W2K8*yy*

exercise instructions accordingly. The Lab Challenge Exercise in Lab 7 requires the creation of a test Organizational Unit (OU) and user accounts for students to test deploying printers through Group Policy. A Group Policy Object (GPO) should be linked to the OU containing the test user accounts that students can use to deploy printer connections.

Lab 8 involves making the following out-of-band downloaded executables available to students:

- Microsoft Network Monitor 3.1
- Microsoft Report Viewer Redistributable 2005
- Windows Server Update Services 3.0 SP1

> **TAKE NOTE** *
>
> If your lab environment does not allow Internet access, you will need an upstream WSUS server available during Lab 8 for students to point their WSUS server to. You will also need to provide configuration specifics on the name or IP address of this server for your students. The Lab 8 instructions assume that the student-created WSUS server has Internet access available.

> **TAKE NOTE** *
>
> If your lab environment requires proxy server configuration in order to access the Internet, you will need to provide this configuration information to your students prior to Project 8.4, Configuring Windows Server Update Services. The Lab 8 instructions assume that the lab environment does not require proxy server configuration.

In Lab 11, performing exercises using Windows Server Backup will require each computer to be configured with a secondary hard drive that is of equal or greater capacity to the system drive configured on each machine.

You have now completed the necessary steps for setup of the labs for the *Windows Server 2008 Network Infrastructure Configuration* Lab Manual. This includes installing Windows Server 2008 as well as configuring the instructor's computer as a DHCP server and as a domain controller in the lucernepublishing.com domain.

Glossary

802.1X enforcement NAP enforcement method that uses 802.1X-aware network access points, such as network switches or wireless assess points, to restrict network access of noncompliant resources

A

Accounting Remote Access component that maintains information about successful and failed connections to a remote access server

Active Directory-integrated zone a DNS zone that stores its data within the Active Directory database

address (a) resource record a DNS resource record that maps an individual host name to an IP address

Address Resolution Protocol (ARP) used to map a known IP address to an unknown MAC address

Administrative Events a built-in custom view in the Windows Server 2008 Event Viewer that collects Critical, Error, and Warning events from all logs on the server

Always Call Back To: the Callback Option that always calls the user back at a pre-configured number

Application Layer the top-most layer of the OSI model, where DHCP and other network applications function

Application Logs records events associated with software that is installed on the server

Applications and Services provides collections of Event Viewer entries associated with server hardware, Internet Explorer, and other Windows-based applications and components

authentication the process of confirming a user's identity

Authentication Exemption a connection security rule used to specify one or more computers that do not need to be authenticated in order to pass traffic

Authentication Header (AH) an IPSec protocol that provides authentication, integrity, and anti-replay for the entire packet

authentication methods a security algorithm and type used for IPSec authentication and key exchange

Authentication Server (AS) an 802.1X component that verifies the supplicant's authentication credentials

authenticator an 802.1X component that requests authentication credentials from supplicants

authoritative a DNS server that hosts a primary or secondary zone for a particular DNS domain

authoritative answer a response from a DNS server that hosts a primary or secondary zone for the DNS domain being queried

authorize the process of enabling an Active Directory DHCP server to provide DHCP services to clients

Autoenrollment PKI feature supported by Windows Server 2003 and later, which allows users and computers to automatically enroll for certificates based on one or more certificate templates

Automatic Private IP Addressing (APIPA) a service in Windows XP, Windows Server 2003, Windows Vista, and Windows Server 2008 that can automatically configure client IP addresses in the absence of a DHCP server; APIPA addresses do not contain a default gateway and can only be used to communicate on the local subnet

automatic restores restores performed by a DHCP server whenever database corruption is detected

automatic updates enables you to obtain critical software updates by automatically interacting with the Windows Update Web site

available address pool the list of TCP/IP addresses within a DHCP scope that can be distributed to DHCP clients

B

Background Intelligent Transfer Service (BITS) Windows service that optimizes network downloads by using idle network bandwidth

background zone loading a new feature in Active Directory–integrated DNS in Windows Server 2008 that allows DNS data to be available more quickly when a server is first booted up

Bandwidth Allocation Protocol (BAP) remote access functionality that automatically adds and drops connections based on client usage

bare-metal restore a restore in which the computer system is restored from "bare metal"; i.e., without any requirements as to previously installed software or operating system

basic disks disks that use partition tables that are recognized by older operating systems such as MS-DOS and Windows 95/98

Basic Encryption (MPPE 40-bit) low (40-bit) encryption used for VPN connections

bits binary sequences of 0s and 1s used to encode traffic onto physical network media

boot volume the volume containing the operating system files

broadcast address reserved IP address used to transmit data to all hosts located on a particular network

C

cache.dns a file containing the root DNS servers

caching-only server a DNS server that hosts no zones

Callback Options a Remote Access setting that will disconnect a connecting client and re-initiate the connection from the server side

canonical name (CNAME) resource record creates an alias to an existing A or AAAA record

Capture Filter a feature of Network Monitor that will capture only the specific network traffic that you specify

Certificate Practice Statement (CPS) an AD CS component that provides a detailed explanation of how a particular Certification Authority manages certificates and keys

Certificate Revocation List (CRL) a PKI component that identifies certificates that have been revoked or terminated, and the corresponding user, computer, or service

Certificate templates a PKI component used by a CA to simplify the administration and issuance of digital certificates

Certification Authority (CA) an entity, such as a Windows Server 2008 server running the AD CS server role, that issues and manages digital certificates for use in a PKI

Certification Authority Web Enrollment a PKI feature that allows users to manually request certificates using a Web interface

certutil a command-line utility for managing Active Directory Certificate Services

Challenge Handshake Authentication Protocol (CHAP) a generic authentication method that offers encryption of authentication data through the MD5 hashing scheme

checkpoint file indicates the last information that was successfully written to a JET database

checksum a mathematical value that is used to provide an integrity check for a network packet

CIDR notation the most common means of expressing a CIDR network address, such as 192.168.1.0/24 or 192.168.1.128/25

cipher suite a collection of cryptographic algorithms used to encrypt data

Class Options DHCP options applied based on type, either vendor classes or user classes

classful addressing a means of segregating TCP/IP networks into Class A, Class B, and Class C networks based on the network address taking up the 1st, 1st and 2nd, or 1st three octets of the IP address

Classless Inter-Domain Routing (CIDR) a means of more granularly segregating TCP/IP networks based on the number of bytes used by the network address versus the host address

client failback a DFS feature that allows clients to be referred to alternate servers if one server is not available, and then be referred back to the most appropriate server when it comes back online

Client Options DHCP options that apply to a single DHCP client; these will override a server option or scope option if one has been configured

collector-initiated a subscription in which the destination computer polls the source computers to pull the relevant information

compact to optimize a DHCP database to reclaim unused space created by deleted records

conditional forwarder a DNS configuration option that refers queries to remote forwarders based on the domain name contained within the query

Configuration information specific configuration data used to determine how a server is configured and whether

changes to that configuration are affecting its performance

connection security rules a Windows Firewall component that requires two peer computers to mutually authenticate before they can pass information between them

content synchronization service a server-side component on your organization's intranet that retrieves the latest critical updates from the Windows Update Web site

cookie text files sent by a server to a Web browser, used for authenticating, tracking, and maintaining specific information about users

cost the deciding factor used by routers when two different routes exist to the same destination; given multiple routes to the same destination network, the router will choose the route with the lowest cost

country code top-level domain names that map to individual countries, such as .uk, .pl, .it

custom filters contains views of all the printers hosted by the print servers listed in the console

Custom view a new feature in the Windows Server 2008 Event Viewer that allows you to create custom views of events that are recorded

D

data collector set a configuration item that allows you to organize a set of performance counters, event traces, and system configuration data into a single "object" that you can reuse on one or more Windows Server 2008 servers

Data collector set templates templates used to create pre-configured data collector sets

data modification an attack in which a network packet that is in transit over a network can be altered to send counterfeit data

Data-Link Layer Layer 2 of the OSI model

default gateway allows a host to communicate with devices that reside on a remote network

Default route a routing table entry that indicates the route that will be used if no other defined routes match a particular destination

demand-dial routing a routing connection that is only initiated when traffic needs to be passed through it

Denial of service attacks (DoS) a type of attack that prevents the normal use of computers or network resources

DFS namespace a DFS component that presents a single unified view of files and folders that are physically stored across multiple computers

DFS namespace server the server responsible for maintaining the list of DFS shared folders and the physical servers that they correspond to

DHCP client a computer that receives its IP address information from a DHCP server

DHCP enforcement a NAP enforcement method that relies on DHCP to enforce client compliance

DHCP lease defines the duration for which a DHCP-assigned IP address is valid

DHCP Relay Agent a host that forwards DHCP requests to a DHCP server on a remote server, eliminating the need to deploy a DHCP server on each subnet

DHCP Server a server that assigns IP address information automatically to DHCP clients

DHCPACK sent by a DHCP server to acknowledge the client's acceptance of a DHCP lease

DHCPDECLINE sent by a DHCP client to a DHCP server to indicate that it is not accepting a DHCP lease that was sent by a DHCPOFFER message

DHCPDISCOVER a broadcast-based DHCP message used by clients to locate available DHCP servers

DHCPINFORM a DHCP message used to detect rogue DHCP servers

DHCPNACK sent by a DHCP server to deny a client's DHCPREQUEST message

DHCPOFFER a broadcast-based DHCP message used by DHCP servers to offer IP address information to a requesting client

DHCPRELEASE sent by a DHCP client to relinquish an IP address and cancel te remaining lease

DHCPREQUEST used by a DHCP client to signal acceptance of a DHCP lease that was sent by a DHCPOFFER message

dial-in properties properties of an individual user account that will allow or deny a remote access connection

dial-on-demand routing see "demand-dial routing"

Dial-Up Networking (DUN) creates a physical connection to a remote network by using a dial-up device such as a POTS modem or a demand-dial ISDN modem

digital certificate a PKI component that contains identifying information about a particular user, computer, or service

directly attached network routes routes to destination networks for which the router in question is directly attached

Discretionary Access Control List (DACL) enables you to specify which users and groups may modify the DNS zones and records

disk quota a limit that is placed on the disk space a user is permitted to consume in a particular volume or folder

Display Filter a feature of Network Monitor that will display only the specific network traffic that you specify

Distributed File System (DFS) a Windows Server 2008 role that allows for a unified file namespace across multiple physical servers, as well as file replication between servers

DNS namespace a hierarchical, tree-structured list of DNS host names and domain names

DNS query the process of requesting DNS information from a Windows server

DNS resolver the DNS client software that submits DNS name resolution queries to DNS servers

DNS round robin a load balancing mechanism used by DNS servers to share and distribute network resource loads

DNS server cache a list of recently resolved DNS queries maintained in RAM by a DNS server to speed subsequent queries for the same information

DNS servers Windows servers that host the DNS server role to provide name resolution to clients

dnscmd a command-line tool used to manage DNS servers, domains, zones, and resource records

DomainDNSZones a DNS replication scope that copies DNS data to all DCs in a domain that are configured as DNS servers

dotted-decimal notation the most common means of expressing an IPv4 address, such as 192.168.1.154

dynamic disks disks that enable more advanced configuration options, but that are not recognized by operating systems prior to Windows 2000

Dynamic Host Configuration Protocol (DHCP) a service used to automate the distribution of TCP/IP addresses and associated configuration information, such as the subnet mask, default gateway and preferred DNS servers.

dynamic rekeying determination of new keying material through a new Diffie-Hellman exchange that takes place on a regular basis

E

EAP-Logoff an 802.1X packet sent from a supplicant to an authenticator, instructing the supplicant to place the port back in an unauthenticated state

EAP-Request an 802.1X packet sent from an authenticator to a supplicant, requesting their EAP information

EAP-Response an 802.1X packet sent from a supplicant to an authenticator, supplying EAP information

Encapsulating Security Payload (ESP) an IPSec protocol that provides confidentiality (in addition to authentication, integrity, and anti-replay) for the IP payload

Enforcement Client a NAP component that enables a particular NAP enforcement mechanism

enforcement method a NAP component that enables administrators to impose consistent client status

enforcement point a server that houses the NAP Enforcement Server component

Enforcement Server (ES) a NAP component that imposes a particular enforcement method

Enhanced Metafile Format (EMF) a default print format used by Windows 2000, Windows XP and Windows Server 2003

enterprise CA a CA that is integrated with Active Directory to allow additional funcitonality

event trace data data is collected over time to provide a real-time view into the behavior and performance of the server operating systems and any applications that it is running

Everyone a special identity group that includes all users of a Windows computer, including anonymous users

exceptions a Windows Firewall configuration item that allows specifically defined traffic to traverse the firewall

exclusion range a portion of an IP address range that will not be distributed to DHCP clients by a DHCP server

extended partition a partition that can host data, but not the computer operating system

Extensible Authentication Protocol (EAP) an 802.1X authentication framework

Extensible Authentication Protocol-Message Digest 5 Challenge Handshake Authentication Protocol (EAP-MD5 CHAP) a version of CHAP that is ported to the EAP framework.

F

File ownership property of a Windows file or folder that indicates which user or group is the owner of the item

File Server Resource Manager (FSRM) an optional role service in the File Service role that enables quotas, file screens, quota templates, and e-mail notifications

file-backed zone see "standard zone"

filter action defines how IPSec should secure network traffic

ForestDNSZones a DNS replication scope that copies DNS data to all DCs in a forest that are configured as a DNS server

forward lookup zone a zone that responds to client requests to map known host names to IP addresses

Forwarded events records events that were forwarded to the Event Viewer on this server

forwarder a DNS configuration option that refers queries that cannot be resolved by the local DNS server to another DNS server on the same network or on a remote network

forwarding-only server a DNS server that will not perform any recursion after forwarders fail; if it cannot resolve a query by using its configured forwarders, it will return a negative response to the query

frames data at Layer 2 of the OSI model (the Data Link Layer) is organized into frames for processing by higher levels of the OSI model

full mesh topology a replication model in which each member server replicates data with every other member server

full zone transfer (AXFR) copying the entire contents of a DNS zone during a zone transfer

fully qualified domain name (FQDN) a DNS name comprised of the host name with the domain name appended to it, such as server1.contoso.com, where server1 is the host name and contoso.com is the domain name

G

gateway NIC that is used to transmit data to a remote network

GUID Partition Table (GPT) a partition style used by dynamic disks

H

hard quota a disk quota that prevents users from saving information if they exceed the defined quota amount

hardware-based router a router running on a dedicated hardware appliance that is only used for performing network routing

hash one-way cryptographic algorithm that takes an input message of arbitrary length and produces a fixed-length digest

hash-based message authentication code (HMAC) see "Integrity Check Value (ICV)"

header information encapsulating the data contained inside of a network packet

health certificate a NAP component used to maintain information about the health compliance (or lack thereof) of a NAP client

health policy server a NAP component that receives health information from NAP enforcement points.

Health Registration Authority (HRA) a NAP component that can obtain health certificates from client computers when the IPSec enforcement method is in use

Health Requirement Server a NAP component that provides current health state information to NPS health policy servers

host a computer, printer, or other physical device configured with a network interface card

host (A) record maps an FQDN to an IPv4 address

host (AAAA) record maps an FQDN to an IPv6 address

host address the portion of an IP address that is unique to an individual device

Host routes a routing table entry that defines a route to a particular destination host rather than a destination network

HOSTS files text files used to provide name resolution for early TCP/IP networks

hub a network device that operates at the Physical Layer (Layer 1) of the OSI model

hub/spoke topology a replication model in which a small number of central servers maintain connections with remote servers, but remote servers to not replicate directly with one another

I

identity spoofing an attack in which an attacker can falsify or "spoof" the identity of either the sending or receiving computer

IGMP Router & Proxy used for multicast forwarding

in-addr.arpa domain a DNS zone used for reverse lookup queries of IPv4 DNS records

incremental zone transfer (IXFR) copying only the contents of a DNS zone that have changed since the last zone transfer to cut down on network traffic

Initial Configuration Tasks a post-installation startup screen that provides a unified administrative interface to configure common items when a server has been newly installed

Integrity Check Value (ICV) a cryptographic checksum that protects each TCP/IP packet protected by IPSec

interface a network interface card

intermediate CA a CA that is subordinate to a root CA within a hierarchical PKI infrastructure

Internet Connection Sharing (ICS) a feature that allows multiple users to share an Internet connection that is directly attached to a single computer

Internet Engineering Task Force (IEFT) an industry standards body that helps define Requests for Comments (RFCs) to define protocols such as FTP and LDAP

Internet Key Exchange (IKE) a standard that defines a mechanism to establish Security Associations

Internet Printing Protocol (IPP) protocol that allows users to send print jobs to printers via an IIS server

Internet Protocol Security (IPSec) enforcement a NAP enforcement method that relies on IPSec to enforce client compliance

Internet Security Association and Key Management Protocol (ISAKMP) a protocol that is used to dynamically negotiate a mutual set of security requirements between two hosts that are attempting to communicate with each other

Internet Service Providers (ISPs) commercial or not-for-profit entities that provide customers with a means of accessing the Internet

IP address a means of identifying a unique host on a TCP/IP network

IP filter a subset of network traffic based on IP address

IP filter list the concatenation of one or more IP filters, which define a range of network traffic

IP version 4 (IPv4) the version of TCP/IP that has been most widely implemented on modern networks

IP version 6 (IPv6) a newer implementation of TCP/IP that includes a much larger address space and numerous security improvements over IPv4

ip6.arpa domain the DNS zone used for reverse lookup queries of IPv6 DNS records

IPSec a suite of protocols used to provide security for TCP/IP hosts at the Internet layer

IPSec policy a shared set of IPSec configuration information that allows multiple computers to communicate

IPSec Policy Agent used to retrieve information about IPSec policies and to pass this information to other IPSec components

ISAKMP SA an IPSec security association used to protect IPSec security negotiations

Isolation a connection security rule used to restrict inbound and outbound connections

iterative query a DNS query sent to a DNS server in which the querying host requests it to return the best answer it can provide using its own information, and without seeking further assistance from other DNS servers

J

Joint Engine Technology (JET) a database format used by the DHCP database

K

key archival the process by which private keys in an Active Directory environment are maintained by the CA for retrieval by a recovery agent

Key Management Service (KMS) a license key that allows you to manage the licensing process using an internal licensing server installed on your own network

key recovery agents user accounts that are configured with a Key Recovery Agent certificate that allows them to recover private keys on behalf of users/computers/services whose private keys have been lost or corrupted

keyed hash a hash that includes the secret key in its calculation

L

Layer 3 devices see "router"

leaf objects host names representing a single physical device such as a computer or printer

limited broadcast address a reserved IP address (255.255.255.255) used as the broadcast address for all networks and routers

LM Authentication the weakest form of NTLM authentication, which has been in use since the earliest days of Windows networking

local print devices a print device that is directly attached to a physical computer

locally-attached print device a print device that is directly attached to a physical computer, such as through a parallel port or USB port

loopback address a reserved IP address (127.0.0.1) used for troubleshooting and testing

M

mail exchanger (MX) record a DNS record that allows e-mail applications to locate e-mail servers

main mode negotiation used to determine encryption key material and security protection for use in protecting subsequent communications

main mode SA see "ISAKMP SA"

Manage Documents a printer permission that allows users to manage all users' documents

Manage Printers a printer permission that allows users to manage user documents as well as manage the configuration of printers

man-in-the-middle attack an attack in which someone between the two communicating computers is actively monitoring, capturing, and controlling the data

manual backup a one-time backup performed using Windows Server Backup, which can be performed by members of the Administrators or Backup Operators group

MBR (Master Boot Record) a partition style used by basic disks

Media Access Control (MAC) address a hard-coded hexadecimal address configured for each Network Interface Card (NIC)

member a single server within a DFS replication group

metric a column in a routing table that indicates the cost of using one route instead of another

mirrored volume a logical unit of disk space comprised of two physical disks, in which the data has been copied exactly from the first disk to the second for fault tolerance

modem bank a collection of multiple physical modems to enable multiple simultaneous dial-up networking connections

modem-pooling equiment see "modem bank"

mount point a logical unit of disk space that will appear as a folder within an existing volume

MS-CHAPv1 an authentication method that relies on one-way authentication to encrypt authentication and connection data

MS-CHAPv2 an authentication method that relies on mutual authentication to encrypt authentication and connection data

multilink a remote access functionality that aggregates multiple dial-up connections to increase the available bandwidth

multinets multiple logical subnets contained within a single network

Multiple Activation Key (MAK) an activation key used for a one-time activation with Microsoft's hosted activation service

Multiple master replication a replication model that can accept data writes from multiple servers, not just a single primary server

multi-port repeater see "hub"

mutual authentication a process used to establish trust between the communicating systems, after which only trusted systems can communicate with each other

N

name resolution the process of mapping an IP address to a human-readable "friendly" name, such as www.lucernepublishing.com

namespace a virtual view of shared folders on different servers as provided by the Distributed File System service

namespace server the DFS server that stores the configuration of a particular DFS namespace

NAP administration server a NAP component that manages NAP server-side components

NAP Agent a NAP component that maintains information about the health of the NAP client computer

NetBIOS the primary method of name resolution on Windows networks prior to the move to DNS within Active Directory

netmask a column in a routing table that indicates the subnet mask of the destination network

network access control a standard for allowing or disallowing network access based on administrator-specified criterion

network access server a server that provides a single point of access for users to access a remote network, such as a RADIUS server or Network Policy Server

network address the portion of an IP address that is shared by all hosts on the same subnet

network address translation (NAT) allows one or more private IP addresses to be mapped to one or more public IP addresses to allow hosts with private IP addresses to communicate on the Internet or another public network

Network and Sharing Center the Control Panel location that allows you to manage and monitor all aspects of Windows Server 2008 networking

network destination a column in a routing table that indicates the remote network that a particular route should be used to reach

Network Device Enrollment Service (NDES) an AD CS service that allows devices, such as hardware-based routers and other network devices and appliances, to enroll for certificates within a Windows Server 2008 PKI

network discovery a network service that locates and queries network resources and shares for information

network interface print device a print device that is connected directly to a Local Area Network (LAN)

Network Layer Layer 3 of the OSI model

network location a configuration setting that allows you to configure one or more network connections to receive unified security settings: you may define different security settings for "home" network locations versus "public" network locations

Network Policy Server (NPS) the Windows Server 2008 implementation of RADIUS

network protocols provide the logical "language" to allow computers to communicate across a physical network medium

network type the type of connection affected by an IPSec policy

network-attached print device a print device that is connected directly to a TCP/IP network

No callback the Callback Option that disables callback functionality

No Encryption a VPN connectivity that does not use any encryption

NPS Network Policy a Remote Access component that maintains information about which users can and cannot access a remote access server

NPS service a NAP component that combines Statement of Health Responses into a single System Statement of Health Response

nslookup a command-line tool used to perform DNS queries

NT LAN Manager (NTLM) a Windows authentication protocol used to authenticate legacy clients and clients configured in a workgroup

NTFS quotas disk quotas that control storage on entire volumes on a per-user basis, for use without the File Server Resource Manager (FSRM) role

NTLM Authentication a user authentication based on the NT LAN Manager authentication protocol

NTLMv2 Authentication the strongest form of NTLM authentication

O

Oakley Key Determination Protocol a protocol used to generate secret key material

octet a portion of an IP address that is 4 bytes in length

online responder an AD CS service that responds to requests from clients concerning the revocation status of a particular certificate, sending back a digitally signed response indicating the certificate's current status

Open Shortest Path First (OSPF) a routing protocol in which individual routers maintained a database of all reachable networks that it was aware of, and shared this database with neighboring routers

Open Systems Interconnection (OSI) model a model for network communications, consisting of seven layers from Physical to Application

P

packet sniffer computer software or computer hardware that can intercept and monitor network traffic in real-time

packet sniffing a network attack that monitors and reads network packets as they traverse a wired or wireless network

Packets data at Layer 3 of the OSI model (the Network Layer) is organized into packets for transmission to local or remote networks

parity additional information added to a RAID-5 volume to provide fault tolerance in the event of a single disk failure

partition see "volume"

partition structure the logical partition structure of one or more physical hard disks

Password Authentication Protocol (PAP) a generic authentication method that does not encrypt authentication data

payload the data contents of a network packet

perfmon a CLI command used to launch the Performance Monitor MMC snap-in

Performance counters specific processes or events that you want to track within the Reliability and Performance Monitor

Performance Log Users a security group that has all the rights of the Performance Monitor Users group, plus the ability to create and modify data collector sets

Performance Monitor a view that provides a visual display of performance counters within Reliability & Performance data

Performance Monitor Users a security group that allows users to view real-time and historical performance and reliability data

persistent policies policies that override Active Directory–based or local IPSec policies, and enhance security during computer startup

Physical Layer Layer 1 of the OSI model, where bits of data interface with the physical network media

pointer (PTR) resource record a DNS resource record that maps a known IP address to a host name

Point-to-Point Tunneling Protocol (PPTP) a legacy VPN protocol that is supported by older operating systems as well as Windows Server 2008

PowerShell a new command-line and task-based scripting technology that is included with Windows Server 2008

primary member the first server installed within a DFS replication group, used to "seed" replication to other members

primary name server a DNS server that hosts a primary zone for one or more DNS domains

primary partition a partition that can host the computer's operating system

Print a printer permission that allows users to print and manage their own documents

print device printer hardware that produces hard copy documents on paper or other print media

Print server a device that receives print jobs from clients and sends them to print devices that are either locally attached or connected to the network

printer the software interface through which a computer communicates with a print device

printer driver a piece of software that converts the print jobs generated by applications into an appropriate string of commands for a specific print device

printer pool a single logical printer connected to multiple physical printers to increase the output of the logical printer

private key a component of public key cryptography that is only known to each individual certificate holder

promiscuous mode a version of Network Monitor that can capture 100 percent of the network traffic available to the network interface

PTR Reousrce Record maps an IP address to an FQDN

public key a component of public key cryptography that is known to the public at large

public key cryptography an encryption method that uses a two-part key: a public key and a private key

Q

quick mode messages ISAKMP messages that are encrypted using the ISAKMP SA

quick mode negotiation the portion of IPSec negotiation in which Security Associations are negotiated, and where the computers negotiate the primary protocols (AH and/or ESP), the hash algorithm, and the encryption algorithm to use for data transfer

quick mode SA an IPSec security association used to protect data sent between the IPSec peers

quota template a collection of settings that defines a number of configuration items for disk quotas

R

RAID-5 volume a logical unit of disk space comprised of three or more physical disks, in which data has been interleaved with additional parity for a balance between performance and fault tolerance

Reconciliation the process of verifying the contents of the DHCP database against the DHCP Registry values

recovery agents configured within a CA to allow one or more users (typically administrators) in an Active Directory environment to recover private keys for users, computers, or services if their keys are lost

Recursion the process of "Tree-walking" used by DNS servers when performing iterative queries

recursive query a DNS query sent to a DNS server in which the querying host asks the DNS server to provide a definitive answer to the query

referral a response from a DFS namespace server that directs clients to the appropriate physical server

Reliability and Performance Monitor a tool located within the Administrative Tools folder that combines features that had previously been spread across a number of tools: Performance Logs and Alerts, Server Performance Advisor, and System Monitor

Reliability Monitor a view within Reliability & Performance Monitor that provides information about system events that can affect a server's stability

Remediation servers a NAP component that allows out-of-compliance clients to regain compliance, by downloading necessary updates/software/etc.

Remote Differential Compression (RDC) a replication protocol used by DFS in Windows Server 2008

Remote network routes routes to destination networks that the router in question is not directly attached to

repair mode an installation option that provides an environment designed to allow you to diagnose and correct a damaged Windows installation

replay a network attack in which network traffic is captured by a packet sniffer and then re-inserted onto the network at a later time to access information or resources

replication group a collection of DFS servers that replicate data between each other

replication scope the number of servers to which DNS information is copied and updated

Requests for Comments (RFC) documents released by the IETF to define protocols such as FTP and LDAP

reservations configures a consistent IP address for a DHCP-enabled host

resource record an element of data that allows DNS servers to resolve client queries

resource record set a list of resource records that matches a particular DNS query

Resource View the default view within Reliability & Performance Monitor

Reverse Address Resolution Protocol (RARP) used to map a known MAC address to an unknown IP address

reverse lookup zone a zone that responds to client requests to map known IP addresses to host names

revocation configuration a PKI configuration item that allows Online Responders to respond to client requests for certificate revocation status

rogue DHCP server a DHCP server that has not been authorized within Active Directory

root CA a Certification Authority that is authoritative for all Certificate Services within a given network

root hints using the top-level Internet DNS servers to resolve a query

router a Layer 3 network device that transmits data between local and remote networks

Router Information Protocol version 2 (RIPv2) a routing protocol supported by the Routing & Remote Access service in Windows Server 2008

router-to-router VPN a secure connection maintained between two router endpoints, to create a secure VPN tunnel between disparate organizations

routes provide destination routers to allow routers to transmit traffic to remote networks

routing the process of transferring data across a network from one LAN to another

routing protocols used in lieu of static routes in more complex network environments to simplify the administration of network routing

S

scavenging the process of removing dynamic DNS records as they become out-of-date

scheduled backup a recurring backup performed using Windows Server Backup that will reformat the destination drive prior to performing the backup

Scope Options DHCP options that apply to a single DHCP scope; these will override a DHCP server option if one has been configured

scopes in DHCP, the portion of the TCP/IP address space that is allocated for a particular group of computers, typically on a single subnet

secondary name server a DNS server that hosts a secondary zone for one or more DNS domains

secondary zone database files the database files used by DNS servers that host secondary DNS zones

second-level domains DNS domains that are registered to individuals or organzations, such as microsoft, hp, dell, etc.

secure dynamic updates allows DNS records to be updated only by the client that first registered the record

security association (SA) a common set of security requirements shared between two hosts

Security logs records events associated with successful or failed access to secured resources on the server

Security Parameters Index (SPI) information stored as a field in the IPSec headers that indicates which SA the destination should use

self-enrollment a feature that enables users to request their own PKI certificates, typically through a Web browser

Server Core an installation option in Windows Server 2008 that provides a minimal installation footprint designed to run only key infrastructure services

Server Options DHCP options that apply to all scopes configured on a DHCP server

Server service a Windows service that allows computers to share files with other network users and computers

Server-to-server a connection security rule that secures traffic between two servers or two groups of servers

Set by Caller the Callback Option that allows the user to specify the callback number at the time the connection is made

Setup log records events associated with server installation, adding and removing server roles, installing applications, etc.

Shadow Copies of Shared Folders a Windows Server 2008 mechanism that automatically retains copies of files on a server volume in multiple versions from specific points in time

shared secret key a cyrptography method in which secret key information is known by both parties

Shiva Password Authentication Protocol (SPAP) a weakly encrypted authentication protocol that offers interoperability with Shiva remote networking products

Simple Certificate Enrollment Protocol (SCEP) a protocol used by the Network Device Enrollment Service

simple volume a logical unit of disk space comprised of space contained on a single physical disk

Single master replication a replication model that can only accept data writes from a single primary server

smart card Small physical devices, usually the size of a credit card or keychain fob, that have a digital certificate installed on them

smart card reader a physical device attached to a workstation that allows users to use a smart card to authenticate to an Active Directory domain, access a Web site, or authenticate to other secured resources

soft quota a disk quota that notifies administrators when a user exceeds the quota limit, but does not prevent the user from saving information in excess of the defined quota

software-based router a router running on a computer running an operating system such as Windows Server 2008 that can also be used for other functions

source computer initiated a subscription in which each source computer must be configured to push the relevant information to the server that has been configured as the repository

spanned volume a logical unit of disk space comprised of space contained on multiple physical disks

standalone CA a CA that is not integrated with an Active Directory environment

standard zone a DNS zone that stores its data in a text file on the DNS server

stateful firewall a firewall that can track and maintain information based on the status of a connection

Statement of Health (SOH) a NAP component that indicates the status of a particular System Health Agent

Statement of Health Response (SoHR) a NAP component generated by an SHV in response to client Statements of Health

static IP address an IP address that has been manually configured by an administrator

Static routes configuration information that manually informs a network router of the destination of network packets destined for remote networks

striped volume a logical unit of disk space comprised of space that has been interleaved across multiple physical disks for improved read performance

Strong Encryption a 56-bit encryption used for VPN connections

Strongest Encryption a 128-bit encryption used for VPN connections

stub zone a DNS zone that contains sufficient information to locate authoritative name servers for a DNS domain

subdomains lower-level domains within a second-level domains, such as sales.lucernepublishing.com

subnet a logical grouping of computers within a TCP/IP network, used to reduce network traffic and streamline administration

subnet mask used to define which portion of an IP address is the network address and which portion is the host address

subnetting the process of subdividing TCP/IP networks into smaller units called "subnets"

superscope an administrative grouping of multiple contiguous DHCP scopes

supplicant an 802.1X device that is seeking access to the network, such as a laptop attempting to access a wireless access point

switch a Layer 2 network device that examines the source and destination MAC address of the network data to determine where the data should be sent

System Health Agent (SHA) a NAP component that maintains information and reporting on one or more elements of the health of a NAP client

System Health Validator (SHV) a NAP component that returns Statement of Health Responses based on client Statements of Health

System log records information associated with operating system events such as server restarts, issues with services, etc.

System Statement of Health (SSOH) a collection of Statements of Health for all SHAs configured on a client computer

System Statement of Health Response (SSOHR) a NAP component that combines individual Statement of Health Responses before returning them to the NAP enforcement client

system volume the volume containing the files necessary to boot a computer

T

T1 represents half of the DHCP lease time

T2 represents 87.5% of the DHCP lease time

targets the physical servers that host data represented within a DFS namespace

Terminal Services Gateway (TS Gateway) enforcement NAP enforcement method that restricts connection attempts by TS Gateway clients

threshold the percentage of a disk quota at which users and administrators can be notified and/or an event logged to the Windows Event Viewer on the server

Time to Live (TTL) the amount of time for which a DNS record is valid before it must be re-verified

top-level domain the top-most domains in the DNS namespace hierarchy, such as .com, .org, or .biz

topology the physical or logical layout of a network

Transmission Control Protocol/Internet Protocol (TCP/IP) the most common network protocol in use today; the network protocol used on the Internet

transport mode an IPSec mode used to provide end-to-end security

Trivial File Transfer Protocol (TFTP) a lightweight version of FTP that uses UDP traffic rather than tCP

tunnel mode an IPSec mode used to provide site-to-site communications that cross the Internet (or other public networks)

tunnel setting the IP address of an IPSec tunnel endpoint

tunnelling protocol a protocol used by VPN software to transmit trafic securely over a non-secure network such as the Internet

U

Unauthenticated access a configuration setting that allows remote access users to connect to a remote access server without providing credentials

User Datagram Protocol (UDP) a connectionless, non-acknowledgement-based TCP/IP protocol used for low-overhead communication

V

Verify Caller ID a Remote Access security setting that will confirm that a remote access connection originates from a specified calling location

Virtual Private Network (VPN) creates a secured logical connection to a remote network over a non-secure network such as the Internet

volume a logical unit of disk space comprised of space contained on one or more physical disks

Volume Activation a process used to manage software activation for multiple installations of Windows within an enterprise network

Volume Activation Management Tool (VMAT) a software tool used to activate software that uses Multiple Activation Keys

Volume Shadow Copies Service (VSS) a Windows service utilized by the Shadow Copies of Shared Folders feature, as well as Windows Server Backup

VPN client software that initiates a secured VPN connection to a public-facing remote access server capable of creating VPN connections

VPN enforcement method a NAP enforcement method that restricts the level of network access that a remote access client can obtain, based on the health information that the client presents when the VPN connection is made

VSS copy backup a Windows Server Backup backup type that will not clear the Application Log on the computer that is being backed up

VSS full backup a Windows Server Backup backup type that will clear the Application Log on the computer that is being backed up

W

wbadmin a command-line tool used to perform Windows Server Backup operations

web enrollment an AD CS feature that allows users to connect to a Windows Server 2008 CA through a Web browser to request certificates and obtain an up-to-date Certificate Revocation List

Windows Event Collector Service allows you to configure a single server as a repository of Event Viewer information for multiple computers

Windows Firewall a software-based firewall that is built into the Windows Server 2008 operating system

Windows Logs the traditional view of the Windows Event Viewer

Windows powerShell see 'Powershell'

Windows Recovery Environment (WinRE) a special Windows boot mode that provides a centralized platform for operating system recovery

Windows Server Backup a Windows Server 2008 feature that allows you to perform one-time and recurring scheduled backups of a Windows server

Windows Server Update Services (WSUS) a Windows service that allows you to centralize the management of critical software updates on a Windows network

Windows Update Catalog a Web site that lists hardware and software designed for use with Windows Vista, Windows XP, Microsoft Windows 2000 Server products, and products in the Windows Server 2003 and Windows Server 2008 family

WINS a Windows networking service that automates the process of NetBIOS name resolution on an enterprise network

WINS server a Windows server providing the WINS server service for automated management and centralization of NetBIOS name resolution

Wireless Networking a Windows Server 2008 feature that installs and configures wireless connections and wireless LAN profiles

WS-Management protocol a protocol used by the Windows Event Collector Service to manage subscriptions and forwarded events

X

XML Printer Specification (XPS) a new, XML-based print format used by Windows Vista and Windows Server 2008

Z

zone a collection of host name-to-IP address mappings stored on a DNS server

zone transfer the process of copying DNS zone data from a server hosting a primary zone to a server hosting a secondary zone

USB. *See* Universal Serial bus (USB)
User Account Properties dialog box, 113–114
User Datagram Protocol (UDP), 38, 112, 204

V

VAMT. *See* Volume Activation Management Tool (VAMT)
Vendor class, 49
Verify Caller ID check box, 114
Virtual Private Network (VPN), 14, 110–112
Volume, types and sizes, 28, 128–130
Volume Activation, 32
Volume Activation Management Tool (VAMT), 32
Volume List, 131
Volume Shadow Copies Service (VSS), 264, 276. *See also* Windows Server Backup
VPN. *See* Virtual Private Network (VPN)
VPN client, 110, 112
VPN connection, 112
VPN enforcement, 253
VPN server, 112
VPN tunnel, 112
VSS. *See* Volume Shadow Copies Service (VSS)

W

Web enrollment, 246
Web Server (IIS), 25
Wide area network (WAN), 128, 141, 205
Wildcard resource record, 78–79
Windows Activation, configuring, 32
Windows Deployment Services, 25
Windows Event Viewer, 88, 186–188, 231
Windows Firewall, 211, 216, 252
    configuring, 23–24, 235–239
    viewing, with Advanced Security node of Group Policy Object (GPO), 227
Windows Firewall Control Panel applet, 235–236
Windows Firewall Remote Management, 237
Windows Firewall with Advanced Security, 216–217
Windows Firewall with Advanced Security MMC snap-in, 35, 227–228, 239
Windows Internet Name Service (WINS), 27, 58
Windows Management Instrumentation (WMI), 237
Windows PowerShell, 276
Windows product key, 19
Windows Recovery Environment (WinRE), 283
Windows Registry, 112
Windows Remote Management, 238
Windows Search Service, 140
Windows Security Configuration Wizard, 238
Windows Server 2008

backing up, 276–282
    restoring, 283–284
Windows Server 2008 Certificate Authority, 251–252
Windows Server 2003 File Services, 140
Windows Server 2008 File Services, 141
Windows Server 2008 Network
    Network Monitor for gathering network data, 188–190
    Reliability and Performance Monitor, 180–186
    Windows Event Viewer, 186–188
Windows Server Administration Tools, 27
Windows Server Backup, 197, 276
    defined, 27, 264
    manual backup, 277–281
    scheduled backup, 277, 281–282
Windows Server Backup MMC snap-in, 283
Windows Server Update Services (WSUS)
    administrative tasks, 196–197
    categories for operating system updates, 190
    client management, 197–199
    components of, 191
    configuring distribution points, 195–196
    defined, 190
    installation management, 196–197
    installing Windows Server Update Services (WSUS) server, 192–199
    software and hardware requirements, 192–193
    Windows Update and Automatic Updates, 191–192
Windows SharePoint Services, 25
Windows Update, 191–192
Windows Update Catalog, 191
WinRE. *See* Windows Recovery Environment (WinRE)
WINS Server, 27. *See also* Windows Internet Name Service (WINS)
WINSservers, 49
Wireless access, 121–122
Wireless Networking, 27
WMI. *See* Windows Management Instrumentation (WMI)
Write ACL, 250
WSUS. *See* Windows Server Update Services (WSUS)

X

XML Paper Specification (XPS), 155
XPS. *See* XML Paper Specification (XPS)

Z

Zone
    benefits of storing, in Active Directory, 66–67
    defined, 61–63
Zone transfer, 63, 68–71

PART II

Excerpts from:

Microsoft® Official Academic Course
Windows Server® 2008
Active Directory® Configuration
Microsoft Certified Technology Specialist Exam 70-640

Microsoft® Official Academic Course

Microsoft® Windows Server® 2008 Active Directory Configuration (70-640)

WILEY

Credits

EXECUTIVE EDITOR	John Kane
DIRECTOR OF MARKETING AND SALES	Mitchell Beaton
MICROSOFT STRATEGIC RELATIONSHIPS MANAGER	Merrick Van Dongen of Microsoft Learning
DEVELOPMENT AND PRODUCTION	Custom Editorial Productions, Inc.
EDITORIAL ASSISTANT	Jennifer Lartz
PRODUCTION MANAGER	Micheline Frederick
PRODUCTION EDITOR	Kerry Weinstein
CREATIVE DIRECTOR	Harry Nolan
COVER DESIGNER	Michael St. Martine
TECHNOLOGY AND MEDIA	Lauren Sapira/Elena Santa Maria

This book was set in Garamond by Aptara, Inc. and printed and bound by Bind Rite Graphics. The covers were printed by Phoenix Color.

Microsoft, ActiveX, Excel, InfoPath, Microsoft Press, MSDN, OneNote, Outlook, PivotChart, PivotTable, PowerPoint, SharePoint SQL Server, Visio, Windows, Windows Mobile, and Windows Vista are either registered trademarks or trademarks of Microsoft Corporation in the United States and/or other countries. Other product and company names mentioned herein may be the trademarks of their respective owners.

The example companies, organizations, products, domain names, e-mail addresses, logos, people, places, and events depicted herein are fictitious. No association with any real company, organization, product, domain name, e-mail address, logo, person, place, or event is intended or should be inferred.

The book expresses the author's views and opinions. The information contained in this book is provided without any express, statutory, or implied warranties. Neither the authors, John Wiley & Sons, Inc., Microsoft Corporation, nor their resellers or distributors will be held liable for any damages caused or alleged to be caused either directly or indirectly by this book.

ISBN 978-0-470-22509-7

Printed in the United States of America

10 9 8 7 6 5 4 3 2 1

Foreword from the Publisher

Wiley's publishing vision for the Microsoft Official Academic Course series is to provide students and instructors with the skills and knowledge they need to use Microsoft technology effectively in all aspects of their personal and professional lives. Quality instruction is required to help both educators and students get the most from Microsoft's software tools and to become more productive. Thus our mission is to make our instructional programs trusted educational companions for life.

To accomplish this mission, Wiley and Microsoft have partnered to develop the highest quality educational programs for Information Workers, IT Professionals, and Developers. Materials created by this partnership carry the brand name "Microsoft Official Academic Course," assuring instructors and students alike that the content of these textbooks is fully endorsed by Microsoft, and that they provide the highest quality information and instruction on Microsoft products. The Microsoft Official Academic Course textbooks are "Official" in still one more way—they are the officially sanctioned courseware for Microsoft IT Academy members.

The Microsoft Official Academic Course series focuses on *workforce development*. These programs are aimed at those students seeking to enter the workforce, change jobs, or embark on new careers as information workers, IT professionals, and developers. Microsoft Official Academic Course programs address their needs by emphasizing authentic workplace scenarios with an abundance of projects, exercises, cases, and assessments.

The Microsoft Official Academic Courses are mapped to Microsoft's extensive research and job-task analysis, the same research and analysis used to create the Microsoft Certified Technology Specialist (MCTS) exam. The textbooks focus on real skills for real jobs. As students work through the projects and exercises in the textbooks they enhance their level of knowledge and their ability to apply the latest Microsoft technology to everyday tasks. These students also gain resume-building credentials that can assist them in finding a job, keeping their current job, or in furthering their education.

The concept of life-long learning is today an utmost necessity. Job roles, and even whole job categories, are changing so quickly that none of us can stay competitive and productive without continuously updating our skills and capabilities. The Microsoft Official Academic Course offerings, and their focus on Microsoft certification exam preparation, provide a means for people to acquire and effectively update their skills and knowledge. Wiley supports students in this endeavor through the development and distribution of these courses as Microsoft's official academic publisher.

Today educational publishing requires attention to providing quality print and robust electronic content. By integrating Microsoft Official Academic Course products, Wiley*PLUS*, and Microsoft certifications, we are better able to deliver efficient learning solutions for students and teachers alike.

Bonnie Lieberman

General Manager and Senior Vice President

Welcome to the Microsoft Official Academic Course (MOAC) program for Microsoft Windows Server 2008. MOAC represents the collaboration between Microsoft Learning and John Wiley & Sons, Inc. publishing company. Microsoft and Wiley teamed up to produce a series of textbooks that deliver compelling and innovative teaching solutions to instructors and superior learning experiences for students. Infused and informed by in-depth knowledge from the creators of Windows Server 2008, and crafted by a publisher known worldwide for the pedagogical quality of its products, these textbooks maximize skills transfer in minimum time. Students are challenged to reach their potential by using their new technical skills as highly productive members of the workforce.

Because this knowledgebase comes directly from Microsoft, architect of the Windows Server operating system and creator of the Microsoft Certified Technology Specialist and Microsoft Certified Professional exams, (www.microsoft.com/learning/mcp/mcts), you are sure to receive the topical coverage that is most relevant to students' personal and professional success. Microsoft's direct participation not only assures you that MOAC textbook content is accurate and current; it also means that students will receive the best instruction possible to enable their success on certification exams and in the workplace.

■ The Microsoft Official Academic Course Program

The *Microsoft Official Academic Course* series is a complete program for instructors and institutions to prepare and deliver great courses on Microsoft software technologies. With MOAC, we recognize that, because of the rapid pace of change in the technology and curriculum developed by Microsoft, there is an ongoing set of needs beyond classroom instruction tools for an instructor to be ready to teach the course. The MOAC program endeavors to provide solutions for all these needs in a systematic manner in order to ensure a successful and rewarding course experience for both instructor and student—technical and curriculum training for instructor readiness with new software releases; the software itself for student use at home for building hands-on skills, assessment, and validation of skill development; and a great set of tools for delivering instruction in the classroom and lab. All are important to the smooth delivery of an interesting course on Microsoft software, and all are provided with the MOAC program. We think about the model below as a gauge for ensuring that we completely support you in your goal of teaching a great course. As you evaluate your instructional materials options, you may wish to use the model for comparison purposes with available products.

■ Pedagogical Features

The MOAC textbook for Microsoft Windows Server 2008 Active Directory is designed to cover all the learning objectives for that MCTS exam, which is referred to as its "objective domain." The Microsoft Certified Technology Specialist (MCTS) exam objectives are high lighted throughout the textbook. Many pedagogical features have been developed specifically for *Microsoft Official Academic Course* programs.

Presenting the extensive procedural information and technical concepts woven throughout the textbook raises challenges for the student and instructor alike. The Illustrated Book Tour that follows provides a guide to the rich features contributing to *Microsoft Official Academic Course* program's pedagogical plan. Following is a list of key features in each lesson designed to prepare students for success on the certification exams and in the workplace:

- Each lesson begins with an **Objective Domain Matrix.** More than a standard list of learning objectives, the Domain Matrix correlates each software skill covered in the lesson to the specific MCTS "objective domain."

- Concise and frequent **Step-by-Step** instructions teach students new features and provide an opportunity for hands-on practice. Numbered steps give detailed, step-by-step instructions to help students learn software skills. The steps also show results and screen images to match what students should see on their computer screens.

- **Illustrations:** Screen images provide visual feedback as students work through the exercises. The images reinforce key concepts, provide visual clues about the steps, and allow students to check their progress.

- **Key Terms:** Important technical vocabulary is listed at the beginning of the lesson. When these terms are used later in the lesson, they appear in bold italic type and are defined. The Glossary contains all of the key terms and their definitions.

- Engaging point-of-use **Reader aids,** located throughout the lessons, tell students why this topic is relevant (*The Bottom Line*), provide students with helpful hints (*Take Note*), or show alternate ways to accomplish tasks (*Another Way*). Reader aids also provide additional relevant or background information that adds value to the lesson.

- **Certification Ready?** features throughout the text signal students where a specific certification objective is covered. They provide students with a chance to check their understanding of that particular MCTS objective and, if necessary, review the section of the lesson where it is covered. MOAC offers complete preparation for MCTS certification.

- **Knowledge Assessments** provide three progressively more challenging lesson-ending activities.

▪ Lesson Features

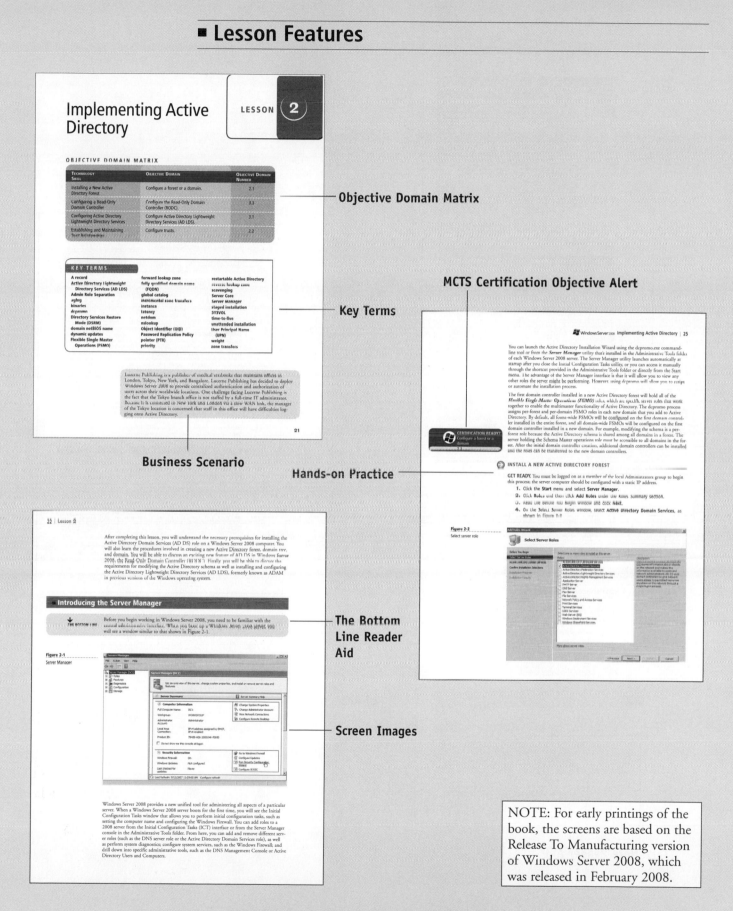

Objective Domain Matrix

Key Terms

MCTS Certification Objective Alert

Business Scenario

Hands-on Practice

The Bottom Line Reader Aid

Screen Images

NOTE: For early printings of the book, the screens are based on the Release To Manufacturing version of Windows Server 2008, which was released in February 2008.

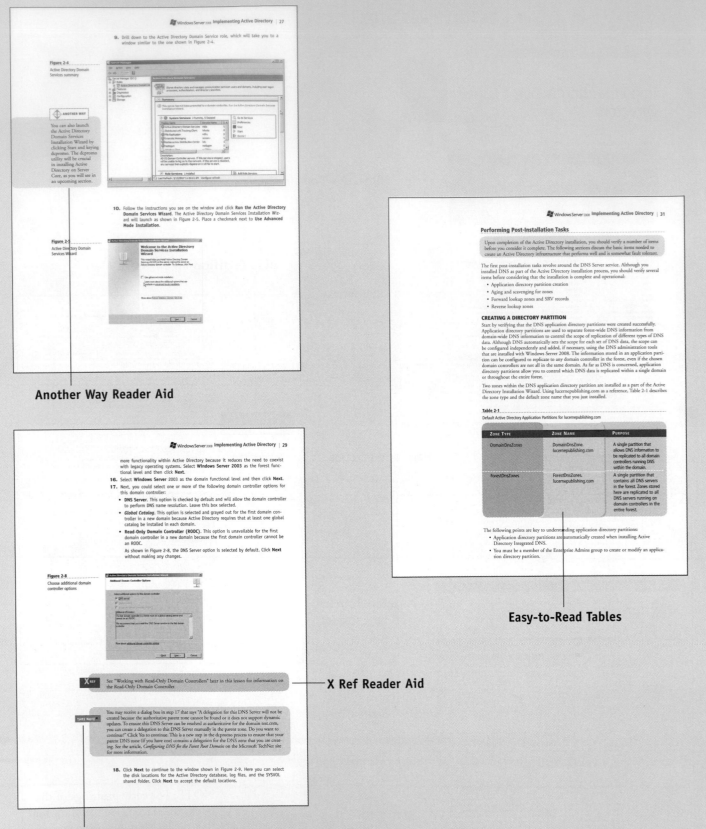

Another Way Reader Aid

Easy-to-Read Tables

X Ref Reader Aid

Take Note Reader Aid

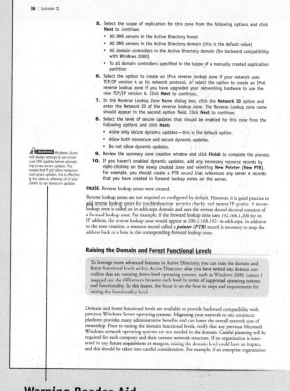

36 | Lesson 2

5. Select the scope of replication for this zone from the following options and click **Next** to continue:
   - All DNS servers in the Active Directory forest
   - All DNS servers in the Active Directory domain (this is the default value)
   - All domain controllers in the Active Directory domain (for backward compatibility with Windows 2000)
   - To all domain controllers specified in the scope of a manually created application partition

6. Select the option to create an IPv4 reverse lookup zone if your network uses TCP/IP version 4 as its network protocol, or select the option to create an IPv6 reverse lookup zone if you have upgraded your networking hardware to use the new TCP/IP version 6. Click **Next** to continue.

7. In the Reverse Lookup Zone Name dialog box, click the **Network ID** option and enter the Network ID of the reverse lookup zone. The Reverse Lookup zone name should appear in the second option field. Click **Next** to continue.

8. Select the level of secure updates that should be enabled for this zone from the following options and click **Next**:
   - Allow only secure dynamic updates—this is the default option.
   - Allow both nonsecure and secure dynamic updates.
   - Do not allow dynamic updates.

9. Review the summary zone creation window and click **Finish** to complete the process.

10. If you haven't enabled dynamic updates, add any necessary resource records by right-clicking on the newly created zone and selecting **New Pointer (New PTR)**. For example, you should create a PTR record that references any server A records that you have created in forward lookup zones on the server.

PAUSE. Reverse lookup zones were created.

Reverse lookup zones are not required or configured by default. However, it is good practice to add reverse lookup zones for troubleshooting, security checks, and reverse IP queries. A reverse lookup zone is called an in-addr.arpa domain and uses the reverse dotted decimal notation of a forward lookup zone. For example, if the forward lookup zone uses 192.168.1.200 for its IP address, the reverse lookup zone would appear as 200.1.168.192-.in-addr.arpa. In addition to the zone creation, a resource record called a *pointer (PTR)* record is necessary to map the address back to a host in the corresponding forward lookup zone.

Raising the Domain and Forest Functional Levels

To leverage more advanced features in Active Directory, you can raise the domain and forest functional levels within Active Directory after you have retired any domain controllers that are running down-level operating systems, such as Windows 2000. Lesson 1 mapped out the differences between each level in terms of supported operating systems and functionality. In this lesson, the focus is on the how-to steps and requirements for raising the functionality level.

Domain and forest functional levels are available to provide backward compatibility with previous Windows Server operating systems. Migrating your network to one consistent platform provides many administrative benefits and can lower the overall network cost of ownership. Prior to raising the domain functional levels, verify that any previous Microsoft Windows network operating systems are not needed in the domain. Careful planning will be required for each company and their current network structure. If an organization is interested in any future acquisitions or mergers, raising the domain level could have an impact, and this should be taken into careful consideration. For example, if an enterprise organization

Warning Reader Aid

Another Way Reader Aid

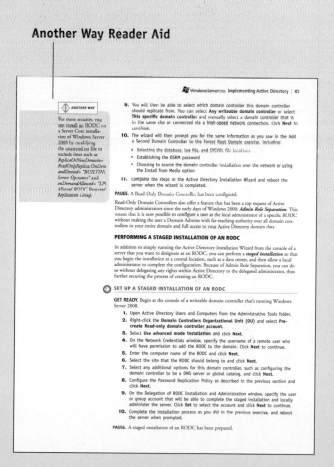

Windows Server 2008 **Implementing Active Directory** | 45

ANOTHER WAY

For more security, you can install an RODC on a Server Core installation of Windows Server 2008 by modifying the unattend.txt file to include lines such as *ReplicaOrNewDomain= ReadOnlyReplica,OnDem andDenied= "BUILTIN\ Server Operators"* and *onDemandAllowed= "LP- Allowed RODC Password Replication Group.*

9. You will then be able to select which domain controller this domain controller should replicate from. You can select **Any writeable domain controller** or select **This specific domain controller** and manually select a domain controller that is in the same site or connected via a high-speed network connection. Click **Next** to continue.

10. The wizard will then prompt you for the same information as you saw in the Add a Second Domain Controller to the Forest Root Domain exercise, including:
    - Selecting the database, log file, and SYSVOL file location
    - Establishing the DSRM password
    - Choosing to source the domain controller installation over the network or using the Install from Media option

11. Complete the steps in the Active Directory Installation Wizard and reboot the server when the wizard is completed.

PAUSE. A Read Only Domain Controller has been configured.

Read-Only Domain Controllers also offer a feature that has been a top request of Active Directory administrators since the early days of Windows 2000: *Admin Role Separation*. This means that it is now possible to configure a user as the local administrator of a specific RODC without making the user a Domain Admins with far-reaching authority over all domain controllers in your entire domain and full access to your Active Directory domain data.

PERFORMING A STAGED INSTALLATION OF AN RODC

In addition to simply running the Active Directory Installation Wizard from the console of a server that you want to designate as an RODC, you can perform a *staged installation* so that you begin the installation at a central location, such as a data center, and then allow a local administrator to complete the configuration. Because of Admin Role Separation, you can do so without delegating any rights within Active Directory to the delegated administrator, thus further securing the process of creating an RODC.

SET UP A STAGED INSTALLATION OF AN RODC

GET READY. Begin at the console of a writeable domain controller that's running Windows Server 2008.

1. Open Active Directory Users and Computers from the Administrative Tools folder.
2. Right-click the **Domain Controllers Organizational Unit (OU)** and select **Pre-create Read-only domain controller account.**
3. Select **Use advanced mode installation** and click **Next.**
4. On the Network Credentials window, specify the username of a remote user who will have permission to add the RODC to the domain. Click **Next** to continue.
5. Enter the computer name of the RODC and click **Next.**
6. Select the site that the RODC should belong to and click **Next.**
7. Select any additional options for this domain controller, such as configuring the domain controller to be a DNS server or global catalog, and click **Next.**
8. Configure the Password Replication Policy as described in the previous section and click **Next.**
9. On the Delegation of RODC Installation and Administration window, specify the user or group account that will be able to complete the staged installation and locally administer the server. Click **Set** to select the account and click **Next** to continue.
10. Complete the installation process as you did in the previous exercise, and reboot the server when prompted.

PAUSE. A staged installation of an RODC has been prepared.

18 | Lesson 1

Beginning at the Windows Server 2003 functional level, you also have the ability to create a new type of trust called a *cross-forest trust*. With Windows NT or Windows 2000 domain controllers in place, it is not possible to create a transitive trust path between forests. Resource access from one forest to another was unsupported. When you are establishing a trust between two forests that are both running at the Windows Server 2003 forest functional level or better, cross-forest trust relationships are transitive in nature and they can be configured as either a one-way or a two-way relationship. This means that every domain in Forest A trusts every resource in Forest B and (in the case of a two-way cross-forest trust) every domain in Forest B trusts every resource in Forest A, as shown in Figure 1-5.

Figure 1-5

Cross-forest trust

WARNING The transitivity of a cross-forest trust does not extend beyond two forests. This means that if you've configured a cross-forest trust between Forest A and Forest B and a second cross-forest trust between Forest B and Forest C, Forest A would not be able to access resources in Forest C unless you configure a third trust relationship directly between Forest A and Forest C.

Once the trust is established, administrators can select users and groups from a trusted forest and include them on the ACL of an object. When a resource is accessed via the cross-forest trust, the user is not required to reenter any logon credentials; you have achieved "single sign-on" across forest boundaries. This advanced feature allows corporations to share resources with partners or new acquisitions without a complete design change or migration.

SUMMARY SKILL MATRIX

IN THIS LESSON YOU LEARNED:

- Active Directory is a database of objects that are used to organize resources according to a logical plan. These objects include containers such as domains and OUs in addition to resources such as users, computers, and printers.
- The Active Directory schema includes definitions of all objects and attributes within a single forest. Each forest maintains its own Active Directory schema.
- Active Directory requires DNS to support SRV records in addition. Microsoft recommends that DNS support dynamic updates.
- Domain and forest functional levels are new features of Windows Server 2008. The levels defined for each of these are based on the type of forest operating systems that are required by the Active Directory design. The Windows Server 2003 forest functional level is the highest functional level available and includes support for all Windows Server 2003 features.
- Two-way transitive trusts are automatically generated within the Active Directory domain structure. Parent and child domains form the trust path by which all domains in the forest can traverse to locate resources. The ISTG is responsible for this process.
- Cross-forest trusts are new to Windows Server 2003 and they are only available when the forest functionality is set to Windows Server 2003. They must be manually created and maintained.

Summary Skill Matrix

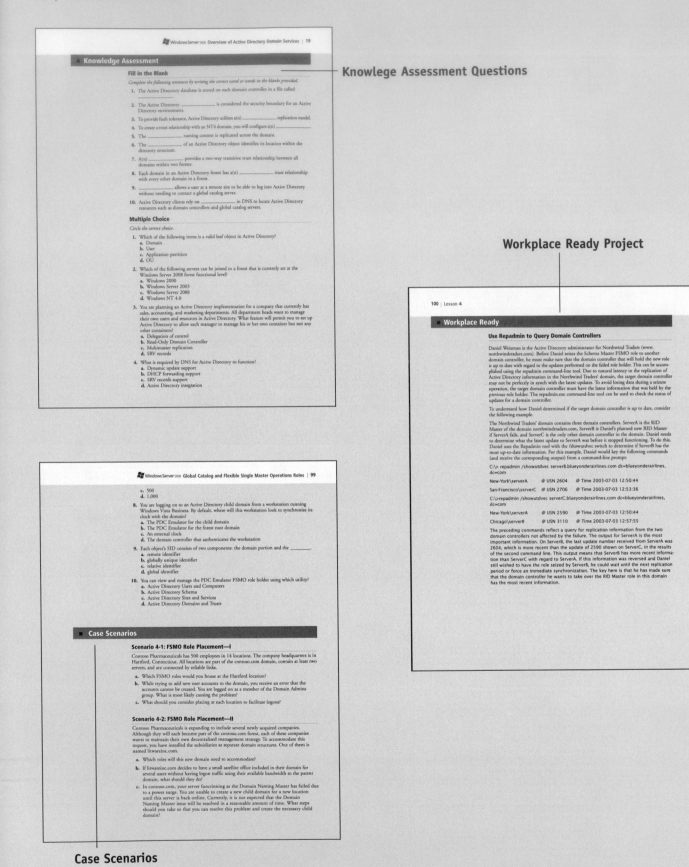

Knowlege Assessment Questions

Workplace Ready Project

Case Scenarios

This book uses particular fonts, symbols, and heading conventions to highlight important information or to call your attention to special steps. For more information about the features in each lesson, refer to the Illustrated Book Tour section.

CONVENTION	MEANING
NEW FEATURE	This icon indicates a new or greatly improved Windows feature in this version of the software.
↓ THE BOTTOM LINE	This feature provides a brief summary of the material to be covered in the section that follows.
CLOSE	Words in all capital letters and in a different font color than the rest of the text indicate instructions for opening, saving, or closing files or programs. They also point out items you should check or actions you should take.
CERTIFICATION READY?	This feature signals the point in the text where a specific certification objective is covered. It provides you with a chance to check your understanding of that particular MCTS objective and, if necessary, review the section of the lesson where it is covered.
TAKE NOTE	Reader aids appear in shaded boxes found in your text. *Take Note* provides helpful hints related to particular tasks or topics.
ANOTHER WAY	*Another Way* provides an alternative procedure for accomplishing a particular task.
X REF	These notes provide pointers to information discussed elsewhere in the textbook or describe interesting features of Windows Server 2008 that are not directly addressed in the current topic or exercise.
Alt + Tab	A plus sign (+) between two key names means that you must press both keys at the same time. Keys that you are instructed to press in an exercise will appear in the font shown here.
A *shared printer* can be used by many individuals on a network.	Key terms appear in bold italic.
Key **My Name is**.	Any text you are asked to key appears in color.
Click **OK**.	Any button on the screen you are supposed to click on or select will also appear in color.

The *Microsoft Official Academic Course* programs are accompanied by a rich array of resources that incorporate the extensive textbook visuals to form a pedagogically cohesive package. These resources provide all the materials instructors need to deploy and deliver their courses. Resources available online for download include:

- The **MSDN Academic Alliance** is designed to provide the easiest and most inexpensive developer tools, products, and technologies available to faculty and students in labs, classrooms, and on student PCs. A free 3-year membership is available to qualified MOAC adopters.

  Note: Microsoft Windows Server 2008 can be downloaded from MSDN AA for use by students in this course

- **Windows Server 2008 Evaluation Software.** DVDs containing an evaluation version of Windows Server 2008 is bundled inside the front cover of this text.

- The **Instructor's Guide** contains Solutions to all the textbook exercises as well as chapter summaries and lecture notes. The Instructor's Guide and Syllabi for various term lengths are available from the Book Companion site (http://www.wiley.com/college/microsoft) and from Wiley*PLUS.*

- The **Test Bank** contains hundreds of questions in multiple-choice, true-false, short answer, and essay formats and is available to download from the Instructor's Book Companion site (http://www.wiley.com/college/microsoft) and from Wiley*PLUS.* A complete answer key is provided.

- **PowerPoint Presentations and Images.** A complete set of PowerPoint presentations is available on the Instructor's Book Companion site (http://www.wiley.com/college/microsoft) and in Wiley*PLUS* to enhance classroom presentations. Tailored to the text's topical coverage and Skills Matrix, these presentations are designed to convey key Windows Server concepts addressed in the text.

  All figures from the text are on the Instructor's Book Companion site (http://www.wiley.com/college/microsoft) and in Wiley*PLUS.* You can incorporate them into your PowerPoint presentations, or create your own overhead transparencies and handouts.

  By using these visuals in class discussions, you can help focus students' attention on key elements of Windows Server and help them understand how to use it effectively in the workplace.

- When it comes to improving the classroom experience, there is no better source of ideas and inspiration than your fellow colleagues. The Wiley Faculty Network connects teachers with technology, facilitates the exchange of best practices, and helps to enhance instructional efficiency and effectiveness. Faculty Network activities include technology training and tutorials, virtual seminars, peer-to-peer exchanges of experiences and ideas, personal consulting, and sharing of resources. For details visit www.WhereFacultyConnect.com.

Wiley*PLUS*

Broad developments in education over the past decade have influenced the instructional approach taken in the Microsoft Official Academic Course programs. The way that students learn, especially about new technologies, has changed dramatically in the Internet era. Electronic learning materials and Internet-based instruction is now as much a part of classroom instruction as printed textbooks. Wiley*PLUS* provides the technology to create an environment where students reach their full potential and experience academic success that will last them a lifetime!

Wiley*PLUS* is a powerful and highly-integrated suite of teaching and learning resources designed to bridge the gap between what happens in the classroom and what happens at home and on the job. Wiley*PLUS* provides instructors with the resources to teach their students new technologies and guide them to reach their goals of getting ahead in the job market by having the skills to become certified and advance in the workforce. For students, Wiley*PLUS* provides the tools for study and practice that are available to them 24/7, wherever and whenever they want to study. Wiley*PLUS* includes a complete online version of the student textbook, PowerPoint presentations, homework and practice assignments and quizzes, image galleries, test bank questions, gradebook, and all the instructor resources in one easy-to-use web site.

Organized around the everyday activities you and your students perform in the class, Wiley*PLUS* helps you:

- **Prepare & Present** outstanding class presentations using relevant PowerPoint slides and other Wiley*PLUS* materials—and you can easily upload and add your own.
- **Create Assignments** by choosing from questions organized by lesson, level of difficulty, and source—and add your own questions. Students' homework and quizzes are automatically graded, and the results are recorded in your gradebook.
- **Offer context-sensitive help to students, 24/7.** When you assign homework or quizzes, you decide if and when students get access to hints, solutions, or answers where appropriate—or they can be linked to relevant sections of their complete, online text for additional help whenever—and wherever they need it most.
- **Track Student Progress:** Analyze students' results and assess their level of understanding on an individual and class level using the Wiley*PLUS* gradebook, or export data to your own personal gradebook.
- **Administer Your Course:** Wiley*PLUS* can easily be integrated with another course management system, gradebook, or other resources you are using in your class, providing you with the flexibility to build your course, your way.

Please view our online demo at **www.wiley.com/college/wileyplus.** Here you will find additional information about the features and benefits of Wiley*PLUS*, how to request a "test drive" of Wiley*PLUS* for this title, and how to adopt it for class use.

MSDN ACADEMIC ALLIANCE—FREE 3-YEAR MEMBERSHIP AVAILABLE TO QUALIFIED ADOPTERS!

The Microsoft Developer Network Academic Alliance (MSDN AA) is designed to provide the easiest and most inexpensive way for universities to make the latest Microsoft developer tools, products, and technologies available in labs, classrooms, and on student PCs. MSDN AA is an annual membership program for departments teaching Science, Technology, Engineering, and Mathematics (STEM) courses. The membership provides a complete solution to keep academic labs, faculty, and students on the leading edge of technology.

Software available in the MSDN AA program is provided at no charge to adopting departments through the Wiley and Microsoft publishing partnership.

As a bonus to this free offer, faculty will be introduced to Microsoft's Faculty Connection and Academic Resource Center. It takes time and preparation to keep students engaged while giving them a fundamental understanding of theory, and the Microsoft Faculty Connection is designed to help STEM professors with this preparation by providing articles, curriculum, and tools that professors can use to engage and inspire today's technology students.

* Contact your Wiley rep for details.

For more information about the MSDN Academic Alliance program, go to:

http://msdn.microsoft.com/academic/

Note: Microsoft Windows Server 2008 can be downloaded from MSDN AA for use by students in this course.

Important Web Addresses and Phone Numbers

To locate the Wiley Higher Education Rep in your area, go to the following Web address and click on the "*Who's My Rep?*" link at the top of the page.

http://www.wiley.com/college

Or Call the MOAC Toll Free Number: 1 + (888) 764-7001 (U.S. & Canada only).

To learn more about becoming a Microsoft Certified Professional and exam availability, visit www.microsoft.com/learning/mcp.

Student Support Program

Book Companion Web Site (www.wiley.com/college/microsoft)

The students' book companion site for the MOAC series includes any resources, exercise files, and Web links that will be used in conjunction with this course.

WileyPLUS

WileyPLUS is a powerful and highly-integrated suite of teaching and learning resources designed to bridge the gap between what happens in the classroom and what happens at home and on the job. For students, WileyPLUS provides the tools for study and practice that are available 24/7, wherever and whenever they want to study. WileyPLUS includes a complete online version of the student textbook, PowerPoint presentations, homework and practice assignments and quizzes, image galleries, test bank questions, gradebook, and all the instructor resources in one easy-to-use web site.

WileyPLUS provides immediate feedback on student assignments and a wealth of support materials. This powerful study tool will help your students develop their conceptual understanding of the class material and increase their ability to answer questions.

- A **Study and Practice** area links directly to text content, allowing students to review the text while they study and answer.

- An **Assignment** area keeps all the work you want your students to complete in one location, making it easy for them to stay on task. Students have access to a variety of interactive self-assessment tools, as well as other resources for building their confidence and understanding. In addition, all of the assignments and quizzes contain a link to the relevant section of the multimedia book, providing students with context-sensitive help that allows them to conquer obstacles as they arise.

- A **Personal Gradebook** for each student allows students to view their results from past assignments at any time.

Please view our online demo at www.wiley.com/college/wileyplus. Here you will find additional information about the features and benefits of WileyPLUS, how to request a "test drive" of WileyPLUS for this title, and how to adopt it for class use.

Wiley Desktop Editions

Wiley MOAC Desktop Editions are innovative, electronic versions of printed textbooks. Students buy the desktop version for 50% off the U.S. price of the printed text, and get the added value of permanence and portability. Wiley Desktop Editions provide students with numerous additional benefits that are not available with other e-text solutions.

Wiley Desktop Editions are NOT subscriptions; students download the Wiley Desktop Edition to their computer desktops. Students own the content they buy to keep for as long as they want. Once a Wiley Desktop Edition is downloaded to the computer desktop, students have instant access to all of the content without being online. Students can also print out the sections they prefer to read in hard copy. Students also have access to fully integrated resources within their Wiley Desktop Edition. From highlighting their e-text to taking and sharing notes, students can easily personalize their Wiley Desktop Edition as they are reading or following along in class.

Windows Server 2008 Evaluation Edition

All MOAC Windows Server 2008 textbooks are packaged with an evaluation edition of Windows Server 2008 on the companion DVDs. Installing the Windows Server Evaluation Edition provides students with the state-of-the-art system software, enabling them to use a full version of Windows Server 2008 for the course exercises. This also promotes the practice of learning by doing, which can be the most effective way to acquire and remember new computing skills.

Evaluating Windows Server 2008 software does not require product activation or entering a product key. The Windows Server 2008 Evaluation Edition provided with this textbook may be installed without activation and evaluated for an initial 60 days. If you need more time to evaluate Windows Server 2008, the 60-day evaluation period may be reset (or re-armed) three times, extending the original 60-day evaluation period by up to 180 days for a total possible evaluation time of 240 days. After this time, you will need to uninstall the software or upgrade to a fully licensed version of Windows Server 2008.

System Requirements

The following are estimated system requirements for Windows Server 2008. If your computer has less than the minimum requirements, you will not be able to install this product correctly. Actual requirements will vary based on your system configuration and the applications and features you install.

PROCESSOR

Processor performance depends not only on the clock frequency of the processor, but also on the number of processor cores and the size of the processor cache. The following are the processor requirements for this product:

> **TAKE NOTE***
>
> An Intel Itanium 2 processor is required for Windows Server 2008 for Itanium-Based Systems.

- Minimum: 1 GHz (for x86 processors) or 1.4 GHz (for x64 processors)
- Recommended: 2 GHz or faster

RAM

The following are the RAM requirements for this product:

- Minimum: 512 MB
- Recommended: 2 GB or more
- Maximum (32-bit systems): 4 GB (for Windows Server 2008 Standard) or 64 GB (for Windows Server 2008 Enterprise or Windows Server 2008 Datacenter)
- Maximum (64-bit systems): 32 GB (for Windows Server 2008 Standard) or 2 TB (for Windows Server 2008 Enterprise, Windows Server 2008 Datacenter, or Windows Server 2008 for Itanium-Based Systems)

www.wiley.com/college/microsoft *or*
call the MOAC Toll-Free Number: 1+(888) 764-7001 (U.S. & Canada only)

Disk space requirements

TAKE NOTE *

Computers with more than 16 GB of RAM will require more disk space for paging, hibernation, and dump files.

The following are the approximate disk space requirements for the system partition. Itanium-based and x64-based operating systems will vary from these estimates. Additional disk space may be required if you install the system over a network. For more information, see http://www.microsoft.com/windowsserver2008.

- Minimum: 10 GB
- Recommended: 40 GB or more
- DVD-ROM drive
- Super VGA (800 x 600) or higher-resolution monitor
- Keyboard and Microsoft mouse (or other compatible pointing device)

Important Considerations for Active Directory Domain Controllers

The upgrade process from Windows Server 2003 to Windows Server 2008 requires free disk space for the new operating system image, for the Setup process, and for any installed server roles.

For the domain controller role, the volume or volumes hosting the following resources also have specific free disk space requirements:

- Application data (%AppData%)
- Program files (%ProgramFiles%)
- Users' data (%SystemDrive%\Documents and Settings)
- Windows directory (%WinDir%)

The free space on the %WinDir% volume must be equal or greater than the current size of the resources listed above and their subordinate folders when they are located on the %WinDir% volume. By default, dcpromo places the Active Directory database and log files under %Windir%—in this case, their size would be included in the free disk space requirements for the %Windir% folder.

However, if the Active Directory database is hosted outside of any of the folders above, then the hosting volume or volumes must only contain additional free space equal to at least 10% of the current database size or 250 MB, whichever is greater. Finally, the free space on the volume that hosts the log files must be at least 50 MB.

A default installation of the Active Directory directory service in Windows Server 2003 has the Active Directory database and log files under %WinDir%\NTDS. With this configuration, the NTDS .DIT database file and all the log files are temporarily copied over to the quarantine location and then copied back to their original location. This is why additional free space is required for those resources. However, the SYSVOL directory, which is also under %WinDir% (%WinDir%\SYSVOL), is moved and not copied. Therefore, it does not require any additional free space.

After the upgrade, the space that was reserved for the copied resources will be returned to the file system.

WARNING Although you can reset the 60-day evaluation period, you cannot extend it beyond 60 days at any time. When you reset the current 60-day evaluation period, you lose whatever time is left on the previous 60-day evaluation period. Therefore, to maximize the total evaluation time, wait until close to the end of the current 60-day evaluation period before you reset the evaluation period.

Installing and Re-Arming Windows Server 2008

Evaluating Windows Server 2008 software does not require product activation. The Windows Server 2008 Evaluation Edition may be installed without activation, and it may be evaluated for 60 days. Additionally, the 60-day evaluation period may be reset (re-armed) three times. This action extends the original 60-day evaluation period by up to 180 days for a total possible evaluation time of 240 days.

How To Install Windows Server 2008 Without Activating It

TAKE NOTE*

After Windows Server 2008 is installed, the edition cannot be changed without reinstalling it.

1. Run the Windows Server 2008 Setup program.

2. When you are prompted to enter a product key for activation, do not enter a key. Click No when Setup asks you to confirm your selection.

3. You may be prompted to select the edition of Windows Server 2008 that you want to evaluate. Select the edition that you want to install.

4. When you are prompted, read the evaluation terms in the Microsoft Software License Terms, and then accept the terms.

5. When the Windows Server 2008 Setup program is finished, your initial 60-day evaluation period starts. To check the time that is left on your current evaluation period, run the Slmgr.vbs script that is in the System32 folder. Use the **-dli** switch to run this script. The **slmgr.vbs -dli** command displays the number of days that are left in the current 60-day evaluation period.

How To Re-Arm the Evaluation Period

This section describes how to extend, or re-arm, the Windows Server 2008 evaluation period. The evaluation period is also known as the "activation grace" period.

When the initial 60-day evaluation period nears its end, you can run the Slmgr.vbs script to reset the evaluation period. To do this, follow these steps:

1. Click **Start**, and then click **Command Prompt**.

2. Type **slmgr.vbs -dli**, and then press **ENTER** to check the current status of your evaluation period.

3. To reset the evaluation period, type **slmgr.vbs —rearm**, and then press **ENTER**.

4. Restart the computer.

This resets the evaluation period to 60 days.

How To Automate the Extension of the Evaluation Period

You may want to set up a process that automatically resets the evaluation period every 60 days. One way to automate this process is by using the Task Scheduler. You can configure the Task Scheduler to run the Slmgr.vbs script and to restart the server at a particular time. To do this, follow these steps:

1. Click **Start**, point to **Administrative Tools**, and then click **Task Scheduler**.

2. Copy the following sample task to the server, and then save it as an .xml file. For example, you can save the file as **Extend.xml**.

```xml
<?xml version="1.0" encoding="UTF-16"?> <Task version="1.2"
xmlns="http://schemas.microsoft.com/windows/2004/02/mit/task">
<RegistrationInfo> <Date>2007-09-17T14:26:04.433</Date>
<Author>Microsoft Corporation</Author> </RegistrationInfo>
<Triggers> <TimeTrigger id="18c4a453-d7aa-4647-916b-
af0c3ea16a6b"> <Repetition> <Interval>P59D</Interval>
<StopAtDurationEnd>false</StopAtDurationEnd> </Repetition>
<StartBoundary>2007-10-05T02:23:24</StartBoundary>
<EndBoundary>2008-09-17T14:23:24.777</EndBoundary>
<Enabled>true</Enabled> </TimeTrigger> </Triggers>
<Principals> <Principal id="Author">
<UserId>domain\alias</UserId>
```

```
<LogonType>Password</LogonType>
<RunLevel>HighestAvailable</RunLevel> </Principal>
</Principals> <Settings> <IdleSettings>
<Duration>PT10M</Duration> <WaitTimeout>PT1H</WaitTimeout>
<StopOnIdleEnd>true</StopOnIdleEnd>
<RestartOnIdle>false</RestartOnIdle> </IdleSettings>
<MultipleInstancesPolicy>IgnoreNew</MultipleInstancesPolicy>
<DisallowStartIfOnBatteries>true</DisallowStartIfOnBatteries>
<StopIfGoingOnBatteries>true</StopIfGoingOnBatteries>
<AllowHardTerminate>true</AllowHardTerminate>
<StartWhenAvailable>false</StartWhenAvailable>
<RunOnlyIfNetworkAvailable>false</RunOnlyIfNetworkAvailable>
<AllowStartOnDemand>true</AllowStartOnDemand>
<Enabled>true</Enabled> <Hidden>false</Hidden>
<RunOnlyIfIdle>false</RunOnlyIfIdle>
<WakeToRun>true</WakeToRun>
<ExecutionTimeLimit>P3D</ExecutionTimeLimit>
<DeleteExpiredTaskAfter>PT0S</DeleteExpiredTaskAfter>
<Priority>7</Priority> <RestartOnFailure>
<Interval>PT1M</Interval> <Count>3</Count>
</RestartOnFailure> </Settings> <Actions Context="Author">
<Exec> <Command>C:\Windows\System32\slmgr.vbs</Command>
<Arguments>-rearm</Arguments> </Exec> <Exec>
<Command>C:\Windows\System32\shutdown.exe</Command>
<Arguments>/r</Arguments> </Exec> </Actions> </Task>
```

3. In the sample task, change the value of the following "UserID" tag to contain your domain and your alias:

   <UserId>domain\alias</UserId>

4. In the Task Scheduler, click **Import Task** on the **Action** menu.

5. Click the sample task .xml file. For example, click **Extend.xml**.

6. Click **Import**.

7. Click the **Triggers** tab.

8. Click the **One Time** trigger, and then click **Edit**.

9. Change the start date of the task to a date just before the end of your current evaluation period.

10. Click **OK**, and then exit the Task Scheduler.

The Task Scheduler will now run the evaluation reset operation on the date that you specified.

Preparing to Take the Microsoft Certified Technology Specialist (MCTS) Exam

The Microsoft Certified Technology Specialist (MCTS) certifications enable professionals to target specific technologies and to distinguish themselves by demonstrating in-depth knowledge and expertise in their specialized technologies. Microsoft Certified Technology Specialists are consistently capable of inplementing, building, troubleshooting, and debugging a particular Microsoft Technology.

For organizations, the new generation of Microsoft certifications provides better skills verification tools that help with assessing not only in-demand skills on Windows Server, but also the ability to quickly complete on-the-job tasks. Individuals will find it easier to identify and work towards the certification credential that meets their personal and professional goals.

To learn more about becoming a Microsoft Certified Professional and exam availability, visit www.microsoft.com/learning/mcp/.

Microsoft Certifications for IT Professionals

The new Microsoft Certified Technology Specialist (MCTS) and Microsoft Certified IT Professional (MCITP) credentials provide IT professionals with a simpler and more targeted framework to showcase their technical skills in addition to the skills that are required for specific developer job roles.

The Microsoft Certified Database Administrator (MCDBA), Microsoft Certified Desktop Support Technician (MCDST), Microsoft Certified System Administrator (MCSA), and Microsoft Certified Systems Engineer (MCSE) credentials continue to provide IT professionals who use Microsoft SQL Server 2000, Windows XP, and Windows Server 2003 with industry recognition and validation of their IT skills and experience.

Microsoft Certified Technology Specialist

The new Microsoft Certified Tehnology Specialist (MCTS) credential highlights your skills using a specific Microsoft technology. You can demonstrate your abilities as an IT professional or developer with in-depth knowledge of the Microsoft technology that you use today or are planning to deploy.

The MCTS certifications enable professionals to target specific technologies and to distinguish themselves by demonstrating in-depth knowledge and expertise in their specialized technologies. Microsoft Certified Technology Specialists are consistently capable of implementing, building, troubleshooting, and debugging a particular Microsoft technology.

You can learn more about the MCTS program at www.microsoft.com/learning/mcp/mcts.

Microsoft Certified IT Professional

The new Microsoft Certified IT Professional (MCITP) credential lets you highlight your specific area of expertise. Now, you can easily distinguish yourself as an expert in database administration, database development, business intelligence, or support.

By becoming certified, you demonstrate to employers that you have achieved a predictable level of skill not only in the use of the Windows Server operating system, but with a comprehensive set of Microsoft technologies. Employers often require certification either as a condition of employment or as a condition of advancement within the company or other organization.

You can learn more about the MCITP program at http://www.microsoft.com/learning/mcp/mcitp/.

The certification examinations are sponsored by Microsoft but administered through Microsoft's exam delivery partner Prometric.

Preparing to Take an Exam

Unless you are a very experienced user, you will need to use a test preparation course to prepare to complete the test correctly and within the time allowed. The *Microsoft Official Academic Course* series is designed to prepare you with a strong knowledge of all exam topics, and with some additional review and practice on your own, you should feel confident in your ability to pass the appropriate exam.

After you decide which exam to take, review the list of objectives for the exam. You can easily identify tasks that are included in the objective list by locating the Objective Domain Matrix at the start of each lesson and the Certification Ready sidebars in the margin of the lessons in this book.

To take the MCTS test, visit www.microsoft.com/learning/mcp/mcts to locate your nearest testing center. Then call the testing center directly to schedule your test. The amount of advance notice you should provide will vary for different testing centers, and it typically depends on the number of computers available at the testing center, the number of other testers who have already been scheduled for the day on which you want to take the test, and the number of times per week that the testing center offers MCTS testing. In general, you should call to schedule your test at least two weeks prior to the date on which you want to take the test.

When you arrive at the testing center, you might be asked for proof of identity. A driver's license or passport is an acceptable form of identification. If you do not have either of these items of documentation, call your testing center and ask what alternative forms of identification will be accepted. If you are retaking a test, bring your MCTS identification number, which will have been given to you when you previously took the test. If you have not prepaid or if your organization has not already arranged to make payment for you, you will need to pay the test-taking fee when you arrive.

Acknowledgments

MOAC Instructor Advisory Board

We would like to thank our Instructor Advisory Board, an elite group of educators who has assisted us every step of the way in building these products. Advisory Board members have acted as our sounding board on key pedagogical and design decisions leading to the development of these compelling and innovative textbooks for future Information Workers. Their dedication to technology education is truly appreciated.

Charles DeSassure, Tarrant County College

Charles DeSassure is Department Chair and Instructor of Computer Science & Information Technology at Tarrant County College Southeast Campus, Arlington, Texas. He has had experience as a MIS Manager, system analyst, field technology analyst, LAN Administrator, microcomputer specialist, and public school teacher in South Carolina. DeSassure has worked in higher education for more than ten years and received the Excellence Award in Teaching from the National Institute for Staff and Organizational Development (NISOD). He currently serves on the Educational Testing Service (ETS) iSkills National Advisory Committee and chaired the Tarrant County College District Student Assessment Committee. He has written proposals and makes presentations at major educational conferences nationwide. DeSassure has served as a textbook reviewer for John Wiley & Sons and Prentice Hall. He teaches courses in information security, networking, distance learning, and computer literacy. DeSassure holds a master's degree in Computer Resources & Information Management from Webster University.

Kim Ehlert, Waukesha County Technical College

Kim Ehlert is the Microsoft Program Coordinator and a Network Specialist instructor at Waukesha County Technical College, teaching the full range of MCSE and networking courses for the past nine years. Prior to joining WCTC, Kim was a professor at the Milwaukee School of Engineering for five years where she oversaw the Novell Academic Education and the Microsoft IT Academy programs. She has a wide variety of industry experience including network design and management for Johnson Controls, local city fire departments, police departments, large church congregations, health departments, and accounting firms. Kim holds many industry certifications including MCDST, MCSE, Security+, Network+, Server+, MCT, and CNE.

Kim has a bachelor's degree in Information Systems and a master's degree in Business Administration from the University of Wisconsin Milwaukee. When she is not busy teaching, she enjoys spending time with her husband Gregg and their two children—Alex, 14, and Courtney, 17.

Penny Gudgeon, Corinthian Colleges, Inc.

Penny Gudgeon is the Program Manager for IT curriculum at Corinthian Colleges, Inc. Previously, she was responsible for computer programming and web curriculum for twenty-seven campuses in Corinthian's Canadian division, CDI College of Business, Technology and Health Care. Penny joined CDI College in 1997 as a computer programming instructor at one of the campuses outside of Toronto. Prior to joining CDI College, Penny taught productivity software at another Canadian college, the Academy of Learning, for four years. Penny has experience in helping students achieve their goals through various learning models from instructor-led to self-directed to online.

Before embarking on a career in education, Penny worked in the fields of advertising, marketing/sales, mechanical and electronic engineering technology, and computer programming. When not working from her home office or indulging her passion for lifelong learning, Penny likes to read mysteries, garden, and relax at home in Hamilton, Ontario, with her Shih-Tzu, Gracie.

Margaret Leary, Northern Virginia Community College

Margaret Leary is Professor of IST at Northern Virginia Community College, teaching Networking and Network Security Courses for the past ten years. She is the co-Principal Investigator on the CyberWATCH initiative, an NSF-funded regional consortium of higher education institutions and businesses working together to increase the number of network security personnel in the workforce. She also serves as a Senior Security Policy Manager and Research Analyst at Nortel Government Solutions and holds a CISSP certification.

Margaret holds a B.S.B.A. and MBA/Technology Management from the University of Phoenix, and is pursuing her Ph.D. in Organization and Management with an IT Specialization at Capella University. Her dissertation is titled "Quantifying the Discoverability of Identity Attributes in Internet-Based Public Records: Impact on Identity Theft and Knowledge-based Authentication." She has several other published articles in various government and industry magazines, notably on identity management and network security.

Wen Liu, ITT Educational Services, Inc.

Wen Liu is Director of Corporate Curriculum Development at ITT Educational Services, Inc. He joined the ITT corporate headquarters in 1998 as a Senior Network Analyst to plan and deploy the corporate WAN infrastructure. A year later he assumed the position of Corporate Curriculum Manager supervising the curriculum development of all IT programs. After he was promoted to the current position three years ago, he continued to manage the curriculum research and development for all the programs offered in the School of Information Technology in addition to supervising the curriculum development in other areas (such as Schools of Drafting and Design and Schools of Electronics Technology). Prior to his employment with ITT Educational Services, Liu was a Telecommunications Analyst at the state government of Indiana working on the state backbone project that provided Internet and telecommunications services to the public users such as K-12 and higher education institutions, government agencies, libraries, and healthcare facilities.

Wen Liu has an M.A. in Student Personnel Administration in Higher Education and an M.S. in Information and Communications Sciences from Ball State University, Indiana. He used to be the director of special projects on the board of directors of the Indiana Telecommunications User Association, and used to serve on Course Technology's IT Advisory Board. He is currently a member of the IEEE and its Computer Society.

Jared Spencer, Westwood College Online

Jared Spencer has been the Lead Faculty for Networking at Westwood College Online since 2006. He began teaching in 2001 and has taught both on-ground and online for a variety of institutions, including Robert Morris University and Point Park University. In addition to his academic background, he has more than fifteen years of industry experience working for companies including the Thomson Corporation and IBM.

Jared has a master's degree in Internet Information Systems and is currently ABD and pursuing his doctorate in Information Systems at Nova Southeastern University. He has authored several papers that have been presented at conferences and appeared in publications such as the Journal of Internet Commerce and the Journal of Information Privacy and Security (JIPC). He holds a number of industry certifications, including AIX (UNIX), A+, Network+, Security+, MCSA on Windows 2000, and MCSA on Windows 2003 Server.

MOAC Windows Server Reviewers

We also thank the many reviewers who pored over the manuscript, providing invaluable feedback in the service of quality instructional materials.

Microsoft® Windows Server® 2008 Active Directory Exam 70-640

Brian Bordelon, Lantec Computer Training Center

Sue Miner, Lehigh Carbon Community College

Bonnie Willy, Ivy Tech

Focus Group and Survey Participants

Finally, we thank the hundreds of instructors who participated in our focus groups and surveys to ensure that the Microsoft Official Academic Courses best met the needs of our customers.

Jean Aguilar, Mt. Hood Community College

Konrad Akens, Zane State College

Michael Albers, University of Memphis

Diana Anderson, Big Sandy Community & Technical College

Phyllis Anderson, Delaware County Community College

Judith Andrews, Feather River College

Damon Antos, American River College

Bridget Archer, Oakton Community College

Linda Arnold, Harrisburg Area Community College–Lebanon Campus

Neha Arya, Fullerton College

Mohammad Bajwa, Katharine Gibbs School–New York

Virginia Baker, University of Alaska Fairbanks

Carla Bannick, Pima Community College

Rita Barkley, Northeast Alabama Community College

Elsa Barr, Central Community College–Hastings

Ronald W. Barry, Ventura County Community College District

Elizabeth Bastedo, Central Carolina Technical College

Karen Baston, Waubonsee Community College

Karen Bean, Blinn College

Scott Beckstrand, Community College of Southern Nevada

Paulette Bell, Santa Rosa Junior College

Liz Bennett, Southeast Technical Institute

Nancy Bermea, Olympic College

Lucy Betz, Milwaukee Area Technical College

Meral Binbasioglu, Hofstra University

Catherine Binder, Strayer University & Katharine Gibbs School–Philadelphia

Terrel Blair, El Centro College

Ruth Blalock, Alamance Community College

Beverly Bohner, Reading Area Community College

Henry Bojack, Farmingdale State University

Matthew Bowie, Luna Community College

Julie Boyles, Portland Community College

Karen Brandt, College of the Albemarle

Stephen Brown, College of San Mateo

Jared Bruckner, Southern Adventist University

Pam Brune, Chattanooga State Technical Community College

Sue Buchholz, Georgia Perimeter College

Roberta Buczyna, Edison College

Angela Butler, Mississippi Gulf Coast Community College

Rebecca Byrd, Augusta Technical College

Kristen Callahan, Mercer County Community College

Judy Cameron, Spokane Community College

Dianne Campbell, Athens Technical College

Gena Casas, Florida Community College at Jacksonville

Jesus Castrejon, Latin Technologies

Gail Chambers, Southwest Tennessee Community College

Jacques Chansavang, Indiana University–Purdue University Fort Wayne

Nancy Chapko, Milwaukee Area Technical College

Rebecca Chavez, Yavapai College

Sanjiv Chopra, Thomas Nelson Community College

Greg Clements, Midland Lutheran College

Dayna Coker, Southwestern Oklahoma State University–Sayre Campus

Tamra Collins, Otero Junior College

Janet Conrey, Gavilan Community College

Carol Cornforth, West Virginia Northern Community College

Gary Cotton, American River College

Edie Cox, Chattahoochee Technical College

Rollie Cox, Madison Area Technical College

David Crawford, Northwestern Michigan College
J.K. Crowley, Victor Valley College
Rosalyn Culver, Washtenaw Community College
Sharon Custer, Huntington University
Sandra Daniels, New River Community College
Anila Das, Cedar Valley College
Brad Davis, Santa Rosa Junior College
Susan Davis, Green River Community College
Mark Dawdy, Lincoln Land Community College
Jennifer Day, Sinclair Community College
Carol Deane, Eastern Idaho Technical College
Julie DeBuhr, Lewis-Clark State College
Janis DeHaven, Central Community College
Drew Dekreon, University of Alaska–Anchorage
Joy DePover, Central Lakes College
Salli DiBartolo, Brevard Community College
Melissa Diegnau, Riverland Community College
Al Dillard, Lansdale School of Business
Marjorie Duffy, Cosumnes River College
Sarah Dunn, Southwest Tennessee Community College
Shahla Durany, Tarrant County College–South Campus
Kay Durden, University of Tennessee at Martin
Dineen Ebert, St. Louis Community College–Meramec
Donna Ehrhart, State University of New York–Brockport
Larry Elias, Montgomery County Community College
Glenda Elser, New Mexico State University at Alamogordo
Angela Evangelinos, Monroe County Community College
Angie Evans, Ivy Tech Community College of Indiana
Linda Farrington, Indian Hills Community College
Dana Fladhammer, Phoenix College
Richard Flores, Citrus College
Connie Fox, Community and Technical College at Institute of Technology West Virginia University
Wanda Freeman, Okefenokee Technical College
Brenda Freeman, Augusta Technical College
Susan Fry, Boise State University
Roger Fulk, Wright State University–Lake Campus
Sue Furnas, Collin County Community College District

Sandy Gabel, Vernon College
Laura Galvan, Fayetteville Technical Community College
Candace Garrod, Red Rocks Community College
Sherrie Geitgey, Northwest State Community College
Chris Gerig, Chattahoochee Technical College
Barb Gillespie, Cuyamaca College
Jessica Gilmore, Highline Community College
Pamela Gilmore, Reedley College
Debbie Glinert, Queensborough Community College
Steven Goldman, Polk Community College
Bettie Goodman, C.S. Mott Community College
Mike Grabill, Katharine Gibbs School–Philadelphia
Francis Green, Penn State University
Walter Griffin, Blinn College
Fillmore Guinn, Odessa College
Helen Haasch, Milwaukee Area Technical College
John Habal, Ventura College
Joy Haerens, Chaffey College
Norman Hahn, Thomas Nelson Community College
Kathy Hall, Alamance Community College
Teri Harbacheck, Boise State University
Linda Harper, Richland Community College
Maureen Harper, Indian Hills Community College
Steve Harris, Katharine Gibbs School–New York
Robyn Hart, Fresno City College
Darien Hartman, Boise State University
Gina Hatcher, Tacoma Community College
Winona T. Hatcher, Aiken Technical College
BJ Hathaway, Northeast Wisconsin Tech College
Cynthia Hauki, West Hills College – Coalinga
Mary L. Haynes, Wayne County Community College
Marcie Hawkins, Zane State College
Steve Hebrock, Ohio State University Agricultural Technical Institute
Sue Heistand, Iowa Central Community College
Heith Hennel, Valencia Community College
Donna Hendricks, South Arkansas Community College
Judy Hendrix, Dyersburg State Community College
Gloria Hensel, Matanuska-Susitna College University of Alaska Anchorage
Gwendolyn Hester, Richland College

Tammarra Holmes, Laramie County Community College

Dee Hobson, Richland College

Keith Hoell, Katharine Gibbs School–New York

Pashia Hogan, Northeast State Technical Community College

Susan Hoggard, Tulsa Community College

Kathleen Holliman, Wallace Community College Selma

Chastity Honchul, Brown Mackie College/Wright State University

Christie Hovey, Lincoln Land Community College

Peggy Hughes, Allegany College of Maryland

Sandra Hume, Chippewa Valley Technical College

John Hutson, Aims Community College

Celia Ing, Sacramento City College

Joan Ivey, Lanier Technical College

Barbara Jaffari, College of the Redwoods

Penny Jakes, University of Montana College of Technology

Eduardo Jaramillo, Peninsula College

Barbara Jauken, Southeast Community College

Susan Jennings, Stephen F. Austin State University

Leslie Jernberg, Eastern Idaho Technical College

Linda Johns, Georgia Perimeter College

Brent Johnson, Okefenokee Technical College

Mary Johnson, Mt. San Antonio College

Shirley Johnson, Trinidad State Junior College–Valley Campus

Sandra M. Jolley, Tarrant County College

Teresa Jolly, South Georgia Technical College

Dr. Deborah Jones, South Georgia Technical College

Margie Jones, Central Virginia Community College

Randall Jones, Marshall Community and Technical College

Diane Karlsbraaten, Lake Region State College

Teresa Keller, Ivy Tech Community College of Indiana

Charles Kemnitz, Pennsylvania College of Technology

Sandra Kinghorn, Ventura College

Bill Klein, Katharine Gibbs School–Philadelphia

Bea Knaapen, Fresno City College

Kit Kofoed, Western Wyoming Community College

Maria Kolatis, County College of Morris

Barry Kolb, Ocean County College

Karen Kuralt, University of Arkansas at Little Rock

Belva-Carole Lamb, Rogue Community College

Betty Lambert, Des Moines Area Community College

Anita Lande, Cabrillo College

Junnae Landry, Pratt Community College

Karen Lankisch, UC Clermont

David Lanzilla, Central Florida Community College

Nora Laredo, Cerritos Community College

Jennifer Larrabee, Chippewa Valley Technical College

Debra Larson, Idaho State University

Barb Lave, Portland Community College

Audrey Lawrence, Tidewater Community College

Deborah Layton, Eastern Oklahoma State College

Larry LeBlanc, Owen Graduate School–Vanderbilt University

Philip Lee, Nashville State Community College

Michael Lehrfeld, Brevard Community College

Vasant Limaye, Southwest Collegiate Institute for the Deaf – Howard College

Anne C. Lewis, Edgecombe Community College

Stephen Linkin, Houston Community College

Peggy Linston, Athens Technical College

Hugh Lofton, Moultrie Technical College

Donna Lohn, Lakeland Community College

Jackie Lou, Lake Tahoe Community College

Donna Love, Gaston College

Curt Lynch, Ozarks Technical Community College

Sheilah Lynn, Florida Community College–Jacksonville

Pat R. Lyon, Tomball College

Bill Madden, Bergen Community College

Heather Madden, Delaware Technical & Community College

Donna Madsen, Kirkwood Community College

Jane Maringer-Cantu, Gavilan College

Suzanne Marks, Bellevue Community College

Carol Martin, Louisiana State University–Alexandria

Cheryl Martucci, Diablo Valley College

Roberta Marvel, Eastern Wyoming College

Tom Mason, Brookdale Community College

Mindy Mass, Santa Barbara City College

Dixie Massaro, Irvine Valley College

Rebekah May, Ashland Community & Technical College

Emma Mays-Reynolds, Dyersburg State Community College

Timothy Mayes, Metropolitan State College of Denver

Reggie McCarthy, Central Lakes College

Matt McCaskill, Brevard Community College

Kevin McFarlane, Front Range Community College

Donna McGill, Yuba Community College

Terri McKeever, Ozarks Technical Community College

Patricia McMahon, South Suburban College

Sally McMillin, Katharine Gibbs School–Philadelphia

Charles McNerney, Bergen Community College

Lisa Mears, Palm Beach Community College

Imran Mehmood, ITT Technical Institute–King of Prussia Campus

Virginia Melvin, Southwest Tennessee Community College

Jeanne Mercer, Texas State Technical College

Denise Merrell, Jefferson Community & Technical College

Catherine Merrikin, Pearl River Community College

Diane D. Mickey, Northern Virginia Community College

Darrelyn Miller, Grays Harbor College

Sue Mitchell, Calhoun Community College

Jacquie Moldenhauer, Front Range Community College

Linda Motonaga, Los Angeles City College

Sam Mryyan, Allen County Community College

Cindy Murphy, Southeastern Community College

Ryan Murphy, Sinclair Community College

Sharon E. Nastav, Johnson County Community College

Christine Naylor, Kent State University Ashtabula

Haji Nazarian, Seattle Central Community College

Nancy Noe, Linn-Benton Community College

Jennie Noriega, San Joaquin Delta College

Linda Nutter, Peninsula College

Thomas Omerza, Middle Bucks Institute of Technology

Edith Orozco, St. Philip's College

Dona Orr, Boise State University

Joanne Osgood, Chaffey College

Janice Owens, Kishwaukee College

Tatyana Pashnyak, Bainbridge College

John Partacz, College of DuPage

Tim Paul, Montana State University–Great Falls

Joseph Perez, South Texas College

Mike Peterson, Chemeketa Community College

Dr. Karen R. Petitto, West Virginia Wesleyan College

Terry Pierce, Onandaga Community College

Ashlee Pieris, Raritan Valley Community College

Jamie Pinchot, Thiel College

Michelle Poertner, Northwestern Michigan College

Betty Posta, University of Toledo

Deborah Powell, West Central Technical College

Mark Pranger, Rogers State University

Carolyn Rainey, Southeast Missouri State University

Linda Raskovich, Hibbing Community College

Leslie Ratliff, Griffin Technical College

Mar-Sue Ratzke, Rio Hondo Community College

Roxy Reissen, Southeastern Community College

Silvio Reyes, Technical Career Institutes

Patricia Rishavy, Anoka Technical College

Jean Robbins, Southeast Technical Institute

Carol Roberts, Eastern Maine Community College and University of Maine

Teresa Roberts, Wilson Technical Community College

Vicki Robertson, Southwest Tennessee Community College

Betty Rogge, Ohio State Agricultural Technical Institute

Lynne Rusley, Missouri Southern State University

Claude Russo, Brevard Community College

Ginger Sabine, Northwestern Technical College

Steven Sachs, Los Angeles Valley College

Joanne Salas, Olympic College

Lloyd Sandmann, Pima Community College–Desert Vista Campus

Beverly Santillo, Georgia Perimeter College

Theresa Savarese, San Diego City College

Sharolyn Sayers, Milwaukee Area Technical College

Judith Scheeren, Westmoreland County Community College

Adolph Scheiwe, Joliet Junior College

Marilyn Schmid, Asheville-Buncombe Technical Community College

Janet Sebesy, Cuyahoga Community College

Phyllis T. Shafer, Brookdale Community College

www.wiley.com/college/microsoft *or*
call the MOAC Toll-Free Number: 1+(888) 764-7001 (U.S. & Canada only)

Ralph Shafer, Truckee Meadows Community College

Anne Marie Shanley, County College of Morris

Shelia Shelton, Surry Community College

Merilyn Shepherd, Danville Area Community College

Susan Sinele, Aims Community College

Beth Sindt, Hawkeye Community College

Andrew Smith, Marian College

Brenda Smith, Southwest Tennessee Community College

Lynne Smith, State University of New York–Delhi

Rob Smith, Katharine Gibbs School–Philadelphia

Tonya Smith, Arkansas State University–Mountain Home

Del Spencer – Trinity Valley Community College

Jeri Spinner, Idaho State University

Eric Stadnik, Santa Rosa Junior College

Karen Stanton, Los Medanos College

Meg Stoner, Santa Rosa Junior College

Beverly Stowers, Ivy Tech Community College of Indiana

Marcia Stranix, Yuba College

Kim Styles, Tri-County Technical College

Sylvia Summers, Tacoma Community College

Beverly Swann, Delaware Technical & Community College

Ann Taff, Tulsa Community College

Mike Theiss, University of Wisconsin–Marathon Campus

Romy Thiele, Cañada College

Sharron Thompson, Portland Community College

Ingrid Thompson-Sellers, Georgia Perimeter College

Barbara Tietsort, University of Cincinnati–Raymond Walters College

Janine Tiffany, Reading Area Community College

Denise Tillery, University of Nevada Las Vegas

Susan Trebelhorn, Normandale Community College

Noel Trout, Santiago Canyon College

Cheryl Turgeon, Asnuntuck Community College

Steve Turner, Ventura College

Sylvia Unwin, Bellevue Community College

Lilly Vigil, Colorado Mountain College

Sabrina Vincent, College of the Mainland

Mary Vitrano, Palm Beach Community College

Brad Vogt, Northeast Community College

Cozell Wagner, Southeastern Community College

Carolyn Walker, Tri-County Technical College

Sherry Walker, Tulsa Community College

Qi Wang, Tacoma Community College

Betty Wanielista, Valencia Community College

Marge Warber, Lanier Technical College–Forsyth Campus

Marjorie Webster, Bergen Community College

Linda Wenn, Central Community College

Mark Westlund, Olympic College

Carolyn Whited, Roane State Community College

Winona Whited, Richland College

Jerry Wilkerson, Scott Community College

Joel Willenbring, Fullerton College

Barbara Williams, WITC Superior

Charlotte Williams, Jones County Junior College

Bonnie Willy, Ivy Tech Community College of Indiana

Diane Wilson, J. Sargeant Reynolds Community College

James Wolfe, Metropolitan Community College

Marjory Wooten, Lanier Technical College

Mark Yanko, Hocking College

Alexis Yusov, Pace University

Naeem Zaman, San Joaquin Delta College

Kathleen Zimmerman, Des Moines Area Community College

We also thank Lutz Ziob, Jim DiIanni, Merrick Van Dongen, Jim LeValley, Bruce Curling, Joe Wilson, Rob Linsky, Jim Clark, and Scott Serna at Microsoft for their encouragement and support in making the Microsoft Official Academic Course programs the finest instructional materials for mastering the newest Microsoft technologies for both students and instructors.

Brief Contents

Contents

Overview of Active Directory Domain Services

KEY TERMS

Active Directory Domain Services (AD DS)	external trust	naming context (NC)
application partition	fault tolerant	object
attribute	forest	organizational unit (OU)
Configuration NC	forest root domain	outbound replication
container object	functional levels	partition
cross-forest trust	globally unique identifier (GUID)	publishing
delegation	inbound replication	Read-Only Domain Controller (RODC)
directory service	IP address	replication
distinguished name (DN)	Knowledge Consistency Checker (KCC)	rolling upgrades
domain	leaf object	schema
domain controller (DC)	Lightweight Directory Access Protocol (LDAP)	Schema NC
Domain Name System (DNS)	link-value replication	shortcut trust
Domain NC	locator service	site
domain tree	loose consistency	SRV record
		trust relationship

Lucerne Publishing is a publisher of medical textbooks that maintains offices in London, Tokyo, New York, and Bangalore. In the past, the Lucerne Publishing staff has used multiple usernames and passwords to access a small number of file servers and applications, but the company has grown significantly in recent years and this growth has made managing this process unwieldy. Lucerne has decided to deploy Windows Server 2008 to provide centralized authentication and authorization of users across its worldwide locations to provide users with a single username and password that will provide access to resources across the enterprise.

After completing this lesson, you will be able to describe the Active Directory Domain Services role in Windows Server 2008 and its functions and benefits. You will also develop an understanding of the components of an Active Directory environment, including forests, sites, domains, domain trees, and organizational units (OUs). We will discuss how to design the physical and logical structure of an Active Directory network and delve into Active Directory's naming standards and their importance to a well-functioning Active Directory environment. Finally, you will understand and assess Active Directory domain and functional levels based on the needs of an organization's network environment as well as the trust models used by Active Directory and the role that Active Directory trusts play in resource accessibility across multiple organizations.

Introducing Active Directory Domain Services

↓
THE BOTTOM LINE

The Active Directory Domain Services (AD DS) service in Windows Server 2008 provides a centralized authentication service for Microsoft networks. Some of the benefits of Active Directory DS include a hierarchical organizational structure, multimaster authentication (the ability to access and modify AD DS from multiple points of administration) to create fault tolerance and redundancy, a single point of access to network resources, and the ability to create trust relationships with external networks running previous versions of Active Directory and even UNIX. Windows Server 2008 includes a number of new features to improve Active Directory, including the introduction of the Read-Only Domain Controller (RODC), fine-grained password policies, an improved graphical user interface (GUI), improved auditing of Active Directory modification and deletions, the ability to start and stop Active Directory as a service without needing to completely restart the domain controller for maintenance, and the introduction of Server Core, a minimal installation of Windows Server 2008 that has a greatly reduced attack footprint relative to a full install of the server operating system.

Identifying Active Directory's Functions and Benefits

Microsoft introduced the Active Directory service in Windows Server 2000 to provide the main repository for information about network users, computers, services, and other resources on a Microsoft network. Although subsequent versions of Active Directory in Windows Server 2003 and Windows Server 2008 have introduced new functionality and security features, the basic premise of the service remains the same: to provide a centralized authentication and authorization repository for large and small organizations alike.

A *directory service* allows businesses to define, manage, access, and secure network resources, including files, printers, people, and applications. Without the efficiency of a directory service, businesses would have difficulty keeping up with demands for fast-paced data exchange. As corporate networks continue to grow in complexity and importance, businesses require more and more from the networks that facilitate this automation. In Windows Server 2008, Microsoft provides two separate roles that can provide directory services:

X REF

For more information about Active Directory Lightweight Directory Services, refer to Lesson 2.

- *Active Directory Domain Services (AD DS)* provides the full-fledged directory service that was referred to as *Active Directory* in Windows Server 2003 and Windows 2000.
- **Active Directory Lightweight Directory Services (AD LDS)** provides a lightweight, flexible directory platform that can be used by Active Directory developers without incurring the overhead of the full-fledged Active Directory DS directory service. For example, an application developer might use AD LDS to provide a directory of employee photographs that integrate with AD DS, without actually needing to store hundreds or thousands of graphics files throughout the company.

A Windows Server 2008 computer that has been configured with the Active Directory DS role is referred to as a *domain controller (DC)*. A domain controller is a server that stores the Active Directory database and authenticates users with the network during logon. Each domain controller actively participates in storing, modifying, and maintaining the Active Directory database information that is stored on each domain controller in a file called ntds.dit. Active Directory is a *multimaster database*, which means that administrators can update the ntds.dit from any domain controller. The process of keeping each domain controller in synch with changes that have been made elsewhere on the network is called *replication*. When a domain controller transmits replication information to other domain controllers on the network, this is called *outbound replication*. Conversely, when a domain controller receives updates to the Active Directory database from other domain controllers on the network, this is called *inbound replication*.

Consider a small network with three domain controllers: DC1, DC2, and DC3. A user changes her password, updating the ntds.dit database on DC1. DC1 must then replicate this change to DC2 and DC3. Domain controllers automatically replicate with other domain controllers in the same domain to ensure that the Active Directory database is consistent. Windows Server 2008 relies on one or more domain controllers to manage access to network services.

Active Directory is designed to enable scalability by handling organizations of any size, from small businesses to global enterprises. In fact, Active Directory is theoretically scalable to holding 4,294,967,041 (2^{32} - 255) separate objects. From a practical standpoint, this means that the maximum size of an Active Directory database is really only limited by the processing power of the hardware that has been deployed onto the domain controllers.

The major benefits of the high-powered Active Directory Domain Services include:

- Centralized resource and security administration
- Single logon for access to global resources
- Fault tolerance and redundancy
- Simplified resource location

Centralizing Resource and Security Administration

Active Directory provides a single point from which administrators can manage network resources and their associated security objects. An organization can administer Active Directory based on an organizational model, a business model, or the types of functions being administered. For example, an organization could choose to administer Active Directory by logically dividing the users according to the departments in which they work, their geographical location, or a combination of these characteristics.

X REF

See "Using Forest and Domain Functional Levels" later in this lesson for information on functional levels.

Active Directory can simplify the security management of all network resources and extend interoperability with a wide range of applications and devices. Management is simplified through centralized access to the administrative tools and to the Active Directory database of network resources. Interoperability with prior versions of Microsoft Windows is available in Windows Server 2008 through the use of *functional levels*.

When Active Directory is installed and configured, it includes a number of GUI and command-line tools that can be used to administer network services, resources, and security at a detailed level. These administrative tools can be accessed from any domain controller in the network or an administrative workstation that has these tools installed. When you configure a Windows 2008 Server as an Active Directory domain controller, you will see the following tools added to the Administrative Tools folder:

TAKE NOTE*

Unlike Active Directory in Windows 2000 and Windows Server 2003, Windows Server 2008 no longer supports the use of Windows NT domain controllers.

- Active Directory Users and Computers
- Active Directory Domains and Trusts
- Active Directory Sites and Services
- ADSI Edit

You will see these administrative tools described throughout this book. As you are introduced to new concepts, the tools that should be used with each associated task will be noted. This will allow you to build your administrative knowledge at a manageable pace.

Providing a Single Point of Access to Resources

Prior to the introduction of directory services into corporate networks, all users were required to log on to many different servers in order to access a variety of different resources. This required users to enter their authentication information multiple times, and an administrator had to maintain duplicate user accounts on every server in the organization. Imagine how enormous the task of managing a separate username and password on each server would be if your organization contained 10 servers and 10 users per server. Now imagine how much *more* difficult that would become with 10 servers and 500 users per server. You would have to create and maintain 5,000 user accounts, with all of the associated security assignments, if you were maintaining separate authentication for each individual server.

Active Directory provides a single point of management for network resources. Active Directory uses a single sign-on to allow access to network resources located on any server within the domain. The user is identified and authenticated by Active Directory once. After this process is complete, the user signs on once to access the network resources that are authorized for the user according to his or her assigned roles and privileges within Active Directory.

Benefiting from Fault Tolerance and Redundancy

A system is said to be *fault tolerant* if it is capable of responding gracefully to a software or hardware failure. For example, a server is fault tolerant if it can continue to function when a power supply or a hard drive suffers a mechanical failure. An authentication system such as Active Directory is considered fault tolerant when it has the ability to continue providing authentication services even if one or more servers that provide authentication services (in the case of AD DS domain controllers) experience hardware failure or a loss of network connectivity. In this way, Active Directory can offer a redundant solution which can continue to provide authentication services without any adverse effects noticed by users, workstations, or other services.

It can take anywhere from a few seconds to several hours for changes to replicate throughout a given environment, which means that each individual domain controller may contain slightly different information until the replication process has been completed. Because of this, the Active Directory database is said to maintain *loose consistency*.

Active Directory builds in fault tolerance through its multimaster domain controller design. This fault tolerance is created due to the fact that all domain controllers in an Active Directory domain share a common database file called ntds.dit; any change that is made on one domain controller is replicated to all other domain controllers in the environment. This ensures that all domain controllers have consistent information about the domain.

Windows Server 2008 introduces the *Read-Only Domain Controller* (**RODC**), a domain controller that contains a copy of the ntds.dit file that cannot be modified and that does not replicate its changes to other domain controllers within Active Directory. Microsoft introduced this type of domain controller as a way to increase security in branch-office deployments because many companies find it necessary to deploy domain controllers in far-removed locations that are not secured as well as a centralized data center. The Read-Only Domain Controller protects Active Directory against unauthorized changes made from these remote locations.

Because the entire Active Directory database is duplicated on all domain controllers, it is still possible for authentication and resource access to take place via another domain controller if one domain controller fails. Because a single-domain-controller environment does not offer the fault tolerance described here, Microsoft recommends configuring at least two domain controllers in every environment.

Simplifying Resource Location

Imagine you are a user in a 10-server environment, where every server has a different set of resources that you need to do your job. If you were in this situation, identifying which server provided each resource would not be an easy task. This is even more complicated when you have mobile users, such as an employee visiting from another site who needs to locate printers and other devices to become productive at the new site.

Active Directory simplifies this process by allowing file and print resources to be published on the network. *Publishing* an object allows users to access network resources by searching the Active Directory database for the desired resource. This search can be based on the resource's name, description, or location. For example, a shared folder can be found by clicking the appropriate search button using My Network Places in Windows XP or Microsoft Windows Server 2003 or the Network and Sharing Center in Windows Vista. Generally, a user can configure the search scope. The shared folder name and keyword do not need to be search criteria. Providing more search information creates more specific results. For example, if you've configured the word "accounting" as a keyword for 100 folders, a search for that keyword will return 100 results that a user would need to sort through to find the desired folder.

Categorizing Active Directory Components

Active Directory consists of a number of components that allow flexibility in the design, scalability, administration, and security of an Active Directory network. Some of these components can be changed and scaled to fit a future design. Others are more difficult to change after the initial configuration, so organizations need to have a clear plan in place for the design of an Active Directory environment before beginning the installation and configuration process.

Each component in Active Directory can be categorized as either a **container object** or a **leaf object**. A container object is one that can have other objects housed within it; these can be additional container objects as well as leaf objects. A leaf object, by contrast, cannot contain other objects and usually refers to a resource such as a printer, folder, user, or group. To begin, let's discuss the following container objects:

- Forests
- Domain trees
- Domains
- OUs

Seeing the Forest

The largest container object within Active Directory is the **forest**. The forest container defines the fundamental security boundary within Active Directory, which means that a user can access resources across an entire Active Directory forest using a single logon/password combination. An additional logon would be required to access resources across more than one forest.

To improve the efficiency of Active Directory, Active Directory divides information into multiple **partitions**, also called **naming contexts (NCs)**. Each domain controller's copy of the ntds.dit database file will contain a minimum of three NCs (sometimes more depending on the configuration of a particular domain controller). The following two NCs are replicated forest-wide and are thus stored in the ntds.dit file on every domain controller in a forest:

- The schema partition, or **Schema NC**, contains the rules and definitions that are used for creating and modifying object classes and attributes within Active Directory.
- The configuration partition, or **Configuration NC**, contains information regarding the physical topology of the network, as well as other configuration data that must be replicated throughout the forest.

Because the Schema NC is replicated forest-wide, each Active Directory forest has a single schema that is shared by every domain and domain tree within the forest. The information in the Configuration NC is similarly shared by all domains in a single forest.

Each domain controller also stores a copy of the **Domain NC**, which is replicated to each DC within a single domain. The Domain NC consists of user, computer, and other resource information for a particular Active Directory domain.

Deploying Domain Trees and Domains

> Within a forest, Active Directory relies on domain trees and domains to create smaller administrative boundaries. These partitions divide the database into manageable pieces that separate forest-wide information from domain-specific information.

An Active Directory *domain tree* is a logical grouping of network resources and devices that can contain one or more *domains* configured in a parent–child relationship. Each Active Directory forest can contain one or more domain trees, each of which can in turn contain one or more domains. Active Directory domains create an administrative boundary of resources that can be managed together as a logical unit. Figure 1-1 depicts a simple Active Directory structure that includes a parent domain, lucernepublishers.com, and a child domain, tokyo.lucernepublishers.com.

Figure 1-1

Simple Active Directory
structure

lucernepublishers.com

tokyo.lucernepublishers.com

TAKE NOTE*

Active Directory domain names most often reflect the registered Internet domain name of the company. Although Windows Server 2003 and Windows Server 2008 allow renaming of domain names, it is best to start with an organization's registered DNS name if possible. Changing a domain name is a nontrivial process, because all references to the domain must also be changed.

Every Active Directory domain has an associated domain partition, or Domain NC, that is replicated to each domain controller within a particular domain. Each domain's Domain NC contains information about the objects that are stored within that domain: users, groups, computers, printers, OUs, and more. This Domain NC is replicated to all domain controllers in a single domain with the forest-wide Schema and Configuration NCs. Active Directory information within a domain is replicated to all domain controllers within the domain to provide redundancy, fault tolerance, and load balancing for resources within the domain.

Although not considered to be a formal partition, the Active Directory global catalog also needs to be replicated throughout the forest. In contrast to the Domain NC, the global catalog does not replicate to all domain controllers. Rather, it replicates only to domain controllers that have been specifically configured to hold the global catalog. These domain controllers are known as global catalog servers.

The example shown in Figure 1-1 would include the following replication information:

X REF

For more information about the global catalog, refer to Lesson 2. For more information about global catalog servers, refer to Lesson 4.

- Each domain controller in the lucernepublishers.com domain replicates a copy of the Schema NC, the Configuration NC, and the lucernepublishers.com Domain NC.
- Each domain controller in the tokyo.lucernepublishers.com domain replicates a copy of the Schema NC, the Configuration NC, and the tokyo.lucernepublishers.com Domain NC.
- Each domain controller in the entire forest that has been configured as a global catalog replicates a copy of the global catalog.

Working with Organizational Units

An Active Directory domain can contain one or more *organizational units (OUs)* that can further subdivide users and resources. An OU is a container that represents a logical grouping of resources that have similar security or administrative guidelines.

Like the parent–child relationships possible with domains, OUs can be nested in a hierarchical fashion in which a parent OU can contain one or more child OUs. Each child OU can be a parent to child OUs of its own. However, although it is possible to create a nested OU structure containing a number of parent–child relationships, you must consider that these subsequent relationships can make the administration of OUs difficult if they are nested too deeply.

An Active Directory OU structure can reflect the logical structure of the organization by modeling the company's organizational chart, depicting employees and their respective departments, or by organizing users according to their resource needs. For example, all users who have similar resource needs can be placed in an OU for ease of management if this best supports the business needs of the organization. By default, security settings that are applied to an OU will be inherited by all child objects of the container. This simplifies management by allowing you to apply a security setting once at the OU level rather than applying a setting individually to dozens or hundreds of user or computer objects contained within that OU.

Administration of an OU also can be delegated to a departmental supervisor or manager and thus can allow that person to manage day-to-day resource access or more mundane tasks, such as resetting passwords. This is referred to as *delegation* of control. Each container or OU can be created with custom security guidelines in mind, allowing detailed administrative control.

OUs can contain the following objects:

- Users
- Groups
- Contacts
- Printers
- Shared folders
- Computers
- OUs
- InetOrgPerson

Beginning in Windows Server 2003, Active Directory also includes a fourth partition type called an *application partition*. Application partitions provide fine control. Administrators can direct where information is replicated to a domain or forest. This results in greater flexibility and better control over replication performance. For example, the DomainDNSZones application partition will replicate information to every DNS server within a single domain; the ForestDNSZones application partition will replicate data to every DNS server in a forest.

Understanding the Schema

The Active Directory schema defines what different types of objects look like within Active Directory. What is a user? What properties does a group have? Active Directory comes with a prepopulated base schema, and it can be modified or extended to meet the needs of custom applications.

Every resource in Active Directory is represented as an *object*, and each object has a set of *attributes* that are associated with it. In Active Directory, each object is defined within the Active Directory *schema*. The schema is a master database that contains definitions of all objects in the Active Directory—in a way, it defines what Active Directory *is*. The schema has two components: object classes and attributes. Each object that is represented in Active Directory—for example, the user John and the printer Laserprinter—is an instance of the user and printer object classes, respectively.

Each object class in the schema is further defined according to a list of attributes that make the object class unique within the database. The list of attributes is defined only once in the schema, but the same attribute can be associated with more than one object class. Some attributes are *required* attributes that are necessary for the object to be created, such as a user account logon name. Other *optional* attributes, such as street address and phone number, provide additional details that can be published for user and administrative purposes.

When Active Directory is installed, a number of object classes are created automatically. Some of these object classes include:

- Users
- Groups
- Computers
- Domain controllers
- Printers

All object classes have a common set of attributes that help to uniquely identify each object within the database. Some of these common attributes are as follows:

- **Unique name.** This name identifies the object in the database. A unique name is given to the object upon its creation and includes references to its location within the directory database. This will be explained later in this lesson.
- *Globally unique identifier (GUID).* The GUID is a 128-bit hexadecimal number that is assigned to every object in the Active Directory forest upon its creation. This number does not change, even when the object itself is renamed. The number is not used again, even if an object is deleted and recreated with the same display name.
- **Required object attributes.** These attributes are required for the object to function. In particular, the user account must have a unique name and a password entered upon creation.
- **Optional object attributes.** These attributes add information that is not critical to the object in terms of functionality. This type of information is "nice to know" as opposed to "need to know." An example of an optional object attribute would be a phone number or street address for a user account.

As you will see, the schema can be modified to include additional objects and attributes when necessary. Each object in the schema is protected by access control lists (ACLs) so that only authorized administrators can access and modify the schema. ACLs are implemented by the administrator and used by the directory to keep track of which users and groups have permission to access specific objects and to what degree they can use or modify them.

Creating Active Directory Sites and Subnets

A *site* is defined as one or more IP subnets that are connected by fast links. In most circumstances, all computers that are connected via a single LAN will constitute a single site. Within Active Directory, sites are used to optimize the replication of Active Directory information across small or large geographic areas.

All domain controllers within the same site will use intrasite replication to replicate information as changes are made to Active Directory, whereas intersite replication takes place at regularly scheduled intervals that are defined by an administrator. An internal Active Directory process known as the *Knowledge Consistency Checker (KCC)* automatically creates and maintains the replication topology. The KCC operates based on the information provided by an administrator in the Active Directory Sites and Services snap-in, which is located in the Administrative Tools folder on a domain controller or an administrative workstation that has had the Administrative Tools installed.

X REF

The Active Directory schema is managed using the *Active Directory Schema* tool. Because modifying the schema is a sensitive operation, this tool does not exist by default in the Administrative Tools folder. The snap-in must be added manually. For more information about adding this tool, refer to Lesson 2.

X REF

For more information about the KCC, replication, and the use of the Active Directory Sites and Services snap-in, refer to Lesson 3.

Figure 1-2

lucernepublishing.com domain, OUs, and leaf objects

lucernepublishers.com

ou = Sales

cn = jsmith

TAKE NOTE *

For further information on the objects defined by LDAP, search for LDAP on the RFC Editor search page at www.rfc-editor.org/rfc-search.html.

Using Active Directory Naming Standards

Active Directory's scalability and integration capabilities result from its use of industry standards for naming formats and directory functions, specifically the *Lightweight Directory Access Protocol (LDAP)*. LDAP was developed in the early 1990s by the Internet Engineering Task Force (IETF) to facilitate the implementation of X.500 in email. (X.500 is the standard that defines how global directories should be structured and organized.)

Since the introduction of LDAP, this protocol has become an industry standard that enables data exchange between directory services and applications. The LDAP standard defines the naming of all objects in the Active Directory database and therefore provides a directory that can be integrated with other directory services, such as Novell *eDirectory*, and Active Directory–aware applications, such as Microsoft Exchange.

Queries and modifications of Active Directory objects take place almost exclusively via LDAP. For this reason, it is necessary to understand how objects are referenced in Active Directory. Consider the following example in Figure 1-2.

LDAP refers to an object using its *distinguished name (DN)*, which references an object in the Active Directory directory structure using its entire hierarchical path, starting with the object itself and including all parent objects up to the root of the domain. LDAP defines the naming attributes that identify each part of the object's name. These attributes are listed in Table 1-1.

Table 1-1

Active Directory Object Classes and Naming Attributes

Object Class	LDAP Naming Attribute	Definition of Naming Attribute
User or any leaf object	Cn	Common name
Organizational unit object	Ou	Organizational unit name
Domain	Dc	Domain components, one for each part of the DNS name

When Figure 1-2 is used as a reference, JSmith has the following distinguished name:

cn=JSmith, ou=sales, dc=lucernepublishing, dc=com

 REF

For more information about performing Active Directory object restores, refer to Lesson 11.

Not all Active Directory management tools require you to specify the full distinguished name of an object to manage it. In many cases, you can specify a shortened account name like "jsmith." However, it is important to understand how a distinguished name is structured for those times when one is required. For example, you might need to restore an object that has been accidentally deleted from the Active Directory database. In this situation, understanding how a distinguished name is structured is critical to accomplishing the desired restore.

 REF

For more information about UPNs, refer to Lesson 2.

In addition to understanding the significance of DNS and LDAP in Active Directory name formats, it is important to understand the use of User Principal Names (UPNs) in Windows Server 2008. UPNs follow the format of *username@lucernepublishing.com*. This convention provides a simple solution to a complex domain structure, in which it can be difficult for users to remember the distinguished name. It also provides an opportunity to create consistency between the user's email name and his or her logon name.

Understanding DNS

You will often hear Active Directory administrators say that "Active Directory lives and dies by DNS." After the introduction of Active Directory in Windows 2000, the *Domain Name System (DNS)* has been Active Directory's default name resolution method. Configuring DNS correctly is a critical task for any Active Directory administrator because the health of an Active Directory environment will largely depend on how well DNS is functioning to support Active Directory.

TAKE NOTE *

This four-octet IP address is an *IP version 4 (IPv4)* address. This refers to version 4 of IP, which is the most widely deployed version of IP at present. Windows Server 2008 and Windows Vista also natively support *IPv6*, which is the next generation of IP. For more details about IPv6, see the MOAC 642 guide.

In most modern networks, TCP/IP is the primary networking protocol used to communicate between systems. All devices on an IP network use a unique number to identify themselves and their location on the network. This is called an IP address. *IP addresses* are four octets long and are commonly expressed in dotted-decimal notation, such as 192.168.10.1.

One way to access a resource is through its IP address. However, when a computer system identifies resources using 32-bit numbers, expecting a user to access a resource by using its IP address would be cumbersome at best. This is where DNS comes into play. DNS is a distributed name resolution service that provides name resolution for an Active Directory domain. In addition to an IP address, all computers are given a DNS host name upon installation. Although the host name helps you define a device's location or purpose, it needs to be translated into a value that computers can understand. This is why you need DNS. DNS maps a computer's host name to its IP address. When a user or application references a computer's host name, DNS provides the translation of the host name to an IP address, thereby allowing the traffic to be routed appropriately to the correct destination.

Integrating DNS and Active Directory

DNS is a foundational requirement for Active Directory; the domain controller role cannot be installed onto a server unless that server can locate an appropriate DNS server on the same machine or somewhere on the network.

In addition to providing computer host name–to–IP address mappings on the network, DNS plays a much larger role in the functionality of Active Directory. Active Directory relies on DNS to provide a *locator service* for clients on the network. This locator service provides direction for clients that need to know which server performs what function. For example, if a user were attempting to log on to the network, the locator service would attempt to provide the client with the host name and IP address of the domain controller located in the same site as the client workstation if possible.

This locator service is necessary within Active Directory because Active Directory is a multimaster directory service. Therefore, network services might not always be provided by the same server. Fault tolerance, load balancing, and redundancy are among the reasons for setting up every network, even a small network, with multiple servers, which makes this locator service essential for clients to be able to access domain controllers and other Active Directory resources.

TAKE NOTE *

SRV records are supported by BIND DNS versions 4.9.7 and later. Dynamic updates are supported by BIND DNS version 8.2.2 and later.

In many cases, organizations will rely on the built-in DNS server role within Windows Server 2008 to provide DNS name resolution for Active Directory. In some cases, though, a company may already have a third-party DNS service in place, such as the BIND DNS service offered by UNIX. When deploying Active Directory with third-party DNS, you need to ensure that the DNS server can support *SRV records*. SRV records are the locator records within DNS that allow clients to locate an Active Directory domain controller or global catalog. Without the ability to resolve SRV records, clients will be unable to authenticate against Active Directory.

In addition to the required support of SRV records, modern DNS implementations also have the ability to support dynamic updates. Dynamic updates permit DNS clients to automatically register and update their information in the DNS database. When a domain controller

For more information about dynamic updates, refer to Lesson 2.

is added to the forest, for example, its SRV and A records can be added dynamically to the DNS database via dynamic updates to keep the DNS locator service up to date. Dynamic DNS provides a convenient method to assist in keeping the database current. Dynamic updates are not required for Active Directory to function, but taking advantage of this feature can make it much simpler to administer.

Using Forest and Domain Functional Levels

Forest and domain functional levels are designed to offer support for Active Directory domain controllers running various supported operating systems. As you decommission legacy domain controllers, you can modify these functional levels to expose new functionality within Active Directory. Some features in Active Directory cannot be activated, for example, until all domain controllers in a forest are upgraded to the Windows Server 2003 family, and some domain-wide Active Directory functionality can only exist in a domain that is at the Windows Server 2008 functional level.

As corporate enterprises expand and update their networks, they typically do not upgrade their entire network at the same time. The upgrade strategy chosen will depend on the size of the network and the impact an upgrade will have on users' productivity and access to the network. Because of this, Microsoft has created functional levels that will allow enterprises to migrate their Active Directory domain controllers gradually, based on the need and desire for the new functionality. You can change the functional level for a single domain within a multi-domain environment without requiring other domains to make the same change. This allows *rolling upgrades* as time, budget, and application compatibility factors permit.

Note that forest and domain functional levels will not change automatically. Even if all domain controllers in a particular domain are running the Windows Server 2008 operating system, for example, the domain functional level will not switch to Windows Server 2008 until an administrator makes the change manually. This is due to the fact that functional level changes are *irreversible*; once you have upgraded a functional level, you cannot return to a previous one without performing a domain- or forest-wide restore of the Active Directory database. Because of the permanent nature of this change, Active Directory requires manual intervention on an administrator's part in order to change the forest or domain functional level of an Active Directory environment.

Raising Domain Functional Levels

Windows Server 2008 supports three domain functional levels, depending on the operating systems of domain controllers that are deployed in the domain. As you raise the domain functional level, additional functionality becomes available within Active Directory.

TAKE NOTE*

The "Windows 2000 mixed" and "Windows Server 2003 interim" domain functional levels are no longer available in Windows Server 2008. These levels were available in Windows Server 2003 to support legacy Windows NT 4.0 Backup Domain Controllers (BDCs).

Within Active Directory, domain functional levels are configured on a per-domain basis. This allows different domains within the forest to be at different phases in the process of transitioning to Windows Server 2008—a parent domain can exist at the Windows Server 2003 domain functional level while a child domain has been raised to the Windows Server 2008 functional level. Windows Server 2008 supports Windows 2000, Windows Server 2003, and Windows Server 2008 domain controllers. Windows NT 4.0 domain controllers are *no longer supported*.

The following domain functional levels are available in Windows Server 2008:

- **Windows 2000 native.** This level allows backward compatibility with Microsoft Windows 2000. It also allows Windows 2000, Windows Server 2003, and Windows Server 2008 domain controllers.
- **Windows Server 2003.** This functional level allows Windows Server 2003 and Windows Server 2008 domain controllers only. It does not allow the presence of Windows 2000 domain controllers.

- **Windows Server 2008.** This functional level allows no backward compatibility. Only Windows Server 2008 domain controllers are supported.

At the Windows 2000 native domain functional level, the following basic Active Directory functionality is available:

- **Install from Media.** This feature, introduced in Windows Server 2003, allows you to promote a server to domain controller status using a backup from an existing domain controller.
- **Application partitions.** As you already learned, application partitions allow you to exert greater control over how application information is replicated throughout Active Directory.
- **Drag-and-drop user interface.** This feature allows you to drag and drop objects from one container to another within tools, such as Active Directory Users and Computers as well as Active Directory Sites and Services. (This feature was not available in Windows 2000.)
- **Global Group nesting and Universal Security groups.** This feature allows greater flexibility in creating Active Directory group objects.
- **SIDHistory.** Each Active Directory user, group, and computer possesses a Security Identifier (SID) that is used to grant or deny access to resources within Active Directory, file servers, and Active Directory–aware applications. SIDHistory allows a user to retain access to these SIDs when an object is migrated from one domain to another.

X REF

For more information about Active Directory group objects, refer to Lessons 7 and 10.

At the Windows Server 2003 domain functional level, a domain can contain Windows Server 2003 and Windows Server 2008 domain controllers. All of the features available in the Windows 2000 native mode are available, as well as the following features:

- **lastLogonTimestamp attribute.** lastLogonTimestamp is an attribute of the user class that allows administrators to keep track of logon times for computers and users within the domain.
- **Passwords for inetOrgPerson objects.** Windows Server 2003 introduced support for the inetOrgPerson object class, which can be used for interoperability with other directory services, such as *openLDAP*. At the Windows Server 2003 domain functional level, inetOrgPerson objects can be configured with passwords and permissions just like Active Directory user objects.
- **Domain rename.** As the name suggests, this feature allows you to rename an Active Directory domain, such as renaming a domain from example.com to cohowinery.com. This operation still has several restrictions placed on it. For example, you cannot use domain rename to restructure a child domain into the parent domain of a separate domain tree. Even in a single-domain environment, renaming a domain is a nontrivial operation that needs to be extensively planned and tested before attempted in a production environment.

At the highest domain functional level of Windows Server 2008, all possible Active Directory features are available to you. To support this advanced functionality, this functional level requires you to have only Windows Server 2008 domain controllers throughout your entire domain. All of the features available in the previous two domain functional levels are available, as well as the following features:

- **SYSVOL replication using DFSR instead of NTFRS.** SYSVOL is a file share that is created on every Active Directory domain controller, the contents of which are replicated to every domain controller in the domain. Windows Server 2008 allows the use of the new Distributed File System Replication (DFSR) replication protocol to replicate SYSVOL instead of the legacy NT File Replication Service (NTFRS) protocol, which has proven cumbersome and difficult to troubleshoot and maintain in previous versions of Active Directory.
- **Additional encryption mechanisms for Active Directory authentication.** This includes support for 256-bit Advanced Encryption Services (AES) encryption for the Kerberos authentication protocol.
- **Improved auditing of user logon information.** This includes recording a user's last successful logon and which computer they logged into, as well as recording the number of failed logon attempts for a user and the time of the last failed logon attempt.

Additionally, the Windows Event Viewer can now capture "before and after" information when a change is made to Active Directory. If you change a user's first name from "William" to "Larry," the Event Viewer can show you the old value ("William") and the value that it was changed to ("Larry").

- **Multiple password policies per domain.** This is an exciting new feature of Windows Server 2008 Active Directory. In previous versions of Active Directory, you could only configure a single password policy per domain. For example, if you configured domain passwords with an eight-character minimum length that would expire every 42 days, you could not configure a more stringent policy setting for administrative accounts in your domain. At the Windows Server 2008 domain functional level, you can now configure multiple password policies within a single domain.

- **Read-Only Domain Controller.** Windows Server 2008 introduces the concept of the Read-Only Domain Controller (RODC), a special type of domain controller that maintains a read-only copy of the Active Directory database and does not perform any outbound replication of its own. To deploy an RODC in a Windows Server 2008 network, your domain must be at the Windows Server 2003 functional level or higher and you need to have at least one writeable 2008 domain controller deployed in the domain.

Before you can raise the domain functional level, you need to ensure that all domain controllers within that domain are running the required version of the Windows operating system. For example, to raise the domain functional level to Windows Server 2003, you must upgrade or retire any remaining Windows 2000 domain controllers in your environment.

Table 1-2 provides a summary of the different functional levels available in Windows Server 2008.

XREF

For more information about password policies, refer to Lesson 6.

TAKE NOTE

To raise the domain functional level, you need to be a member of the Domain Admins group for the domain in question.

Table 1-2

Summary of Domain Functional Levels

Domain Functional Level	Supported Operating Systems	Windows Server 2003 Features
Windows 2000 native	Windows 2000 Windows Server 2003 Windows Server 2008	Install from Media Application Directory partitions Drag-and-drop user interface Universal groups
Windows Server 2003	Windows Server 2003 Windows Server 2008	All Windows 2000 native features and the following: Replicated lastLogonTimestamp attribute User password on inetOrgPerson Domain rename
Windows Server 2008	Windows Server 2008	All Windows Server 2003 native features and the following: Improved SYSVOL replication Improved encryption for authentication methods Improved auditing of user logons Multiple password policies per domain

Using Forest Functional Levels

In most respects, forest functional levels are treated like domain functional levels. Advancing from a lower to a higher forest functional level is a one-way process that cannot be reversed.

Note that although domain functional levels can be independent of other domains in the forest, the forest functional level applies to all domains within that forest. Three forest functional levels are available within Windows Server 2008: Windows 2000, Windows Server 2003, and Windows Server 2008. As when dealing with domain functional levels, Windows Server 2008 Active Directory supports only domain controllers that are running Windows 2000, Windows Server 2003, and Windows Server 2008. Windows NT 4.0 domain controllers are *no longer supported.*

Windows 2000 is the default forest functionality enabled when the first Windows Server 2008 domain controller is introduced into the network. Just as in Windows 2000 native domain functionality, Windows 2000 forest functionality supports domain controllers running Windows 2000, Windows Server 2003, and Windows Server 2008. Windows 2000 is the default forest functional level for installations of new Windows Server 2008 Active Directory forests. The Windows 2000 forest functional features include:

- **Install from Media.** This is the same feature that was described in the Windows 2000 native domain functional level. It allows servers to be promoted to domain controllers using a backup replica from another domain controller.
- **Universal group caching.** This feature allows users to log on to a domain at a remote site without having a global catalog server present in that site.
- **Application Directory partitions.** Like the Windows 2000 native domain functionality, this allows a separate replication partition for application data that does not need to be globally available. It allows greater control over the scope of replication within a network.

The next forest functional level is Windows Server 2003, which requires that all domain controllers have Windows Server 2003 or Windows Server 2008 installed. Before raising the forest functional level, it is important to ensure that support for Windows 2000 domain controllers is no longer required. Raising the forest functional level is an irreversible procedure like raising the domain functional level. The Windows Server 2003 forest functional level includes all Windows Server 2000 features, as well as the following features:

- **Improved replication of group objects.** In Windows 2000, whenever you make a change to the member list of a group object, the entire member list is replicated throughout the domain. By raising the forest functional level to Windows Server 2003, Active Directory can take advantage of *link-value replication*, which will replicate only the portions of the member list that have actually been added, modified, or deleted.
- **Dynamic auxiliary class objects.** This is a new schema modification option that provides support for dynamically linking auxiliary classes to individual objects. Prior to this functionality, an auxiliary class object could be linked only to an entire class of objects.
- **User objects can be converted to inetOrgPerson objects.** The inetOrgPerson object is used by non–Microsoft LDAP directory services, such as Novell. This new base object in Windows Server 2003 allows easier migration of objects from these other platforms.
- **Schema deactivations.** Windows Server 2003 allows you to deactivate (though not delete) classes or attributes that have been added to the schema.
- **Domain rename.** Domains can be renamed within this functional level to accommodate major design changes on your network.
- **Cross-forest trusts permitted.** This trust type was introduced in Windows Server 2003 and allows resources to be shared between Active Directory forests. Trust relationships are described in the next section.
- **Improved Intersite Topology Generator (ISTG).** ISTG is the process used to initiate the creation and management of the replication topology between sites. In Windows 2000, this feature was limited by the number of sites in the forest. In Windows Server 2003, this feature scales to allow a greater number of sites.

TAKE NOTE*

In a forest that is configured at the Windows Server 2003 forest functional level, any new child domains will automatically be created at the Windows Server 2003 domain functional level.

The Windows Server 2003 forest functional level assumes that all domains have been raised to Windows Server 2003 before the forest is raised. All new features and enhancements become available. However, note that all new domain controllers introduced into the domain must be installed as a Windows Server 2003 product.

The highest available forest functional level is Windows Server 2008. In the present release of Active Directory, the Windows Server 2008 functional level does not unlock any new functionality within Active Directory. Its primary purpose is to ensure that once the forest functional level has been raised to Windows Server 2008, any new child domains that are added to the forest will automatically be created at the Windows Server 2008 domain functional level. This ensures that all new child domains have immediate access to the advanced functionality of the Windows Server 2008 domain functional level, as well as preventing any down-level domain controllers from being added to the forest.

Use the following guidelines to raise the forest functional level:

- To raise the functional level of a forest, you must be logged on as a member of the Enterprise Admins group.
- The functional level of a forest can be raised only by connecting to the DC that holds the Schema Master role. This server is the authority for all schema changes.
- All domain controllers in the entire forest must be running an operating system supported by the targeted forest functional level.
- Raising the forest functional level to the highest level, Windows Server 2008, requires that all domains within the forest be at the Windows Server 2008 functional level.
- During a forest functional level advancement, all domains will automatically be raised to support the new forest functional level.
- Raising the forest functional level is an irreversible procedure.

Table 1-3 provides a summary of the forest functional levels and the included features.

For more information about the Schema Master role, refer to Lesson 4.

Table 1-3

Summary of Forest Functional Levels

FOREST FUNCTIONAL LEVEL	SUPPORTED OPERATING SYSTEMS	WINDOWS SERVER 2003 FEATURES
Windows 2000	Windows 2000 Windows Server 2003 Windows Server 2008	Install from Media Universal group caching Application Directory partitions Enhanced user interface
Windows Server 2003	Windows Server 2003 Windows Server 2008	All Windows 2000 functionality and the following: Linked-value replication Improved ISTG functionality User objects can be converted to inetOrgPerson objects Schema modifications to attributes and classes Can create instances of Dynamic Auxiliary class objects called dynamicObjects Domain renaming Cross-forest trusts All new domains will be created at the Windows Server 2003 domain functional level
Windows Server 2008	Windows Server 2008	All new domains will be created at the Windows Server 2008 domain functional level

Understanding Active Directory Trust Models

X REF

You can find more information about trust relationships in Lesson 2.

Active Directory uses *trust relationships* to allow access between multiple domains and/or forests, either within a single forest or across multiple enterprise networks. As the name implies, a trust relationship allows administrators from a particular domain to grant access to their domain's resources to users in other domains.

To see trust relationships in action, consider this example. A book publisher called Lucerne Publishing has entered into a business agreement with Wingtip Toys, a child's toy manufacturer, in preparation for an anticipated merger. To allow the Wingtip Toys R&D department to access design files on the Lucerne Publishing file servers, the administrators of the Lucerne Publishing domain need to establish a trust relationship with the Wingtip Toys Active Directory.

To ease the Active Directory administrative process, certain trust relationships are created automatically during the Active Directory installation process. A two-way trust means that users from Domain A can access resources in Domain B, and users in Domain B can simultaneously access resources in Domain A. A transitive trust relationship harkens back to days of middle-school mathematics—it means that if Domain A trusts Domain B and Domain B trusts Domain C, then Domain A automatically trusts Domain C. The trust relationships in an Active Directory forest are structured as follows:

- When a child domain is created, it automatically receives a two-way transitive trust with its parent domain. So the sales.tokyo.lucernepublishers.com child domain has a two-way transitive trust with its tokyo.lucernepublishers.com parent domain. And, because of trust transitivity (tokyo.lucernepublishers.com has a two-way transitive trust with its lucernepublishers.com parent domain), the users in the sales "grandchild" domain can access resources in the lucernepublishers.com "grandparent" domain and vice versa.

- When a new domain tree is created, the root domain in the new tree automatically receives a two-way transitive trust with the root domain. So, if the graphicdesigninstitute.com forest includes a separate domain tree called fineartschool.net, a two-way transitive trust is configured between the root domains. Due to the transitive nature of the trust, any child domains in the graphicdesigninstitute.com tree will be able to access resources in child domains in the fineartschool.net tree and vice versa. Likewise, any additional domain trees will receive a two-way transitive trust with the forest root domain.

Figure 1-3 illustrates the transitive nature of trust relationships between domains in an Active Directory forest. Note that each child domain is linked to its parent domain, continuing up

Figure 1-3

Domain trust model

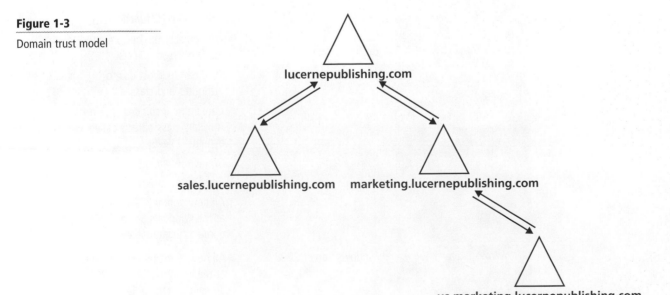

to the forest root domain. If a user in sales.lucernepublishing.com needs access to a resource in us.marketing.lucernepublishing.com, the request is sent up from the sales child domain to the lucernepublishing root domain. From there, it is sent to the marketing child domain and finally to its destination in the us.marketing.lucernepublishing.com domain. This process is called tree-walking.

If the domains within a forest are separated by slow WAN links and this tree-walking process takes an exceedingly long time to allow user authentication across domains, you can configure a *shortcut trust* along a commonly used "trust path." Therefore, if users in tokyo.lucernepublishing.com require frequent access to resources in marketing.us.tailspintoys.com, you can create a shortcut trust to "short-circuit" the tree-walking process and form a direct trust path between the two domains, as shown in Figure 1-4. These shortcut trusts are transitive and can be one-way or two-way in nature.

Figure 1-4

Shortcut trust

Another type of trust that you can create is an *external trust* with a Windows NT domain or a Windows 2000 domain in a separate forest. Similar to shortcut trusts, external trusts are one-way, nontransitive trusts. If users in your domain are able to access resources in a remote domain, users in the remote domain will *not* be able to access resources in your domain unless you create a second trust relationship in the opposite direction. Similarly, if your organization creates a trust with Vendor A and Vendor A subsequently creates a trust relationship with Vendor B, your users will *not* be able to access resources on Vendor B's network. You would need to create a separate trust directly linking your Active Directory with Vendor B's Active Directory. Also, in the case of a remote Windows 2000 Active Directory domain, because an external trust is nontransitive, you will only have access to the specific domain for which the trust has been configured. If you configure a trust with the tokyo.lucernepublishing.com domain, you will not be able to access resources in the lucernepublishing.com domain without configuring a separate trust with lucernepublishing.com directly.

Beginning at the Windows Server 2003 functional level, you also have the ability to create a new type of trust called a ***cross-forest trust***. With Windows NT or Windows 2000 domain controllers in place, it is not possible to create a transitive trust path between forests. Resource access from one forest to another was unsupported. When you are establishing a trust between two forests that are both running at the Windows Server 2003 forest functional level or better, cross-forest trust relationships are transitive in nature and they can be configured as either a one-way or two-way relationship. This means that every domain in Forest A trusts every resource in Forest B and (in the case of a two-way cross-forest trust) every domain in Forest B trusts every resource in Forest A, as shown in Figure 1-5.

Figure 1-5

Cross-forest trust

lucernepublishing.com   wingtiptoys.com

sales.lucernepublishing.com   sales.wingtiptoys.com   marketing.wingtiptoys.com

 WARNING The transitivity of a cross-forest trust does not extend beyond two forests. This means that if you've configured a cross-forest trust between Forest A and Forest B and a second cross-forest trust between Forest B and Forest C, Forest A would *not* be able to access resources in Forest C unless you configure a third trust relationship directly between Forest A and Forest C.

Once the trust is established, administrators can select users and groups from a trusted forest and include them on the ACL of an object. When a resource is accessed via the cross-forest trust, the user is not required to reenter any logon credentials; you have achieved "single sign-on" across forest boundaries. This advanced feature allows corporations to share resources with partners or new acquisitions without a complete design change or migration.

SUMMARY SKILL MATRIX

IN THIS LESSON YOU LEARNED:

- Active Directory is a database of objects that are used to organize resources according to a logical plan. These objects include containers such as domains and OUs in addition to resources such as users, computers, and printers.

- The Active Directory schema includes definitions of all objects and attributes within a single forest. Each forest maintains its own Active Directory schema.

- Active Directory requires DNS to support SRV records. In addition, Microsoft recommends that DNS support dynamic updates.

- Domain and forest functional levels are new features of Windows Server 2008. The levels defined for each of these are based on the type of server operating systems that are required by the Active Directory design. The Windows Server 2003 forest functional level is the highest functional level available and includes support for all Windows Server 2003 features.

- Two-way transitive trusts are automatically generated within the Active Directory domain structure. Parent and child domains form the trust path by which all domains in the forest can traverse to locate resources. The ISTG is responsible for this process.

- Cross-forest trusts are new to Windows Server 2003, and they are only available when the forest functionality is set to Windows Server 2003. They must be manually created and maintained.

Knowledge Assessment

Fill in the Blank

Complete the following sentences by writing the correct word or words in the blanks provided.

1. The Active Directory database is stored on each domain controller in a file called
   _____.

2. The Active Directory _____ is considered the security boundary for an Active Directory environment.

3. To provide fault tolerance, Active Directory utilizes a(n) _____ replication model.

4. To create a trust relationship with an NT4 domain, you will configure a(n) _____.

5. The _____ naming context is replicated across the domain.

6. The _____ of an Active Directory object identifies its location within the directory structure.

7. A(n) _____ provides a two-way transitive trust relationship between all domains within two forests.

8. Each domain in an Active Directory forest has a(n) _____ trust relationship with every other domain in a forest.

9. _____ allows a user at a remote site to be able to log into Active Directory without needing to contact a global catalog server.

10. Active Directory clients rely on _____ in DNS to locate Active Directory resources such as domain controllers and global catalog servers.

Multiple Choice

Circle the correct choice.

1. Which of the following items is a valid leaf object in Active Directory?
   a. Domain
   b. User
   c. Application partition
   d. OU

2. Which of the following domain controllers can be joined to a forest that is currently set at the Windows Server 2008 forest functional level?
   a. Windows 2000
   b. Windows Server 2003
   c. Windows Server 2008
   d. Windows NT 4.0

3. You are planning an Active Directory implementation for a company that currently has sales, accounting, and marketing departments. All department heads want to manage their own users and resources in Active Directory. What feature will permit you to set up Active Directory to allow each manager to manage his or her own container but not any other containers?
   a. Delegation of control
   b. Read-Only Domain Controller
   c. Multimaster replication
   d. SRV records

4. What is required by DNS for Active Directory to function?
   a. Dynamic update support
   b. DHCP forwarding support
   c. SRV records support
   d. Active Directory integration

5. If the user named Amy is located in the sales OU of the central.cohowinery.com domain, what is the correct syntax for referencing this user in a command-line utility?
   a. amy.cohowinery.com
   b. cn=amy.ou=sales.dc=cohowinery.com
   c. cn=amy,ou=sales,dc=central,dc=cohowinery,dc=com
   d. dc=com,dn=cohowinery,ou=sales,cn=amy

6. RODCs do not participate in which of the following?
   a. Replication
   b. Cross-forest trusts
   c. Outbound replication
   d. External trusts

7. Which naming context contains forest-wide data about the physical topology of an Active Directory forest?
   a. Schema
   b. ForestDNSZones
   c. Configuration
   d. DomainDNSZones

8. Which of the following is a container object within Active Directory?
   a. Folder
   b. Group
   c. User
   d. OU

9. What is the first domain installed in a new Active Directory forest called?
   a. Forest root domain
   b. Parent root domain
   c. Domain tree root
   d. Domain root

10. Which of the following is the security boundary within Active Directory?
    a. Forest
    b. Domain
    c. Domain tree
    d. OU

■ Workplace Ready

Deploying Windows Server 2008

You are the manager for the IT department of a large organization. Your company currently has a mixed environment of Novell, Microsoft Windows NT, and Windows 2000 servers. You are working with a network designer to assist in planning an upgrade of all servers to Windows Server 2008 over the next six months. Consider that the rollout will take place in phases and that the goal is minimal downtime. Which new features in Windows Server 2008 will help you with this migration? Why will these new features assist you in your migration of the network?

In addition, your company recently acquired another company. The new acquisition company already has a Windows Server 2008 network in place that you want to maintain. However, you would like to provide access to resources in both networks. What should you do to establish a path between the two networks? What do you need to check before doing so?

Implementing Active Directory

OBJECTIVE DOMAIN MATRIX

Technology Skill	Objective Domain	Objective Domain Number
Installing a New Active Directory Forest	Configure a forest or a domain.	2.1
Configuring a Read-Only Domain Controller	Configure the Read-Only Domain Controller (RODC).	3.3
Configuring Active Directory Lightweight Directory Services	Configure Active Directory Lightweight Directory Services (AD LDS).	3.1
Establishing and Maintaining Trust Relationships	Configure trusts.	2.2

KEY TERMS

A record
Active Directory Lightweight Directory Services (AD LDS)
Admin Role Separation
aging
binaries
dcpromo
Directory Services Restore Mode (DSRM)
domain netBIOS name
dynamic updates
Flexible Single Master Operations (FSMO)

forward lookup zone
fully qualified domain name (FQDN)
global catalog
incremental zone transfers
instance
latency
netdom
nslookup
Object Identifier (OID)
Password Replication Policy
pointer (PTR)
priority

restartable Active Directory
reverse lookup zone
scavenging
Server Core
Server Manager
staged installation
SYSVOL
time-to-live
unattended installation
User Principal Name (UPN)
weight
zone transfers

Lucerne Publishing is a publisher of medical textbooks that maintains offices in London, Tokyo, New York, and Bangalore. Lucerne Publishing has decided to deploy Windows Server 2008 to provide centralized authentication and authorization of users across their worldwide locations. One challenge facing Lucerne Publishing is the fact that the Tokyo branch office is not staffed by a full-time IT administrator. Because it is connected to New York and London via a slow WAN link, the manager of the Tokyo location is concerned that staff in this office will have difficulties logging onto Active Directory.

After completing this lesson, you will understand the necessary prerequisites for installing the Active Directory Domain Services (AD DS) role on a Windows Server 2008 computer. You will also learn the procedures involved in creating a new Active Directory forest, domain tree, and domain. You will be able to discuss an exciting new feature of AD DS in Windows Server 2008, the Read-Only Domain Controller (RODC). Finally, you will be able to discuss the requirements for modifying the Active Directory schema as well as installing and configuring the Active Directory Lightweight Directory Services (AD LDS), formerly known as ADAM in previous versions of the Windows operating system.

■ Introducing the Server Manager

THE BOTTOM LINE

Before you begin working in Windows Server 2008, you need to be familiar with the central administrative interface. When you boot up a Windows Server 2008 server, you will see a window similar to that shown in Figure 2-1.

Figure 2-1

Server Manager

Windows Server 2008 provides a new unified tool for administering all aspects of a particular server. When a Windows Server 2008 server boots for the first time, you will see the Initial Configuration Tasks window that allows you to perform initial configuration tasks, such as setting the computer name and configuring the Windows Firewall. You can add roles to a 2008 server from the Initial Configuration Tasks (ICT) interface or from the Server Manager console in the Administrative Tools folder. From here, you can add and remove different server roles (such as the DNS server role or the Active Directory Domain Services role), as well as perform system diagnostics; configure system services, such as the Windows Firewall; and drill down into specific administrative tools, such as the DNS Management Console or Active Directory Users and Computers.

Designing an Active Directory Implementation

↓ THE BOTTOM LINE

This lesson focuses on the process used to install and configure Active Directory, including the important points you must understand to prepare for installation and key post-installation tasks. In particular, this lesson describes the key concepts involved in deploying the Microsoft Windows Server 2008 Active Directory forest.

Understanding the Requirements for Active Directory

You will install Active Directory by configuring one or more domain controllers within your Windows Server 2008 network and then configuring your clients to authenticate against these domain controllers. Before you begin, you need to understand the hardware requirements for installing Active Directory. In addition, you need to be able to size your domain controller hardware appropriately to support the size and scope of your organization's Active Directory requirements.

Generally speaking, you can configure Active Directory on any server that has been configured with a Windows 2000, Windows Server 2003, or Windows Server 2008–based operating system that has been secured with the most up-to-date service packs and hot fixes. The Active Directory Installation Wizard, *dcpromo*, will guide you through any of the following installation scenarios:

- Adding a domain controller to an existing environment
- Creating an entirely new forest structure
- Adding a child domain to an existing domain
- Adding a new domain tree to an existing forest
- Demoting domain controllers and eventually removing a domain or forest

Before installing a Windows Server 2008 Active Directory, consider the following hardware, software, and administrative requirements:

- A server running Windows Server 2008 Standard Edition, Windows Server 2008 Enterprise Edition, or Windows Server 2008 Datacenter Edition. You can install Active Directory on the full version of Windows Server 2008 as well as Server Core, a new installation option in Windows Server 2008.
- An administrator account and password on the local machine.
- An NT file system (NTFS) partition for the **SYSVOL** folder structure. The SYSVOL shared folder exists on all domain controllers and is used to store Group Policy Objects, login scripts, and other files that are replicated domain-wide.
- 200 MB minimum free space on the previously mentioned NTFS partition for Active Directory database files.
- 50 MB minimum free space for the transaction log files. These files can be located on the same partition as the database files or elsewhere. However, to achieve optimal performance, these files should be located on a physical drive other than the one holding the operating system. Placing the database and log files on separate hard drives results in better performance because they do not need to compete for the input/output (I/O) processes of a single drive.
- Transmission Control Protocol/Internet Protocol (TCP/IP) must be installed and configured to use DNS.
- An authoritative DNS server for the DNS domain that supports service resource (SRV) records. Microsoft also recommends that the server providing DNS for Active Directory be able to support *incremental zone transfers* and dynamic updates. A *zone transfer* is the process of replicating DNS information from one DNS server to another. With an

TAKE NOTE*

Keep in mind that these are minimum installation requirements; in a real deployment, you should configure domain controllers with sufficient capacity to allow current requirements as well as any future expansion.

incremental zone transfer, bandwidth is conserved because the entire zone does not have to be transferred. Only the changes are transferred. When the Internet Protocol (IP) address of a host changes, *dynamic updates* allow the DNS database to be updated with the changed information. This allows more efficiency in the maintenance of the database, resulting in fewer resolution problems for clients.

Before you can install Active Directory, you will also need to know the potential size of the Active Directory database. Active Directory space requirements per object are much smaller than you might think. The approximate sizes of objects and attributes in Active Directory are as follows:

- Security principal (User, Group, Computer) = 3,600 bytes
- Organizational unit (OU) = 1,100 bytes
- Security certificates mapped to a user = 1,500 bytes
- Object attributes = ~100 bytes
- Access Control Entry (ACE) = 70 bytes per ACE

Taking these sizing requirements into consideration, a user account having 20 attributes and a certificate will take up approximately 7100 bytes of space. When planning space requirements, you need to know the approximate number and types of objects you need to accommodate. After doing some simple math, you will find that the Active Directory database takes up relatively little space considering the amount of information it contains. Always be prepared to pad your final number to ensure that you are not caught short in case you need to expand beyond your original projections.

Prior to running the Active Directory Installation Wizard, you should gather all of the information you will need during the installation process, which includes the following:

- Local administrator password
- Domain controller type
- Domain name
- Location for the Active Directory database and log files. This defaults to C:\WINDOWS\NTDS, but for larger Active Directory installations you can improve performance by moving these files to a separate disk controller.
- Desired location for the SYSVOL folder structure, which is used to store administrative items such as Group Policy Objects and login scripts. This defaults to C:\WINDOWS\SYSVOL, but can also be moved to improve performance on larger installs.
- DNS information, such as whether DNS will be installed on the same server as Active Directory. If not, then you need to have the IP addresses of one or more DNS servers.
- *Directory Services Restore Mode (DSRM)* password. This is a separate password that is used to access Active Directory during data restore or disaster-recovery scenarios.
- The installation CD-ROM or the location of the installation files if you are installing from a network folder.
- Ensure that you have installed the most up-to-date service packs and hot fixes on the server.

After you have gathered this prerequisite information, you can start the installation process as described in the following section.

TAKE NOTE *

Windows Server 2008 provides a new *restartable Active Directory* feature, which allows you to place the ntds.dit file in an offline mode without rebooting the domain controller outright.

Installing a New Active Directory Forest

The first Active Directory domain on the network is the forest root domain. The forest root domain is critical to the functioning of Active Directory because it needs to remain online and in place for the lifetime of an Active Directory installation. You can add and remove child domains and additional domain trees as the needs of your organization grow and change, but the forest root domain must remain in place.

You can launch the Active Directory Installation Wizard using the dcpromo.exe command-line tool or from the ***Server Manager*** utility that's installed in the Administrative Tools folder of each Windows Server 2008 server. The Server Manager utility launches automatically at startup after you close the Initial Configuration Tasks utility, or you can access it manually through the shortcut provided in the Administrative Tools folder or directly from the Start menu. The advantage of the Server Manager interface is that it will allow you to view any other roles the server might be performing. However, using dcpromo will allow you to script or automate the installation process.

The first domain controller installed in a new Active Directory forest will hold all of the ***Flexible Single Master Operations (FSMO)*** roles, which are specific server roles that work together to enable the multimaster functionality of Active Directory. The dcpromo process assigns per-forest and per-domain FSMO roles in each new domain that you add to Active Directory. By default, all forest-wide FSMOs will be configured on the first domain controller installed in the entire forest, and all domain-wide FSMOs will be configured on the first domain controller installed in a new domain. For example, modifying the schema is a per-forest role because the Active Directory schema is shared among all domains in a forest. The server holding the Schema Master operations role must be accessible to all domains in the forest. After the initial domain controller creation, additional domain controllers can be installed and the roles can be transferred to the new domain controllers.

CERTIFICATION READY?
Configure a forest or a domain
2.1

INSTALL A NEW ACTIVE DIRECTORY FOREST

GET READY. You must be logged on as a member of the local Administrators group to begin this process; the server computer should be configured with a static IP address.

1. Click the **Start** menu and select **Server Manager**.
2. Click **Roles** and then click **Add Roles** under the Roles Summary section.
3. Read the Before You Begin window and click **Next**.
4. On the Select Server Roles window, select **Active Directory Domain Services**, as shown in Figure 2-2.

Figure 2-2

Select server role

Add Roles Wizard

Select Server Roles

Before You Begin
Select Server Roles
Active Directory Domain Services
Confirm Installation Selections
Installation Progress
Installation Results

Select one or more roles to install on this server.

Roles:

- [ ] Active Directory Certificate Services
- [x] Active Directory Domain Services
- [ ] Active Directory Federation Services
- [ ] Active Directory Lightweight Directory Services
- [ ] Active Directory Rights Management Services
- [ ] Application Server
- [ ] DHCP Server
- [ ] DNS Server
- [ ] Fax Server
- [ ] File Services
- [ ] Network Policy and Access Services
- [ ] Print Services
- [ ] Terminal Services
- [ ] UDDI Services
- [ ] Web Server (IIS)
- [ ] Windows Deployment Services
- [ ] Windows SharePoint Services

Description:
Active Directory Domain Services (AD DS) stores information about objects on the network and makes this information available to users and network administrators. AD DS uses domain controllers to give network users access to permitted resources anywhere on the network through a single logon process.

More about server roles

< Previous   Next >   Install   Cancel

5. Click **Next** to continue. You are presented with an introduction to Active Directory Domain Services that provides a number of helpful hints for installing and administering Active Directory. The tips include the following points:

   • Be sure to install more than one domain controller in each Active Directory domain so that clients can log on even if a single domain controller fails.

   • Active Directory requires an available DNS server on the network.

   • Installing Active Directory will also add the following prerequisite services to the server: *DFS Namespace, DFS Replication*, and the *File Replication Service*.

6. Click **Next** after you read the Introduction to AD Domain Services window.

7. Click **Install** to begin the installation process. The Server Manager will appear to pause for a few minutes because the actual executable files or *binaries* that are needed to install Active Directory are being copied to the system drive. A significant security improvement in Windows Server 2008 is that these binaries (installation files) are not actually installed until you choose to install Active Directory; this prevents any viruses or worms from targeting these files if the server is not configured as a domain controller because the files in question are not present on the hard disk.

8. After the AD DS binaries have installed, click **Close**. You are returned to Server Manager, which will now resemble the window shown in Figure 2-3. Notice that the Active Directory Domain Services role is listed, but it has a red 'X' next to it. This indicates that the AD DS binaries have been installed on the server, but Active Directory has not been completely configured.

Figure 2-3

Active Directory Domain Services role installed but not configured

9. Drill down to the Active Directory Domain Service role, which will take you to a window similar to the one shown in Figure 2-4.

Figure 2-4

Active Directory Domain Services summary

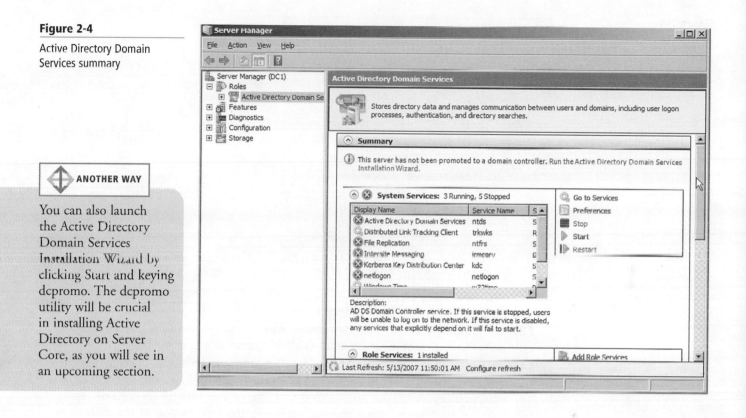

ANOTHER WAY

You can also launch the Active Directory Domain Services Installation Wizard by clicking Start and keying dcpromo. The dcpromo utility will be crucial in installing Active Directory on Server Core, as you will see in an upcoming section.

10. Follow the instructions you see on the window and click **Run the Active Directory Domain Services Wizard**. The Active Directory Domain Services Installation Wizard will launch as shown in Figure 2-5. Place a checkmark next to **Use Advanced Mode Installation**.

Figure 2-5

Active Directory Domain Services Wizard

11. Read the information and click **Next** in two windows to display the window shown in Figure 2-6.

Figure 2-6

Choose a deployment configuration

12. To create the first domain controller in a new Active Directory forest, select **Create a new domain in a new forest** and click **Next.**

13. You are prompted to enter the domain name of the Active Directory forest root domain. In this case, key **lucernepublishing.com** and click **Next.**

14. You are prompted to fill in the *domain netBIOS name* for this domain. The domain netBIOS name is limited to 15 characters and is maintained for legacy compatibility with older applications that cannot use DNS for their name resolution. In most cases, this name will simply be the first portion of the *fully qualified domain name (FQDN)*—LUCERNEPUBLISHING in the case of the lucernepublishing.com FQDN or SALES in the case of sales.lucernepublishing.com. However, because LUCERNEPUBLISHING is longer than 15 characters, you must select a shorter name. Enter **LP** as the domain netBIOS name as shown Figure 2-7 and click **Next.**

Figure 2-7

Enter the Domain NetBIOS name

15. You are prompted to select the forest functional level (FFL) and domain functional level (DFL) of the new domain and the new forest. As discussed in Lesson 1, the FFL and DFL are used to control what operating systems can be installed as domain controllers within a domain or forest. Raising the DFL or FFL will enable more functionality within Active Directory because it reduces the need to coexist with legacy operating systems. Select **Windows Server 2003** as the forest functional level and then click **Next**.

16. Select **Windows Server** 2003 as the domain functional level and then click **Next**.

17. Next, you could select one or more of the following domain controller options for this domain controller:

   • **DNS Server**. This option is checked by default and will allow the domain controller to perform DNS name resolution. Leave this box selected.

   • *Global Catalog*. This option is selected and grayed out for the first domain controller in a new domain because Active Directory requires that at least one global catalog be installed in each domain.

   • **Read-Only Domain Controller (RODC)**. This option is unavailable for the first domain controller in a new domain because the first domain controller cannot be an RODC.

   As shown in Figure 2-8, the DNS Server option is selected by default. Click **Next** without making any changes.

Figure 2-8

Choose additional domain controller options

See "Working with Read-Only Domain Controllers" later in this lesson for information on the Read-Only Domain Controller.

TAKE NOTE* You may receive a dialog box in step 17 that says "A delegation for this DNS Server will not be created because the authoritative parent zone cannot be found or it does not support dynamic updates. To ensure this DNS Server can be resolved as authoritative for the domain test.com, you can create a delegation to this DNS Server manually in the parent zone. Do you want to continue?" Click Yes to continue. This is a new step in the dcpromo process to ensure that your parent DNS zone (if you have one) contains a delegation for the DNS zone that you are creating. See the article, *Configuring DNS for the Forest Root Domain* on the Microsoft TechNet site for more information.

18. In the window shown in Figure 2-9, you can select the disk locations for the Active Directory database, log files, and the SYSVOL shared folder. Click **Next** to accept the default locations.

Figure 2-9

Choose disk locations

![Active Directory Domain Services Installation Wizard - Location for Database, Log Files, and SYSVOL]

Active Directory Domain Services Installation Wizard

Location for Database, Log Files, and SYSVOL
Specify the folders that will contain the Active Directory domain controller database, log files, and SYSVOL.

For best performance and recoverability, store the database and log files on separate volumes.

Database folder:
C:\Windows\NTDS   Browse...

Log files folder:
C:\Windows\NTDS   Browse...

SYSVOL folder:
C:\Windows\SYSVOL   Browse...

More about placing Active Directory Domain Services files

< Back   Next >   Cancel

TAKE NOTE *

The DSRM password is not stored in Active Directory. Be sure to keep a record of this password in a secure location for later access.

19. You are prompted to enter the Directory Services Restore Mode (DSRM) password that is used to access Directory Services Restore Mode to perform maintenance and disaster-recovery operations on your domain controller. Enter a strong password and click **Next** to continue.

20. In Figure 2-10, you see the Summary window, which will allow you to review your configuration choices before configuring this server as a domain controller. Pay special attention to the Export Settings button on this window. You can use this button to create a text file that can be used to automate the installation of additional domain controllers from the command line. For now, click **Next** to begin the installation process.

> **X REF**
> See "Installing Active Directory on Server Core" later in this lesson for information on the automation process used to configure a domain controller on Server Core.

Figure 2-10

Review selections

![Active Directory Domain Services Installation Wizard - Summary]

Active Directory Domain Services Installation Wizard

Summary

Review your selections:

Configure this server as the first Active Directory domain controller in a new forest of domain trees.

The new domain name is lucernepublishing.com. This is also the name of the new forest.

The NetBIOS name of the domain is LP

Forest Functional Level: Windows Server 2003

Domain Functional Level: Windows Server 2003

Site: Default-First-Site-Name

To change an option, click Back. To begin the operation, click Next.

These settings can be exported to an answer file for use with other unattended operations.
More about using an answer file   Export settings...

< Back   Next >   Cancel

PAUSE. After the installation process has completed, click **Finish** and **Restart Now to** reboot the newly configured domain controller when prompted.

You have just created the first domain controller in an Active Directory forest root domain. You will build on this exercise to create additional domain controllers, including Read-Only Domain Controllers and domain controllers running Server Core.

Performing Post-Installation Tasks

Upon completion of the Active Directory installation, you should verify a number of items before you consider it complete. The following sections discuss the basic items needed to create an Active Directory infrastructure that performs well and is somewhat fault tolerant.

The first post-installation tasks revolve around the DNS Server service. Although you installed DNS as part of the Active Directory installation process, you should verify several items before considering that the installation is complete and operational:

- Application directory partition creation
- Aging and scavenging for zones
- Forward lookup zones and SRV records
- Reverse lookup zones

CREATING A DIRECTORY PARTITION

Start by verifying that the DNS application directory partitions were created successfully. Application directory partitions are used to separate forest-wide DNS information from domain-wide DNS information to control the scope of replication of different types of DNS data. Although DNS automatically sets the scope for each set of DNS data, the scope can be configured independently and added, if necessary, using the DNS administration tools that are installed with Windows Server 2008. The information stored in an application partition can be configured to replicate to any domain controller in the forest, even if the chosen domain controllers are not all in the same domain. As far as DNS is concerned, application directory partitions allow you to control which DNS data is replicated within a single domain or throughout the entire forest.

Two zones within the DNS application directory partition are installed as a part of the Active Directory Installation Wizard. Using lucernepublishing.com as a reference, Table 2-1 describes the zone type and the default zone name that you just installed.

Table 2-1

Default Active Directory Application Partitions for lucernepublishing.com

Zone Type	Zone Name	Purpose
DomainDnsZones	DomainDnsZone. lucernepublishing.com	A single partition that allows DNS information to be replicated to all domain controllers running DNS within the domain.
ForestDnsZones	ForestDnsZones. lucernepublishing.com	A single partition that contains all DNS servers in the forest. Zones stored here are replicated to all DNS servers running on domain controllers in the entire forest.

The following points are key to understanding application directory partitions:

- Application directory partitions are automatically created when installing Active Directory Integrated DNS.
- You must be a member of the Enterprise Admins group to create or modify an application directory partition.

- If you were unable to create an application directory partition during the Active Directory Installation Wizard, you can do so manually at a later time; if this partition already exists, the option to create an application directory partition will not exist.

CONFIGURING AGING AND SCAVENGING

The next task relating to DNS is setting up *aging* and *scavenging* of DNS records on your DNS servers. Although not enabled by default, aging and scavenging are processes that can be used by Windows Server 2008 DNS to clean up the DNS database after DNS records become "stale" or out of date. Without this process, the DNS database would require manual maintenance to prevent server performance degradation and potential disk-space issues.

CONFIGURE AGING AND SCAVENGING

GET READY. You must be a member of the local Administrators or the DNS Admins group to perform these steps.

1. Select the **DNS** tool from the Administrative Tools folder.
2. Right-click the desired DNS server, and click **Set Aging/Scavenging** for all zones. The window shown in Figure 2-11 is displayed.

Figure 2-11

Server Aging/Scavenging Properties dialog box

3. Select the **Scavenge Stale Resource Records** checkbox.
4. Click **OK** to save your changes. You will then see the window shown in Figure 2-12, which allows you to automatically enable scavenging for all existing Active Directory–integrated DNS zones.

Figure 2-12

Server Aging/Scavenging Confirmation dialog box

TAKE NOTE*

The remaining steps configure an individual DNS zone for aging and scavenging.

5. Place a checkmark next to **Apply these settings to the existing Active Directory–integrated zones**. Click **OK** to continue.
6. Open DNS in the Administrative Tools folder.
7. Right-click the desired zone and select **Properties** from the submenu.

8. Click the **General** tab and click **Aging**.

9. Select the **Scavenge Stale Resource Records** checkbox.

10. Modify any other desired properties and click **Apply** to save any changes.

PAUSE. Aging and scavenging has been configured.

The dynamic update feature of Windows Server 2008 DNS allows computers using Windows 2000, Windows XP, Windows 2003, or Windows Server 2008 to add their IP addresses and names to the DNS database automatically. Manual intervention from an IT administrator is not needed. When the IP address is added, a timestamp is placed on the record based on the current server time.

Scavenging is the process of removing records that were not refreshed or updated within specified time intervals, which will occur naturally with machines that are removed from the network. Because their records will not be updated or refreshed, all timers will expire. Aging and scavenging must be configured for the DNS server and all desired zones on the server. To configure the DNS server for aging and scavenging, complete the steps in the following section.

VERIFYING THE CREATION OF A FORWARD LOOKUP ZONE

Next, you will verify that the appropriate DNS records were created during the Active Directory Installation Wizard process. *Forward lookup zones* are necessary for computer hostname–to–IP address mappings, which are used for name resolution by a variety of services. For example, when a user requests access to a server based on its host name, the request is passed to a DNS server to resolve the host name to an IP address. Most queries are based on forward lookups.

VERIFY THE CREATION OF A FORWARD LOOKUP ZONE

GET READY. Following the Active Directory installation, perform the following steps on the DNS server that your domain controller is pointing to for name resolution.

1. Open DNS from the Administrative Tools folder.

2. Under DNS, expand your server.

3. Expand the Forward Lookup Zones heading. You should see the currently configured forward lookup zones.

   - ._msdcs.lucernepublishing.com
   - lucernepublishing.com

PAUSE. The forward lookup zone has been created.

Support for SRV records is required by Active Directory in Windows 2000, Windows Server 2003, and Windows Server 2008. SRV records are used by DNS to provide mappings of services to the computers that provide them. For example, when Active Directory is installed on a server, the server becomes a domain controller as well as a Netlogon server. Clients attempting to authenticate to an Active Directory network need to locate a Netlogon server. If a server named Server2 in the lucernepublishing.com domain is configured as a domain controller, it dynamically registers itself with DNS at startup. This registration includes an *A record* for the server name and any appropriate SRV records for services running on the server. An A record is the building block of DNS that maps a single IP address to a DNS host name. For example, an A record might map the IP address 192.168.1.142 to the host name server1.lucernepublishing.com. One SRV record is registered for each service the server is configured to provide. Clients attempting to authenticate to the network will use DNS to help them find an appropriate domain controller based on the requested service. SRV records can be found by default in the forward lookup zone of DNS.

When Active Directory is installed, a DNS domain named .msdcs.*DnsDomainName* is created. This domain contains records that reflect the specific services provided and the servers to which these services are mapped. Each SRV record follows a specific format beginning with the service being provided, and each record includes the following information:

- **Protocol.** Either TCP or UDP
- **Domain name.** The domain name corresponding to this record. In this case, lucernepublishing.com is the domain name.
- *Time-to-live.* The length of time for which this record is valid, after which it needs to be reregistered
- *Priority.* A mechanism to set up load balancing between multiple servers that are advertising the same SRV records. Clients will always use the record with the lower-numbered priority first. They will only use an SRV record with a higher-numbered priority if the server corresponding to the lower-numbered priority record is unavailable.
- *Weight.* A relative weighting for SRV records that have the same priority. For example, consider three SRV records with the same priority with relative weights of 60, 20, and 20. Because 60 + 20 + 20 = 100, the record with the weight of 60 will be used 60/100, or 60 percent, of the time, whereas each of the other two records will be used 20/100, or 20 percent, of the time.
- **Port.** The TCP or UDP port that this service listens on, such as TCP port 88 for the _kerberos SRV record

As you can see, clients use the priority and weight fields to help determine which server is the most appropriate connection for the requested services. Two methods can be used to verify the SRV records:

- DNS Manager in the Administrative Tools folder
- Nslookup utility from the command line

Verifying Zone and Record Creation

Using the DNS Manager tool, you can verify that the appropriate zone has been created. You can also verify the individual records by completing the following steps.

 VERIFY ZONE AND RECORD CREATION

GET READY. The Active Directory installation must be performed on a DNS server.

1. Open DNS from the Administrative Tools folder.
2. Expand the desired DNS server and expand the DNS domain you wish to view; for example, lucernepublishing.com. You should see the following entries:

   _msdcs

   _sites

   _tcp

   _udp

   In addition, you may see the following zones created for application directory partition information:

   DomainDnsZones

   ForestDnsZones

PAUSE. Zone and record creation has been verified.

Nslookup, which is a command-line tool, is somewhat cumbersome at first use, but it is a powerful tool, and it is well worth taking the time to become familiar with it. Because the GUI tools available in Server Core are limited, developing an understanding of the nslookup utility is critical for working with DNS on Server Core.

VERIFYING THAT DYNAMIC UPDATES ARE SELECTED

For domain controllers to register their records with DNS at startup, dynamic updates must be allowed. By default, when a DNS zone is Active Directory integrated, Secure Dynamic Updates are enabled. In this case, a client must be authenticated before attempting to update or add information to the DNS database. This prevents unwanted or unnecessary records from being added to the database, ultimately creating performance, space, and potential security issues.

VERIFY THAT DYNAMIC UPDATES ARE SELECTED

GET READY. The Active Directory installation must be performed on a DNS server.

1. Right-click the desired zone and select **Properties**.
2. View the selected type of updates for this zone. By default, if the zone is Active Directory integrated, it will be set to *Secure only*.

PAUSE. Dynamic updates are selected.

In the previous exercise, you configured a DNS zone to allow dynamic DNS updates only from members of the same Active Directory infrastructure.

Creating a Reverse Lookup Zone

In addition to forward lookup zones, which are automatically created by the Active Directory Installation Wizard, you should also configure a *reverse lookup zone* for full DNS functionality. Reverse lookup zones answer queries in which a client provides an IP address and DNS resolves the IP address to a host name.

CREATE A REVERSE LOOKUP ZONE

GET READY. The Active Directory installation must be performed on a DNS server.

1. Open DNS from the Administrative Tools folder.
2. Expand the desired server and right-click **Reverse Lookup Zone**.
3. Click **New Zone** to begin the wizard and then click **Next** to bypass the initial Welcome window.
4. Select the type of zone you wish to create. If this is the first reverse lookup zone, select **Primary Zone**. If this zone is to be stored on a domain controller running Active Directory-integrated DNS, select **Store the zone in Active Directory**, as shown in Figure 2-13. Click **Next** to continue.

Figure 2-13

New Zone Wizard

5. Select the scope of replication for this zone from the following options and click **Next** to continue:

   • All DNS servers in the Active Directory forest

   • All DNS servers in the Active Directory domain (this is the default value)

   • All domain controllers in the Active Directory domain (for backward compatibility with Windows 2000)

   • To all domain controllers specified in the scope of a manually created application partition

6. Select the option to create an IPv4 reverse lookup zone if your network uses TCP/IP version 4 as its network protocol, or select the option to create an IPv6 reverse lookup zone if you have upgraded your networking hardware to use the new TCP/IP version 6. Click **Next** to continue.

7. In the Reverse Lookup Zone Name dialog box, click the **Network ID** option and enter the Network ID of the reverse lookup zone. The Reverse Lookup zone name should appear in the second option field. Click **Next** to continue.

8. Select the level of secure updates that should be enabled for this zone from the following options and click **Next**:

   • Allow only secure dynamic updates—this is the default option.

   • Allow both nonsecure and secure dynamic updates.

   • Do not allow dynamic updates.

9. Review the summary zone creation window and click **Finish** to complete the process.

10. If you haven't enabled dynamic updates, add any necessary resource records by right-clicking on the newly created zone and selecting **New Pointer (New PTR)**. For example, you should create a PTR record that references any server A records that you have created in forward lookup zones on the server.

PAUSE. Reverse lookup zones were created.

Reverse lookup zones are not required or configured by default. However, it is good practice to add reverse lookup zones for troubleshooting, security checks, and reverse IP queries. A reverse lookup zone is called an in-addr.arpa domain and uses the reverse dotted decimal notation of a forward lookup zone. For example, if the forward lookup zone uses 192.168.1.200 for its IP address, the reverse lookup zone would appear as 200.1.168.192- in-addr.arpa. In addition to the zone creation, a resource record called a *pointer (PTR)* record is necessary to map the address back to a host in the corresponding forward lookup zone.

Raising the Domain and Forest Functional Levels

To leverage more advanced features in Active Directory, you can raise the domain and forest functional levels within Active Directory after you have retired any domain controllers that are running down-level operating systems, such as Windows 2000. Lesson 1 mapped out the differences between each level in terms of supported operating systems and functionality. In this lesson, the focus is on the how-to steps and requirements for raising the functionality level.

Domain and forest functional levels are available to provide backward compatibility with previous Windows Server operating systems. Migrating your network to one consistent platform provides many administrative benefits and can lower the overall network cost of ownership. Prior to raising the domain functional levels, verify that any previous Microsoft Windows network operating systems are not needed in the domain. Careful planning will be required for each company and their current network structure. If an organization is interested in any future acquisitions or mergers, raising the domain level could have an impact, and this should be taken into careful consideration. For example, if an enterprise organization

> **WARNING** Windows clients will always attempt to use nonsecure DNS updates before attempting to use secure updates. This means that if you allow nonsecure and secure updates, this is effectively the same as allowing all of your clients to use nonsecure updates.

is growing rapidly by buying up the competition, it would be safe to assume that not all of the new acquisitions are running Windows Server 2008. Deciding how to integrate network structures into your corporate enterprise will be a challenge because many networks will have a mixed bag of operating systems. The Windows Server 2008 family provides several new enhancements to assist in making the transition easier. Note the following key facts and requirements for raising domain and forest functional levels:

- This is a one-way operation. Raising the domain and forest functional levels cannot be reversed without a complete reinstallation of the domain or forest.
- Each domain can be handled independently, thereby allowing a phased approach to increasing functionality. This allows corporations sufficient transition time to upgrade each location or domain. Some locations may need to purchase new hardware or upgrade existing infrastructure prior to a migration.
- The forest functional level cannot be raised until all domains in a forest have been raised to at least the corresponding Domain Functional Level.
- You must be logged on as a member of the Domain Admins group to raise the domain functional level.
- You must be logged on as a member of the Enterprise Admins group to raise the forest functional level.

> **TAKE NOTE***
>
> You can raise the domain or forest functionality by using Active Directory Domains and Trusts.

RAISE THE DOMAIN FUNCTIONAL LEVEL

GET READY. Before you begin these steps, you must be logged on as a member of the Domain Admins group.

1. Open Active Directory Domains and Trusts from the Administrative Tools folder.
2. Right-click the domain you wish to raise and select **Raise Domain Functional Level**, as shown in Figure 2-14.

Figure 2-14

Raise Domain Functional Level

3. Choose the level you wish to achieve from Select An Available Domain Functional Level and then click **Raise**. You will be presented with the dialog box shown in Figure 2-15, which explains the irreversible nature of this procedure. Click **OK** to acknowledge this warning and raise the functional level of the domain, and then click **OK** to acknowledge that the change was made.

Figure 2-15

Warning about raising domain functional level

PAUSE. You raised the domain functional level.

In the previous exercise, you raised the domain functional level of an Active Directory domain to the Windows Server 2008 functional level. Next, you will raise the forest functional level.

⊘ RAISE THE FOREST FUNCTIONAL LEVEL

GET READY. Before you begin these steps, you must be logged on as a member of the Enterprise Admins group.

1. Open Active Directory Domains and Trusts from the Administrative Tools folder.
2. Right-click the **Active Directory Domains and Trusts** icon in the console tree and select **Raise Forest Functional Level**.
3. If your domains have not all been raised to at least Windows Server 2008, you will receive an error indicating that raising the forest functional level cannot take place yet. If all domains have met the domain functionality criteria of Windows Server 2008, you can click **Raise** to proceed.
4. A warning message explaining the irreversible nature of this procedure is displayed. Click **OK** to acknowledge this warning and raise the functional level of the forest, and then click **OK** to acknowledge that the change was made.

PAUSE. You raised the forest functional level.

In the previous exercise, you raised the forest functional level of your forest to Windows Server 2008.

Adding a Second Domain Controller to the Forest Root Domain

During your planning of the Active Directory infrastructure, a second domain controller should be added to each domain for fault tolerance. This provides some redundancy in case one of the domain controllers fails. In addition, because the first domain controller in the forest holds all FSMO roles, adding a second domain controller allows you to offload some of the work to another domain controller.

⊘ ADD A SECOND DOMAIN CONTROLLER TO THE FOREST ROOT DOMAIN

GET READY. You must have administrative credentials on the existing Active Directory domain to add a second domain controller; the server computer should be configured with a static IP address.

1. Install the server operating system. You can configure the server as a member of a workgroup or as a member server within the existing domain.
2. Ensure that the new domain controller can resolve SRV records within the domain that you are joining it to. The simplest way to accomplish this is by configuring the new server with the IP address of a DNS server within the existing domain. If the new server is running the DNS server service, you can configure the new server with a DNS forwarder, secondary zone, or stub zone of an existing DNS server within the Active Directory environment that you are joining.
3. Add the Active Directory Domain Services role to this server and configure it as an additional domain controller in an existing domain. This is the first suboption on the Choose a Deployment Configuration page in the Active Directory Installation

X REF

For more information about configuring DNS, refer to Lesson 12.

Wizard, as shown in Figure 2-16. The wizard prompts you for the following information to add a second domain controller to an existing domain:

- The DNS name of the domain that you wish to join (if the server is not already configured as a member server)
- Administrative credentials for the domain
- The name of the Active Directory site that the new domain controller should be placed in
- Configuration of the server as a DNS server, global catalog, and/or Read-Only Domain Controller
- The location for the Active Directory database, log files, and SYSVOL folder
- The DSRM password
- Choose to replicate the database over the network from an existing domain controller or select the *Install from Media* feature which allows you to use a System State backup from an existing domain controller to create the new domain controller

For more information about the process of transferring FSMO roles from one server to another, refer to Lesson 4.

Figure 2-16

Adding a second domain controller

4. Transfer single operations master roles as necessary to this server.

PAUSE. A second domain controller has been added.

In the previous exercise, you added a domain controller to an existing Active Directory domain.

Installing Active Directory on Server Core

One of the key new features of Windows Server 2008 is **Server Core**, a special installation option that creates a minimal environment for running only specific services and roles. Server Core runs almost entirely without a graphical user interface (GUI), which means that it needs to be administered exclusively from the command line. Where Active Directory is concerned, Server Core provides a useful way to deploy a domain controller with an extremely small security footprint, improving the security of domain controllers in branch offices or other remote environments.

When you log on to a Server Core computer, you will see a single command-line window, as shown in Figure 2-17. Because Server Core does not support many graphical utilities, including Server Manager and the Active Directory Installation Wizard, you will need to run dcpromo from the command line using an *unattended installation*, which uses a specially formatted text file to specify the necessary installation options.

Figure 2-17

Command-line window

INSTALL ACTIVE DIRECTORY ON SERVER CORE

GET READY. You must have administrative credentials on the existing Active Directory domain to install Active Directory on Server Core; the server computer should be configured with a static IP address.

1. Key **notepad** from the Server Core command-prompt window and press (Enter). When the Notepad window opens, key the following content:

; DCPROMO unattend file

; Usage:

[DCInstall]

; Replica DC promotion

ReplicaOrNewDomain=Replica

ReplicaDomainDNSName=lucernepublishing.com

SiteName=Default-First-Site-Name

InstallDNS=Yes

ConfirmGc=Yes

UserDomain=lucernepublishing.com

UserName=lucernepublishing.com\administrator

Password=Password1

DatabasePath=C:\Windows\NTDS

LogPath=C:\Windows\NTDS

SafeModeAdminPassword=MySafeModePassword

RebootOnCompletion=Yes

TransferIMRoleIfNecessary=No

2. Save the text file to the root of C:\ as *unattend.txt.*

3. Enter the following command from the Server Core console:

dcpromo /unattend:c:\unattend.txt

PAUSE. A second domain controller running Windows Server 2008 Server Core has been added.

By reading through the values listed in the unattend.txt file, you can see how the target domain control is to be configured. You can modify the behavior of the dcpromo process by modifying one or more lines in the text file. For example, you can modify the database path by changing

    DatabasePath=C:\Windows\NTDS

to

    DatabasePath=D:\NTDS

Removing Active Directory

Removing Active Directory from a domain controller demotes that computer to a member server within an Active Directory domain. You will use this to decommission older hardware or to remove Active Directory so that you can perform troubleshooting or extensive maintenance on that server.

➔ REMOVE ACTIVE DIRECTORY

GET READY. You must have administrative credentials on the existing Active Directory domain to remove an existing domain controller.

1. Click the **Start** menu, key **dcpromo**, and then press **Enter**.
2. Click **Next** to bypass the initial Welcome window. If you see a message warning you that the domain controller is also a global catalog server, click **OK** to continue.
3. The window shown in Figure 2-18 is displayed. Click **Next** to continue.

Figure 2-18

Delete the Domain

4. Enter a local administrator password for the newly demoted server in the Password field, then enter it again in the Confirm password field. Click **Next** to continue.
5. On the Summary window, review your choices and click **Next** to begin the uninstall process.

PAUSE. Active Directory is removed.

The Active Directory Installation Wizard can also be used to remove the Active Directory database from an existing domain controller. If the domain controller in question is the last domain controller in a domain, demoting the server will remove all Active Directory components and destroy any existing database files for that domain. If the server is the last server in the forest, the entire forest will be removed when the domain controller is uninstalled. The outcome of this procedure is that all Active Directory services, including Netlogon, will not function. This procedure should be done only when a complete reinstallation of the Active Directory is required.

Working with Read-Only Domain Controllers

Another exciting new feature of Windows Server 2008 is the Read-Only Domain Controller (RODC). The RODC can greatly improve the security of a domain controller that's deployed in a branch office or another hard-to-secure location.

In Windows 2000 and Windows Server 2003, all domain controllers participated in Active Directory's multimaster replication scheme, which meant that an administrator could make a change on any domain controller and it would be replicated throughout the rest of Active Directory. This created issues for businesses that needed to deploy domain controllers in offices that had limited physical security, such as a remote branch office with only a few employees. As the name suggests, Read-Only Domain Controllers now allow you to deploy a domain controller that will host a *read-only* copy of the Active Directory database. This means that an administrator will need to connect to a writeable domain controller to make any changes to Active Directory.

One of the key features of RODCs is that they do not perform any outbound replication whatsoever. They only accept inbound replication connections from writeable domain controllers. To deploy an RODC, you need to have at least one writeable Windows Server 2008 domain controller deployed in your environment, and you need to be at the Windows Server 2003 domain and forest functional levels.

Another key feature of an RODC is that each RODC can be configured with its own *Password Replication Policy*. On writeable domain controllers, information about every Active Directory password is stored locally within the ntds.dit file. If a writeable domain controller is compromised or stolen, all username and password information in your environment is at risk. By contrast, you can specify a particular list of user or group accounts whose password information should be stored (or cached) on a particular RODC. For example, if you deploy an RODC in lucernepublishing's Tokyo branch, you can configure the RODC so that it will only cache password information for members of the TokyoUsers security group. Conversely, you can also configure specific users or groups whose password information should *not* be cached on an RODC. For example, high-level administrative accounts, such as Domain Admins and Enterprise Admins, are configured by default so that their password information *cannot* be cached on any RODCs within an environment. Microsoft recommends that you do not change these settings. To allow enterprise-wide configuration of the RODC Password Replication Policy, Windows Server 2008 creates the following security groups:

- **Denied RODC Password Replication Group.** Members of this group will be placed in the Deny list of the Password Replication Policies of all RODCs by default. This group contains the following members when Windows Server 2008 is first installed: Cert Publishers, Domain Admins, Domain Controllers, Enterprise Admins, Group Policy Creator Owners, Read-Only Domain Controllers, Schema Admins, and kerbtgt.

- **Allowed RODC Password Replication Group.** Members of this group will be placed in the Allow list of the Password Replication Policies of all RODCs by default. This group has *no members* when Windows Server 2008 is first installed.

CONFIGURING A READ-ONLY DOMAIN CONTROLLER

To configure users whose password information will or will not be cached on all RODCs in your organization, the most efficient method is to add those users to the Allowed RODC Password Replication Group or the Denied RODC Password Replication Group, respectively. You can also configure users or groups so that their password information will only be cached on a single RODC. For example, you may want to have the Tokyo branch office users' password information cached on *only* the Tokyo RODC and not on other RODCs that those users will rarely, if ever, log on to.

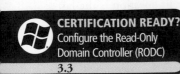

CERTIFICATION READY?
Configure the Read-Only
Domain Controller (RODC)
3.3

⊕ **CONFIGURE A READ-ONLY DOMAIN CONTROLLER**

GET READY. You must have administrative credentials on the domain to add an RODC; the server computer should be configured with a static IP address.

1. Click the **Start** menu and select **Server Manager.**

2. Select **Roles** and then click **Add Role.**

3. Add the Active Directory Domain Services role to this server and configure it as an additional domain controller in an existing domain, using the advanced mode installation option. The wizard prompts you for the following information to add a domain controller to an existing domain:

   • The DNS name of the domain that you wish to join (if the server is not already configured as a member server)

   • Administrative credentials for the domain

   • The name of the Active Directory site where the new domain controller should be placed

4. Step through the installation process until you reach the Additional Domain Controller Options window, which provides the DNS Server, Global Catalog and Read-Only Domain Controller (RODC) options. Select the **Read-Only Domain Controller (RODC)** option.

5. Click **Next** to begin configuring the Read-Only Domain Controller. The window shown in Figure 2-19 is displayed. Here you see the Password Replication Policy in action, where you can configure specific user or group accounts that should or should not have their passwords cached on the RODC. As you can see, the following security groups are set to *Deny* in the default Password Replication Policy:

   • Administrators

   • Server Operators

   • Backup Operators

   • Account Operators

   • Denied RODC Password Replication Group

   The only group that is configured to *Deny* in the default Password Replication Policy is the Allowed RODC Password Replication Group.

Figure 2-19

Specify the Password Replication Policy

6. To configure users who will (or will not) have their password information cached only on this particular RODC, click the **Add or Remove** button, select one of the following options, and then click **OK**, as shown in Figure 2-20:

- Allow passwords for the account to replicate to this RODC
- Deny passwords for the account from replicating to this RODC

Figure 2-20

Add Groups, Users, and Computers dialog box

7. On the window shown in Figure 2-21, you can specify a user or group object for Admin Role Separation. This user or group will have local administrator rights to the RODC without receiving any administrative rights within Active Directory. Key the group or user in the Group or User field and click the **Set** button to select a local administrator for the RODC. Click **Next**.

Figure 2-21

Delegation of RODC Installation and Administration window

8. On the Install from Media window shown in Figure 2-22, you can choose to replicate the ntds.dit file over the network or perform the initial installation from local source media. Make your selection and click **Next**.

Figure 2-22

Install from Media

9. You will then be able to select which domain controller this domain controller should replicate from. You can select **Any writeable domain controller** or select **This specific domain controller** and manually select a domain controller that is in the same site or connected via a high-speed network connection. Click **Next** to continue.

10. The wizard will then prompt you for the same information as you saw in the Add a Second Domain Controller to the Forest Root Domain exercise, including:

    • Selecting the database, log file, and SYSVOL file locations

    • Establishing the DSRM password

    • Choosing to source the domain controller installation over the network or using the Install from Media option

11. Complete the steps in the Active Directory Installation Wizard and reboot the server when the wizard is completed.

PAUSE. A Read-Only Domain Controller has been configured.

Read-Only Domain Controllers also offer a feature that has been a top request of Active Directory administrators since the early days of Windows 2000: *Admin Role Separation*. This means that it is now possible to configure a user as the local administrator of a specific RODC without making the user a Domain Admins with far-reaching authority over all domain controllers in your entire domain and full access to your Active Directory domain data.

PERFORMING A STAGED INSTALLATION OF AN RODC

In addition to simply running the Active Directory Installation Wizard from the console of a server that you want to designate as an RODC, you can perform a *staged installation* so that you begin the installation at a central location, such as a data center, and then allow a local administrator to complete the configuration. Because of Admin Role Separation, you can do so without delegating any rights within Active Directory to the delegated administrator, thus further securing the process of creating an RODC.

 SET UP A STAGED INSTALLATION OF AN RODC

GET READY. Begin at the console of a writeable domain controller that's running Windows Server 2008.

1. Open Active Directory Users and Computers from the Administrative Tools folder.

2. Right-click the **Domain Controllers Organizational Unit (OU)** and select **Pre-create Read-only domain controller account**.

3. Select **Use advanced mode installation** and click **Next** twice to continue.

4. On the Network Credentials window, specify the username of a remote user who will have permission to add the RODC to the domain. Click **Next** to continue.

5. Enter the computer name of the RODC and click **Next**.

6. Select the site that the RODC should belong to and click **Next**.

7. Select any additional options for this domain controller, such as configuring the domain controller to be a DNS server or global catalog, and click **Next**.

8. Configure the Password Replication Policy as described in the previous section and click **Next**.

9. On the Delegation of RODC Installation and Administration window, specify the user or group account that will be able to complete the staged installation and locally administer the server. Click **Set** to select the account and click **Next** to continue.

10. Complete the installation process as you did in the previous exercise, and reboot the server when prompted.

PAUSE. A staged installation of an RODC has been prepared.

ANOTHER WAY

For more security, you can install an RODC on a Server Core installation of Windows Server 2008 by modifying the unattend.txt file to include lines such as *ReplicaOrNewDomain= ReadOnlyReplica, OnDem andDenied= "BUILTIN\ Server Operators"* and *onDemandAllowed= "LP\ Allowed RODC Password Replication Group."*

At this point, the local administrator will launch the Active Directory Installation Wizard from the target server. It is important that you follow these two steps when preparing the target computer:

- The target server needs to be configured with the same name as the one you specified in the first phase of the installation. If the server currently has a different name, you need to rename it before beginning the second phase.
- The target server needs to be configured as part of a workgroup. The target server can't be already joined to the domain. If you have already joined the server to the domain as a member server, disjoin the server from the domain and delete its computer account before proceeding.

⊖ COMPLETE A STAGED INSTALLATION OF AN RODC

GET READY. The remote administrator will proceed with the second phase of the installation by launching the Active Directory Installation Wizard from the remote server that has been designated to be configured as an RODC; the server computer should be configured with a static IP address.

1. Click **Next** twice to bypass the initial Welcome and informational windows.
2. On the Choose a Deployment Configuration window, select **Existing Forest**, and then select **Add a domain controller to an existing domain**. Click **Next** to continue.
3. Enter the name of the target domain and then click **Set** to specify the credentials of the remote user on the window shown in Figure 2-23. Click **Next** to continue.

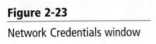

Figure 2-23

Network Credentials window

4. Select the target domain and click **Next** again.
5. If the remote administrator does not have administrative rights within Active Directory, you will see the warning shown in Figure 2-24. Click **Yes** to continue.

Figure 2-24

Warning dialog box indicating that a user does not have administrative rights

6. You will then see the message shown in Figure 2-25, indicating that the Installation Wizard has found a precreated account for an RODC that matches the name of the remote computer. Click **OK** and follow the prompts to complete the configuration of the RODC as usual.

Figure 2-25

Warning dialog box indicating that a match was found

TAKE NOTE*

RODCs do not participate in any form of outbound replication within Active Directory.

PAUSE. A staged installation of an RODC has been completed.

In the previous exercise, the remote administrator completed the second phase of a staged installation of a Read-Only Domain Controller. This two-stage process allows remote administrators to deploy an RODC in an Active Directory domain without requiring elevated administrative privileges on the domain.

Decommissioning an RODC

If you are ever in the unfortunate situation where a writeable domain controller in your environment is compromised or stolen, you are faced with the daunting task of resetting every password for every user in your environment because they are all subject to compromise on the stolen domain controller. RODC helps to minimize the fallout in a "stolen domain controller" situation because only the users specified in the Password Replication Policy will have password information stored on an RODC.

With the introduction of RODCs, Windows Server 2008 also introduces a new procedure for removing an RODC from the network. When you delete an RODC's computer object from the Domain Controllers OU in Active Directory Users and Computers, you are presented with the selections shown in Figure 2-26:

Figure 2-26

Available options when removing an RODC from Active Directory

- **Reset all passwords for user accounts that were cached on this Read-only Domain Controller.** This forces all of these users to contact your help desk to regain access to the network.

- **Reset all passwords for computer accounts that were cached on this Read-only Domain Controller.** This requires you to remove and re-add each affected workstation in the domain.

- **Export the list of accounts that were cached on this Read-only Domain Controller to this file**. This exports the names of all affected user and computer accounts to a text file so that you can manage them more pro-actively.

Modifying the Active Directory Schema

The Active Directory schema will probably be modified at some time during the life of your implementation plan. Many applications used as common tools, such as email, will require modification to add necessary objects to the Active Directory database. Being able to safely and correctly modify the schema is a key task for any Active Directory administrator.

Numerous commercial applications require the ability to extend the Active Directory schema, or you may wish to create custom schema extensions to support in-house applications that you have developed internally. For example, Microsoft Exchange 2003 adds over 1,000 classes and attributes to the schema to support its operation. Each class or attribute that you add to the schema should have a valid *Object Identifier (OID)*. As part of the X.500 structure on which Active Directory is based, OIDs must be globally unique, and they are represented by a hierarchical dotted-decimal notation string. If you are familiar with the Simple Network Management Protocol (SNMP) namespace, you will recognize the OID structure. An example of a complete OID might be 1.55678.5.15. OIDs can be obtained directly from the ISO at www.iso.org or from the American National Standards Institute (ANSI) at www.ansi.org.

The Active Directory schema is replicated to every domain controller within a forest, which means that each Active Directory forest can only have a single schema. Modifications to the schema are managed by the domain controller that is assigned the Schema Master FSMO role. By default, the Schema Master FSMO is assigned to the first domain controller that's installed in the forest. Any changes to the schema are then replicated to all domain controllers in the forest during the Active Directory replication process. Planning for these changes involves an understanding of the following points:

- Schema extensions are replicated to all domain controllers in the forest and have a global effect on the modified objects and attributes.
- Default system classes cannot be modified, but additional classes can be added and changed. The best example of this occurs when an application modifies the schema.
- Any class and attribute that you add to the schema cannot be removed; extending the schema is a *one-way operation*. However, beginning in Windows Server 2003, schema additions can be deactivated, which reduces the overhead created by unwanted schema modifications.
- When the schema is modified, it triggers replication within the forest. Planning modification of the schema may require sensitivity to the time of day and the possible performance impact. If modifications are made during peak usage hours, users may experience some significant performance issues. In particular, an application like Microsoft Exchange 2003 can add over 1,000 attributes to the schema at once.
- A certain amount of *latency* can be expected before all domain controllers contain consistent schema information. As discussed in Lesson 1, latency describes the amount of time it takes for an Active Directory change to be replicated to all domain controllers in the forest. This latency can be a matter of a few minutes or significantly longer in a larger organization in which replication schedules are carefully controlled.

Because of the ramifications of extending the schema improperly, you should only make these modifications if the change is specifically required. Many things in the schema can go awry if changes are made incorrectly. To protect against possible midnight restores of a corrupted Active Directory, be sure you fully understand the ramifications of a change prior to making it. For example, if a change is made that renames an object attribute, it will be difficult to reverse the change after the fact. If the original attribute is called by another script or program, that script or program will not function properly until the issue is resolved. In addition, Microsoft recommends adding administrators to the Schema Admins group only for the duration of the task. Also, be sure to test any modifications in an isolated environment that closely matches your actual production environment before releasing the changes to the production network. Planning modifications can sometimes delay the deployment of a desired application or feature, but it is well worth the effort if something does not function as designed in the test environment. You may want to institute a change management process (CMP) infrastructure prior to beginning modifications. The CMP will permit you to track exactly which changes were made to the schema and who made those changes.

INSTALLING THE SCHEMA MANAGEMENT SNAP-IN

As discussed, some commercial applications such as Microsoft Exchange will modify the schema as a part of their installation process. You can also extend the schema manually using the Active Directory Schema snap-in. To modify the schema manually, you must meet the following requirements:

- You must be a member of the Schema Admins group.
- The Active Directory Schema snap-in should be installed on the domain controller holding the Schema Master Operations role.

⊕ INSTALL THE SCHEMA MANAGEMENT SNAP-IN

GET READY. Before you begin these steps, you must be logged on as a member of the Schema Admins group.

>
> The Schema Management snap-in is not installed by default in Windows Server 2008. To enable any edits of the Active Directory schema, it is necessary to have the snap-in available. Adding the Active Directory Schema snap-in to a Microsoft Management Console (MMC) window is the simplest way to modify the schema. The MMC is a graphic tool similar to other tools included with Windows Server 2008. It allows you to customize a set of tools you wish to have available for easy management.

1. From a command prompt, key **regsvr32 schmmgmt.dll** to register the necessary DLL file needed to run the Active Directory Schema MMC snap-in.
2. Close the Command Prompt window, click **Start**, and then select **Run**.
3. Key **mmc/a** in the dialog box and click **OK**.
4. Click the **File** menu and select **Add/Remove Snap-in**.
5. Click **Add** to see the list of available snap-ins.
6. Double-click **Active Directory Schema** in the list.
7. Click **OK**.
8. If you want to save this console for future use, click **File** and then click **Save**. By adding this step, you can simply open the console or create a shortcut on your desktop for easy accessibility.

PAUSE. The Schema Management snap-in has been installed.

In the previous exercise, you added the Schema Management snap-in by registering the associated DLL file. This DLL is not registered by default in Windows Server 2008 and needs to be added manually to run the Schema Management MMC snap-in.

> When performing administrative tasks, you should not log on to the console of a domain controller. Instead, it is recommended that administrative tasks be performed from an administrative workstation running Windows XP or Windows Vista, using a normal user account and the Run As program. Details on the Run As program and the security issues surrounding this warning are explained further in Lesson 6.

CONFIGURING ACTIVE DIRECTORY LIGHTWEIGHT DIRECTORY SERVICES

Windows Server 2008 includes a new *Active Directory Lightweight Directory Services (AD LDS)* role that provides developers the ability to store data for directory-enabled applications without incurring the overhead of extending the Active Directory schema to support their applications. Each AD LDS *instance* has its own schema, which allows developers to create, deploy, and upgrade directory-enabled applications without worrying about the one-way nature of Active Directory schema modifications.

CONFIGURE ACTIVE DIRECTORY LIGHTWEIGHT DIRECTORY SERVICES

GET READY. You must be logged on as a member of the local Administrators group to begin this process.

1. Click the **Start** menu and select **Server Manager**.
2. Click **Roles** and then click **Add Roles** under the Roles Summary section.
3. Read the Before You Begin window and click **Next**.
4. On the Select Server Roles window, place a checkmark next to **Active Directory Lightweight Directory Services**. Click **Next** to continue.
5. You will be presented with an introduction to Active Directory Lightweight Directory Services that provides a number of helpful hints for installing and administering AD LDS. Some of these tips include the following items:
   - After installing AD LDS, instances of AD LDS can be created using the AD LDS Setup Wizard in the Administrative Tools folder.
   - Before removing the AD LDS role, you need to remove all instances of AD LDS that you have configured on this server.

   Click **Next** after you read the Introduction to AD LDS window.
6. Click **Install** to begin the installation process. The Server Manager will appear to pause for a few minutes while the AD LDS binaries are installed.
7. After the AD LDS binaries have installed, click **Close**.
8. Click **Start**, click **Administrative Tools**, and then click **Active Directory Lightweight Directory Services Setup**.
9. Click **Next** to bypass the initial Welcome window.
10. The window shown in Figure 2-27 is displayed. Click **A unique instance** to create a new AD LDS instance, and click **Next** to continue.

Figure 2-27

Create a new AD LDS instance

> **Active Directory Lightweight Directory Services Setup Wizard**
>
> **Setup Options**
> An AD LDS instance is created each time AD LDS is installed.
>
> You can create a unique instance, or you can install a replica of an existing instance.
>
> Select the type of instance you want to install.
>
> ⦿ A unique instance
> This option automatically creates a new instance of AD LDS that uses the default configuration and schema partitions. The new instance will not be able to replicate with existing instances.
>
> ○ A replica of an existing instance
> This option creates a new instance of AD LDS that uses the configuration and schema partitions replicated from another instance of AD LDS. You can also select the application partitions to replicate.
>
> < Back   Next >   Cancel   Help

11. On the Instance Name window, key **LP-APP** as a unique name for the AD LDS instance. Click **Next** to continue.

12. The window shown in Figure 2-28 is displayed. The default ports used to communicate with an AD LDS instance are TCP port 389 for LDAP and TCP port 636 for SSL-secured communications. Click **Next** to continue.

Figure 2-28

Select ports for AD LDS

⚠ **WARNING** If you are installing an AD LDS instance on a server that is already configured as a domain controller, ports 389 and 636 will not be available here; you will need to select alternate ports, such as 50000 and 50001.

13. On the Application Directory Partition window, select **No, do not create an application directory partition**. By selecting this option, all AD LDS data will be stored on the local server. If you select the option to create an application directory partition, you can store and replicate AD LDS data inside a custom application directory partition within Active Directory. Click **Next** to continue.

14. On the File Locations window, select a directory to store the AD LDS data files and data recovery files, as shown in Figure 2-29. Click **Next** to continue.

Figure 2-29

Select File Locations for an AD LDS instance

15. On the Service Account Selection window, select the account that this AD LDS instance should run under. The default is the Network service account. Maintain this default selection and click **Next** to continue.

16. On the AD LDS Administrators window, select the user or group that will have administrative rights to this LDS instance. The default value is the currently logged-on user. Or, click **This account** and click **Browse** to select another user or group. Click **Next** to continue.

17. On the Importing LDIF Files window, select one or more predefined LDIF files to import into the schema of this AD LDS instance, as shown in Figure 2-30. Click **Next** to continue.

Figure 2-30

Importing LDIF files into an AD LDS instance

18. On the Ready to Install window, confirm your selections and click **Next** to begin the configuration of this LDS instance.

19. Click **Finish** when the installation is complete.

PAUSE. The AD LDS has been configured.

In the previous exercise, you configured the AD LDS. LDS instances can contain any type of Active Directory object that is not a security principal: in other words, any type of object except Active Directory user, group, or computer objects.

Establishing and Maintaining Trust Relationships

Trust relationships exist to make resource accessibility easier between domains and forests. As discussed in Lesson 1, many trust relationships are established by default during the creation of the Active Directory forest structure, as well as other trusts that you can create manually.

In addition to the default trust relationships that exist between parent and child domains and between root domains of domain trees within a forest, four trust types can be manually established in Windows Server 2008:

- **Shortcut trusts.** As discussed in Lesson 1, shortcut trusts can be used to shorten the "tree-walking" process for users who require frequent access to resources elsewhere in the forest.

- **Cross-forest trusts.** This trust relationship was introduced in Windows Server 2003; it allows you to create two-way transitive trusts between separate forests.

- **External trusts.** External trusts are used to configure a one-way nontransitive trust with a Windows 2000 domain or a single domain in an external organization.

- **Realm trusts.** These trusts allow you to configure trust relationships between Windows Server 2008 Active Directory and a UNIX MIT Kerberos realm, which is the UNIX equivalent to an Active Directory domain allowing centralized user and password administration on a UNIX network.

Use the Active Directory Domains and Trusts MMC snap-in to establish manual trust relationships. When using the New Trust Wizard in this utility, you can decide if the trust will be one-way incoming, one-way outgoing, or two-way. A one-way incoming trust establishes that users from another domain, external trust source, or realm can gain access to resources in your domain. However, users in your source domain would not be able to gain access to resources in the trusted external domain. For example, suppose a company wishes to allow a vendor or other subsidiary to gain access to certain resources, such as product lists or order information. Generally, the access would be limited, but allow the vendor or supplier to gain access to necessary business-related data. It may not be necessary or desirable for the vendor to allow the same permissions for your company to access their data. A one-way trust allows this type of situation to take place securely.

A one-way outgoing trust is the exact opposite of a one-way incoming trust. The vendor or supplier wishes to allow your organization accessibility, but you do not want them to gain access to your resources. If both organizations choose to allow access, a two-way trust is available and would achieve the same goal as establishing a one-way incoming *and* a one-way outgoing trust.

CERTIFICATION READY?
Configure trusts

2.2

CREATING A TRUST RELATIONSHIP

If you have the appropriate administrative privileges in the source and target forest or domain, you can create both sides of the trust relationship. To create a cross-forest trust, each forest must be able to resolve the DNS names and SRV records contained in the other forest through the use of secondary zones, stub zones, or conditional forwarding.

⊘ CREATE A TRUST RELATIONSHIP

GET READY. Before you begin these steps, you must be logged on as a member of the Domain Admins group of the local domain. You also need to have a second Active Directory domain configured and have administrative credentials available for the remote domain.

1. Open Active Directory Domains and Trusts from the Administrative Tools folder.
2. In the console tree on the left, right-click the domain for which you wish to establish a trust and select **Properties**.
3. Click the **Trusts** tab and click **New Trust** to begin the New Trust Wizard. Click **Next** to continue.
4. On the Trust Name page, key the DNS name of the domain and click **Next**.
5. On the Trust page, select the desired trust type.
6. On the Direction of Trust page, select the type and direction of the desired trust. On the Sides of Trust page, select whether you wish to create both sides of the trust simultaneously. (You must have administrative credentials on both the source and remote domains.) On the Trust Password page, enter a strong password to confirm the trust relationship; the same password must be entered when creating the other side of the trust on the remote domain. As a final step, you will be prompted to confirm the outgoing and incoming trusts; only perform these steps if the trust relationship has also been created on the remote domain.

TAKE NOTE *

When creating a forest trust, you will be prompted to configure permissions for the trust, to either allow authentication for all resources in the local domain or to allow authentication for only selected resources in the local domain.

PAUSE. You created a trust relationship.

In the previous exercise, you created a trust relationship between an Active Directory domain and an external network.

VERIFYING A TRUST RELATIONSHIP

After you establish a manual trust, you can verify the trust using either Active Directory Domains and Trusts or the *netdom* command-line tool that is used to create, delete, verify, and reset trust relationships from the Windows Server 2008 command line. Because automatic trusts are part of the default functionality provided by Active Directory, you can only use this process to verify shortcut, external, and cross-forest trusts.

⊘ VERIFY A TRUST RELATIONSHIP USING ACTIVE DIRECTORY

GET READY. Before you begin these steps, you must be logged on as a member of the Domain Admins group.

1. In Active Directory Domains and Trusts, right-click the domain for which you want to verify trusts, and select **Properties**.

2. On the Trusts tab, select **Domains Trusted By This Domain (Outgoing)** or **Domains that Trust This Domain (Incoming)**. Select the appropriate trust and click **Properties**.

3. Click **Validate**. You will be prompted to choose to validate only one side of the trust or validate both sides of the trust simultaneously. Select **Yes** to validate both sides of the trust. You will be prompted to supply an administrative user account and password on the target domain. Select **No** to manually log on to the target domain to validate the other side of the trust relationship.

PAUSE. You used Active Directory Domains and Trusts to verify a trust relationship.

In the previous exercise, you verified the validity of a trust relationship within the Active Directory Domains and Trusts MMC snap-in.

 VERIFY A TRUST RELATIONSHIP USING NETDOM

GET READY. Before you begin these steps, you must be logged on as a member of the Domain Admins group.

1. Open a command prompt and key the following text:

    netdom trust *TrustingDomainName***/d:***TrustedDomainName***/verify**

    Replace *TrustingDomainName* with the domain that is allowing access to resources. *TrustedDomainName* is the domain that needs to gain access.

2. Press **Enter**.

PAUSE. You used netdom to verify a trust relationship.

In the previous exercise, you verified the validity of an Active Directory trust relationship from the command line using the netdom tool.

REVOKING A TRUST RELATIONSHIP

In some cases, it may be necessary to remove an established trust. If a corporation relinquishes its business relationship with a supplier that was trusted, you will need to revoke the trust to prevent unwanted access to network resources. Just like creating trust relationships, you can use Active Directory Domains and Trusts or netdom to revoke a trust.

 REVOKE A TRUST USING ACTIVE DIRECTORY DOMAINS AND TRUSTS

GET READY. Before you begin these steps, you must be logged on as a member of the Domain Admins group.

1. In Active Directory Domains and Trusts, right-click the domain for which you want to verify trusts and select **Properties**.

2. On the Trusts tab, select **Domains Trusted By This Domain (Outgoing)** or **Domains That Trust This Domain (Incoming)**. Select the appropriate trust and click **Properties**.

3. Click **Remove** and follow the prompts to revoke the trust relationship.

4. Repeat steps 1 through 3 for the other end of the trust relationship.

PAUSE. You used Active Directory Domains and Trusts to revoke a trust relationship.

In the previous exercise, you removed an Active Directory trust relationship using the Active Directory Domains and Trusts MMC snap-in.

 REVOKE A TRUST USING NETDOM

GET READY. Before you begin these steps, you must be logged on as a member of the Domain Admins group.

1. Open a command prompt and enter the following text:

    netdom trust *TrustingDomainName***/d:***TrustedDomainName***/remove**

2. Press (Enter).

3. Repeat steps 1 and 2 for the other end of the trust relationship.

PAUSE. You used netdom to revoke a trust relationship.

In the previous exercise, you removed an Active Directory trust relationship using the netdom command-line tool.

Changing the Default Suffix for User Principal Names

As your organization grows due to normal expansion, acquisitions, mergers, and new geographic locations, the Active Directory structure can become difficult to navigate. Users needing access to more than one tree structure within the forest can find it cumbersome to recall what is contained in each domain. The distributed system can be cumbersome to navigate. To alleviate this confusion and provide a simple means for users to gain global access to the forest structure, Active Directory supports User Principal Names.

A ***User Principal Name (UPN)*** is stored in the global catalog, which allows the UPNs to be available forest-wide. In addition, if a cross-forest trust exists, a UPN can be used to gain access to resources in a trusting forest. A UPN follows a naming convention that can reflect the forest root domain or another alias that you configure that follows the format of *username@domainname*. One common practice is to configure the UPN to match the email ID of the user. In the case of a company with different internal and external domain names, using the external name for the UPN is preferred so that entering the correct UPN is simpler to the user. In larger organizations, this may mean that you will need to modify the default UPN suffix when creating users. To modify the default suffix for a UPN, you must have Enterprise Administrator credentials because this is a forest-wide operation.

CHANGE THE DEFAULT SUFFIX FOR USER PRINCIPAL NAMES

GET READY. Before you begin these steps, you must be logged on as a member of the Enterprise Admins group

1. Open Active Directory Domains and Trusts from the Administrative Tools folder.

2. Right-click **Active Directory Domains and Trusts** and choose **Properties**.

3. Click the **UPN Suffix** tab, key the new suffix, and click **Add**. The window shown in Figure 2-31 is displayed.

Figure 2-31

UPN Suffixes window

4. Key more than one suffix if your forest has more than one tree. Click **OK**.

END. You changed the default UPN suffix.

When creating a new user account, the new suffixes will be available for you to assign to users, as shown in Figure 2-32.

Figure 2-32

New Object—User window

⚠️ **WARNING** Removing a UPN suffix that is in use will cause users to be unable to log on to the domain. You will receive a warning message if you attempt to remove a UPN.

SUMMARY SKILL MATRIX

IN THIS LESSON YOU LEARNED:

- Active Directory requires DNS to be installed. DNS does not have to be installed on a Windows Server 2008 machine, but the version of DNS used does need to support SRV records for Active Directory to function.

- Planning the forest and domain structure should include a checklist that can be referenced for dialog information required by the Active Directory Installation Wizard.

- Verification of a solid Active Directory installation includes verifying DNS zones and the creation of SRV records. Additional items, such as reverse lookups, aging, and scavenging, also should be configured.

- Application directory partitions are automatically created when Active Directory integrated zones are configured in DNS. These partitions allow replica placement within the forest structure.

- System classes of the schema cannot be modified, but additional classes can be added. Classes and attributes cannot be deleted, but they can be deactivated.

- Planning forest and domain functionality is dependent on the need for down-level operating system compatibility. Raising a forest or domain functional level is a procedure that cannot be reversed.

- Four types of manual trusts can be created: shortcut, external, cross-forest, and realm trusts. Manual trusts can be created by using Active Directory Domains and Trusts or netdom at a command line.

- UPNs provide a mechanism to make access to resources in multiple domains user friendly. UPNs follow a naming format similar to email addresses. You must be a member of the Enterprise Admins group to add additional suffixes that can be assigned at user object creation.

■ Knowledge Assessment

Fill in the Blank

Complete the following sentences by writing the correct word or words in the blanks provided.

1. You can install Active Directory from the Windows command line using the _____ utility.

2. The _____ will configure which user accounts will or will not have their password information cached on an RODC.

3. The _____ command allows you to troubleshoot DNS information from the command line.

4. To install Active Directory on a Server Core computer, you will need to use a(n) _____.

5. You can use _____ to ease the user logon process in a large, multidomain environment.

6. The _____ shared folder is replicated to each domain controller and stores domain-wide information such as Group Policy Objects and login scripts.

7. Active Directory _____ refers to the amount of time it takes for changes to replicate to every domain controller in an environment.

8. _____ zone transfers allow modern DNS servers to replicate only records that have been changed rather than the contents of an entire zone.

9. The Active Directory Domain Services _____ are not installed on a Windows Server 2008 computer until you add the AD DS role to the computer.

10. If two SRV records have the same priority, the frequency by which they are accessed by clients will be determined by their relative _____.

Multiple Choice

Select the correct answer for each of the following questions. Choose all answers that are correct.

1. What mechanism within DNS is used to set up load balancing between multiple servers that are advertising the same SRV records?
   a. Protocol
   b. Domain name
   c. Port
   d. Priority

2. What security improvement allows you to begin the installation of an RODC from a secure central location before completing it at the remote site where the RODC will be housed?
   a. Staged installation
   b. Two-part installation
   c. Part I installation
   d. Multi-part installation

3. What does each class or attribute that you add to the Active Directory schema need to have?
   a. Protocol
   b. Object Identifier
   c. Priority
   d. Port

4. Which Windows Server 2008 feature enables you to perform certain Active Directory maintenance functions without needing to reboot the domain controller?
   a. Directory Services Restore Mode
   b. Safe Mode
   c. Safe Mode with Networking
   d. Restartable Active Directory

5. Which utility allows you to create, remove, and maintain Active Directory trust relationships from the command line?
   a. Repadmin
   b. Nslookup
   c. Netdom
   d. Shstat

6. What is the new unified tool, introduced by Windows Server 2008, for managing numerous aspects of a 2008 server?
   a. Computer Management
   b. Server Manager
   c. Active Directory Users & Computers
   d. Active Directory Domains & Trusts

7. Although all writeable domain controllers use multimaster replication, there are certain sensitive operations that can only be controlled by one DC at a time. What is this functionality called?
   a. Flexible Single Master Operations (FSMO) roles
   b. Flexible Multiple Master Operations (FMMO) roles
   c. Flexible Single Operations Master (FSOM) roles
   d. Flexible Multiple Operations Master (FMOM) roles

8. What Windows Server 2008 feature allows you to configure a user or group as the local administrator of an RODC without delegating any rights to the user or group within Active Directory?
   a. Flexible Single Master Operations (FSMO) roles
   b. Admin Role Separation
   c. Staged Installations
   d. Active Directory Lightweight Domain Services (AD LDS)

9. What is a new installation option in Windows Server 2008 that features a minimal installation footprint designed to run specific infrastructure services?
   a. RODC
   b. FSMO
   c. Server Core
   d. Web Server Edition

10. What term describes the length of time for which a DNS record is valid, after which it needs to be re-registered?
    a. Protocol
    b. Priority
    c. Weight
    d. Time-to-Live

■ Case Scenarios

Scenario 2-1: Designing Active Directory

Margie's Travel has decided to install a Windows Server 2008 network. They plan to use the name margiestravel.com as their DNS name because it is already registered with the InterNic. The corporate headquarters is located in Detroit and branches are located in Chicago, Dallas, and Phoenix. Margie's Travel wants to maintain a separate child domain in the forest representing each of the branches for ease of management. Create a pen and paper drawing of how you would design this forest structure. Be sure to include the recommended domain names within the forest.

Scenario 2-2: Configuring Access Across Networks

The management of Margie's Travel has just released the names of several vendors that you must allow access to network resources. These vendors have Microsoft Windows 2000, Windows Server 2003, or Windows Server 2008 domains. You have established a domain that holds all the information that vendors will need to access within your forest. The vendors want to be able to gain access to these resources without permitting access for your company to their network. What do you need to do to make this happen?

Scenario 2-3: Planning a Migration

You are an IT consultant working with a mid-sized corporation to improve its network. Currently the company is running six Windows 2000 servers in three separate domains. The workstations run various versions of Microsoft Windows, including Windows 2000 Professional and Windows XP Professional. Several new Windows Vista Business machines are being used by management. The company has decided to migrate to Windows Server 2008 using Active Directory to take advantage of centralized administration and better security. To help you consult with your customer, answer the following questions:

1. What considerations should you make during the migration planning?
2. What recommendations will you make?
3. What functional level should be set initially?

Scenario 2-4: DNS Naming

The same client discussed in Scenario 2-3 already has a DNS name registered with the Internet. The client uses it for the company's Web site, which allows customers to access the product database and place orders online. Your client would like to use the same name for its internal network, but you have been advised that using the internal network may affect network security. What options would you suggest they explore to allow some naming consistency while providing internal network security?

Working with Active Directory Sites

OBJECTIVE DOMAIN MATRIX

TECHNOLOGY SKILL	OBJECTIVE DOMAIN	OBJECTIVE DOMAIN NUMBER
Introducing Active Directory Sites	Configure sites.	2.3
Configuring Active Directory Replication	Configure Active Directory replication.	2.4

KEY TERMS

asynchronous replication
bridgehead server
change notification
Classless Inter-Domain Routing (CIDR)
compressed
connection objects
convergence
cost
dcdiag
dual counter-rotating ring
frequency

intersite replication
Intersite Topology Generator (ISTG)
intrasite replication
linked-value replication (LVR)
preferred bridgehead servers
Remote Procedure Calls over Internet Protocol (RPC over IP)
repadmin
replication partners
replication topology

schedule
Simple Mail Transport Protocol (SMTP)
site link bridge
site links
timestamp
transitive
update sequence number (USN)
urgent replication
version ID
well-connected

Woodgrove Bank is a mid-sized community bank in the northeastern United States that is in the process of expanding its branch locations by acquiring smaller banks in nearby areas. Woodgrove Bank relies on Active Directory to provide a single authentication store for its current assets, and it is in the process of migrating its new acquisitions into its existing Active Directory to provide a streamlined logon experience. To manage bandwidth usage between Woodgrove's corporate headquarters and its new acquisitions, its Active Directory design team has created multiple Active Directory sites to control how replication traffic is transmitted between locations.

After completing this lesson, you will have a firm understanding of the Active Directory replication process, which is used to communicate changes from one domain controller to all other domain controllers in a domain or forest. You will be able to discuss the differences between intrasite replication, which takes place within a single well-connected location, and intersite replication, which allows Active Directory changes to be communicated across WAN links to remote locations. You will understand how to implement a plan for creating and managing Active Directory sites as well as managing and monitoring the AD replication process. Because Active Directory Domain Services allows updates to the Active Directory database to be made from any writeable domain controller, replication is a key concept in maintaining a healthy and functional Active Directory environment.

■ Introducing Active Directory Sites

THE BOTTOM LINE

Active Directory replication is the process of duplicating Active Directory information between domain controllers for the purposes of fault tolerance and redundancy. The multimaster replication model within Active Directory requires that domain controllers from each domain participate in the replication process for that domain, as well as replicating forest-wide schema and configuration information. The process of replicating the database and ensuring that updates occur in a timely manner requires you to define how this information is replicated within a domain and throughout the forest. Active Directory sites are the means by which administrators can control replication traffic. Domain controllers that reside within the same site participate in *intrasite replication*. Domain controllers located in different sites will participate in *intersite replication*. Intrasite replication will transmit changes to the Active Directory database almost as soon as they occur; intersite replication occurs on a scheduled basis (every 15 minutes by default). Intersite replication traffic is also *compressed* by default to decrease the use of network bandwidth; intrasite replication traffic is not. This lesson focuses on the details regarding the creation, configuration, replication, and monitoring of Active Directory sites.

Active Directory is made up of separate logical and physical structures. The logical structure of Active Directory defines the logical grouping of Active Directory resources, consisting of forests, domains, trees, and OUs. In contrast, the physical structure of Active Directory defines how information passes through the underlying local area network (LAN) and wide area network (WAN) topology of the network, specifically defining how Active Directory sites and domain controllers map to this physical structure. You can view and manage Active Directory's logical structure with Active Directory Users and Computers and its physical structure with Active Directory Sites and Services. As discussed in Lesson 1, Active Directory sites are based on IP subnets within a physical network. You will create these subnets within Active Directory based on the physical design of your network. When clients log on to Active Directory, they use DNS to query the Active Directory site topology to locate the closest available domain controller and other network resources. Domain controllers use the site topology to establish replication partners that provide efficiency and keep the Active Directory database consistent.

CERTIFICATION READY?
Configure sites
2.3

When you install the forest root domain controller in an Active Directory forest, the Active Directory Installation Wizard creates a single site called Default-First-Site-Name, which you can see in the Active Directory Sites and Services tool, as shown in Figure 3-1. The forest root domain controller server object is placed within the Servers folder of this site. As you will see later, the site can be renamed to more accurately reflect a physical location.

Figure 3-1

Viewing the Active Directory Sites and Services tool

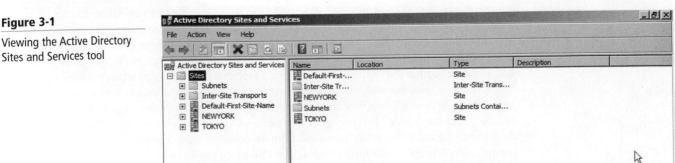

After you installed the first Active Directory domain controller within the Default-First-Site-Name container, you can (and should) customize the site configuration of Active Directory to allow replication to take place between appropriate domain controllers. In general, Active Directory sites have the following characteristics:

- Sites are defined by IP subnets that are ***well-connected***, which means that network infrastructure between them is fast and reliable. In most cases, an Active Directory site will map to a single LAN.

- Multiple sites will be joined together by site links. Intersite replication takes place along site links that you defined within Active Directory Sites and Services. In most cases, your Active Directory site links map to the WAN connections on your network.

- Sites organize the replication process by defining groups of servers that will replicate with each another using intrasite or intersite replication.

- During the logon process, each client queries site information within DNS to assist in determining appropriate domain controllers to be used for Active Directory authentication.

- Active Directory sites are independent of the logical structure of Active Directory. This means that a single site can contain multiple domains, as shown in Figure 3-2, or a single domain can span multiple sites, as shown in Figure 3-3.

Figure 3-2

Configuring multiple domains in a single site

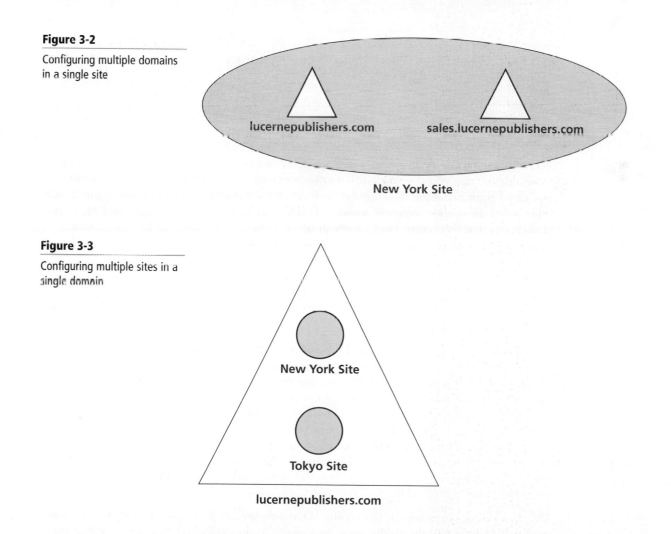

New York Site

Figure 3-3

Configuring multiple sites in a single domain

New York Site

Tokyo Site

lucernepublishers.com

Planning your site topology should be a fundamental component of the Active Directory design process, and it should take place before any actual Active Directory deployment. Because sites are based on IP subnets and on LAN and WAN connections, establishing a site topology prior to installing domain controllers allows you to take advantage of the automatic placement of a domain controller in its appropriate site. During the installation of a new domain controller, the domain controller will automatically be placed in the site corresponding to the network address portion of the domain controller's IP address. However, if the appropriate sites haven't been created prior to installing a new DC, the domain controller will be placed in the Default-First-Site-Name container, and you will need to move it later manually; this can lead to Active Directory clients attempting to authenticate against DCs that may reside in a remote physical location or be separated by slow WAN links. Creating sites according to your IP topology design before the Active Directory rollout saves time and effort and delivers a more robust Active Directory implementation to your end users.

Understanding the Replication Process

Active Directory creates a *replication topology* with the idea that all writeable domain controllers in a domain should communicate Active Directory information to each other, in addition to communicating forest-wide information with other domains. Sites and subnets defined within Active Directory will dictate the path used by replication traffic on the network, as well as form the basis for how Active Directory information is distributed.

Active Directory replication is designed to efficiently track changes and provide fault tolerance to the Active Directory database. Replication within Active Directory will occur when one of the following conditions is met:

- An object is added or removed from Active Directory
- The value of an attribute has changed
- The name of an object has changed

Because changes can be made from any writeable domain controller, Active Directory needs to be able to track changes from different sources and determine which objects need to be replicated from one domain controller to another. Each domain controller maintains a local value called an *update sequence number (USN)* that keeps track of changes that are made at each DC and thus keeps track of which updates should be replicated to other domain controllers. Consider a simple domain consisting of two domain controllers: DC1 and DC2. DC1 currently has a USN of 1000 and DC2 has a USN of 2000. An administrator logs on to DC1 and changes the last name on jsmith's user account, thus incrementing DC1's USN to 1001. When DC2 requests replication changes from DC1, DC1 will transmit the change in jsmith's last name, which DC2 will apply to its local copy of the ntds.dit file.

In addition to the USN, each Active Directory attribute has a *version ID* associated with it that keeps track of how many times that attribute has been changed. So, if the version ID of jsmith's last name attribute is 3 and an administrator changes it from Smith to Arnold to Smith-Arnold and back to Smith again, the new version ID of jsmith's last name attribute is now 6. If the same attribute is modified on two domain controllers at the same time, Active Directory will use the version ID as the first tie-breaker to determine which value to keep and which one to discard. So, if jsmith's last name attribute on DC1 has a value of Smith and a version ID of 6, while DC2's copy of the jsmith object has been updated with a last name of Smith-Arnold with a version ID of 5, Active Directory will retain the value of Smith because it has the higher version ID.

If Active Directory cannot use the version ID as a tie-breaker, the next tie-breaker is the *timestamp*, the time when the modification took place. In the case where two conflicting changes have the same version ID, the modification that took place later will be retained by Active Directory.

TAKE NOTE*

In the extremely
unlikely event that the
version ID *and* the
timestamp are the same,
Active Directory will
use the globally unique
identifier (GUID) of the
domain controller where
the conflicting modifica-
tions took place. The
domain controller with
the *lower* GUID will
win the third, and final,
replication tie-breaker.

When replicating information between sites, Active Directory will designate a ***bridgehead server*** in each site to act as a gatekeeper in managing site-to-site replication. This allows intersite replication to update only one domain controller within a site. After a bridge-head server is updated, it updates the remainder of its domain controller partners with the newly replicated information. For example, suppose the WAN link is down for several hours between two locations of a corporate network. During this time, changes are made to objects and attributes on both sides of the WAN link. When the WAN link comes back online, Active Directory compares the USNs, version IDs, and timestamps of the changes on the bridgehead server on both sides of the WAN link. After determining which updates "win" any tie-breakers that occurred, the bridgehead server in each site contacts its partner bridgehead servers and replicates the new Active Directory changes. After the bridgehead servers in each site have received all the latest replication updates, they will, in turn, con-tinue to replicate the newly obtained information with other partner domain controllers in the same site. Active Directory ***convergence*** describes the amount of time that it takes for this process to take place so that all domain controllers in the environment contain the most up-to-date information.

Working with Intrasite Replication

To understand the details of how replication actually works, you need to understand the difference between intrasite replication and intersite replication. The functional details and roles provided by these replication methods are described in the following sections.

Intrasite replication takes place between domain controllers that are located in the same site, as shown in Figure 3-4. Each domain controller uses an internal process called the Knowledge Consistency Checker (KCC) to map the logical network topology between the domain con-trollers. For each domain controller in the site, the KCC will select one or more ***replication partners*** for that domain controller and will create ***connection objects*** between the domain controller and its new replication partners. Each connection object is a one-way connection. Therefore, in a site with three domain controllers, DC1 might have a connection object to DC2, but DC2 might not have a connection object with DC1.

Figure 3-4

Viewing intrasite replication connections

NEW YORK

TAKE NOTE*

Prior to Windows Server 2003 and Windows Server 2008, any changes to the membership of an Active Directory group forced the entire group member list to be replicated because the member list attribute was considered to be one attribute. A simultaneous change made by multiple administrators to the same group membership list caused some of the updates to be lost due to conflict resolution. The fact that the entire list had to be replicated also required more processing time and higher bandwidth utilization. After you have raised the forest functional level to Windows Server 2003 or higher, a single membership change to a group triggers the replication of only this change to each member in the list rather than the entire membership list. This improvement to replication is called ***linked-value replication (LVR)***.

The guiding principle involved in the KCC's selection of replication partners and its creation of replication objects is the "Rule of Three," which states that no single domain controller should be more than three network hops away from any domain controller that can originate a change to the Active Directory database to minimize the amount of time required for a change to reach all DCs. The KCC is fully automated and does not require administrator intervention unless you have a definite business reason for manually configuring the KCC topology. In fact, there is a significant disadvantage to configuring Active Directory replication links manually, which you'll see in the next section.

Because Active Directory consists of multiple partitions—the domain, schema, configuration partitions, and any application partitions that have been configured—information within each of these partitions is replicated within Active Directory. Domain partition information is replicated to all domain controllers within a domain, and application partition information is replicated based on how the partition in question has been configured. Forest-wide information, such as the content of the schema and configuration partitions, is replicated to all domain controllers in all domains in the forest. Each partition is referred to as a *naming context,* and Active Directory will create a separate replication topology for each partition. This topology defines which servers will replicate the information contained within each naming context.

As you add domain controllers to a site, they become part of the intrasite replication within that site. The KCC will adjust the intrasite replication topology by creating new connection objects to reflect the addition of the newly added DC. You can view these connection objects within the NTDS Settings section within the Active Directory Sites and Services snap-in for each server object.

The KCC runs every 15 minutes and analyzes the best path and placement for connection objects. If a domain controller or a link between domain controllers has failed, the KCC automatically updates the topology by removing this connection from the list of possible replication paths. Consider a single domain containing 2 sites: SiteA and SiteB. SiteA contains two DCs: DC1 and DC2. SiteB contains a single DC, DC3, with a replication connection between DC2 and DC3. In this scenario, if DC2 fails, the KCC will detect this failure and create a new connection object between DC1 and DC3.

By default, intrasite replication is configured to minimize latency to allow changes to take place quickly. Latency is the amount of time or delay it takes for changes to be replicated to all participating domain controllers. The KCC minimizes latency in intrasite replication in a number of ways, including:

- The KCC creates a ***dual counter-rotating ring*** for the replication path. If one domain controller in the ring fails, traffic is routed in the opposite direction to allow replication to continue.

- As the site grows, additional connection objects are created to ensure that no more than three hops for replication exist between domain controllers.

- Intrasite replication traffic is not compressed, resulting in fewer CPU cycles at each domain controller during a replication event.

- Domain controllers use ***change notification*** to inform one another when changes need to be replicated. Each domain controller will hold a change for 15 seconds before forwarding it, after which it will transmit the change to each of its replication partners in 3-second intervals. Because the maximum number of hops between domain controllers is three, the maximum replication latency for changes to reach their final destination is 15 seconds plus 3 seconds per replication partner. Certain operations, such as a password change or an account lockout, will be transmitted using ***urgent replication***, which means that the change will be placed at the "beginning of the line" and will be applied before any other changes that are waiting to be replicated.

Although the KCC process of creating a replication path is fully automatic, it is nonetheless possible to create manual connection objects between domain controllers within the same domain. Creating manual replication connections will allow you to override the replication topology created by the KCC. However, once a manual connection object is created, all automatic connection objects are ignored. Creating manual connection objects also removes the KCC's ability to perform on-the-fly modifications to the replication topology if a domain controller or site link becomes unavailable.

When multiple domains are used within a single site, each domain maintains its own independent replication topology, although schema and configuration naming context information from all domains will still be replicated forest-wide. Consider the example in Figure 3-5. Domain A and Domain B coexist within the same site. All domain information for Domain A replicates with Domain A servers only. The same is true of Domain B. However, the schema and configuration information replicates to all domain controllers in both domains due to the forest-wide nature of the information in both partitions.

Figure 3-5

Viewing intersite replication connections

VIEW ACTIVE DIRECTORY CONNECTION OBJECTS

GET READY. Before you begin these steps, log on to the console of a domain controller using an account with administrative privileges.

1. Open the Active Directory Sites and Services MMC snap-in.
2. Click the **Sites** folder, select the desired site, and then click the **Servers** folder.
3. Expand the server name for which you wish to view connection objects, and right-click **NTDS Settings**. Click **Properties**.
4. Select the **Connections** tab, as shown in Figure 3-6, and view the replication partners that have been configured for this domain controller.

Figure 3-6

Connections tab

5. Click **Cancel** to close the dialog box.

PAUSE. You can close the Active Directory Sites and Services snap-in or leave it open for future exercises.

In the previous exercise, you viewed the replication connections that were configured for a domain controller for intrasite replication.

Implementing and Managing a Site Plan

You will create and manage Active Directory sites using the Active Directory Sites and Services MMC snap-in. In addition to the first site that is automatically configured when you create an Active Directory forest, you can create and manage additional sites to better control replication traffic on your network. The following sections discuss the steps necessary to create, configure, and manage your site plan.

RENAME THE DEFAULT-FIRST-SITE-NAME

GET READY. Before you begin these steps, log on to the console of a domain controller or an administrative workstation that has the Active Directory Administrative Tools installed.

1. Open Active Directory Sites and Services and expand the Sites folder.
2. Right-click the **Default-First-Site-Name** site object, and click **Rename**.
3. Key a site name that is appropriate for your environment (Redmond-Site, for example) and press (**Enter**).

PAUSE. LEAVE the MMC console open to use in the next exercise.

It is not uncommon to rename the Default-First-Site-Name to reflect your overall site strategy. The goal here is to name all elements intuitively, making it easy to understand how they correlate. When naming sites and other related objects, it is best to use only letters, numbers, and the hyphen character.

CREATE A NEW SITE

GET READY. Before you begin these steps, log on to the console of a domain controller or an administrative workstation that has the Active Directory Administrative Tools installed.

1. In Active Directory Sites and Services, right-click the **Sites** folder, and select **New Site**.
2. In the New Object-Site dialog box, key a site name for the new site that is appropriate for your environment.
3. Select **DefaultIPSiteLink** from the list of site names, and click **OK** to complete the site creation. If prompted with an additional information message, read the information presented and then click **OK**.

PAUSE. LEAVE the MMC console open to use in the next exercise.

After all sites and subnets are created, you associate the appropriate site link with the site. The procedure for this is outlined in the next section.

Creating a New Subnet

Each subnet should correspond to a physical network segment. After you have defined the subnets for your network, you will associate them with the appropriate sites.

⊕ **CREATE A NEW SUBNET**

GET READY. Before you begin these steps, log on to the console of a domain controller or an administrative workstation that has the Active Directory Administrative Tools installed.

1. In Active Directory Sites and Services, right-click the **Subnets** folder.
2. Select **New Subnet** from the menu.
3. In the New Object-Subnet dialog box, enter the IP address and subnet in ***Class-less Inter-Domain Routing (CIDR)*** notation in the Name field, as shown in Figure 3-7. This form of notation shows the number of bits being used for the subnet mask. For example, if you are using an IP address of 192.168.64.0 with a mask of 255.255.255.0, the CIDR representation of this would be 192.168.64.0/24.

Figure 3-7

New Object-Subnet dialog box

```
New Object - Subnet                                              ×

   ▮▮   Create in:   lucernepublishing.com/Configuration/Sites/Subnets
  ─────────────────────────────────────────────────────────────────

   Enter the address prefix using network prefix notation (address/prefix
   length), where the prefix length indicates the number of fixed bits. You
   can enter either an IPv4 or an IPv6 subnet prefix.
   Learn more about entering address prefixes.

   IPv4 example:   157.54.208.0/20

   IPv6 example:   3FFE:FFFF:0:C000::/64

   Prefix::
   ┌──────────────────────────────────────────────────────────────┐
   │ 192.168.52.0/24                                                │
   └──────────────────────────────────────────────────────────────┘

   Prefix name in Active Directory Domain Services:
   ┌──────────────────────────────────────────────────────────────┐
   │ 192.168.52.0/24                                                │
   └──────────────────────────────────────────────────────────────┘

   Select a site object for this prefix.
   Site Name
   ┌──────────────────────────────────────────────────────────────┐
   │ 🖳 Default-First-Site-Name                                      │
   │                                                                │
   │                                                                │
   │                                                                │
   └──────────────────────────────────────────────────────────────┘

                         [   OK   ]   [ Cancel ]   [  Help  ]
```

4. Select the site you wish to associate with this subnet and click **OK**.

PAUSE. LEAVE the MMC console open to use in the next exercise.

In this exercise, you created a subnet to associate with a particular site object within Active Directory Sites and Services. By default, no subnets are created through the Active Directory installation process. You need to define all subnets manually within Active Directory Sites and Services. You should create subnets that reflect your physical infrastructure based on the TCP/IP scheme.

Configuring Intersite Replication

If Active Directory information were only replicated within a single site, there would be no way to share object information in the global network. The enterprise network would be made up of many separate LANs that could not share resources, and the idea of centralized administration and single sign-on from anywhere on the network would not be feasible. Recalling that each site consists of one or more IP subnets connected by fast and reliable links, you can now look at how these sites communicate with each other to form one enterprise network.

Active Directory site names generally reflect the name of a physical location and include domain controllers that participate in the domain replication process. Each site contains one or more subnets contained within that site. Consider a computer training company that has a network located in Chicago with four buildings connected by high-speed links. The subnets within these buildings could all be part of the same site. If you add to this network a remote training site located in Minneapolis, you would need to create an additional site with subnets that reflect the location's IP address scheme. When you install a domain controller at the Minneapolis location within the same domain as the Chicago domain controllers, you will need to create a site link in order for replication to take place between Chicago and Minneapolis. A *site link* is a logical, transitive connection between two sites that mirrors the routed connections between networks and allows replication to occur. To create a replication topology in a multisite network, one domain controller within each site runs the *Intersite Topology Generator* (ISTG), which is a process that is responsible for selecting a bridgehead server and mapping the topology to be used for replication between sites.

With the exception of the DEFAULTIPSITELINK, which is created automatically when you install Active Directory, all Active Directory site links need to be created manually. All site link objects possess the following characteristics:

- Site links connect two sites that communicate using the same protocol.
- Site link objects are defined manually.
- Site link objects correspond to the WAN links connecting the sites.
- The ISTG uses site links to establish an intersite replication topology.

The primary goal of intersite replication is to minimize bandwidth usage. Unlike intrasite replication, intersite replication will compress data that is replicated between sites, thus reducing the amount of network traffic used by Active Directory replication.

When you create a site link object, configure the following three attributes to control the behavior of replication traffic over the site link:

- *Cost.* Assigning a cost to a site link object allows the administrator to define the path that replication will take. If more than one path can be used to replicate information, cost assignments will determine which path is chosen first. A lower-numbered cost value will be chosen over a higher-numbered cost value. Cost values can use a value of 1 to 99,999. No absolute numbering scheme is used here. Instead, the values are chosen by the Active Directory administrator and are relational only to one another. For example, a site link with a cost of 2 will be selected over one with a cost of 5, and a site link with a cost of 1,000 will be selected over one with a cost of 10,000. The default cost of a newly created site link object is 100.

- *Schedule.* The schedule of the site link object determines when the link is available to replicate information. For example, you may configure a site link's schedule so that it can only transmit replication traffic between midnight and 5 AM Monday through Friday. You will typically configure this value to reflect off-peak business hours for slow or heavily utilized WAN links to ensure that link bandwidth is not bogged down by replication traffic. By default, newly created site link objects are available for replication 24/7.

- *Frequency.* A site link's frequency determines how often information will be replicated over a particular site link. Replication will take place only during scheduled hours. However, within that scheduled time it can take place as often as the frequency attribute permits. The default replication frequency for a new site link is 180 minutes, but it can be configured to take place as frequently as every 15 minutes and as infrequently as once per week.

CERTIFICATION READY?
Configure Active Directory replication
2.4

CREATE A NEW SITE LINK OBJECT

GET READY. Before you begin these steps, log on to the console of a domain controller or an administrative workstation that has the Active Directory Administrative Tools installed.

1. In Active Directory Sites and Services, expand the Inter-Site Transports folder as shown in Figure 3-8.

Figure 3-8

Inter-Site Transports folder

2. Right-click the desired protocol, either IP or SMTP, and select **New Site Link**.

3. In the New Object-Site Link dialog box, key the name of the site link. This name should reflect the locations that will be connected using this link.

4. From the Sites Not In This Site Link list, select the sites you wish to associate with this link and click **Add**. They will appear on the right side of the dialog box under Sites In This Site Link. Click **OK** to complete the link creation.

5. Right-click the site link you just created and select **Properties**. The site link cost is set to 100 by default; modify this number, if necessary, according to your site link plan. Remember that a lower number indicates a preferred path.

6. If you wish to change the replication frequency to something other than the default of 180, modify the Replicate Every xx Minutes field.

7. To modify the schedule to allow replication to take place only during the hours you specify, click **Change Schedule**.

8. Select the days and hours you wish to disallow or allow replication and adjust the option button at the right of the schedule chart to show the appropriate color. Days and hours highlighted in blue indicate that replication is allowed. When finished, select **OK** to close the Schedule dialog box.

9. Upon completing all desired link configurations, click **OK**.

PAUSE. LEAVE the Sites and Services MMC snap-in open to complete the next exercise.

When designing your site link topology, the values that you assign to these attributes must be considered carefully for maximum replication performance. Use the following guidelines when setting link properties:

* Cost attribute values should consider the speed and reliability of the links in use. For example, you would assign a relatively lower cost to a reliable T-1 link than to a 128-Kbps ISDN link that is only utilized when the T-1 is unavailable.

* Schedule attribute values should consider the tradeoff between replicating during off-peak hours and having the most up-to-date information at all sites.

* Short frequency attribute values consume less bandwidth due to frequent small replication cycles, as well as providing more up-to-date information. Longer replication intervals may require more bandwidth during replication and less up-to-date information between replication cycles.

Selecting a Replication Protocol

When configuring replication, you can choose between two possible protocols: RPC over IP and SMTP. In this section, we'll discuss the differences between these two replication protocols. We will also look at situations in which you might choose one over the other, based on the advantages and disadvantages of each.

TAKE NOTE*

After you have created a site or a site link object, you can go to the Properties sheet for that object and place a checkmark next to Protect from Accidental Deletion on the Object tab. As the name implies, this will protect you against an administrator deleting a critical object, like a site, by mistake; with this checkbox selected, Active Directory will not allow the deletion and will instead raise an error message alerting the administrator that the object has been protected against deletion.

For both intrasite and intersite replication, Active Directory uses *Remote Procedure Calls over Internet Protocol (RPC over IP)* by default for all replication traffic. RPC is commonly used to communicate with network services on various computers, whereas IP is responsible for the addressing and routing of the data. RPC over IP replication keeps data secure while in transit by using both authentication and encryption.

Simple Mail Transport Protocol (SMTP) is an alternative solution for intersite replication when a direct or reliable IP connection is not available. SMTP, a member of the Transmission Control Protocol/Internet Protocol (TCP/IP) suite, is the standard protocol used for message transfer such as email. SMTP site links use *asynchronous replication*, meaning that each replication transaction does not need to complete before another can start because the transaction can be stored until the destination server is available. This protocol provides limited replication functionality because it can only replicate configuration, schema, and application directory partitions. SMTP cannot replicate domain directory partitions, and it requires an enterprise certification authority (CA) that is fully integrated with Active Directory. The CA signs SMTP messages exchanged between domain controllers, thereby ensuring the authenticity of directory updates. A CA is responsible for issuing digital certificates that allow two computers to communicate securely.

Unlike RPC over IP, SMTP does not adhere to schedules and should be used only when replicating between different domains over an extremely slow or unreliable WAN link. Table 3-1 summarizes the differences between intrasite and intersite replication.

X REF

You will find a complete discussion of Active Directory Certificate Services in Lesson 13.

Table 3-1

Intrasite and Intersite Replication

INTRASITE REPLICATION	INTERSITE REPLICATION
Replication within sites is not compressed. It is optimized to reduce latency.	Replication between sites is compressed to optimize WAN bandwidth utilization.
Replication partners notify each other of the changes that need to be made.	Bridgehead servers are responsible for collecting replication data, compressing it, and sending it across site links.
Normal replication takes place at 15-minute intervals. Security-sensitive changes trigger immediate replication.	Site links must be configured for replication to take place between sites.
The KCC checks for site topology changes every 15 minutes.	The default replication schedule is set for every 180 minutes, seven days a week.
Replication uses the RPC over IP protocol within a site.	If two or more site links are configured for fault tolerance, the cost settings determine the preferred path.
RPC over IP is used as the transport protocol.	RPC over IP or SMTP can be used as the transport protocol. RPC over IP is the preferred choice for most situations.

Designating a Bridgehead Server

Although all domain controllers within the same site will participate in the replication process with each other, not all domain controllers will replicate with other sites simultaneously. This is because replicating Active Directory data between sites using all available domain controllers can be an extremely bandwidth-intensive operation. To further minimize the bandwidth implications of intersite replications, Active Directory will designate a bridgehead server within each site.

All traffic within a site is replicated to that site's bridgehead server. The bridgehead server is then responsible for replicating all changes that have taken place within that site to other bridgehead servers in remote sites. The Inter-Site Topology Generator (ISTG) automatically assigns one server in each site as the bridgehead server unless you override this by establishing a list of *preferred bridgehead servers*. The advantage of administratively assigning a preferred bridgehead server list is that you can determine which servers have the best processing power and available network bandwidth for handling replication traffic. Remember that intersite replication traffic is compressed by default, so the bridgehead servers will be responsible for decompressing, compressing, sending, and receiving all replication traffic within the site and between sites. Configuring more than one preferred bridgehead server allows administrative control over the task of replicating between sites using the most efficient machines. When more than one preferred bridgehead server is configured and the preferred bridgehead server fails, the KCC will choose another server from the list.

When planning the use of bridgehead servers, consider the following guidelines:

- Configure a list of preferred bridgehead servers to assist in better performance from site to site. Servers should be chosen based on processing capabilities. Bridgehead servers must compress and decompress replication data efficiently. The server with the slowest processor on your network would not be the best choice for the role of bridgehead server.
- Configure multiple bridgehead servers for multiple partitions.
- If a server that has been designated by the ISTG as a preferred bridgehead server fails, the ISTG will assign a new bridgehead server from the configured list. This assumes that you have configured more than one server in the list. Microsoft, therefore, recommends that you configure multiple preferred bridgehead servers whenever possible.

DESIGNATE PREFERRED BRIDGEHEAD SERVERS

GET READY. Before you begin these steps, log on to the console of a domain controller using an account that has administrative privileges.

1. In Active Directory Sites and Services, expand the desired Sites folder, and then expand the Servers folder containing the server you wish to add to the bridgehead server list.

2. Right-click the domain controller you wish to configure and select **Properties**, as shown in Figure 3-9.

Figure 3-9

General tab of the Properties window

3. From the list of transports on the left side, choose the appropriate protocol for replication, and then click **Add.** The protocol will appear on the right side, showing that this server will be added to the list of Preferred Bridgehead Servers for the chosen protocol.

PAUSE. LEAVE the Sites and Services MMC snap-in open to complete the next exercise.

A *site link bridge* defines a chain of site links by which domain controllers from different sites can communicate. In the case where there is a centralized site that connects two branch sites via site links, the site link bridge creates a direct link between the branch sites using the total cost of both site links to the central site.

All site links that use the same transport protocol are considered to be *transitive* by default, which means that a domain controller in any site can connect to a domain controller in any other site by navigating a chain of site links. In a fully routed IP network, this feature generally follows your routing topology. The ISTG uses this information when creating the replication topology to automatically bridge all site links, thereby allowing two or more sites to replicate in any direction using this automatic site link bridging. However, if your network is not fully routed, it is recommended that you disable automatic site link bridging and instead configure manual site link bridges according to your network infrastructure. This allows the ISTG to create paths that are most appropriate for your topology and link speeds. The following situations warrant the manual creation of site link bridges:

- When your network is not fully routed, manually created site link bridges allow better performance by creating a shortcut between sites that are not directly connected.
- If there are many sites and the forest functional level has not been raised to the Windows Server 2003 forest level or better, creating manual site link bridges may be necessary to prevent the ISTG from becoming overloaded.

CONFIGURING MANUAL SITE LINK BRIDGING

Site link bridging is enabled by default and works well in a fully routed network. However, disabling site link bridging in a network that is not fully connected will allow you to create the site links according to your network infrastructure or business guidelines.

➔ DISABLE AUTOMATIC SITE LINK BRIDGING

GET READY. Before you begin these steps, log on to the console of a domain controller or an administrative workstation that has the Active Directory Administrative Tools installed.

1. In Active Directory Sites and Services, expand the Inter-Site Transports folder.
2. Right-click the protocol you wish to configure and select **Properties.**
3. Remove the checkmark next to the **Bridge All Site Links** checkbox and click **OK.**

PAUSE. LEAVE the Sites and Services MMC snap-in open to complete the next exercise.

In the previous exercise, you disabled automatic site link bridging within the Active Directory Sites and Services MMC snap-in. The next step in this situation would be to create one or more manual site link bridges to match the topology of your physical network.

➔ CREATE A MANUAL SITE LINK BRIDGE

GET READY. Before you begin these steps, log on to the console of a domain controller or an administrative workstation that has the Active Directory Administrative Tools installed. Be sure that you have disabled automatic site link bridging, as described in the previous exercise.

1. In Active Directory Sites and Services, expand the Inter-Site Transports folder.
2. Right-click the protocol you wish to bridge and select **New Site Link Bridge.**

3. Select the site links you wish to bridge and click **Add.** Key a description for the bridge and click **OK** to finish.

PAUSE. LEAVE the Sites and Services MMC snap-in open to complete the next exercise.

In the previous exercise, you created a manual site link bridge for a network in which automatic site link bridging has been disabled. This is a necessary step for a company that has a physical network that is not fully routed or in situations where you wish to exert more granular control over the path taken by Active Directory replication traffic.

Managing Replication

When monitoring Active Directory replication, any errors that occur will be logged to the Directory Services Event Viewer on each domain controller. For example, when simultaneous changes are made to an object's attributes from different domain controllers and the change cannot be updated due to a collision, the error is logged to the Event Viewer. Some of these errors may be for informational purposes, whereas others may warrant some investigation and corrective action. This section describes some of the methods used to determine which domain controllers contribute to the problems.

In many cases, after an Active Directory problem is isolated, it is necessary to initiate a forced replication to help get Active Directory up to date and consistent. Refreshing the replication topology is accomplished by forcing the KCC to run. Depending on whether you wish to refresh the intrasite topology or the intersite topology, the steps are slightly different. Refreshing the topology within a site requires the KCC to be triggered on one of the domain controllers within the site.

REFRESH THE INTRASITE REPLICATION TOPOLOGY

GET READY. Before you begin these steps, log on to the console of a domain controller or an administrative workstation that has the Active Directory Administrative Tools installed.

1. In Active Directory Sites and Services, expand Sites, followed by the site where you wish to run the KCC.
2. Expand Servers, and double-click one of the domain controllers.
3. In the details pane, right-click **NTDS Settings**, click **All Tasks**, and select **Check Replication Topology.**

PAUSE. LEAVE the MMC console open to use in the next exercise.

To refresh the intersite replication topology, follow the steps listed in the previous exercise on the domain controller that has been designated as the ISTG for a particular site.

DETERMINE WHICH SERVER HOLDS THE ISTG ROLE

GET READY. Before you begin these steps, log on to the console of a domain controller or an administrative workstation that has the Active Directory Administrative Tools installed.

1. In Active Directory Sites and Services, expand the Sites folder, and then expand the appropriate site.
2. In the Details pane, right-click **NTDS Site Settings**, and then select **Properties**. The Properties page displays the server holding the ISTG role.
3. To force the KCC to regenerate the intersite topology, right-click **NTDS Settings**, click **All Tasks**, and then select **Check Replication Topology.**

PAUSE. LEAVE the MMC console open to use in the next exercise.

The ISTG role is held by one domain controller at each site. The ISTG is designated automatically, and it is responsible for the intersite topology and the designation of bridgehead servers if you have not defined them manually. Determining which server is running the ISTG service allows you to force the KCC to run so that you can refresh the intersite replication topology.

TRIGGERING MANUAL REPLICATION

When troubleshooting Active Directory replication, you may wish to manually force replication between two DCs in an attempt to correct any inconsistencies or errors that you have found. You may also wish to force replication to occur when you make chang es, such as disabling user accounts, that you wish to replicate immediately throughout the enterprise without waiting for the next replication interval.

⊖ FORCE MANUAL REPLICATION

GET READY. Before you begin these steps, log on to the console of a domain controller or an administrative workstation that has the Active Directory Administrative Tools installed.

1. In Active Directory Sites and Services, expand Sites, followed by the site that contains the connection for which you wish to force replication.
2. Locate the server in the Servers container that provides the connection object.
3. Click **NTDS Settings** in the console tree.
4. In the details pane, right-click the connection for which you want replication to occur and select **Replicate Now**.

PAUSE. LEAVE the MMC console open to use in the next exercise.

In the previous exercise, you used the Active Directory Sites and Services MMC snap-in to force Active Directory replication to occur. You can also perform this task using the repadmin command-line tool, which we will discuss in the following section.

Monitoring Replication

Monitoring replication is a vital part of managing your Active Directory network because many Active Directory issues can be prevented by monitoring replication activity on your network. Windows Server 2008 provides a number of tools that allow problem discovery, diagnosis, and resolution. In addition to the directory service event log available in the Event Viewer, Windows Server 2008 provides several additional monitoring tools that are installed when you add the Active Directory Domain Services role to a 2008 server. The tools discussed here were formerly part of the Support Tools available on the Windows Server 2003 CD, but are now supported natively within the Windows Server 2008 operating system.

The monitoring tools that you will focus on here are dcdiag and repadmin both of which can be run from the command-line of the domain controller as well as remotely from an administrative workstation.

Dcdiag is a command-line tool used for monitoring Active Directory. When run from a command prompt, this tool can do the following:

- Perform connectivity and replication tests, reporting errors that occur
- Report DNS registration problems
- Analyze the permissions required for replication
- Analyze the state of domain controllers within the forest

To view all of the options and syntax for dcdiag, use the /? option from a command prompt as follows:

```
dcdiag /?
```

An example of the syntax required to check replication connections using dcdiag is as follows:

```
dcdiag /test:replications
```

Repadmin is a command-line tool used for the following:

- To view the replication topology from the perspective of each domain controller. This aids in understanding how information is transferred, ultimately assisting in the isolation of replication problems.

- To manually create a replication topology if site link bridging is disabled because the network is not fully routed.

- To force replication between domain controllers when you need updates to occur immediately without waiting for the next replication cycle.

- To view the replication metadata, which is the combination of the actual data and the up-to-date vector or USN information. This is helpful in determining the most up-to-date information prior to seizing an operations master role.

Like dcdiag, you can view a complete list of syntax options for repadmin by using the / ? switch. The following example illustrates this:

```
repadmin /?
```

The following is an example of the syntax to show all replication partners for server1 in the cohowinery.com domain:

```
repadmin /showreps server1.cohowinery.com
```

SUMMARY SKILL MATRIX

IN THIS LESSON YOU LEARNED:

- To define and manage sites and site links.

- To determine a site strategy based on the physical network infrastructure.

- To use Active Directory Sites and Services to configure replication.

- To understand the differences between intrasite and intersite replication.

- To describe the role of the Intersite Topology Generator (ISTG) and Knowledge Consistency Checker (KCC) in site replication.

- To optimize replication by configuring bridgehead servers and site link bridging.

- To monitor replication using dcdiag and repadmin.

Knowledge Assessment

Fill in the Blank

Complete the following sentences by writing the correct word or words in the blanks provided.

1. The amount of time that it takes for a change to be replicated to all domain controllers in an environment is called _____.

2. The default _____ of any new site link is 100.

3. Intersite replication uses _____ traffic to reduce the impact to bandwidth on corporate WAN links.

4. The KCC creates a(n) _____ to allow replication to take place in the opposite direction in the event that a single domain controller in the replication topology fails.

5. The purpose of the KCC is to create a(n) _____ between multiple domain controllers within a site as well as between sites.

6. By default, all Active Directory site links are _____.

7. When Active Directory detects a replication conflict in which two objects have been modified nearly simultaneously, the first attribute that Active Directory will use as a tie-breaker is the _____.

8. Active Directory will designate a(n) _____ within each site to manage inter-site replication activity.

9. The minimum _____ that you can assign to a site link is 15 minutes.

10. Within a single site, domain controllers will use _____ to inform other DCs that intrasite replication needs to take place.

Multiple Choice

Circle the correct choice.

1. The KCC is responsible for calculating intrasite replication partners. During this process, what is the maximum number of hops that the KCC will allow between domain controllers?
   a. 2
   b. 3
   c. 4
   d. 5

2. Replication that occurs between sites is called _____ replication.
   a. Local
   b. Remote
   c. Intersite
   d. Intrasite

3. Company XYZ is a national company with locations in Detroit, Minneapolis, Phoenix, and Dallas. There are two connections between Detroit and Minneapolis. The first is a T-1 link and the second is a 128-Kbps link. When setting up the site links for replication, what should you do to ensure that the 128-Kbps link is used only if the T-1 is unavailable?
   a. Set a cost of 1 for the T-1 and a cost of 5 for the 128-Kbps link.
   b. Set a cost of 5 for the T-1 and 1 for the 128-Kbps link.
   c. Leave the costs at their default value of 100.
   d. Change the schedule manually to disallow replication on the 128-Kbps link until it is needed.

4. You are the administrator for a network that has several sites. There is a site link from the main headquarters to each remote site for file transfer and replication purposes. You have been asked to create five new users on the network, and several of the users need immediate access to network applications. When asked by your manager how long replication of these new accounts will take, what is your response?
   a. Replication occurs every 180 minutes by default.
   b. Replication occurs at 15-minute intervals.
   c. Replication occurs as soon as the account is added.
   d. Replication occurs only between 12:00 AM and 6:00 AM.

5. Given the scenario in question 4, how long would it take for other DCs within the head-quarters site to replicate the accounts belonging to the new users?
   a. Replication occurs every 180 minutes by default.
   b. Replication occurs at 15-minute intervals.
   c. Replication occurs within 15 seconds of the account being added.
   d. Replication occurs only between 12:00 AM and 6:00 AM.

6. What mechanism is used by an Active Directory domain controller to indicate that it has unreplicated changes to communicate to its replication partners?
   a. Preferred bridgehead servers
   b. Change notification
   c. Site link bridges
   d. Intersite replication

7. When would you disable automatic site link bridging within Active Directory Sites and Services?
   a. When you need to configure intersite replication
   b. When you wish to configure different costs for your site links
   c. When your physical network is not fully routed
   d. When you wish to control the hours during which intersite replication will occur

8. To optimize client authentication and location of resources, which kind of object should each Active Directory site contain?
   a. Site links
   b. Costs
   c. Connection objects
   d. Subnets

9. Which of the following naming contexts are replicated across an entire Active Directory forest?
   a. Configuration and Schema
   b. Schema and DomainDNSZones
   c. Configuration and ForestDNSZones
   d. Schema and ForestDNSZones

10. When creating a site link, you can configure it to use which of the following protocols?
    a. TCP/IP or RPC over IP
    b. RPC over IP or SMTP
    c. SMTP or TCP/IP
    d. SMTP or CIDR

■ Case Scenarios

Scenario 3-1: Adding a New Site to a Network

Your company is located in the United States, and it has just added a location in Canada that will need to become part of your Active Directory network. Your network designer has provided you with the following configuration information regarding the new location servers and the connections that have been procured.

Three new servers will be installed in the Canada facility with the following specifications:

- Server 1: 2.4-GHz processor with 2 GB RAM will be installed as a domain controller.
- Server 2: 2.0-GHz processor with 1 GB RAM will be installed as a domain controller.
- Server 3: 2.0-GHz processor with 2 GB RAM will be installed as an application server.

Two links between the United States and Canada facilities will be available. They are as follows:

- A T-1 link for the primary connection
- A 256-Kbps link for a backup connection

Bandwidth should be used during the day mainly for file transfers and email. Any network maintenance that requires bandwidth should be done only between 11:00 PM and 4:00 AM on weekdays. Weekends are available anytime for maintenance procedures.

Sketch a design that will meet the previous requirements and consider the following questions:

1. Should you configure a bridgehead server at the Canada facility? If so, which server would you recommend?

2. What will you configure the costs for on each link?

3. What should the replication schedule and interval be set for?

Scenario 3-2: Improving Replication Efficiency

You are the administrator for a mid-sized company network that consists of Windows Server 2008 domain controllers. The five sites you have are not fully routed, and there have been some problems replicating Active Directory data. You know your budget will not allow you to add additional links or purchase additional equipment. What can you do to improve the efficiency of replication within your network?

Global Catalog and Flexible Single Master Operations (FSMO) Roles

OBJECTIVE DOMAIN MATRIX

TECHNOLOGY SKILL	OBJECTIVE DOMAIN	OBJECTIVE DOMAIN NUMBER
Configuring Additional Global Catalog Servers	Configure the global catalog.	2.5
Placing FSMO Role Holders	Configure operations masters.	2.6

KEY TERMS

cached credentials

clock skew

Domain Naming Master

_gc

Indexed

Infrastructure Master

partial attribute set (PAS)

Primary Domain Controller (PDC)
  Emulator

relative Identifier (RID)

Relative Identifier (RID) Master

Schema Master

security identifier (SID)

seize

transfer

universal group

universal group membership
  caching

Margie's Travel is a national chain of booking agencies for resort hotels throughout Europe and the Caribbean. It relies heavily on Active Directory to provide authentication for its many database and intranet applications. Margie's Travel uses a multidomain Active Directory forest containing an empty forest root domain and several child domains representing the geographical regions served by the different offices. Because of the multidomain nature of the Margie's Travel Active Directory infrastructure, the Margie's Travel IT staff needs to strictly maintain access to global catalog servers and Flexible Single Master Operations (FSMO) role holders across the entire organization.

After completing this lesson, you will be able to discuss the global catalog server and the critical role that it plays within Active Directory. You will understand the importance of proper placement of global catalog servers within an Active Directory forest and how to add and remove global catalogs from your network. You will also be able to discuss a feature known as universal group caching, which can reduce the reliance on global catalog servers in certain environments where it might not be feasible to deploy as many as you require. Finally, you will be able to describe the Flexible Single Master Operations (FSMO) roles, and the functions that they perform within an Active Directory domain and forest. Through the exercises and information presented in this lesson, you will be able to plan the optimum placement of FSMO roles within your environment as well as deploy, transfer, and seize FSMO roles in the event of the temporary or permanent failure of one or more domain controllers within your Active Directory domain or forest.

Understanding the Global Catalog

THE BOTTOM LINE

Although the global catalog is not one of the five FSMO roles, the services it provides are of critical importance to the functionality of the Active Directory network. The global catalog holds a subset of forest-wide Active Directory objects and acts as a central repository by holding a complete copy of all objects from the host server's local domain along with a partial copy of all objects from other domains within the same forest, called the *partial attribute set (PAS)*. This partial copy of forest-wide data includes a subset of each object's attributes. The attributes included in this subset are necessary to provide functionality such as logon, object searches, and universal group memberships.

Understanding the Functions of the Global Catalog

By default, the first domain controller installed in the forest root domain is designated as a global catalog server. However, any or all domain controllers in a domain can be designated as global catalog servers. As an Active Directory administrator, you need to carefully weigh the benefits of designating additional domain controllers in your environment as global catalogs against the resulting performance implications.

X REF

For more information about Active Directory's need for SRV record support in DNS, refer to Lesson 2.

The global catalog has four main functions in an Active Directory environment:

- **Facilitating searches for objects in the forest.** When a user initiates a search for an object in Active Directory, the request is automatically sent to TCP port 3268, which is used by Active Directory to direct these requests to a global catalog server. One of the SRV records used by Active Directory refers to the global catalog, or _gc, service, which listens on port 3268 to respond to these requests.

- **Resolving User Principal Names (UPNs).** UPNs allow users to log on to domains across the forest using a standardized naming format that matches the format used for email addresses, such as jsmith@lucernepublishing.com. When a local domain controller receives a request for logon via a UPN, it contacts a global catalog server to complete the logon process. For example, assume the user account for jsmith resides in the lucernepublishing.com domain, and jsmith is currently working from the tokyo. lucernepublishing.com location. Because jsmith travels frequently between the various corporate locations, he uses the UPN, jsmith@lucernepublishing.com, to log on to his network account and his email account. Upon receiving a logon attempt from jsmith, a local domain controller searches for a global catalog server to resolve jsmith@ lucernepublishing.com to a username. The global catalog server stores enough information about the user to permit or deny the logon request. For example, if a time restriction allows logons only during business hours and jsmith is attempting to log on after hours, the global catalog will have a copy of that information and, therefore, jsmith's logon request will be denied. Because of this need to allow user authentication across domains, Active Directory must be able to contact a global catalog (or have a mechanism to cache global catalog information as you will see shortly) to process any user logon, even in a single-domain environment.

TAKE NOTE ✱ UPN logons also are possible between forests that have a cross-forest trust established.

- **Maintaining universal group membership information.** Active Directory users can be permitted or denied access to a resource based on their group memberships. This information is an important part of a user's security token, which is used to determine which resources a user can and cannot access. Domain local and global group memberships are stored at the domain level; universal group memberships are stored in the global catalog. A *universal group* can contain users, groups, and computers from any domain in the forest. In addition, universal groups, through their membership in domain local groups, can receive permissions for any resource anywhere in the forest. A user who is a member of a universal group can be granted or denied permission to access resources throughout the forest. This presents another reason why a global catalog is required for a successful first-time logon to Active Directory. Without the global catalog available to query universal group memberships, a complete picture of the user's group memberships cannot be created and the logon process would be incomplete.

- **Maintaining a copy of all objects in the domain.** A domain controller that has been configured as a global catalog will contain a copy of its own domain NC, as well as a copy of the partial attribute set (PAS) of every other domain NC in the forest. Each object class has a certain list of attributes that are included in the PAS. This is defined within the Active Directory schema. You can add attributes to the PAS by modifying the attribute so that it is *indexed*, which means that it will be stored in the PAS and replicated to all global catalog servers in the forest.

For sites that do not have a global catalog server available, Windows Server 2003 and 2008 offer a feature called *universal group membership caching*. This stores universal group memberships on a local domain controller that can be used for logon to the domain, eliminating the need for frequent access to a global catalog server. The universal group membership caching feature allows domain controllers to process a logon or resource request without the presence of a global catalog server. For universal group membership caching to function, a user must have successfully logged on when a global catalog server was available and universal group membership caching was enabled. Universal membership caching records each user's information individually. For example, if universal group caching is not available to record the user's information into cache and the global catalog server goes offline, the logon attempt will fail.

Universal group membership caching is enabled on a per-site basis. The information in the cache is refreshed every eight hours, by default, using a confirmation request sent by the local domain controller to a global catalog server. Universal group caching has the following benefits:

- It eliminates the need to place a global catalog in a remote location where the link speed is slow or unreliable.

- It provides better logon performance for users with cached information. If the global catalog is located across a WAN link, cached credentials can replace the need to have logon traffic sent across a slow or unreliable link.

- It minimizes WAN usage for replication traffic because the domain controller does not have to hold information about forest-wide objects. In addition, these remote domain controllers are not listed in DNS as providers of global catalog services for the forest, further reducing bandwidth constraints.

WARNING If the user has successfully logged on in the past and you have enabled *cached credentials* in your environment, a user will be able to log on using a cached copy of his or her logon credentials that have been stored on his or her local workstation. Allowing these credentials to be cached on a local computer can pose a security threat for certain companies. For example, if you have a computer that is shared by multiple users with different access permissions, cached credentials could be used for an account to allow an unauthorized user to gain access to a resource.

REF

Group policies allow cached logons to be disabled on a local computer. For more information about the use of group policies for security purposes, refer to Lessons 7 through 10.

Table 4-1 summarizes the logon process with regard to the global catalog and universal group membership caching.

Table 4-1

Logon Process Summary

LOGON REQUEST SCENARIO	RESPONSE
The forest mode is set to Windows 2000 or above. A global catalog server is available.	The domain controller receiving the authentication request attempts to locate a global catalog server. A global catalog server is queried for the user's universal group memberships. The user is granted or denied access based on supplied credentials and the associated ACLs.
The forest mode is set to Windows 2000 or above. A global catalog server is not available. It is not functioning or inaccessible due to a connectivity problem or a down WAN link. Universal group membership caching is not enabled.	The domain controller receiving the authentication request attempts to locate a global catalog. The user logon is denied because the global catalog server cannot be contacted.
The forest mode is set to Windows 2000 or above. A global catalog server is not available. Universal group membership caching is enabled.	The domain controller receiving the authentication request attempts to locate a global catalog server. This query fails. If the user has successfully logged on in the past when the global catalog server was online and universal group membership caching was enabled, the logon is processed and the user is granted or denied access based on supplied credentials and ACLs. If the user has not logged on in the past when a global catalog server was available and universal group membership caching was enabled, the logon will be denied.

 ENABLE UNIVERSAL GROUP MEMBERSHIP CACHING

GET READY. Before you begin these steps, you must be logged on as a member of the Domain Admins group in the forest root domain or as an Enterprise Admin.

1. Open Active Directory Sites and Services.
2. Select the site from the console tree for which you want to enable universal group membership caching.
3. In the details window, right-click **NTDS Site Settings** and select **Properties**.

4. Select the **Enable Universal Group Membership Caching** checkbox, as shown in Figure 4-1.

Figure 4-1

Enabling universal group membership caching

5. In the Refresh Cache From field, select a site that you wish this site to receive updates from or leave it at <Default> to refresh from the nearest site that contains a global catalog server. Click **OK**.

PAUSE. CLOSE the Active Directory Sites and Services MMC snap-in.

You have just enabled universal group membership caching for a single site within Active Directory. This setting must be enabled for each site that you wish to configure for universal group membership caching.

Configuring Additional Global Catalog Servers

By default, the first domain controller in a forest is a global catalog server. Therefore, your initial site will already contain a global catalog server.

The following guidelines will help you decide when you should add a global catalog server.

- Each site should contain a global catalog server to facilitate user logons. If a remote site is located across an unreliable or slow WAN link, a locally deployed global catalog server will allow logons and Active Directory searches to take place regardless of the state of the WAN link. If this is not possible, consider enabling universal group membership caching.

- When placing a global catalog at a remote site, consider the amount of bandwidth necessary to replicate global catalog information. Responding to logon requests from other sites increases the demands on bandwidth for the remote site.

- The domain controller that hosts the global catalog must have enough space on the hard drive to house the global catalog. As a rule of thumb, you should estimate 50 percent of the size of the ntds.dit file of every other domain in the forest when sizing hardware for a global catalog server.

- A site that contains an application using port 3268 for global catalog queries should contain a global catalog server. Port 3268 is used for Active Directory object searches.

CONFIGURE AN ADDITIONAL GLOBAL CATALOG SERVER

GET READY. Before you begin these steps, you must be logged on as a member of the Domain Admins group.

1. On the domain controller where you want the new global catalog, open **Active Directory Sites and Services** from the Administrative Tools folder.

2. In the console tree, double-click **Sites**, and then double-click the site name that contains the domain controller for which you wish to add the global catalog.

3. Double-click the **Servers** folder and select your domain controller. Right-click **NTDS Settings** and select **Properties**.

4. On the General tab, select the **Global Catalog** checkbox, as shown in Figure 4-2, to assign the role of global catalog to this server. Click **OK**.

Figure 4-2

Configuring an additional global catalog server

PAUSE. CLOSE the Active Directory Sites and Services MMC snap-in.

TAKE NOTE*

You also have the option to configure an RODC to host the Global Catalog Server role.

You have just configured a domain controller as an additional global catalog within an Active Directory domain. You can enable some or all domain controllers in a forest as additional global catalog servers in your environment. You will need to allow sufficient time for the account and schema information to replicate to the new global catalog server. The length of time this process takes will vary depending on the number of objects to be replicated and the speed of the link used for the transfer. The Directory Services Event Viewer will display Event ID 1119 when the computer is ready to advertise itself as a global catalog server.

■ Understanding Flexible Single Master Operations (FSMO) Roles

THE BOTTOM LINE

As discussed previously, Active Directory is a multimaster database, which means that updates to the Active Directory database can be made by any writeable domain controller in your environment. However, some sensitive operations need to be controlled more stringently than others, such as schema management and adding or removing additional domains from an Active Directory forest. These specialized roles are called Flexible Single Master Operations (FSMO) roles. Beyond acting as a normal domain controller in the replica ring, the domain controllers that hold these FSMO roles are responsible for providing services classified as single-master operations. This means only one domain controller in each domain or, in some cases, one domain controller in each forest can provide a particular operation. By employing single-master operations servers, you can more closely control the kinds of operations that might create issues in Active Directory if more than one domain controller were able to perform them at one time.

As you have already learned, writeable Active Directory domain controllers follow a multi-master replication model. This multimaster model ensures that multiple copies of all domain objects provide ease of accessibility and fault tolerance. In addition, any domain controller can update the contents of the database when changes occur. This multimaster model provides a fast and efficient directory service when the implementation guidelines are followed.

Although Active Directory has mechanisms, such as version IDs and timestamps, to assist in possible conflict resolution, critical functions need to have the assurance of little or no risk of errors. An example of a task that should not be subject to more than one simultaneous change is illustrated in the following scenario.

You are the network administrator for Margie's Travel. Your company has seven locations scattered throughout the world. As part of the application deployment team, you are assigned the job of installing a newly developed application on the network. Part of the instructions for the installation requires that you add a custom attribute to several objects in Active Directory. Unknown to you or your manager, another administrator at a different location has been assigned the same task. You and the other administrator are working on the task at the same time.

Assuming you are attempting to do the tasks simultaneously on a multimaster platform, you could end up with a corrupted Active Directory schema due to conflicting simultaneous changes. However, in Server 2008, Active Directory this type of situation will not occur because Microsoft has implemented FSMO roles to avoid this type of corruption. These roles are performed by only one specific server, which eliminates the risk associated with database corruption due to these kinds of sensitive tasks.

Active Directory supports five FSMO roles. Their functionality is divided between domain-wide and forest-wide FSMOs. In a small-business scenario, where there may be only one domain and a single domain controller, all of the roles can exist on the same domain controller. If you deploy a second domain controller for fault tolerance, you can *transfer* some of these FSMO roles to the new domain controller. This offers not only fault tolerance, but also performance improvements because processing these tasks is balanced between more than one server.

Three roles are domain specific.

- *Relative Identifier (RID) Master.* Responsible for assigning relative identifiers to domain controllers in the domain. Relative identifiers are variable-length numbers assigned by a domain controller when a new object is created.

- *Infrastructure Master.* Responsible for reference updates from its domain objects to other domains. This assists in tracking which domains own which objects.

- *Primary Domain Controller (PDC) Emulator.* Provides backward compatibility with Microsoft Windows NT 4.0 domains and other down-level clients. Password changes, account lockouts, and time synchronization for the domain will also be managed by the PDC Emulator. The domain controller that initiates a password change will send the change to the PDC Emulator, which in turn updates the global catalog server and provides immediate replication to other domain controllers in the domain.

Let's examine these three FSMO roles in more detail.

The domain controller that is assigned the RID Master role in a domain is responsible for generating a pool of identifiers that are used when new accounts, groups, and computers are created. These identifiers are called *relative identifiers (RID)* because they are related to the domain in which they are created. The RID is a variable-length number that is assigned to objects at creation and becomes part of the object's *security identifier (SID)*. A SID is used to uniquely identify an object throughout the Active Directory domain. Part of the SID identifies the domain to which the object belongs, and the other part is the RID.

Each domain can have only one RID Master. When two or more domain controllers exist in a domain, the RID Master assigns a block of 500 identifiers to each domain controller. When a new object is created, the domain controller where the object is created assigns a RID to it from its RID pool. When a domain controller has used 50 percent of the supply of RIDs that it originally received from the RID Master, it must contact the RID Master and request a new supply. If any domain controller cannot contact the RID Master for any reason to retrieve a new supply of RIDs, that DC will be unable to create any new objects until the problem is resolved.

If the server functioning as the RID Master goes down, another domain controller can be assigned this role. The absence of a RID Master is transparent to users on the network. When an object needs to be moved from one domain to another, you must be logged on to the RID Master in the source domain, and the move operation must be performed against the RID Master in the destination domain.

The possible effects of the RID Master being unavailable are as follows:

- The possible inability to create new objects. This would be the case only if a domain controller did not have any remaining RIDs and attempted to contact an inaccessible RID Master to obtain additional identifiers.
- The inability to move objects between domains.

The domain controller functioning as the Infrastructure Master is responsible for replicating changes to an object's SID or distinguished name (DN). Because the SID is domain specific and the distinguished name reflects where the object is located in the forest, an object's SID and DN can change when the object is moved to another domain. However, the object's globally unique identifier (GUID) does not change. The GUID is a 128-bit hexadecimal number that is assigned to each object at the time that it is created in the Active Directory forest. This number is a combination of the date and time the object was created, a unique identifier, and a sequence number. This number never changes, even if the account is moved from one domain to another domain within the same forest. This number also is never repeated, so any object deleted destroys the GUID and it is never used again, even if a new object of the same name and type is created in the same domain.

If an object is moved or renamed, the Infrastructure Master replicates the change in name or location to all domains that have trust relationships with the source domain. This process ensures that the object maintains access to resources in other domains. The Infrastructure Master and the global catalog work closely together. The Infrastructure Master compares its objects to those in the global catalog. If it finds the global catalog has a newer copy of an object, it requests an update and then sends the updated information to other domain controllers in the domain. Because the global catalog and the Infrastructure Master work so closely with one another in a forest consisting of more than one domain and multiple domain controllers, these roles cannot be serviced by the same domain controller. When they are located on the same domain controller within a domain that is part of a multiple domain forest, they share the same database information, making it impossible for the Infrastructure Master to know what information has changed. In a large forest, this will cause the domain controllers to be out of synch with the global catalog contents. (In a single-domain environment or in a multidomain environment in which all domain controllers have been configured as global catalog servers, the Infrastructure Master placement would not matter.) If you configure the domain controller that holds the Infrastructure Master as a global catalog, Event ID number 1419 will be logged in Directory Services Event Viewer.

The PDC Emulator is responsible for the following tasks:

- Managing time synchronization within an Active Directory domain
- Managing edits to Group Policy Objects (GPOs)
- Managing replication of security-sensitive account replication events, such as password changes and account lockouts

As discussed, Active Directory updates include a timestamp to assist in conflict resolution. These timestamps are based on the time setting on the domain controller that originated the change. This means that if all domain controllers do not agree on a time, it nullifies the importance of timestamps. By default, Active Directory only permits a 5-minute *clock skew* between any client or member server and the domain controllers in a domain. If the clock setting between a client and a server are off by more than 5 minutes, users might not be able to log on until the issue is corrected. The Active Directory time synchronization process is hierarchical and adheres to the following model:

The default maximum tolerance for computer clock synchronization can be changed through a group policy. For more information about group policy implementation, refer to Lessons 7 through 10.

1. Clients and member servers within a domain will synchronize their clocks against the domain controller that authenticated them.
2. Domain controllers in each domain will synchronize their time against the PDC Emulator for their domain.
3. The PDC Emulator of each domain in the forest will synchronize its time against the PDC Emulator of the forest root domain.
4. The PDC Emulator of the forest root domain can obtain its time from an internal clock or, as a best practice, it can be configured to obtain its time from an external time source, such as the U.S. Navy Internet Time Service.

In addition to managing time synchronization within a domain, the PDC Emulator also receives preferential replication of password changes from other domain controllers. When a password change takes place, that change will take time to be replicated to all domain controllers. However, the password change is replicated to the PDC Emulator immediately. If a logon request on another domain controller fails due to a bad password, the domain controller that receives the request will forward the request to the PDC Emulator before returning an error message to the client. This will ensure that users do not receive a password error if a recently changed password has not had time to replicate throughout the domain.

Like the RID Master and the Infrastructure Master, there can be only one PDC Emulator in each domain. Unlike domain-wide FSMOs, the forest-wide FSMO roles provide functionality that must be unique across all domains. The forest-wide FSMO roles keep track of adding and removing domain names within an Active Directory forest, as well as managing modifications to the Active Directory schema, which is replicated forest-wide.

The two roles in Active Directory that have forest-wide authority are:

• *Domain Naming Master.* Has the authority to manage the creation and deletion of domains, domain trees, and application data partitions in the forest. When any of these is created, the Domain Naming Master ensures that the name assigned is unique to the forest.
• *Schema Master.* Is responsible for managing changes to the Active Directory schema.

Let's discuss each of these roles in further detail. The Domain Naming Master role is held by only one domain controller in the forest. When you create a new domain, domain tree, or application data partition, Active Directory contacts the Domain Naming Master to make sure the name is unique to the forest. If the Domain Naming Master server is down, you will not be able to create or delete any child domains, domain trees, or application data partitions.

Finally, the domain controller that holds the Schema Master role manages all schema modifications that take place within Active Directory. When an object class or attribute is modified within the schema, it is the responsibility of the Schema Master to make sure the change is replicated to all domains in the forest.

Placing FSMO Role Holders

When you install the first domain controller in a new forest, that domain controller holds both of the forest-wide FSMOs as well as the three domain-wide FSMOs for the forest root domain. Although this default location may be sufficient for a single-site design, a forest containing numerous domain controllers or sites may require you to transfer some of the roles to different domain controllers.

CERTIFICATION READY?
Configure operations
masters
2.6

Planning the appropriate locations for FSMO role holders requires that you consider the following design aspects:

- The number of domains that are or will be part of the forest
- The physical structure of the network
- The number of domain controllers that will be available in each domain

Each of these factors will assist you in deciding where to place FSMO roles to achieve the best possible performance, accessibility, and fault tolerance for your Active Directory environment. In addition, you must know which domain controllers might be able to take over a FSMO role for a server if the server is temporarily or permanently offline.

As discussed, when you create the first domain in a new forest, all of the FSMO roles are automatically assigned to the first domain controller in that domain. Figure 4-3 shows a simple design and the default locations for the global catalog and all five FSMO roles.

Figure 4-3

Default FSMO placement in a single-domain forest

DC1 roles:
Global Catalog
PDC Emulator
RID Master
Infrastructure Master
Domain Naming Master
Schema Master

DC2   DC3

Figure 4-4 illustrates the result of creating a new child domain or the root domain of a new domain tree within an existing forest. The forest-wide FSMOs and the domain-wide FSMOs for the forest root domain remain in place, and the first domain controller in the new domain is automatically assigned the RID Master, PDC Emulator, and Infrastructure Master roles.

Figure 4-4

Default FSMO placement in a forest with one child domain

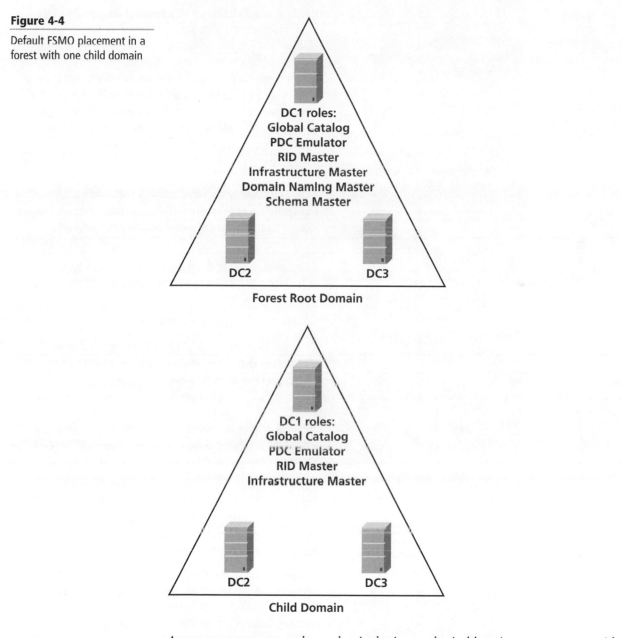

As your company grows beyond a single site or physical location, you must consider placement of the FSMO roles that will accommodate growth without compromising accessibility, fault tolerance, or performance. Table 4-2 shows a breakdown of each FSMO role and the recommended guidelines for placement. In this table, two attributes are used to describe a domain controller: highly available and high capacity. As applied to domain controllers operating as FSMO servers, these terms are defined as follows:

- **Highly available.** This domain controller is centrally located if possible and contains additional hardware, such as a redundant array of independent disks (RAID) controller. RAID allows a server to keep functioning even if one of the drives in the array experiences a failure.

- **High capacity.** This domain controller has a greater processing ability relative to the other domain controllers available. A high-capacity server generally has a faster central processing unit (CPU), more memory, and faster network access.

Table 4-2

Breakdown of FSMO Roles

ROLE	SCOPE	GUIDELINES
Schema Master	Forest	One per forest.
		Highly available because all schema changes take place from this domain controller.
Domain Naming Master	Forest	One per forest.
		Highly available because all domain creations and deletions must go through this domain controller. For smaller environments, you can place the Schema Master and the Domain Naming Master on the same server, which has been configured as a global catalog server.
PDC Emulator	Domain	One per domain.
		Highly available because all domain controllers access this server for time synchronization, mismatched password logon attempts, and password changes. All BDCs and down-level clients require this role to log on to the domain.
		High capacity due to the increased load placed on this server for logon traffic and the aforementioned bulleted items.
		Separate this domain controller from the global catalog server when possible to provide higher capacity.
		Consider lowering the SRV record's weight and priority to allow other domain controllers to have a higher priority to clients seeking authentication.
RID Master	Domain	One per domain.
		Highly available so that domain controllers requesting identifiers for their pools have access. These RIDs are dispensed in blocks of 500 at a time.
		Place this role in a site from which most of the objects are created. This allows object creation to continue even if a network link has failed. If all account administration does not take place from one location, place this role on a centrally located domain controller.
		If possible, configure the PDC Emulator and the RID Master on the same domain controller because the PDC Emulator is a major consumer of RIDs within an Active Directory domain. This minimizes the latency during replication if the role needs to be seized later. Role seizure will be discussed later in this lesson.
Infrastructure Master	Domain	Does not need to be placed on a high-capacity or highly available server.
		Avoid placing this role on the same domain controller as the global catalog so that it can function properly in its role. Exceptions to this rule occur when you are working in a single-domain forest or each domain controller in your forest is also configured as a global catalog server.
		Place in the same site as a global catalog server so they can communicate efficiently with regard to object updates.

Managing FSMO Roles

Now that you have an understanding of each FSMO role and its function, we will discuss what to do when a server that holds one of these roles is not accessible.

When managing FSMO role outages, whether planned or unplanned, two techniques can be used to manage existing roles or recover from a failed role:

- **Role transfer.** This process is used when you move a FSMO role gracefully from one domain controller to another. You can transfer FSMO roles from one domain controller to another to improve Active Directory performance or as a temporary measure when a domain controller will be taken offline for maintenance.
- **Role seizure.** This procedure is used only when you have experienced a failure of a domain controller that holds a FSMO role. *Seizing* a role can be defined as a forced, ungraceful transfer. This procedure assumes that you cannot restore the domain controller that previously held the role. Seizing a role is a drastic measure that should be done only if the original domain controller holding the role will not be brought back online. For example, if a role holder has become inaccessible due to a WAN link failure, usually you should wait for the role holder to become available again. The decision to seize a role also depends on the network impact of not having it available. Table 4-3 shows the impact of an unavailable FSMO role and several alternate corrective actions that you can take.

Table 4-3

Corrective Actions When the FSMO Role Is Not Available

ROLE	IMPACT OF UNAVAILABILITY	ACTION
Schema Master	Temporary outage will not be visible to users or administrators. Outage will only be noticeable when you need to perform a schema modification or to raise the forest functional level of an Active Directory forest.	If failure is deemed permanent, seize the role to a chosen standby Schema Master. After you seize the Schema Master to another domain controller, the original role holder must be removed from Active Directory before being returned to the network.
Domain Naming Master	Temporary outage will not be visible to users or administrators. Outage will only be noticeable when an attempt is made to create or delete a domain or add or remove a domain controller.	If failure is deemed permanent, seize the role to a chosen standby Domain Naming Master. After you seize the Domain Naming Master to another domain controller, the original role holder must be removed from Active Directory before being returned to the network.
RID Master	Temporary outage will not be visible to users or administrators. Outage will be noticeable when attempt is made to create objects, such as users or group objects on a domain controller that has exhausted its relative identifiers.	If failure is deemed permanent, seize the role to a chosen standby Domain Naming Master. After you seize the RID Master to another domain controller, the original role holder must be removed from Active Directory before being returned to the network.

(continued)

Table 4-3

(continued)

ROLE	IMPACT OF UNAVAILABILITY	ACTION
PDC Emulator	Affects network users who are attempting to log on from down-level workstations. An outage of the PDC Emulator will be quite visible because clients will be unable to log on to the domain or change their passwords. You will also be unable to raise the domain functional level of a domain.	Immediately seize the role to an alternate domain controller if users are affected. If the failure is not permanent, the role can be returned to the original domain controller when it comes back online.
Infrastructure Master	Temporary outage will not be visible to users or administrators. Outage will be noticeable if a recent request is made to rename or move a large number of objects, as well as inconsistencies with universal group memberships if the outage lasts an extended period of time.	If failure is deemed permanent, seize the role to a chosen standby Infrastructure Master that is not a global catalog server in the same site. If the failure is not permanent, the role may be seized and then returned to its original provider when it comes back online.

VIEWING THE FSMO ROLE HOLDERS

To view the domain-wide roles of RID Master, PDC Emulator, or Infrastructure Master, complete the following procedure. To view the forest-wide FSMO role holders, complete the second and third procedure in this section.

VIEW THE RID MASTER, PDC EMULATOR, OR INFRASTRUCTURE MASTER FSMO ROLE HOLDERS

GET READY. Before you begin these steps, you must be logged on as a member of the Domain Admins group of the domain that you are querying.

1. Open the Active Directory Users and Computers MMC snap-in.
2. Right-click the **Active Directory Users and Computers** node, click **All Tasks**, and select **Operations Masters**, as shown in Figure 4-5.

Figure 4-5

Operations Masters dialog box

```
Operations Masters                                    ? X
┌─────┬─────┬──────────────┐
│ RID │ PDC │ Infrastructure │
└─────┴─────┴──────────────┘

The operations master manages the allocation of RID pools to other Domain
Controllers. Only one server in the domain performs this role.

Operations master:
┌─────────────────────────────────────────┐
│ RWDC02.margiestravel.com                  │
└─────────────────────────────────────────┘

To transfer the operations master role to the following    ┌─────────┐
computer, click Change.                                    │ Change...│
                                                           └─────────┘
┌─────────────────────────────────────────┐
│ RWDC02.margiestravel.com                  │
└─────────────────────────────────────────┘




                              ┌───────┐  ┌────────┐
                              │ Close │  │ Cancel │
                              └───────┘  └────────┘
```

ANOTHER WAY

You can also view the FSMO role holders using the following command-line syntax: dcdiag /test: Knowsofroleholders /v.

3. In the Operations Master dialog box, select the tab that represents the FSMO you wish to view. The name of the server holding your chosen role is displayed.

4. Close the Operations Master dialog box.

PAUSE. CLOSE the Active Directory Users and Computers MMC snap-in before continuing.

In the previous exercise, you viewed the domain-wide FSMO roles (RID Master, PDC Emulator, and Infrastructure Master) using the Active Directory Users and Computers MMC snap-in.

VIEW THE DOMAIN NAMING MASTER FSMO ROLE HOLDER

GET READY. Before you begin these steps, you must be logged on as a member of the Domain Admins group of forest root domain.

1. In Active Directory Domains and Trusts, right-click the **Active Directory Domains and Trusts** node, and select **Operations Master**, as shown in Figure 4-6. In the Operations Master dialog box, the name of the current Domain Naming Master will be displayed.

Figure 4-6

Operations Master dialog box

2. Close the Operations Master dialog box.

PAUSE. CLOSE the Active Directory Users and Computers MMC snap-in before continuing.

In the previous exercise, you viewed the Domain Naming Master forest-wide FSMO role using the Active Directory Domains and Trusts MMC snap-in. In the following exercise, you will view the Schema Master FSMO role holder.

VIEW THE SCHEMA MASTER FSMO ROLE HOLDER

GET READY. Before you begin these steps, you must be logged on as a member of the Domain Admins group of forest root domain.

1. Open the Active Directory Schema snap-in.

2. Right-click **Active Directory Schema** from the console tree and select **Change Operations Master**. The name of the current Schema Master role holder is displayed in the Current Schema Master (Online) box.

3. Close the Change Schema Master dialog box.

PAUSE. CLOSE the Active Directory Users and Computers MMC snap-in before continuing.

TAKE NOTE*

Remember that before you can access the Active Directory Schema snap-in, you need to register the schmmgmt.dll DLL file using the following syntax: regsvr32 schmmgmt.dll.

In the previous exercise, you viewed the Schema Master forest-wide FSMO role using the Active Directory Schema MMC snap-in.

Transferring a FSMO Role Holder

Transferring a FSMO role requires that the source domain controller *and* the target domain controller be online. Table 4-4 lists the various FSMO roles and the Active Directory console that you will use to transfer each one. These are the same tools that were used to view the current role holders in the previously listed procedures.

Table 4-4

FSMO Roles and the Active Directory Console

ROLE	CONSOLE USED
RID Master, PDC Emulator, Infrastructure Master	Active Directory Users and Computers
Domain Naming Master	Active Directory Domains and Trusts
Schema Master	Active Directory Schema

TRANSFER THE RID MASTER, PDC EMULATOR, OR INFRASTRUCTURE MASTER

GET READY. Before you begin these steps, you must be logged on as a member of the Domain Admins group of the target domain.

1. Open the Active Directory Users and Computers MMC snap-in.
2. In the console tree, right-click the **Active Directory Users and Computers** node and select **Change Domain Controller**, as shown in Figure 4-7.

Figure 4-7

Changing the domain controller

![Active Directory Users and Computers console with right-click context menu showing Change Domain..., Change Domain Controller..., All Tasks, View, Refresh, Export List..., and Help options]

3. Complete this dialog box by selecting the name of the domain controller that you want to become the new role holder from the dropdown list. Click **OK**.
4. In the console tree, right-click the **Active Directory Users and Computers** node, point to **All Tasks**, and select **Operations Masters**.
5. Select the tab that reflects the role you are transferring: **PDC Emulator**, **RID Master**, or **Infrastructure Master**. Click **Change**.

6. In the confirmation message box, click **Yes** to confirm the change in roles. In the next message box, click **OK**.

7. Close the Operations Master dialog box.

PAUSE. CLOSE the Active Directory Users and Computers MMC snap-in before continuing.

In the previous exercise, you transferred the domain-wide FSMO role holders from the current role holder to another domain controller within the domain. For a FSMO role to be transferred from one domain controller to another, the current role holder needs to be online and accessible.

 TRANSFER THE DOMAIN NAMING MASTER FSMO ROLE

GET READY. Before you begin these steps, you must be logged on as a member of the Domain Admins group of the forest root domain.

1. Open the Active Directory Domains and Trusts snap-in.

2. Right-click the **Active Directory Domains and Trusts** node and select **Connect To Domain Controller**.

3. Complete this dialog box by selecting the name of the domain controller you wish to become the new Domain Naming Master from the dropdown list. Click **OK**.

4. In the console tree, right-click the **Active Directory Domains and Trusts** node and select **Operations Master**.

5. In the Change Operations Master dialog box, click **Change**.

6. Click **Close** to close the Change Operations Master dialog box.

PAUSE. CLOSE the Active Directory Users and Computers MMC snap-in before continuing.

In the previous exercise, you transferred the forest-wide Domain Naming Master FSMO role from the current role holder to another domain controller within the forest. For a FSMO role to be transferred from one domain controller to another, the current role holder needs to be online and accessible.

 TRANSFER THE SCHEMA MASTER FSMO ROLE

GET READY. Before you begin these steps, you must be logged on as a member of the Domain Admins group of the target domain.

1. Open the Active Directory Schema snap-in.

2. Right-click **Active Directory Schema** and select **Change Domain Controller**.

3. In the Change Domain Controller dialog box, choose from the following options.

   - **Any Domain Controller.** This option allows Active Directory to select the new Schema Master FSMO holder.

   - **Specify Name.** This option allows you to enter the name of the server to be assigned the Schema Master FSMO role.

4. Click **OK**.

5. In the console tree, right-click **Active Directory Schema** and select **Operations Master**.

6. In the Change Schema Master dialog box, click **Change**.

7. Click **OK** to close the Change Schema Master dialog box.

PAUSE. CLOSE the Active Directory Schema MMC snap-in before continuing.

In the previous exercise, you transferred the forest-wide Schema Master FSMO role from the current role holder to another domain controller within the forest. For a FSMO role to be transferred from one domain controller to another, the current role holder needs to be online and accessible.

SEIZING A FSMO ROLE

An unrecoverable failure to the original FSMO server is usually the reason for seizing a FSMO role. If the original FSMO role server is still functioning, the role should be transferred, not seized. Seizing a FSMO role is a drastic measure that should be performed only in the event of a permanent role holder failure. The ntdsutil utility allows you to transfer and seize FSMO roles. When you use this tool to seize a FSMO role, the tool attempts a transfer from the current role owner first. Ntdsutil will only actually seize the role if the existing FSMO holder is unavailable.

 SEIZE A FSMO ROLE

GET READY. Before you begin these steps, you must be logged on as a member of the Domain Admins group of the target domain.

1. Click **Start**. Key **cmd** and press (Enter).
2. From the Command Prompt, key **ntdsutil** and press (Enter).
3. At the ntdsutil prompt, key **roles** and press (Enter).
4. At the fsmo maintenance prompt, key **connections** and press (Enter).
5. At the server connections prompt, key **connect to server**, followed by the fully qualified domain name of the desired role holder, and press (Enter). For example, key **connect to server dc3.lucernepublishing.com** and press (Enter).
6. At the server connections prompt, key **quit** and press (Enter).
7. At the fsmo maintenance prompt, key one of the following options:
   • **seize schema master** and press (Enter)
   • **seize domain naming master** and press (Enter)
   • **seize RID master** and press (Enter)
   • **seize PDC** and press (Enter)
   • **seize infrastructure master** and press (Enter)
8. If an "Are you sure?" dialog box is displayed, click **Yes** to continue.
9. At the fsmo maintenance prompt, key **quit** and press (Enter).
10. At the ntdsutil prompt, key **quit** and press (Enter).

END. CLOSE the Windows command prompt snap-in.

In the previous exercise, you forcibly seized a FSMO role from one domain controller to another. FSMO role seizure should only take place if the original role holder has completely failed and will not return to the network for an extended period of time.

SUMMARY SKILL MATRIX

IN THIS LESSON YOU LEARNED:

- The global catalog server acts as a central repository for Active Directory by holding a complete copy of all objects within its local domain and a partial copy of all objects from other domains within the same forest. The global catalog has three main functions: the facilitation of searches for objects in the forest, resolution of UPN names, and provision of universal group membership information.

- A global catalog should be placed in each site when possible. As an alternate solution when a site is across an unreliable WAN link, universal group membership caching can be enabled for the site to facilitate logon requests.

- Global catalog placement considerations include the speed and reliability of the WAN link, the amount of traffic that will be generated by replication, the size of the global catalog database, and the applications that might require use of port 3268 for resolution.

- Operations master roles are assigned to domain controllers to perform single-master operations.

- The Schema Master and Domain Naming Master roles are forest-wide. Every forest must have one and only one of each of these roles.

- The RID Master, PDC Emulator, and Infrastructure Master roles are domain-wide. Every domain must have only one of each of these roles.

- The default placement of FSMO roles is sufficient for a single-site environment. However, as your network expands, these roles should be divided to increase performance and reliability. Table 4-2 provides detailed guidelines.

- FSMO roles can be managed in two ways: role transfer and role seizure. Transfer a FSMO role to other domain controllers in the domain or forest to balance the load among domain controllers or to accommodate domain controller maintenance and hardware upgrades. Seize a FSMO role assignment when a server holding the role fails and you do not intend to restore it. Seizing a FSMO role is a drastic step that should be considered only if the current FSMO role holder will never be available again.

- Use repadmin to check the status of the update sequence numbers (USNs) when seizing the FSMO role from the current role holder. Use ntdsutil to actually perform a seizure of the FSMO role.

■ Knowledge Assessment

Fill in the Blank

Complete the following sentences by writing the correct word or words in the blanks provided.

1. Active Directory will tolerate a maximum of a 5-minute _____ between a client and the domain controller that authenticates it.

2. The _____ is responsible for managing time synchronization within a domain.

3. You can improve login times in a site that does not contain a global catalog server by implementing _____.

4. To add or remove an application directory partition from Active Directory, the _____ _____ needs to be accessible.

5. If a domain controller that holds a FSMO role fails and will not be returned to the network, you can _____ the FSMO role to another domain controller.

6. You can add additional attributes to the _____ by modifying the Active Directory schema.

7. The _____ uniquely identifies an object within an Active Directory domain, but will change if an object is moved from one domain to another.

8. The _____ FSMO role should not be housed on a domain controller that has been configured as a global catalog.

9. You can transfer the _____ FSMO from one domain controller to another using the Active Directory Domains and Trusts MMC snap-in.

10. Membership information for a(n) _____ is stored on the global catalog.

Multiple Choice

Circle the correct choice.

1. What is the Active Directory component that contains a reference to all objects within Active Directory called?
   a. Main database
   b. Central catalog
   c. Global database
   d. Global catalog

2. Which of the following roles is a forest-wide FSMO role?
   a. PDC Emulator
   b. Infrastructure Master
   c. Schema Master
   d. Global catalog

3. To which port does the _gc SRV record listen?
   a. TCP 445
   b. UDP 137
   c. TCP 3268
   d. UDP 445

4. You are the administrator of an Active Directory forest that contains a forest root domain with three child domains. How many of each FSMO does this forest contain?
   a. 1 Domain Naming Master, 1 Schema Master, 3 PDC Emulators, 3 Infrastructure Masters, 3 RID Masters
   b. 3 Domain Naming Masters, 3 Schema Masters, 3 PDC Emulators, 3 Infrastructure Masters, 3 RID Masters
   c. 1 Domain Naming Master, 1 Schema Master, 4 PDC Emulators, 4 Infrastructure Masters, 4 RID Masters
   d. 1 Domain Naming Master, 1 Schema Master, 1 PDC Emulator, 1 Infrastructure Master, 1 RID Master

5. The Schema Master FSMO for your forest will be taken offline for a few hours so that your hardware vendor can replace the motherboard of the server. To allow your clients to continue to log in, what is the minimum that you need to do?
   a. Transfer the Schema Master FSMO to another domain controller before taking it offline.
   b. Seize the Schema Master FSMO to another domain controller before taking it offline.
   c. Do nothing. Your clients will still be able to log in while the Schema Master is offline.
   d. Disable the domain controller's computer account from Active Directory Users and Computers before taking it offline.

6. You are a member of the Domain Admins group of a child domain on an Active Directory network. You have an application that requires you to configure an application directory partition, but you find that you are unable to do so. What could be preventing you from creating an application directory partition in your domain?
   a. You must be a member of the Enterprise Admins group to create an application directory partition.
   b. You must be a member of the Schema Admins group to create an application directory partition.
   c. You must be a member of the Forest Admins group to create an application directory partition.
   d. You must be a member of the DNS Admins group to create an application directory partition.

7. The RID Master FSMO distributes RIDs to domain controllers in increments of ____.
   a. 100
   b. 250

       c. 500

       d. 1,000

  8. You are logging on to an Active Directory child domain from a workstation running Windows Vista Business. By default, where will this workstation look to synchronize its clock with the domain?

       a. The PDC Emulator for the child domain

       b. The PDC Emulator for the forest root domain

       c. An external clock

       d. The domain controller that authenticates the workstation

  9. Each object's SID consists of two components: the domain portion and the _____.

       a. remote identifier

       b. globally unique identifier

       c. relative identifier

       d. global identifier

  10. You can view and manage the PDC Emulator FSMO role holder using which utility?

       a. Active Directory Users and Computers

       b. Active Directory Schema

       c. Active Directory Sites and Services

       d. Active Directory Domains and Trusts

■ Case Scenarios

Scenario 4-1: FSMO Role Placement—I

Contoso Pharmaceuticals has 500 employees in 14 locations. The company headquarters is in Hartford, Connecticut. All locations are part of the contoso.com domain, contain at least two servers, and are connected by reliable links.

  a. Which FSMO roles would you house at the Hartford location?

  b. While trying to add new user accounts to the domain, you receive an error that the accounts cannot be created. You are logged on as a member of the Domain Admins group. What is most likely causing the problem?

  c. What should you consider placing at each location to facilitate logons?

Scenario 4-2: FSMO Role Placement—II

Contoso Pharmaceuticals is expanding to include several newly acquired companies. Although they will each become part of the contoso.com forest, each of these companies wants to maintain their own decentralized management strategy. To accommodate this request, you have installed the subsidiaries as separate domain structures. One of them is named litwareinc.com.

  a. Which roles will this new domain need to accommodate?

  b. If litwareinc.com decides to have a small satellite office included in their domain for several users without having logon traffic using their available bandwidth to the parent domain, what should they do?

  c. In contoso.com, your server functioning as the Domain Naming Master has failed due to a power surge. You are unable to create a new child domain for a new location until this server is back online. Currently, it is not expected that the Domain Naming Master issue will be resolved in a reasonable amount of time. What steps should you take so that you can resolve this problem and create the necessary child domain?

■ Workplace Ready

Use Repadmin to Query Domain Controllers

Daniel Weisman is the Active Directory administrator for Northwind Traders (www. northwindtraders.com). Before Daniel seizes the Schema Master FSMO role to another domain controller, he must make sure that the domain controller that will hold the new role is up to date with regard to the updates performed on the failed role holder. This can be accomplished using the repadmin command-line tool. Due to natural latency in the replication of Active Directory information in the Northwind Traders' domain, the target domain controller may not be perfectly in synch with the latest updates. To avoid losing data during a seizure operation, the target domain controller must have the latest information that was held by the previous role holder. The repadmin.exe command-line tool can be used to check the status of updates for a domain controller.

To understand how Daniel determined if the target domain controller is up to date, consider the following example.

The Northwind Traders' domain contains three domain controllers. ServerA is the RID Master of the domain northwindtraders.com, ServerB is Daniel's planned new RID Master if ServerA fails, and ServerC is the only other domain controller in the domain. Daniel needs to determine what the latest update to ServerA was before it stopped functioning. To do this, Daniel uses the Repadmin tool with the /showutdvec switch to determine if ServerB has the most up-to-date information. For this example, Daniel would key the following commands (and receive the corresponding output) from a command-line prompt:

```
C:\> repadmin /showutdvec serverB.blueyonderairlines.com dc=blueyonderairlines,
dc=com

New-York\serverA        @ USN 2604      @ Time 2003-07-03 12:50:44

San-Francisco\serverC   @ USN 2706      @ Time 2003-07-03 12:53:36

C:\>repadmin /showutdvec serverC.blueyonderairlines.com dc=blueyonderairlines,
dc=com

New-York\serverA        @ USN 2590      @ Time 2003-07-03 12:50:44

Chicago\serverB         @ USN 3110      @ Time 2003-07-03 12:57:55
```

The preceding commands reflect a query for replication information from the two domain controllers not affected by the failure. The output for ServerA is the most important information. On ServerB, the last update number received from ServerA was 2604, which is more recent than the update of 2590 shown on ServerC, in the results of the second command line. This output means that ServerB has more recent information than ServerC with regard to ServerA. If this information was reversed and Daniel still wished to have the role seized by ServerB, he could wait until the next replication period or force an immediate synchronization. The key here is that he has made sure that the domain controller he wants to take over the RID Master role in this domain has the most recent information.

Active Directory Administration

OBJECTIVE DOMAIN MATRIX

TECHNOLOGY SKILL	OBJECTIVE DOMAIN	OBJECTIVE DOMAIN NUMBER
Creating Users, Computers, and Groups	Maintain Active Directory accounts.	4.2
Creating Users, Computers, and Groups	Automate creation of Active Directory accounts.	4.1

KEY TERMS

access token
Anonymous Logon
authenticate
authentication
authorization
batch file
built-In user accounts
Comma-Separated Value
    Directory Exchange (CSVDE)
Comma-Separated Values (CSV)
distribution group
domain account
domain local group

dsadd
Everyone
global group
group
group nesting
group scope
group type
header record
LDAP Data Interchange Format
    (LDIF)
LDAP Data Interchange Format
    Directory Exchange (LDIFDE)

local account
local group
nested
nested membership
SAM account name
Security Account Manager
    (SAM)
security group
special identity group
Windows Script Host
    (WSH)

Lucerne Publishing has recently configured an Active Directory forest to support its critical business operations. Now that the underpinnings of Active Directory are in place, the network administrators need to determine a strategy for configuring user and group accounts within the new Active Directory infrastructure. At present, Lucerne Publishing users rely on multiple user accounts to access individual file servers, which create numerous troubleshooting tickets for the members of the deskside support team. By leveraging domain-wide user and group objects, the Active Directory administrators for Lucerne Publishing will create a more seamless experience for end users who need to access critical resources.

After completing this lesson, you will be able to discuss one of the most common administrative tasks performed when working with Active Directory Domain Services: administering user and group accounts. You will have the essential ability to properly configure and maintain these user accounts. They are the means by which your users will be able to access any resources within an Active Directory domain or forest. You will use Active Directory group accounts to address email messages to groups of users as well as secure resources such as files, folders, and other items. You will understand the different types of user and group accounts that can be configured, and you will be able to develop an implementation plan to deploy group security in an efficient and scalable manner. You will also be able to discuss ways in which you can automate the creation of user and group accounts using batch files, scripts, and utilities that are built into the Windows Server 2008 operating system. This will assist you in working with larger organizations that require the ability to automate repetitive tasks.

■ Understanding User Accounts

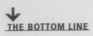

THE BOTTOM LINE

The user account is the primary means by which people using an Active Directory network will access resources. Resource access for individuals takes place through their individual user accounts. To gain access to the network, prospective network users must *authenticate* to a network using a specific user account. This is known as *authentication*. Authentication is the process of confirming a user's identity using a known value such as a password, the pin number on a smart card, or the user's fingerprint or handprint in the case of biometric authentication. When a username and password are used, authentication is accomplished by validating the username and password supplied in the logon dialog box against information that has been stored within the Active Directory database. (Authentication should not be confused with *authorization*, which is the process of confirming that an authenticated user has the correct permissions to access one or more network resources.)

Three types of user accounts can be created and configured in Windows Server 2008:

- *Local accounts.* These accounts are used to access the local computer only and are stored in the local *Security Account Manager (SAM)* database on the computer where they reside. Local accounts are never replicated to other computers, nor do these accounts have domain access. This means that a local account configured on one server cannot be used to access resources on a second server; you would need to configure a second local account in that case.

- *Domain accounts.* These accounts are used to access Active Directory or network-based resources, such as shared folders or printers. Account information for these users is stored in the Active Directory database and replicated to all domain controllers within the same domain. A subset of the domain user account information is replicated to the global catalog, which is then replicated to other global catalog servers throughout the forest.

- *Built-in user accounts.* These accounts are automatically created when Microsoft Windows Server 2008 is installed. Built-in user accounts are created on a member server or a standalone server. However, when you install Windows Server 2008 as a domain controller, the ability to create and manipulate these accounts is disabled. By default, two built-in user accounts are created on a Windows Server 2008 computer: the Administrator account and the Guest account. Built-in user accounts can be local accounts or domain accounts, depending on whether the server is configured as a standalone server or a domain controller. In the case of a standalone server, the built-in accounts are local accounts on the server itself. On a domain controller, the built-in accounts are domain accounts that are replicated to each domain controller.

On a member server or standalone server, the built-in local Administrator account has full control of all files as well as complete management permissions for the local computer. On a domain controller, the built-in Administrator account created in Active Directory has full control of the domain in which it was created. By default, there is only one built-in administrator account per domain. Neither the local Administrator account on a member server or standalone server nor a domain Administrator account can be deleted; however, they can be renamed.

The following list summarizes several security guidelines you should consider regarding the Administrator account:

REF

For more information about configuring strong passwords, refer to Lesson 6.

- **Rename the Administrator account.** This will stave off attacks that are targeted specifically at the 'administrator' username on a server or domain. This will only protect against fairly unsophisticated attacks though, and you should not rely on this as the only means of protecting the accounts on your network.

- **Set a strong password.** Make sure that the password is at least seven characters in length and contains uppercase and lowercase letters, numbers, and alphanumeric characters.

- **Limit knowledge of administrator passwords to only a few individuals.** Limiting the distribution of administrator passwords limits the risk of security breaches using this account.
- **Do not use the Administrator account for daily non-administrative tasks.** Microsoft recommends using a non-administrative user account for normal work and using the Run As command when administrative tasks need to be performed.

The built-in Guest account is used to provide temporary access to the network for a user, such as a vendor representative or a temporary employee. Like the Administrator account, this account cannot be deleted, but it can and should be renamed. In addition, the Guest account is disabled by default and is not assigned a default password. In most environments, you should consider creating unique accounts for temporary user access rather than relying on the Guest account. In this way, you can be sure the account follows corporate security guidelines defined for temporary users. However, if you decide to use the Guest account, review the following guidelines:

- **Rename the Guest account after enabling it for use.** As we discussed with the Administrator account, this will deny intruders a username, which is half of the information necessary to gain access to your domain.
- **Set a strong password.** The Guest account, by default, is configured with a blank password. For security reasons, you should not allow a blank password. Make sure that the password is at least seven characters in length and contains uppercase and lowercase letters, numbers, and alphanumeric characters.

Understanding Group Accounts

Since the very early days of the Microsoft server operating system, *groups* have been used to make network permissions easier to administer. Groups are implemented to allow administrators to assign permissions to multiple users simultaneously. A group can be defined as a collection of user or computer accounts that is used to simplify the assignment of permissions to network resources.

Group memberships act like memberships in a physical fitness center. Suppose the fitness center offers several different membership levels and associated privileges. For example, if you simply want to use the weight machines, treadmills, and stationary bicycles, you pay for a first level membership. If you wish to use the swimming pool and spa privileges, you pay for the second level. You assume that when you purchase your membership level, you receive an access card that allows you to enter the parts of the building where these activities take place. This card contains a magnetic strip that is read at the door of the facility. If your card does not contain the appropriate permissions, access to that part of the building is denied. Similarly, all members who belong to a particular membership level receive the same benefits. The access card for your fitness center serves as proof that you have paid for certain usage privileges.

In Windows Server 2008, group membership functions in much the same way as the aforementioned health club membership. When a user logs on, an *access token* is created that identifies the user and all of the user's group memberships. This access token, like a club membership card, is used to verify a user's permissions when the user attempts to access a local or network resource. By using groups, multiple users can be given the same permission level for resources on the network. Suppose, for example, that you have 25 users in the graphics department of your company who need access to print to a color printer. Either you can assign each user the appropriate printing permissions for the printer, or you can create a group containing the 25 users and assign the appropriate permissions to the group. By using a group object to access a resource, you have accomplished the following:

- Users who need access to the printer can simply be added to the group. Once added, the user receives all permissions assigned to this group. Similarly, you can remove users from the group when you no longer wish to allow them access to the printer.

TAKE NOTE*

A user's access token is only generated when they first log on to the network from their workstation. If you add a user to a group, they will need to log off and log back on again for that change to take effect.

- The users' level of access for the printer needs to be changed only once for all users. Changing the group's permissions changes the permission level for all group members. Without the group, all 25 user accounts would need to be modified individually.

Users can be members of more than one group. In addition, groups can contain other Active Directory objects, such as computers, and other groups in a technique called *group nesting*. Group nesting describes the process of configuring one or more groups as members of another group. For example, consider a company that has two groups: marketing and graphic design. A group object is created for both groups, and each group object contains the users in their respective department. Graphic design group members have access to a high-resolution color laser printer that the marketing group personnel use. To simplify the assignment of permissions for the color laser printer to the marketing group, the marketing group object could simply be added as a member of the graphic design group. This would give the marketing group members the same permission to the color laser printer as the members of the graphic design group. When you added the marketing group to the graphic design group, the users who were members of the marketing group also became members of the graphic design group by way of *nested membership*.

When configuring groups on a Windows Server 2008 network, be aware of two defining characteristics: *group type* and *group scope*. Group type defines how a group is to be used within Active Directory. Only two group types can be created and stored in the Active Directory database:

- *Distribution groups.* Nonsecurity-related groups created for the distribution of information to one or more persons
- *Security groups.* Security-related groups created for purposes of granting resource access permissions to multiple users

TAKE NOTE*

A security group can be used to grant permissions to resources as well as to enable email access. A distribution group, however, can only be used for email purposes; it cannot be used to secure any resources on your network.

Active Directory–aware applications can use distribution groups for nonsecurity-related functions. For example, a distribution group might be created to allow an email application, such as Microsoft Exchange, to send messages to multiple users or allow a software distribution program, such as Microsoft System Center Configuration Manager 2007, to inform users of upcoming maintenance on their desktops. Only applications that are designed to work with Active Directory can make use of distribution groups in this manner.

Groups that can be assigned permissions to resources are referred to as *security groups*. Multiple users that need access to a particular resource can be made members of a security group. The security group, such as the Marketing group shown in Figure 5-1, is then given permission to access the resource. After a group is created, it can be converted from a security group to a distribution group, and vice versa, at any time.

Figure 5-1

Granting permissions to users via security groups

Folder A

Marketing Group

User A   User B   User C

In addition to security and distribution group types, several *group scopes* are available within Active Directory. The group scope controls which objects the group can contain, limiting the objects to the same domain or permitting objects from remote domains as well, and controls the location in the domain or forest where the group can be used. Group scopes available in an Active Directory domain include domain local groups, global groups, and universal groups. We'll discuss each of these in turn.

Domain local groups can contain user accounts, computer accounts, global groups, and universal groups from any domain, in addition to other domain local groups from the same domain. Domain local groups are used to assign permissions to resources that reside only in the same domain as the domain local group. Domain local groups can make permission assignment and maintenance easier to manage. For example, if you have 10 users that need access to a shared folder, you can create a domain local group that has the appropriate permissions to this shared folder. Next, you would create a global or universal group and add the 10 user accounts as members of this group. Finally, you add the global group to the domain local group. The 10 users will have access to the shared folder via their membership in the global group. Any additional users that need access to this shared folder can simply be added to the global group, and they will automatically receive the necessary permissions.

Global groups can contain user accounts, computer accounts, and/or other global groups only from within the same domain as the global group. Global groups can be used to grant or deny permissions to any resource located in any domain in the forest. This is accomplished by placing the global group into a domain local group that has been given the desired permissions. Global group memberships are replicated only to domain controllers within the same domain. Users with common resource needs should be placed in a global group to facilitate the assignment of permissions to resources. Changes to the group membership list can be as frequent as necessary to allow users the necessary resource permissions.

Universal groups can contain user accounts, computer accounts, and/or other global or universal groups from anywhere in the forest. If a cross-forest trust exists, universal groups can contain similar accounts from a trusted forest. Universal groups, like global groups, are used to organize users according to their resource access needs. They can be used to organize users to facilitate access to any resource located in any domain in the forest through the use of domain local groups.

Universal groups are used to consolidate groups and accounts that either span multiple domains or span the entire forest. A key point in the application and utilization of universal groups is that group memberships in universal groups should not change frequently because these groups are stored in the global catalog. Changes to universal group membership lists are replicated to all global catalog servers throughout the domain. If these changes occur frequently, a significant amount of bandwidth could be used for replication traffic.

When you create a group, you must choose the group type and the group scope. Figure 5-2 shows the New Object - Group dialog box in Active Directory Users and Computers. All options discussed thus far are available for selection in this dialog box.

Figure 5-2

Creating a group in Windows Server 2008 Active Directory

As we've discussed previously, *group nesting* is the term used when groups are added as members of other groups. For example, when a global group is made a member of a universal group, it is said to be **nested** within the universal group. Group nesting reduces the number of times you need to assign permissions to users in different domains in a multidomain forest. For example, assume you have multiple child domains in your company, and the users in each domain need to access an enterprise database application located in the parent domain. The simplest way to set up access to this application is as follows:

1. Create global groups in each domain that contain all users needing access to the enterprise database.

2. Create a universal group in the parent domain. Include each location's global group as a member.

3. Add the universal group to the required domain local group to assign the necessary permission to access and use the enterprise database.

WORKING WITH DEFAULT GROUPS

Although many situations exist in which you create groups to organize users or computers and then assign permissions, several built-in security groups are created when Windows Server 2008 Active Directory is installed. Many of the built-in groups are assigned a set of predefined rights that allow members to perform certain network-related tasks, such as backup and restore. Accounts added to the membership of these default groups receive all of the rights to perform associated tasks, in addition to any resource access permissions to which the group is assigned.

The users and built-in container objects in Active Directory Users and Computers hold these default groups. The list of predefined groups you see in these containers varies depending on the installed services. For example, when the Dynamic Host Configuration Protocol (DHCP) service is installed, two new groups appear in the Users container: the DHCP Administrators group and the DHCP Users group. The DHCP Administrators group has full control to manage the DHCP server; the DHCP Users group can be used to view the DHCP server information.

All default groups are security groups. Active Directory does not include any default distribution groups. Table 5-1 explains all of the default groups created when Active Directory is installed. You can view the groups described in the table by viewing their respective containers in the Active Directory Users and Computers snap-in.

Table 5-1

Default Groups Created When Active Directory Is Installed

Group Name	Group Scope	Location in Active Directory	Default Members	Purpose	Special Notes
Account Operators	Domain local	Built-in container	None	Members can administer domain user and group accounts. By default, members can create, modify, and delete accounts for users, groups, and computers in all containers and organizational units (OUs) of Active Directory, except the Built-in folder and the Domain Controller's OU.	Members do not have permission to modify the Administrators, Domain Admins, and Enterprise Admins groups. They do not have permission to modify the accounts for members of those groups.

(continued)

Table 5-1 (*continued*)

Group Name	Group Scope	Location in Active Directory	Default Members	Purpose	Special Notes
Adminis-trators	Domain local	Built-in container	Administrator account, Domain Admins global group from the specific domain, and the Enterprise Admins universal group	Members have complete and unrestricted access to the computer or domain controller locally, including the right to change their own permissions.	None
Backup Operators	Domain local	Built-in container	None	Members can back up and restore all files on a computer, regardless of the permissions that protect those files. Members can log on to the computer and shut it down.	None
Certificate Service DCOM Access	Domain local	Built-in container	None	Members are allowed to connect to Certification Authorities across the Active Directory forest.	None
Cryptographic Operators	Domain local	Built-in container	None	Members are allowed to perform cryptographic operations.	None
Distributed COM Users	Domain local	Built-in container	None	Members are permitted to use Distributed COM objects on all domain controllers.	None
Event Log Readers	Domain local	Built-in container	None	Members are permitted to read event logs from all domain controllers.	None
Guests	Domain local	Built-in container	Domain Guests global group and the Guests user account	Members have the same privileges as members of the Users group.	The Guest account is disabled by default.
IIS_IUSRS	Domain local	Built-in container	IUSR special identity	Built-in group used by IIS.	None
Incoming Forest Trust Builders	Domain local	Built-in container	None	Members can create incoming, one-way trusts to this forest.	None
Network Configuration Operators	Domain local	Built-in container	None	Members have the same default rights as members of the Users group. Members can perform all tasks related to the client side of network configuration, except for installing and removing drivers and services.	Members cannot configure network server services, such as the Domain Name System (DNS) and DHCP server services.

(*continued*)

Table 5-1 (*continued*)

Group Name	Group Scope	Location in Active Directory	Default Members	Purpose	Special Notes
Performance Log Users	Domain local	Built-in container	None	Members have remote access to schedule logging of performance counters on this computer.	None
Performance Monitor Users	Domain local	Built-in container	Network Service from the NT Authority folder. This is a placeholder account that may or may not be used.	Members have remote access to monitor this computer.	None
Pre–Windows 2000 Compatible Access	Domain local	Built-in container	Authenticated Users from the NT Authority folder. This is a place-holder account that may or may not be used.	Members have read access on all users and groups in the domain. This group is provided for backward compatibility for computers running Microsoft Windows NT Server 4.0 and earlier.	None
Print Operators	Domain local	Built-in container	None	Members can manage printers and document queues.	None
Remote Desktop Users	Domain local	Built-in container	None	Members can log on to a computer from a remote location.	None
Replicator	Domain local	Built-in container	None	This group supports directory replication functions and is used by the file replication service on domain controllers. The only member should be a domain user account that is used to log on to the replicator services of the domain controller.	Do not add users to this group. They are added automatically by the system.
Server Operators	Domain local	Built-in container	None	Members can do the following: Log on to a server interactively. Create and delete network shares. Start and stop some services. Back up and restore files. Format the hard disk. Shut down the computer. Modify the system date and time.	This group exists only on domain controllers.
Terminal Server License Servers	Domain local	Built-in container	None	Members of this group can update Active Directory user accounts with information about licensing usage.	None

(continued)

Table 5-1 (continued)

Group Name	Group Scope	Location in Active Directory	Default Members	Purpose	Special Notes
Users	Domain local	Built-in container	Domain Users global group, Authenticated Users Special Identity group, and Interactive Special Identity group	Used to allow general access. Members can run applications, use printers, shut down and start the computer, and use network shares for which they are assigned permissions.	None
Windows Authorization Access Group	Domain local	Built-in container	Enterprise Domain Controllers special identity	Members of this group can view the token Groups Global And Universal attribute on User objects to determine their rights to a given resource.	None
Allowed RODC Password Replication Group	Domain local	Users container	None	Members of this group are eligible to have their passwords stored on any RODC in the domain.	Each RODC will have an analagous local group that will allow users' passwords to be stored only on a single DC.
Cert Publishers	Domain local	Users container	None	Members of this group are permitted to publish certificates to Active Directory.	None
Denied RODC Password Replication Group	Domain local	Users container	Cert Publishers, Domain Admins, Domain Controllers, Enterprise Admins, Group Policy Creator Owners, krbtgt, Read Only Domain Controllers, Schema Admins	Members of this group are *not* eligible to have their passwords stored on any RODC in the domain.	Each RODC will have an analagous local group that will prevent users' passwords from being stored only on a single DC.
DnsAdmins (installed with DNS)	Domain local	Users container	None	Members of this group are permitted administrative access to the DNS server service.	None
DnsUpdate-Proxy (installed with DNS)	Global	Users container	None	Members of this group are DNS clients permitted to perform dynamic updates on behalf of some other clients, such as DHCP servers.	None
Domain Admins	Global	Users container	Administrator user account for the domain	Members of this group can perform administrative tasks on any computer anywhere in the domain.	None

(continued)

Table 5-1 (*continued*)

Group Name	Group Scope	Location in Active Directory	Default Members	Purpose	Special Notes
Domain Computers	Global	Users container	Members include all workstations and servers joined to the domain and any computer accounts manually created.	Any computer account created in a domain is automatically added to this group. The group can be used to make computer management easier through group policies. (Refer to Lessons 7 through 10.)	None
Domain Controllers	Global	Users container	Members include all domain controllers within the respective domain	All computers installed in the domain as domain controllers are automatically added to this group.	None
Domain Guests	Global	Users container	Guest account	Members include all domain guests.	None
Domain Users	Global	Users container	User account created in a domain is automatically added to this group	Members include all domain users. This group can be used to assign permissions to all users in the domain.	None
Enterprise Admins (appears only on forest root domain controllers)	Universal	Users container	Administrator user account for the forest root domain	This group is added to the Administrators group on all domain controllers in the forest. This allows the global administrative privileges associated with this group, such as the ability to create and delete domains.	None
Enterprise Read-Only Domain Controllers	Universal	Users container	None	This group contains all Read-Only Domain Controllers within an entire forest.	None
Group Policy Creator Owners	Global	Users container	Administrator user account for the domain	Members can modify group policy for the domain.	None
RAS and IAS Servers	Domain local	Users container	None	Servers in this group—for the Remote Access Service (RAS) and Internet Authentication Service (IAS)—are permitted access to the users' remote access properties.	None

(*continued*)

Table 5-1 (*continued*)

Group Name	Group Scope	Location in Active Directory	Default Members	Purpose	Special Notes
Read-Only Domain Controllers	Global	Users container	None	This group contains the computer accounts for all Read-Only Domain Controllers within a single domain.	None
Schema Admins (appears only on forest root domain controllers)	Universal	Users container	Administrator user account for the forest root domain	Members can manage and modify the Active Directory schema.	None

UNDERSTANDING SPECIAL IDENTITY GROUPS AND LOCAL GROUPS

You may also encounter several additional groups when reviewing permission assignments. These are called *special identity groups*. You cannot manually modify the group membership of special identity groups, nor can you view their membership lists. Another group type that you will encounter is a *local group*, which is a collection of user accounts that are local to one specific workstation or member server. It is important to understand that local groups are very different from the previously described domain local groups. Local groups are created in the security database of a local computer and are not replicated to Active Directory or to any other computers on the network.

Windows Server 2008 uses special identity groups to represent a class of users or the system itself. For example, the *Everyone* group is a special identity group that contains all authenticated users and domain guests.

One of the security enhancements present in Windows Server 2008 is a strict rule set determining how the Anonymous Logon group should be treated. Prior to Windows Server 2003, the special identity *Anonymous Logon*, referring to users who had not supplied a username and password, was a member of the Everyone group. By default, the Everyone group was granted full control to newly created network resources and, therefore, so was the Anonymous Logon group. To disallow unauthorized access to resources intended for authenticated users, the administrator in a Windows NT or Windows 2000 network needed to manually remove the Everyone group from the ACL of resources. If they forgot this step, it created an obvious security risk for those resources.

In Windows Server 2003 and Windows Server 2008, the Anonymous Logon group is no longer a member of the Everyone group. Resources for which you want to allow anonymous access must be specifically configured with the Anonymous Logon group as a member of the ACL for that resource. Table 5-2 describes the Everyone group and the other special identity groups that you will encounter in Windows Server 2008.

Table 5-2

Special Identity Groups

Group Name	Members	Purpose
Anonymous Logon	All users who log on without a username and password	Used to allow anonymous users access to resources. Windows Server 2008 no longer includes the Anonymous Logon group as a member of the Everyone group. This security enhancement prevents the potential for unauthorized access to resources that can occur if a Windows 2000 or earlier administrator forgets to remove the Everyone group from a resource.
Authenticated Users	All users who log on with a valid username and password combination that is stored in the Active Directory database	Used to allow controlled access to resources throughout the forest or domain.
Batch	Users who are logging on to a server as a batch job.	Used to facilitate users who need to log on as a batch job (i.e., to run a scheduled task on a Windows Server 2008 computer).
Creator Group	The primary group that is configured for the creator of an object.	Used as a placeholder for the primary group of an object's creator.
Creator Owner	The user that created a particular object.	Used to grant permissions to the creator of an object.
Dial-Up	Includes users currently logged on using a dial-up connection	Used to allow access to resources from a remote location.
Digest Authentication	Users who are authenticating using Digest authentication	Used to controll access to a resource based on the type of authentication being used.
Enterprise Domain Controllers	All domain controllers in the forest	Used to facilitate access to forest-wide Active Directory services.
Everyone	On Windows Server 2003 and later computers: Authenticated Users Domain Guests On Windows NT Server 4.0 and Windows 2000 computers: Authenticated Users Domain Guests Anonymous Logon	Used to provide access to resources for all users and guests. Do not assign this group to resources. Instead, use groups that require authentication and have membership lists that can be administratively modified.
Interactive	Includes the user account that is currently logged on to the local computer either directly or through a Remote Desktop connection	Provides access to physically local resources. Users logged on from across the network are not included in this group membership.
IUSR	N/A	Used as the built-in account for Internet Information Services (IIS).
Local Service	N/A	Used as a reduced-privilege account to allow applications to run on a server without requiring administrative access. The Local Service does not have any permissions to network resources, only the local server.
Network	Includes any user that currently has a connection from another computer to a network resource, such as a shared folder, on this computer.	Used to allow access to shared resources or services from across the network. Users logged on interactively are not included in this group membership.

(continued)

Table 5-2 (*continued*)

Group Name	Members	Purpose
Network Service	N/A	Used as a reduced-privilege account to allow applications to run on a server without requiring administrative access. Similar to the Local Service account, but it can access network resources.
Remote Interactive Logon	All users who log on to a computer using a Remote Desktop Connection session	Used to control access to resources based on how a user is connecting to the network; in this case, via an RDC session.
Restricted	N/A	Used to control processes that have been assigned the "restrictive" security level in a Software Restriction Policy.
Self	N/A	Used as a placeholder for the current user.
Service	Includes all security principals: users, groups, or computers that are currently logged on as a service	Used by the system to allow permission to protected system files for services to function properly.
System	Used by the operating system and any processes that run using LocalSystem	Any process that runs as System has full administrative rights to the computer where it is running.
Terminal Server User	When Terminal Services is installed in application serving mode, this group contains any users who are currently logged on to the system using a terminal server.	Used to allow access to applications via a terminal services connection.

As we discussed briefly at the beginning of this section, you can also create local groups that exist in the local security database of a Windows workstation or a member server. These groups are used to assign permissions to resources that are found only on the computer in which they are created. They cannot be given access to resources within an Active Directory domain, nor can they become members of any other group. Local groups have the potential to inhibit your ability to centralize administration of computer resources and, therefore, should be used only if there are no other options.

DEVELOPING A GROUP IMPLEMENTATION PLAN

Now that you have learned the concepts behind group usage in Windows Server 2008, we will discuss the development of a plan for group implementation that considers the business goals of a company. A group implementation plan should serve current resource access needs and allow easy revisions when changes arise.

Today's corporate environments often impose frequent changes on network administrators due to acquisitions and organizational changes. When users move between departments and change responsibilities, resource access needs change as well. A user may need more or less access to a particular resource than in a previous job position. In addition, an entirely new set of resources may be needed.

In a newly installed network, you have the opportunity to implement a plan that can be revised easily when changes, such as user departmental moves, occur. A plan that is created without goals and good practice guidelines in mind can cause problems in the future regarding security access. For example, consider the following scenario.

Lucerne Publishing, a mid-sized publishing firm, decided to upgrade from Windows 2003 to Windows Server 2008 as its network operating system. Over the last several months, the company has gone through a major restructuring of employees and their responsibilities. Each time a request is made to remove a user's resource access permissions or add a user to a new resource, the change is, at best, difficult to implement without negative ramifications. Either the user loses privileges to a resource that was needed or the groups that have privileges to the new resource have more permissions than they should. When the company brings in a consultant to assess the situation, she determines that most resource ACLs consist of individual user accounts only and the group objects that exist do not seem to have any relationship to the current organizational structure.

Such a scenario can be all too common in some organizations. Generally, these types of situations arise when a solid plan that includes group and user implementation guidelines is not in place. When you develop a plan for implementing groups, you should include the following documented information:

- A plan that states who has the ability and responsibility to create, delete, and manage groups
- A written policy that states how domain local, global, and universal groups are to be used
- A written policy that states guidelines for creating new groups and deleting old groups
- A naming standards document to keep group names consistent
- A standard for group nesting

After your plan is documented, it is important for you to take the time to periodically evaluate the plan to make sure there are no new surprises that might cause problems. Distributing copies of your implementation plan to all administrators that have responsibility for creating and managing groups helps to keep new group creations in line with your plan.

Creating Users, Computers, and Groups

One of the most common tasks for administrators is the creation of Active Directory objects. Windows Server 2008 includes several tools you can use to create objects. The specific tool you use depends on how many objects you need to create, the time frame available for the creation of these groups, and any special circumstances that are encountered, such as importing users from an existing database.

Generally, when creating a single user or group, most administrators use the Active Directory Users and Computers tool. However, when you need to create many users or groups in a short time frame or you have an existing database from which to import these objects, you will want to choose a more efficient tool. Windows Server 2008 provides a number of tools you can choose according to what you want to accomplish. The following list describes the most commonly used methods for creating multiple users and groups. Each method will be detailed in the upcoming pages.

- *Batch files.* These files, typically configured with either a .bat extension or a .cmd extension, can be used to automate many routine or repetitive tasks. To create or delete user and group objects, batch files are frequently used with various command-line tools available in Windows Server 2008.
- *Comma-Separated Value Directory Exchange (CSVDE).* This command-line utility is used to import or export Active Directory information from a comma-separated value (.csv) file. These files can be created in any text editor. This command-line utility only imports or exports new objects; it cannot modify or delete existing objects.
- *LDAP Data Interchange Format Directory Exchange (LDIFDE).* Like CSVDE, this utility can be used to import or export Active Directory information. It can be used to add, delete, or modify objects in Active Directory, in addition to modifying the schema,

if necessary. It also can be used to import data from other directory services, such as Novell NetWare.

- *Windows Script Host (WSH).* Script engines run script files created using Microsoft Visual Basic Scripting Edition (VBScript) or JScript. WSH allows the scripts to be run from a Windows desktop or a command prompt. The runtime programs provided to do this are WScript.exe and CScript.exe, respectively.

These tools all have their roles in network administration; it is up to you to select the best tool for a particular situation. For example, you might have two tools that can accomplish a job, but your first choice might be the tool that you are most familiar with or the one that can accomplish the task in a shorter amount of time. In the following exercise, you will see some step-by-step examples of creating users, computers, and groups using the GUI and command-line utilities. The sections following the exercise will present scenarios and examples for using these tools.

CERTIFICATION READY?
Maintain Active Directory accounts
4.2

CREATE USERS, COMPUTERS, AND GROUPS

GET READY. Part A of this exercise assumes that you are signed on to a Windows Server 2008 computer with local administrator credentials. Part B of this exercise covers domain accounts and assumes that you are signed on to a Windows Server 2008 Active Directory domain controller using Domain Administrator credentials.

Part A – Working with Local User and Group Objects

1. Log on to the member server using local administrator credentials.
2. Click the **Start** button, click **Administrative Tools**, and then click **Computer Management**.
3. Browse to **System Tools, Local Users and Groups**, and then **Users**, as shown in Figure 5-3.

Figure 5-3

Users selected

4. To add a new local user account, right-click the **Users** folder and click **New User**. The New User window is displayed, as shown in Figure 5-4.

Figure 5-4

New User window

Figure 5-4

New User window

New User

User name: LocalUser

Full name: New Local User Account

Description: New Local User Account

Password: •••••••••

Confirm password: •••••••••

☑ User must change password at next logon
☐ User cannot change password
☐ Password never expires
☐ Account is disabled

Help   Create   Close

5. Enter the appropriate values in the following fields and then click **Create**.
   a. User name
   b. Full name
   c. Description
   d. Password
   e. Confirm password

6. To create a new group object, right-click the **Groups** folder in the left pane and click **New Group**. The New Group window is displayed, as shown in Figure 5-5. Enter the appropriate values in the following fields:
   a. Group name
   b. Description

Figure 5-5

New Group window

New Group

Group name: FinanceGroup

Description: Finance Users

Members:

LocalUser

Add...   Remove

Help   Create   Close

7. To add users to the group, click **Add**. The Select Users screen is displayed.

8. Enter the name of the user account that you wish to add, and then click **OK**.

9. Click **Create** and then close the Computer Management console.

10. Close all open windows and then log out of the member server.

Part B – Working with Domain User and Group Objects

1. Log on to the domain controller using Domain Admin credentials.

2. Click the **Start** button, click **Administrative Tools**, and then click **Active Directory Users and Computers**.

3. Expand the <domain name> node; in this case, expand lucernepublishing.com.

4. Right-click **Users** and select **New → User.** The New Object – User screen is displayed, as shown in Figure 5-6. Enter the appropriate values in the following fields and click **Next:**

   a. First name

   b. Last name

   c. User logon name

Figure 5-6

New Object - User window

5. Key an initial password for the user in the Password field. Key the same initial password in the Confirm password field. Click **Next.**

6. Click **Finish.**

7. Right-click **Users**, click **New**, and then click **Group.** The New Object – Group window is displayed, as shown in Figure 5-7.

Figure 5-7

Creating a group

8. Enter the appropriate values in the following fields and click **OK** to create the group; the Group name (pre–Windows 2000) field will populate automatically:

   a. Group name: FinanceUsers

   b. Group scope: Global

   c. Group type: Security

9. To create objects from the command prompt, click the **Start** button, key **cmd**, and then press (**Enter**).

10. At the command prompt, key the following command and then press (Enter), substituting the appropriate domain distinguished name, such as dc=lucernepublishing, dc=com:

```
Dsadd user "cn=Robert Brown,cn=Users,<domain dn>" -samid rbrown
-pwd MSPress#1 -mustchpwd yes -disabled no
```

11. To create a group object at the command line, key the following command and then press (Enter), substituting the appropriate domain distinguished name, such as dc=lucernepublishing,dc=com:

```
Dsadd group cn=Accounting,cn=Users,<domain dn> -desc
"Accounting Users" -secgrp yes -scope g
```

12. In the Active Directory Users and Computers MMC console, click **Users** in the left pane. Press (F5) to refresh the listing in the right pane to confirm that the user and group objects that you just created at the command line are present.

STOP. Close all open windows and log out of the Active Directory domain controller.

In the previous exercise you created a single user and group object using the graphical user interface (GUI) and some of the available command-line tools in Windows Server 2008. In the upcoming sections we will examine some of the available mechanisms for automating the creation of large numbers of Active Directory objects.

CERTIFICATION READY?
Automate creation of Active Directory accounts
4.1

USING BATCH FILES

Batch files are commonly used files that can be written using any text editor. You can write a batch file to create objects in Active Directory by following standard batch file rules and using the dsadd command, which is available in Windows Server 2003 and later. *Dsadd* can be used to create, delete, view, and modify Active Directory objects, including users, groups, and OUs.

To create a user using the dsadd utility, you need to know the distinguished name for the user and the user's login ID, also known as the **SAM account name** attribute within Active Directory. The distinguished name of an object signifies its relative location within an Active Directory OU structure. For example, the distinguished name **cn=jsmith,ou=accounts, dc=lucernepublishing,dc=com** refers to the jsmith account, which resides in the Accounts OU, which resides in the lucernepublishing.com Active Directory domain. Each object has a unique DN, but this DN can change if you move the object to different locations within the Active Directory structure. If you create a separate OU for individual departments within Lucerne Publishing, the previous DN might change to **cn=jsmith,ou=Marketing,ou=Accounts,dc=lucernepublishing,dc=com**, even though it is the same user object with the same rights and permissions. The SAM account name refers to each user's login name—the portion to the left of the '@' within a User Principal Name—which is **jsmith** in **jsmith@lucernepublishing.com**. The SAM account name must be unique across a domain.

When you have both of these items, you can create a user with the dsadd utility using the following syntax:

```
dsadd user username DN -samid SAM account name
```

For example, you can create the jsmith account referenced above as follows:

```
dsadd user

cn=jsmith,ou=Marketing,ou=Accounts,dc=lucernepublishing,dc=com -samid
jsmith
```

You can also add fields with the dsadd tool. The following syntax specifies MySecretC0de as a password for jsmith's account:

```
dsadd user

cn=jsmith,ou=Marketing,ou=Accounts,dc=lucernepublishing,dc=com -samid
jsmith -pwd MySecretC0de
```

In addition, you can use dsadd to create computer objects. The only required syntax to create a computer with dsadd is the distinguished name of the computer object, as shown in the following example:

```
dsadd computer

cn=workstation1,ou=Marketing,ou=Workstations,dc=lucernepublishing,dc=com
```

TAKE NOTE *

In addition to creating user and group objects, you can use dsadd to create computer objects, contact objects, and organizational units.

Finally, you can also create a group object using dsadd. In addition to the distinguished name and SAM account name of the group, you can specify the scope of the group (local, global, or universal) and whether the group is a security or distribution group. To create a global security group called Trainers, for example, use the following syntax:

```
Dsadd group

cn=Trainers,ou=HR,dc=lucernepublishing,dc=com -scope g  secgroup yes
-samid trainers
```

To create multiple objects (including users, groups, or any other object type) using a batch file, open Notepad and use the syntax in these examples, placing a single command on each line. After all commands have been entered, save the file and name it using a .cmd or .bat extension. Files with .cmd or .bat extensions are processed line by line when you enter the name of the batch file at a command prompt or double-click on the file within Windows Explorer.

USING CSVDE

Microsoft Excel and Microsoft Exchange are two common applications where you can have a number of usernames, addresses, and contact information to add to the Active Directory database. In this case, you can import and export information from these applications by saving it to a file in *Comma-Separated Values (CSV)* format. CSV format also can be used to import and export information from other third-party applications. For example, you may have the need to export user account information to a file for use in another third-party application, such as a UNIX database. CSVDE can provide this capability as well.

The CSVDE command-line utility allows an administrator to import or export Active Directory objects. It uses a .csv file that is based on a header record, which describes each part of the data. A *header record* is simply the first line of the text file that uses proper attribute names. The attribute names must match the attributes allowed by the Active Directory schema. For example, if you have a list of people and telephone numbers you want to import as users into the Active Directory database, you will need to create a header record that accurately reflects the object names and attributes you want to create. Review the following common attributes used for creating a user account:

- **dn.** Refers to the distinguished name of the object so that the object can be properly placed in Active Directory.
- **sAMAccountName.** Populates the SAM account field for the pre–Windows 2000 logon name.
- **objectClass.** Determines the type of object to be created, such as user, group, or OU.
- **telephoneNumber.** Populates the Telephone Number field.
- **userPrincipalName** Populates the User Principal Name field for the account.

As you create your database file, order the data to reflect the sequence of the attributes in the header record. If fields and data are out of order, either you will encounter an error when running the CSVDE utility or you might not get accurate results in the created objects. The following example of a header record uses the previously listed attributes to create a user object.

```
dn,sAMAccountName,userPrincipalName,telephoneNumber, objectClass
```

A data record using this header record would appear as follows:

```
"cn=Scott
Seely,ou=Sales,dc=cohowinery,dc=com",SSeely,SSeely@cohowinery.com,
        586-555-1234,user
```

After you have added a record for each account you want to create, save the file using .csv as the extension. Assuming that you create a file named Newusers.csv, key the following command to execute the creation of the user accounts.

```
csvde.exe -i -f newusers.csv
```

The -i switch tells CSVDE that this operation will import users into the Active Directory database. The -f switch is used to specify the .csv file containing the records to be imported.

USING LDIFDE

LDIFDE is a utility that has the same basic functionality as CSVDE and provides the ability to modify existing records in Active Directory. For this reason, LDIFDE is a more flexible option. Consider an example where you have to import 200 new users into your Active Directory structure. In this case, you can use CSVDE or LDIFDE to import the users. However, you can use LDIFDE to modify or delete these objects later, whereas CSVDE does not provide this option.

You can use any text editor to create the LDIFDE input file, which is formatted according to the *LDAP Data Interchange Format (LDIF)* standard. The format for the data file containing the object records you wish to create is significantly different from that of CSVDE. The following example shows the syntax for a data file to create the same jsmith user account discussed in the CSVDE section.

```
Dn:
cn=jsmith,ou=Marketing,ou=Accounts,dc=lucernepublishing,dc=com

changetype: add
ObjectClass: user
SAMAccountName: jsmith
UserPrincipalName: jsmith@lucernepublishing.com
telephoneNumber: 586-555-1234
```

Using LDIFDE, you can specify one of three actions that will be performed by the LDIF file:

- **Add.** Specifies that the record contains a new object.
- **Modify.** Specifies that existing object attributes will be modified.
- **Delete.** Specifies that the record will delete the specified object.

After creating the data file and saving it using the .LDF file extension, key the following syntax to execute the LDIFDE script and modify the Active Directory object.

```
ldifde -i -f newobjects.ldf
```

The next example illustrates the required syntax to modify the telephone number for the previously created user object. Note that the hyphen in the last line is required for the file to function correctly.

```
Dn:
cn=jsmith,ou=Marketing,ou=Accounts,dc=cohowinery,dc=com

changetype: modify

replace: telephoneNumber

telephoneNumber: 586-555-1111

-
```

USING WINDOWS SCRIPTING HOST

Windows Script Host (WSH) supports Microsoft VBScript and JScript engines. It has the flexibility of running scripts from a Windows interface or a command prompt. WSH is built into all editions of Windows Vista, Windows 2000, Windows XP, Windows Server 2003, and Windows Server 2008. It provides a robust scripting method that supports a multitude of administrative tasks, including creating Active Directory objects, mapping drives, connecting to printers, modifying environment variables, and modifying registry keys.

The following example is a VBScript that creates a user account for Scott Seely using WSH. You can use any text editor to write and edit the script. The script should be saved with a .vbs extension. Notice that the first few lines prepare the script to create a user object in the Sales OU of cohowinery.com. The fourth line of text begins the information that specifies Scott Seely and the Active Directory information for his account. Blank lines are used for visual purposes and are ignored during file processing.

```
Option Explicit

Dim ldapP, acctUser


Set ldapP = GetObject ("LDAP://OU=sales,DC=cohowinery,DC=com")


Set acctUser = ldapP.Create("user", "CN=" & "Scott Seely")

Call acctUser.Put("sAMAccountName", "sseely")

Call acctUser.Put("userPrincipalName", "sseely" & "@cohowinery.com")

Call acctUser.Put("TelephoneNumber", "586-555-1234")

Call acctUser.Put("userAccountControl", &H200)

acctUser.SetPassword ("MSpress#1")

acctUser.SetInfo

Set acctUser = Nothing
```

Assuming the name of the previous script file is Newusers.vbs, key the following command from a command prompt to run it.

```
cscript c:\newusers.vbs
```

SUMMARY SKILL MATRIX

IN THIS LESSON YOU LEARNED:

- Three types of user accounts exist in Windows Server 2008: local user accounts, domain user accounts, and built-in user accounts. Local user accounts reside on a local computer and are not replicated to other computers by Active Directory. Domain user accounts are created and stored in Active Directory and replicated to all domain controllers within a domain. Built-in user accounts are automatically created when the operating system is installed and when a member server is promoted to a domain controller.

- The Administrator account is a built-in domain account that serves as the primary supervisory account in Windows Server 2008. It can be renamed, but it cannot be deleted. The Guest account is a built-in account used to assign temporary access to resources. It can be renamed, but it cannot be deleted. This account is disabled by default and the password can be left blank.

- Windows Server 2008 group options include two types, security and distribution, and three scopes, domain local, global, and universal.

- Domain local groups are placed on the ACL of resources and assigned permissions. They typically contain global groups in their membership list.

- Global groups are used to organize domain users according to their resource access needs. Global groups are placed in the membership list of domain local groups, which are then assigned the desired permissions to resources.

- Universal groups are used to provide access to resources anywhere in the forest. Their membership lists can contain global groups and users from any domain. Changes to universal group membership lists are replicated to all global catalog servers throughout the forest.

- The recommended permission assignment strategy places users needing access permissions in a global group, the global group in a universal group, and the universal group in a domain local group and then assigns permissions to the domain local group.

- Group nesting is the process of placing group accounts in the membership of other group accounts for the purpose of simplifying permission assignments.

- Multiple users and groups can be created in Active Directory using several methods. Windows Server 2008 offers the ability to use batch files, CSVDE, LDIFDE, and WSH to accomplish your administrative goals.

Knowledge Assessment

Fill in the Blank

Complete the following sentences by writing the correct word or words in the blanks provided.

1. A(n) _____ can only contain members from within the same domain.

2. You can use the _____ utility to import data from Comma-Separated Values (CSV) files.

3. Each user and group object has a(n) _____, which must be unique across an entire Active Directory domain.

4. The Anonymous Logon group is an example of a(n) _____.

5. You can use the _____ command-line utility to create and modify Active Directory objects.

6. When users log on to Active Directory, they receive a(n) _____ consisting of all of their security group memberships.

7. A local user is stored in the _____ database of the computer on which it was created.

8. Each CSV file needs to begin with a(n) _____ when used with the CSVDE command-line tool.

9. A(n) _____ can only be used to send and receive email, not to secure network resources.

10. _____ is the practice of adding one group as a member of another group.

Multiple Choice

Circle the correct choice.

1. Which special identity group controls anonymous access to resources in Windows Server 2008?
   a. Everyone
   b. Network
   c. Interactive
   d. Anonymous Logon

2. What defines the types of objects that can belong to a particular group and the types of resources that group can be used to secure?
   a. Group scope
   b. Group security
   c. Special Identity group
   d. Security group

3. What technique is used to configure one security group as a member of another security group?
   a. Group security
   b. Group nesting
   c. Group overloading
   d. Group scope

4. The Administrator and Guest user accounts are examples of
   a. Special identity user accounts
   b. Administrative user accounts
   c. Built-in user accounts
   d. Domain user accounts

5. Which command-line tool can be used to create various object types within Active Directory?
   a. dsget
   b. dsquery
   c. dsadd
   d. dsmove

6. Which input file format allows you to create, modify, and delete objects within Active Directory?
   a. LDAP Data Interchange Format (LDIF)
   b. Comma Separated Value (CSV)
   c. Tab-delimited Text (TXT)
   d. Microsoft Excel (XLS)

7. Which group type allows you to assign permissions to resources as well as receive messages via Active Directory-enabled email applications such as Microsoft Exchange?
   a. Distribution group
   b. Exchange group
   c. Permissions group
   d. Security group

8. Which group scope can contain users and groups from any domain within an Active Directory forest, but can be used only to secure resources located within the same domain as the group itself?
   a. Domain group
   b. Global group
   c. Domain local group
   d. Universal group

9. Which account type is configured on an Active Directory domain controller and can be used to grant access to resources on any domain-joined computer?
   a. Domain local account
   b. Global account
   c. Domain account
   d. Local account

10. What can be used to run script files using VBScript or JScript from the Windows desktop or from a command prompt?
    a. Visual Basic
    b. Windows Scripting Host (WSH)
    c. Visual Basic Express
    d. Windows Scripting Engine

■ Case Scenarios

Scenario 5-1: Administering Groups for Humongous Insurance

You are a network administrator for Humongous Insurance. Humongous Insurance has a multidomain forest. The forest root is humongousinsurance.com. There are also two child domains named west.humongousinsurance.com and east.humongousinsurance.com. The company has approximately 7,000 users, 7,000 client workstations, and 100 servers.

All domains are Windows Server 2008 domains. The forest root domain has 10 domain controllers. Five of those domain controllers are configured as DNS servers and two are configured as global catalog servers. The West domain has three domain controllers. Two of those domain controllers are configured as DNS servers. One of those domain controllers is configured as a global catalog server. The East domain has two Windows Server 2008 domain controllers and three Windows 2003 domain controllers.

The forest root domain is located in College Station, Texas. The East domain is located in Gainesville, Florida. The West domain is located in San Diego, California. An Active Directory site is configured for each of these locations. The site for College Station is named Main_Site. The Gainesville site is named East_Site. The San Diego site is named West_Site.

You are one of several network administrators assigned to handle the forest root domain and College Station site. Your manager, Jean Trenary, has called a meeting of all network and desktop administrators. She wants to address several issues.

1. Jean says four internal auditors are in the forest root domain. Two internal auditors are in each of the child domains. Each set of internal auditors has been placed in a global group within each domain. These groups are named IA_Main, IA_East, and IA_West after their respective locations. Jean wants all of the members of these groups to be able to access a common set of resources in the Main domain, while still segregating the auditors' ability to access other resources in domains other than their own. What is the recommended way to configure the groups to allow the desired functionality?

2. The network administrators from the West domain want to know why everyone always recommends placing global groups into universal groups instead of placing the users directly into the universal groups. What should you tell them?

3. Jean approves a plan to hire assistants for each domain to create and manage user accounts. How can you give the assistants the immediate ability to help in this way without making them domain administrators?

4. Two employees have been hired to back up data and manage printers for the Main_Site. Which built-in groups will give these users the permissions they require to manage the domain controllers? How should you set up their accounts and group memberships?

Scenario 5-2: Evaluating Scripts

This scenario will help you to find and evaluate one of the script types discussed in this lesson.

1. Describe each type of scripting that can add users to Active Directory. Provide an example of a scenario using each one.

2. Using the Internet as your resource, find an example of one of the script types and write a short description of the script and what it accomplishes.

Security Planning and Administrative Delegation

OBJECTIVE DOMAIN MATRIX

TECHNOLOGY SKILL	OBJECTIVE DOMAIN	OBJECTIVE DOMAIN NUMBER
Creating an OU Structure	Maintain Active Directory accounts.	4.2

KEY TERMS

Active Directory Migration
   Tool (ADMT)
Delegation of Control Wizard
dictionary attack
drag-and-drop

dsmove
password
password-cracking
personal identification number
   (PIN)

Run as administrator
runas
Secondary Logon
strong password

Contoso Pharmaceuticals is a global biomedical firm specializing in the research and marketing of new vaccines. Each research office is largely autonomous and staffs one or more local personnel to take care of day-to-day IT support activities such as password resets. In addition, certain Contoso offices perform highly sensitive research activities, and the vice president of the research wing is concerned about the security of the data stored in these locations. The Contoso Active Directory team has deployed a highly developed OU structure to allow delegated administration of the various Contoso offices.

After completing this lesson, you will be able to perform the critical task of implementing account security for users in your Active Directory environment. This includes developing a cohesive naming standard for users and computers to ease the administration process, as well as creating a strong password policy and educating users on the importance of establishing and maintaining good passwords to protect themselves and their network resources. You will also be able to discuss the importance of securing access to Active Directory. This consists of securing the administrative process through the use of separate administrative accounts, as well as deploying an Organizational Unit (OU) structure that allows secure administration of Active Directory resources.

■ Planning and Implementing Account Security

THE BOTTOM LINE

One of the most significant considerations to take into account when planning a secure network is user account security. After all, access to network resources begins with a user account and password that is used for authentication purposes. After this authentication is established, users can gain access to the network resources to which they were granted permission. Because user authentication is so crucial to network security, it is critical that this process be carefully planned and configured on a Windows Server 2008 Active Directory network.

User logon names will typically follow a corporate naming standard set forth during the planning stages of an Active Directory deployment. You will usually create a naming standards document to outline the rules for naming all Active Directory objects. This document will specify conventions such as the number and type of characters to use when creating a new object in Active Directory. Table 6-1 contains an example of a naming standard for user accounts.

Table 6-1

Sample Naming Standards for User Accounts

NAMING STANDARD	EXAMPLE	EXPLANATION
FLLLLLxx	JSmith01	First initial followed by first five characters of the last name, appended with a number to ensure uniqueness when duplicate names may exist.
LLLLLFFM	SmithJoS or SmithJo1	First five characters of the last name followed by the first two characters of the first name, appended with a middle initial. If a middle initial is not applicable, a unique number is used instead.

Because user accounts in a corporate network will typically follow the organization's corporate naming standard or some other agreed-upon guideline, a user's logon name can sometimes be guessed easily. Because the user account name is 50 percent of the information required for a successful logon, this makes protecting user password information even more crucial.

Using Passwords

By default, Microsoft Windows Server 2008 requires a password for all user accounts. Most organizations will implement passwords for their user accounts, but many fail to then educate users on good practices to follow when choosing and protecting their passwords. In this section, we will discuss the following methods for securing user accounts:

- Educating users
- Configuring strong passwords
- Implementing smart cards

X REF

For more information
about smart cards, refer
to Lesson 13.

Educating Users on the Importance of Passwords

Passwords and *personal identification numbers (PINs)* are becoming common in
many areas of life, including banking, email, voice mail, and keyless entry systems such
as garage door openers. A password is an alphanumeric sequence of characters that you
enter with a username to access a server, workstation, or shared resource. A PIN typically
consists of at least four characters or digits that are entered while presenting a physical
access token, such as an ATM card or a smart card. For example, accessing your account
at an automated teller machine (ATM) at a bank requires a PIN. The combination of
the magnetic strip on the back of your ATM card and the PIN are matched against
the credentials for your account. If you enter an incorrect PIN, you cannot access your
account. Your PIN thereby serves as a password for your account.

The primary function of a password is to protect a user's authentication information, thus
ensuring that no one can impersonate a particular user and thereby gain access to resources
that the user has been authorized to view or edit. Therefore, when you create an account for
an Active Directory user, you should make the user aware of the security risks associated with
sharing his or her logon information with others. Share the following list of password protection best practices with your users:

- When documenting passwords on paper, keep the document in a secure location, such
  as a manager's safe. Do not leave the document out in the open where others can see it.
- Do not share your password with anyone. If you feel your password has been compromised some reason, change it immediately.
- In higher security networks, do not save passwords to your computer for activities such
  as easy logon to Internet sites. Although many secure sites that require authentication
  offer an option to store the password on your computer, storing any passwords on your
  computer poses a potential security risk.
- When creating or changing your password, use the guidelines for creating strong passwords, which are discussed in the next section.

Educating users can become part of your network security defense system. Distributing this
information is easy when it is made part of new employee training programs or professional
development sessions.

Configuring Strong Passwords

A *strong password* can be simply defined as a password that follows guidelines that
make it difficult for a potential hacker to determine the user's password. Configuring
strong passwords on a Windows Server 2008 network is a combination of creating a
minimum required password length, a password history, requiring multiple types of
characters within a password, and setting minimum password age.

Password-cracking is an attempt to discover a user's password. Password-cracking tools are
widely available on the Internet for download by even the least skilled attacker, and their ability to crack user passwords improves on almost a daily basis. Password-cracking can be accomplished by intelligent guessing on the part of the hacker or through the use of an automated
dictionary attack. Automated password-cracking tools will try every possible combination
of characters until the correct sequence of characters is finally discovered. The goal of implementing a strong password is to deter these types of attacks by implementing passwords that
require more time and processing abilities to crack.

In Windows Server 2008, strong passwords are required when Active Directory is installed. If the local Administrator password is blank when you begin the Active Directory installation process, a dialog box appears warning you of the risks of not using a strong password for this account, similar to the warning shown in Figure 6-1.

Figure 6-1

Warning message displayed when using a blank password

> **Active Directory Domain Services Installation Wizard**
>
> ⚠ The local Administrator account becomes the domain Administrator account when you create a new domain.
>
> Currently, the local Administrator password is blank, which might lead to security issues. We recommend that you press Ctrl+Alt+Delete, use the net user command-line tool, or use Local Users and Groups to set a strong password for the local Administrator account before you create the new domain.
>
> Do you want to continue?
>
> [Yes] [No]

X REF

For more information about a password policy, refer to Lesson 8.

The Administrator account should not be the only account for which you configure a strong password. All Active Directory user accounts should require strong passwords as well. You can define a strong password policy to force users to use strong passwords when they create or change their passwords. For now, it is necessary to understand what constitutes a strong password.

A strong password has the following characteristics:

- At least eight characters in length
- Contains uppercase and lowercase letters, numbers, and nonalphabetic characters
- At least one character from each of the previous character types
- Differs significantly from other previously used passwords

A strong password should not be left blank or contain any of the following information:

- Your user name, real name, or company name
- A complete dictionary word

Windows passwords for Windows Server 2008, Windows Vista, Windows Server 2003, and Microsoft Windows XP clients can be up to 127 characters in length. Using the criteria for creating strong passwords will help in developing a more secure network environment. *MspR3s5#1* is an example of a strong password based on these criteria.

Securing Administrative Access to Active Directory

> Setting user account guidelines is an important part of securing your network. However, a hacker who has access to a standard user account cannot damage your network nearly as much as a hacker with administrative permissions. Therefore, securing the use of any administrative account is a critical security task for an Active Directory administrator.

X REF

For more information about guidelines for securing the Administrator account, refer to Lesson 5.

As discussed in Lesson 5, you should not use an account possessing administrative privileges for daily tasks such as browsing the Web or monitoring email. Administrative accounts should be reserved for tasks that require administrator privileges. Using the Administrator account or an account that is a member of Domain Admins, Enterprise Admins, or Schema Admins for daily tasks offers an opportunity for hackers to attack your network and potentially cause severe and irreversible damage. For example, accessing an Internet site or opening a virus-infected email message can lead to accounts or files being deleted or hard drives being reformatted, or it can allow malicious attackers to take complete control of your server or workstation. Limiting the use of the Administrator account for daily tasks, such as email, application use, and access to the Internet, reduces the potential for this type of damage.

The recommended solution for reducing the risks associated with the Administrator account is to use a standard user account and the ***Run as administrator*** option in the GUI or the ***runas*** command-line tool when it is necessary to perform an administrative task. The following list identifies characteristics of the Run as administrator or runas option:

- The Run as administrator or runas option allows you to maintain your primary logon as a standard user and creates a secondary session for access to an administrative tool.
- During the use of a program or tool opened using Run as administrator or runas, your administrative credentials are valid only until you close that program or tool.
- Run as administrator or runas can be used from the command line or from the GUI.
- Some tasks, such as upgrading the operating system and configuring system parameters, do not support the use of Run as administrator or runas. You must be logged on interactively to perform such tasks.
- Run as administrator and runas require the ***Secondary Logon*** service to be running. The Secondary Logon service provides the ability to log on with an alternate set of credentials to that of the primary logon.
- Run as administrator and runas can be used to start two separate instances of an administrative application, such as Active Directory Domains and Trusts or Active Directory Users and Computers. Each instance can be directed at a different domain or forest. This allows you to perform interdomain or interforest administration tasks more efficiently.
- The runas command-line tool is not limited to administrator accounts. You can use runas to log on with separate credentials from any account. This can be a valuable tool in testing resource access permissions.

USE RUN AS FROM THE GUI

GET READY. This exercise assumes that you are signed onto a Windows Server 2008 member server or a Windows Vista workstation that has been joined to a Windows Server 2008 domain.

1. From the Start button, navigate to the application you wish to run, such as note-pad.exe. Press and hold the (**Shift**) key, right-click the desired application, and select the **Run as administrator** option.

2. If you are already logged on as an administrative user, you will be presented with a User Account Control confirmation dialog. Click **Continue** to launch the selected program using administrative credentials.

   or

   If you are logged in as a nonadministrative user, you will be prompted to enter the username and password of an administrative user to continue.

   PAUSE. You can close the application that you just opened using the Run as administrator option.

You have just launched an application from a workstation or member server using the Run as administrator option. This allows you to run a program with secondary credentials from your Windows desktop.

USE RUNAS FROM THE COMMAND LINE

GET READY. To run the DNS Management snap-in using a domain administrator account named domainadmin in the lucernepublishing.com domain, complete the following steps.

1. Open a command prompt window.

2. At the command prompt, key

   ```
   runas /user:lucernepublishing.com\domainadmin "mmc %windir%\
   system32\dnsmgmt.msc"
   ```

3. When prompted, enter the password for the domainadmin account and press (Enter).

PAUSE. You can close the application that you just opened using the Run as administrator option.

You have just launched an application from a Windows Vista workstation using the runas command-line tool. Running a program based on secondary credentials using the command-line utility works in much the same way as using the GUI.

■ Planning an Organizational Unit Strategy

↓ **THE BOTTOM LINE**

Lesson 1 discussed the concept of OUs, including the objects they can contain and how they can be created to represent your company's functional or geographical model as a foundation. This section expands on that foundation to include additional benefits of planning an OU structure.

You will create OUs in your Active Directory structure for several reasons:

- OUs represent the functional or geographical model of your company so that resources can be placed according to the users who need them. OUs can be created to represent geographic locations or functional needs of a company. For example, if you have a company that has three locations in a single domain, you may choose to represent these locations by creating an OU for each location. To organize your structure even further, you may wish to nest OUs for each department beneath their respective locations.

- OUs delegate administrative control over a container's resources to lower-level or branch office administrators. When creating OUs that represent locations and departments, you may find that administrative tasks would be easier to accomplish if an administrator from that location was designated to perform them. For example, if you have a department that tends to have high turnover in employees and job responsibilities, it might be easier to allow the manager of that department to create and delete user accounts as necessary. In addition, a local administrator could add and remove his or her users from the groups that give them resource access. Some administrators create OUs specifically for the delegation of administrative tasks. This allows some of the daily tasks, such as account creation and password resets, to be offloaded to lower-level administrators.

For more information about the specifics of Group Policy creation and management, refer to Lessons 7 through 10.

- OUs apply consistent configurations to client computers, users, and member servers through the application of Group Policy Objects. When group policies are created for an OU, the policies are applied to that OU and all child OUs within the hierarchy by default. Designing an OU structure with this in mind will simplify such things as application deployments and account logon policies. Because there are multiple ways to manage Group Policies but only one way to manage OU delegation, plan your OU structure with administrative delegation as your first priority, above Group Policy implementation.

Creating an OU Structure

OUs can be nested to create a design that allows administrators to take advantage of the benefits of the solid OU design listed previously. As with groups, you should limit the number of OUs that are nested, because nesting too many levels of OUs can slow the response time to resource requests and complicate the application of Group Policy settings.

As shown in Figure 6-2, when Active Directory is installed, only one OU is created by default: the Domain Controllers OU. An OU is represented in Active Directory Users and Computers by a folder with an icon of an open book on it. All other OUs must be created by a domain administrator. The other containers that are created during the installation, such as the Users container, appear as folders with no icons on them. The principal difference between these containers and OUs is that you cannot apply Group Policy Objects to these objects.

Figure 6-2

Viewing the default OU structure

OUs are not considered security principals. This means that you cannot assign access permissions to a resource based on membership to an OU. Herein lies the difference between OUs and global, domain local, and universal groups. Groups are used for assigning access permissions, whereas OUs are used for organizing resources and delegating permissions.

Using OUs to Delegate Active Directory Management Tasks

Creating OUs to support a decentralized administration model gives you the ability to allow others to manage portions of your Active Directory structure, without affecting the rest of the structure. Delegating authority at a site level affects all domains and users within the site. Delegating authority at a domain level affects the entire domain. However, delegating authority at the OU level affects only that OU and its hierarchy.

By allowing administrative authority over an OU structure, as opposed to an entire domain or site, you gain the following advantages:

- Minimize the number of administrators with global privileges. By creating a hierarchy of administrative levels, you limit the number of people who require global access.
- Limit the scope of errors. Administrative mistakes such as a container deletion or group object deletion affect only the respective OU structure.

CERTIFICATION READY?
Maintain Active Directory Accounts
4.2

Using the ***Delegation of Control Wizard***, you utilize a simple interface to delegate permissions for domains, OUs, or containers. The interface allows you to specify to which users or groups you want to delegate management permissions and the specific tasks you wish them to be able to perform. You can delegate predefined tasks, or you can create custom tasks that allow you to be more specific.

DELEGATE ADMINISTRATIVE CONTROL OF AN OU

GET READY. To complete this exercise, you must be logged on as a member of the Domain Admins group.

1. Open Active Directory Users and Computers, right-click the object to which you wish to delegate control, and click **Delegate Control**.
2. Click **Next** on the Welcome to the Delegation of Control Wizard page.

3. As shown in Figure 6-3, click **Add** on the Users or Groups page.

Figure 6-3

Delegating control to a specified user or group

4. In the Select Users, Computers, or Groups dialog box, key the user or group to
which you want to delegate administration in the *Enter the object names to select*
box, and click **OK**. (If you have not created user or group objects, select a built-in
group such as Domain Users or Server Operators.) Click **Next** to proceed.

5. On the Tasks to Delegate page shown in Figure 6-4, you will see the following
options:

Figure 6-4

Selecting a task to delegate

- **Delegate the following common tasks.** This option allows you to choose from a
  list of predefined tasks.
- **Create a custom task to delegate.** This option allows you to be more specific
  about the task delegation.

6. Click **Create a custom task to delegate** and click **Next**.

7. On the Active Directory Object Type page shown in Figure 6-5, the following
options are displayed:

- **This folder, existing objects in this folder, and creation of new objects in this
  folder.** This option delegates control of the container, including all of its current
  and future objects.
- **Only the following objects in the folder.** This option allows you to select specific
  objects to be controlled. You can select **Create selected objects in this folder**
  to allow selected object types to be created, or select **Delete selected objects in
  this folder** to allow selected object types to be deleted.

Click **This folder, existing objects in this folder, and creation of new objects in this folder.** Click **Next** to proceed.

Figure 6-5

Selecting objects to delegate

8. On the Permissions page shown in Figure 6-6, set the delegated permissions according to your needs for the user or group that has delegated control. You can combine permissions from all three of the bulleted options:

Figure 6-6

Selecting permissions to delegate

- **General.** Displays general permissions, which are equal to those displayed on the Security tab in an object's properties. For example, selecting Full Control for general permissions is inclusive of all property rights as well.
- **Property-specific.** Displays permissions that apply to specific attributes or properties of an object. If you select the Read permission using the General option, all read-specific properties are selected.
- **Creation/deletion of specific child objects.** Displays permissions that apply to creation and deletion permissions for specified object types.

9. After selecting the appropriate permissions, click **Next** to proceed.
10. The Completing the Delegation of Control Wizard page is displayed. Review your choices carefully and click **Finish**.

PAUSE. You can close the Active Directory Users and Computers MMC snap-in now or leave it open for the next exercise.

In the previous exercise, you granted permissions over a portion of Active Directory to a delegated administrator or group of administrators. Although the Delegation of Control Wizard can be used to give permissions to users or groups, it cannot be used to verify or remove permissions. To verify or remove permissions that were delegated, you must use the Security tab in the Properties dialog box of the delegated object.

⊕ VERIFY AND REMOVE DELEGATED PERMISSIONS

GET READY. To complete this exercise, you must be logged on as a member of the Domain Admins group.

1. In Active Directory Users and Computers, click the **View** menu, and then click **Advanced Features**. This allows you to see the Security tab as required in step 3.

2. Navigate in the left pane to the object for which you wish to verify delegated permissions, right-click the object, and select **Properties**.

3. On the Security tab, click **Advanced**.

4. On the Permissions tab, under Permissions entries, view the assigned permissions.

5. Select the user or group for which you wish to remove delegated control privileges and click **Remove**. Click **OK** twice to exit the Properties window.

PAUSE. You can close the Active Directory Users and Computers MMC snap-in.

In the previous exercise, you viewed and removed delegated permissions using the Advanced view of the Active Directory Users and Computers MMC snap-in.

Moving Objects Between OUs

You can move objects from one OU to another for administrative or business purposes. For example, consider a scenario where you are a consultant who has been called in to analyze and recommend changes to make network administration simpler and more effective. If all users are created in the Users container, it probably would be best to restructure these users according to resource needs and administrative goals, because you cannot link Group Policy Objects to the Users container.

Windows Server 2008 allows you to restructure your Active Directory database by moving leaf objects such as users, computers, and printers between OUs, in addition to moving OUs into other OUs to create a nested structure. When you move objects between OUs in a domain, permissions that are assigned directly to objects remain the same and the objects inherit permissions from the new OU. All permissions that were inherited previously from the old OU no longer affect the objects. Windows Server 2008 provides two methods for moving objects between OUs in the same domain:

- *Drag-and-drop* within Active Directory Users and Computers. The drag-and-drop feature was introduced in Windows Server 2003. This ability is welcomed by administrators of the previous version of Active Directory, which did not support it. The drag-and-drop feature functions the same way as it does in Windows Explorer, the main file management system within all Windows-based operating systems.

- Use the Move menu option within Active Directory Users and Computers. Using the drag-and-drop feature can be cumbersome and sometimes produces undesired results if you are not accurate with the mouse. The Move option in Active Directory Users and Computers offers a safer method than the drag-and-drop feature, but has the same results.

TAKE NOTE* To move objects between domains, use the *Active Directory Migration Tool (ADMT)*, a free download from the Microsoft Web site.

→ MOVE AN OBJECT BETWEEN OUS USING DRAG-AND-DROP

GET READY. To complete this exercise, you must be logged on as a member of the Domain Admins group.

1. In Active Directory Users and Computers, select the object you wish to move. If you wish to move multiple objects, press and hold the (**Ctrl**) key while selecting the objects you wish to move.

2. While holding down the left mouse button, drag the object to the desired destination OU and release the mouse. The object will appear in its new location.

PAUSE. You can close the Active Directory Users and Computers MMC snap-in now, or leave it open for the next exercise.

In the previous exercise, you moved one or more objects between OUs by using the drag-and-drop feature of the Active Directory Users and Computers MMC snap-in.

→ MOVE AN OBJECT BETWEEN OUS USING THE MOVE OPTION

GET READY. To complete this exercise, you must be logged on as a member of the Domain Admins group.

1. In Active Directory Users and Computers, select the object you wish to move. If you wish to move multiple objects, press and hold the (**Ctrl**) key while selecting the objects you wish to move.

2. Right-click the selected object(s) and select **Move** from the shortcut menu. In the Move dialog box, select the container object that is the destination for the selected objects and click **OK.** Active Directory will refresh and the objects will appear in their new location.

PAUSE. You can close the Active Directory Users and Computers MMC snap-in.

In the previous exercise, you moved one or more objects between OUs by using the Move feature of the Active Directory Users and Computers MMC snap-in.

 ANOTHER WAY

You can also move an object from one location to another using the *dsmove* command-line utility

SUMMARY SKILL MATRIX

IN THIS LESSON YOU LEARNED:

- Creating a naming standards document will assist in planning a consistent Active Directory environment that is easier to manage.

- Securing user accounts includes educating users to the risks of attacks, implementing a strong password policy, and possibly introducing a smart card infrastructure into your environment.

- As part of creating a secure environment, you should create standard user accounts for administrators and direct them to use Run as administrator or runas when performing administrative tasks.

- When planning your OU structure, consider the business function, organizational structure, and administrative goals for your network. Delegation of administrative tasks should be a consideration in your plan.

- Administrative tasks can be delegated for a domain, OU, or container to achieve a decentralized management structure. Permissions can be delegated using the Delegation of Control Wizard. Verification or removal of these permissions must be achieved through the Security tab in the Properties dialog box of the affected container.

- Moving objects between containers and OUs within a domain can be achieved using the Move menu command, the drag-and-drop feature in Active Directory Users and Computers, or the dsmove utility from a command line.

■ Knowledge Assessment

Matching

Match the following definitions with the appropriate term.

   a. Active Directory Migration Tool
   b. Delegation of Control Wizard
   c. dictionary attack
   d. drag-and-drop
   e. dsmove
   f. password-cracking
   g. personal identification number (PIN)
   h. runas
   i. Secondary Logon
   j. strong password

_____ **1.** This service is required to use the runas feature.

_____ **2.** This command-line tool can be used to move an object from one OU to another.

_____ **3.** This tool is used to move objects from one domain to another.

_____ **4.** Hackers will use this attack to identify a user's password by trying numerous words and word combinations until they find a match.

_____ **5.** When you create this item do not use words from the dictionary.

_____ **6.** This can be used to run a single command using administrative privileges while logging onto a workstation or server using a Domain User account.

_____ **7.** This can be used for authentication in lieu of a password when used with an ATM or a smart card.

_____ **8.** Use this tool to grant authority to a user or group of users over a portion of the Active Directory tree.

_____ **9.** This method of moving objects from one OU to another was introduced in Windows Server 2003.

_____ **10.** A dictionary attack is one type of this attack.

Multiple Choice

Circle the correct choice.

1. Which interface allows you to grant limited permissions within Active Directory to individual users or groups to adhere to a principle of least privilege in administering Active Directory?
   a. Delegation of Authority Wizard   **b.** Delegation of Control Wizard
   c. Control Wizard   **d.** Authority Wizard

2. Which program allows you to use the Secondary Logon service to launch individual programs and utilities using administrative privileges?
   a. Runas   **b.** Wscript
   c. Cscript   **d.** Secwiz

3. Which command-line utility can be used to move an Active Directory object from one container to another?
   a. Dsget   **b.** Dsrm
   c. Dsmove   **d.** Admt

4. What is a numeric or alphanumeric character sequence that you enter with a smart card to access a server or other Active Directory resource?
   a. Personal Identification Number (PIN)
   b. Password Identification Number (PIN)

   c. Smart card password
   d. Smart card identifier

5. What is a password that has sufficient length and complexity to make it difficult for a hacker or other malicious user to hack?
   a. Long password
   b. Smart card password
   c. Strong password
   d. Personal identification password

6. Which service enables you to use the runas command-line utility?
   a. Secondary Service
   b. Secondary Logon
   c. Runas Service
   d. Alternate Credentials Service

7. What is the recommended method for moving Active Directory objects from one domain to another?
   a. Movetree.exe
   b. Dsmove
   c. Active Directory Migration Tool (ADMT)
   d. Drag-and-drop

8. Which password-cracking attack functions by attempting every possible combination of alphanumeric characters until it finds a match?
   a. Trojan horse
   b. Dictionary attack
   c. Rootkit
   d. Boot virus

9. What is a new GUI option in Windows Server 2008 and Windows Vista that allows you to launch a specific application using elevated privileges?
   a. Delegation of Control Wizard
   b. Active Directory Administrative Credentials
   c. Run as Administrator
   d. Delegation of Privilege Wizard

10. With a username, what is needed to access network resources in a default Active Directory environment?
   a. Password
   b. Access Token
   c. Smart card
   d. PIN

Case Scenarios

Case Scenario 6-1: Planning Active Directory for Contoso Pharmaceuticals

You are a consultant working with Contoso Pharmaceuticals to assist them in planning their Active Directory infrastructure. Contoso Pharmaceuticals is a medical research and experimental drug company that participates in government projects. The information on the company's network is very sensitive and, therefore, security is the CEO's primary concern. The plan that is implemented should have the strongest precautions against attacks from the outside.

The company currently is using a Microsoft Windows 2000 domain and will be transitioning to Active Directory with the migration of their network to Windows Server 2008. The company has a single domain and will be expanding to include a single forest and one domain for each of its five locations when the new network is installed. An administrator has been designated for each location. In addition, the accounting and human resource departments, which are located at the main site, want to be able to manage their own containers.

  a. Based on this scenario, should administration be centralized or decentralized? Explain.
  b. How will you achieve the goal set forth by the accounting and human resource departments?
  c. What will you propose for a secure logon method?

Introduction to Group Policy

OBJECTIVE DOMAIN MATRIX

TECHNOLOGY SKILL	OBJECTIVE DOMAIN	OBJECTIVE DOMAIN NUMBER
Using the Group Policy Management Console	Create and apply Group Policy Objects (GPOs).	4.3
Configuring Group Policy Settings	Configure GPO templates.	4.4

KEY TERMS

Administrative Templates
ADMX
asynchronous processing
Block Policy Inheritance
Central Store
Computer Configuration
Default Domain Controller Policy
Default Domain Policy
domain GPO
Enforce
folder redirection
GPO inheritance
Group Policy container (GPC)
Group Policy Management Console (GPMC)

Group Policy Management Editor
Group Policy Object (GPO)
Group Policy template (GPT)
linking
local GPO
Loopback Processing
LSDOU
Merge
multiple local GPOs
node
offline file storage
registry-based policies
Replace
return on investment (ROI)

scripts
security group filtering
software installation policies
Software Settings
starter GPO
synchronous processing
total cost of ownership (TCO)
User Configuration
Windows Deployment Services (WDS)
Windows Settings

Lucerne Publishing has recently deployed its Active Directory environment. Network administrators have created an Active Directory site to correspond to each of Lucerne Publishing's physical locations, as well as OUs representing each department, including Marketing, Human Resources, Finance, and Administration. Each department has requested different settings to control their Windows desktops. Also, the Marketing and Finance departments have specialized applications that must be deployed to every desktop in their departments. To meet these needs, the Lucerne Publishing Active Directory administrators have decided to create multiple Group Policy Objects (GPOs) to configure consistent settings across the various departments and locations.

After completing this lesson, you will understand the benefits and overall architecture of Group Policy Objects (GPOs). You will be able to describe the Group Policy Container and Group Policy Templates, as well as the use of the Group Policy Management Console (GPMC). You will be able to configure Group Policy settings, understand how GPOs are processed, and fine-tune the application of GPOs.

■ Introducing Group Policy

↓ THE BOTTOM LINE

Group Policy is a method of controlling settings across your network. Group Policy consists of user and computer settings on the Windows Server 2008, Windows Server 2003 family, Microsoft Windows 2000 family, Window Vista, and Microsoft Windows XP Professional platforms that can be implemented during computer startup and shutdown and user logon and logoff. You can configure one or more GPOs within a domain and then use a process called *linking*, which applies these settings to various containers within Active Directory. You can link multiple GPOs to a single container or link one GPO to multiple containers throughout the Active Directory structure.

The following managed settings can be defined or changed through Group Policies:

- *Registry-based policies*, such as user desktop settings and environment variables, provide a consistent, secure, manageable environment that addresses the users' needs and the organization's administrative goals. As the name implies, these settings modify the Windows Registry.

- *Software installation policies* can be used to ensure that users always have the latest versions of applications. If application files are inadvertently deleted, repairs are made without user intervention.

- *Folder redirection* allows files to be redirected to a network drive for backup and makes them accessible from anywhere on the network.

- *Offline file storage* works with folder redirection to provide the ability to cache files locally. This allows files to be available even when the network is inaccessible.

- *Scripts* including logon, logoff, startup, and shutdown scripts, can assist in configuring the user environment.

- *Windows Deployment Services (WDS)* assists in rebuilding or deploying workstations quickly and efficiently in an enterprise environment.

- Microsoft Internet Explorer settings provide quick links and bookmarks for user accessibility, in addition to browser options such as proxy use, acceptance of cookies, and caching options.

- Security settings protect resources on computers in the enterprise.

Depending on the organization's needs, you can choose which features and settings you wish to implement. For example, you may need to create a policy for a public access computer in a library that configures the desktop environment with a proprietary library-access system. In addition, you might wish to disable the ability to write to the computer's hard drive. As you determine the needs of different users and address those needs within corporate security and computing policies, you can plan the best methods to implement Group Policy.

Although the name *Group Policy Object* implies that policies are linked directly to groups, this is not the case. Group Policies can be linked to sites, domains, or OUs to apply those settings to all users and computers within these Active Directory containers. However, an advanced technique, called *security group filtering*, will allow you to apply GPO settings to only one or more users or groups within a container by selectively granting the "Apply Group Policy" permission to one or more users or security groups.

In the next section, you will learn some of the benefits that Group Policy offers to Active Directory administrators and the users and computers they support.

Understanding the Benefits of Group Policy

For the most part, corporations no longer use the pen-and-paper method of recording their accounting activities. Conversely, they also do not want to spend money needlessly in the implementation and management of their corporate computing systems. Rather, corporations always consider two criteria when evaluating technologies such as Group Policy: *return on investment (ROI)* and *total cost of ownership (TCO)*.

Return on investment (ROI) can be measured by tangible benefits, such as implementation costs and ongoing support. In addition, it can be measured by intangible benefits, such as increased user productivity, and other factors that are difficult to measure from a financial standpoint. In financial terms, ROI is the amount of money gained (or lost) relative to the amount of money that was invested in a particular project or technology. Total cost of ownership (TCO) is designed to assess the cost of implementing computer software or hardware, both in terms of direct and indirect costs. TCO can be calculated based on how much ownership costs over the lifetime of a business resource. For example, the TCO of a network includes costs such as the original purchases of equipment, upgrades, implementation costs, and management costs, spread out over the life of the network. The goals of implementing Group Policies are to increase a company's ROI and decrease its TCO in terms of managing end-user workstations. These two benefits can be achieved by carefully planning your Group Policies to align with company policies and administrative goals.

Users may initially view Group Policies as a heavy-handed management tactic to keep them from using certain computer functions. However, if the concept is presented appropriately, users will understand that they also benefit from Group Policies. The following are just some of the benefits to users of Group Policy implementation:

- Users can access their files, even when network connectivity is intermittent. This is accomplished by using folder redirection and offline files.
- The user environment can be set up to be consistent, regardless of which workstation or location is used as the login computer.
- User files can be redirected to a server location that allows them to be backed up regularly, saving users from the headaches of lost data due to the failure of their workstations.
- Applications that become damaged or need to be updated can be maintained automatically.

Group Policies probably have their largest impact on reducing TCO due to their administrative benefits. Administrators find that Group Policy implementation helps them to achieve centralized management. The following list identifies administrative benefits of Group Policy implementation:

- Administrators have control over centralized configuration of user settings, application installation, and desktop configuration.
- Problems due to missing application files and other minor application errors often can be alleviated by the automation of application repairs.
- Centralized administration of user files eliminates the need for and cost of trying to recover files from a damaged drive. (Note, however, that this does not eliminate the need to establish a regular backup schedule for server data.)
- The need to manually make security changes is reduced by the rapid deployment of new settings through Group Policy.

Defining Group Policy Architecture

> *Group Policy Objects (GPOs)* contain all of the Group Policy settings that you wish to implement to user and computer objects within a site, domain, or OU. The GPO must be associated with the container to which it is applied. This association occurs by linking the Group Policy to the desired Active Directory object. You will learn how to link GPOs to containers after you learn how to define GPOs and specify where they are stored.

There are three types of GPOs: *local GPOs*, *domain GPOs,* and *starter GPOs*. Each computer running Windows Server 2008, Windows Server 2003, Windows XP Professional, or Windows 2000 has only one local GPO, and the settings in that local GPO will apply to all users who log on to the computer. The local GPO settings are stored on the local computer in the %systemroot%/System32/GroupPolicy folder.

A local GPO has the following characteristics:

- Local GPOs contain fewer options. They do not support folder redirection or Group Policy software installation. Fewer security settings are available.
- When a local and a nonlocal (Active Directory–based) GPO have conflicting settings, the local GPO is overwritten by the nonlocal GPO.

As a new feature in Windows Vista, workstations can have *multiple local GPOs*. This allows you to specify a different local GPO for administrators and to create specific GPO settings for one or more local users configured on a workstation.

Nonlocal GPOs are created in Active Directory. They are linked to sites, domains, or OUs. Once linked to a container, the GPO is applied to all users and computers within that container by default. The content of each nonlocal GPO is actually stored in two locations. These locations are as follows:

- *Group Policy container (GPC)*—an Active Directory object that stores the properties of the GPO.
- *Group Policy template (GPT)*—located in the Policies subfolder of the SYSVOL share, the GPT is a folder that stores policy settings, such as security settings and script files.

Starter GPOs are a new feature in Windows Server 2008. They are used as GPO templates within Active Directory. Starter GPOs allow you to configure a standard set of items that will be configured by default in any GPO that is derived from a starter GPO, as shown in Figure 7-1.

Figure 7-1

Using starter GPOs in Windows Server 2008

Viewing the Group Policy Container

The Group Policy container (GPC) directory object includes subcontainers that hold GPO policy information. By default, when Active Directory is installed, two policies are placed in this container. Each Active Directory GPC is named according to the globally unique identifier (GUID) that is assigned to it when it is created.

Default GPC containers are created when the Active Directory Domain Services role is installed. A new GPC is created to store policy information and settings. The GPC contains two subcontainers—one for computer configuration information and another for user configuration information. The more specific information included in each GPC is as follows:

X REF

See "Configuring Group Policy Settings" later in this lesson for information on default policies.

- Status information that indicates whether the GPO is enabled or disabled
- Version information to ensure that the GPC is synchronized and up to date with the most current information
- A list of components that have settings in this GPO

⊖ VIEW THE GROUP POLICY CONTAINER

GET READY. To perform this exercise, you should be logged on with Domain Administrator credentials.

1. In Active Directory Users and Computers, click the **View** menu and then select **Advanced Features**. This allows you to see additional objects in Active Directory.

TAKE NOTE*

If Advanced Features already has a checkmark next to it, clicking it again hides the Advanced Features view options. Verify that a checkmark is displayed next to Advanced Features before proceeding to step 2.

2. In the left console pane, expand the *<domain name>* folder (for example, lucernepublishing.com), and then expand the System folder, as shown in Figure 7-2.

Figure 7-2

Expanded System folder

For more information about globally unique identifiers, refer to Lesson 1.

3. In the System folder, locate the Policies folder and expand it by clicking the plus sign (+). This opens the folder, displaying the two default policies named using its GUID.

PAUSE. CLOSE the Active Directory Users and Computers MMC snap-in.

Computers access the GPC to locate Group Policy templates via a link or connection reference to the Group Policy template. Domain controllers access the GPC to get version information. If the version information for a GPO is not current, replication occurs to update the GPO with the latest version. The GPC can be found in Active Directory Users And Computers using Advanced View. Figure 7-3 shows the GPC discussed in this section.

Figure 7-3

Viewing the Group Policy container

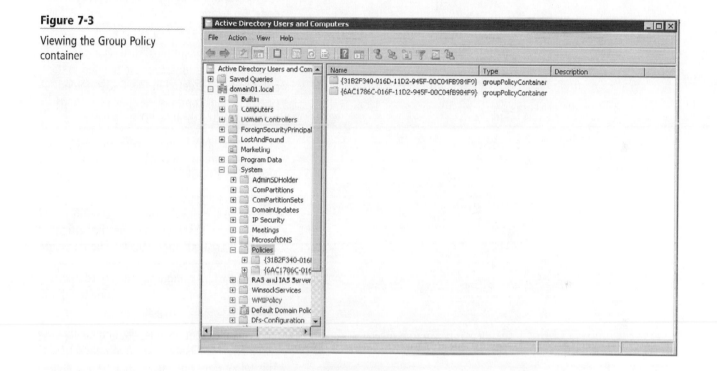

Viewing Group Policy Templates

The Group Policy templates (GPT) folder structure is located in the shared SYSVOL folder on a domain controller. By default, two folders that refer to the default domain policies are named when they are created by Active Directory. These GUIDs should be the same as those described for the GPCs. When additional GPOs are created, a corresponding GPT folder structure is created that contains all of the policy's settings and information. As with the GPC, computers connect to the GPT folder structure to read these settings.

The path to the default GPT structure for the lucernepublishing.com domain is %systemroot%\sysvol\sysvol\<*domain name*>\Policies\ (for example, C:\WINDOWS\SYSVOL\SYSVOL\lucernepublishing.com\Policies). Replace %systemroot% with the folder location for the operating system files. In a default Windows Server 2008 installation, this is the C:\Windows folder. Notice that the name of the domain (lucernepublishing.com in this case) is included as part of the path.

For each GUID that refers to a policy in the GPT structure, there are several subfolders and a gpt.ini file. Every Group Policy that is created has a gpt.ini file. This file contains the version and status information regarding the specific GPO. The subfolders contain more specific settings that are defined within the policy. Table 7-1 identifies several of the subfolders that are part of the GPT structure and describes their contents. (This table is not all-inclusive; some folders and their contents are created when policy settings are defined.)

Table 7-1

GPT Subfolders

FOLDER	CONTENT
\Machine	Contains a Registry.pol file that makes changes to the HKEY_LOCAL_MACHINE hive in the registry based on machine-specific settings. This file is created automatically when a policy has used the Administrative Templates option within the Computer Configuration node. For example, enabling Disk Quotas for a machine creates a Registry.pol file.
\Machine\Microsoft \WindowsNT\SecEdit	Contains security settings, such as account lockout specifications, that are defined in the policy. A file is created in this folder named GptTmpl.inf. It contains the specific settings to be applied with the GPO.
\Machine\Scripts	Contains settings for any startup or shutdown scripts that are in effect when the computer affected by this GPO is started or shut down.
\User	Contains a Registry.pol file that makes changes to the HKEY_CURRENT_USER hive in the registry based on user-specific settings. This file is created automatically when a policy has used the Administrative Templates option under the User Configuration node. For example, setting a user's account to autoenroll for a certificate creates a Registry.pol file.
\User\Applications	Contains files that include instructions for assigned or published application packages. This folder does not exist until package files used to deploy software applications have been assigned to the User Configuration node of the GPO.
\User\Scripts	Contains settings for logon and logoff scripts that are applied when a user affected by this GPO logs on or off the network.

X REF

For more information about disk quotas refer to Lesson 8.

TAKE NOTE*

To assist you in troubleshooting, memorize the first few digits of each of the Default Domain Policy and the Default Domain Controller Policy GUIDs so that you will recognize them on sight.

When Active Directory is installed, two domain GPOs are created by default. These two GPOs are named by their GUIDs, and they can be found in Active Directory Users and Computers and in the SYSVOL folder structure, as demonstrated earlier. These GUIDs represent the following default GPOs: {31B2F340-016D-11D2-945F-00C04FB984F9} represents the **Default Domain Policy**. It is linked to the domain, and its settings affect all users and computers in the domain. {6AC1786C-016F-11D2-945F-00C04FB984F9} represents the **Default Domain Controller Policy**. It is linked to the Domain Controllers OU, and its settings affect all domain controllers in the domain. As domain controllers are added to the domain, they are automatically placed in this OU and are affected by any settings applied with this policy. These two policies are very important in your domain. Settings in these policies can affect security and your administrative abilities throughout the domain. We will discuss these two policies and several of the main settings that are important in subsequent lessons. For now, you need to understand what they are and the extent of their effects.

Using the Group Policy Management Console

The *Group Policy Management Console (GPMC)* is the Microsoft Management Console (MMC) snap-in that is used to create and modify Group Policies and their settings. The *Group Policy Management Editor* can be opened several different ways, depending on what you wish to accomplish. You can create a GPO and then link it to a domain, site or OU, or create and link a GPO in a single step. The GPMC was not pre-installed in Windows Server 2003; it needed to be downloaded manually from the Microsoft Web site. However, it is now included in Windows Server 2008 by default.

CERTIFICATION READY?
Create and Apply Group
Policy objects (GPOs)
4.3

➔ CREATE AND LINK A GPO TO AN OU

GET READY. To complete this exercise, you must be logged on using Domain Administrator credentials.

1. To create an OU for this exercise, go to a command prompt and key **dsadd ou ou=Training,<DomainDN>**. (For the lucernepublishing.com domain, for example, key *dsadd ou ou=Training,dc=lucernepublishing,dc com*), as shown in Figure 7-4.

Figure 7-4

Creating an OU

2. Click **Start**, click **Administrative Tools**, and then click **Group Policy Management Console**. Click the plus sign (+) next to lucernepublishing.com.
3. Right-click the **Training** OU and select **Create a GPO in this domain, and link it here**, as shown in Figure 7-5.

Figure 7-5

Creating an OU

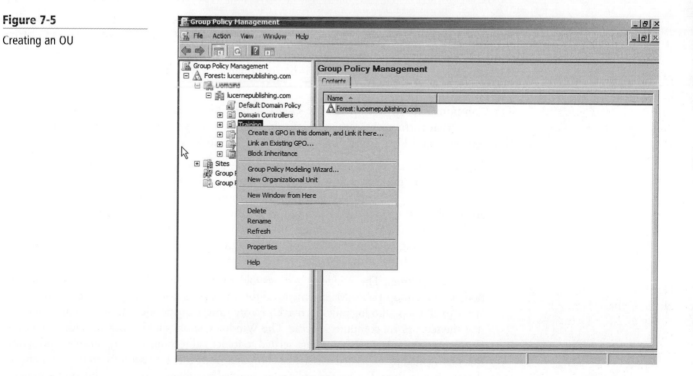

4. Key a name for your GPO and click **OK**.

5. Expand the Group Policy Objects node. Right-click the GPO that you just created and click **Edit**. The Group Policy Management Editor opens, and you can proceed with defining your policy settings, as shown in Figure 7-6.

Figure 7-6

Viewing the Group Policy Management Editor

PAUSE. CLOSE the Group Policy Management Editor and the Group Policy Management Console.

When you link a GPO to a domain, site, or OU or create and link a GPO to one of these containers in a single step, the settings within that GPO apply to all child objects within the object. For example, if you create a GPO from the domain object in Active Directory Users and Computers, it applies to all users and computers in the domain. On a larger scale, if a GPO is created for a site that contains multiple domains, the Group Policy is applied to all domains and the child objects contained within them. This process is referred to as *GPO inheritance*.

Configuring Group Policy Settings

Configuring Group Policy settings enables you to customize the configuration of a user's desktop, environment, and security settings. The actual settings are divided into two subcategories: *Computer Configuration* and *User Configuration*. The subcategories are referred to as Group Policy *nodes*. A node is simply a parent structure that holds all related settings. In this case, the node is specific to computer configurations and user configurations.

Group Policy nodes provide a way to organize the settings according to where they are applied. Defined settings can be applied to client computers, users, or member servers and domain controllers. The application of settings depends on the container to which the GPO is linked. By default, all objects within the container with which the GPO is associated are affected by the GPO's settings.

The Computer Configuration and the User Configuration nodes contain three subnodes, or extensions, that further organize the available Group Policy settings. Within the Computer Configuration and User Configuration nodes, the subnodes are as follows:

* *Software Settings.* The Software Settings folder located under the Computer Configuration node contains settings that apply to all users who log on from that specific computer. Settings modified here are computer specific, meaning that these settings are applied before any user is allowed to log on to the desktop. Rather than being computer specific, the Software Settings folder located under the User Configuration node contains settings that are applied to users designated by the Group Policy, regardless of the computer from which they log on to Active Directory.

* *Windows Settings.* The Windows Settings folder located under the Computer Configuration node in the Group Policy Management Editor contains security settings and scripts that apply to all users who log on to Active Directory from that specific computer. This means that the settings are computer specific. The Windows Settings folder located under the User Configuration node contains settings related to folder redirection, security settings, and scripts that are applied to associated users. The computer from which a user logs on does not affect these policy settings. Rather, the policies are applied regardless of the user's log on location.

* *Administrative Templates.* Windows Server 2008 includes thousands of Administrative Template policies, which contain all registry-based policy settings. Administrative

TAKE NOTE*

Over 100 ADMX files are installed by default when you promote a Windows Server 2008 domain controller.

Templates are files with the .admx extension. They are used to generate the user interface for the Group Policy settings that you can set using the Group Policy Management Editor. The Windows Server 2008 .admx files are based on the eXtensible Markup Language (XML), unlike the Windows 2003 .adm files, which are Unicode-based text files. *ADMX* files can be stored in a single location called the *Central Store* in the SYSVOL directory.

Because Administrative Templates is an area of Group Policy where many commonly used administrative settings reside, it is important to be familiar with how you can determine the purpose of each setting. In the Group Policy Management Editor, you can view descriptions of policy settings using the Explain tab; an example of a GPO setting configuring client DNS settings is shown in Figure 7-7. This comprehensive help feature describes the function of the policy setting. Additionally, the Group Policy Management Editor console itself includes a Requirements section for each setting that indicates the minimum operating system revision that will support it.

Figure 7-7

Viewing explanations of Group Policy settings

To work with Administrative Template settings, you need to understand the three different states of each setting. Figure 7-8 shows the available options to configure a representative GPO setting configuring client DNS settings. First, a setting can be *Not Configured*, which means that no modification to the registry from its default state occurs. Not Configured is the default setting for the majority of GPO settings. When a GPO with a Not Configured setting is processed, the registry key affected by the setting is not modified or overwritten. Next, a setting can be *Enabled*, which means the registry key is modified by this setting. Last, a setting can be *Disabled*, which means the policy setting is not selected. A Disabled setting will undo a change made by a prior Enabled setting.

Figure 7-8

Viewing Group Policy settings

One new feature of Group Policy management in Windows Server 2008 is the ability to search for a particular GPO setting under the Administrative Tempates folder based on elements such as keywords or the minimum operating system level. This is a convenience to administrators, because literally hundreds of settings are available under any number of nodes and subnodes within the Administrative Templates folder. Figure 7-9 shows the Filter Options screen in the Group Policy Management Editor. In addition, each individual Administrative Templates setting now includes a Comment tab that allows you to enter free-form text to describe the entry. You can search against the text in these comments fields using the Filter Options window. Finally, you will also see the All Settings node below the Administrative Templates node for User Configuration and Computer Configuration, which allows you to browse and sort all available policies alphabetically or by state (i.e., Enabled, Disabled, or Not Configured).

Figure 7-9

Viewing the Filter Options window in Windows Server 2008

CERTIFICATION READY?
Configure GPO templates
4.4

Understanding Group Policy Processing

As discussed earlier, you can have local policies, site policies, domain policies, and OU policies within your domain structure. To learn how to best implement Group Policies to serve the organization, you need to understand the order in which the policies are applied.

Nonlocal GPOs are created in Active Directory and linked to container objects. Nonlocal GPOs can be linked to Active Directory sites, domains, or OUs. They cannot be linked to built-in containers, such as the default Users, Builtin, or Computers containers. These containers can receive policies only through domain or site-linked policies that flow down to all objects within them. Policies affect the containers to which they are linked in the following ways:

- Site-linked policies affect all domains within a site.
- Domain-linked policies affect all users and computers within a domain and within any containers within a domain. This includes objects in built-in containers, as well as objects within OUs and sub-OUs within the domain structure.
- OU-linked policies affect all objects within the OU and any other OU structures nested within them.

To begin, policies are processed in the following order, typically referred to as *LSDOU*:

1. Local policies
2. Site policies

3. Domain policies
4. OU policies

Following the order of processing from steps 1 to 4, the settings in the policies that are processed last, that is, those that are assigned to an OU in step 4, override any conflicting settings in the policies that were processed in the previous steps. For example, suppose you have a policy setting that is applied to the site and affects all domains and their contents. If you have modified the same setting to produce a different result in an OU policy, the OU policy settings prevail. This behavior is intentional and provides administrators with flexibility in Group Policy application. In addition, as policies are applied, each container inherits the settings of the parent container policies by default.

Domains, sites, and OUs can have multiple group policies linked to them. Expanding on the previous example, you might have more than one policy linked to the Education department's OU. In this situation, the top GPO in the list is processed last. When multiple GPOs are linked to a container, the first GPO in the list has the highest priority. In other words, by default, the list of linked GPOs is processed from the bottom to the top.

Policies can be applied to containers and the user and computer objects that reside in them. Computer Configuration settings are processed when a computer starts, followed by User Configuration settings, which are processed during user logon. Computer startup scripts and user logon scripts can run during startup. In addition, user logoff scripts and computer shutdown scripts can run during shutdown.

The following steps describe the process of implementing the settings of the assigned GPOs for a computer and user:

1. When a computer is initialized during startup, it establishes a secure link between the computer and a domain controller. Then, the computer obtains a list of GPOs to be applied.

2. Computer configuration settings are applied synchronously during computer startup before the Logon dialog box is presented to the user. **Synchronous processing** of policies means that each policy must be read and applied completely before the next policy can be invoked. The default synchronous behavior can be modified by the system administrator if necessary, although such modification is discouraged. No user interface is displayed during this process with the exception of a Startup dialog box indicating that policies are being applied. The policies are read and applied in the LSDOU sequence described earlier.

3. Any startup scripts set to run during computer startup are processed. These scripts also run synchronously and have a default timeout of 600 seconds (10 minutes) to complete. This process is hidden from the user.

4. When the Computer Configuration scripts and startup scripts are complete, the user is prompted to press Ctrl+Alt+Del to log on.

5. Upon successful authentication, the user profile is loaded, based on the Group Policy settings in effect.

6. A list of GPOs specific for the user is obtained from the domain controller. User Configuration settings also are processed in the LSDOU sequence. The GPO processing is again transparent to the user, and the policies are processed synchronously.

7. After the user policies run, any logon scripts run. These scripts, unlike the startup scripts, run asynchronously by default. **Asynchronous processing** allows multiple scripts to be processed at the same time, without waiting for the outcome of a previously launched script to occur. However, the user object script runs last.

8. The user's desktop appears after all policies and scripts have been processed.

Configuring Exceptions to GPO Processing

As with most rules, there are usually exceptions, and this is true of Group Policy processing and inheritance. The purpose of having exceptions to the default processing of Group Policy options is to allow greater control and flexibility over the final settings that are applied. In this section, we will discuss several options that provide exceptions to the Group Policy processing rules.

The exceptions to the default Group Policy processing rules include the following:

- *Enforce.* Configuring this setting on an individual GPO link forces a particular GPO's settings to flow down through the Active Directory, without being blocked by any child OUs.

- *Block Policy Inheritance.* Configuring this setting on a container object such as a site, domain, or OU will block all policies from parent containers from flowing to this container. It is not policy specific; it applies to all policies that are applied at parent levels. GPO links that are set to Enforce are not affected by this setting; they are still applied.

- *Loopback Processing.* This is a Group Policy option that provides an alternative method of obtaining the ordered list of GPOs to be processed for the user. When set to Enabled, this setting has two options: *Merge* and *Replace*.

Now let's examine each of these options in detail. As we discussed earlier, if you assign a GPO policy at a site level, it is inherited by all domains within that site. The inheritance process takes place in the same order as Group Policies are applied. Specifically, this process results in sites obtaining GPO settings from site-linked GPOs; domains inheriting policies from site-linked GPOs, as well as obtaining settings from domain-linked GPOs; OUs inheriting GPO settings from both site-linked and domain-linked GPOs, as well as settings from OU-linked GPOs; and child OUs inheriting settings from all of the above. *Inheritance* then means that all objects within each of these containers inherit the GPO settings from higher up in the hierarchy. Because child container settings can overwrite the settings that were invoked at a parent container, you can assign the Enforce attribute to a GPO link to force a parent setting, preventing it from being overwritten by a conflicting child setting. The Enforce option denies the ability of child objects to apply the Block Policy Inheritance setting, as we will discuss next. Figure 7-10 shows the Enforce option for a Group Policy link.

Figure 7-10

Configuring Enforce for a GPO link

The second setting that can affect policy processing is the Block Policy Inheritance setting. As shown in Figure 7-11, this setting is applied to an entire container rather than a single policy. This setting is useful when you wish to start a new level of policy inheritance or when you do not want a parent policy to affect objects in a particular container.

The Block Policy Inheritance setting can be useful. However, when a parent policy is set to Enforce, the Block Policy Inheritance feature does not block settings from this particular parent policy.

Figure 7-11

Configuring Block Policy
Inheritance

Finally, there is the notion of Loopback Processing. When a computer starts up and its Active Directory container object is located, a list of GPOs that apply to the computer is generated and processed. Similarly, when a user logs on, a list of GPOs based on the user object's Active Directory location is processed. In certain situations, you might not want user-specific settings applied to certain computers. For example, when you log on to a domain controller or member server computer, you probably do not want a software application that is associated with your user object to be installed on that computer. Because user policies are applied after computer policies, you can alter this situation. This is where Loopback Processing comes into play.

As the name implies, Loopback Processing allows the Group Policy processing order to circle back and reapply the computer policies after all user policies and logon scripts run. When it is enabled, you can choose the Merge option or the Replace option. When the Merge option is selected, after all user policies run, the computer policy settings are reapplied, which allows all current GPO settings to merge with the reapplied computer policy settings. In instances where conflicts arise between computer and user settings, the computer policy supercedes the user policy. This occurs before the desktop is presented to the user. The settings here are simply appended to the settings that were already processed. Merging may not overwrite all of the settings implemented by the User Configuration settings.

The Replace option overwrites the GPO list for a user object with the GPO list for the user's logon computer. This means that the computer policy settings remove any conflicting user policy settings.

In addition, the Loopback Processing setting is a very valuable tool for managing computers shared by more than one user, as in a kiosk, classroom, or public library. Using the Replace option can greatly reduce the need for you to undo actions, such as application installs and desktop changes, that are made based on the settings associated with a user object. For example, consider an academic environment in which administrative accounts, such as teachers and staff, are placed in an Admin OU and student user accounts are placed in student OUs named for the students' graduation year. All computers are located in a Lab OU. In the computer labs, anyone can log on to the network. However, when users in the Admin OU log on, they are configured to print on printers located in their offices, and applications that are assigned to them are installed on the lab computers. Teachers complain that they have to walk back to their offices to pick up print jobs that should be printing on the printers located in the lab. In addition, applications that should not reside on the lab computers have been installed and now need to be removed. One solution to the problem outlined here is to use Loopback's Replace option. When the Replace option is set, only the user settings from the Lab OU will be applied. This resolves the issue of applying unwanted settings on shared computers from other locations in the Active Directory hierarchy.

SUMMARY SKILL MATRIX

IN THIS LESSON YOU LEARNED:

- Group Policy consists of user and computer settings that can be implemented during computer startup and user logon. These settings can be used to customize the user environment, to implement security guidelines, and to assist in simplifying user and desktop administration. Group Policies can be beneficial to users and administrators. They can be used to increase a company's return on investment and to decrease the overall total cost of ownership for the network.

- In Active Directory, Group Policies can be assigned to sites, domains, and OUs. By default, there is one local policy per computer. Local policy settings are overwritten by Active Directory policy settings.

- Group Policy content is stored in an Active Directory GPC and in a GPT. Whereas the GPC can be seen by using the Advanced Features view in Active Directory Users and Computers, the GPT is a GUID-named folder located in the systemroot\sysvol\SYSVOL\ *domain_name*\Policies folder.

- The Default Domain Policy and the Default Domain Controller Policy are created by default when Active Directory is installed.

- The Group Policy Management Console is the tool used to create and modify Group Policies and their settings.

- GPO nodes contain three subnodes, including Software Settings, Windows Settings, and Administrative Templates. Administrative templates are XML files with the .admx file extension. Over 100 ADMX files are included with Windows Server 2008.

- The order of Group Policy processing can be remembered using the acronym LSDOU: local policies are processed first, followed by site, domain, and, finally, OU policies. This order is an important part of understanding how to implement Group Policies for an object.

- Group Policies applied to parent containers are inherited by all child containers and objects. Inheritance can be altered by using the Enforce, Block Policy Inheritance, or Loopback settings.

■ Knowledge Assessment

Matching

Match the following definitions with the appropriate term.

a. Administrative Templates	**b.** asynchronous processing
c. Block Policy Inheritance	**d.** Default Domain Controller Policy
e. Enforce	**f.** GPO Inheritance
g. local GPO	**h.** Loopback Processing
i. LSDOU	**j.** multiple local GPOs

_____ 1. Configuring this setting will prevent a GPO's settings from being overwritten by another GPO that is applied later in the inheritance process.

_____ 2. By default, GPOs are applied in this order.

_____ 3. Computers in child OUs will receive GPO settings applied to a parent OU through this process.

_____ 4. User logon scripts are applied in this manner.

_____ 5. These are used to define registry-based policy settings in the User Configuration and Computer Configuration nodes.

_____ **6.** Use this option to configure GPO settings for a particular user based on the location in Active Directory of the user's computer.

_____ **7.** This option will allow you to configure separate local GPOs for administrators and non-administrators on a Windows Vista computer.

_____ **8.** This setting is configured at the container level and prevents default GPO inheritance.

_____ **9.** This GPO is linked to the Domain Controllers OU by default in a Windows Server 2008 domain.

_____ **10.** This is the first GPO applied during normal GPO processing.

Multiple Choice

Circle the correct choice.

1. What is the process of applying a Group Policy Object to a particular container, such as a site, domain, or an organizational unit?
   - **a.** Linking
   - **b.** Inheriting
   - **c.** Configuring
   - **d.** Applying

2. Which folder stores policy settings, such as security settings and script files?
   - **a.** Group Policy Container (GPC)
   - **b.** Group Policy Object (GPO)
   - **c.** SYSVOL
   - **d.** Group Policy Template (GPT)

3. Which technique allows you to specify individual users or groups within a container who should or should not receive the settings configured in a particular GPO?
   - **a.** Block Policy Inheritance
   - **b.** Security group filtering
   - **c.** Linking
   - **d.** No Override

4. Which utility is used to edit the settings contained in an individual Active Directory Group Policy Object?
   - **a.** Group Policy Management Editor
   - **b.** Group Policy Management Console
   - **c.** GPResult
   - **d.** Resultant Set of Policy

5. What is a new feature in Windows Server 2008 that allows you to configure a GPO "pattern" that you can use to create additional GPOs beginning with the same settings in the pattern?
   - **a.** Group Policy Container (GPC)
   - **b.** Group Policy Template (GPT)
   - **c.** Starter GPO
   - **d.** Central Store

6. Which type of GPO processing requires that each GPO must be read and applied completely before the next policy can be processed?
   - **a.** Synchronous processing
   - **b.** Asynchronous processing
   - **c.** Multisynchronous processing
   - **d.** Unisynchronous processing

7. Which GPO setting automates the process of presenting user files from a network folder rather than an individual user's desktop, thus making them accessible from anywhere on the network?
   - **a.** Roaming profiles
   - **b.** Roaming documents
   - **c.** Folder redirection
   - **d.** Document redirection

8. Which file extension identifies Administrative templates in Windows Server 2008?
   - **a.** ADM
   - **b.** ADMX
   - **c.** INF
   - **d.** POL

9. Which feature, new to Windows Server 2008, allows you to install workstation operating systems and software in an enterprise environment?
   - **a.** Remote Installation Service (RIS)
   - **b.** Folder redirection
   - **c.** Windows Deployment Services (WDS)
   - **d.** Offline file storage

10. What is the single location within the SYSVOL share where ADMX files can be stored?
    - **a.** Central Store
    - **b.** Group Policy Container (GPC)
    - **c.** Group Policy Template (GPT)
    - **d.** Folder Redirection Store

■ Case Scenarios

Scenario 7-1: Determining Group Policy Placement

You are the main administrator for Contoso Pharmaceuticals. The Active Directory structure is shown in Figure 7-12. You are beginning to plan the Group Policy implementation, and your supervisor has several key policies that you need to decide where to place. Using the figure, complete the table, documenting how you can accommodate the following goals.

- You need to have an email application installed and configured on all desktops throughout the company.
- The workstations in the US site should all point to a single WSUS server; the workstations in the MX site should point to a separate WSUS server.
- All locations in the West OU should have several options in Internet Explorer modified.

Figure 7-12

Contoso.com domain

Contoso.com domain

LOCATION	POLICY GOALS AND SPECIAL SETTINGS

Scenario 7-2: Understanding Group Policy Planning

You are the administrator for Coho Winery, Inc., a large wine distribution company that has locations in the United States and Canada. In the last six months, Coho Winery, Inc. has purchased several smaller distribution companies. As you integrate them into your forest, you want to allow them to remain autonomous in their management of desktops and security. In the process of making their domains part of your corporate network, you have some policies that you want to become part of their environment, and others that you do not want to implement at this time. As you discuss this with your IT team, your manager asks you to explain which features in Windows Server 2008 allow you to provide the Group Policy flexibility needed by the new Active Directory structure. List several of the features in Windows Server 2008 Group Policy that will allow Coho Winery, Inc. to achieve its postacquisition goals. Be prepared to discuss your answers in class.

Configuring the User and Computer Environment Using Group Policy

OBJECTIVE DOMAIN MATRIX

TECHNOLOGY SKILL	OBJECTIVE DOMAIN	OBJECTIVE DOMAIN NUMBER
Configuring Account Policies	Configure account policies.	4.6
Planning and Configuring an Audit Policy	Configure audit policy by using GPOs.	4.7

KEY TERMS

Account Lockout Policies
account logon events
account management events
Audit Policy
auditing
disk quotas
Enforce Password History
Fine-Grained Password Policies (FGPP)
gpupdate.exe

Kerberos Policies
Key Distribution Center (KDC)
Local Policies
logon events
msDS-PasswordSettings
Offline Files
Password Policies
Password Settings Object (PSO)
policy change events

refresh interval
Restricted Groups
Security Options
system events
System Services
tattooing
User Rights Assignment

Lucerne Publishing has created an OU structure that allows administrators to group users and computers by department: Training, HR, Finance, and so on. To improve security on the network, the administrators will use GPOs to configure password and account lockout policies to prevent security breaches caused by weak passwords or repeated password-cracking attempts. In addition, they will configure additional password policies that require administrators to have significantly longer passwords to protect accounts possessing elevated privileges, such as Domain Admins and Enterprise Admins. The administrators of Lucerne Publishing wish to configure consistent security settings for Windows Registry, File System, and System Services across the domain controllers and application servers, which will also be implemented using Group Policy.

After completing this lesson, you will be able to configure user and computer environments through the use of Group Policy Objects (GPOs). You will be able to configure account policies in a Windows Server 2008 domain, including Fine-Grained Password Policies, a new Windows Server 2008 feature that allows you to configure more than one password policy within a single domain. You will also be able to perform the steps needed to configure audit policies in Windows Server 2008, as well as uniform settings for the Windows Event Viewer, System Services, and Registry and File System settings. Finally, you will be able to maintain and optimize Group Policy processing within a Windows Server 2008 environment.

■ Configuring Security Policies Using Group Policy Objects

↓
THE BOTTOM LINE

The previous lesson focused on familiarizing you with Group Policy concepts, terminology, features, and benefits. In this lesson, you will take a closer look at account security policies, folder redirection, offline file abilities, and disk quotas that can be implemented using Group Policy. It is important for you to know the difference between user and computer settings. In addition to learning about these settings and categorizing them based on where they are applied, you will also look at the default policy refresh process. Specifically, this lesson discusses how the policy refresh process works and how to invoke a manual refresh of Group Policies when necessary.

Centralized management of security settings for users and computers can be accomplished using Group Policy. Most of the settings that pertain to security are found in the Windows Settings folder within the Policies node in the Computer Configuration node of a Group Policy Object (GPO). Security settings can be used to govern how users are authenticated to the network, the resources they are permitted to use, group membership policies, and events related to user and group actions recorded in the event logs. Table 8-1 briefly describes some of the security settings that can be configured within the Policies node in the Computer Configuration node.

Table 8-1

Policies Node in the Computer Configuration Node Security Settings

SETTING	DESCRIPTION
Account Policies	Includes settings for Password Policy, Account Lockout Policy, and Kerberos Policy. A domain-wide policy, such as the Default Domain Policy GPO, also includes Kerberos Policy settings. In Windows 2000 and Windows Server 2003, the Password Policy and Account Lockout Policy could only be configured at the domain level. In Windows Server 2008, you can configure Fine-Grained Password Policies to allow multiple password policies in a single domain.
Local Policies	Contains three subcategories that pertain to the local computer policies. These subcategories include Audit Policy, User Rights Assignment, and Security Options.
Event Log Policy	These settings pertain to Event Viewer logs, their maximum size, retention settings, and accessibility.
Restricted Groups Policy	This setting gives administrators control over the Members property and Members Of property within a security group.
System Services Policy	These settings can be used to define the startup mode and access permissions for all system services. Each service can be configured as disabled, start automatically, or start manually. Also, the access permissions can be set to Start, Stop, or Pause.

Table 8-1 (continued)

SETTING	DESCRIPTION
Registry and File System Policies	These settings can be used to set access permissions and audit settings for specific registry keys or file system objects.
Wireless Network (IEEE 802.11) Policies	Allows definition of a policy for an IEEE 802.11 wireless network. Settings include preferred networks and authentication types, in addition to several other security-related options.
Public Key Policies	This node includes options to create an Encrypted File System (EFS), automatic certificate request, trusted root certificates, and an enterprise trust list.
Software Restriction Policies	This policy can specify software that you wish to run on computers. Also, it can prevent applications from running that might pose a security risk to the computer or organization.
IPSec Policy on Active Directory	Includes policy settings that allow an administrator to define mandatory rules applicable to computers on an IP-based network.

In the previous lesson, you learned that policy settings created within the Policies node in the Computer Configuration node apply to a computer; it does not matter who is logging on to it. More security settings can be applied to a specific computer than can be applied to a specific user. Table 8-2 describes the security settings that can be applied within the Policies node in the User Configuration node of Group Policy.

Table 8 2

Security Settings Applied in the Policies Node in the User Configuration Node

SETTING	DESCRIPTION
Public Key Policies	Includes the Enterprise Trust policy that allows an administrator to list the trusted sources for certificates. Also, auto-enrollment settings can be specified for the user within this node.
Software Restriction Policies	This policy can be used to specify software that you wish to run for the user. Specifically, it can be used to disallow applications that might pose a security risk if run.

The next several sections discuss many of these settings in detail. In addition, examples will be presented to help you understand when and how to implement these policy settings.

Configuring Account Policies

Account policies influence how a user interacts with a computer or a domain. They are specified within the Policies node in the Computer Configuration node of a GPO that is linked to a particular domain, either the Default Domain Policy or one that you create manually. This account policy is applied to all accounts throughout the domain by default, unless you create one or more *Fine-Grained Password Policies (FGPP)* that override the domain-wide policy. These Fine-Grained Password Policies can be applied to one or more users or groups of users, allowing you to specify a more or less stringent password policy for this subset than the password policy defined for the entire domain. Fine-Grained Password Policies are a new feature in Windows Server 2008; in Windows 2000 and Windows Server 2003, you could only configure a single password policy and a single account lockout policy within each Active Directory domain.

The three subcategories within the Account Policies category of the security settings are *Password Policies*, *Account Lockout Policies*, and *Kerberos Policies*. Figure 8-1 shows the expanded Password Policy category within the security settings of the Default Domain Policy GPO for lucernepublishing.com. Note that the figure shows default settings for this policy. Settings in this category focus on enforcing password length, password history, and so on. Password Policies can be applied to domain and local user accounts.

Figure 8-1

The Default Domain Password
Policy in Windows Server 2008

[figure: Group Policy Management Editor showing the Default Domain Policy password settings]

Policy	Policy Setting
Enforce password history	24 passwords remembered
Maximum password age	42 days
Minimum password age	1 days
Minimum password length	7 characters
Password must meet complexity requirements	Enabled
Store passwords using reversible encryption	Disabled

DEFINE A DOMAIN-WIDE ACCOUNT POLICY

1. **OPEN** the GPMC. Click **Forest: <Forest Name>**, click **Domains**, click **<Domain Name>**, and then click **Group Policy Objects**.

2. Right-click the Default Domain Policy and click **Edit**. A Group Policy Management Editor window for this policy is displayed.

3. In the left window pane, expand the Computer Configuration node, expand the Policies node, and expand the Windows Settings folder. Then, expand the Security Settings node. In the Security Settings node, expand Account Policies and select **Password Policy**. This displays the available settings for this category of the GPO, similar to what you saw in Figure 8-1. All settings reflect the implemented defaults when the domain was created.

4. To modify a setting, double-click the setting in the right window pane to open the Properties dialog box for the setting. Then, make the desired value changes. For example, double-click the **Enforce password history** setting, change the value to **22** and then click **OK** to change the domain-wide password history from 24 remembered passwords to 22.

5. Click **OK** to close the setting's Properties dialog box.

6. Close the Group Policy Management Editor window for this policy.

PAUSE. You can close the GPMC MMC snap-in or leave it open for the next exercise.

Figure 8-2 illustrates the expanded Account Lockout Policy category within the security settings of the Default Domain Policy GPO for lucernepublishing.com. Account Lockout Policies can be used for domain and local user accounts. An Account Lockout Policy specifies the number of unsuccessful logon attempts that, if made within a contiguous time frame, may constitute a potential security threat from an intruder. An Account Lockout Policy can be set to lock the account in question after a specified number of invalid attempts. Additionally, the policy specifies the duration that the account remains locked.

Figure 8-2

The Default Domain Account Lockout Policy in Windows Server 2008

[Screenshot of Group Policy Management Editor]

Group Policy Management Editor

File   Action   View   Help

Default Domain Policy [DC1.con...
Computer Configuration
  Policies
    Software Settings
    Windows Settings
      Scripts (Startup
      Security Setting
        Account Pol
          Passwo
          Accoun
          Kerberc
        Local Policie
        Event Log
        Restricted (
        System Ser
        Registry
        File System

Policy ▲	Policy Setting
Account lockout duration	Not Defined
Account lockout threshold	0 invalid logon attempts
Reset account lockout counter after	Not Defined

CONFIGURE A DOMAIN-WIDE ACCOUNT LOCKOUT POLICY

1. **OPEN** the GPMC. Click **Forest: <Forest Name>**, click **Domains**, click **<Domain Name>**, and then click **Group Policy Objects**.

2. Right-click the Default Domain Policy and click **Edit.** A Group Policy Management Editor window for this policy is displayed.

3. In the left window pane, expand the Computer Configuration node, expand the Policies node, and expand the Windows Settings folder. Then, expand the Security Settings node. In the Security Settings node, expand Account Policies and select **Account Lockout Policy**. The available settings for this category of the GPO are displayed.

4. In the right window pane, double-click the **Account lockout duration** policy setting to view the Properties dialog box.

5. Select the **Define This Policy Setting** checkbox. Note the default setting of 30 minutes for Account Lockout Duration. If you want to change the account lockout duration, you may do so here.

6. Click **OK** to accept the specified lockout duration. The Suggested Value Changes dialog box, which indicates other related settings and their defaults, is displayed.

7. Click **OK** to automatically enable these other settings or click **Cancel** to go back to the Account Lockout Duration Properties dialog box.

8. Click **OK** to accept the additional setting defaults.

9. Make any additional changes, as necessary, to the other individual Account Lockout Policy settings.

10. Close the Group Policy Management Editor window for this policy.

PAUSE. **LEAVE** the GPMC open for the following exercise.

You have now configured a domain-wide password policy that will configure consistent password settings across an entire domain.

Configuring Fine-Grained Password Policies

Prior to Windows Server 2008, an Active Directory administrator was only able to configure a single Password Policy and Account Lockout Policy for any Active Directory domain. If you were faced with a subset of users whose password policy requirements were different, you were left with the choice of configuring a separate domain or forcing all users within the domain to conform to a single password policy. Beginning in Windows Server 2008, you can configure Fine-Grained Password Policies, which allow you to define multiple password policies within a single domain.

To enable Fine-Grained Password Policies, Windows Server 2008 introduces a new object type called *msds-PasswordSettings*, also called a ***Password Settings Object (PSO)***. Each PSO has the following mandatory attributes:

- **cn.** The common name for the PSO, such as "ServiceAccountNoLockout."

- **msDS-PasswordSettingsPrecedence.** In a case where multiple PSOs apply, this attribute of the PSO is used as a tie-breaker to determine which PSO should apply: a PSO with a precedence of 1 will be applied over a PSO with a precedence of 5, a PSO with a precedence of 10 will be applied over a PSO with a precedence of 100, and so on.

- **msDS-PasswordReversibleEncryptionEnabled.** This attribute indicates whether the PSO allows passwords to be stored in Active Directory using reversible encryption. This setting should only be enabled if a particular application requires it, because it presents a significant security risk.

- **msDS-PasswordHistoryLength.** This attribute indicates the number of passwords that Active Directory should retain in memory before allowing someone to reuse a previously used password. Setting this attribute to a value of "2," for example, would prevent someone from reusing the previous two passwords that they had configured for their user account. This setting corresponds to the ***Enforce Password History*** setting in Group Policy.

- **msDS-PasswordComplexityEnabled.** This attribute indicates whether the PSO requires a complex password; that is, a password that uses a mixture of uppercase and lowercase letters, numbers, and symbols. The default password policy in Windows Server 2008 requires the use of complex passwords.

- **msDS-MinimumPasswordLength.** This attribute indicates the minimum length of a password defined by this PSO.

- **msDS-MinimumPasswordAge.** This attribute is a negative number that indicates the number of milliseconds old a password must be before it can be changed. The default value is -864000000000, which equates to one day.

- **msDS-MaximumPasswordLength.** As the name indicates, this attribute identifies the maximum length of a password defined by this PSO.

- **msDS-MaximumPasswordAge.** This attribute is a negative number that indicates in milliseconds when a password will expire. The default value is −36288000000000, or 42 days.

- **msDS-LockoutThreshold.** This attribute indicates the number of bad login attempts permitted before an account is locked out.

- **msDS-LockoutObservationWindow.** This attribute is a negative number that indicates the number of milliseconds that must pass before the counter for failed logon attempts should be reset.

- **msDS-LockoutDuration.** This attribute is a negative number expressed in milliseconds that indicates how long an account will remain locked out. A value of "0" indicates that the account will stay locked out until it is manually unlocked by an administrator.

You can create one or more PSOs within a domain and then configure each PSO to apply to one or more user or group accounts within the domain; these objects are not created using the Group Policy Management Editor, but by manually creating the object using ADSIEdit or LDIFDE. When a user logs on to the domain, Windows Server 2008 uses the following steps to determine the user's effective password requirements:

1. Are one or more PSOs assigned to the individual user account? If so, use the PSO that has the winning precedence. If not, continue to step 2.

2. Are one or more PSOs assigned to a group that has the user account as a member, either directly or through nested group membership? If so, use the PSO that has the winning precedence. If not, continue to step 3.

3. If PSOs are not assigned to the user or to any group that has the user as a member, apply the domain-wide password policy and account lockout requirements.

Configuring the Kerberos Policy

X REF

For more information about the importance of time synchronization in Active Directory and client clock synchronization, refer to Lesson 4.

For domain accounts only, the Kerberos Policy allows you to configure settings that govern how Active Directory authentication functions. Several settings are available within this security setting on a domain-linked GPO.

Kerberos is the default mechanism for authenticating domain users in Windows Server 2008, Windows Server 2003, and Microsoft Windows 2000. Kerberos is a ticket-based system that allows domain access by using a ***Key Distribution Center (KDC),*** which is used to issue Kerberos tickets to users, computers, or network services. These tickets have a finite lifetime and are based in part on system time clocks. Note that Kerberos has a 5-minute clock skew tolerance between the client and the domain controller. If the clocks are off by more than 5 minutes, the client will not be able to log on. Another main setting, Enforce User Logon Restrictions, is enabled by default, as shown in Figure 8-3. This setting tells Windows Server 2008 to validate each request for a session ticket against the rights associated with the user account. Although this process can slow the response time for user access to resources, it is an important security feature that should not be overlooked or disabled.

Figure 8-3

Configuring the domain-wide Kerberos Policy

CONFIGURE THE KERBEROS POLICY

1. **OPEN** the GPMC. Click **Forest: <Forest Name>**, click **Domains**, click **<Domain Name>**, and then click **Group Policy Objects**.

2. Right-click the Default Domain Policy and click **Edit**. A Group Policy Management Editor window for this policy is displayed.

3. In the left window pane, expand the Computer Configuration node, expand the Policies folder and expand the Windows Settings folder. Then, expand the Security Settings node. In the Security Settings node, expand Account Policies and select **Kerberos Policy**. The available settings for this category of the GPO are displayed. All settings reflect the defaults that were implemented when the domain was created.

4. To modify a setting, double-click the setting in the right window pane to open the Properties dialog box for the setting. Make the desired value changes. For example, double-click **Maximum lifetime for service ticket** and change the existing setting to 480 minutes to change the maximum Kerberos ticket lifetime from 10 hours to 8 hours.

5. Click **OK** to close the setting's Properties dialog box.

6. Close the Group Policy Management Editor window for this policy.

PAUSE. You can close the GPMC or leave it open for the following exercise.

You have now configured the Kerberos Policy for a Windows Server 2008 domain, including configuring the maximum ticket lifetime for a Kerberos ticket and the maximum clock skew that can be tolerated by a 2008 Active Directory network.

Defining Local Policies

Local Policies allow administrators to set user privileges on the local computer that govern what users can do on the computer and determine if these actions are tracked within an event log. Tracking events that take place on the local computer, a process referred to as *auditing*, is another important part of monitoring and managing activities on a Windows Server 2008 computer.

The Local Policies setting area of a GPO has three subcategories: *User Rights Assignment*, *Security Options,* and *Audit Policy*. As discussed in each of the following sections, keep in mind that Local Policies are local to a computer. When they are part of a GPO in Active Directory, they affect the local security settings of computer accounts to which the GPO is applied.

As shown in Figure 8-4, the User Rights Assignment settings are extensive and include settings for items that pertain to rights needed by users to perform system-related tasks. For example, logging on locally to a domain controller requires that a user has the Log On Locally right assigned to his or her account or be a member of the Account Operators, Administrators, Backup Operators, Print Operators, or Server Operators group on the domain controller. Other similar settings included in this collection are related to user rights associated with system shutdown, taking ownership privileges of files or objects, restoring files and directories, and synchronizing directory service data.

Figure 8-4

User Rights Assignments in Group Policy

The Security Options category includes security settings related to interactive log on, digital signing of data, restrictions for access to floppy and CD-ROM drives, unsigned driver installation behavior, and logon dialog box behavior. The Security Options category also includes options to configure authentication and communication security within Active Directory through the use of the following settings:

- **Domain controller: LDAP server signing requirements** controls whether LDAP traffic between domain controllers and clients must be signed. This setting can be configured with a value of **None** or **Require signing**.

- **Domain member: Digitally sign or encrypt or sign secure channel data (always)** controls whether traffic between domain members and the domain controllers will be signed and encrypted at all times.

- **Domain member: Digitally encrypt secure channel data (when client agrees)** indicates that traffic between domain members and the domain controllers will be encrypted only if the client workstations are able to do so.

- **Domain member: Digitally sign secure channel data (when client agrees)** indicates that traffic between domain members and the domain controllers will be signed only if the client services are able to do so.

- **Microsoft network client: Digitally sign communications (always)** indicates that Server Message Block (SMB) signing will be enabled by the SMB signing component of the SMB client at all times.

- **Microsoft network client: Digitally sign communications (If server agrees)** indicates that SMB signing will be enabled by the SMB signing component of the SMB client only if the corresponding server service is able to do so.

- **Microsoft network server: Digitally sign communications (always)** indicates that SMB signing will be enabled by the SMB signing component of the SMB server at all times.

- **Microsoft network server: Digitally sign communications (if server agrees)** indicates that SMB signing will be enabled by the SMB signing component of the SMB server only if the corresponding client service is able to do so.

From this section, you can also enforce the level of NT LAN Manager (NTLM) authentication that will be allowed on your network. Although Kerberos is the default authentication protocol in an Active Directory network, NTLM authentication will be used in certain situations. The original incarnation of NTLM authentication was called LAN Manager (LM) authentication, which is now considered a weak authentication protocol that can easily be decoded by network traffic analyzers. Microsoft has improved NTLM authentication over the years by introducing first NTLM and subsequently NTLMv2. NTLM authentication levels are controlled by the Network security: NTLM authentication levels security setting, which allows you to select one of the following options:

- **Send LM and NTLM responses**
- **Send LM and NTLM—use NTLMv2 session security if negotiated**
- **Send NTLM response only**
- **Send NTLMv2 response only**
- **Send NTLMv2 response only. Refuse LM**
- **Send NTLMv2 response only. Refuse LM and NTLM**

By allowing only the most stringent levels of NTLM authentication on your network, you can improve the overall communications security of Active Directory. The final key component in defining Local Policies is planning and configuring an *Audit Policy* for a Windows Server 2008 Active Directory network, which we will discuss in-depth in the following section.

Planning and Configuring an Audit Policy

The Audit Policy section of GPO Local Policies allows administrators to log successful and failed security events, such as logon events, account access, and object access. Auditing can be used to track user activities and system activities. Planning to audit requires that you determine the computers to be audited and the types of events you wish to track.

When you specify an event to audit, such as account logon events, you determine whether you wish to audit success events, failure events, or both. Tracking successful events allows you to find out how often resources are accessed. This information can be valuable in planning your resource usage and budgeting for new resources when necessary. Tracking failed events can help you determine when security breaches should be resolved. For example, if you notice frequent failed logon attempts using a specific user account, you may want to investigate further. Figure 8-5 illustrates the policy settings available for auditing.

Figure 8-5

Audit Policies in the Default Domain Policy

When an audited event occurs, Windows Server 2008 writes an event to the security log on the domain controller or computer where the event took place. If it is an account logon attempt or other Active Directory–related event, the event is written to the domain controller. If it is a computer event, such as floppy drive access, the event is written to the local computer's event log.

Auditing is turned off by default and, as a result, you must decide which computers, resources, and events you want to audit. It is important to balance the need for auditing against the potential information overload that would be created if you audited every possible event type. The following guidelines will help you plan your audit policy:

- **Audit only pertinent items.** Determine the events you want to audit and consider whether it is more important to track successes or failures of these events. You should only plan to audit events that will help you gather network information. When auditing object access, be specific about the type of access you want to track. For example, if you want to audit read access to a file or folder, only audit the read events, not Full Control. Auditing of Full Control would trigger writes to the log for every action on the file or folder. Auditing does use system resources to process and store events. Therefore, auditing unnecessary events will create overhead on your server and make it more difficult to monitor.

- **Archive security logs to provide a documented history.** Keeping a history of event occurrences can provide you with supporting documentation. Such documentation can be used to support the need for additional resources based on the usage of a particular resource. In addition, it provides a history of events that might indicate past security breach attempts. If intruders have administrative privileges, they can clear the log, leaving you without a history of events that document the breach.

- **Configure the size of your security logs carefully**. You need to plan the size of your security logs based on the number of events that you anticipate logging. Event Log Policy settings can be configured under the Computer Configuration\Policies\Windows Settings\Security Settings\Event Log node of a GPO.

Security logs are viewed using the Event Viewer and can be configured to monitor any number of event categories, including the following:

- *System events.* Events that trigger a log entry in this category include system startups and shutdowns; system time changes; system event resources exhaustion, such as when an event log is filled and can no longer append entries; security log cleaning; or any event that affects system security or the security log. In the Default Domain Controllers GPO, this setting is set to log successes by default.

- *Policy change events.* By default, this policy is set to audit successes in the Default Domain Controllers GPO. Policy change audit log entries are triggered by events such as user rights assignment changes, establishment or removal of trust relationships, IPSec policy agent changes, and grants or removals of system access privileges.

- *Account management events.* This policy setting is set to audit successes in the Default Domain Controllers GPO. This setting triggers an event that is written based on changes to account properties and group properties. Log entries written due to this policy setting reflect events related to user or group account creation, deletion, renaming, enabling, or disabling.

- *Logon events.* This setting logs events related to successful user logons on a computer. The event is logged to the Event Viewer Security Log on the computer that processes the request. The default setting is to log successes in the Default Domain Controllers GPO.

- *Account logon events.* This setting logs events related to successful user logons to a domain. The event is logged to the domain controller that processes the request. The default setting is to log successes in the Default Domain Controllers GPO.

Implementation of your plan requires awareness of several factors that can affect the success of your Audit Policy. You must be aware of the administrative requirements to create and administer a policy plan. Two main requirements are necessary to set up and administer an Audit Policy. First, you must have the Manage Auditing and Security Log user right for the computer on which you want to configure a policy or review a log. This right is granted by default to the Administrators group. However, if you wish to delegate this task to a subadministrator, such as a container administrator, the subadministrator must possess the specific right. Second, any files or folders to be audited must be located on NTFS volumes. This requirement is carried over from prior Windows operating system versions, such as Windows 2000 and Windows Server 2003.

CERTIFICATION READY?
Configure an audit policy by using GPOs
4.7

Implementation of your plan requires that you specify the categories to be audited and, if necessary, configure objects for auditing. Configuring objects for auditing is necessary when you have configured either of the two following event categories:

- **Audit Directory Service Access.** This event category logs user access to Active Directory objects, such as other user objects or OUs.

- **Audit Object Access.** This event category logs user access to files, folders, registry keys, and printers.

Each of these event categories requires additional setup steps, which are described in the following exercise.

⊘ CONFIGURE AN AUDIT POLICY

GET READY. To perform this exercise, you will need to be logged on to the Active Directory domain using Domain Administrator credentials.

1. **OPEN** the GPMC. Click **Forest: <Forest Name>**, click **Domains**, click **<Domain Name>**, and then click **Group Policy Objects**.

2. Right-click the Default Domain Policy and click **Edit**. A Group Policy Management Editor window for this policy is displayed.

3. In the left window pane, expand the Computer Configuration node, expand the Policies node, and expand the Windows Settings folder. Then, expand the Security Settings node.

In the Security Settings node, expand Local Policies, and select **Audit Policy**. The available settings for this category of the GPO are displayed.

4. In the right window pane, double-click the Audit Policy setting you want to modify; for example, double-click **Audit system events**. The Properties dialog box for the chosen setting is displayed. Select the **Define This Policy Setting** checkbox.

5. Select the appropriate checkboxes to audit Success, Failure, or both under the Audit These Attempts heading.

6. Click **OK** to close the setting's Properties dialog box.

7. Close the Group Policy Management Editor window for this policy.

PAUSE. LEAVE the GPMC open for the following exercise.

You have now configured an Audit Policy within the GPMC.

→ **CONFIGURE AN ACTIVE DIRECTORY OBJECT FOR AUDITING**

GET READY. To perform this exercise, you will need to be logged on to the Active Directory domain using Domain Administrator credentials.

1. In Active Directory Users and Computers (MMC snap-in), click the **View** menu, and then click **Advanced Features**.

2. Navigate to the object that you wish to audit. Right-click the object and select **Properties**.

3. Click the **Security** tab, and then click **Advanced**. The Advanced Security Settings dialog box for the object is displayed.

4. On the Auditing tab, click **Add**.

5. Select the users or groups to be audited for Active Directory object access and click **OK**. The Auditing Entry dialog box for the object is displayed.

6. Select the events you want to audit on this object. Select the tab for object access or property access. Select the **Successful** checkbox, the **Failed** checkbox, or both checkboxes, depending on what you want to track.

7. In the Apply Onto list, specify which objects are audited. By default, *This Object And All Child Objects* is selected.

8. Click **OK** to return to the Advanced Security Settings dialog box for the object.

9. Choose whether you wish auditing entries from parent objects to be inherited to this object by selecting or clearing the **Allow Inheritable Auditing Entries From Parent To Propagate To This Object** checkbox. If the checkboxes in the Access box are shaded in the Auditing Entry dialog box for the object, or if Remove is unavailable in the Advanced Security Settings dialog box for the object, auditing has been inherited from the parent object.

10. Click **OK** to complete this process.

11. Open a command prompt and enter the following command to enable auditing for Active Directory changes, as shown in Figure 8-6:

```
auditpol /set /subcategory: "directory service changes" /success: enable
```

PAUSE. CLOSE the Active Directory Users and Computers MMC snap-in.

Figure 8-6

Enable auditing for Active Directory changes

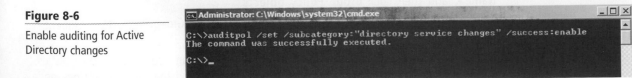

```
C:\>auditpol /set /subcategory:"directory service changes" /success:enable
The command was successfully executed.

C:\>_
```

Beginning in Windows Server 2008, new options are available for Active Directory auditing that will indicate that a change has occurred and provide the old value and the new value. For example, if you change a user's description from "Marketing" to "Training," the Directory Services Event Log will record two events containing the original value and the new value.

CONFIGURE FILES AND FOLDERS FOR AUDITING

GET READY. To perform this exercise, you must be logged on to the Active Directory domain using Domain Administrator credentials.

1. In Windows Explorer, right-click the file or folder you want to audit and select **Properties**.
2. On the Security tab in the Properties dialog box for the selected file or folder, click **Advanced**.
3. In the Advanced Security Settings dialog box for the file or folder, select the **Auditing** tab, and then click **Add**. Select the users and groups to be audited for file or folder access and then click **OK**. The Auditing Entry dialog box for the file or folder is displayed.
4. Select **Successful**, **Failed**, or both checkboxes for the events you wish to audit.
5. In the Apply Onto list, specify which objects are to be audited. This box is set to *This Folder, Subfolder And Files* by default. This means that changes you make are inherited to lower levels in the file system directory.
6. Click **OK** to return to the Advanced Security Settings dialog box for the object.
7. Choose whether you wish auditing entries from parent objects to be inherited to this object by selecting or deselecting the **Allow Inheritable Auditing Entries From Parent To Propagate To This Object And All Child Objects** check box. If the checkboxes in the Access box are shaded in the Auditing Entry dialog box for the object or if Remove is unavailable in the Advanced Security Settings dialog box for the object, auditing has been inherited from the parent object.
8. Click **OK** to complete this process.
9. Close the Group Policy Management Editor window for this policy.

PAUSE. CLOSE the Windows Explorer window.

You have now configured auditing for files and folders within the Windows operating system.

Customizing Event Log Policies

The Event Log Policy settings area allows administrators to configure settings that control the maximum log size, retention, and access rights for each log. Depending on the services you install, the number of logs you have can vary on Windows Server 2008. For example, if your server is configured as a domain controller, you will have a Directory Service log that contains Active Directory–related entries. In addition, if your server is configured as a Domain Name System (DNS) server you will have a DNS log that contains entries specifically related to DNS.

The Event Log Policy settings area includes settings for the three primary log files: the Application, Security, and System logs. In addition to using Event Log Group Policy settings to modify the default log sizes, you can also manually configure the log sizes and actions to be taken when the log reaches its maximum size.

⊙ **CUSTOMIZE EVENT LOG POLICIES**

GET READY. To perform this exercise, you must be logged onto the Active Directory domain using Domain Administrator credentials.

1. From the Administrative Tools menu, open Event Viewer.
2. Right-click the log for which you want to view or modify the settings, and select **Properties**.
3. Modify the desired settings and click **OK**.

PAUSE. CLOSE the Event Viewer before continuing to the next exercise.

In the previous exercise, you configured Event Log Policies for a Windows Server 2008 computer.

X REF

See "Maintaining and Optimizing Group Policy" later in this lesson for information on the refresh process for restricted groups.

Understanding Restricted Groups

The **Restricted Groups** policy setting allows an administrator to specify group membership lists. Using this policy setting, you can control membership in important groups, such as the local Administrators and Backup Operators groups. This policy setting allows you to configure the group members and the groups in which the specified group is nested.

Consider an example: You wish to configure the default administrator account, Scott Seely and John Smith, as members of the built-in Administrators group. As shown in Figure 8-7, you would add these users to the Members Of section of this group list for the restricted Administrators group. If another user is added to the Administrators group using Active Directory Users and Computers (MMC snap-in) for malicious or other reasons, the manually added users are removed when the Group Policy is reapplied during the refresh cycle. Only those users who are part of the Restricted Group membership list within the policy setting will be applied.

Figure 8-7

Configuring Restricted Groups

In addition, the Restricted Groups setting can be used to populate a local group's membership list with a domain group, such as Domain Administrators. This allows administrative privileges to be transferred to the local workstations, making management and access to resources easier. This "Member of" functionality is nondestructive, in that it will add users or groups to the membership of a particular group without removing any existing group members that have been configured.

Customizing System Services, Registry, and File System Settings

The *System Services* category is used to configure the startup and security settings for services running on a computer. Figure 8-8 shows this policy area within the Default Domain Controllers Policy GPO. The service startup options are Automatic, Manual, and Disabled. Each functions as follows: *Automatic* starts a service automatically during system startup; *Manual* starts a service only by user intervention; and *Disabled* configures the service so that it cannot start.

Figure 8-8

Configuring System Services

When using the Automatic setting for service startup, you should test the setting to make sure that the service starts automatically as expected. If certain services do not start as expected, users may not have the desired network functionality, and this may result in unnecessary downtime for users.

In addition to startup settings, the System Services Policy area also allows administrators to determine who has permissions to a particular service. For example, you may need to give certain users the ability to stop and restart a service that is malfunctioning, which includes start, stop, and pause permissions to the service. Permissions are defined by clicking Edit

Security after defining the policy. Figure 8-9 shows the Security page for a System Services Policy setting.

The Registry and File System areas of Group Policy are discussed together because they are similar in function. The Registry security area is used to configure security on registry keys. The File System security area is used to configure security for file system objects. Both of these areas allow administrators to set user permissions that reflect certain registry keys or files and the permissions users have to view and modify them. In addition, you can also set auditing on both of these items so that changes can be tracked for reference later.

Configuring Folder Redirection

Folder Redirection is a Group Policy folder located within the User Configuration node of a Group Policy linked to an Active Directory container object. Folder redirection provides administrators with the ability to redirect the contents of certain folders to a network location or to another location on the user's local computer. Contents of folders on a local computer located in the Documents and Settings folder, including the Documents, Application Data, Desktop, and Start Menu folders, can be redirected.

Depending on the folder being redirected, user data can be redirected to a dynamically created folder, a specified folder created by the administrator, the user's home directory, or the local user profile location. Redirection of the data from a user's local computer to a network location provides the following benefits:

- Files can be backed up during the normal network server backup process. Note that typical users do not back up their own data. Folder redirection eliminates the problems that arise when a local computer fails and a user has stored all documents on the local hard drive. When the data is redirected to a server hard drive, the data is backed up, and therefore is not lost due to hardware failure.

- When users log on to the network from a workstation other than their own, they have access to their files, because files are stored on a network server rather than on the local computer.

Redirecting a folder and files to a separate drive on the local computer can allow administrators to automatically redirect data files to a location separate from the operating system files. In this case, if the operating system must be reinstalled, the data files would not need to be

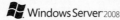

deleted, nor would they be automatically overwritten by anything else. Figure 8-10 shows the Folder Redirection Policy setting within the User Configuration node of a GPO.

Figure 8-10

Viewing Folder Redirection settings

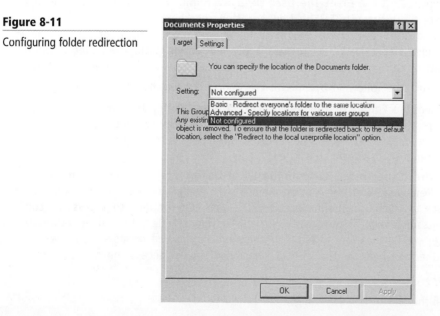

CONFIGURE FOLDER REDIRECTION

GET READY. Before you begin these steps, you must be logged on using an account with Domain Admin credentials.

1. Create a GPO or modify an existing GPO with the necessary Folder Redirection Policy setting. Using the Group Policy Management Editor for the desired GPO, locate the Folder Redirection policy extension in the User Configuration/Policies/Windows Settings/node.

2. Right-click the **Documents** folder in the left window pane and select **Properties**.

3. As shown in Figure 8-11, use the Setting drop-down box of the Target tab to select one of the following options in the My Documents Properties dialog box:

   • **Basic–Redirect Everyone's Folder To The Same Location.** If you select this option, you must create a shared folder to which all subfolders are appended. This will be discussed in further detail later in this section. If this setting is chosen, proceed to step 4 now.

   • **Advanced–Specify Locations For Various User Groups.** Select this option to redirect folders to specified locations based on security group membership. For example, use this option to redirect the Application Data folder for accounting group users to one location and the Application Data folder for engineering group users to a different location. If you select this setting, proceed to step 5 now.

Figure 8-11

Configuring folder redirection

4. If you chose *Basic–Redirect Everyone's Folder To The Same Location*, you must specify the Target folder location in the Settings dialog box. Choose from the following options:

- **Create A Folder For Each User Under The Root Path.** This option is the default. When a user's folders are redirected using this setting, a subfolder is automatically created using the username based on the %username% variable and the folder name of the redirected folder. Allowing the system to create the subfolder structure automatically ensures that the appropriate user permissions are implemented. However, for the subfolder structure creation to work, each user must have appropriate permissions on the shared folder to create a folder. For the root path, use a Universal Naming Convention (UNC) name, rather than a drive letter–referenced path, which may change.

- **Redirect To The Following Location.** This option allows you to specify the path used to redirect the Documents folder. Use this option to redirect the folder to a server share or to another valid local path. When specifying a path, use a UNC name, rather than a drive letter–referenced path, which may change.

- **Redirect To The User's Home Directory.** This option redirects the Documents folder to a preconfigured home directory for the user. This setting is not recommended unless you have already deployed home directories in your organization and wish to maintain them. Security is not checked automatically using this option, and the assumption is made that the administrator has placed appropriate permissions on the folders. Administrators have full control over the users' My Documents folders when they are redirected to the user's home directory, even if the *Grant The User Exclusive Rights To Documents* checkbox is selected.

- **Redirect To The Local User Profile Location.** This option allows administrators to return redirected folders to their original default locations. This setting copies the contents of the redirected folder back to the user profile location. The redirected folder contents are not deleted. The user continues to have access to the content of the redirected folder, but access is provided from the local computer, instead of the redirected location.

5. If you chose *Advanced–Specify Locations For Various User Groups* in step 3, you must specify the target folder location for each group that you add in the Settings dialog box. The choices are the same as those outlined in step 4; however, you need to associate each group selected with a specific target location. Click **Add** to select the groups and choose the target folder location for redirected files.

6. The Settings tab for the Documents Properties dialog box provides several additional selections. Select the **Grant The User Exclusive Rights To Documents** and **Move The Contents Of Documents To The New Location** checkboxes, if necessary. If you will be supporting down-level clients running Windows 2000, Windows XP, or Windows Server 2003, place a checkmark next to **Also apply redirection policy to Windows 2000, Windows 2000 Server, Windows XP, and Windows Server 2003 operating systems**.

7. Select from the following options in the Policy Removal box of the Settings tab:

- **Leave The Folder In The New Location When Policy Is Removed.** This option keeps the redirected folder in its redirected location, without doing anything to the data. If the policy is removed, the user continues to have access to the contents at the redirected folder.

- **Redirect The Folder Back To The Local Userprofile Location When Policy Is Removed.** With this option enabled, the folder and its contents are copied back to their user profile location. The user can continue to access the contents on the local computer. With this option disabled, the folder returns to its user profile location, but the contents are not copied or moved back with the redirection process. The user can no longer see or access the files.

8. Click **OK**.

PAUSE. CLOSE the Group Policy Management Editor window.

If the policy is changed to Not Configured, it will have no bearing on the redirection of user data. Data continues to be redirected until the policy removal setting is changed to redirect the folder to the user profile location. This is an example of *tattooing* with Group Policy. Tattooing means that the setting continues to apply until it is reversed using a policy that overwrites the setting.

Configuring Offline Files

Offline Files is a separate Group Policy category that can allow files to be available to users, even when the users are disconnected from the network. The Offline Files feature works well with Folder Redirection: When Offline Files is enabled, users can access necessary files as if they were connected to the network. When the network connection is restored, changes made to any documents are updated to the server. Folders can be configured so that either all files or only selected files within the folder are available for offline use. When it is combined with Folder Redirection, users have the benefits of being able to redirect files to a network location and still have access to the files when the network connection is not present.

Offline Files is configured on the Sharing tab of a folder. As shown in Figure 8-12, on a Windows XP or Windows 2000 Professional workstation, shared folders can be set for Manual Caching Of Documents, Automatic Caching Of Documents, or Automatic Caching Of Programs And Documents. In contrast, as shown in Figure 8-13, on a Windows Server 2003 or Windows Server 2008 family computer, the following options are available:

Figure 8-12

Offline Files in Windows 2000 and Windows XP

Figure 8-13

Offline Files in Windows Server 2003 and Windows Server 2008

- **Only The Files That Users Specify Will Be Available Offline.** This option is equivalent to the previously mentioned Manual Caching feature. As the default selection, it provides offline caching of only those files that have been selected. Users can choose the files they wish to have available when they are disconnected from the network.

- **All Files And Programs That Users Open From The Share Will Be Automatically Available Offline.** This option replaces the previously mentioned Automatic Caching Of Programs And Documents and the Automatic Caching Of Documents options. All files that have been previously opened in the shared folder are available for offline use.
- **Files Or Programs From The Share Will Not Be Available Offline.** This option stops any files in a shared folder from being available offline. This setting is particularly useful in preventing users from storing files for offline use.

Group Policy allows administrators to define the behavior of offline files for users in an Active Directory domain. For example, in Windows XP, Windows Server 2003, and Windows Server 2008, all redirected folders are automatically cached by default. This default behavior can be changed by enabling the Do Not Automatically Make Redirected Folders Available Offline policy setting in the User Configuration\Policies\Administrative Templates\Network\Offline Files extension. When this policy setting is enabled, users must manually choose which files to cache for offline use. Figure 8-14 displays the available User Configuration node Group Policy settings for Offline Files. Note that most of the policy settings are available in both the User Configuration and Computer Configuration nodes of Group Policy.

Figure 8-14

Configuring Offline Files in Group Policy

⚠️ **WARNING** Allowing users to choose the files they want to cache locally can be a security concern. In high-security networks, offline file caching is disabled to prevent the possibility of sensitive data leaving the corporate environment. Consider exploring policy settings such as At Logoff, Delete Local Copy Of Users Offline Files, and Prohibit User Configuration Of Offline Files.

Using Disk Quotas

Use ***disk quotas*** to limit the amount of space available on the server for user data. By implementing disk quotas when folder redirection is also configured, administrators can control the amount of information that is stored on the server. This is important for a couple of reasons. For example, when information is stored on a server, your backup strategy and the amount of resources that it takes to implement it must take into account the amount of data that needs to be backed up. Disk quotas can minimize the resources required in this regard.

TAKE NOTE*

If a user compresses a file using the compression utility in Windows 2000, Windows XP, Server 2003, or Server 2008, the original uncompressed size of the file is used to determine the amount of data utilizing quota space because Windows will need at least that amount of space to uncompress the file.

Backup resources include the hardware involved, such as a tape backup device, and tapes or media to store the data. A network backup strategy usually takes into consideration the time required to back up information, the amount of media that is used, and the time it takes to restore the information if necessary. Considering all of this, disk quotas allow administrators to have control over the amount of information that is backed up for each user. When a disk quota limit is reached, the users cannot store additional data until either their limit is increased or they clean up allocated space by deleting unnecessary files or archiving old files to make room for new data.

Disk quotas can be implemented manually through the Properties dialog box of a drive volume, as shown in Figure 8-15. This requires individual configuration of quotas for each volume that the administrator wishes to limit. The disk quota feature is only available on volumes formatted with the NTFS file system.

Figure 8-15

Configuring disk quotas at the volume level

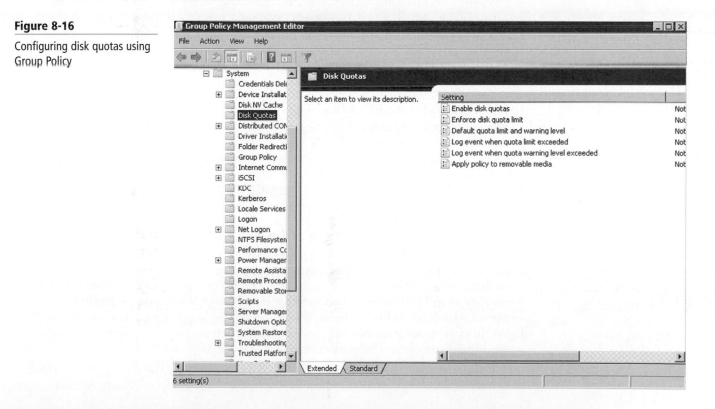

Using Group Policy to configure disk quotas enables all NTFS volumes on all computers running Windows 2000, Windows XP, Windows Server 2003, Windows Vista, and Windows Server 2008 affected by the GPO to be configured with consistent disk quota settings. This policy setting is located in the Computer Configuration\Policies\Administrative Templates\System\Disk Quotas extension of a GPO. Figure 8-16 shows the available settings within this GPO extension.

Figure 8-16

Configuring disk quotas using Group Policy

The following list describes each policy setting within this GPO area:

- **Enable Disk Quotas.** This setting enables or disables disk quota management on all NTFS volumes of computers affected by the GPO.
- **Enforce Disk Quota Limit.** Enabling this setting enforces the space limitations designated by the Default Quota Limit and Warning Level setting for all users on the volume from that point forward. Existing files on the volume owned by the user are not counted against the user's quota limit. When a limit is set, the same limit applies to all users on all volumes. If this setting is not configured and disk quotas are enabled, users are able to write data to the volume until it is full. Allowing this to occur defeats the purpose of enabling disk quotas.
- **Default Quota Limit And Warning Level.** This setting requires that the previous setting of Enforce Disk Quota Limit is enabled. This setting allows administrators to determine the space limitation and warning settings when the limit is reached.
- **Log Event When Quota Limit Exceeded.** When enabled, this setting allows quota limit events to be logged to the Application log in Event Viewer. This setting requires that the Default Quota Limit and Warning Level setting is configured.
- **Log Event When Quota Warning Level Exceeded.** When enabled, this setting writes an event to the Application log that indicates when a user is approaching the user's disk quota limits.
- **Apply Policy To Removable Media.** This setting allows the policy settings to be applied to NTFS volumes located on removable media such as external drives.

When applying disk quotas to your network, careful planning of the necessary amount of disk space required by each user is very important. Realistic expectations of drive usage should be calculated. Because the Group Policy settings for disk quotas enforce the same limits to all users, it is better to plan for a larger space limit than to inconvenience users who need more space with error messages stating that the drive is full. When disk quota policy changes are made, you need to restart the server for them to take effect.

Maintaining and Optimizing Group Policy

The final sections of this lesson will discuss the Group Policy refresh process, manual policy refresh procedures, and recommendations for policy settings to increase performance. This includes understanding and configuring the Group Policy refresh rate for member servers and domain controllers, as well as modifying the configuration of GPOs to optimize logon performance for your users and workstations.

Computer Configuration policies are applied by default when a computer starts up. User Configuration policies are applied during user logon. Both of these policies are also refreshed at regular points throughout the day. When a policy is refreshed, all settings are reprocessed, enforcing all of their policy settings. For example, settings that were previously enabled and are set to disabled are overwritten by the new setting and vice versa. In addition, settings that were previously enabled and set to Not Configured are simply ignored, leaving the setting in the registry unchanged. Each policy type has a default refresh cycle that takes place in the background to ensure that the most recent policy changes are applied, even if the system is not restarted or the user does not log off and back on. Although this is generally true, some policy settings will only process on initial startup or during user logon. For example, a policy that is used to install an application may interfere with another application's files for a program that is currently running on the user's computer. This could cause the installation to be incomplete or to fail. For this reason, software installation policies are only processed during computer startup. In addition, Folder Redirection policies are only processed during user logon. In the next sections, you will look at each policy type, the default refresh period, and where administrators can change the default refresh period.

- **Computer Configuration Group Policy Refresh Interval.** The setting for the refresh interval for computers is located in the Computer Configuration\Policies\Administrative

Templates\System\Group Policy node in the Group Policy Object Editor window for a GPO. By default, computer policies are updated in the background every 90 minutes, with a random offset of 0 to 30 minutes.

- **Domain Controllers Group Policy Refresh Interval.** The setting for the refresh interval for domain controllers is located in the Computer Configuration\Policies\Administrative Templates\System\Group Policy node in the Group Policy Object Editor. By default, domain controller group policies are updated in the background every 2 minutes.

- **User Configuration Group Policy Refresh Interval.** The setting for the refresh interval for user policy settings is located in the User Configuration\Policies\Administrative Templates\System\Group Policy node in Group Policy Object Editor for a GPO.

The available period that each background refresh process can be set to ranges from 0 to 64,800 minutes (45 days). If you set the *refresh interval* to zero, the system attempts to update the policy every 7 seconds. This can cause a significant amount of traffic and overhead on a production network and should be avoided except in a lab or test environment. However, setting a policy refresh interval to 45 days is also extreme and should not be implemented unless network bandwidth is at a premium. It is also possible to turn off the background refresh of a Group Policy entirely. This setting is available in the Computer Configuration\Policies\Administrative Templates\System\Group Policy node. This setting prevents any policy refreshes, except when a computer is restarted.

Manually Refreshing Group Policy

When you modify settings that you wish to be immediately invoked without requiring a restart, a new logon session, or waiting for the next refresh period, you can force a manual refresh. This process uses the *gpupdate.exe* tool. This command-line tool was introduced in Windows Server 2003, and it is used in Windows Server 2003 and Windows Server 2008 to replace the secedit /refreshpolicy command that was used in Windows 2000.

An example of the syntax necessary for *gpupdate.exe* to refresh all the user settings affected by the User Configuration node of the Default Domain GPO is as follows:

```
gpupdate/target:user
```

To refresh the Computer Configuration node policy settings, the syntax would be as follows:

```
gpupdate/target:computer
```

Without the /target switch, both the user and computer configuration policy settings are refreshed.

Optimizing Group Policy Processing

When processing a policy that uses computer or user settings, but not both, the setting area that is not configured should be disabled for faster processing. For example, if you wish to configure a computer policy that applies to all computers within an OU, you should disable the User Configuration node settings so that the policy processing is faster. When one part of the policy is disabled, that section is ignored and the settings are disregarded. This speeds up the completion of the policy processing, because each setting does not need to be read for changes.

⊙ **OPTIMIZE GROUP POLICY PROCESSING**

GET READY. To perform this exercise, you must be logged on to the Active Directory domain using Domain Administrator credentials.

1. Open the Group Policy Management Console (GPMC). Click **Forest: <Forest Name>**, click **Domains**, click **<Domain Name>**, and then click **Group Policy Objects**.

2. Select the Default Domain Policy and click **Edit**.

3. Right-click the Default Domain Policy node at the top of the left window pane. Click **GPO Status**, and place a checkmark next to **User Configuration Settings Disabled**, **Computer Configuration Settings Disabled**, or **All Settings Disabled**.

PAUSE. CLOSE the GPMC.

You have now modified a GPO to optimize its performance at computer startup and shutdown or user logon and logoff.

SUMMARY SKILL MATRIX

IN THIS LESSON YOU LEARNED:

- Most security-related settings are found within the Windows Settings node of the Policies node in the Computer Configuration node of a GPO.

- Policy settings that you wish to apply to all computers or users within a domain should be made within the Default Domain Policy GPO. Generally, domain-wide account policies, such as password policies, account lockout, and Kerberos settings, are modified here.

- Windows Server 2008 provides the ability to configure Fine-Grained Password Policies, which allow multiple password and account lockout policies within a single domain.

- Local policy settings govern the actions users can perform on a specific computer and determine if the actions are recorded in an event log. Create audit policies here.

- Auditing can be configured to audit successes, failures, or both. Plan auditing carefully before implementation. Events that are not important to your documentation and information needs can cause unnecessary overhead when audited. Auditing can be a very important security tool when used prudently.

- Because audited events are recorded in the appropriate event log, it is necessary to understand the Event Log Policy setting area. This area allows control over maximum log sizes, log retention, and access rights to each log.

- Restrictions on group memberships can be accomplished using the Group Restriction Policy setting. Implementing this policy removes group members who are not part of the configured group membership list or adds group members according to a preconfigured list.

- Folder Redirection can be configured for folders located on a local computer within the Documents and Settings folder. The Offline Files settings allow redirected folders to be available when a network connection is not present. These two setting areas complement each other.

- Disk quotas can be used to control storage space on a network drive. Implementing disk quotas allows administrators to have tighter control over drive usage, which can affect tape backup and restore functionality.

- Computer configuration group policies are refreshed every 90 minutes by default. Domain controller group policies are refreshed every 2 minutes. These settings can be altered based on the frequency in which policy changes occur.

- Disabling unused portions of a GPO decreases the time it takes to complete policy processing.

Fill in the Blank

Complete the following sentences by writing the correct word or words in the blanks provided.

1. In a case where multiple PSOs are configured for a particular user, Active Directory will determine which one to apply by using the PSO's _____.

2. You can automatically add a technical support user to the local Administrators group of each domain workstation by using _____.

3. The _____ command allows you to manually refresh Group Policy settings on a particular computer.

4. _____ refers to a Group Policy setting that is not removed when the GPO setting reverts to "Not Configured."

5. You would audit _____ to determine who is authenticating against your Active Directory domain controllers.

6. Each Active Directory domain controller acts as a(n) _____ to enable the distribution of Kerberos tickets.

7. _____ allows you to configure a user's Documents, Desktop, and other folders so that they are stored on a network drive rather than the local computer.

8. Settings in the _____ section of Group Policy allow you to configure the maximum allowable clock skew between a client and a domain controller.

9. Auditing for _____ will alert you when a change is made to User Rights assignments, IPSec policies, or trust relationships.

10. You can create a consistent service startup configuration for multiple computers by using the _____ node in Group Policy.

Multiple Choice

Circle the correct choice.

1. What type of object would you create to enable multiple password policies within a Windows Server 2008 domain?
   a. msDS-MinimumPasswordLength   b. msDS-MultiplePasswordPolicies
   c. PasswordSettingsObject (PSO)   d. msDS-PasswordObject

2. Which configuration item has a default value of 90 minutes for workstations and member servers, with a random offset of 0 to 30 minutes to optimize network performance?
   a. Refresh time   b. Refresh interval
   c. Clock skew   d. Clock interval

3. To determine which users are accessing resources on a particular member server in an Active Directory domain, which event type would you audit?
   a. Account logon event   b. Policy change event
   c. Account management event   d. Logon event

4. Monitoring a system such as Active Directory for the success and/or failure of specific user actions is called
   a. auditing   b. inspecting
   c. scanning   d. sniffing

5. Which audit category includes events such as server startup and shutdown, time changes, and clearing the security log within the Windows Event Viewer?
   a. Process tracking   b. Privileged use
   c. System Events   d. Policy management

6. Which feature allows you to control how much space a user can take on a particular hard drive volume, configurable via Group Policy?
   a. Disk quotas
   b. Folder redirection
   c. Offline files
   d. Object access auditing

7. To prevent users from re-using a certain number of network passwords, what can you configure as part of a domain-wide policy or as part of a Fine-Grained Password Policy?
   a. Minimum password length
   b. Minimum password age
   c. Maximum password age
   d. Enforce password history

8. A PasswordSettingsObject (PSO) within Active Directory is also known as which type of object?
   a. msDS-PasswordSettingsPrecedence
   b. msDS-PasswordSettings
   c. msDS-PasswordComplexityEnabled
   d. msDS-MinimumPasswordLength

9. Which Group Policy feature allows users to access user files when the user is disconnected from the corporate network?
   a. Folder redirection
   b. Disk quotas
   c. Offline files
   d. Object access auditing

10. Which audit event type is triggered when user or group accounts are created, deleted, renamed, enabled, or disabled?
    a. Account logon events
    b. Account management events
    c. Privileged use events
    d. Policy management events

■ Case Scenarios

Scenario 8-1: Lucerne Publishing and Offline Files

You are a computer consultant. Linda Randall, Chief Information Officer of Lucerne Publishing, has asked for your help. The Lucerne Publishing network consists of a single Active Directory domain with four domain controllers running Windows Server 2008, three file servers, and 300 clients that are evenly divided between Windows XP Professional and Windows Vista.

Recently, several publishing projects stored in electronic format were lost when an employee's laptop was stolen from a publishing convention. Previously, another employee lost important publishing project files during a fire sprinkler system incident in which the employee's computer was destroyed.

Employees typically store documents in the Documents folder on their local systems. Linda wants all employees to store their data on the network servers. The data on the network servers is backed up regularly. Linda tells you that her editors tend to work on sensitive data that requires special handling. She is especially worried that the data is backed up and secured.

All client computers have P drive mappings that are supposed to be used for storing files. However, many employees do not understand drive mappings. They often store files in their Documents folder and then copy them over to the P drive. This is also an issue because many employees forget to copy their files to the server until something occurs, such as a data loss.

Given Lucerne Publishing's concerns, answer the following questions:

a. How would you address Linda's concern that some employees do not understand drive mappings and others forget to store their data on the server?

b. How can you address the situation concerning the sensitive data editors use?

c. How would you address the users with mobile computers so that they could work on their files while traveling?

d. Linda warns that some users may have huge amounts of data already stored in the My Documents folder on their local computer. How might this affect your recommendations?

Performing Software Installation with Group Policy

OBJECTIVE DOMAIN MATRIX

TECHNOLOGY SKILL	OBJECTIVE DOMAIN	OBJECTIVE DOMAIN NUMBER
Managing Software through Group Policy	Configure software deployment GPOs.	4.5

KEY TERMS

Assign
Basic User
certificate rule
Disallowed
distribution share
file-activated installation
hash
hash algorithm

hash rule
hash value
Install This Application At
 Logon
.msi file
network zone rule
patch files
path rule

Publish
repackaging
self-healing
software life cycle
System Development Life
 Cycle (SDLC)
Unrestricted
.zap file

Lucerne Publishing has created a series of GPOs to configure password and account lockout policies and similar security-related settings on the Lucerne Publishing corporate network. Management wants to extend Active Directory to further automate the desktop management process by allowing automated software deployments. Certain applications are required across the entire enterprise; the layout artists and graphic designers use different graphics applications that they switch between, depending on the needs of a particular project. Finally, Lucerne Publishing's Human Resources department wants to restrict the use of peer-to-peer file sharing applications on the Lucerne Publishing network because of copyright and intellectual property issues.

After completing this lesson, you will be able to discuss the tasks necessary to configure Software Installation via Group Policy. This includes the steps needed to package software installers into a format that can be leveraged by Group Policy Objects, as well as determining the appropriate means of deploying software installation GPOs within your organization. You will also be able to deploy Software Restriction Policies (SRPs) to control which software can and cannot be installed and run from user workstations and servers within an Active Directory domain.

■ Managing Software through Group Policy

Group Policy can be used to install, upgrade, patch, or remove software applications when a computer is started, when a user logs on to the network, or when a user accesses a file associated with a program that is not currently on the user's computer. In addition, Group Policy can be used to fix problems associated with applications. For example, if a user inadvertently deletes a file from an application, Group Policy can be used to launch a repair process that will fix the application. To understand how Group Policy can be used to perform all of these tasks, we will discuss the Windows Installer Service and its purpose. We will also discuss Software Restriction Policies, their benefits, and how you configure them to meet the needs of your organization.

CERTIFICATION READY?
Configure software
deployment GPOs
4.5

The process that takes place from the time an application is evaluated for deployment in an organization until the time when it is deemed old or not suitable for use is referred to as the *software life cycle*. The software life cycle is a derivative of the *System Development Life Cycle (SDLC)*. The SDLC is used to develop information systems software, projects, or components through a structured process that includes analysis, design, implementation, and maintenance. The software life cycle consists of four phases that are derived from the SDLC model, as follows:

- **Planning.** This phase defines all planning activities, including the analysis of the software to be installed, verification of its compatibility, supported methods of installation, and the identification of any risks associated with the software and the desired deployment method.

- **Implementation.** This phase is used to prepare for deployment. Using Group Policy as a tool, the implementation phase includes a set of steps for a deployment, such as creating a shared access location for files and creating or using the appropriate package files. After all of the deployment steps have been achieved, the actual deployment takes place in this phase.

- **Maintenance.** The maintenance phase includes the elements that are required to keep the software running smoothly. Examples of this include upgrading software to the latest version, installing patches when necessary, and a *self-healing* function that allows the software to detect and correct problems such as missing or deleted files.

- **Removal.** The removal phase is the final phase before the software life cycle begins again with a new software deployment plan. When software is scheduled to be retired due to obsolescence or software requirement changes, this phase requires a clean removal of the software to be performed.

This lesson describes how Group Policy can be used to accomplish the latter three phases. Understanding how to use Group Policy to implement, maintain, and remove software is extremely helpful in streamlining the management of software across your enterprise.

Microsoft Windows Server 2008 uses the Windows Installer with Group Policy to install and manage software that is packaged into an *.msi file*. Windows Installer consists of two components: one for the client-side component and another for the server-side component. The client-side component is called the *Windows Installer Service*. This client-side component is responsible for automating the installation and configuration of the designated software. The Windows Installer Service requires a package file that contains all of the pertinent information about the software. This package file consists of the following information:

- An .msi file, which is a relational database file that is copied to the target computer system with the program files it deploys. In addition to providing installation information, this database file assists in the self-healing process for damaged applications and clean application removal.

- External source files that may be required for the installation or removal of software.

- Summary information about the software and the package.

- A reference point to the path where the installation files are located.

Windows Installer–enabled applications must be used to install software through Group Policy. An application that has an approval stamp from Microsoft on its packaging, including the Designed for Windows Server 2008, Windows Server 2003, Windows Vista, Windows XP, or Windows 2000 logos, is Windows Installer–enabled by default. This means the application provides support for Group Policy deployments using an .msi file.

At times, you may need to modify Windows Installer files to better suit the needs of your corporate network. Modifications to .msi files require transform files, which have an .mst extension. Consider an example where you are the administrator of a corporate network in which you use .msi files to deploy your desktop applications. Users at each location require all of the Microsoft Office 2003 applications except for Microsoft Access. Office 2003 contains an .msi file that installs all of the Office 2003 applications. However, because you do not wish to install Access, you will need to create an .mst file to modify the .msi file by using the Custom Installation Wizard included with Office 2003. When the .mst file is placed in the same directory as the original .msi file, it customizes the installation by installing all of the Office XP applications, with the exception of Access. In addition, transform files can be created to add new features to the package, such as document templates for Microsoft Word, that are specific to your organization.

Windows Installer files with the .msp extension serve as patch files. *Patch files* are used to apply service packs and hot fixes to installed software. Unlike an .msi file, a patch package does not include a complete database. Instead, it contains, at minimum, a database transform procedure that adds patching information to the target installation package database. For this reason, .msp files should be located in the same folder as the original .msi file when you want the patch to be applied as part of the Group Policy software installation. This allows the patch file to be applied to the original package or .msi file.

Repackaging Software

Not all software on the market provides .msi support. Therefore, you might not be able to take advantage of Windows Installer with all of your enterprise applications. To remedy this, you might want to consider *repackaging* some software packages to take advantage of the Windows Installer technology.

Several third-party package-creation applications on the market, including Wyse, Altiris, and others, allow you to repackage software. Repackaged software does not support some of the features of an original .msi, such as self-healing. For this reason, you should consider the long-term cost of implementing software within your organization that does not conform to the Microsoft Logo program.

In the simplest case, the process of repackaging software for .msi distribution includes taking a snapshot of a clean computer system before the application is installed, installing the application as desired, and taking a snapshot of the computer after the application is installed. A clean computer system is defined as a system with no other applications installed and only those service packs, hot fixes, and operating system patches that are required for operating system functionality. The repackaged application takes into account the changes to the registry, system settings, and file system caused by the installation itself. When you repackage an application, you are creating a relational database that tracks the installation parameters associated with the application.

The Windows Installer uses the database to find these items at installation time. Windows Installer does not create the repackaged file; this must be done by using a third-party application. Generally, application manufacturers do not support the reengineering of their .msi packages. However, you can use the .mst process to modify manufacturer-supplied .msi packages to reflect the needs of your organization. After the process is understood, it provides a well-documented and reliable method of software deployment.

When repackaging an application is not an option and a Windows Installer file is not available, you can use a *.zap file* to publish an application. A .zap file is a non–Windows Installer package that can be created in a text editor. A .zap file looks and functions very similar to an .ini file. The disadvantages of creating .zap files are as follows:

- They can be published, but not assigned. These two options will be discussed in detail later in this lesson.
- Deployments require user intervention, instead of being fully unattended.
- Local administrator permissions might be required to perform the installation.
- They do not support custom installations or automatic repair.
- They do not support the removal of applications that are no longer needed or applications that failed to install properly.

Determining which applications you wish to deploy and assessing the type of files that are necessary to provide functionality with Windows Installer should be included as part of the planning phase of your deployment plan. After these needs have been researched, analyzed, and documented, you can move into the implementation phase of your plan.

Implementing Software Using Group Policy

Group Policy allows administrators to deploy required user software when the computer starts, when the user logs on, or on demand based on file associations. From the user's perspective, applications are available and functional when they are needed. From the administrator's perspective, the applications for each user do not have to be installed manually. Once again, note that the total cost of ownership (TCO) for applications is reduced when the time to install each application for each user is eliminated or significantly lessened. The Software Installation extension in Group Policy can be used to deploy software to computers running any version of the Microsoft Windows 2000, Microsoft Windows XP, Windows Server 2003, Windows Vista, or Windows Server 2008 operating systems.

Before deploying software using Group Policy, you must create a *distribution share*. This shared folder, also named the *software distribution point,* is a network location from which users can download the software that they need. In Windows Server 2008, the network location can include software distribution points located in other forests when two-way forest trusts have been established on your network. This shared folder contains any related package files and all of the application files that are required for installation. Each application that you wish to install should have a separate subfolder in the parent shared folder. For example, if you wish to create a distribution point called SharedApps and include a word processing program, a spreadsheet program, and a database program, you should create a subfolder for each of these applications, such as ~\SharedApps\Word, ~\SharedApps\Excel, and ~\SharedApps\Access. Windows Installer uses this directory to locate and copy files to the workstation. Users who are affected by the Group Policy assignment should be assigned NTFS Read permission to the folder containing the application and package files.

After a software distribution point is created, you must create a GPO or modify an existing GPO to include the software installation settings. As part of configuring a GPO for software installation, you have to decide whether you are going to use the *Assign* or *Publish* option for deploying the application. The Assign option is helpful when you are deploying required applications to pertinent users and computers. The Publish option allows users to install the applications that they consider useful to them. If you use the Assign option, you must also decide whether you will assign the application to a computer or a user account. Choosing the appropriate deployment option is an important part of configuring your GPO settings to meet your business needs; we'll discuss the available options in the next sections.

Assigning an Application to a User or Computer

> When an application is assigned to a user, the application is advertised on the Start menu of the user's workstation. The actual installation of the application is triggered when the user attempts to access it through the Start menu. This allows the software to be installed on demand.

To understand the process of assigning an application to a user, consider this example: Suppose the Sales department needs to have all users running Microsoft Excel to complete their daily sales reports. Using a Group Policy linked to the Sales OU, you can modify the settings to include the assignment of the Excel package file. When a member of the Sales OU logs on, Windows Installer adds Excel as a selection on the Start menu and changes the registry to associate .xls files with Excel. When the user attempts to access the program for the first time using the Start menu selection, the installation process begins. Additionally, if the user attempts to open a file named with an .xls extension and Excel is not already installed, Windows Installer automatically begins the installation, and the file that was originally accessed will be opened upon completion. As we will discuss later in this lesson, installations can be configured to be totally automated or they can require some user input.

The behavior of assigning an application using the Computer Configuration\Policies\Software Settings\Software Installation node of Group Policy is somewhat different than assigning it within the User Configuration node. When you use the Computer Configuration node, the application is installed during startup. This is a safe method, because a minimum number of processes compete for utilization and few, if any, other applications are running that could cause conflicts.

Publishing an Application

> Publishing an application is only available under the User Configuration\Policies\Software Settings\Software Installation extension. When an application is published, it is advertised in Add Or Remove Programs in the Control Panel. A published application is not listed as an option on the Start Menu or on the desktop as it is when an application is assigned. Using the Publish option instead of Assign might be preferred when users are allowed to choose their applications, rather than forcing them to use a specific application.

 WARNING If you have blocked the availability of the Add Or Remove Programs application in Control Panel through Group Policy, users cannot access published applications. Prior to publishing applications, be sure to check that access to Control Panel or Add Or Remove Programs has not been blocked.

To understand the Publish option in Group Policy, consider the example of a company that has many graphic artists. Because the graphic artists have different software preferences, it has been determined that three applications will be available and users can install the application they prefer to use. Publishing a list of available applications allows users to install their preferred application or they can install all of them, if desired.

Using the Publish method of distributing applications also allows a *file-activated installation* to take place. This functionality is identical to the assigned application functionality discussed earlier. When a user opens a file associated with an application that does not currently exist on the user's workstation, the application is installed.

WARNING As a precautionary step, you should test the available applications to ensure that they can function together if the user opts to install them all. With certain application types, such as multimedia applications, conflicts in the required versions of supporting files may cause a malfunction. It is always prudent to test each application and its compatibility before it is distributed to the users. In addition, testing the deployment to be sure that applications are distributed only to the intended recipients is equally important.

CONFIGURE SOFTWARE INSTALLATION DEFAULTS

GET READY. To configure a GPO to assign or publish an application, complete the following steps:

1. **OPEN** the Group Policy Management Editor window for an existing GPO, and expand the User Configuration or the Computer Configuration node, followed by Policies, followed by Software Settings.

2. As shown in Figure 9-1, right-click the appropriate Software Installation node and then click **Properties**.

Figure 9-1

Viewing Software Installation
Properties

3. In the General tab of the Software Installation Properties dialog box, key the Uniform Naming Convention (UNC) path (\\servername\sharename) to the software distribution point for the Windows Installer packages (.msi files) in the GPO in the Default Package Location box.

4. In the New Packages section on the General tab, select one of the following:

- **Display The Deploy Software Dialog Box.** Use this option to specify that the Deploy Software dialog box displays when you add new packages to the GPO, allowing you to choose whether to assign, publish, or configure package properties. This is the default setting.

- **Publish.** Use this option to specify that the applications will be published by default with standard package properties when you add new packages to the GPO. Packages can be published only to users, not computers. If this is an installation under the Computer Configuration node of the Group Policy Object Editor console, the Publish choice is unavailable.

- **Assign.** Use this option to specify that the applications will be assigned by default with standard package properties when you add new packages to the GPO. Packages can be assigned to users and computers.

- **Advanced.** Use this option to specify that the Properties dialog box for the package will display when you add new packages to the GPO, allowing you to configure all properties for the package.

5. In the Installation User Interface Options section, select one of the following:

- **Basic.** Use this option to provide only a basic display for users during all package installation in the GPO.

- **Maximum.** Use this option to provide all installation messages and screens for users during the installation of all packages in the GPO.

6. Click the **Advanced** tab, as shown in Figure 9-2, and select any of the following options to apply the options to all packages in the GPO:

Figure 9-2

Configuring Advanced Software Installation Properties

• **Uninstall The Applications When They Fall Out Of The Scope Of Management.** Use this option to remove the application when it no longer applies to users or computers.

• **Include OLE Information When Deploying Applications.** Use this option to specify whether to deploy information about Component Object Model (COM) components with the package.

• **Make 32-Bit X86 Windows Installer Applications Available To Win64 Machines.** Use this option to specify whether 32-bit Windows Installer Applications (.msi files) can be assigned or published to 64-bit computers.

• **Make 32-Bit X86 Down-Level (ZAP) Applications Available To Win64 Machines.** Use this option to specify whether 32-bit application files (.zap files) can be assigned or published to 64-bit computers.

7. In the Application Precedence list box, move the application with the highest precedence to the top of the list using the Up or Down buttons. The application at the top of the list is automatically installed if the user invokes a document with the related filename extension and the application has not yet been installed.

8. Click the **Categories** tab, and then click **Add**. The Enter new category dialog box is displayed, as shown in Figure 9-3.

Figure 9-3

Configuring software categories

TAKE NOTE*

The application categories that you establish are per domain, not per GPO. You need to define them only once for the whole domain, not once for each GPO.

10. Key the name of the application category to be used for the domain in the Category box, and click **OK**.

11. Click **OK** to save your changes.

PAUSE. LEAVE the Group Policy Management Editor open for the next exercise.

You have now configured default Software Installation settings for GPOs in Windows Server 2008 Active Directory.

CREATE A NEW SOFTWARE INSTALLATION PACKAGE

GET READY. To create a new Windows Installer package within a GPO, complete the following steps:

1. **OPEN** the Group Policy Management Editor for the GPO you wish to configure. In the Computer Configuration or User Configuration node, drill down to Policies and then Software Settings.

2. Right-click the **Software Installation node**, select **New**, and then click **Package**. The Open dialog box is displayed.

3. In the File Name list, key the UNC path to the software distribution point for the Windows Installer packages (.msi files), and then click **Open**. The UNC path is very important. If you do not use a UNC path to the software distribution point, clients will not be able to find the package files.

4. As shown in the Deploy Software dialog box in Figure 9-4, select one of the following:

   • **Published.** Use this option to publish the Windows Installer package to users, without applying modifications to the package. It is only available if the policy was configured under the User Configuration node of Group Policy. Publishing cannot occur in a computer-based policy.

   • **Assigned.** Use this option to assign the Windows Installer package to users or computers, without applying modifications to the package.

   • **Advanced.** Use this option to set properties for the Windows Installer package, including published or assigned options and modifications.

Figure 9-4

Publishing or assigning a software package

5. Click **OK** and then choose from the following options:

   • If you selected Published or Assigned, the Windows Installer package has been successfully added to the GPO and appears in the Details pane.

   • If you selected Advanced, the Properties dialog box for the Windows Installer package opens to permit you to set properties for the Windows Installer package, including deployment options and modifications. Make the necessary modification and click **OK**.

PAUSE. LEAVE the Group Policy Management Editor open for later exercises.

You have now created a Software Installation package within Active Directory Group Policy.

Customizing Software Installation Packages

In the Properties window for each Windows Installer package, additional settings can be associated with the package, such as modification or transform (.mst) files and upgrade settings. Modifications to the previously assigned deployment settings can also be made. Figure 9-5 shows the Properties window for a Windows Installer package.

Figure 9-5

Properties of a Windows Installer package

The following list explains the tabs in the package Properties window:

- **General.** This tab allows you to change the default name of the package. In addition, a Uniform Resource Locator (URL) can be added to point to a support Web page. Some packages already contain a URL to the support Web page from the manufacturer of the software. Web sites used as support sites can contain valuable user instructions and answers to common questions.

- **Deployment.** As shown in Figure 9-6, this tab contains all of the deployment options discussed previously, including the Deployment Type (Published or Assigned), Deployment Options (Auto-install when the associated document is activated, Uninstall when the application falls out of scope, and Control Panel display selection), and Installation User Interface Options (Basic or Maximum). An Advanced button contains additional deployment information, such as advanced deployment options and diagnostics information.

Figure 9-6

Deployment Options for software installation packages

TAKE NOTE *

If the package is set to Assigned, the ***Install This Application At Logon*** option is available. This option allows the application to be installed immediately, rather than advertised on the Start menu. If users have slow links between their workstations and the software distribution point, this option should be avoided. Installation can take a lot of time when performed using a slow link.

- **Upgrades.** Use this tab, shown in Figure 9-7, to configure any upgrades that will be applied to a package. This tab will not appear on .zap package files.

Figure 9-7

Upgrade configuration for software installation packages

- **Categories.** As shown in Figure 9-8, use this tab to configure software categories in the Add/Remove Programs option of Control Panel.

Figure 9-8

Assigning categories to software installation packages

- **Modifications.** Use this tab to specify the transform (.mst) files or patch (.msp) files that are to be applied to the package. You can also modify the order in which these files will be applied to the package, as shown in Figure 9-9.

Figure 9-9

Assigning modifications to software installation packages

⚠ **WARNING** When adding the transform or patch files that you want to apply to an application, be sure that you complete all aspects of this tab before clicking **OK**. After you select **OK**, the application is assigned or published immediately. If all of the proper configurations have not been made on this tab, you may have to uninstall or upgrade the package to make the proper changes.

- **Security** As shown in Figure 9-10, this tab is used to specify who has permissions to install the software using this package.

Figure 9-10

Assigning security to software installation packages

Using Software Categories

Allowing users to choose the applications they prefer provides them with some level of control over their working environment. It is possible to publish all of the available applications to give the users complete control over their environment. However, when a larger number of applications are published, the users may get confused and have difficulty understanding the purpose of each application. In addition, they may have difficulty locating the programs they need from a long list of selections. This type of situation can be resolved by creating software categories.

Software categories allow published applications to be organized within specific groupings for easy navigation. For example, an administrator could create categories for each type of application, such as word processing applications, spreadsheet applications, database applications, graphics applications, and so on. Alternatively, the administrator could create categories that are used within different departments in an organization. These categories would contain the appropriate applications on a per-department basis. When publishing many different applications, software categories facilitate user navigation and help the user to select the applications that are appropriate for their needs. When you create or add software categories, they apply to the entire domain and are not GPO-specific.

Configuring Software Restriction Policies

First introduced in Windows Server 2003 and Windows XP operating systems, the options in the Software Restriction Policies node provide organizations greater control in preventing potentially dangerous applications from running. Software restriction policies are designed to identify software and control its execution. In addition, administrators can control who will be affected by the policies.

The Software Restriction Policies node is found in the Policies\Windows Settings\Security Settings node of the User Configuration or the Computer Configuration node of a Group Policy. By default, the Software Restriction Policies folder is empty. As shown in Figure 9-11, two subfolders are created when you create a new policy: Security Levels and Additional Rules. The Security Levels folder allows you to define the default behavior from which all rules will be created. The criteria for each executable program are defined in the Additional Rules folder.

Figure 9-11

Creating a new software restriction policy

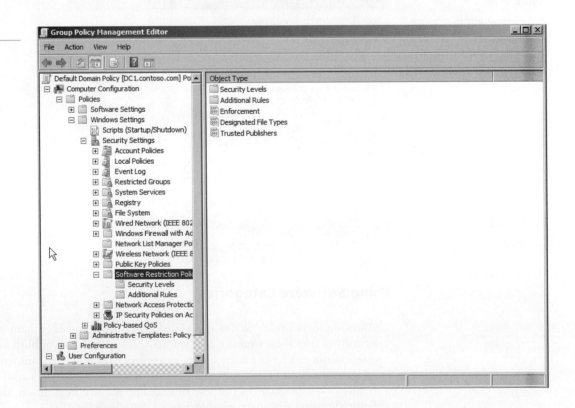

In the following sections, you will learn how to set the security level for a software restriction policy and how to define rules that will govern the execution of program files.

Prior to creating any rules that govern the restriction or allowance of executable files, it is important to understand how the rules work by default. If a policy does not enforce restrictions, executable files run based on the permissions that users or groups have in the file system. When considering the use of software restriction policies, you must determine your approach to enforcing restrictions. The three basic strategies for enforcing restrictions are:

- *Unrestricted.* This allows all applications to run except those that are specifically excluded.
- *Disallowed.* This prevents all applications from running except those that are specifically allowed.
- *Basic User.* This prevents any application from running that requires administrative rights, but allows programs to run that only require resources that are accessible by normal users.

The approach you take depends on the needs of your particular organization. By default, the Software Restriction Policies area has an Unrestricted value in the Default Security Level setting.

For example, you may wish to allow only specified applications to run in a high-security environment. In this case, you would set the Default Security Level to Disallowed. By contrast, in a less secure network, you might want to allow all executables to run unless you have specified otherwise. This would require you to leave the Default Security Level as Unrestricted. In this case, you would have to create a rule to identify an application before you could disable it. These rules will be discussed in a subsequent section.

The Default Security Level can be modified to reflect the Disallowed setting. Because the Disallowed setting assumes that all programs will be denied unless a specific rule permits them to run, this setting can cause administrative headaches if not thoroughly tested. All applications you wish to run should be tested to ensure that they will function properly.

⊙ MODIFY THE DEFAULT SECURITY LEVEL

GET READY. To modify the Default Security Level setting to reflect the Disallowed setting, complete the following steps:

1. In the Group Policy Management Editor window for the desired policy, expand the Software Restriction Policies node from either the Computer Configuration\Policies\ Windows Settings\Security Settings or User Configuration\Policies\Windows Settings\ Security Settings node. If a software restriction policy is not already defined, right-click Software Restriction Policies and select **New Software Restriction Policies**.
2. In the details pane, double-click **Security Levels**. Note the checkmark on the Unrestricted icon, which is the default setting.
3. Right-click the security level that you want to set as the default, and then click **Set As Default**. When you change the default settings to Disallowed, the dialog box shown in Figure 9-12 is displayed.

Figure 9-12

Configuring the Default Security Level of a software restriction policy

PAUSE. LEAVE the Group Policy Management Editor open for subsequent exercises.

You have now modified the Default Security Level for a software restriction policy on a Windows Server 2008 Active Directory network.

Configuring Software Restriction Rules

The functionality of software restriction policies depends on the rules that identify software, followed by the rules that govern its usage. When a new software restriction policy is created, the Additional Rules subfolder is displayed. This folder allows you to create rules that specify the conditions under which programs can be executed or denied. The rules that are applied can override the Default Security Level setting when necessary.

Four types of software restriction rules can be used to govern which programs can or cannot run on your network:

- *Hash rule*
- *Certificate rule*
- *Path rule*
- *Network zone rule*

We will discuss each of these in the following pages.

A ***hash*** is a series of bytes with a fixed length that uniquely identifies a program or file. A ***hash value*** is generated by a formula that makes it nearly impossible for another program to have the same hash. A hash is computed by a ***hash algorithm***, which in effect creates a fingerprint of the file. If a hash rule is used and a user attempts to run a program affected by the rule, the hash value of the executable file is checked. If the hash value of the executable file matches the hash value of the executable file governed by a software restriction policy, the policy settings will apply. Therefore, using a ***hash rule*** on an application executable will check the file's hash value and prevent the application from running if the hash value is not correct. Because the hash value is based on the file itself, the file can be moved from one location to another and still be affected by the hash rule. If the file is altered in any way, such as if it is altered or replaced by a worm or virus, the rules in the software restriction policy will prevent the file from running.

A ***certificate rule*** uses the signing certificate of an application. Certificate rules can be used to allow software from a trusted source to run or prevent software that does not come from a trusted source from running. Certificate rules can also be used to run programs in disallowed areas of the operating system.

A ***path rule*** identifies software by specifying the directory path where the application is stored in the file system. Path rules can be used to create an exception rule to allow an application to execute when the Default Security Level for software restriction policies is set to Disallowed, or they can be used to prevent an application from executing when the Default Security Level for software restriction policies is set to Unrestricted.

Path rules can specify either a location in the file system directory to application files or a registry path setting. Registry path rules provide assurance that the application executables will be found. For example, suppose an administrator used a path rule to define a file system path for an application. In this case, if the application were moved from its original file system path to a new location, such as during a restructuring of your network, the original path specified by the path rule would no longer be valid. If the rule specified that the application does not function except if located in a particular path, the program would not be allowed to run from its new path. This could cause a significant security breach opportunity if the program references confidential information. In contrast, if a path rule is defined using a registry key location, any change to the location of the application files will not affect the outcome of the rule. This is because when an application is relocated, the registry key that points to the application's files is updated automatically.

Network zone rules apply only to Windows Installer packages that attempt to install from a specified zone, such as a local computer, a local intranet, trusted sites, restricted sites, or the Internet. This type of rule can be applied to allow only Windows Installer packages to be installed if they come from a trusted area of the network. For example, an Internet zone rule could restrict Windows Installer packages from being downloaded and installed from the Internet or other network locations.

By default, two path rules that allow operating system files to run are located in the Additional Rules folder, as shown in Figure 9-13. Note the use of variables such as the percent sign (%) and the wildcard asterisk symbol (*). Paths that are specified here support the use of common variables such as: %userprofile%, %windir%, %appdata%, %programfiles%, or %temp%.

Figure 9-13

Default software restriction
policy rules

A software restriction policy can be defined using multiple rule types to allow and disallow
program execution. Using multiple rule types, it is possible to have a variety of security levels. For example, you may wish to specify a path rule that disallows programs to run from
the \\Server1\Accounting shared folder and a path rule that allows programs to run from the
\\Server1\Application shared folder. You can also choose to incorporate certificate rules and
hash rules into your policy. When you implement multiple rule types, rules are applied in the
following order:

1. Hash rules

2. Certificate rules

3. Network zone rules

4. Path rules

When a conflict occurs between rule types, such as between a hash rule and a path rule, the
hash rule prevails because it is higher in the order of preference. If a conflict occurs between
two rules of the same type and the same identification settings, such as two path rules that
identify software from the same directory, the most restrictive setting will apply. In this case,
if one of the path rules were set to Unrestricted and the other to Disallowed, the policy would
enforce the Disallowed setting.

Within the Software Restriction Policies folder, three specific properties can be configured to
provide additional settings that apply to all policies when implemented: enforcement, designated file types, and trusted publishers.

As shown in Figure 9-14, Enforcement properties allow you to determine whether the policies
apply to all files or whether library files, such as Dynamic Link Library (DLL), are excluded.

Figure 9-14

Configuring Enforcement
properties

Excluding DLLs is the default. This is the most practical method of enforcement. For example, if the Default Security Level for the policy is set to Disallowed and the Enforcement properties are set to All Software Files, you would have to create a rule that would allow every DLL to be checked before the program is allowed or denied. By contrast, excluding DLL files by using the default Enforcement property would not require an administrator to define individual rules for each DLL file.

The Designated File Types properties within the Software Restriction Policies folder, as shown in Figure 9-15, are used to specify file types that are considered executable. File types that are designated as executable or program files will be shared by all rules, although you can specify a list for a computer policy that is different from one that is specified for a user policy.

Figure 9-15

Configuring Designated File Types properties

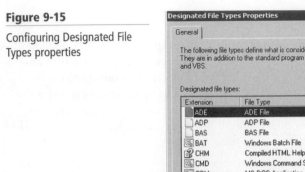

Finally, the Trusted Publishers properties allow an administrator to control how certificate rules are handled. As shown in Figure 9-16, in the Properties dialog box for Trusted Publishers, the first setting enables you to determine which users are allowed to decide on trusted certificate sources. By default, local computer administrators have the right to specify trusted publishers on the local computer, and enterprise administrators have the right to specify trusted publishers in an OU. From a security standpoint, in a high-security network, users should not be allowed to determine the sources from which certificates can be obtained.

Figure 9-16

Configuring Trusted Publishers properties

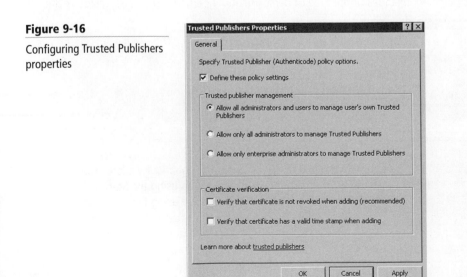

In addition, the Trusted Publisher Properties dialog box lets you decide if you wish to verify that a certificate has not been revoked. If a certificate has been revoked, the user should not be allowed to gain access to network resources. You have the option of checking either the Publisher or the Timestamp of the certificate to determine if it has been revoked.

Software restriction policies can be an asset to your organization's security strategy when they are understood and implemented properly. Planning how you want to use software restriction policies is your best defense in preventing problems. Microsoft has several recommendations that can help you to plan and implement software restriction policies, including the following:

- Software restriction policies should be used with standard access control permissions. Combining these two security features allows you to have tighter control over program usage.

- The Disallowed Default Security Level should be used cautiously, because all applications will be restricted unless explicitly allowed.

- If policies that cause undesirable restrictions on a workstation are applied, reboot the computer in Safe mode to troubleshoot and make changes, because software restriction policies cannot be applied in Safe mode. Rebooting in Safe mode is a temporary solution, because the policies remain in effect until they are modified or removed.

- When editing software restriction policies, you should disable the policy so that a partially complete policy does not cause undesirable results on a computer. After the policy modifications have been made, the policy can be enabled and refreshed.

- Creating a separate GPO for software restriction policies allows you to disable or remove them without affecting other policy settings.

- Test all policies before deploying them to the users. Very restrictive policies can cause problems with files that are required for the operating system to function properly.

SUMMARY SKILL MATRIX

IN THIS LESSON YOU LEARNED:

- Group Policy can be used to deploy new software on your network and remove or repair software originally deployed by a GPO from your network. This functionality is provided by the Windows Installer service within the Software Installation extension of either the User Configuration\Policies\Software Settings or Computer Configuration\Policies\Software Settings node.

- Three types of package files are used with the Windows Installer service: .msi files for standard software installation, .mst files for customized software installation, and .msp files for patching .msi files at the time of deployment. All pertinent files must reside in the same file system directory.

- A .zap file can be written to allow non–Windows Installer–compliant applications to be deployed. A .zap file does not support automatic repair, customized installations, or automatic software removal. In addition, these files must be published.

- A shared folder named a software distribution point must be created to store application installation and package files that are to be deployed using Group Policy. Users must have the NTFS Read permission to this folder for software installation policies to function.

- Software to be deployed using Group Policy can either be Assigned or Published. Assigning software using the User Configuration node of a Group Policy allows the application to be installed when the user accesses the program using the Start menu or an associated file. Assigning software can also be performed using the Computer Configuration node of a Group Policy, which forces the application to be installed during computer startup. Publishing an application allows the application to be available through Add Or Remove Programs in Control Panel. In addition, published applications can be divided into domain-wide software categories for ease of use.

- Software restriction policies were introduced in Windows Server 2003 and allow the software's executable code to be identified and either allowed or disallowed on the network.

- The three Default Security Levels within software restriction policies are Unrestricted, which means all applications function based on user permissions; Disallowed, which means all applications are denied execution regardless of the user permissions; and Basic User, which allows only executables to be run that can be run by normal users

- Four rule types can be defined within a software restriction policy. They include, in order of precedence; hash, certificate, network zone, and path rules. The security level set on a specific rule supersedes the Default Security Level of the policy.

- Enforcement properties within software restriction policies allow the administrator to control users affected by the policy. Administrators can be excluded from the policy application so that it does not hamper their administrative capabilities.

- Certificate rules require enabling the System settings: Use Certificate Rules on Windows Executables for Software Restriction Policies located in Computer Configuration\Policies\ Windows Settings\Security Settings\Local Policies \Security Options.

- Path rules can point to either a file system directory location or a registry path location. The registry path location is the more secure option of the two choices because the registry key location changes automatically if the software is reinstalled. In contrast, if a file system directory is blocked for executables, the program can still run from an alternate location if it is moved or copied there, allowing the possibility of a security breach.

■ Knowledge Assessment

Matching

Match the following definitions with the appropriate term.

a. .zap file
b. Assign
c. Basic User
d. hash
e. path rule

f. Publish
g. self-healing
h. distribution share
i. .msi file
j. hash rule

_____ 1. This feature of Group Policy software installation will automatically reinstall critical application files if they are accidentally or maliciously deleted.

_____ 2. Group Policy software installations rely on this file type to create an installation package that can be cleanly Assigned and Published and that has self-healing capabilities.

_____ 3. This Default Security Level in Software Restriction Policies will disallow any executable that requires administrative rights to run.

_____ 4. This Group Policy software installation option is not available in the Computer Configuration node.

_____ 5. When deploying software with Group Policy, you need to create one or more of these to house the installation files for the applications that you wish to deploy.

_____ 6. This software restriction policy rule will prevent executables from running if they have been modified in any way by a user, virus, or piece of malware.

_____ 7. If you need to deploy a software installation package that does not have an .msi file available, you can create one of these as an alternative.

_____ 8. This describes a series of bytes with a fixed length that uniquely identifies a program or file.

_____ 9. This software restriction policy rule will allow or prevent applications from running that are located within a particular folder or subfolder.

_____ 10. This GPO software installation method can be used to automatically install an application when a computer starts up or a user logs in.

Multiple Choice

Circle the correct choice.

1. Which of the following rule types apply only to Windows Installer packages?
   a. Hash rules
   b. Certificate rules
   c. Internet zone rules
   d. Path rules

2. Which file type is used by Windows Installer?
   a. .inf
   b. .bat
   c. .msf
   d. .msi

3. Which of the following is not one of the Default Security Levels that can be used with a software restriction policy?
   a. Basic User
   b. Unrestricted
   c. Restricted
   d. Disallowed

4. As part of your efforts to deploy all new applications using Group Policy, you discover that several of the applications you wish to deploy do not include the necessary installer files. What can you use to deploy these applications?
   a. Software restriction policies
   b. .msi files
   c. .mdb files
   d. .zap files

5. Which of the following describes the mathematical equation that creates a digital "fingerprint" of a particular file?
   a. Hash rule
   b. Hash algorithm
   c. Software restriction policy
   d. Path rule

6. Which of the following rules will allow or disallow a script or a Windows Installer file to run on the basis of how the file has been signed?
   a. Path rule
   b. Hash rule
   c. Network zone rule
   d. Certificate rule

7. You wish to deploy several software applications using Group Policy, such that the applications can be manually installed by the users from the Add/Remove Programs applet in their local Control Panel. Which installation option should you select?
   a. Assign
   b. Disallowed
   c. Publish
   d. Unrestricted

8. You have assigned several applications using GPOs. Users have complained that there is a delay when they double-click the application icon, which you know is the result of the application being installed in the background. What option can you use to pre-install assigned applications when users log on or power on their computers?
   a. Uninstall when the application falls out of scope
   b. Install This Application At Logon
   c. Advanced Installation Mode
   d. Path rule

9. Which of the following is used to develop information systems software through a structured process that includes analysis, design, implementation, and maintenance?
   a. Hash algorithm
   b. System Development Life Cycle
   c. Software Restriction Policy
   d. Group Policy Object

10. Which of the following Default Security Levels in Software Restriction Policies will disallow any executable from running that has not been explicitly enabled by the Active Directory administrator?
    a. Basic User
    b. Restricted
    c. Disallowed
    d. Power User

■ Case Scenarios

Scenario 9-1: Planning Group Policy Software Deployments

Your company, a healthcare organization, is currently working toward compliance with new government standards on patient confidentiality. Your IT department has decided that using software restriction policies with standard user access permissions will help to fulfill the necessary security requirements. You are preparing an implementation plan that is based on user needs and security requirements. Users should not be able to access any programs with the exception of those that are pertinent to their jobs. In addition, the user needs within the organization are as follows:

- Users only need access to email and a patient database.
- The patient database has its own built-in security access system that is configured for each user based on the user's needs within the program.
- All user accounts are located in containers based on the user's office location.

In addition, the following points should be considered in your implementation plan:

- Software restriction policy settings should not affect settings that are already in place within existing GPOs. If problems arise with software restriction policies, they should be easy to rectify, without affecting other security areas.
- Administrator accounts should not be affected by software restrictions.
- Other applications should not be affected by any of the restrictions.

List the key points that should be part of your implementation plan based on the information provided here.

Scenario 9-2: Consulting with Wide World Importers

You have been asked by Max Benson, CEO of Wide World Importers, to advise the company on the software deployment issues they are facing. Wide World Importers is an import/export company handling primarily clothing and textile products. It has offices in New York, New York; San Diego, California; and Fort Lauderdale, Florida. Wide World's network is configured as a single Active Directory domain with sites and OUs for each location. Below each top-level OU is a second layer of OUs representing the functional areas of Shipping, Finance, and Marketing. The users and client computers are distributed as shown in Table 9-1.

Table 9-1

Wide World Importers' Network Structure

Office/OU	Users	Computers	Operating Systems Used
NY/Shipping	15	8	Windows 2000 Professional
NY/Finance	60	60	Windows 2000 Professional and Windows XP Professional
NY/Marketing	175	185	Windows 2000 Professional and Windows XP Professional
CA/Shipping	55	40	Windows 2000 Professional and Microsoft Windows NT version 4.0 Workstation
CA/Finance	110	110	Windows XP Professional
CA/Marketing	210	210	Windows 2000 Professional and Windows XP Professional
FL/Shipping	25	15	Windows NT version 4.0 Workstation
FL/Finance	20	20	Windows 2000 Professional
FL/Marketing	140	150	Windows 2000 Professional and Windows XP Professional

The California and New York offices are connected by a dedicated T-1 line. Dedicated 256-Kbps fractional T-1 lines connect the Florida office to the California and New York offices. Several of the Marketing users have mobile computers, and a portion of their time is spent traveling the world. Access to the main network is accomplished by dialing in to a local Internet service provider (ISP) and then establishing a Layer Two Tunneling Protocol (L2TP) virtual private network (VPN) to the California office. Each location has three domain controllers and one file server. The wide area network (WAN) links are used heavily during the day, but Wide World does not plan to upgrade them any time soon. It is important that the software deployment strategy you suggest does not adversely affect the WAN links during business hours.

Max has indicated that he wants more control over software deployment and wants to leverage his investment in Windows Server 2008. The main software requirements of the company include Office 2003 for all users, a third-party program used by Marketing, an application used by Finance for billing and accounting, and a proprietary shipping application developed for Wide World Importers. Although all users utilize Office 2003, they do not all use the same applications. Many users utilize only Outlook and Word, whereas others also make use of Access and PowerPoint. Still others use Excel on a daily basis.

Given the concerns of Wide World Importers, answer the following questions:

1. Utilizing GPO for software deployment, how can you configure the network in a way that will not negatively impact the business by saturating the WAN links during deployment?

2. With respect to the marketing, finance, and shipping applications, what are some of the options and considerations when deciding how to deploy these applications?

3. How do you recommend resolving the issue that many users utilize different parts of the Office 2003 suite of applications?

4. The shipping application is a proprietary application that does not have an .msi file associated with it. How would you recommend using Group Policy to deploy this application to the Shipping department?

10 LESSON

Planning a Group Policy Management and Implementation Strategy

OBJECTIVE DOMAIN MATRIX

TECHNOLOGY SKILL	OBJECTIVE DOMAIN	OBJECTIVE DOMAIN NUMBER
Introducing the Group Policy Management MMC Snap-In	Configure GPO templates.	4.4

KEY TERMS

Common Information
  Management Object Model
  (CIMOM)
GPResult
Group Policy Modeling

Group Policy Results
Logging mode
Planning mode
Resultant Set of Policy
  (RSoP)

Windows Management
  Instrumentation (WMI)
WMI Filtering
WMI Query Language
  (WQL)

Lucerne Publishing has established a number of GPOs to enforce a consistent security configuration across its environment, in addition to implementing communication security and software installation for users in various departments. The Group Policy infrastructure at Lucerne Publishing has grown substantially, and now the Lucerne Publishing administrators are documenting procedures for optimizing and troubleshooting GPOs on the network. In particular, administrators must find a way to prevent certain restrictive GPOs from applying to individual users within departmental OUs who require more open access to the desktop and applications. Additionally, Lucerne Publishing has recently purchased upgrades for all of the major desktop publishing applications, but administrators must ensure that these upgrades are only deployed to users whose workstations have sufficient RAM and hard drive space to support the installation.

After completing this lesson, you will be able to discuss Group Policy management by focusing on planning an overall implementation strategy for GPOs within a Windows Server 2008 Active Directory environment. You will be able to use the Group Policy Management Console (GPMC), a unified management console that allows you to view GPO settings across an organization as well as report on existing GPO configurations and run "what-if" planning scenarios to test potential changes to your GPO environment. You will be able to fine-tune the application of GPOs using Security Group Filtering and WMI filters to better control which users and computers will (and will not) receive a particular GPO. You will troubleshoot GPOs, using built-in utilities such as the Resultant Set of Policy Wizard and Group Policy Modeling and Results queries.

Managing Group Policy

THE BOTTOM LINE

This lesson focuses on expanding your knowledge of Group Policy. Specifically, you will learn how to plan and manage group policies. In addition to other management tools, we will discuss Group Policy Management, a new Windows Server 2008 MMC snap-in that can assist you in planning, implementing, and troubleshooting group policies. As you have learned, Group Policy is a powerful security tool that can provide administrative benefits when properly used and administered. It is important to be familiar with the tool and have a working ability to analyze and obtain information about applying Group Policy settings. As discussed in previous lessons, the policy-application process can be complex. When multiple policies are applied to a computer and to a user, it is important to understand which policy settings will be in effect after the policies have finished processing.

Although we have discussed the use of methods such as Block Policy Inheritance and Enforce to alter the flow of group policies within the Active Directory structure, several other methods can be used to filter policy application. These methods will be discussed in this lesson. In addition to defining policy-filtering methods, you will learn how to use various tools to identify the final effective GPO settings that are applied to a user or computer at any given time. Finally, we will discuss the key points to be considered when planning an effective Group Policy structure.

Introducing the Group Policy Management MMC Snap-In

The Group Policy Management MMC snap-in is a tool for managing Windows Server 2008, Windows Server 2003, and Windows 2000 Active Directory domains. The Group Policy Management MMC provides a single access point to all aspects of Group Policy that were previously spread across other tools, such as Active Directory Users and Computers, Active Directory Sites and Services, Resultant Set of Policy (RSoP), and the Group Policy Management Editor.

The simplified Group Policy Management user interface offers administrators a single point of administration for creating and modifying Group Policy. It also offers the following functionality:

- **Importing and copying GPO settings to and from the file system.** This functionality works within a domain, across domains, or across forests. The Import Settings feature allows you to bring settings from a file system GPO into an existing GPO. The Copy feature allows you to copy settings from an existing GPO to a new GPO. Links to the

GPO are not modified during an import or copy operation. Table 10-1 details the differences between Import and Copy within the Group Policy Management snap-in.

Table 10-1

GPMC Copy Versus Import

COPY	IMPORT
Source: An existing GPO within Active Directory.	Source: Any GPO that was backed up and stored in the file system.
Destination: Creates a new GPO in Active Directory. This new GPO will have a unique GUID.	Destination: Erases the existing settings of an existing GPO in Active Directory.
ACL: Can use the default ACL for new GPOs or copy the ACL from the source GPO.	ACL: Not modified in the destination GPO.
Required Permissions: The right to create GPOs in the target location and Read access to the source GPO are required.	Required Permissions: Read permission to the source GPO and edit rights to the destination GPO.

- **Backup and restoration of GPOs is available in Group Policy Management.** The Group Policy Management Backup feature allows a GPO to be exported to the file system and stored for disaster recovery or testing. Multiple versions of the same GPO can be backed up to the same file system directory. The Restore feature allows a specific GPO to be restored to a prior state. If multiple settings are modified that produce undesirable results, the Restore feature provides a contingency solution. It restores all attributes, settings, Access Control Lists (ACLs), GUIDs, and links to any Windows Management Instrumentation (WMI) filters.

- *Resultant Set of Policy (RSoP)* **functionality integration includes Group Policy Modeling and Group Policy Results.** RSoP is a query engine that looks at GPOs and then reports its findings. Use this tool to determine the effective settings for a user or a computer based on the combination of the local, site, domain, domain controller, and OU policies. RSoP was originally created as a separate MMC snap-in. The two modes, planning and logging, are renamed in GPMC to Group Policy Modeling and Group Policy Results. We will discuss RSoP in further detail later in this lesson.

- **Hypertext Markup Language (HTML) reports allow read-only views of GPO settings and RSoP information.** This information is easily acquired and easy to save or print for documentation or analysis purposes.

- **Search for GPOs based on name, permissions, WMI filter, GUID, or policy extensions set in the GPOs.**

- **Search for individual settings within a GPO by keyword and search for only those settings that have been configured.**

- **GPMC is natively installed with Windows Server 2008.** In previous versions of the operating system, it needed to be manually downloaded from the Microsoft Web site.

In addition to the primary capabilities listed previously and the new management interface, the GPMC provides a simplified method of delegating GPO management. We will discuss GPO delegation and the remaining GPO topics within the context of this new management tool.

Group Policy Management is located in the Administrative Tools folder of the Start menu. Figure 10-1 illustrates the default view of Group Policy Management when it is launched from the Administrative Tools folder.

Figure 10-1

Viewing the Group Policy Management MMC snap-in

Expanding the Forest node in the left console pane allows you to see the subnodes, which include Domains, Sites, Group Policy Modeling, and Group Policy Results. When you expand the node that refers to a specific site, domain, or OU, you will see three main tabs in the right console pane:

- **Linked Group Policy Objects.** As shown in Figure 10-2, this tab allows an administrator to change the order of policies, create new policies, edit existing policies, create policy links, and view and change the enabled status.

Figure 10-2

Viewing the Linked Group Policy Objects tab

- **Group Policy Inheritance.** As shown in Figure 10-3, this tab displays the order of precedence for the policies set on this container.

Figure 10-3

Viewing the Group Policy Inheritance tab

- **Delegation.** The Delegation tab, shown in Figure 10-4, displays groups and users with permission to link, perform modeling analyses, or read group policy results information. Modeling is the same as planning mode using RSoP. Reading results data is the same as RSoP's logging mode. Also located on this tab is an Advanced button that allows administrators to access the Group Policy Object's Security tab.

Figure 10-4

Viewing the Group Policy Delegation tab

Managing an Individual GPO

As illustrated previously, Group Policy Management allows administrators to create and modify policies from the container on which they are linked. Additionally, all aspects of each individual policy, including the scope of its application, filtering methods, enabled or disabled status, effective settings, and delegation of application and management, can be managed using Group Policy Management. The tabbed display interface is organized logically, easy to navigate, and simplifies modifications.

The following list explains and illustrates the features available on each tab when a GPO is selected in the Group Policy Management interface:

- **Scope.** As shown in Figure 10-5, this tab allows administrators to view the locations to which the policy is linked. In addition, security filtering using permissions and WMI are available for viewing, editing, or creating. When a WMI filter is applied to the policy, it appears in the list with an Open button that allows filter modification. If a WMI filter is not applied to the policy, the button will allow a new filter to be created or linked to the GPO.

- **Details.** This tab, shown in Figure 10-6, allows the GPO to be enabled or disabled. It also displays read-only information that includes the owner, GUID, creation date, and last modification date.

- **Settings.** When this tab is activated, an HTML report is generated that allows administrators to view GPO settings that do not have the original default values. Links on the right side of the report allow detailed information to be displayed or hidden. Right-clicking within this view allows administrators to print or save the report.

- **Delegation.** Like the previously discussed Delegation tab for a container object, this tab lists the users and groups that have access to this GPO and the permissions that apply to them. The Advanced button allows access to the Security tab to directly view the GPO's ACL.

Now that you have a clearer picture of the Group Policy Management tool and its interface, we will discuss several policy management techniques and how to accomplish them using this tool.

Figure 10-5

Viewing the Scope of a GPO

Figure 10-6

Viewing the Details of a GPO

Configuring Starter GPOs

A new Group Policy management feature in Windows Server 2008 is the ability to create Starter GPOs that can act as templates when creating new GPOs for your organization. You can configure a common list of settings within a Starter GPO, and any GPOs that you create based on that Starter GPO will receive those settings.

CONFIGURE A STARTER GPO

GET READY. To complete this exercise, you must be logged on with Domain Admins or Group Policy Creator Owner credentials.

1. **OPEN** the Group Policy Management MMC console.
2. Drill down to *<forest name>*, click *<domain name>*, and then click **Starter GPOs**.

3. If this is the first time you have used Starter GPOs, the Contents tab is gray. Click **Create Starter GPOs Folder**.

4. Right-click the **Starter GPOs** node and click **New**. The New Starter GPO dialog is displayed. Enter a name and description for the Starter GPO and click **OK**.

5. Right-click the Starter GPO that you just created and click **Edit**. The Group Policy Starter GPO Editor will open. Make any modifications to this Starter GPO and then close the Group Policy Starter GPO Editor.

6. To create a new GPO that is based on this Starter GPO, navigate to the Group Policy Objects node. Right-click **Group Policy Objects** and click **New**. The window shown in Figure 10-7 is displayed. Enter a name for the new GPO. In the Source Starter GPO dropdown list, select the Starter GPO that you want to use as the source of the new GPO and click **OK**.

Figure 10-7

Creating a new GPO based on a Starter GPO

PAUSE. CLOSE the Group Policy Management MMC snap-in and any open Group Policy Management Editor windows.

You have now configured a Starter GPO to use as a template for new GPOs and created a new GPO based on that Starter GPO. Any GPOs that you create based on a Starter GPO will begin with the settings contained within that Starter GPO.

Filtering Group Policy Scope

By default, Group Policy settings will apply to all child objects within the domain, site, or OU to which they are linked. In addition, the settings will be inherited down through the Active Directory structure unless policy inheritance has been blocked. Using the Block Policy Inheritance policy setting, you can prevent policy settings from applying to all child objects at the current level and all subordinate levels. Although the Block Policy Inheritance setting is useful in some circumstances, it may be necessary to have a policy apply only when certain conditions exist or only to a certain group of people.

To meet the need for refined control over the application of group policies, two additional filtering methods, discussed in the following sections, can be used. They include the following:

- **Security Group Filtering.** This method uses the GPO's Security tab to determine user and group account access to the policy.
- *WMI Filtering.* This method uses filters written in the *WMI Query Language (WQL)*, which is similar to structured query language (SQL), to control GPO application.

Configuring Security Group Filtering

Security Group Filtering refines the application of a GPO to include or exclude certain users, groups, or computers based on the ACL that is applied to the GPO. For example, consider a GPO that prevents users from accessing a command prompt and prohibits access to the Control Panel. When applied to general users, the restrictive nature of the policy may be appropriate. However, when applied to administrators it might hinder their ability to perform their job responsibilities, such as troubleshooting or making configuration changes. Security Group Filtering can be implemented to allow a policy to be applied to some users without applying it to others.

As shown in Figure 10-8, the Delegation tab on a GPO within the Group Policy Management console allows you to select who can read or make changes to the policy. By default, the Authenticated Users group has the Read and Apply Group Policy Access Control Entry (ACE) permissions set to Allow. These two permissions are required for policy settings to take effect on a user or group account. Although administrators have Full Control permissions by default, they also are members of the Authenticated Users special identity group. They will be affected by the policy settings applied through the policy. To prevent restrictive policies from applying to administrators or other accounts for which they are not intended, you have two options:

- Remove the ACE entry for the Authenticated Users group that grants Read and Apply Group Policy permissions, and grant these two permissions to only the groups that you want the GPO to affect.

- Set the Apply Group Policy ACE to Deny for the specific group or groups that you want to exclude from the Group Policy; the GPO will still apply to all other users because of the Authenticated Users ACE.

Figure 10-8

Viewing Security Settings on a GPO

Setting the Apply Group Policy ACE to Deny for a specific group can also impact users who are members of more than one group. The Deny setting will supersede any Allow setting that is granted to a user through membership to another group. It is important to make sure you know to which groups the affected users belong.

CONFIGURE SECURITY GROUP FILTERING

GET READY. The following steps outline how to set a GPO's permissions so that the GPO will not be applied to users in the Administrators group.

1. **OPEN** the Group Policy Management MMC snap-in.

2. Navigate to the GPO you wish to modify. Click the **Delegation** tab, and then click **Advanced**.

3. If the Administrators group is not listed in the Group or User Names window, click **Add** and key **Administrators** in the Enter Object Names to Select box. Click **OK**.

4. Make sure that **Administrators** is selected and click the **Deny** checkbox for the Apply Group Policy permission.

5. Click **OK**. The dialog box shown in Figure 10-9 is displayed. Read the dialog box and click **Yes** to continue.

Figure 10-9

Applying a deny permission to a GPO

6. Click **OK** to close the Properties dialog box for the GPO.

PAUSE. LEAVE the Group Policy Management Console and the Group Policy Management Editor open for the next exercise.

You just modified the default security settings for a Group Policy object. It is important to note that Group Policy permission settings apply to the entire policy; in other words, there is no way to set permissions for individual policy settings.

Configuring WMI Filtering

Windows Management Instrumentation (WMI) is a component of the Microsoft Windows operating system that provides management information and control in an enterprise environment. It allows administrators to create queries based on hardware, software, operating systems, and services. These queries can be used to gather data or to determine where items, such as GPOs, will be applied. WMI filters can be used to control which users or computers will be affected by a GPO based on defined criteria. For example, a WMI filter can be created for a software installation GPO so that only computers that have enough free space on the drive and a processor capable of running the application will receive the application. The filter is evaluated at the time the policy is processed.

The following list details the key points that should be considered when using WMI filters:

- At least one domain controller running Windows Server 2003 or Windows Server 2008 must be present to use WMI filters.
- Filters will only be evaluated on Windows Vista, Windows XP Professional, or Windows Server 2003 computers. Windows 2000–based computers will ignore WMI filters.
- All filter criteria must have an outcome of true for the GPO to be applied. Any criteria with an outcome of false after evaluation will negate the application of the GPO.
- Only one WMI filter can be configured per GPO. After it is created, a WMI filter can be linked to multiple GPOs.

Now that you understand the key points regarding the functionality of WMI filters, it is important that you also have examples that illustrate the type of queries that can be performed using WMI filters. Because WMI essentially evaluates data from a destination computer and determines if that data matches the criteria within the filter, administrators can use WMI filters to apply group policies based on this information. Table 10-2 lists examples of query types that might be useful for determining policy application rules.

Table 10-2

WMI Filter Examples

TARGET COMPUTER	SAMPLE WMI FILTER STRING
All computers that are running Windows XP Professional	Select * from Win32_OperatingSystem where Caption = "Microsoft Windows XP Professional"
All computers that have more than 10MB of available drive space on a C: NTFS partition	Select * from Win32_LogicalDisk WHERE Name= "C:" AND DriveType = 3 AND FreeSpace > 10485760 AND FileSystem = "NTFS"
All computers that have a modem installed	Select * from Win32_POTSModem Where Name – "MyModem"

Do not to overuse WMI filters within a production environment. As a tool for deploying GPOs to the appropriate users and computers, they are very powerful. However, it is important to consider the impact that they will have on the performance of startup and logon processes. WMI filter evaluation creates an additional impact on performance due to the time required to evaluate the criteria. Combining WMI filter evaluation and actual policy application increases the time it takes to deliver a working environment to the user. WMI filters can be created using the Group Policy Management console.

CONFIGURE WMI FILTERING

GET READY. In this exercise you will create a WMI filter, and then apply that filter to a Group Policy Object.

1. **OPEN** the Group Policy Management MMC snap-in. Drill down to <*forest name*>, click <*domain name*>, and then click **WMI Filters**.

2. Right-click the **WMI Filters** node and click **New**. In the Name and Description fields, enter a name and description for the new WMI filter.

3. In the Queries section, click **Add**. The WMI Query window will be displayed. Enter the desired query information and click **OK**.

4. Click **Save** to create the WMI filter.

5. Navigate to the Group Policy Objects node. Select the GPO to be assigned this WMI filter.

6. On the Scope tab, select the name of the WMI filter you just created from the WMI Filtering dropdown box. Click **Yes** to confirm your changes.

PAUSE. LEAVE the Group Policy Management console open for the next exercise.

You have just created a new WMI filter and configured a GPO to apply only to users or computers that fit the criteria of the filter. It is important to not overuse WMI filters, because they can have a negative impact on the performance of your client workstations when logging onto Active Directory.

Determining and Troubleshooting Effective Policy Settings

Resultant Set of Policy (RSoP) is the sum of the policies applied to a user or computer after all filters, security group permissions, and inheritance settings, such as Block Policy Inheritance and Enforce, have finished processing. As the application of group policies becomes more complex within your Active Directory structure, it can become difficult to predict what the final policy settings will be when all processing is complete. In addition, it may be difficult to trace the origin of a particular outcome due to policy inheritance, policy links, and permission settings.

To help alleviate the possibly daunting task of determining where policy settings came from and the results of all cumulative policies, Microsoft provides several tools:

- Resultant Set of Policy Wizard
- Group Policy Results and Group Policy Modeling components of Group Policy Management
- GPResult command-line tool

Each of these tools provides value in assisting with policy planning and troubleshooting. However, each has a different level of functionality. We will discuss these tools in the next sections.

Using the Resultant Set of Policy Wizard

The Resultant Set of Policy Wizard is provided in Windows Server 2008 to assist administrators in determining the effects of policies on users and computers. In addition to assisting in debugging and reporting on existing policies, the wizard allows administrators to simulate policy effects prior to implementing them on the production network.

Two modes within RSoP allow the previous functionality. These modes are as follows:

- *Planning mode.* This mode allows administrators to simulate the effect of policy settings prior to implementing them on a computer or user. This mode is beneficial when planning due to growth or changes to your organization. You can use planning mode to test the effects of changes to group policies on your organization prior to deployment. You can use planning mode to simulate the results of a slow link on a GPO in addition to simulating the loopback process.

- *Logging mode.* This mode queries existing policies in the hierarchy that are linked to sites, domains, domain controllers, and OUs. This mode is useful for documenting and understanding how combined policies are affecting users and computers. The results are returned in an MMC window that can be saved for later reference.

RSoP is available as an MMC snap-in. It is also available through Group Policy Management. In Group Policy Management, the functionalities of planning and logging are renamed, respectively, to Group Policy Modeling and Group Policy Results. You will learn each method of obtaining RSoP information beginning with the Resultant Set Of Policy MMC snap-in.

As shown in Figure 10-10, in the Resultant Set of Policy snap-in you must generate data that will serve your query needs. The RSoP Wizard will allow you to specify the extent of your query after determining the mode.

Figure 10-10

The Resultant Set of Policy MMC Snap-In

RSoP uses information that is part of the ***Common Information Management Object Model (CIMOM)*** database. The CIMOM database is used through WMI and contains information that is gathered when a computer starts and becomes part of the network. This information includes hardware, Group Policy Software Installation Settings, Internet Explorer Maintenance settings, scripts, Folder Redirection settings, and Security settings. When RSoP is started in Planning or Logging mode, information in the CIMOM database is used to assist in producing the desired reports.

USE THE RESULTANT SET OF POLICY WIZARD

GET READY. This exercise will create an RSoP Planning mode report, and then create an RSoP Logging mode report.

1. Click **Start**, click **Run**, key **mmc**, and press (**Enter**). From the File menu, select **Add/Remove Snap-in**, and then click the **Add** button.

2. Select the **Resultant Set of Policy** snap-in from the Add Standalone Snap-in windows, click **Add**, and then click **Close**.

3. Click **OK** to finish creating the new console window.

4. In the left console pane, select **Resultant Set of Policy**.

5. From the Action menu, select **Generate RSoP Data** to launch the RSoP Wizard. Click **Next**.

6. In the Mode selection page, select **Planning Mode** and click **Next** to continue.

7. In the User and Computer Selection page, complete the appropriate fields to select the user or computer for which you wish to simulate policy settings. Click **Next** to proceed.

8. In the Advanced Simulation Options page, you can choose to simulate your policy with additional conditions, such as slow links and loopback processing. The settings in this window are optional. The Loopback processing option is only available if you chose to simulate settings for a user and computer. Click **Next** to continue.

9. On the User Security Groups page, you can choose to simulate the effect of changing the user's security group memberships. The settings on this page are optional. Click **Next** to continue.

10. On the Computer Security Groups page, you can simulate changes to the computer's security groups. The settings on this page are optional. Click **Next** to continue.

11. On the WMI Filters for Users page, select any filters that you would like to include in your simulation. The page settings here are optional. Click **Next** to continue.

12. On the WMI Filters for Computers page, select any filters that you would like to include in your simulation. The page settings here are optional. Click **Next** to continue.

13. On the Summary Of Selections page, review your simulation query information, change the domain controller on which you wish to process the simulation if necessary, and click **Next** to generate the report.

14. Click **Finish** to close the wizard. The results of your query will be displayed in an MMC window that looks similar to a Group Policy Object Editor window. The MMC can be saved with the results of the query.

15. In the left console pane, select **Resultant Set of Policy**.

16. From the Action menu, select **Generate RSoP Data** to launch the RSoP Wizard. Click **Next**.

17. From the Mode Selection page, select **Logging Mode** and click **Next** to continue.

18. On the Computer Selection page, you can select **This Computer** or select **Another Computer** and key the name of the computer. If you are not sure of the computer name, you can click **Browse** to find the computer for which you wish to perform the query. The other option on this page is to click the **Do Not Display Policy Settings for the Selected Computer in the Results Display** checkbox. This will eliminate the computer policy settings from the results window. Click **Next** to continue.

19. On the User Selection page, select the appropriate bullet for the user for which you wish to display query results. If you chose a computer in step 7 and do not wish to have user policy settings displayed in the final results, you can click the **Do Not Display User Policy Settings in the Results** checkbox. Click **Next** to continue.

20. On the Summary of Selections page, verify your desired query information, click the checkbox to show error information, and click **Next** to begin the analysis. Click **Finish** to close the wizard. The MMC window will display the results of your request.

PAUSE. CLOSE the MMC console before continuing.

To create an RSoP query for an existing computer or user, you must be logged on to the local computer as a user, be a member of the local Administrators, Domain Administrators, or Enterprise Administrator group, or have permission to generate an RSoP for the domain or OU in which the user and computer accounts are contained. If the RSoP query includes site GPOs that cross domain boundaries in the same forest, you must be logged on as an Enterprise Administrator. The results that are displayed for the RSoP query look very similar to the information available when editing or creating a GPO using the Group Policy Object Editor. However, only the settings that have been altered from the default will be displayed. Changes to a policy will not be reflected unless the RSoP query is run again after a GPO has been refreshed by a computer restart, user logon, or the use of gpupdate.exe.

Creating a Group Policy Modeling Query

The same information that is gathered and reported using the Resultant Set of Policy snap-in can be gathered and reported using the Group Policy Management utility. In fact, it is even simpler to use the Group Policy Management utility to obtain information than to use the Resultant Set of Policy snap-in. Individual settings that affect the user are easy to find, and multiple queries can be created and stored within one interface. To view query results using the Resultant Set of Policy MMC snap-in, it is necessary to save each individual console window. You must run multiple instances of the Resultant Set of Policy MMC snap-in to compare results. In contrast, using the Group Policy Management tool permits multiple queries available within the same interface for comparison purposes. In addition, the interface allows administrators to save the reports for future reference and print them directly from the HTML window pane.

This section will demonstrate how to use the Group Policy Modeling and Group Policy Results features of Group Policy Management to obtain RSoP information. *Group Policy Modeling*, referred to as *Planning mode* using the Resultant Set of Policy snap-in, is used to simulate the effect of a policy on the user environment.

⊘ **CREATE A GROUP POLICY MODELING QUERY**

GET READY. To create a query, complete the following steps using Group Policy Management.

1. From the Administrative Tools folder on the Start menu, open **Group Policy Management** and browse to the forest or domain in which you want to create a Group Policy Modeling query.
2. Right-click **Group Policy Modeling** and then click **Group Policy Modeling Wizard**.
3. On the Welcome to the Group Policy Modeling Wizard page, click **Next**.
4. Complete the remaining pages, entering the information that will build the appropriate simulation criteria. These remaining pages are the same as those you completed using the Resultant Set of Policy MMC in Planning mode.

PAUSE. View the generated report.

The generated report contains three tabs to organize and display important information about the query. The Summary tab in the newly created Group Policy Modeling query report will show a summary of information collected during the simulation process. Figure 10-11 shows an example of a Summary report.

Figure 10-11

Group Policy Modeling Wizard Summary tab

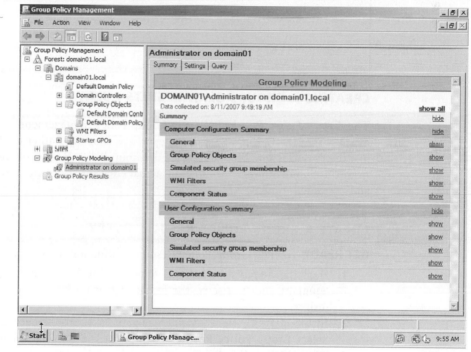

The Settings tab provides comprehensive information that includes individual policy settings areas and the effects each would have in a live deployment. Click the *show all* link in the top right corner of the display to expand the report's contents. This report can be printed or saved by right-clicking in the display window area and selecting the desired choice.

The Query tab, shown in Figure 10-12, displays the criteria for the modeling query. This information can be helpful when comparing multiple modeling scenarios during the planning phase of your group policy structure.

Figure 10-12

Group Policy Modeling Wizard Query tab

CREATING A GROUP POLICY RESULTS QUERY

The *Group Policy Results* feature in Group Policy Management is equivalent to the Logging mode within the Resultant Set of Policy MMC snap-in. Rather than simulating policy effects like the Group Policy Modeling Wizard, Group Policy Results obtains RSoP information from the client computer to show the actual effects that policies have on the client computer and user environment.

CREATE A GROUP POLICY RESULTS QUERY

GET READY. To view Group Policy Results information, complete the following steps.

1. From the Administrative Tools folder on the Start Menu, open **Group Policy Management** and browse to the forest or domain from which you want to view query results.
2. In Group Policy Management, navigate to and right-click **Group Policy Results**. Select **Group Policy Results Wizard**. On the Welcome to Group Policy Results Wizard page, click **Next**.
3. On the Computer Selection page, select the current computer or click **Browse** to select another computer. Click **Next** to continue.
4. On the User Selection page, select the current user or specify another user for which you wish to obtain policy results and click **Next**.
5. On the Summary of Selections page, verify your criteria and click **Next**.
6. Click **Finish** to close the Completing the Group Policy Results Wizard page.

STOP. CLOSE the Group Policy Management console before continuing. View and close the report. Close all open windows.

Like the Group Policy Modeling Wizard, the generated report based on the Group Policy Results criteria includes three tabs. Similar to the Group Policy Modeling Wizard, the Summary tab gives an overall summary of the applied policy settings. The Settings tab provides comprehensive information that includes individual policy settings areas and their resulting effects. Also like the Group Policy Modeling Wizard, clicking the Show All link in the top right corner of the display expands the report's contents. This report can be printed or saved by right-clicking in the display window area and selecting the desired action.

The Policy Events tab, shown in Figure 10-13, collects all policy-related events and stores them in one convenient location. The information provided here can be extremely valuable in troubleshooting policy application and consolidating group policy events that are directly related to the queried objects. Double-click any item on this tab to display the Event Properties window, providing additional information.

Figure 10-13

Group Policy Modeling Wizard Policy Events tab

In addition to having all of the previously discussed tabs available, the individual policy settings can be viewed in the Resultant Set of Policy results window.

Using GPRESULT

> Although not as easy to read as the Group Policy Results information that can be obtained using GPMC, *GPResult* is a command-line tool that allows you to create and display an RSoP query from the command line. It provides comprehensive information about the operating system, the user, and the computer.

Although not quite as broad in its capabilities, GPResult provides a valuable method of obtaining information efficiently. The following information is included in a GPResult query:

- The last time a group policy was applied and the domain controller responsible for its application
- A complete list of applied GPOs
- Applied registry settings
- Redirected folders
- Information on assigned and published applications
- Disk quota information
- IP security settings
- Scripts

GPResult uses syntax to obtain information from the previous list that is similar to the syntax of other command-line utilities. This syntax consists of the command followed by switches that enable flexibility in defining the output. The following examples list the syntax necessary to obtain a variety of RSoP information outputs for the user Sseely.

To obtain RSoP information on computer and user policies that will affect Sseely, key the following command from a command line:

```
gpresult /user sseely /v
```

To narrow the results of the previous command to include only the computer policy information that will affect Sseely, modify the previous command string to include the /scope option. The following example illustrates the required command to do this:

```
gpresult /user sseely /scope computer /v
```

If you are logged on with a standard user account, you need to supply administrative credentials to allow GPResult to function. The following example modifies the command string to include the /u switch to specify a user account with administrative privileges. The /p switch is used to supply the password for the user account.

```
gpresult /u cohowinery.com/Admin01 /p MSPr3ss#1 /user sseely /scope computer /v
```

SUMMARY SKILL MATRIX

IN THIS LESSON YOU LEARNED:

- Application of group policies can be filtered by using Block Policy Inheritance, No Override, permissions, and WMI filters.

- WMI filters allow administrative control over group policy implementation based on criteria defined in the filter. After evaluation, all filter criteria must return a value of true for the policy to be applied. Any criteria that return a value of false after evaluation will prevent the policy from being applied.

- Only one WMI filter can be applied to each GPO.

- GPMC can be used to manage all aspects of Group Policy, including the following: creation, linking, editing, reporting, modeling, backup, restore, copying, importing, and scripting.

- Determining effective group policies can be accomplished using RSoP, GPMC, or GPResult.

- RSoP is an MMC snap-in that has two modes: Planning and Logging. Planning mode allows administrators to simulate policy settings prior to their deployment. Logging mode reports on the results of existing policies.

- Delegating administrative control of Group Policy management tasks is an important feature when planning a decentralized administrative approach. GPMC is a comprehensive tool that simplifies delegation of all aspects of Group Policy management.

■ Knowledge Assessment

Matching

Match the following definitions with the appropriate term.

- **a.** Common Information Management (CMOM)
- **b.** GPResult
- **c.** Group Policy Modeling
- **d.** Group Policy Results
- **e.** Logging mode
- **f.** Planning mode
- **g.** Resultant Set of Policy (RSoP)

h. Windows Management Instrumentation (WMI)

i. WMI Filtering

j. WMI Query Language (WQL)

_____ 1. This RSoP mode allows administrators to simulate the effect of policy settings prior to implementing them on a computer or user.

_____ 2. This command-line utility allows you to create and display an RSoP query from the command line.

_____ 3. This GPMC node is used to simulate the effect of a policy on the user and computer environment and replaces Planning mode in RSoP.

_____ 4. This method of controlling GPO application uses filters written in the WMI Query Language (WQL) to determine whether a particular computer should have a GPO applied to it.

_____ 5. This MMC snap-in can be used in two possible modes to report actual or planned GPO settings for a particular user/computer combination.

_____ 6. This GPMC node is used to report on the actual GPO settings that are applied to a particular user and computer, and replaces Logging mode in RSoP.

_____ 7. This language, similar to Structured Query Language (SQL), is used to create WMI filters to control the application of Group Policy.

_____ 8. This RSoP mode queries existing policies in Active Directory to determine the effective GPO settings that are being applied to a user or computer.

_____ 9. This is used by WMI to retrieve information about computer configuration, including hardware, Group Policy Software Installation Settings, Internet Explorer Maintenance settings, scripts, Folder Redirection settings, and Security settings.

_____ 10. This is a component of the Microsoft Windows operating system that provides management information and control in an enterprise environment.

Multiple Choice

Circle the correct choice.

1. Which Resultant Set of Policy mode queries existing GPOs linked to sites, domains, and OUs to report on currently-applied GPO settings?
  a. Planning mode
  b. Logging mode
  c. Extant mode
  d. Event Viewer mode

2. What provides a common framework that can be used to query servers and workstations for information about specific hardware or software, such as RAM, hard drive space, running services, and installed software?
  a. Common Information Management Object Model (CIMOM)
  b. Resultant Set of Policy (RSoP)
  c. Windows Management Instrumentation (WMI)
  d. Group Policy Objects

3. Which GPMC component provides information analogous to Planning Mode in the Resultant Set of Policy MMC snap-in?
  a. Group Policy Modeling
  b. Group Policy Results
  c. Group Policy Management Editor
  d. Group Policy Object Editor

4. Which tool can be used to obtain effective Group Policy information from the command line?
  a. Gpupdate
  b. Secedit
  c. Netsh
  d. GPresult

5. Which Resultant Set of Policy mode can be used to obtain Group Policy Modeling information?
   a. Logging mode
   b. Planning mode
   c. Event Viewer mode
   d. Design mode

6. Which database contains information used by Windows Management Instrumentation?
   a. Resultant Set of Policy (RSoP)
   b. SYSVOL
   c. Common Information Management Object Model (CIMOM)
   d. Group Policy Container (GPC)

7. What is a GUI-based query engine that looks at a configured GPO in a forest and then reports its findings?
   a. Resultant Set of Policy (RSoP)
   b. Gpresult
   c. Gpupdate
   d. Group Policy Management Editor

8. What language is used to write WMI queries?
   a. SQL
   b. T-SQL
   c. VBScript
   d. WQL

9. Which node within the Group Policy Management Console provides the effective policy settings applied to a particular user/computer combination?
   a. Group Policy Modeling
   b. Group Policy Results
   c. Group Policy Management Editor
   d. Group Policy Object Editor

10. You have a Group Policy Object used to install a particular software application. Because this is a resource-intensive application, you want the software to be installed only on computers that have at least 1GB of RAM. What feature can you use to restrict the application of this GPO to computers that meet this criterion?
    a. Security group filtering
    b. WQL filtering
    c. WMI filtering
    d. CIMOM filtering

■ Case Scenarios

Scenario 10-1: Planning GPOs for Tailspin Toys

Tailspin Toys is running a single Windows Server 2008 Active Directory domain with multiple OUs configured for each of its 12 locations. An administrator at each location is responsible for managing GPOs and user accounts. You are the enterprise administrator responsible for planning the infrastructure. For each of the following challenges, document your options and be prepared to share them with other students.

1. Administrators located at each location should be able to create new GPOs and edit any that they have created. They should not be able to change or delete GPOs that they have not created. What are your options for providing this functionality?

2. All users in each location are currently in one OU. Certain group policies should only apply to users in some departments and not others. What options should you consider that will allow group policies to be applied to only the necessary users?

3. Although you have created a domain-wide policy that enforces restrictions on administrative tools, you do not want those settings to apply to users for which you have delegated administrative permissions on each location's OU. What are your options to solve this?

Active Directory Maintenance, Troubleshooting, and Disaster Recovery

OBJECTIVE DOMAIN MATRIX

TECHNOLOGY SKILL	OBJECTIVE DOMAIN	OBJECTIVE DOMAIN NUMBER
Maintaining Active Directory	Perform offline maintenance.	5.2
Backing Up Active Directory	Configure backup and recovery.	5.1
Using the Reliability and Performance Monitor	Monitor Active Directory.	5.3

KEY TERMS

ADSIEdit
authoritative restore
back-links
bcdedit
Boot Configuration Data (BCD)
boot volume
bootmgr.exe
checkpoint file
copy backup
critical volumes
defragmentation
Directory Services Restore Mode

dsacls
edb.log
Extensible Storage Engine (ESE)
fragmentation
garbage collection
LDP
manual backup
nltest
nonauthoritative restore
offline defragmentation
online defragmentation
performance counters
performance objects

Reliability and Performance Monitor
Repadmin
Restartable Active Directory Domain Services
scheduled backup
system volume
tombstone
transaction buffer
VSS full backup
wbadmin
Windows PowerShell
Windows Server Backup

Lucerne Publishing is a global publishing firm with offices in North America, Europe, and India. Over the past several weeks, the IT staff at Lucerne Publishing has designed and implemented a Windows Server 2008 Active Directory network containing multiple sites, OUs, and GPOs. To maintain the Active Directory network, Lucerne Publishing needs to develop a backup and recovery plan for Active Directory to protect against the loss of a single domain controller, object, or container. Additionally, the IT staff at Lucerne Publishing needs to implement an ongoing monitoring scheme to ensure that the new Active Directory environment remains available for all users, workstations, and member servers.

After completing this lesson, you will be able to monitor, troubleshoot, back up, and restore Active Directory Domain Services in Windows Server 2008. You will be able to discuss the new Windows Server Backup technology, which is used to perform backups and restores of the Active Directory database. You will be able to monitor Active Directory, including monitoring the Windows Event Viewer and using the new Windows Server 2008 Reliability and Performance Monitor tool. Finally, you will use several tools and techniques to troubleshoot the AD DS service, as well as diagnostic tools that determine the cause of an error and resolve the error.

■ Maintaining Active Directory

THE BOTTOM LINE

After successfully implementing a Microsoft Windows Server 2008 environment, it is important to develop maintenance procedures to keep it running smoothly. A solid monitoring and maintenance plan can prevent potential problems.

When maintenance and monitoring procedures are in place to identify possible issues and proactively manage the environment, it is no longer necessary to troubleshoot problems *after* they occur. This lesson presents guidelines for monitoring and maintaining Active Directory. It also describes the tools used to monitor, maintain, and troubleshoot Active Directory. Finally, it offers appropriate methods for backing up, restoring, and defragmenting the Active Directory database.

CERTIFICATION READY?
Perform offline
maintenance
5.2

Active Directory is a database based on the ***Extensible Storage Engine (ESE)*** format. The ESE is responsible for managing changes to the Active Directory database. Changes are referred to as *transactions*. Transactions can contain more than one change, such as the addition of a new object and the modification of an existing object's properties. As requests for the creation or modification of database objects are made, the ESE carries the requests through the following process:

1. Active Directory writes the transaction to a ***transaction buffer*** located in memory on the server. This transaction buffer stores the data in server RAM before it is actually written to the server's hard drive so that all data in the transaction can be written to disk at once.

2. Active Directory writes the transaction to the Transaction log file. The default log file is named ***edb.log.*** The log file allows the transaction to be stored until it can be written to the actual database. A transaction log file has a default size of 10 MB. When the default edb.log file is full, it is renamed to include a sequential number as a suffix, such as edb1.log. When the edb.log file reaches its 10-MB capacity, it is renamed to edbx.log, where x is replaced with the next sequential number.

3. Active Directory writes the transaction from the transaction buffer to the ntds.dit database.

X REF

For more information about ntds.dit, refer to Lesson 1.

4. Active Directory compares the database with the change to the edbx.log file from step 2 to ensure that the transaction written matches the log file transaction.

5. Active Directory updates the edb.chk ***checkpoint file***. The checkpoint file is used as a reference for database information written to disk. In a case where Active Directory needs to be recovered from a failure, the checkpoint file is used as a starting point. It contains references to the point in the log file from which a recovery must take place.

The caching in step 1, in addition to the logging discussed in step 2, allows Active Directory to process multiple additional transactions before writing them to the database. When transactions are written to the database, it is more efficient to write multiple simultaneous transactions stored in the log file than to write each transaction individually.

Like any database, modifications and changes to the Active Directory database can affect database performance and data integrity. As modifications are made to the database, fragmentation can occur. *Fragmentation* refers to the condition of a disk when data from the database is divided into pieces scattered across the disk. As the database becomes more fragmented, searches for database information slow down and performance deteriorates. In addition, the potential exists for database corruption. A process called *defragmentation* is used to rearrange the information, making it easier to find during access requests and searches. *Defragmentation* is the process of taking fragmented database pieces and rearranging them contiguously to make the entire database more efficient. Depending on the method used, the size of the database can be reduced, making room for additional objects. Active Directory has two defragmentation methods: *online defragmentation* and *offline defragmentation*.

- *Online Defragmentation.* Online defragmentation is an automatic process that occurs during the *garbage collection* process. The garbage collection process runs by default every 12 hours on all domain controllers in the forest. When the garbage collection process begins, it removes all tombstones from the database. A *tombstone* is what is left of an object that has been deleted. Deleted objects are not completely removed from the Active Directory database; rather, they are marked for deletion. Tombstone objects have a lifetime of 180 days, by default. When the lifetime expires, the objects are permanently deleted during the garbage collection process. Additional free space is reclaimed during the garbage collection process through the deletion of tombstone objects and unnecessary log files. The advantage of an online defragmentation is that it occurs automatically and does not require the server to be offline to run. An online defragmentation does not reduce the actual size of the Active Directory database.

- *Offline Defragmentation.* Offline defragmentation is a manual process that defragments the Active Directory database in addition to reducing its size. Performing an offline defragmentation is not considered to be a regular maintenance task. You should only perform an offline defragmentation if you need to recover a significant amount of disk space. For example, if your domain controller no longer provides global catalog services in a forest, you might want to recover the disk space that once held the global catalog information. As its name suggests, offline defragmentation requires that the server be taken offline so that the Active Directory database is closed and not in use. An offline defragmentation cannot run while the AD DS service is running. In previous versions of Active Directory, this meant that you needed to restart a domain controller in a special startup mode called *Directory Services Restore Mode (DSRM)* to run an offline defrag. When a domain controller is restarted in DSRM, the Active Directory database is offline and the DC cannot service any client logon requests. In Windows Server 2008, Active Directory can now be started, stopped, and restarted, similar to any other service on a server, in a feature called *Restartable Active Directory Domain Services*. This allows administrators to perform certain operations, such as an offline defragmentation, without rebooting the domain controller in DSRM.

The following tasks should be performed before running an offline defragmentation:
- Back up the volume containing the Active Directory database, thereby backing up the current Active Directory database. Backup is discussed later in this lesson.
- Create a folder to temporarily store the compacted database.
- Verify that you have free space equivalent to the size of the current database, plus at least an additional 15 percent. This ensures that there is enough space for temporary storage during the defragmentation process and space for the newly compacted database.

PERFORM AN OFFLINE DEFRAGMENTATION

GET READY. To perform these steps, you must have the Directory Services Restore Mode password available.

1. Restart your domain controller and press (F8) after the BIOS information is displayed.

2. Select **Directory Services Restore Mode (Windows Server 2008 domain controllers only)** and press (Enter).

3. Select the Windows Server 2008 operating system and press (Enter).

4. Log on to Windows Server 2008 with the local Administrator account. This account is defined in the local computer database, not the Domain Administrator account.

5. From the Start menu, key **cmd** to open a Command Prompt window.

6. Key **ntdsutil** and press (Enter).

7. From the Ntdsutil menu, key **activate instance NTDS** and press (Enter). You will return to the Ntdsutil menu.

8. Key **files** and press (Enter).

9. Key **info** and press (Enter) to view the current location of the Active Directory data files.

10. At the files prompt, key the following command, replacing *drive* and *directory* with the destination path for the compacted database:

    compact to *drive:\directory*

11. Press (Enter) to initiate the creation of a new ntds.dit file in the specified directory.

12. Key **quit** and press (Enter) to exit the Ntdsutil utility. Key **quit** again to return to the Command Prompt window.

13. Copy the new ntds.dit file from the directory you specified in step 9 to the current Active Directory database path, which by default is C:\Windows\Ntds.

PAUSE. Restart your domain controller in normal mode.

You just performed an offline defragmentation of the Active Directory database. Next, we discuss the benefits and procedures for moving the database to a new location.

The decision to move the Active Directory database is usually driven by a need for additional disk space. The working database file system location must be updated in the registry—Ntdsutil does this automatically. If you are low on disk space on the drive where the original Active Directory database is stored, you can move the database to a different drive that has sufficient space. The difference in the outcome between the procedure for compacting the database, as discussed previously, and the procedure for moving the database is that when you move the database you must ensure that the registry keys used to provide the Active Directory database location are updated. If the registry keys that point to the file system location of Active Directory are not updated, Active Directory is not able to start. When the database is compacted, it is compacted to a new location. On completion, it is moved to the working database location. The registry keys pointing to the path in the file system for the working database do not change.

Moving the database and the associated log files requires two separate move procedures. These procedures are discussed next.

TAKE NOTE*

When specifying a path that contains spaces at the command line, enclose the entire path in quotes. For example, if the destination path is D:\New Database, the path that should be keyed at the command line is "D:\New Database."

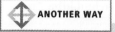

MOVE THE ACTIVE DIRECTORY DATABASE AND LOG FILES

GET READY. To perform these steps, you must have the Directory Services Restore Mode password available.

1. As a precaution, back up the volume containing the Active Directory database. (Backup is discussed later in this lesson.)

2. Click **Start**, click **Administrative Tools**, and then click **Services**. The Services MMC snap-in is displayed.

3. Right-click **Active Directory Domain Services** and click **Stop**. The Stop Other Services window is displayed, indicating that if you stop the Active Directory Domain Services service, you will also stop additional services on the Windows Server 2008 computer.

4. Click **Yes** to stop these additional services.

5. From the Start menu, key **cmd** to open a command prompt window.

6. Key **ntdsutil** and press (Enter).

7. From the Ntdsutil menu, key **activate instance NTDS** and press (Enter). You will return to the Ntdsutil menu.

8. Key **files** and press (Enter).

9. Key **info** and press (Enter) to see the current file information for the Active Directory database and logs.

10. At the files prompt, key the following command, replacing *drive* and *directory* with the destination path where you will move the database:

    move DB to *drive:\directory*

11. Press (Enter) to move the database to the new location.

12. To move the Transaction log files, key the following command at the files prompt:

    move logs to *drive:\directory*

13. Press (Enter) to complete the command. Key **quit** and press (Enter), then key **quit** and press (Enter) a second time to exit the Ntdsutil utility and command line.

14. From the Services MMC snap-in, right-click **Active Directory Domain Services** and click **Start**.

15. Wait a few seconds and then refresh the Services MMC snap-in to confirm that the additional services have restarted successfully.

PAUSE. CLOSE the Services MMC snap-in before continuing.

After the database has been moved, you will need to back up the new volume containing the Active Directory database to ensure that you can restore the database to the correct path if a failure occurs. Backup and restore procedures will be covered in upcoming sections.

Backing Up Active Directory

One of the most essential duties of an administrator is ensuring that data and operating system information is backed up in case of a failure. Procedures that include the frequency of backups in addition to the type of information that needs to be backed up should be planned and implemented in every organization.

Depending on the number of servers in your organization, your plan may vary. For example, if you have only one domain controller in your environment that services logons and stores data, then you must back up this computer frequently in case of a failure. In another scenario that includes one domain controller and several member servers that are storing data and delivering applications, the domain controller's Active Directory database should be backed up frequently, and the data stored on each member server backed up separately. Although backing up data is extremely important, this section covers the procedures necessary to back up Active Directory. Without a backup of Active Directory, if your domain controller fails users will not be able to access shared resources and it will be necessary to rebuild the database manually.

To back up Active Directory, you must install the *Windows Server Backup* feature from the Server Manager console. If you wish to perform backups from the command line, you will also need to install *Windows PowerShell*, which is a new command-line and task-based scripting technology that is included with Windows Server 2008, although in the present release of Windows Server 2008 PowerShell cannot be installed on Server Core. Windows Server Backup supports the use of CD and DVD drives as backup destinations, but does not support magnetic tapes as backup media. Additionally, you cannot perform backups to dynamic volumes.

Windows Server 2008 supports two types of backup:

- *Manual backup.* This backup can be initiated by using Server Backup or the Wbadmin.exe command-line tool when a backup is needed. You must be a member of the Administrators group or the Backup Operators group to launch a manual backup.
- *Scheduled backup.* Members of the local Administrators group can schedule backups using the Windows Server Backup utility or the Wbadmin.exe command-line tool. Scheduled backups will reformat the target drive that hosts the backup files, and thus can only be performed on a local physical drive that does not host any critical volumes.

Windows Server 2008 does not back up or recover System State data in the same way as servers that run Windows Server 2003 or Windows Server 2000. In Windows Server 2008, you must back up *critical volumes* rather than only backing up the System State data. Backing up critical volumes involves backing up the following data:

- The *system volume*, which hosts the boot files, which consist of *bootmgr.exe* (the Windows boot loader) and the *Boot Configuration Data (BCD)* store, which describes boot applications and boot application settings and replaces the boot.ini file in previous versions of Windows.
- The *boot volume*, which hosts the Windows operating system and the Registry.
- The volume that hosts the SYSVOL share.
- The volume that hosts the Active Directory database (Ntds.dit).
- The volume that hosts the Active Directory database log files.

In Windows Server 2008, the system components that make up System State data depend on the roles installed on a particular computer and which volumes host the critical files used by the operating system and its installed roles. At a minimum, the System State consists of the following data, plus any additional data, depending on the server roles that are installed:

- Registry
- COM+ Class Registration database
- Boot files described earlier in this topic
- Active Directory Certificate Services database
- Active Directory Domain Services database
- SYSVOL directory
- Cluster service information
- Microsoft Internet Information Services (IIS) metadirectory
- System files that are under Windows Resource Protection

WARNING The new Windows Server Backup tool does not allow you to back up individual files or directories; you must back up the entire volume that hosts the files that you want to protect. This means that you must configure a backup destination that is at least as large as the volume or volumes that you wish to back up.

TAKE NOTE*

The ntldr file from previous versions of Windows has been replaced by bootmgr.exe and a set of system-specific boot loaders.

➔ PERFORM A MANUAL ACTIVE DIRECTORY BACKUP

GET READY. To perform this backup, you must have a second hard drive volume available that is at least 1MB larger than the critical volumes of the server that you are backing up. These steps assume that you are backing up to a local volume. You must also have the Window Server Backup feature installed on the Windows Server 2008 computer; this can be installed from the Server Manager console if you have not done so already.

1. Log on to the domain controller as the default Administrator or a member of the Backup Operators group. On the Start menu, click **Administrative Tools** and select **Windows Server Backup**. The Windows Server Backup window is displayed.

2. In the right pane, select **Backup Once**. The Backup options window is displayed, as shown in Figure 11-1.

Figure 11-1

Configuring one-time backup options

3. Because you have not configured scheduled backups, the only available option is the Different Options radio button. Click **Next** to continue. The Select backup configuration window is displayed, as shown in Figure 11-2.

Figure 11-2

Specifying the backup type

4. If you are backing up to a local device, select **Custom** and click **Next**. The Select backup items window is displayed, as shown in Figure 11-3.

Figure 11-3

Selecting volumes to be backed up

5. Ensure that the destination volume has been deselected and click **Next**. The Specify destination type window is displayed, as shown in Figure 11-4.

Figure 11-4

Specifying the destination type

6. Select a local drive or a remote shared folder to store this backup and click **Next**. The Select backup destination window is displayed, as shown in Figure 11-5.

Figure 11-5

Selecting the backup destination

> **Backup Once Wizard** ☒
>
> 💿 **Select backup destination**
>
> | | |
> |---|---|
> | Backup options | Select a volume to store the backup. An external disk attached to this computer is listed as a volume. |
> | Specify backup type | |
> | Select backup items | Backup item size: 6.12 GB |
> | Specify destination type | Backup destination: BACKUPS (E:) ▾ |
> | **Select backup destination** | |
> | Specify VSS backup type | Total space in backup destination: 15.98 GB |
> | Confirmation | Free space in backup destination: 11.02 GB |
> | Backup progress | |
>
> [< Previous] [Next >] [Backup] [Cancel]

7. In the Backup destination dropdown box, select the appropriate backup destination and click **Next**. The Specify advanced option window is displayed, as shown in Figure 11-6.

Figure 11-6

Specify advanced option window

> **Backup Once Wizard** ☒
>
> 💿 **Specify VSS backup type**
>
> | | |
> |---|---|
> | Backup options | Choose what type of Volume Shadow Copy Service (VSS) backup you want to create. |
> | Specify backup type | |
> | Select backup items | ⦿ Copy backup (recommended) |
> | Specify destination type | Choose this option if you are using another backup product to back up applications that are on Volumes included in the current backup. This option retains the application log files. |
> | Select backup destination | |
> | **Specify VSS backup type** | ⦾ VSS full backup |
> | Confirmation | Choose this option if you are not using any other backup product to back up your applications. This option updates each file's backup history and clears the application log files. |
> | Backup progress | |
>
> More about backup types and VSS
>
> [< Previous] [Next >] [Backup] [Cancel]

8. Select one of the following backup types and click **Next**. The Confirmation window is displayed, as shown in Figure 11-7.

   a. *Copy backup.* This backup type will retain the Application log files on the local server. Select this backup type if you will be using a third-party backup tool in addition to Windows Server Backup.

   b. *VSS full backup.* This backup type will update each file's backup history and will clear the Application Log files.

Figure 11-7

Confirming backup selections

9. To begin the backup process, click **Backup**. The Backup progress window is displayed, as shown in Figure 11-8.

Figure 11-8

Viewing an in-progress backup

10. When the backup is complete, click **Close**.

PAUSE. LEAVE the Windows Server Backup window open for the next exercise.

You have just configured a one-time backup of the critical volumes on a Windows Server 2008 domain controller. In the next exercise, you will configure a backup schedule to provide regular backup protection for your domain controller.

CONFIGURE SCHEDULED ACTIVE DIRECTORY BACKUPS

GET READY. To perform this exercise you must be logged into the server as a member of the Administrators group. To perform this backup, you must have a second hard drive volume available that is at least 1 MB larger than the critical volumes of the server that you are backing up. These steps assume that you are backing up to a local volume. You must also have the Window Server Backup feature installed on the Windows Server 2008 computer; this can be installed from the Server Manager console if you have not done so already.

1. Log on to the domain controller as the default Administrator or a member of the Backup Operators group. On the Start menu, click **Administrative Tools** and select **Windows Server Backup**. The Windows Server Backup window is displayed.

2. In the right pane, select **Backup Schedule**. The Getting Started window is displayed.

3. Click **Next**. The Specify Backup Type window is displayed.

4. If you are backing up to a local device, select **Custom** and click **Next**. The Select Backup Items window is displayed.

5. Verify that the destination volume has not been selected and click **Next**. The Specify backup time window is displayed, as shown in Figure 11-9.

Figure 11-9

Specifying a backup time

6. Select the time that you want the backups to take place and click **Next**. The Select Destination Disk window is displayed.

7. If your backup destination disk does not appear automatically, click **Show All Available Disks**, place a checkmark next to the destination, and click **OK**.

8. Place a checkmark next to the desired destination disk and click **Next**. A Windows Server Backup warning is displayed, as shown in Figure 11-10.

Figure 11-10

Confirming the backup destination

TAKE NOTE *

Backing up your System State data frequently prevents you from losing changes that occurred after the last backup. It is a good practice to back up System State data after any major configuration changes so that the changes are not lost if a restoration is necessary.

9. Read the warning and click **Yes** to continue. The Label Destination Disk window is displayed.

10. Click **Next** to continue. The Confirmation window is displayed.

11. Click **Finish** to schedule the backup. The destination disk will be formatted automatically. Click **Close** to return to the Windows Server Backup window.

PAUSE. CLOSE the Windows Server Backup MMC snap-in.

You have now configured scheduled backups of a Windows Server 2008 computer. To modify or delete the scheduled job, use the Task Scheduler. To access the Task Scheduler, click All Programs, click Accessories, and then click the System Tools menu. In the next section, we will discuss restoring the Active Directory database.

Restoring Active Directory

Windows Server 2008 offers the ability to restore the Active Directory database.

Depending on your environment and the situation from which you need to recover, several options for restoring the Active Directory database to a domain controller are available. These restoration methods are discussed next.

RESTORING ACTIVE DIRECTORY USING NORMAL REPLICATION

As discussed in Lesson 3, when a domain has multiple domain controllers, the Active Directory database is replicated within each domain controller. This replication ensures availability, accessibility, and fault tolerance.

The Active Directory replication process provides fault tolerance in cases where one of the domain controllers experiences a hardware or software failure. For example, if one of the domain controllers fails and requires a clean installation of the operating system, you can reinstall Active Directory as you normally would through the dcpromo tool. After this is finished, you can allow normal replication to repopulate the domain controller with database information from the other domain controllers.

RESTORING ACTIVE DIRECTORY USING WBADMIN AND NTDSUTIL

Windows Server 2008 allows several different restoration methods, depending on the goals for your restore. You can use *wbadmin*, which is the command-line component of the Windows Server Backup snap-in, to perform a *nonauthoritative restore* of Active Directory, which restores a single Active Directory domain controller to its state before the backup. This method can be used to restore a single domain controller to a point in time when it was considered to be good. If the domain has other domain controllers, the replication process will update the domain controller with the most recent information after the restore is complete.

In addition to the two methods provided by the wbadmin utility, the Ntdsutil command-line utility allows you to perform an authoritative restore. An authoritative restore cannot be performed using any other Windows Server 2008 tool. This method is used with the normal restore to allow certain database information to be marked as authoritative, or most current, so that the replication process will not overwrite this data. This type of restore is helpful in correcting administrative mistakes that have been replicated to all domain controllers in the domain. For example, if an OU that contains multiple users is mistakenly deleted, that deletion replicates to all domain controllers, causing users in that OU to no longer exist. Using an authoritative restore, you can obtain a backup from a date prior to the errant deletion and mark the OU as current. When the OU is restored, it is replicated to the rest of the domain, allowing you to recover the user accounts it originally contained.

WARNING Active Directory cannot be restored from a backup that is older than the tombstone lifetime of 180 days, by default, because Active Directory domain controllers only keep track of deleted objects for the duration of the tombstone's lifetime.

In addition to the ability to assist with performing an authoritative restore, the Ntdsutil tool offers the ability to assist with other Active Directory repairs. The following list includes several of these important options:

- **Ntdsutil's Files menu.** Allows you to move, recover, and compact the Active Directory database.
- **Ntdsutil's semantic database analysis menu.** Allows you to verify and repair the Active Directory database.
- **Ntdsutil's metadata cleanup menu.** Allows you to remove objects, such as domains, naming contexts, and servers, from the Active Directory database.

A nonauthoritative restore will restore Active Directory objects with their original Update Sequence Number (USN), which is the number that each domain controller assigns to every transaction that is either originated on the DC or replicated in from another domain controller. Any other domain controller with a higher USN for a particular object overwrites the object during the replication interval to ensure that all domain controllers have the most recent object information.

To perform a System State restore in Windows Server 2008, you will boot the DC into Directory Services Restore Mode, and then use the wbadmin command-line utility with the following syntax, where the –version switch indicates the date and time of the backup that you wish to recover from:

```
wbadmin start sysstaterecovery -version:MM/DD/YYYY-HH:MM-backuptarget:targetDrive:
-machine:BackupComputerName-quiet
```

PERFORMING AN AUTHORITATIVE RESTORE

If you find yourself in a position where you need to restore an object or container within Active Directory that has been inadvertently deleted, you will need to perform an *authoritative restore*. A normal restore will not be sufficient in this case, because a normal restore will allow post-restore updates to be replicated into the restored DC. This means that a normal restore would simply delete the questionable objects again, because they have been tombstoned on any other DC in your environment. Performing an authoritative restore will mark the object or container as the authoritative source of the objects in question, which will overwrite the tombstones that have been replicated to other DCs and effectively revive the deleted objects. To do an authoritative restore, perform a normal restore using the wbadmin tool and then increment the versionID of the objects in question by an extremely high number (100,000 by default) using the Ntdsutil command-line utility.

To perform an authoritative restore of an object or subtree, you need to know the distinguished name of the object. For example, the user object for jsmith in the Marketing OU of the lucernepublishing.com domain will have a distinguished name of cn=jsmith,ou=marketing, dc=lucernepublishing,dc=com.

The authoritative restore process will also create a file that allows you to restore *back-links* for any object that you have authoritatively restored. A **back-link** is a reference to an attribute within another object that will also need to be restored with the object. For example, if you have authoritatively restored a user object that was a member of five Active Directory groups, a back-link to each of those groups will need to be restored so that the user will be added again to each group appropriately. The authoritative restore process will create an LDIF file containing each back-link that needs to be restored; after the authoritative restore has completed, you will need to use the LDIFDE command-line utility to restore the back-links contained within that file.

PERFORM AN AUTHORITATIVE RESTORE

GET READY. This exercise assumes that you have rebooted your domain controller into Directory Services Restore Mode, and that you have already performed a nonauthoritative restore using wbadmin.

1. Open a command prompt window.
2. Key **ntdsutil** and press (Enter).

3. From the Ntdsutil menu, key **activate instance NTDS** and press (Enter). You will return to the Ntdsutil menu.

4. Still working from the Ntdsutil menu, key **authoritative restore** and press (Enter).

   a. To restore a single object, key **restore object** *<ObjectDN>* and press (Enter).

   b. To restore a container and the objects it contains, key **restore subtree** **<ContainerDN>** and press (Enter). The Authoritative Restore Confirmation Dialog window is displayed.

5. Click **Yes** to perform the authoritative restore. After the authoritative restore has completed, you will see the window shown in Figure 11-11. As you can see, this indicates that a text file was created containing information about each object that was authoritatively restored, as well as listing the name of the LDF file containing any back-link information that needs to be restored.

Figure 11-11

Performing an authoritative restore

6. Key **quit** and press (Enter) twice to return to the command prompt.

7. If back-links need to be restored, restart the domain controller in normal mode. Open a command prompt, key **ldifde –i –f <LDIF file name> -s <FQDN of the local DC>** and press (Enter).

8. Close the command prompt window.

PAUSE. Restart the domain controller in normal mode if you did not do so in step 7.

You just performed an authoritative restore of one or more Active Directory objects. When the restored domain controller is online and connected to the network, normal replication synchronizes the restored domain controller with any changes from the additional domain controllers that were not overwritten by the authoritative restore. Replication also propagates the authoritatively restored objects to other domain controllers in the forest. The deleted objects that were marked as authoritative are replicated from the restored domain controller to the additional domain controllers. Because the restored objects have the same object GUID and object SID, security remains intact, and object dependencies are maintained.

■ Monitoring Active Directory

↓
THE BOTTOM LINE

Monitoring the Active Directory service is an important part of network administration. Monitoring enables you to take a proactive approach to network management. By raising the awareness of possible network problems before they occur, you have better control over their impact.

Creating a monitoring plan can help you flag minor processes or configuration issues before they turn into something potentially catastrophic to your network. For example, monitoring the disk space use on the drive that holds the ntds.dit file and discovering that you are low on available disk space can lead you to resolve this situation before all the free space is used.

Monitoring Active Directory can provide the following benefits:

- Early alerts to potential problems
- Improved system reliability
- Fewer support calls to the helpdesk
- Improved system performance

Several important items must be considered when developing your monitoring plan. In addition, you need to know which tools are available to assist you in monitoring the Active Directory system. The next sections discuss how to collect and locate information related to Active Directory errors and warnings by using Event Viewer and System Monitor.

Understanding Event Logs

Windows Server 2008 uses the Windows Event Viewer to record system events, such as security, application, and directory service events. Events related to Active Directory are recorded in the Directory Service log. The Directory Service log is created when Active Directory is installed. It logs informational events such as service start and stop messages, errors, and warnings. This log should be the first place you look when you suspect a problem with Active Directory.

Figure 11-12 shows the Directory Service log on a Windows Server 2003 computer. Because Event Viewer shows logs for informational and error messages, it is important to monitor the logs for some basic events that can indicate the system's overall health. In the Type field of any of the log files in Event Viewer, you should monitor and filter events that indicate a warning or stop error. A warning is indicated by a yellow triangle with an exclamation mark, and a stop error is indicated by a red circle with an X on it. The event details will provide additional information that pertain to possible reasons for the entry in addition to resources that can provide possible solutions. Error codes reported by the Event Viewer can also be researched in the Microsoft Knowledge Base on the Microsoft Web site.

Figure 11-12

Viewing the Directory Services Event Log

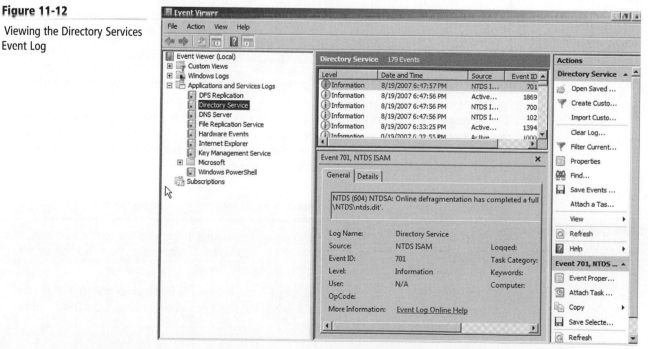

Using the Reliability and Performance Monitor

The *Reliability and Performance Monitor* is a tool located within the Administrative Tools folder. Reliability and Performance Monitor in Windows Server 2008 allows you to collect real-time information on your local computer or from a specific computer to which you have permissions. This information can be viewed in a number of different formats that include charts, graphs, and histograms. The reports can be saved or printed for documentation purposes. You can also customize the parameters that you want to track and store them in an MMC snap-in so that they can be used on other computers within your network.

CERTIFICATION READY?
Monitor Active
Directory
5.3

Before you can effectively use the Reliability and Performance Monitor shown in Figure 11-13, you need to understand how to configure it so that you can obtain the desired information. The Reliability and Performance Monitor uses categories to organize the items that can be monitored. These categories are referred to as *performance objects*. Performance objects contain *performance counters* associated with the category that you want to monitor. Performance counters are the specific processes or events that you want to track. For example, within the NTDS performance object, the Directory Replication (DRA) Inbound Bytes Compressed counter will monitor the size of compressed data that was replicated from other sites.

Figure 11-13

Viewing the Reliability and Performance Monitor

The DirectoryServices performance object contains over 120 performance counters that pertain to Active Directory. It is important for you to determine which of these counters suit your purposes. Table 11-1 provides a breakdown of some representative counters that you should consider adding to your basic monitoring plan.

Table 11-1

Representative NTDS Performance Object Counters

COUNTER	DESCRIPTION
DRA Inbound Bytes Compressed (Between Sites, After Compression)/Sec	The compressed size, in bytes, of inbound compressed replication data. This is the size, after compression, from Directory System Agents [DSAs] in other sites.
DRA Inbound Bytes Compressed (Between Sites, Before Compression)/Sec	The original size, in bytes, of inbound compressed replication data. This is the size, before compression, from DSAs in other sites.

DRA Inbound Bytes Not Compressed (Within Site)/Sec	The number of bytes received through inbound replication that were not compressed at the source from other DSAs in the same site.
DRA Inbound Bytes Total/Sec	The total number of bytes received through replication per second. It is the sum of the number of uncompressed bytes and the number of compressed bytes.
DRA Inbound Full Sync Objects Remaining	The number of objects remaining until the full synchronization process is completed or set.
DRA Inbound Objects/Sec	The number of objects received, per second, from replication partners through inbound replication.
DRA Inbound Objects Applied/ Sec	The rate per second at which replication updates are received from replication partners and applied by the local directory service. This count excludes changes that are received but not applied, such as when the change is already present. This indicates how much replication update activity is occurring on the server due to changes generated on other servers.
DRA Inbound Object Updates Remaining in Packet	The number of object updates received in the current directory replication update packet that have not been applied to the local server. This tells you when the monitored server is receiving changes and taking a long time applying them to the database.
DRA Outbound Bytes Compressed (Between Sites, After Compression)/Sec	The compressed size, in bytes, of outbound compressed replication data, after compression, from DSAs in other sites.
DRA Outbound Bytes Compressed (Between Sites, Before Compression)/Sec	The original size, in bytes, of outbound compressed replication data, before compression, from DSAs in other sites.
DRA Outbound Bytes Not Compressed (Within Site)/Sec	The number of bytes replicated that were not compressed from DSAs in the same site.
DRA Outbound Bytes Total/Sec	The total number of bytes replicated per second. This is the sum of the number of uncompressed bytes and the number of compressed bytes.
DRA Pending Replication Synchronizations	The number of directory synchronizations that are queued for this server but not yet processed. This helps in determining replication backlog. A larger number indicates a larger backlog.
DRA Sync Requests Made	The number of synchronization requests made to replication partners.
DS Directory Reads/Sec	The number of directory reads per second.
DS Directory Writes/Sec	The number of directory writes per second.
DS Search Suboperations/Sec	Number of search suboperations per second. One search operation is made up of many suboperations. A suboperation corresponds roughly to an object the search causes the DS to consider.
LDAP Client Sessions	The number of connected LDAP client sessions.
LDAP Searches/Sec	The number of search operations per second performed by LDAP clients.
NTLM Binds/Sec	The number of Windows NT LAN Manager (NTLM) authentications per second serviced by this domain controller.

After you have determined the counters you want to monitor, you must add them to the Reliability and Performance Monitor console. To add performance counters and display options to your System Monitor console, complete the following exercise.

→ **USE THE RELIABILITY AND PERFORMANCE MONITOR**

GET READY To perform these steps, log on to your domain controller using an account with administrative credentials.

1. Click **Start**, click **Administrative Tools**, and then click **Reliability and Performance Monitor**. Drill down to **Monitoring Tools** and click **Performance Monitor**.

2. From the Performance Monitoring console, click the green plus sign (+) on the menu bar. The Add Counters dialog box opens.

3. In the Add Counters dialog box, select the computer from which you want to obtain data. If you select Use Local Computer Counters, data is collected from the local computer. If you choose Select Counters From Computer, you can use an IP address or the Universal Naming Convention (UNC) name of the computer from which you want to collect data, like \\server1.adatum.com. Figure 11-14 shows the Add Counters dialog box with the DirectoryServices object selected, showing the various counters you can add.

Figure 11-14

Adding a performance counter

4. In the Performance Object list, select the performance object you want to monitor. For example, to monitor Active Directory, select the Directory Services collection.

5. Select the counters you want to monitor. If you want to monitor all counters, select the **All Instances** button from the Instances of Select Object dialog. If you want to monitor only particular counters, select the appropriate instance; you can select multiple counters by holding the (CTRL) key and clicking on the counters. (For most Directory Services counters, the only instance available will be the NTDS instance.)

6. Click the **Add** button.

7. When you are finished adding counters, click **OK**. The chosen counters are displayed in the lower part of the Reliability and Performance Monitor. Each counter is represented by a different color.

8. On the toolbar, you can change the display output to reflect graph, histogram, or report display by choosing the appropriate tool. It is easiest to use a graph format if you are monitoring performance over extended periods of time. Reports and histograms only reflect the most recent values and averages and might not reflect the information you need for long-term reporting.

PAUSE. LEAVE the Reliability and Performance Monitor open for the next exercise.

You just configured monitoring of Active Directory performance thresholds using the Reliability and Performance Monitor.

■ Diagnosing and Troubleshooting Active Directory

▼
THE BOTTOM LINE

After you collect information through your monitoring process, you must understand the tools and techniques used to further investigate a potential problem. For example, the logs available in Event Viewer only record critical events and errors in the Directory Service log. In some cases, by the time the error is recorded, the problem may be serious. To assist you with obtaining more detailed information in the event logs, you can set the event logs to record diagnostic information specific to processes related to Active Directory.

Configuring Active Directory diagnostic event logging requires that you edit the registry. The following key contains the additional areas that can be logged into the Directory Service log:

    HKEY_LOCAL_MACHINE\SYSTEM\CurrentControlSet\Services\NTDS\Diagnostics

Numerous values are present within the Diagnostics key. Values can be modified to increase or decrease the amount of data that is logged for each event type shown in Figure 11-15.

Figure 11-15

Configuring diagnostics logging levels

Registry Editor		
File Edit View Favorites Help		
Name	**Type**	**Data**
(Default)	REG_SZ	(value not set)
1 Knowledge Consistency Checker	REG_DWORD	0x00000000 (0)
10 Performance Counters	REG_DWORD	0x00000000 (0)
11 Initialization/Termination	REG_DWORD	0x00000000 (0)
12 Service Control	REG_DWORD	0x00000000 (0)
13 Name Resolution	REG_DWORD	0x00000000 (0)
14 Backup	REG_DWORD	0x00000000 (0)
15 Field Engineering	REG_DWORD	0x00000000 (0)
16 LDAP Interface Events	REG_DWORD	0x00000000 (0)
17 Setup	REG_DWORD	0x00000000 (0)
18 Global Catalog	REG_DWORD	0x00000000 (0)
19 Inter-site Messaging	REG_DWORD	0x00000000 (0)
2 Security Events	REG_DWORD	0x00000000 (0)
20 Group Caching	REG_DWORD	0x00000000 (0)
21 Linked-Value Replication	REG_DWORD	0x00000000 (0)
22 DS RPC Client	REG_DWORD	0x00000000 (0)
23 DS RPC Server	REG_DWORD	0x00000000 (0)
24 DS Schema	REG_DWORD	0x00000000 (0)
3 ExDS Interface Events	REG_DWORD	0x00000000 (0)
4 MAPI Interface Events	REG_DWORD	0x00000000 (0)
5 Replication Events	REG_DWORD	0x00000000 (0)
6 Garbage Collection	REG_DWORD	0x00000000 (0)
7 Internal Configuration	REG_DWORD	0x00000000 (0)
8 Directory Access	REG_DWORD	0x00000000 (0)
9 Internal Processing	REG_DWORD	0x00000000 (0)

Computer\HKEY_LOCAL_MACHINE\SYSTEM\CurrentControlSet\Services\NTDS\Diagnostics

To increase the level of logging for any event category, double-click a key and modify its value to one of the following:

- **0 (None).** Only critical events and error events are logged at this level. This is the default setting for all entries, and it should be modified only if a problem occurs that you want to investigate.
- **1 (Minimal).** Very high-level events are recorded in the event log at this setting. Events may include one message for each major task that is performed by the service. Use this setting to start an investigation when you do not know the location of the problem.
- **2 (Basic).** This level records slightly more detailed information than the lowest level. Use this setting if Minimal logging is not producing sufficient error messages to allow you to troubleshoot a particular issue.

- **3 (Extensive).** This level records more detailed information than the lower levels, such as steps that are performed to complete a task. Use this setting when you have narrowed the problem to a service or a group of categories.

- **4 (Verbose).** Verbose logging records significantly more detail than the four previous levels. Use this setting when you have narrowed the problem to a specific service, but still need more information to determine the exact cause of the problem.

- **5 (Internal).** This level logs all events, including debug strings and configuration changes. A complete log of the service is recorded. Use this setting when you have traced the problem to a particular category of a small set of categories.

TAKE NOTE★

Each event category is set to a value of 0 (None) by default.

If you decide to configure any of these additional processes for logging in Event Viewer, then consider increasing the size of the log files. Additional entries may cause your logs to fill up faster than you originally anticipated, and therefore you need to make adjustments so that data is not overwritten when the log is full. Also, increasing monitoring can impact performance. You should monitor only those items that you suspect might be causing problems.

In addition to monitoring the Event Viewer and the Reliability and Performance Monitor, many of the tools previously mentioned are helpful in diagnosing and troubleshooting problems related to Active Directory. Table 11- 2 lists these tools and describes how they can assist in diagnosing problems in Active Directory.

Table 11-2

Active Directory Diagnostic Tools

Tool	Description
Dcdiag	This command-line tool can analyze the state of the domain controllers in the forest or enterprise and report any problems to assist in troubleshooting.
Repadmin	This command-line tool can check replication consistency between replication partners, monitor replication status, display replication metadata, and force replication events and knowledge consistency checker (KCC) recalculation.
Netdom	This command-line tool can manage and verify trusts, join computers to domains, and verify replication ability and permissions between partners.
ADSIEdit	This graphical tool is an MMC snap-in that can be used to verify the current functional level and perform low-level Active Directory editing. Use this tool to add, delete, and edit Active Directory objects.
LDP	This graphical support tool provides a much more detailed method of adding, removing, searching, and modifying the Active Directory database.
Nltest	This command-line tool is typically used to verify trusts and check replication.
Dsacls	This command-line tool can be used to display or modify permissions of an Active Directory object. In effect, it is equivalent to an object's Security tab.

SUMMARY SKILL MATRIX

IN THIS LESSON YOU LEARNED:

- Active Directory has two defragmentation methods: online defragmentation and offline defragmentation. Online defragmentation is an automatic process triggered by the garbage collection process. Offline defragmentation is a manual process that requires the server to be restarted in Directory Services Restore mode. The Ntdsutil command-line utility is used to perform the offline defragmentation.

- The Active Directory database can be moved to a new location if you decide that there is a need to relocate it due to space limitations. This is accomplished with the Ntdsutil command-line utility.

- When you back up Active Directory, you must include the System State data. The System State data includes operating system-specific information needed for installed services and operating system components to function.

- In the event of a domain controller failure, two restore options are available in Windows Server 2008: nonauthoritative and authoritative. The nonauthoritative restore method restores the Active Directory database to its state before the backup. After a normal restore, replication of more recent object information from other domain controllers is used to update the database to match all other domain controllers. An authoritative restore uses the Ntdsutil command-line utility and allows you to mark records that supersede any existing records during replication.

- Active Directory cannot be restored from a backup that is older than the default tombstone lifetime of 180 days. Domain controllers keep track of deleted objects only for the duration of the tombstone lifetime.

- When monitoring the health of Active Directory, you can examine the Directory Service log to obtain information. The Directory Service log is created when Active Directory is installed. By default, It logs informational events, such as service start and stop messages, errors, and warnings. Additional diagnostic logging can be achieved by modifying the registry.

- Reliability and Performance Monitor in Windows Server 2008 allows you to collect real-time information on your local computer or from a specific computer to which you have permissions. This information can be viewed in a number of different formats that include charts, graphs, and histograms.

- Reliability and Performance Monitor uses performance objects, or categories, and performance counters to organize performance information. Performance counters are the specific processes to monitor. Many counters are available.

Knowledge Assessment

Matching

a.	authoritative restore	f.	LDP
b.	checkpoint file	g.	system volume
c.	Directory Services Restore Mode	h.	tombstone
d.	fragmentation	i.	transaction buffer
e.	garbage collection	j.	Windows PowerShell

_____ 1. This object is created when an object is deleted within Active Directory.

_____ 2. Active Directory changes are written here before they are committed to disk.

_____ 3. This is a new advanced command-line and scripting interface included in Windows Server 2008.

_____ 4. This volume houses the boot files for a Windows Server 2008 computer.

_____ 5. This describes the process of removing trombstoned objects from the NTDS.DIT file.

_____ 6. You will need to perform this operation if you have inadvertently deleted one or more Active Directory objects.

_____ 7. This is a graphical user interface that will allow you to query Active Directory as part of the troubleshooting process.

_____ 8. This is used as a reference file in case the Active Directory database needs to be recovered from a system failure to ensure that no transactions are lost.

_____ 9. To perform many Active Directory maintenance operations, you will need to restart your domain controller in this startup mode.

_____ 10. This can decrease database performance because updates are made to the Active Directory over time.

Multiple Choice

Circle the correct choice.

1. Which of the following backup types can be initiated by a member of the local Administrators group or a member of the local Backup Operators group on a Windows Server 2008 computer?
   a. Manual backup
   b. Scheduled backup
   c. Full backup
   d. Differential backup

2. The NTDS.DIT file is based on which database technology?
   a. Structured Query Language (SQL)
   b. Oracle
   c. Extensible Storage Engine (ESE)
   d. My*SQL

3. Which of the following commands can be used to configure Active Directory permissions from the command line?
   a. LDP
   b. Dsacls
   c. Dcdiag
   d. ADSI Edit

4. What runs automatically on a domain controller every 12 hours by default during the garbage collection process?
   a. Offline defragmentation
   b. Authoritative restore
   c. Nonauthoritative restore
   d. Online defragmentation

5. Which tool can you use to force a domain controller to start in Directory Services Restore Mode on its next reboot?
   a. cmd.exe
   b. bootmgr.exe
   c. bcdedit.exe
   d. dcpromo.exe

6. Which operation requires the Active Directory Domain Service to be taken offline?
   a. Offline defragmentation
   b. Online defragmentation
   c. Garbage Collection
   d. Transaction Buffering

7. Which of the following backup types can be initiated only by a member of the local Administrators group on a Windows Server 2008 computer?
   a. Manual backup
   b. Scheduled backup

    c. Full backup

    d. Differential backup

8. Which backup type will empty the Application log on the server that is being backed up?

    a. Copy backup

    b. Differential backup

    c. Normal backup

    d. VSS full backup

9. Which of the following volumes hosts the Windows operating system?

    a. Boot volume

    b. Shared volume

    c. System volume

    d. Host volume

10. When performing an authoritative restore of a user object that belongs to multiple Active Directory groups, what is restored by the LDF file that is generated by Ntdsutil?

    a. Optional attributes

    b. Mandatory attributes

    c. Back-links

    d. Security Identifier (SID)

■ Case Scenarios

Scenario 11-1: Consulting for Margie's Travel

You are a computer consultant for Margie Shoop, the owner of Margie's Travel. Margie has a single Active Directory domain structure with the domain margiestravel.com. Margie has travel agencies worldwide, at 50 locations in 7 countries. All locations are connected to a satellite array. Margie has signed a 10-year contract to provide satellite access to her 50 locations. Connectivity to the satellite array varies from 57 Kbps to 128 Kbps. Although her locations vary greatly in the number of computer and user accounts, each location with more than 15 users has its own domain controller, global catalog server, and DNS server, all typically configured on the same computer. The margiestravel.com Active Directory infrastructure has nine sites. Given this information about Margie's Travel, answer the following questions:

1. You discuss performance monitoring with Margie. During your conversation, you learn no one has ever used Replication and Performance Monitor to check the performance of her domain controllers. Margie wants to know why anyone would even bother. What do you say to her?

2. Margie tells you that some of her domain controllers have multiple hard disks. She tells you that the additional physical hard disks are not being used. She wants to know if they can be used to improve the performance of Active Directory. What would you tell her?

3. Margie sends you to Cairo, Egypt, to troubleshoot a few domain controllers in her Egypt location. You find some event messages concerning replication events, but you would like to see more detailed information than the data in the log now. What can you do?

Appendix A
Microsoft Windows Server 2008 Active Directory Configuration: Exam 70-640

Matrix Skill	Skill Number	Lesson Number
Configure zones.	1.1	12
Configure DNS server settings.	1.2	12
Configure zone transfers and replication.	1.3	12
Configure a forest or a domain.	2.1	2
Configure trusts.	2.2	2
Configure sites.	2.3	3
Configure Active Directory replication.	2.4	3
Configure the global catalog.	2.5	4
Configure operations masters.	2.6	4
Configure Active Directory Lightweight Directory Service (AD LDS).	3.1	2
Configure Active Directory Rights Management Service (AD RMS).	3.2	12
Configure the read-only domain controller (RODC).	3.3	2
Configure Active Directory Federation Services (AD FS).	3.4	12
Automate creation of Active Directory accounts.	4.1	5
Maintain Active Directory accounts.	4.2	5, 6
Create and apply Group Policy objects (GPOs).	4.3	7
Configure GPO templates.	4.4	7, 10
Configure software deployment GPOs.	4.5	9
Configure account policies.	4.6	8
Configure audit policy by using GPOs.	4.7	8
Configure backup and recovery.	5.1	11
Perform offline maintenance.	5.2	11
Monitor Active Directory.	5.3	11
Install Active Directory Certificate Services.	6.1	13
Configure CA server settings.	6.2	13
Manage certificate templates.	6.3	13
Manage enrollments.	6.4	13
Manage certificate revocations.	6.5	13

■ Getting Started

The *Windows Server 2008 Active Directory Configuration* title of the Microsoft Official Academic Course (MOAC) series includes two books: a textbook and a lab manual. The exercises in the lab manual are designed for classroom use under the supervision of an instructor or a lab aide. In an academic setting, the computer classroom might be used by a variety of classes each day, so you must plan your setup procedure accordingly. For example, consider automating the classroom setup procedure and using removable fixed disks in the classroom. Use the automated setup procedure to rapidly configure the classroom environment and remove the fixed disks after teaching this class each day.

■ Classroom Setup

This course should be taught in a classroom containing networked computers where students can develop their skills through hands-on experience with Microsoft Windows Server 2008. The exercises in the lab manual require the computers to be installed and configured in a specific manner. Failure to adhere to the setup instructions in this document can produce unanticipated results when the students perform the exercises.

TAKE NOTE＊

You can either use multiple physical machines for each student or you can install the server and client as virtual machines on a single physical machine using Microsoft Virtual PC. If you use Virtual PC, your physical machine must comply with the minimum requirements for Windows Server 2008. Virtual PC also requires 1.6GHz processor speed or faster and 640MB RAM (1GB recommended) over and above the RAM required by the hosting operating system.

Windows Server 2008 Requirements

The computers running Windows Server 2003 require the following hardware and software.

HARDWARE REQUIREMENTS

All hardware must be on the Microsoft Windows Server 2008 Windows Catalog.
- One 1Ghz processor (2Ghz or greater recommended)
- 512MB RAM (2GB or greater recommended)
- 10GB hard disk minimum (40GB or greater recommended)
- One DVD-ROM drive
- One mouse
- One Super VGA display adapter and monitor
- One Ethernet network interface adapter

SOFTWARE REQUIREMENTS

The software listed below is required for the course.

- Microsoft Windows Server 2008 (evaluation edition available as a free download from Microsoft's Web site at http://technet.microsoft.com/)

Classroom Configuration and Network Considerations

Each student's server is configured as a Windows Server 2008 stand-alone server in a workgroup configuration. The instructor's computer is configured as a Windows Server 2008 domain controller for the purposes of the first Lab exercise, using the following configuration:

- Active Directory domain name: lucernepublishing.com
- Computer name: INSTRUCTOR01
- Fully qualified domain name (FQDN): instructor01.lucernepublishing.com

For several optional exercises, each student will require two additional server computers, one running Server Core and one full installation of Windows Server 2008 to function as a Read-Only Domain Controller.

In Lab 11, performing exercises using Windows Server Backup will require each computer to be configured with a secondary hard drive that is of equal or greater in capacity to the system drive configured on each machine.

Installing Windows Server 2008

If your computer has an existing 32-bit operating system installed, start the computer as usual and insert the Windows Server 2008 Installation disk. The Microsoft Windows 2008 window opens automatically. In the left pane of the window, select Install Windows Server 2008. If the Microsoft Windows 2008 window does not open automatically, double-click the CD-ROM drive in Windows Explorer to launch the auto-play feature.

If your computer does not have an operating system installed, you will need to boot your computer from the Windows Server 2008 Installation disk. When you boot from the disk, the Windows Server 2008 Setup program starts automatically.

After Windows Server 2008 Setup is launched, follow the steps below to continue the installation.

⊘ **INSTALLING WINDOWS SERVER 2008**

1. Insert a bootable Windows Server 2008 CD and power on the physical or virtual server.
2. You will see the initial installation screen. Here you are prompted to configure the following three items:
   - Language to install: for example, English or German
   - Time and currency format: for example, English (United States) or French (Switzerland)
   - Keyboard/input layout: for example, US or United Kingdom
3. Click **Next**, followed by **Install Now**.
4. Next you will be prompted to enter the Windows product key. Enter a legitimate windows product key and click **Next**.

TAKE NOTE *

Depending on how your school's network is set up, you might need to use different values for settings, such as IP addresses, to match your actual networking environment.

5. Next you will be prompted to install either the full version of Windows Server 2008 or Server Core. Select a full install or a Server Core install as appropriate for the particular image that you are building. Click **Next** to continue.

6. On the following screen, you will be prompted to accept the Windows Server 2008 license terms. Read the licensing terms and then place a checkmark next to *I accept the license terms*. Click **Next** to continue the installation.

7. You will be prompted to select an upgrade installation or a clean install. If you are installing Windows onto brand-new hardware, you will notice that the Upgrade option is grayed out and only the Custom option is available. Select the **Custom** installation option.

8. On the following screen, you will be prompted to select the hard drive partition on which to install Windows. Select the appropriate partition and click **Next**. At this point the installation process will begin. The remainder of the installation is largely automated. To improve the security of a Windows Server 2008 installation, you will be prompted to establish a complex password on the final reboot.

> **TAKE NOTE***
>
> After Windows Server 2008 Setup restarts, the computer might try to boot from the Windows Server 2008 disk. If this happens, you should be prompted to press a key to boot from the disk. However, if Setup restarts automatically, simply remove the disk, and then restart the computer.

In the previous exercise, you performed the initial installation of the Windows Server 2008 operating system on a newly formatted computer. In the following section, you will install the Virtual Machine Additions onto the Virtual PC instance in question. (If you are using separate physical machines rather than VM instances, you can skip this section.)

COMPLETE POST-INSTALLATION TASKS ON THE SERVER

1. After the installation is complete and the computer has restarted, you should see the Welcome To Windows dialog box. Press **Ctrl+Alt+Delete** and enter the username and password you specified earlier to log on (*Administrator/MSPress#1*). The Initial Configuration Tasks dialog box is displayed. Leave this page displayed, because students will use this interface during the first lab exercise.

2. If you are using Virtual PC, install Virtual Machine Additions. To do so, select **Install Or Update Virtual Machine Additions** from the Actions menu, and then follow the prompts. After the installation, you will be prompted to restart Windows Server 2008. After restarting, repeat step 1 of this section to log on.

> **TAKE NOTE***
>
> At some point the operating system will prompt you to activate the server. When that happens, follow the steps to activate the server.

In the previous exercise, you installed the Virtual Machine Additions onto one or more Virtual PC or Microsoft Virtual Server instances of the Windows Server 2008 operating system.

Installing Active Directory on the Instructor's Computer

> In the following exercise, you will install and configure the Active Directory Domain Services role on the instructor computer, for use as part of early lab exercises in the manual.

INSTALL ACTIVE DIRECTORY ON THE INSTRUCTOR'S COMPUTER

1. Press **Ctrl+Alt+Delete** on the instructor's computer and log on as the default administrator of the local computer. Your username will be *Administrator*. The password will be *MSPress#1* or the password that you configured when the server was built. The Server Manager screen will be displayed automatically.

2. Expand the Server Manager window to full screen if necessary.

3. In the left pane of Server Manager, double-click **Roles**.

4. Click **Add Role**. Click **Next** to bypass the initial Welcome screen. The Select Server Roles screen is displayed.

5. Place a checkmark next to *Active Directory Domain Services*. Click **Next**. The Active Directory Domain Services screen is displayed.

6. Read the introductory information to Active Directory Domain Services and click **Next**. The Confirm Installation Selections screen is displayed.

7. Read the confirmation information to prepare for the installation. Click **Install** to install the AD Domain Services role. The Installation Results screen is displayed.

8. Click **Close this wizard and launch the Active Directory Domain Services Installation Wizard (dcpromo.exe)**. The Welcome to the Active Directory Domain Services Installation Wizard screen is displayed.

9. Click **Next**. The Choose a Deployment Configuration screen is displayed.

10. Click the **Create a new domain in a new forest** radio button. The Name the Forest Root domain screen is displayed.

11. Key **lucernepublishing.com** as the name of the new domain and click **Next**. The Set Forest Functional Level screen is displayed.

12. Select **Windows Server 2008** and click **Next**. The Additional Domain Controller Options screen is displayed.

13. Verify that the DNS Server checkbox is selected, and then click **Next**. A warning message is displayed concerning DNS delegations. Read the warning message and click **Yes** to continue. The Location for Database, Log Files, and SYSVOL screen is displayed.

14. Accept the default selections and click **Next** to continue. The Directory Services Restore Mode Administrator Password screen is displayed.

15. Enter **MSPress#1** into the Password and Confirm Password text boxes and click **Next** to continue. The Summary screen is displayed.

16. Review your installation choices and click **Next** to continue. The Active Directory Domain Services Installation Wizard screen is displayed, indicating that the Active Directory DS service is being installed. The Completing the Active Directory Domain Services Installation Wizard is displayed.

17. Click **Finish**. When prompted, click **Restart now** to restart the newly configured domain controller.

18. When the domain controller reboots, log onto the instructor's computer as the default administrator of lucernepublishing.com.

In the previous exercise, you configured the instructor's computer as a domain controller in the lucernepublishing.com domain. In the following section, you will configure a DHCP server to allow the lab computers to obtain IP addresses automatically. If your lab network uses DHCP through another mechanism; that is, a hardware-based router, you can skip this section.

INSTALL AND CONFIGURE THE DHCP SERVER

1. Press **Ctrl+Alt+Delete** on the instructor's computer and log on as the default administrator of the local computer. Your username will be *Administrator*. The password will be *MSPress#1* or the password that you configured when the server was built. The Server Manager screen will be displayed automatically.

2. Expand the Server Manager window to full screen if necessary.

3. In the left pane of Server Manager, double-click **Roles**.

4. Click **Add Role**. Click **Next** to bypass the initial Welcome screen. The Select Server Roles screen is displayed.

5. Place a checkmark next to *DHCP Server*. Click **Next**. The Introduction to DHCP Server screen is displayed.

6. Read the information about the DHCP Server role and click **Next**. The Specify IPv4 DNS Server Settings screen is displayed.

7. Leave all text boxes blank and click **Next**. The Specify IPv4 WINS Server Settings screen is displayed.

8. Leave the default radio button selected and click **Next**. The Add or Edit DHCP Scopes screen is displayed.

9. Click **Add** to create a DHCP scope for your network. The Add Scope screen is displayed.

10. Enter the following information, customized as appropriate for your classroom setup:

    - Name: 70-640 Lab
    - Starting IP address: 192.168.1.100
    - Ending IP address: 192.168.1.254
    - Subnet mask: 255.255.255.0
    - Default gateway: 192.168.1.1
    - Subnet type: Wired

11. Verify that there is a checkmark next to *Activate this scope*, and then click **OK**.

12. Click **Next**. The Configure DHCPv6 Classless Mode screen is displayed.

13. Leave the default radio button selected and click **Next**. The Specify IPv6 DNS Server Settings screen is displayed.

14. Leave all text boxes blank and click **Next**. The Authorize DHCP Server screen is displayed.

15. Leave the default radio button selected and click **Next**. The Confirm Installation Selections screen is displayed.

16. Click **Install**. When the installation is completed, click **Close**.

You have now completed all the necessary steps to complete the setup of the instructor's computer and all the student computers to use the *Windows Server 2008 Active Directory Configuration* Lab Manual. This includes installing Windows Server 2008 on all student computers, as well as configuring the instructor's computer as a DHCP server and as a domain controller in the lucernepublishing.com domain.

Glossary

298

A

A record The building block of the DNS that maps a single IP address to a DNS hostname.

access token Created when a user logs on, this value identifies the user and all of the user's group memberships. Like a club membership card, it verifies a user's permissions when the user attempts to access a local or network resource.

Account Lockout Policies A subcategory in the Account Policies category that specifies the number of unsuccessful logon attempts that, if made within a contiguous timeframe, might constitute a potential security threat from an intruder. An Account Lockout Policy can be set to lock the account in question after a specified number of invalid attempts. Additionally, the policy specifies how long the account will remain locked.

account logon events Setting that logs events related to successful user logons to a domain.

account management events Setting that triggers an event that is written based on changes to account properties and group properties. Log entries written due to this policy setting reflect events related to user or group account creation, deletion, renaming, enabling, or disabling.

account organizations The organizations that contain the user accounts accessing the resources controlled by resource organizations, similar to a trusted domain in a traditional Windows trust relationship.

Active Directory Certificate Services (AD CS) A server role available in Windows Server 2008 that enables administrators to create and administer PKI certificates for users, computers, and applications.

Active Directory Domain Services (AD DS) Windows Server 2008 service that provides a centralized authentication service for Microsoft networks. Provides the full-fledged directory service that is called Active Directory in Windows Server 2008 and previous versions of Windows Server.

Active Directory Federation Services (AD FS) Role that enables administrators to configure Single Sign-On (SSO) for Web-based applications across multiple organizations without requiring users to remember multiple usernames and passwords.

Active Directory Lightweight Directory Services (AD LDS) Role that provides developers the ability to store data for directory-enabled applications without incurring the overhead of extending the Active Directory schema to support their applications. This feature was introduced in Windows Server 2008.

Active Directory Migration Tool (ADMT) A free tool used to move objects between domains.

Active Directory Rights Management Service (AD RMS) A Windows Server 2008 service that administrators can use to protect sensitive data on a Windows network. In particular, it enables owners of data stored within RMS–capable applications (such as word processing or spreadsheet applications) to control who can open, modify, or print a document, and even who can print or forward confidential email messages.

AD FS Federation Service Service that enables administrators to route authentication requests from user accounts in one organization to Web-based application resources in another.

AD FS Federation Services Proxy Service that creates a proxy to the Federation Service that can be deployed in a perimeter network or demilitarized zone (DMZ).

AD–integrated zone Zone in which the DNS data is stored within the Active Directory database.

Admin Role Separation Feature offered by Read-Only Domain Controllers (RODCs) that enables an administrator to configure a user as the local administrator of a specific RODC without making the user a Domain Admins with far-reaching authority over all domain controllers in the entire domain and full access to the Active Directory domain data.

Administrative Templates Files used to generate the user interface for the Group Policy settings that can be set using the Group Policy Management Editor.

ADMX Windows Server 2008 Administrative Templates using the .admx extension.

ADSIEdit An MMC snap-in that is a graphical tool used to verify the current functional level and perform low-level Active Directory editing. This tool can be used to add, delete, and edit Active Directory objects.

aging The dynamic update feature that places a timestamp on record, based on the current server time, when the IP address is added. This is part of the aging and scavenging process.

Alias Canonical Name (CNAME) A resource record, sometimes called an Alias record, that is used to specify an alias, or alternative name, for the system specified in the Name field.

Anonymous Logon Special identity that refers to users who have not supplied a username and password.

application partition A partition that allows information to be replicated to administratively chosen domain controllers. An example of information that is commonly stored in an application partition is DNS data. Application partitions offer control over the scope and placement of information that is to be replicated.

Assign An option used to deploy required applications to pertinent users and computers.

asynchronous processing A method of processing multiple scripts at the same time, without waiting for the outcome of a previously launched script to occur.

asynchronous replication Each replication transaction does not need to complete before another can start because the transaction can be stored until the destination server is available.

attribute Characteristics associated with an object class in Active Directory that make the object class unique within the database. The list of attributes is defined only once in the schema, but the same attribute can be associated with more than one object class.

Audit Policy The section of GPO Local Policies that enables administrators to log successful and failed security events, such as logon events, account access, and object access.

auditing Tracking events that take place on the local computer.

authenticate To gain access to the network, prospective network users must identify themselves to a network using specific user accounts.

authentication The process of confirming a user's identity using a known value, such as a password, a pin number on a smart card, or, in the case of biometric authentication, the user's fingerprint or handprint.

authoritative restore A restore operation that marks the object or container as the authoritative source of the objects in question, which will overwrite the tombstones that have been replicated to other domain controllers and effectively revive the deleted objects.

authorization The process of confirming that an authenticated user has the correct permissions to access one or more network resources.

autoenrollment A PKI feature supported by Windows Server 2003 and later, which allows users and computers to automatically enroll for certificates based on one or more certificate templates, as well as using Group Policy settings in Active Directory.

Automatic Certificate Request A Public Key Policies setting that enables computers to automatically submit a request for a certificate from an Enterprise Certification Authority (CA) and install that certificate.

B

back-links A reference to an attribute within another object that will also need to be restored with the object.

Basic User Strategy for enforcing restrictions that prevents any application from running that requires administrative rights but allows programs to run that only require resources that are accessible by normal users.

batch file Files, typically configured with either a .bat extension or a .cmd extension, that can be used to automate many routine or repetitive tasks.

bcdedit A command-line utility used to manage Boot Configuration Data (BCD) stores.

binaries The executable files needed to install Windows.

Block Policy Inheritance A setting on a container object, such as a site, domain, or Organizational Unit, that will block all policies from parent containers from flowing to this container. It is not policy specific; it applies to all policies applied at parent levels.

Boot Configuration Data (BCD) The store that describes boot applications and boot application settings and replaces the boot.ini file in previous versions of Windows.

boot volume The volume that hosts the Windows operating system and the registry.

bootmgr.exe The Windows boot loader.

bridgehead server The server at each site that acts as a gatekeeper in managing site-to-site replication. This allows intersite replication to update only one domain controller within a site. After a bridgehead server is updated, it updates the remainder of its domain controller partners with the newly replicated information.

built-in user accounts The accounts automatically created when Microsoft Windows Server 2008 is installed. By default, two built-in user accounts are created on a Windows Server 2008 computer: the Administrator account and the Guest account.

C

cached credentials A cached copy of a user's logon credentials that have been stored on the user's local workstation.

caching only servers A DNS server that contains no zones and hosts no domains.

Central Store Single location in the SYSVOL directory containing Administrative Templates with the .admx extension.

certificate A digital document that contains identifying information about a particular user, computer, service, and so on. The digital certificate contains the certificate holder's name and public key, the digital signature of the Certificate Authority that issued the certificate, as well as the certificate's expiration date. Also known as a *digital certificate*.

Certificate Practice Statement (CPS) Provides a detailed explanation of how a particular Certification Authority manages certificates and keys.

Certificate Request Wizard Enables a user to manually create a certificate request file using the Certificates MMC snap-in; this wizard creates a request file that can be used by the Certification Authority MMC to generate a certificate based on the request.

Certificate Revocation List (CRL) List that identifies certificates that have been revoked or terminated, and the corresponding user, computer, or service.

certificate rule A software restriction rule that uses the signing certificate of an application to allow software from a trusted source to run or to prevent software that does not come from a trusted source from running. Certificate rules also can be used to run programs in disallowed areas of the operating system.

Certificate Services Client Auto-Enrollment A Public Key Policies setting that allows an administrator to enable or disable the automatic enrollment of computer and user certificates, in addition to renewing and requesting certificates based on certificate templates.

certificate template Templates used by a CA to simplify the administration and issuance of digital certificates.

certification authority (CA) An entity, such as a Windows Server 2008 server running the AD CS server role, that issues and manages digital certificates used by companies to sign SMTP messages exchanged between domain controllers, thereby ensuring the authenticity of directory updates.

Certification Authority Web Enrollment Enables users to manually request certificates using a Web interface, located by default at https://<CA Name/certsrv on a CA that is running the Certification Authority Web Enrollment role service.

certutil An extremely flexible command-line utility for administering Active Directory Certificate Services.

change notification Method used by domain controllers to inform one another of when changes need to be replicated. Each domain controller will hold a change for 45 seconds before forwarding it, after which it will transmit the change to each of its replication partners in 3-second intervals.

checkpoint file A file used as a reference for database information written to disk. In a case where Active Directory needs to be recovered from a failure, the checkpoint file is used as a starting point.

claims based A characteristic of AD FS–enabled applications, which allows a much more scalable authentication model for Internet-facing applications.

claims-aware agent An agent installed on a Web server that hosts a claims-based application to enable it to query A D FS security claims.

Classless Inter-Domain Routing (CIDR) Form of notation that shows the number of bits being used for the subnet mask. For example, for an IP address of 192.168.64.0 with a mask of 255.255.255.0, the CIDR representation would be 192.168.64.0/24.

clock skew The time difference between any client or member server and the domain controllers in a domain.

Comma-Separated Value Directory Exchange (CSVDE) The command-line utility used to import or export Active Directory information from a comma-separated value (.csv) file.

Comma-Separated Values (CSV) Format that contains a comma between each value. The CSV format can be used to import and export information from other third-party applications.

Common Information Management Object Model (CIMOM) A database used through Windows Management Instrumentation that contains information gathered when a computer starts and becomes part of the network. This information includes hardware, Group Policy Software Installation settings, Internet Explorer Maintenance settings, scripts, Folder Redirection settings, and Security settings.

compressed To reduce the size of transmitted data to decrease the use of network bandwidth.

Computer Configuration A Group Policy setting that enables administrators to customize the configuration of a user's desktop, environment, and security settings. Enforced policies are based on the computer used.

conditional forwarders A server that will forward queries selectively based on the domain specified in the name resolution request.

Configuration NC The configuration partition contains information regarding the physical topology of the network, as well as other configuration data that must be replicated throughout the forest.

connection objects The link, created by the Knowledge Consistency Checker, between domain controllers that replicate with one another in a site.

container object An object, such as a domain or an Organizational Unit, that is used to organize other objects. Also known as a *leaf object*.

convergence The amount of time required for replication so that all domain controllers in the environment contain the most up-to-date information.

copy backup A backup type that retains the Application log files on the local server. This backup type should be implemented if a third-party backup tool is used in addition to Windows Server Backup.

cost Value assigned to a site link object to define the path that replication will take. If more than one path can be used to replicate information, cost assignments will determine which path is chosen first. A lower-numbered cost value will be chosen over a higher-numbered cost value.

critical volumes Volumes that should be backed up.

cross-forest trust Trust type that allows resources to be shared between Active Directory forests.

D

dcdiag A command-line tool used for monitoring Active Directory.

dcpromo The Active Directory Installation Wizard.

Default Domain Controller Policy A policy linked to the Domain Controllers OU; its settings affect all domain controllers in the domain.

Default Domain Policy A policy linked to the domain; its settings affect all users and computers in the domain.

defragmentation The process of taking fragmented database pieces and rearranging them contiguously to make the database more efficient.

delegation Administration of an Organizational Unit is tasked to a departmental supervisor or manager, thus allowing that person to manage day-to-day resource access as well as more mundane tasks, such as resetting passwords.

Delegation of Control Wizard A simple interface used to delegate permissions for domains, Organizational Units, and containers.

dictionary attack Automated password-cracking tools that try every possible com-bination of characters until the correct sequence of characters is finally discovered.

digital certificate A digital document that contains identifying information about a particular user, computer, service, and so on. The digital certificate contains the certificate holder's name and public key, the digital signature of the Certificate Authority that issued the certificate, as well as the certificate's expiration date. Also known as a *certificate*.

digital signature This electronic signature (created by a mathematical equation) proves the identity of the entity which has signed a particular document.

directory service Allows businesses to define, manage, access, and secure network resources, including files, printers, people, and applications.

Directory Services Restore Mode A special startup mode used to run an offline defragmentation.

Disallowed Strategy for enforcing restrictions that prevents all applications from running except those that are specifically allowed.

disk quotas A setting that limits the amount of space available on the server for user data.

distinguished name (DN) The full name of an object that includes all hierarchical containers leading up to the root domain. The distinguished name begins with the object's common name and appends each succeeding parent container object, reflecting the object's location in the Active Directory structure.

distribution group Non-security-related groups created for the distribution of information to one or more persons.

distribution share The shared folder that is a network location from which users can download software. Also known as the *software distribution point*.

DNS domain An administrative entity that consists of a group of hosts, usually a combination of computers, routers, printers, and other TCP/IP–enabled devices.

DNS namespace Consists of a hierarchy of domains. Each domain has DNS name servers that are responsible for supplying information about the hosts in that domain.

domain A grouping of objects in Active Directory that can be managed together. A domain can function as a security boundary for access to resources, such as computers, printers, servers, applications, and file systems.

domain account The accounts used to access Active Directory or network-based resources, such as shared folders or printers.

domain controller (DC) A server that stores the Active Directory database and authenticates users with the network during logon.

domain GPO A type of Group Policy Object associated with a domain.

domain local group A group used to assign permissions to resources that reside only in the same domain as the domain local group. They can contain user accounts, computer accounts, global groups, and universal groups from any domain, in addition to other domain local groups from the same domain.

Domain Name System (DNS) The name resolution mechanism computers use for all Internet communications and for private networks that use the Active Directory domain services included with Microsoft Windows Server 2008, Windows Server 2003, and Windows 2000 Server.

Domain Naming Master A role that has the authority to manage the creation and deletion of domains, domain trees, and application data partitions in the forest. Upon creation of any of these, the Domain Naming Master ensures that the name assigned is unique to the forest.

Domain NC Active Directory domain partition that is replicated to each domain controller within a particular domain. Each domain's Domain NC contains information about the objects that are stored within that domain: users, groups, computers, printers, Organizational Units, and more.

domain netBIOS name Domain name limited to 15 characters that is maintained for legacy compatibility with older applications that cannot use DNS for their name resolution.

domain tree In Active Directory, a logical grouping of network resources and devices that can contain one or more domains configured in a parent–child relationship. Each Active Directory forest can contain one or more domain trees, each of which can, in turn, contain one or more domains.

DomainDNSZones The application partition that is replicated to all domain controllers that are running the DNS server service in the domain.

drag-and-drop User interface enabling the user to drag an object and drop it on a target. This feature was introduced in Windows Server 2003.

dsacls A command-line tool that can be used to display or modify permissions of an Active Directory object. In effect, it is equivalent to an object's Security tab.

dsadd A command-line tool used to create, delete, view, and modify Active Directory objects, including users, groups, and Organizational Units.

dsmove A command-line utility used to move an object from one location to another.

dual counter-rotating ring Created by the Knowledge Consistency Checker for the replication path. If one domain controller in the ring fails, traffic is routed in the opposite direction to allow replication to continue.

dynamic updates Enables the DNS database to be updated with the changed information when the Internet Protocol (IP) address of a host changes.

E

edb.log A log file that stores a transaction until it can be written to the actual database. A transaction log file has a default size of 10 MB.

Encrypting File System (EFS) A Public Key Policies setting that enables an administrator to modify the list of recovery agents by adding other accounts as recovery agents. This setting is only available in the Computer Configuration node.

Enforce A setting on an individual GPO link that forces a particular GPO's settings to flow down through the Active Directory, without being blocked by any child Organizational Units.

Enforce Password History Group Policy setting that indicates the number of passwords that Active Directory should retain in memory before allowing someone to reuse a previously used password.

enrollment agent A certificate generated by the enterprise CA that is used to generate a smart card logon certificate for users in the organization.

enterprise CA An entity that can issue certificates only to users and computers in its own forest.

Enterprise Trust A Public Keys Policies setting that allows an administrator to define and distribute a certificate trust list (CTL) for external root certificate authorities (CAs). A CTL is a list of root CAs that the administrator has deemed to be reputable sources.

Everyone A special identity group that contains all authenticated users and domain guests.

Exchange The field that contains the name of a computer capable of acting as an email server for the domain specified in the Name field.

Extensible Storage Engine (ESE) A database engine responsible for managing changes to the Active Directory database.

external trust A one-way, nontransitive trust that is established with a Windows NT domain or a Windows 2000 domain in a separate forest.

F

fault tolerant The ability to respond gracefully to a software or hardware failure. In particular, a system is considered to be fault tolerant when it has the ability to continue providing authentication services after the failure of a domain controller.

file-activated installation A method of distributing applications whereby an application is installed when a user opens a file associated with an application that does not currently exist on the user's workstation.

Fine-Grained Password Policies (FGPP) A policy that can be applied to one or more users or groups of users, allowing the administrator to specify a more or less stringent password policy for the subset than the password policy defined for the entire domain.

Flexible Single Master Operations (FSMO) The specific server roles that work together to enable the multimaster functionality of Active Directory.

folder redirection A setting that allows files to be redirected to a network drive for backup and makes them accessible from anywhere on the network.

forest The largest container object within Active Directory. The forest container defines the fundamental security boundary within Active Directory, which means that a user can access resources across an entire Active Directory forest using a single logon/password combination.

forest root domain The first domain created within an Active Directory forest.

ForestDNSZones The application partition that consists of all domain controllers configured as DNS servers within the entire forest.

forward lookup zone Zones necessary for computer hostname–to–IP address mappings, which are used for name resolution by a variety of services.

forwarder A DNS server that receives queries from other DNS servers that are explicitly configured to send them.

fragmentation The condition of a disk when data from the database is divided into pieces scattered across the disk.

frequency A value assigned to a site link that determines how often information will be replicated over the site link.

fully qualified domain name (FQDN) The complete DNS name used to reference a host's location in the DNS structure; for example, LUCERNEPUBLISHING.

functional levels Designed to offer support for Active Directory domain controllers running various supported operating systems by limiting functionality to specific software versions. As legacy domain controllers are decommissioned, administrators can modify the functional levels to expose new functionality within Active Directory. Some features in Active Directory cannot be activated, for example, until all domain controllers in a forest are upgraded to a specific level.

G

garbage collection A process that removes all tombstones from the database.

_gc Global catalog service that listens on port 3268 to respond to requests to search for an object in Active Directory.

global catalog A domain controller that contains a partial replica of every domain in Active Directory. The global catalog stores those attributes most frequently used in search operations (such as a user's first and last names) and those attributes required to locate a full replica of the object. The Active Directory replication system builds the global catalog automatically.

global group A group used to grant or deny permissions to any resource located in any domain in the forest. Global groups can contain user accounts, computer accounts, and/or other global groups only from within the same domain as the global group.

globally unique identifier (GUID) A 128-bit hexadecimal number that is assigned to every object in the Active Directory forest upon its creation. This number does not change even when the object itself is renamed.

GPO inheritance The process of applying Group Policy to all domains and the child objects contained within them.

GPResult A command-line tool that enables administrators to create and display a Resultant Set of Policy (RSoP) query from the command line.

gpupdate.exe A command-line tool used to force a manual Group Policy refresh. This tool was introduced in Windows Server 2003, and it is used in Windows Server 2003 and Windows Server 2008 to replace the secedit/refreshpolicy command that was used in Windows 2000.

group A collection of user or computer accounts that is used to simplify the assignment of permissions to network resources.

group nesting The process of configuring one or more groups as members of another group.

Group Policy container (GPC) An Active Directory object that stores the properties of the GPO.

Group Policy Management Console (GPMC) The Microsoft Management Console (MMC) snap-in that is used to create and modify Group Policies and their settings.

Group Policy Management Editor The Microsoft Management Console (MMC) snap-in that is used to create and modify Group Policies and their settings.

Group Policy Modeling A Group Policy Management feature that uses the Resultant Set of Policy snap-in to simulate the effect of a policy on the user environment.

Group Policy Object (GPO) Objects that contain all of the Group Policy settings that will be implemented on all user and computer objects within a site, domain, or OU.

Group Policy Results A feature in Group Policy Management that is equivalent to the Logging mode within the Resultant Set of Policy MMC snap-in. Rather than simulating policy effects like the Group Policy Modeling Wizard, Group Policy Results obtains Resultant Set of Policy (RSoP) information from the client computer to show the actual effects that policies have on the client computer and user environment.

Group Policy template (GPT) A folder located in the Policies subfolder of the SYSVOL share that stores policy settings, such as security settings and script files.

group scope Group characteristic that controls which objects the group can contain, limiting the objects to the same domain or permitting objects from remote domains as well, and controls the location in the domain or forest where the group can be used.

group type Group characteristic that defines how a group is to be used within Active Directory.

H

hash A series of bytes with a fixed length that uniquely identifies a program or file.

hash algorithm A formula that generates a hash value.

hash rule A software-restriction rule applied to an application executable that will check the file's hash value and prevent the application from running if the hash value is incorrect.

hash value A value generated by a formula that makes it nearly impossible for another program to have the same hash.

header record The first line of the imported or exported text file that uses proper attribute names.

hierarchical Related to a series of graded levels. When applied to a certification authority (CA), it means that you can have many subordinate CAs within an organization that chain upwards to a single root CA that is authoritative for all Certificate Services within a given network.

host (A) The fundamental data unit of the DNS. This resource record has a single Address field that contains the IP address associated with the system identified in the Name field.

host (AAAA) The resource record for an IPv6 host; an AAAA record is the IPv6 equivalent of an A record in IPv4.

Host Information (HINFO) The resource record contains two fields, CPU and OS, which contain values identifying the processor type and operating system used by the listed host.

host name A one-word friendly name assigned to a computer.

I

in-addr.arpa A special domain that is specifically designed for reverse name resolution.

inbound replication Occurs when a domain controller receives updates to the Active Directory database from other domain controllers on the network.

incremental zone transfers Method of conserving bandwidth by transferring part of a zone.

indexed An attribute has been stored in the partial attribute set and replicated to all global catalog servers in the forest.

Infrastructure Master A domain-specific role that is responsible for reference updates from its domain objects to other domains. This assists in tracking which domains own which objects.

Install This Application At Logon A deployment option that allows the application to be installed immediately, rather than advertised on the Start menu.

instance A single occurrence of an element.

intermediate CA In a hierarchy of certification authorities (CA), a single root CA issues certificates to several of these certification authorities.

intersite replication The process of replicating Active Directory information from one site to another.

Intersite Topology Generator (ISTG) A process that selects a bridgehead server and maps the topology to be used for intersite replication.

intrasite replication The process of replicating Active Directory information between domain controllers within a site.

IP address A unique number used to identify all devices on an IP network. IP addresses are four octets long and are commonly expressed in dotted-decimal notation, such as 192.168.10.1.

issuing CA A certification authority (CA) that issues certificates to users or computers.

iterative query The server that receives the name resolution request immediately responds to the requester with the best information it possesses. This information can be cached or authoritative, and it can be a resource record containing a fully resolved name or a reference to another DNS server.

K

Kerberos Policies For domain accounts only, this policy enables administrators to configure settings that govern how Active Directory authentication functions.

key archival The process by which private keys are maintained by the certification authority (CA) for retrieval by a recovery agent, if at all.

Key Distribution Center (KDC) Used to issue Kerberos tickets to users for domain access.

key recovery agent User accounts that are configured with a Key Recovery Agent certificate that allows them to restore an escrow copy of a private key.

Knowledge Consistency Checker (KCC) An internal Active Directory process that automatically creates and maintains the replication topology. The KCC operates based on the information provided by an administrator in the Active Directory Sites and Services snap-in, which is located in the Administrative Tools folder on a domain controller, or an administrative workstation that has the Administrative Tools installed.

L

latency The amount of time or delay it takes to replicate information throughout the network.

LDAP Data Interchange Format (LDIF) The format for the data file containing the object records to be created.

LDAP Data Interchange Format Directory Exchange (LDIFDE) A command-line utility used to import or export Active Directory information and create, modify, and delete Active Directory objects.

LDP A graphical support tool that provides a much more detailed method of adding, removing, searching, and modifying the Active Directory database.

leaf object An object, such as a domain or an Organizational Unit, that is used to organize other objects. Also known as a *container object*.

Lightweight Directory Access Protocol (LDAP) The protocol that has become an industry standard that enables data exchange between directory services and applications. The LDAP standard defines the naming of all objects in the Active Directory database and, therefore, provides a directory that can be integrated with other directory services, such as Novell eDirectory, and Active Directory–aware applications, such as Microsoft Exchange.

linked-value replication (LVR) An improvement to replication that is available for use after the forest functional level has been raised to Windows Server 2003 or higher, enabling a single membership change to a group to trigger the replication of only this change to each member in the list, rather than the entire membership list.

linking A process that applies Group Policy settings to various containers within Active Directory.

link-value replication When a change is made to the member list of a group object, only the portion of the member list that has been added, modified, or deleted will be replicated.

local account The accounts used to access the local computer only. They are stored in the local Security Account Manager (SAM) database on the computer where they reside. Local accounts are never replicated to other computers, nor do these accounts have domain access.

local GPO A type of Group Policy Object associated with the local computer.

local group A collection of user accounts that are local to one specific workstation or member server. Local groups are created in the security database of a local computer and are not replicated to Active Directory or to any other computers on the network.

Local Policies Policies that enable administrators to set user privileges on the local computer that govern what users can do on the computer and determine if these actions are tracked within an event log.

locator service Active Directory DNS provides direction for network clients that need to know which server performs what function.

Logging mode The Resultant Set of Policy (RSoP) mode that queries existing policies in the hierarchy that are linked to sites, domains, domain controllers, and Organizational Units. This mode is useful for documenting and understanding how combined policies are affecting users and computers. The results are returned in an MMC window that can be saved for later reference.

logon events This setting logs events related to successful user logons on a computer.

Loopback Processing A Group Policy option that provides an alternative method of obtaining the ordered list of GPOs to be processed for the user. When set to Enabled, this setting has two options: Merge and Replace.

loose consistency Individual domain controllers in an Active Directory database may contain slightly different information, because it can take anywhere from a few seconds to several hours for changes to replicate throughout a given environment.

LSDOU The sequence used to process policies: local policies, site policies, domain policies, and then Organizational Unit policies.

M

Mail Exchanger (MX) A DNS function that directs email messages to the appropriate mail server.

manual backup A backup initiated by using Server Backup or the Wbadmin. exe command-line tool.

Merge A Loopback Processing option. After all user policies run, the computer policy settings are reapplied, which allows all current GPO settings to merge with the reapplied computer policy settings. In instances where conflicts arise between computer and user settings, the computer policy supersedes the user policy. This occurs before the desktop is presented to the user.

msDS-PasswordSettings A new object type in Windows Server 2008 that enables the use of Fine-Grained Password Policies. Also known as a *Password Settings Object* (PSO).

.msi file A relational database file that is copied to the target computer system, with the program files it deploys. In addition to providing installation information, this database file assists in the self-healing process for damaged applications and clean application removal.

multiple local GPOs (MLGPO) A new feature in Windows Vista whereby administrators can specify a different local GPO for administrators and create specific GPO settings for one or more local users configured on a workstation.

N

Name Server (NS) The NS resource record identifies the name server that is the authority for the particular zone or domain; that is, the server that can provide an authoritative name-to-IP address mapping for a zone or domain.

name servers Applications running on server computers maintain information about the domain tree structure and contain authoritative information about specific areas of that structure.

naming context (NC) An Active Directory partition.

nested An object placed inside another object of the same type.

nested membership When a group is placed in a second group, the members of the first group become members of the second group.

NetBIOS name The name assigned to a computer during the operating system installation.

netdom A command-line tool that is used to create, delete, verify, and reset trust relationships from the Windows Server 2008 command line.

Network Device Enrollment Service (NDES) This service allows devices, such as hardware-based routers and other network devices and appliances, to enroll for certificates within a Windows Server 2008 PKI that might not otherwise be able to do so.

network zone rule A software restriction rule that allows only Windows

Installer packages to be installed if they come from a trusted area of the network.

nltest A command-line tool that is typically used to verify trusts and check replication.

node A subcategory of Group Policy settings.

nonauthoritative restore Restores a single Active Directory domain controller to its state before the backup. This method can be used to restore a single domain controller to a point in time when it was considered to be good.

notify list A list that allows the server hosting a primary zone to notify secondary zones when changes have occurred.

nslookup A command-line tool that is critical for working with DNS on Server Core.

O

object An element in Active Directory that refers to a resource. Objects can be container objects or leaf objects. Containers are used to organize resources for security or organizational purposes; leaf objects refer to the end-node resources, such as users, computers, and printers.

Object Identifier (OID) A unique string used to identify every class or attribute added to a schema. OIDs must be globally unique, and they are represented by a hierarchical dotted-decimal notation string.

OCSP Response Signing certificate Template that enables digital signatures, which are required for Online Certificate Status Protocol (OCSP) transactions. The template is located on any CA that will be used as an Online Responder.

offline defragmentation A manual process that defragments the Active Directory database in addition to reducing its size.

offline file storage This feature works with folder redirection to provide the ability to cache files locally. This allows files to be available even when the network is inaccessible.

Offline Files A separate Group Policy category that can allow files to be available to users, even when users are disconnected from the network.

Online Certificate Status Protocol (OCSP) Protocol used by the Online Responder to respond to queries from clients requesting data about the status of a PKI certificate that has been issued by a particular CA.

online defragmentation The automatic process of taking fragmented database pieces and rearranging them contiguously that occurs during the garbage-collection process.

Online Responder Service that responds to requests from clients concerning the revocation status of a particular certificate, returning a digitally signed response indicating the certificate's current status.

organizational unit (OU) A container that represents a logical grouping of resources that have similar security or administrative guidelines.

outbound replication Occurs when a domain controller transmits replication information to other domain controllers on the network.

P

partial attribute set (PAS) A partial copy of all objects from other domains within the same forest. This partial copy of forest-wide data includes a subset of each object's attributes.

partition Portion of Active Directory database used to divide the database into manageable pieces.

password An alphanumeric sequence of characters entered with a username to access a server, workstation, or shared resource.

Password Policies A subcategory in the Account Policies category that enforces password length, password history, and so on. Password Policies can be applied to domain and local user accounts.

Password Replication Policy A list of user or group accounts whose passwords should be stored on a particular Read-Only Domain Controller (RODC) or should not be stored on the specific RODC.

Password Settings Object (PSO) A new object type in Windows Server 2008 that enables the use of Fine-Grained Password Policies. Also known as *msDS-PasswordSettings*.

password-cracking An attempt to discover a user's password.

patch files Windows Installer files with the .msp extension that are used to apply service packs and hotfixes to installed software.

path rule A software restriction rule that identifies software by specifying the directory path where the application is stored in the file system.

performance counters A data item associated with a performance object to monitor the specific process or event to be tracked.

performance objects Reliability and Performance Monitor categories used to organize items that can be monitored.

personal identification number (PIN) Typically consists of at least four characters or digits that are entered while presenting a physical access token, such as an ATM card or a smart card.

Planning mode The Resultant Set of Policy (RSoP) mode that allows administrators to simulate the effect of policy settings prior to implementing them on a computer or user.

pointer (PTR) The resource record that is the functional opposite of the A record, providing an IP address to name mapping for the system identified in the Name field using the in-addr.arpa domain name.

policy change events By default, this policy is set to audit successes in the Default Domain Controllers GPO. Policy change audit log entries are triggered by events such as user rights assignment changes, establishment or removal of trust relationships, IPSec policy agent changes, and grants or removals of system access privileges.

precedence An attribute of the Password Settings Object (PSO) used as a tiebreaker to determine which PSO should apply: a PSO with a precedence of 1 will be applied over a PSO with a precedence of 5

Preference The field that contains an integer value indicating the relative priority of this resource record compared to others of the same type and class in the same domain. The lower the value, the higher the priority.

preferred bridgehead servers The administrator's list of servers to be used as bridgehead servers. A bridgehead server is the server at each site that acts as a gatekeeper in managing site-to-site replication.

Primary Domain Controller (PDC) Emulator A role that provides backward compatibility with Microsoft Windows NT 4.0 domains and other down-level clients.

primary zone A zone that contains the master copy of the zone database, in which administrators make all changes to the zone's resource records.

principle of least privilege A security best practice which dictates that users should receive only the minimum amount of privileges needed to perform a particular task.

priority A mechanism to set up load balancing between multiple servers that are advertising the same SRV records. Clients will always use the record with the lower-numbered priority first. They will only use an SRV record with a higher-numbered priority if the lower-numbered priority record is unavailable.

private key A piece of information, used as part of the public key infrastructure (PKI), that is known only to the individual user or computer.

public key A piece of information, used as part of the public key infrastructure (PKI).

public key cryptography A mathematical algorithm, utilizing public keys and private keys, used by public key infrastructure (PKI) to communicate securely.

public key infrastructure (PKI) A system of digital certificates, certification authorities (CAs), and other registration authorities (RAs) that verify and authenticate the validity of each party involved in an electronic transaction using public key cryptography.

Public Key Policies The area of Group Policy that offers greater administrative control in establishing rules and governing the issuance, maintenance, and guidelines within a public key infrastructure (PKI).

Publish 1) An option that allows users to access network resources by searching the Active Directory database for the desired resource. (See Lesson 1.) 2) An option used to deploy applications. It allows users to install the applications that they consider useful to them. (See Lesson 9.)

R

Read-Only Domain Controller (RODC) A domain controller that contains a copy of the ntds.dit file that cannot be modified and that does not replicate its changes to other domain controllers within Active Directory. This feature was introduced in Windows Server 2008.

recovery agent Configured within a CA to allow one or more users (typically administrators) to recover private keys for users, computers, or services if their keys are lost.

recursive query The DNS server receiving the name resolution request takes full responsibility for resolving the name.

referral The process by which one DNS server sends a name resolution request to another DNS server.

refresh interval The available period that each background refresh process that can be set to ranges from 0 to 64,800 minutes (45 days).

registry-based policies Settings that provide a consistent, secure, manageable environment that addresses the users' needs and the organization's administrative goals.

relative identifier (RID) A variable-length number that is assigned to objects at creation and becomes part of the object's security identifier (SID).

Relative Identifier (RID) Master Role that is responsible for assigning relative identifiers to domain controllers in the domain. Relative identifiers are variable length numbers assigned by a domain controller when a new object is created.

Reliability and Performance Monitor Tool located within the Administrative Tools folder that enables administrators to collect real-time information on the local computer or from a specific computer that they have permission to access.

Remote Procedure Calls over Internet Protocol (RPC over IP) Default protocol used for all replication traffic.

repackaging The process of preparing software for .msi distribution, which includes taking a snapshot of a clean computer system before the application is installed, installing the application as desired, and taking a snapshot of the computer after the application is installed.

repadmin A command-line tool that can check replication consistency between replication partners, monitor replication status, display replication metadata, and force replication events and Knowledge Consistency Checker (KCC) recalculation.

Replace A Loopback Processing option. This option overwrites the GPO list for a user object with the GPO list for the user's logon computer. This means that the computer policy settings remove any conflicting user policy settings.

replication The process of keeping each domain controller in sync with changes made elsewhere on the network.

replication partners Servers that inform each other when updates are necessary. The Knowledge Consistency Checker (KCC) selects one or more replication partners for each domain controller in the site.

replication topology Defines the path used by replication traffic.

resolvers Client programs generate requests for DNS information and send them to name servers for fulfillment. A resolver has direct access to at least one name server and can process referrals to direct its queries to other name servers when necessary.

resource organizations The organizations that own the resources or data accessible from the AD FS–enabled application, similar to a trusting domain in a traditional Windows trust relationship.

resource record The fundamental data storage unit in all DNS servers. When DNS clients and servers exchange name and address information, they do so in the form of resource records.

Responder array Multiple Online Responders linked together to process status requests.

restartable Active Directory Feature that enables administrators to place the NTDS.DIT file in an offline mode without rebooting the domain controller outright. This feature was introduced in Windows Server 2008.

Restartable Active Directory Domain Services (Restartable AD DS) Windows Server 2008 feature that enables administrators to start, stop, and restart Active Directory, similar to any other service on a server.

restricted enrollment agent Limits the permissions required for an enrollment agent to configure smart cards on behalf of other users.

Restricted Groups Policy setting that enables an administrator to specify group membership lists.

Resultant Set of Policy (RSoP) Query engine that looks at GPOs and then reports its findings. Use this tool to determine the effective settings for a user or a computer based on the combination of the local, site, domain, domain controller, and OU policies.

return on investment (ROI) The amount of money gained (or lost) relative to the amount of money that was invested in a particular project or technology. Can be measured by tangible benefits, such as implementation costs and ongoing support. In addition, it can also be measured by intangible benefits, such as increased user productivity, and other factors that are difficult to measure from a financial standpoint.

reverse lookup zone Zone that answers queries in which a client provides an IP address and DNS resolves the IP address to a hostname.

rolling upgrades Upgrade strategy based on functional levels that allows enterprises to migrate their Active Directory domain controllers gradually, based on the need and desire for the new functionality.

root CA In a hierarchy of certification authorities (CA), this CA issues certificates to several of intermediate CAs.

root name servers The highest level DNS servers in the entire namespace.

Run as Administrator Option that enables administrators to maintain their primary logon as a standard user and create a secondary session for access to an administrative tool.

runas A command-line tool that enables administrators to log on with alternate credentials.

S

SAM account name Each user's login name—the portion to the left of the '@' within a User Principal Name. The SAM account name must be unique across a domain.

scavenging The process of removing records that were not refreshed or updated within specified time intervals.

schedule Determines the time when a site link object is available to replicate information.

scheduled backup A backup using the Windows Server Backup utility or the Wbadmin.exe command-line tool. Scheduled backups will reformat the target drive that hosts the backup files, and thus can only be performed on a local physical drive that does not host any critical volumes.

schema Master database that contains definitions of all objects in the Active Directory.

Schema Master An Active Directory role that has forest-wide authority to manage changes to the Active Directory schema.

Schema NC The partition that contains the rules and definitions used for creating and modifying object classes and attributes within Active Directory.

scripts A managed setting that can be defined or changed through Group Policies. Scripts, including logon, logoff, startup, and shutdown commands, can assist in configuring the user environment.

Secondary Logon A feature that provides the ability to log on with an alternate set of credentials to that of the primary logon.

secondary zone A read-only copy of the data that is stored within a primary zone on another server.

Security Account Manager (SAM) A database containing user accounts and security information that is located on a server.

security group Security-related groups created for purposes of granting resource access permissions to multiple users.

security group filtering An advanced technique that enables you to apply GPO settings to only one or more users or groups within a container by selectively granting the "Apply Group Policy" permission to one or more users or security groups.

security identifier (SID) A variable-length number used to uniquely identify an object throughout the Active Directory domain. Part of the SID identifies the domain to which the object belongs, and the other part is the RID.

Security Options A subcategory of the Local Policies setting area of a Group Policy Object that includes security settings related to interactive log on, digital signing of data, restrictions for access to floppy and CD-ROM drives, unsigned driver installation behavior, and logon dialog box behavior.

seize A forced, ungraceful transfer of a role. This procedure is used only in the event of a catastrophic failure of a domain controller that holds a FSMO role.

self-enrollment Feature that enables users to request their own PKI certificates, typically through a Web browser.

self-healing A function that allows software to detect and correct problems, such as missing or deleted files.

Server Core A special installation option that creates a minimal environment for running only specific services and roles. Server Core runs without the Windows Desktop shell, which means that it must be administered exclusively from the command line or using Group Policy. This feature was introduced in Windows Server 2008.

Server Manager A utility that enables administrators to view any other roles the server might be performing. The Server Manager utility launches automatically at startup after the Initial Configuration Tasks utility is closed. It can be accessed manually through the shortcut provided in the Administrative Tools folder or directly from the Start menu.

service record (SRV) The record that enables clients to locate servers providing a particular service.

shared secret key A secret piece of information shared between two parties prior to being able to communicate securely.

shortcut trust A manually created nontransitive trust that allows child domains in separate trees to communicate more efficiently by eliminating the tree-walking of a trust path.

signed Certifies that the document originated from the person or entity in question. In cases where a digital signature is used to sign something like an email message, a digital signature also indicates that the message is authentic and has not been tampered with since it left the sender's Outbox.

Simple Certificate Enrollment Protocol (SCEP) A network protocol that allows network devices to enroll for PKI certificates.

Simple Mail Transport Protocol (SMTP) Transport protocol used for intersite replication when a direct or reliable IP connection is unavailable.

Single Sign-On (SSO) For Web-based applications across multiple organizations, this feature allows user access without requiring the users to remember multiple usernames and passwords.

site One or more IP subnets connected by fast links.

site link bridge Defines a chain of site links by which domain controllers from different sites can communicate.

site links A connection between two or more sites that enables intersite replication.

smart card A small physical devices, usually the size of a credit card or keychain fob, that has a digital certificate installed. Used with a PIN to enable logon to a secure resource.

smart card enrollment station A dedicated workstation from which an administrator or another authorized user can preconfigure certificates and smart cards on behalf of a user or workstation.

smart card reader A physical device attached to a workstation that enables users to utilize a smart card to authenticate to an Active Directory domain, access a Website, or authenticate to other secured resources.

software installation policies A managed setting that can be defined or changed through Group Policies. This setting can be used to ensure that users always have the latest versions of applications. If application files are inadvertently deleted, repairs are made without user intervention.

software life cycle The process that takes place from the time an application is evaluated for deployment in an organization until the time when it is deemed old or no longer suitable for use.

Software Settings A subnode within the Computer Configuration and User Configuration nodes. The Software Settings folder located under the Computer Configuration node contains settings that apply to all users who log on from that specific computer. The Software Settings folder located under the User Configuration node contains settings that are applied to users designated by the Group Policy, regardless of the computer from which they log on to Active Directory.

special identity group Group used to define permission assignments. Administrators cannot manually modify the group membership of special identity groups, nor can they view their membership lists.

SRV record The locator records within DNS that allows clients to locate an Active Directory domain controller or global catalog.

staged installation To begin the Active Directory installation at a central location, such as a data center, and then allow a local administrator to complete the configuration.

standalone CA An entity that can issue certificates only to users and computers in its own forest. Standalone CAs are not integrated with Active Directory.

standard zone A primary master zone database file on the local drive.

Start of Authority (SOA) The resource record that identifies which name server is the authoritative source of information for data within this domain. The first record in the zone database file must be an SOA record.

starter GPO A type of Group Policy that enables administrators to configure a standard set of items that will be configured by default in any GPO that is derived from a starter GPO. Starter GPOs are a new feature in Windows Server 2008.

strong password A password that follows guidelines that make it difficult for a potential hacker to determine the user's password. Password guidelines include a minimum required password length, a password history, requiring multiple types of characters within a password, and setting a minimum password age.

stub zone A copy of a primary zone that contains Start of Authority (SOA) and Name Server (NS) resource records, plus the Host (A) resource records that identify the authoritative servers for the zone.

subordinate CA A CA within an organization that chains upwards to a single root CA that is authoritative for all Certificate Services within a given network.

synchronous processing Processing method whereby each policy must be read and applied completely before the next policy can be invoked.

System Development Life Cycle (SDLC) A structured process used to develop information systems software, projects, or components; phases include analysis, design, implementation, and maintenance.

system events Events that trigger a log entry in this category include system startups and shutdowns; system time changes, system event resources exhaustion, such as when an event log is filled and can no longer append entries; security log cleaning; or any event that affects system security or the security log. In the Default Domain Controllers GPO, this setting is set to log successes by default.

System Services The category that is used to configure the startup and security settings for services running on a computer.

system volume The volume that hosts the boot files.

SYSVOL A shared folder that exists on all domain controllers and is used to store Group Policy Objects, login scripts, and other files that are replicated domain-wide.

T

tattooing An Administrative Template setting that continues to apply until it is reversed using a policy that overwrites the setting.

timestamp An attribute set on an object to indicate when it was last updated. Timestamps are used to assist in the resolution of conflicts during replication. If a change was made to an attribute of the same object, the timestamp can help determine which object is the most up-to-date.

time-to-live The length of time a record is valid, after which it needs to be reregistered.

tombstone What is left of an object that has been deleted. Deleted objects are not completely removed from the Active Directory database; rather, they are marked for deletion. Tombstone objects have a lifetime of 180 days, by default.

total cost of ownership (TCO) A value used to assess the cost of implementing computer software or hardware, both in terms of direct and indirect costs. TCO can be calculated based on how much ownership costs over the lifetime of a business resource.

transaction buffer Server RAM that stores data before it is actually written to the server's hard drive so that all data in the transaction can be written to disk at the same time.

transfer Move a role to a new domain controller.

transitive Default characteristic of site links that use the same transport protocol. A domain controller in any site can connect to a domain controller in any other site by navigating a chain of site links.

trust relationship Enables administrators from a particular domain to grant access to their domain's resources to users in other domains.

Trusted Root Certification Authorities A Public Key Policies setting that determines whether users can choose to trust root CAs and the criteria that must be met by the CA to fulfill user requests.

two-factor authentication An authentication method that requires a smart card and a PIN to provide more secure access to company resources.

U

unattended installation Running dcpromo from the command line using a specially formatted text file to specify the necessary installation options.

universal group Memberships stored in the global catalog. A universal group can contain users, groups, and computers from any domain in the forest. In addition, universal groups, through their membership in domain local groups, can receive permissions for any resource anywhere in the forest.

universal group membership caching This feature stores universal group memberships on a local domain con-

troller that can be used for logon to the domain, eliminating the need for frequent access to a global catalog server.

Unrestricted Strategy for enforcing restrictions that allows all applications to run, except those that are specifically excluded.

update sequence number (USN) A local value, maintained by each domain controller, that tracks the changes that are made at each DC, thus tracking which updates should be replicated to other domain controllers.

urgent replication The change will be placed at the "beginning of the line" and it will be applied before any other changes that are waiting to be replicated.

User Configuration A Group Policy setting that enables administrators to customize the configuration of a user's desktop, environment, and security settings. Enforced policies are based on the user rather than on the computer used.

User Principal Name (UPN) A naming format that simplifies access to multiple services such as Active Directory and email. A UPN follows a naming convention that can reflect the forest root domain or another alias that follows the format of username@domainname.

User Rights Assignment A subcategory of the Local Policies setting area of a Group Policy Object that includes settings for items that pertain to rights needed by users to perform system-related tasks.

V

version ID A value associated with each Active Directory attribute that keeps track of how many times that attribute has been changed.

VSS full backup A backup type that updates each file's backup history and clears the Application Log files.

W

wbadmin The command-line component of the Windows Server Backup snap-in.

Web enrollment Feature that enables users to connect to a Windows Server 2008 CA through a Web browser to request certificates and obtain an up-to-date Certificate Revocation List.

weight A relative weighting for SRV records that have the same priority. For example, consider three SRV

records with the same priority with relative weights of 60, 20, and 20. Because $60 + 20 + 20 = 100$, the record with the weight of 60 will be used 60/100, or 60 percent, of the time, whereas each of the other two records will be used 20/100, or 20 percent, of the time.

well-connected The network infrastructure between sites defined by fast and reliable IP subnets.

Windows Deployment Services (WDS) A managed setting that can be defined or changed through Group Policies. This setting assists in rebuilding or deploying workstations quickly and efficiently in an enterprise environment.

Windows Internet Naming Service (WINS) A name resolution mechanisms for NetBIOS names.

Windows Management Instrumentation (WMI) A component of the Microsoft Windows operating system that provides management information and control in an enterprise environment. It allows administrators to create queries based on hardware, software, operating systems, and services.

Windows PowerShell A command-line and task-based scripting technology introduced in Windows Server 2008.

Windows Script Host (WSH) Allows scripts to be run from a Windows desktop or a command prompt. The runtime programs provided to do this are WScript.exe and CScript.exe, respectively.

Windows Server Backup A feature used to back up Active Directory. It supports the use of CD and DVD drives as backup destinations, but does not support magnetic tapes as backup media.

Windows Settings A subnode within the Computer Configuration and User Configuration nodes. The Windows Settings folder located under the Computer Configuration node in the Group Policy Management Editor contains security settings and scripts that apply to all users who log on to Active Directory from that specific computer. The Windows Settings folder located under the User Configuration node contains settings related to folder redirection, security settings, and scripts that are applied to associated users.

Windows token-based agent An agent installed on a Web server that hosts traditional Windows NT token-based applications so that administrators can convert these tokens from AD FS tokens into Windows NT tokens.

WMI Filtering A filtering method that method uses filters written in the WMI Query Language (WQL) to control GPO application.

WMI Query Language (WQL) A language that is similar to structured query language (SQL).

Z

.zap file A non–Windows Installer package that can be created in a text editor.

zone transfers The process of replicating DNS information from one DNS server to another.

Index